The Norton
Field Guide
to Writing

with readings

Richard Bullock

WRIGHT STATE UNIVERSITY

Maureen Daly Goggin

ARIZONA STATE UNIVERSITY

W. W. NORTON & COMPANY

New York • London

W. W. Norton & Company has been independent since its founding in 1923, when William Warder Norton and Mary D. Herter Norton first published lectures delivered at the People's Institute, the adult education division of New York City's Cooper Union. The Nortons soon expanded their program beyond the Institute, publishing books by celebrated academics from America and abroad. By mid-century, the two major pillars of Norton's publishing program — trade books and college texts — were firmly established. In the 1950s, the Norton family transferred control of the company to its employees, and today — with a staff of four hundred and a comparable number of trade, college, and professional titles published each year — W. W. Norton & Company stands as the largest and oldest publishing house owned wholly by its employees.

Composition: Matrix Publishing Services
Manufacturing: R. R. Donnelley, Crawfordsville
Text Design: Anna Palchik
Cover Design: Debra Morton Hoyt
Production Manager: Diane O'Connor

Library of Congress Cataloging-in-Publication Data

Bullock, Richard H.
    The Norton field guide to writing, with readings / Richard Bullock, Maureen Daly Goggin.
      p. cm.
    Includes bibliographical references and index.
    ISBN-13: 978-0-393-92662-0 (pbk.)
    ISBN-10: 0-393-92662-1 (pbk.)
    1. English language—Rhetoric—Handbooks, manuals, etc.   2. English language—
Grammar—Handbooks, manuals, etc.   3. Report writing—Handbooks, manuals,
etc.   4. College readers.   I. Goggin, Maureen Daly.   II. Title.
PE1408.B883825 2006
808'.0427—dc22   2006047157

W. W. Norton & Company, Inc., 500 Fifth Avenue, New York, N.Y. 10110
www.wwnorton.com

W. W. Norton & Company Ltd., Castle House, 75/76 Wells Street, London W1T 3QT

3 4 5 6 7 8 9 0

Preface

The Norton Field Guide to Writing began as an attempt to offer the kind of writing guidelines found in the best rhetorics in a format as user-friendly as the most popular handbooks, and on top of that to be as brief as could be. It was to be a handy guide to help college students with all their written work. Just as there are field guides for bird watchers and accountants, this would be one for writers. The book touched a chord with many instructors, and it quickly became the most widely used brief rhetoric. At the same time, many instructors asked for more readings. So we are happy now to offer a version that includes an anthology of 51 more readings.

    The Norton Field Guide aims to offer the guidance new teachers and first-year writers need and the flexibility many experienced teachers want. From our experiences as teachers and WPAs, we know that books with explicit writing guides work well for students and novice teachers. At the same time, many instructors chafe at the structure imposed by such books, and students complain about having to buy books that have much more detail than they need. So we've tried to provide enough structure without too much detail — to give the information college writers need to know, and to resist the temptation to tell them everything there is to know.

    Most of all, we've tried to make the book easy to use. To that end, we've designed *The Norton Field Guide to Writing, with readings* as two books in one, the rhetoric in front and the anthology in back — and used color-coded links to make it easy to navigate between the two. Color-coded links are also the key to making the rhetoric brief: most chapters are short, but links send students to specific pages elsewhere in the book where they can find more detail *if they need more detail*.

    Finally, part of the *Field Guide* is on the Web, so that students can access materials from the book online. A Writing Toolbar — color-coded, of course, to match the book — provides students with online access to these materials when they most need them, *as they write*.

An Overview of the Book

The Norton Field Guide covers fifteen kinds of writing often assigned to college students. Much of the book is in the form of guidelines, designed to help students consider the choices they have as writers. Most chapters are brief, in response to students' complaints about books with too much detail — but color-coded links send them to places in the book where they can find more information if they need it. The book is organized in seven parts:

- **RHETORICAL SITUATIONS.** Chapters 1–5 focus on purpose, audience, genre, stance, and media and design. In addition, almost every chapter includes a short list of tips to help students focus on their particular rhetorical situation.

- **GENRES.** Chapters 6–20 offer guidelines for fifteen kinds of writing, from abstracts to lab reports to memoirs. Literacy narrative, textual analysis, report, and argument are treated in greater detail.

- **PROCESSES.** Chapters 21–27 offer advice for generating ideas and text, drafting, revising and rewriting, editing, proofreading, compiling a portfolio, and collaborating with others.

- **STRATEGIES.** Chapters 28–37 cover familiar ways of developing and organizing text — writing effective beginnings and endings, coming up with good titles and developing effective thesis statements, comparing, describing, using dialogue, and other essential writing strategies. Chapter 38 offers a catalog of useful reading strategies.

- **RESEARCH / DOCUMENTATION.** Chapters 39–46 offer advice on how to do academic research; work with sources; quote, paraphrase, and summarize source materials; and document sources using MLA and APA styles.

- **MEDIA / DESIGN.** Chapters 47–49 give general guidance on designing and presenting texts for print, spoken, and electronic media.

- **READINGS.** Chapters 50–59 provide additional readings in ten of the genres. Discussion questions help students engage with the text — to read purposefully and to mine the texts rhetorically — and are color-coded to refer students to relevant details elsewhere in the book if they need more explanation.

An Overview of the Web Site

The companion site provides instant access to parts of *The Norton Field Guide* online. A Writing Toolbar provides easy access to useful materials from the *Field Guide*, and a Portfolio Space allows students to submit drafts electronically. Visit the site at **wwnorton.com/write/fieldguide**.

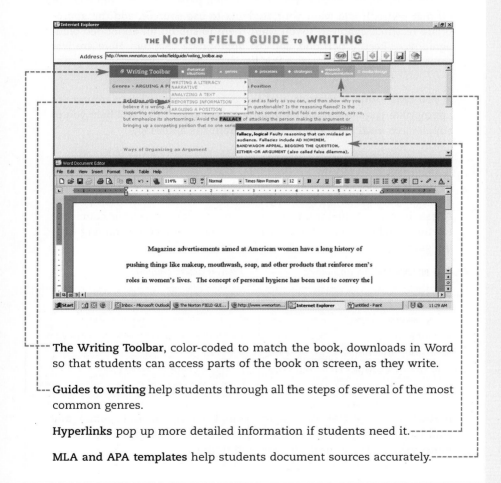

The Writing Toolbar, color-coded to match the book, downloads in Word so that students can access parts of the book on screen, as they write.

Guides to writing help students through all the steps of several of the most common genres.

Hyperlinks pop up more detailed information if students need it.

MLA and APA templates help students document sources accurately.

Ways of Teaching with *The Norton Field Guide*

The Norton Field Guide has been designed to be easy for you to use, and to give you complete flexibility about how you use it. The two-books-in-one format allows you to teach from the rhetoric or from readings. There are clear assignment sequences if you want them, or you can create your own. If, for example, you wish to assign a position paper, there's a full chapter on that genre. If you want your students to use sources, add the appropriate research chapters. If you want them to submit an annotated bibliography, or keep a portfolio, add the appropriate chapters. Here are just some of the ways you can use this book:

If you teach with a rhetoric, you can organize your syllabus around the appropriate chapters in the *Field Guide*. Color-coded links will help you to supplement with appropriate readings from the anthology.

If you base your course on readings, you'll find more than 70 readings in this book. You can assign readings in particular genres in the anthology; or if you take a thematic approach, the Thematic Guide will lead you to readings on 18 themes. In either case, you can focus your course on readings, and color-coded links will refer students to corresponding writing guidelines elsewhere in the book — as shown here:

From a **READING** *in the anthology:*   *From a* **GENRE** *chapter:*

Engaging with the Text

154-55

1. According to Nicholas Howe, how has High Street changed over the years? What **BACKGROUND** and **CONTEXT** does Howe supply to help his readers understand the changes? How can the character of High Street be described today?

154
255-59

2. A good profile generally focuses on an unusual subject, or on something very ordinary shown in an interesting way. How does Howe make a fairly ordinary street in Columbus, Ohio, an **INTERESTING SUBJECT**?

3. According to Howe, what has **CAUSED** the various changes on High Street? Why do you think he addresses these causes in his profile of High Street? What do they contribute to the overall profile?

Key Features / Profiles

An interesting subject.   The subject may be something unusual, or it may be something very ordinary shown in an intriguing way. You might profile an interesting person (Shirley Barnes, for example, is someone who does something unusual), a place (Barnes's garage, perhaps), an event (a convention or rally for owners of Nash Metropolitans), or an activity (the workshops for other "Metheads").

Any necessary background or context.   A profile usually includes just enough information to let readers know where the subject comes from or why it is what it is. For example, Merlis gives us minimal background on

If you focus on genres, you will find complete chapters on 15 genres, and additional readings for 10 of those genres in the anthology. Color-coded links make it easy to navigate back and forth.

If you organize your course thematically, you can start with the Thematic Guide, which will lead you to readings on 18 themes. Each reading is followed by a number of writing suggestions, or you can assign the chapter on generating ideas to get students thinking about the theme. You can also assign them to do research on the theme, starting with the chapter on finding sources. Whatever genre they eventually decide on, there's likely to be a chapter to guide them.

If you want your students doing research, there are 7 chapters on the research process, including guidelines and sample papers demonstrating MLA and APA documentation. You can also assign any of the genre chapters, for the guides to writing in those chapters refer students to appropriate research chapters, with color-coded links and specific page numbers.

If you focus on particular strategies, you'll find full chapters on narration, description, comparison, and other strategies. These chapters focus on each pattern as a strategy that a writer might use for many writing purposes, and each chapter points out genres where that strategy is particularly useful. If you wish to assign students to write an essay organized entirely around a particular strategy, each of these chapters ends with links that will lead students through the process of doing so.

If you teach online, you will likely want to use the Field Guide Web Site, where you will find complete guides for literacy narratives, textual analyses, reports, and arguments, and many of the other chapters in this book, including MLA and APA guidelines and sample papers. You'll especially want to take advantage of the portfolio space, which allows you to receive and respond to student work electronically, using the Word commenting feature, and to sort papers by assignment, class, student, and date.

Acknowledgments

Writing never takes place in isolation; from start to finish, it is always a collaborative venture. In writing our acknowledgments, we struggled thinking about whom to include and how far back we should go in recognizing the many people who have influenced what we do as writers and teachers, and as authors of this book. Even as we offer our gratitude here by naming those who have most directly contributed to making *The Norton Field Guide to Writing, with readings* a reality, we are aware that many others have been instrumental as well.

Marilyn Moller, the editor of the *Field Guide*, tops our list of those we want to thank. She deserves great praise and our heartfelt appreciation for her keen instincts, creative thinking, and unflagging assistance. She is one of the finest editors we've had the good fortune to work with. The quality of this book is due in large part to her knowledge of the field of composition, her formidable editing and writing skills, and her sometimes uncanny ability to see the future of the teaching of writing.

We also want to commend and thank heartily Erin Granville, our talented associate editor who kept us and the text on track with insightful suggestions and steadfast help. Many others at Norton contributed to this version of the *Field Guide*, starting with Steve Dunn, who had the foresight to get us thinking about this new version even before teachers began asking for it. We also thank Marian Johnson, whose sensitivity to language and eye for detail improved almost every page, and Diane O'Connor for transforming the manuscript into a finished product in record time. We thank Anna Palchik for the user-friendly interior design and Debra Morton Hoyt for the whimsical cover. Mike Fleming copyedited and Maura Burnett proofread, both with careful attention to detail, and Cat Spencer helped us in ways large and small. Katrina Washington and Rivka Genesen deserve mention for their tenacious efforts to secure permissions for the readings, as does Stephanie Romeo for researching the images. We owe a special debt to Mike Wright for promoting this book so enthusiastically and skillfully. The success of the *Field Guide* is due in no small part to his efforts. In fact, we want to thank the entire Norton sales staff; it's good to have you with us at the composition end of the hall.

We also wish to acknowledge the generous support we've enjoyed at Wright State and Arizona State. At Wright State, Rich has many, many people to thank for their support and assistance over the many years he's been working on the *Norton Field Guide*; among them Brady Allen, Debbie Bertsch (now at Columbus State Community College), Vicki Burke, Jane

Blakelock, Adrienne Cassel (now at Sinclair Community College), Jimmy Chesire, Carol Cornett, Byron Crews, Catherine Crowley, Deborah Crusan, Sally DeThomas, Stephanie Dickie, Scott Geisel, Beth Klaisner, Peggy Lindsey, Nancy Mack, Marty Maner, Cynthia Marshall, Sarah McGinley, Michelle Metzner, Kristie Rowe, Bobby Rubin, Cathy Sayer, David Seitz, Caroline Simmons, Tracy Smith, Rick Strader, Mary Van Loveren, and A.J. Williams. He also thanks Henry Limouze, chair of the English Department, and Lynn Morgan, secretary to the writing programs. And thanks especially to the more than 100 graduate teaching assistants and 6,000 first-year students who have class-tested, taught, and studied with the various editions of the *Field Guide* and whose experiences have helped shape it.

At Arizona State, Maureen wants to acknowledge the support of Neal A. Lester, chair of the English Department, and the assistance of Jason Diller, her graduate research assistant — and to thank all her colleagues, all exemplary teachers and mentors, for creating a supportive intellectual environment, especially Philip Bernick, Sharon Crowley, Gregory Glau, Peter Goggin, Keith Miller, Camille Newton, Duane Roen, and Patricia Webb. Finally, Maureen wants to pay tribute to her students, who themselves are among her best teachers.

We are grateful to the many teachers across the country who reviewed the manuscript and offered valuable input and encouragement: Jonathan Alexander, University of Cincinnati; Cathryn Amdahl, Harrisburg Area Community College; Anne Beaufort, State University of New York at Stony Brook; Sue Beebe, Texas State University; Patrick Bizzaro, East Carolina University; Kevin Brooks, North Dakota State University; Ron Christiansen, Salt Lake Community College; Pat Dansby, San Jacinto College Central; Marvin Diogenes, Stanford University; Sarah Duerdan, Arizona State University; Russel Durst, University of Cincinnati; Sylvia Edwards, Longview Community College; Karen Fitts, West Chester University; Lloren A. Foster, Hampton University; Ivonne M. Garcia, Ohio State University; Gregory Glau, Arizona State University; Susanmarie Harrington, Indiana University-Purdue University Indianapolis; Paul Heilker, Virginia Polytechnic Institute and State University; Michael Hennessy, Texas State University; Maurice Hunt, Baylor University; Mitzi Walker Jones, University of Arkansas, Fort Smith; Rhonda Kyncl, the University of Oklahoma; Sally Lahmon, Sinclair

Community College; T. Michael Mackey, Community College of Denver; Magdalena Maczynska, Catholic University of America; Susan Miller, Mesa Community College; Thomas Miller, University of Arizona; Bryan Moore, Arkansas State University; Irv Peckham, Louisiana State University; Donna Qualley, Western Washington University; Nedra Reynolds, University of Rhode Island; Althea Rhodes, University of Arkansas, Fort Smith; Gardner Rogers, University of Illinois, Urbana/Champaign; William H. Smith, Weatherford College; Jeffrey Larsen Snodgrass, Prince George's Community College; Mary Stripling, Dallas Baptist University; John M. Thomson, Johnson County Community College; Monica Parrish Trent, Montgomery College, Rockville Campus; and Jarica Watts, University of Utah.

Rich has been grateful for the opportunity to meet with faculty at several schools using the *Field Guide* this past year and has learned a lot from discussions with the many teachers who attended. Thanks especially to those who organized these meetings and workshops: Susan Miller and Maureen Mathison at the University of Utah; Jeanne McDonald at Waubonsee Community College; Anne Dvorak and Diana Grahn at Longview Community College; Lori Gallinger, Rose Hawkins, and Jennifer Nelson at the Community College of Southern Nevada; and Stuart Blythe at Indiana University-Purdue University Fort Wayne.

It's customary to conclude by expressing gratitude to one's spouse and family, and for good reason. Writing and revising *The Norton Field Guide* over the past several years, we have enjoyed the loving and unconditional support of our spouses, Barb and Peter, who provide the foundation for all we do. Thank you. We couldn't have done it without you.

How to Use This Book

There's no one way to do anything, and writing is no exception. Some people need to do a lot of planning on paper; others write entire drafts in their heads. Some writers compose quickly and loosely, going back later to revise; others work on one sentence until they're satisfied with it, then move on to the next. And writers' needs vary from task to task, too: sometimes you know what you're going to write about and why, but need to figure out how to do it; other times your first job is to come up with a topic. *The Norton Field Guide to Writing* is designed to allow you to chart your own course as a writer—to offer you guidelines that suit your writing processes and needs. It is organized in seven parts:

1. **RHETORICAL SITUATIONS**: No matter what you're writing, it will always have some purpose, audience, genre, stance, and medium and design. This part will help you to consider each of these elements.

2. **GENRES**: Use these chapters for help with specific kinds of writing, from abstracts to lab reports to memoirs and more. You'll find more detailed guidance for four especially common assignments: literacy narratives, analyzing texts, reporting information, and arguing a position.

3. **PROCESSES**: These chapters offer general advice for all writing situations—how to go about generating ideas and text, drafting, revising and rewriting, editing, proofreading, compiling a portfolio—and collaborating productively with others.

4. **STRATEGIES**: Use the advice in this part to develop and organize your writing—to write effective beginnings and endings, to guide readers through your text, and to use comparison, description, dialogue, and other strategies as appropriate.

5. RESEARCH / DOCUMENTATION: Use this section for advice on how to do research, work with sources, and compose and document research-based texts using MLA and APA styles.

6. MEDIA / DESIGN: This section offers guidance in designing your work and working with visuals, and in delivering what you write on paper, on screen, or in person.

7. READINGS: Here you'll find more than 50 readings in 10 of the genres, all providing good examples of the kinds of writing you yourself may be assigned to do.

Ways into the Book

The Norton Field Guide gives you the writing advice you need, along with the flexibility to write in the way that works best for you. Here are some of the ways you can find what you need in the book.

Brief menus.   Inside the front cover you'll find a list of all the chapters; start here if you are looking for a chapter on a certain kind of writing or a general writing issue. Inside the back cover is a list of all the readings in the ANTHOLOGY part of the book.

Complete contents.   Pages xv–xxxiv contain a detailed table of contents. Look here if you need to find a reading or a specific section in a chapter.

Guides to writing.   If you know the kind of writing you need to do, you'll find guides to writing fifteen common genres in Part 2. These guides are designed to help you through all the decisions you have to make — from coming up with a topic to organizing your materials to editing and proof reading your final draft.

Color-coding.   The parts of this book are color-coded for easy reference: red for RHETORICAL SITUATIONS, green for GENRES, lavender for PROCESSES, orange for STRATEGIES, blue for RESEARCH / DOCUMENTATION, yellow for MEDIA / DESIGN, and apple green for READINGS. You'll find a key to the colors on the front cover flap and also at the foot of each left-hand page. When you see a word screened in a color, that tells you where you can find additional detail on the topic.

Glossary / index. At the back of the book is a combined glossary and index, where you'll find full definitions of key terms and topics, along with a list of the pages where everything is covered in detail.

Directories to MLA and APA documentation. A brief directory inside the back cover will lead you to guidelines on citing sources and composing a list of references or works cited. The documentation models are color-coded so you can easily see the key details.

The Web site. You can also start at wwnorton.com/write/fieldguide. There you'll find a Writing Toolbar that provides electronic access to some of what's in the book, including writing guides for several genres, MLA and APA guidelines, the glossary, a portfolio space for submitting writing to your teacher electronically, and more.

Ways of Getting Started

If you know your genre, simply turn to the appropriate genre chapter. There you'll find model readings, a description of the genre's Key Features, and a Guide to Writing that will help you come up with a topic, generate text, organize and write a draft, get response, revise, edit, and proofread. The genre chapters also point out places where you might need to do research, use certain writing strategies (comparison, description, and so on), design your text a certain way—and direct you to the exact pages in the book where you can find help doing so.

If you know your topic, you might start with some of the activities in Chapter 22, Generating Ideas and Text. From there, you might turn to Chapter 40, for help Finding Sources on the topic. When it comes time to narrow your topic and come up with a thesis statement, Chapter 29 can help. If your assignment or your thesis defines your genre, turn to that chapter; if not, consult Chapter 3 for help determining the appropriate genre, and then turn to that genre chapter. The genre chapters point out places where you might need to do more research, use certain writing strategies (comparison, description, and so on), design your text a certain way—and direct you to the exact pages in the book where you can find help doing so.

Contents

Part 2   Genres   19

Part 3   Processes   *193*

Part 4 Strategies *237*

Part 7   Readings   *485*

50 Literacy Narratives   *487*

56 Memoirs   *715*

57 Profiles   *747*

58 Proposals   *776*

Thematic Guide to the Readings

History

Home and Family

Identity

Language and Literacy

Science and Technology

World Cultures and Global Issues

part 1

Rhetorical Situations

Whenever we write, whether it's email to a friend or a toast for a wedding, an English essay or a résumé, we face some kind of rhetorical situation. We have a **PURPOSE**, a certain **AUDIENCE**, a particular **STANCE**, a **GENRE**, and a **MEDIUM** to consider — and often as not a **DESIGN**. All are important elements that we need to think about carefully. The following chapters offer brief discussions of those elements of the rhetorical situation, along with questions that can help you make the choices you need to as you write. See also the fifteen **GENRES** chapters for guidelines for considering your rhetorical situation in specific kinds of writing.

Rhetorical Situations

Purpose   1

All writing has a purpose. We write to explore our thoughts and emotions, to express ourselves, to entertain; we write to record words and events, to communicate with others, to try to persuade others to believe as we do or to behave in certain ways. In fact, we often have several purposes at the same time. We may write an essay in which we try to persuade an audience of something, but as we write, we may also be exploring our thoughts on the subject. Look, for example, at this passage from a 2002 *New York Time's Magazine* essay about the compensation of chief executive officers by economist and editorial columnist Paul Krugman:

> Is it news that C.E.O.'s of large American corporations make a lot of money? Actually, it is. They were always well paid compared with the average worker, but there is simply no comparison between what executives got a generation ago and what they are paid today.
>
> Over the past 30 years most people have seen only modest salary increases: the average annual salary in America, expressed in 1998 dollars (that is, adjusted for inflation), rose from $32,522 in 1970 to $35,864 in 1999. That's about a 10 percent increase over 29 years — progress, but not much. Over the same period, however, according to *Fortune* magazine, the average real annual compensation of the top 100 C.E.O.'s went from $1.3 million — 39 times the pay of an average worker — to $37.5 million, more than 1,000 times the pay of ordinary workers.
>
> The explosion in C.E.O. pay over the past 30 years is an amazing story in its own right, and an important one. But it is only the most spectacular indicator of a broader story, the reconcentration of income and wealth in the U.S. The rich have always been different from you and me, but they are far more different now than they were not long ago — indeed, they are as different now as they were when F. Scott Fitzgerald made his famous remark.
>
> —Paul Krugman, "For Richer"

Krugman is reporting information here, outlining how top business executives' pay has increased over the last thirty years. He is also making an argument, that their pay is far greater than it was not too long ago and that this difference in income resembles the disparity that characterized the United States right before the Great Depression. (Krugman, writing for a magazine, is also using a style—dashes, contractions, rhetorical questions that he then answers—that strives to be entertaining while it informs and argues.)

Even though our purposes may be many, knowing our primary reason for writing can help us shape that writing and understand how to proceed with it. Our purpose can determine the genre we choose, our audience, even the way we design what we write.

Identify your purpose. While writing often has many purposes, we usually focus on one. When you get an assignment or see a need to write, ask yourself what the primary purpose of the writing task is: to entertain? to inform? to persuade? to demonstrate your knowledge or your writing ability? What are your own goals? What are your audience's expectations, and do they affect the way you define your purpose?

Thinking about Purpose

- *What do you want your audience to do, think, or feel?* How will they use what you tell them?

- *What does this writing task call on you to do?* Do you need to show that you have mastered certain content or skills? Do you have an assignment that specifies a particular **STRATEGY** or **GENRE**—to compare two things, perhaps, or to argue a position?

- *What are the best ways to achieve your purpose?* What kind of **STANCE** should you take? Should you write in a particular genre? Do you have a choice of **MEDIUM,** and does your text require any special **DESIGN** elements?

237–328 ◆
19–192 ▲
12–14 ■
451–84 □

Audience 2

Who will read (or hear) what you are writing? A seemingly obvious but crucially important question. Your audience affects your writing in various ways. Consider a piece of writing as simple as a note left on the kitchen table:

Jon —
Please take the chicken out to thaw,
and don't forget to feed Annye.
Remember: Dr. Wong at 4.
Love,
Mom

On the surface, this brief note is a straightforward reminder to do three things. But in fact it is a complex message filled with compressed information for a specific audience. The writer (Mom) counts on the reader (her son) to know a lot that can be left unsaid. She expects that Jon knows that the chicken is in the freezer and needs to thaw in time to be cooked for dinner; she knows that he knows who Annye is (a pet?), what he or she is fed, and how much; she assumes that Jon knows who (and where) Dr. Wong is. She doesn't need to spell any of that out because she knows what Jon knows and what he needs to know—and in her note she can be brief. She understands her audience. Think how different such a reminder would be were it written to another audience—a babysitter, perhaps, or a friend helping out while Mom is out of town.

What you write, how much you write, how you phrase it, even your choice of genre (memo, essay, email, note, speech)—all are influenced by the audience you envision. And your audience will interpret your writing according to their expectations and experiences.

When you are a student, your teachers are most often your audience, so you need to be aware of their expectations and know the conventions (rules, often unstated) for writing in specific academic fields. You may make statements that seem obvious to you, not realizing that your instructors may consider them assertions that must be proved with evidence of one sort or another. Or you may write more or less formally than teachers expect. Understanding your audience's expectations — by asking outright, by reading materials in a related field, by trial and error — is important to your success as a writer.

This point is worth dwelling on. You are probably reading this text for a writing course. As a student, you will be expected to produce essays with few or no errors. If you have a job in an office or correspond using email, you may question such standards; after all, much of the email you get at work or from friends is not grammatically perfect. But in a writing class, the instructor needs to see your best work. Whatever the rhetorical situation, your writing must meet the expectations of your audience.

Identify your audience. Audiences may be defined as *known, multiple,* or *unknown. Known audiences* can include people with whom you're familiar as well as people you don't know personally but whose needs and expectations you do know. You yourself are a known, familiar audience, and you write to and for yourself often. Class notes, to-do lists, reminders, and journals are all written primarily for an audience of one: you. For that reason, they are often in shorthand, full of references and code that you alone understand. Other known, familiar audiences include anyone you actually know — friends, relatives, teachers, classmates — and whose needs and expectations you understand. You can also know what certain readers want and need, even if you've never met them personally, if you write for them within a specific shared context. Such a known audience might include computer gamers who read instructions for beating a game that you have posted on the Internet; you don't know those people, but you know roughly what they know about the game and what they need to know, and you know how to write about it in ways they will understand.

You often have to write for *multiple audiences.* Business memos or reports may be written initially for a supervisor, but he or she may pass them along to others. Grant proposals are a good example: the National Cancer Institute Web site advises scientists applying for grants to bear in mind that the application may have six levels of readers—each, of course, with its own expectations and perspectives. Even writing for a class might involve multiple audiences: your instructor and your classmates.

Unknown audiences can be the most difficult to address since you can't be sure what they know, what they need to know, how they'll react. Such an audience could be your downstairs neighbor, whom you say hello to but with whom you've never had a real conversation; how will she respond to your letter asking her to sponsor you in an upcoming charity walk? Another unknown audience—perhaps surprisingly—might be many of your instructors, who want—and expect!—you to write in ways that are new to you. While you can benefit from analyzing any audience, you need to think most carefully about those you don't know.

Thinking about Audience

- *Whom do you want to reach?* To whom are you writing (or speaking)?

- *What is your audience's background—their education and life experiences?* It may be important for you to know, for example, whether your readers attended college, fought in a war, or have young children.

- *What are their interests?* What do they like? What motivates them? What do they care about?

- *Is there any demographic information that you should keep in mind?* Consider whether race, gender, sexual orientation, disabilities, occupations, religious beliefs, economic status, and so on, should affect what or how you write. For example, writers for *Men's Health*, *InStyle*, and *Out* must consider the particular interests of each magazine's readers.

- *What political circumstances may affect their reading?* What attitudes—opinions, special interests, biases—may affect the way your audience reads your piece? Are your readers conservative, liberal, or middle of the road? Politics may take many other forms as well—retirees on a fixed income may object to increased school taxes, so a letter arguing for such an increase would need to appeal to them differently than would a similar letter sent to parents of young children.

- *What does your audience already know — or believe — about your topic? What do you need to tell them? What is the best way to do so?* Those retirees who oppose school taxes already know that taxes are a burden for them; they may need to know why schools are justified in asking for more money every few years when other government organizations do not. A good way to explain this may be with a bar graph showing how good schools with adequate funding benefit property values. Consider which STRATEGIES will be effective — narrative, comparison, something else?

237–328 ◆

- *What's your relationship with your audience, and how does it affect your language and tone?* Do you know them, or not? Are they friends? colleagues? mentors? adversaries? completely unknown to you? Will they likely share your STANCE? In general, you need to write more formally when you're addressing readers you don't know, and you may address friends and colleagues more informally than you would a boss.

12–14 ■

- *What does your audience need and expect from you?* Your history professor, for example, may need to know how well you can discuss the economy of the late Middle Ages in order to assess your learning; that same professor may expect you to write a carefully reasoned argument, drawing conclusions from various sources, with a readily identifiable thesis in the first paragraph. Your boss, on the other hand, may need an informal email that briefly lists your sales contacts for the day; she may expect that you list the contacts in the order in which you saw them, that you clearly identify each one, and that you give a few words about how well each contact went. What GENRE is most appropriate?

19–192 ▲

- *What kind of response do you want?* Do you want to persuade readers to do or believe something? to accept your information on a topic? to understand why an experience you once had matters to you?

- *How can you best appeal to your audience?* Is there a particular MEDIUM that will best reach them? Are there any DESIGN requirements? (Elderly readers may need larger type, for instance.)

451–84 ☐
451–84 ☐

■ rhetorical situations ▲ genres ○ processes ◆ strategies ● research mla/apa ☐ media/design

Genres are kinds of writing. Letters, profiles, reports, position papers, poems, Web pages, instructions, parodies — even jokes — are genres. Genres have particular conventions for presenting information that help writers write and readers read. For example, here is the beginning of a profile of a mechanic who repairs a specific kind of automobile:

> Her business card reads Shirley Barnes, M.D., and she's a doctor, all right — a Metropolitan Doctor. Her passion is the Nash Metropolitan, the little car produced by Austin of England for American Motors between 1954 and 1962. Barnes is a legend among southern California Met lovers — an icon, a beacon, and a font of useful knowledge and freely offered opinions.

A profile offers a written portrait of someone or something that informs and sometimes entertains, often examining its subject from a particular angle — in this case, as a female mechanic who fixes Nash Metropolitans. While the language in this example is informal and lively ("she's a doctor, all right"), the focus is on the subject, Shirley Barnes, "M.D." If this same excerpt were presented as a poem, however, the new genre would change our reading:

> Her business card reads
> Shirley Barnes, M.D.,
> and she's a doctor, all right
> — a Metropolitan Doctor.
> Her passion is the Nash Metropolitan,
> the little car produced by Austin of England
> for American Motors between 1954 and 1962.
> Barnes is a legend
> among southern California Met lovers
> — an icon,

a beacon,
and a font of useful knowledge and
freely offered opinions.

The content and words haven't changed, but the presentation invites us to read not only to learn about Shirley Barnes but also to explore the significance of the words and phrases on each line, to read for deeper meaning and greater appreciation of language. The genre thus determines how we read and how we interpret what we read.

Genres help us write by defining features for conveying certain kinds of information. They give readers clues about what sort of information they're likely to find and so help them figure out how to read ("Ah! A letter from Brit!" or "Thank goodness! I found the instructions for programming this DVD player"). At the same time, writers sometimes challenge genre conventions, reshaping them as communicative needs and technologies change. For example, computers have enabled us to add visuals to texts that we never before thought to illustrate.

19–192 ▲ **Identify your genre.**   Does your writing situation call for a certain **GENRE?** A memo? A report? A proposal? A letter? Academic assignments generally specify the genre ("take a position," "analyze the text"), but if the genre isn't clear, ask your instructor.

Thinking about Genre

- *What is your genre, and does it affect what content you can or should include?* Objective information? Researched source material? Your own opinions? Personal experience?

237–328 ◆ - *Does your genre call for any specific* **STRATEGIES?** Profiles, for example, usually include some narration; lab reports often explain a process.

- *Does your genre require a certain organization?* Most proposals, for instance, first identify a problem and then offer a solution. Some genres leave room for choice. Business letters delivering good news might be organized differently than those making sales pitches.

rhetorical situations   genres   processes   strategies   research mla/apa   media/ design

- *Does your genre affect your tone?* An abstract of a scholarly paper calls for a different tone than a memoir. Should your words sound serious and scholarly? brisk and to the point? objective? opinionated? Sometimes your genre affects the way you communicate your **STANCE.**

12–14

- *Does the genre require formal (or informal) language?* A letter to the mother of a friend asking for a summer job in her bookstore calls for more formal language than does an email to the friend thanking him for the lead.

- *Do you have a choice of medium?* Some genres call for print; others for an electronic medium. Sometimes you have a choice: a résumé, for instance, can be mailed (in which case it must be printed), or it may be emailed. Some teachers want reports turned in on paper; others prefer that they be emailed or posted to a class Web site. If you're not sure what **MEDIUM** you can use, ask.

451–84

- *Does your genre have any design requirements?* Some genres call for paragraphs; others require lists. Some require certain kinds of typefaces—you wouldn't use **Impact** for a personal narrative, nor would you likely use **DrSeuss** for an invitation to Grandma's sixty-fifth birthday party. Different genres call for different **DESIGN** elements.

451–84

4 Stance

Whenever you write, you have a certain stance, an attitude toward your topic. The way you express that stance affects the way you come across as a writer and a person. This email from a college student to his father, for example, shows a thoughtful, reasonable stance for a carefully researched argument:

> Hi Dad,
> I'll get right to the point: I'd like to buy a car. I saved over $2500 from working this summer, and I've found three different cars that I can get for under $2000. That'll leave me $400 to cover the insurance. I can park in Lot J, over behind Monte Hall, for $75 for both semesters. And I can earn gas and repair money by upping my hours at the cafeteria. It won't cost you any more, and if I have a car, you won't have to come and pick me up when I want to come home.
> Love,
> Michael

While such a stance can't guarantee that Dad will give permission, it's more likely to produce results than this version:

> Hi Dad,
> I'm buying a car. A guy in my Western Civ course has a cool Chevy he wants to get rid of. I've got $2500 saved from working this summer, it's mine, and I'm going to use it to get some wheels. Mom said you'd blow your top if I did, but I want this car.
> Michael

The writer of the first email respects his reader and offers reasoned arguments and evidence of research to convince him that buying a car is an action that will benefit them both. The writer of the second, by contrast, seems impulsive, ready to buy the first car that comes along, and

rhetorical situations ▪ genres ▲ processes ○ strategies ◆ research mla/apa ● media/ design □

defiant—he's picking a fight. Each email reflects a certain stance that shows the writer as a certain kind of person dealing with a situation in a certain way and establishing a certain relationship with his audience.

Identify your stance.   What is your attitude about your topic? Critical? Curious? Opinionated? Objective? Passionate? Indifferent? You convey your attitude about your topic (and your audience) in the tone your writing takes. And your tone may be affected by your relationship to your audience. How do you want them to see you? As a colleague sharing information? As a good student showing what you can do? As an advocate for a position? Often your stance is affected by your GENRE; for example, lab reports require an objective, unemotional stance that emphasizes the content and minimizes the writer's own attitudes. Memoir, by comparison, allows you to reveal your feelings about your topic. As a writer, you communicate your stance through your tone, in the words you choose.

▲ 19–192

Just as you likely alter what you say depending on whether you're speaking to a boss, an instructor, a parent, or a good friend, so you need to make similar adjustments as a writer. It's a question of appropriateness: we behave in certain ways in various social situations, and writing is a social situation. You might sign email to a friend with an x and an o, but in an email to your supervisor you'll likely sign off with a "Many thanks" or "Regards." To write well, you need to write with integrity, to say what you wish to say, yet you also must understand that in writing, as in speaking, your voice needs to suit your purpose, your relationship to your audience, the way in which you wish your audience to perceive you, and your medium. In writing as in other aspects of life, the Golden Rule applies: "Do unto audiences as you would have them do unto you." Address readers respectfully if you want them to respond to your words with respect.

Thinking about Stance

- *What is your stance, and how can you present it best to achieve your purpose?* If you're writing about something you take very seriously, be

sure that your language and even your typeface reflect that seriousness. Make sure your stance is appropriate to your **PURPOSE.**

3–4

- *What tone will best convey your stance?* Do you want to be seen as reasonable? angry? thoughtful? gentle? funny? ironic? What aspects of your
personality do you want to project? Check your writing for words that
reflect that tone — and for ones that do not (and revise as necessary).

- *How is your stance likely to be received by your audience?* Your tone and
especially your attitude toward your **AUDIENCE** will affect how willing
they are to take your argument seriously.

5–8

- *Should you openly reveal your stance?* Do you want or need to announce
your own perspective on your topic? Will doing so help you reach your
audience, or would it be better to make your argument without saying directly where you're coming from?

Media/Design 5

In its broadest sense, a *medium* is a go-between: a way for information to be conveyed from one person to another. We communicate through many media, verbal and nonverbal: our bodies (we catch someone's eye, wave, nod), our voices (we whisper, talk, shout, groan), and various technologies, including handwriting, print, telephone, radio, CD, film, and computer.

Each medium has unique characteristics that influence both what and how we communicate. As an example, consider this message: "I haven't told you this before, but I love you." Most of the time, we communicate messages like that one in person, using the medium of voice (with, presumably, help from eye contact and touch). A phone call will do, though most of us would think it a poor second choice, and a handwritten letter or note would be acceptable, if necessary. Few of us would break such news on a Web site or during a radio call-in program.

By contrast, imagine whispering the following sentence in a darkened room: "By the last decades of the nineteenth century, the territorial expansion of the United States had left almost all Indians confined to reservations." That sentence starts a chapter in a history textbook, and it would be strange indeed to whisper it into someone's ear. It is available in the medium of print, in the textbook, but it may also be read on a Web site, in promotional material for the book, or on a PowerPoint slide accompanying an oral presentation. Each medium has different uses and takes different forms, and each has distinctive characteristics. As you can see, we can choose various media depending on our purpose and audience. *The Norton Field Guide* focuses mostly on three media: **PRINT**, **SPOKEN**, and **ELECTRONIC**.

453–63
464–75
476–84

Because we now do most of our writing on computers, we are increasingly expected to pay close attention to the look of the material we write. No matter the medium, a text's *design* affects the way it is received and understood. A typed letter on official letterhead sends a different message than the same letter handwritten on pastel stationery, whatever the words on the page. Classic type sends a different message than *flowery italics*. Some genres and media (and audiences) demand photos, diagrams, color. Some information is easier to explain—and read—in the form of a pie chart or a bar graph than in the form of a paragraph. Some reports and documents are so long and complex that they need to be divided into sections, which are then best labeled with headings. Those are some of the elements to consider when you are thinking about how to design what you write.

Identify your media and design needs.   Does your writing situation call for a certain medium and design? A printed essay? An oral report with visual aids? A Web site? Academic assignments often assume a particular medium and design, but if you're unsure about your options or the degree of flexibility you have, check with your instructor.

Thinking about Media

453–63
464–75
476–84

- *What medium are you using—* PRINT? SPOKEN? ELECTRONIC?—*and how does it affect the way you will write your text?* A printed résumé is usually no more than one page long; a scannable résumé sent via email has no length limits. An oral presentation should contain detailed information; accompanying PowerPoint slides should provide only an outline.

237–328

- *Does your medium affect your organization and* STRATEGIES? Long paragraphs are fine on paper but don't work well on the Web. On Power-Point slides, phrases or key words work better than sentences. In print, you need to define unfamiliar terms; on the Web, you can sometimes just add a link to a definition found elsewhere.

- *How does your medium affect your language?* Some print documents require a more formal voice than spoken media; email often invites greater informality.

- *Should you use a combination of media?* Should you include audio or video in Web text? Do you need PowerPoint slides, handouts, or other visuals to accompany an oral presentation?

rhetorical situations · genres · processes · strategies · research mla/apa · media/design

Thinking about Design

- *What's the appropriate look for your* RHETORICAL SITUATION? Should your text look serious? whimsical? personal? something else? What design elements will suit your audience, purpose, genre, and medium?

1–17

- *Does your text have any elements that need to be designed?* Is there any information you would like to highlight by putting it in a box? Are there any key terms that should be bold?

- *What typeface(s) are appropriate* to your audience, purpose, genre, and medium?

- *Are you including any illustrations?* Should you? Is there any information in your text that would be easier to understand as a chart or graph? Will your AUDIENCE expect or need any?

5–8

- *Should you include headings?* Would they help you organize your materials and help readers follow the text? Does your GENRE require them?

9–11

part 2

Genres

When we make a shopping list, we automatically write each item we need in a single column. When we email a friend, we begin with a salutation: "Hi, Brian." Whether we are writing a letter, a résumé, a lab report, or a proposal, we know generally what it should contain and what it should look like because we are familiar with each of those genres. Genres are kinds of writing, and texts in any given genre share goals and features—a proposal, for instance, generally starts out by identifying a problem and then suggests a certain solution. The chapters in this part provide guidelines for writing in fifteen common academic genres. First come detailed chapters on four genres often assigned in writing classes: LITERACY NARRATIVES, essays ANALYZING TEXTS, REPORTS, and ARGUMENTS, followed by brief chapters on ELEVEN OTHER GENRES.

Genres

Narratives are stories, and we read and tell them for many different purposes. Parents read their children bedtime stories as an evening ritual. Preachers base their Sunday sermons on Bible stories to teach the importance of religious faith. Grandparents tell how things used to be (sometimes the same stories year after year). Schoolchildren tell teachers that their dog ate their homework. College applicants write about significant moments in their lives. Writing students are often called upon to compose literacy narratives to explore how they learned to read or write. This chapter provides detailed guidelines for writing a literacy narrative. We'll begin with three good examples.

Readings

RICK BRAGG
All Over But the Shoutin'

This narrative is from All Over But the Shoutin,' *a 1997 autobiography by Rick Bragg, a former reporter for the* New York Times *and author of* I Am a Soldier, Too: The Jessica Lynch Story *(2003). Bragg grew up in Alabama, and in this narrative he recalls when, as a teenager, he paid a final visit to his dying father.*

> He was living in a little house in Jacksonville, Alabama, a college and mill town that was the closest urban center—with its stoplights and a high school and two supermarkets—to the country roads we roamed in our raggedy cars. He lived in the mill village, in one of those houses the mills subsidized for their workers, back when companies still did things like

that. It was not much of a place, but better than anything we had ever lived in as a family. I knocked and a voice like an old woman's, punctuated with a cough that sounded like it came from deep in the guts, told me to come on in, it ain't locked. It was dark inside, but light enough to see what looked like a bundle of quilts on the corner of a sofa. Deep inside them was a ghost of a man, his hair and beard long and going dirty gray, his face pale and cut with deep grooves. I knew I was in the right house because my daddy's only real possessions, a velvet-covered board pinned with medals, sat inside a glass cabinet on a table. But this couldn't be him.

He coughed again, spit into a can and struggled to his feet, but stopped somewhere short of standing straight up, as if a stoop was all he could manage. "Hey, Cotton Top," he said, and then I knew. My daddy, who was supposed to be a still-young man, looked like the walking dead, not just old but damaged, poisoned, used up, crumpled up and thrown in a corner to die. I thought that the man I would see would be the trim, swaggering, high-toned little rooster of a man who stared back at me from the pages of my mother's photo album, the young soldier clowning around in Korea, the arrow-straight, good-looking boy who posed beside my mother back before the fields and mophandle and the rest of it took her looks. The man I remembered had always dressed nice even when there was no cornmeal left, whose black hair always shone with oil, whose chin, even when it wobbled from the beer, was always angled up, high.

I thought he would greet me with that strong voice that sounded so fine when he laughed and so evil when, slurred by a quart of corn likker, he whirled through the house and cried and shrieked, tormented by things we could not see or even imagine. I thought he would be the man and monster of my childhood. But that man was as dead as a man could be, and this was what remained, like when a snake sheds its skin and leaves a dry and brittle husk of itself hanging in the Johnson grass.

"It's all over but the shoutin' now, ain't it, boy," he said, and when he let the quilt slide from his shoulders I saw how he had wasted away, how the bones seemed to poke out of his clothes, and I could see how it killed his pride to look this way, unclean, and he looked away from me for a moment, ashamed.

He made a halfhearted try to shake my hand but had a coughing fit again that lasted a minute, coughing up his life, his lungs, and after

5

that I did not want to touch him. I stared at the tops of my sneakers, ashamed to look at his face. He had a dark streak in his beard below his lip, and I wondered why, because he had never liked snuff. Now I know it was blood.

I remember much of what he had to say that day. When you don't see someone for eight, nine years, when you see that person's life red on their lips and know that you will never see them beyond this day, you listen close, even if what you want most of all is to run away.

"Your momma, she alright?" he said.

I said I reckon so.

"The other boys? They alright?"

I said I reckon so. 10

Then he was quiet for a minute, as if trying to find the words to a question to which he did not really want an answer.

"They ain't never come to see me. How come?"

I remember thinking, fool, why do you think? But I just choked down my words, and in doing so I gave up the only real chance I would ever have to accuse him, to attack him with the facts of his own sorry nature and the price it had cost us all. The opportunity hung perfectly still in the air in front of my face and fists, and I held my temper and let it float on by. I could have no more challenged him, berated him, hurt him, than I could have kicked some three-legged dog. Life had kicked his ass pretty good.

"How come?"

I just shrugged. 15

For the next few hours—unless I was mistaken, having never had one before—he tried to be my father. Between coughing and long pauses when he fought for air to generate his words, he asked me if I liked school, if I had ever gotten any better at math, the one thing that just flat evaded me. He asked me if I ever got even with the boy who blacked my eye ten years ago, and nodded his head, approvingly, as I described how I followed him into the boys' bathroom and knocked his dick string up to his watch pocket, and would have dunked his head in the urinal if the aging principal, Mr. Hand, had not had to pee and caught me dragging him across the concrete floor.

He asked me about basketball and baseball, said he had heard I had a good game against Cedar Springs, and I said pretty good, but it was two years ago, anyway. He asked if I had a girlfriend and I said,

"One," and he said, "Just one?" For the slimmest of seconds he almost grinned and the young, swaggering man peeked through, but disappeared again in the disease that cloaked him. He talked and talked and never said a word, at least not the words I wanted.

He never said he was sorry.

He never said he wished things had turned out different.

He never acted like he did anything wrong.

Part of it, I know, was culture. Men did not talk about their feelings in his hard world. I did not expect, even for a second, that he would bare his soul. All I wanted was a simple acknowledgment that he was wrong, or at least too drunk to notice that he left his pretty wife and sons alone again and again, with no food, no money, no way to get any, short of begging, because when she tried to find work he yelled, screamed, refused. No, I didn't expect much.

After a while he motioned for me to follow him into a back room where he had my present, and I planned to take it and run. He handed me a long, thin box, and inside was a brand-new, well-oiled Remington .22 rifle. He said he had bought it some time back, just kept forgetting to give it to me. It was a fine gun, and for a moment we were just like anybody else in the culture of that place, where a father's gift of a gun to his son is a rite. He said, with absolute seriousness, not to shoot my brothers.

I thanked him and made to leave, but he stopped me with a hand on my arm and said wait, that ain't all, that he had some other things for me. He motioned to three big cardboard egg cartons stacked against one wall.

Inside was the only treasure I truly have ever known.

I had grown up in a house in which there were only two books, the King James Bible and the spring seed catalog. But here, in these boxes, were dozens of hardback copies of everything from Mark Twain to Sir Arthur Conan Doyle. There was a water-damaged Faulkner, and the nearly complete set of Edgar Rice Burroughs's Tarzan. There was poetry and trash, Zane Grey's Riders of the Purple Sage, and a paperback with two naked women on the cover. There was a tiny, old copy of Arabian Nights, threadbare Hardy Boys, and one Hemingway. He had bought most of them at a yard sale, by the box or pound, and some at a flea market. He did not even know what he was giving me, did not recognize most of the writers. "Your momma said you still liked to read," he said.

rhetorical situations   genres   processes   strategies   research mla/apa   media/ design

There was Shakespeare. My father did not know who he was, exactly, but he had heard the name. He wanted them because they were pretty, because they were wrapped in fake leather, because they looked like rich folks' books. I do not love Shakespeare, but I still have those books. I would not trade them for a gold monkey.

"They's maybe some dirty books in there, by mistake, but I know you ain't interested in them, so just throw 'em away," he said. "Or at least, throw 'em away before your momma sees 'em." And then I swear to God he winked.

I guess my heart should have broken then, and maybe it did, a little. I guess I should have done something, anything, besides mumble "Thank you, Daddy." I guess that would have been fine, would not have betrayed in some way my mother, my brothers, myself. But I just stood there, trapped somewhere between my long-standing, comfortable hatred, and what might have been forgiveness. I am trapped there still.

Bragg's narrative illustrates all the features that make a narrative good: how the son and father react to each other creates the kind of suspense that keeps us reading; vivid details and rich dialogue bring the scene to life. His later reflections make the significance of that final meeting very clear—and the carton of books reveals the story's complex connection to Bragg's literacy.

RICHARD BULLOCK

How I Learned about the Power of Writing

I wrote this literacy narrative, about my own experience learning to read, as a model for my students in a first-year writing course.

When I was little, my grandmother and grandfather lived with us in a big house on a busy street in Willoughby, Ohio. My grandmother spent a lot of time reading to me. She mostly read the standards, like *The Little Engine That Could,* over and over and over again. She also let me help her plant African violets (I stood on a chair in her kitchen, carefully placing fuzzy violet leaves into small pots of soil) and taught me to tell time (again in her kitchen, where I watched the minute hand move slowly around the dial and tried in vain to see the hour hand move). All that attention and time spent studying the pages as Grandma read them again and again led me to start reading when I was around three years old.

My family was blue-collar, working-class, and—my grandmother excepted—not very interested in books or reading. But my parents took pride in my achievement and told stories about my precocious literacy, such as the time at a restaurant when the waitress bent over as I sat in my booster chair and asked, "What would you like, little boy?" I'm told I gave her a withering look and said, "I'd like to see a menu."

There was a more serious aspect to reading so young, however. At that time the murder trial of Dr. Sam Sheppard, a physician whose wife had been bludgeoned to death in their house, was the focus of lurid coverage in the Cleveland newspapers. Daily news stories recounted the grisly details of both the murder and the trial testimony, in which Sheppard maintained his innocence. (The story would serve as the inspiration for both *The Fugitive* TV series and the Harrison Ford movie of the same name.) Apparently I would get up early in the morning, climb over the side of my crib, go downstairs and fetch the paper, take it back upstairs to my crib, and be found reading about the trial when my parents got up. They learned that they had to beat me to the paper in the morning and remove the offending sections before my youthful eyes could see them.

The story of the Sheppard murder had a profound effect on me: it demonstrated the power of writing, for if my parents were so concerned that I not see certain things in print, those things must have had great importance. At the same time, adults' amazement that I could read was itself an inducement to continue: like any three-year-old, I liked attention, and if reading menus and the *Plain Dealer* would do it, well then, I'd keep reading.

As I got older, I also came to realize the great gift my grandmother had given me. While part of her motivation for spending so much time with me was undoubtedly to keep me entertained in a house isolated from other children at a time when I was too young for nursery school, another part of her motivation was a desire to shape me in a certain way. As the middle child in a large family in rural West Virginia, my grandmother had received a formal education only through the eighth grade, after which she had come alone to Cleveland to make a life for herself, working as a seamstress while reading the ancient Greeks and Etruscans on her own. She had had hopes that her daughter (my mother) would continue her education as she herself hadn't been able to, but Mom chose instead to marry Dad shortly after graduating from high school, and Dad hadn't even gotten that far—he had dropped out of school three days before graduation. So Grandma decided that I was going to be different, and she took over much of my preschool life to promote the love of learning that she herself had always had. It worked, and at ninety she got to see me graduate from college, the first in our family to do so.

In my literacy narrative, the disconnect between my age and my ability to read provides a frame for several anecdotes. The narrative's significance comes through in the final paragraph, in which I explore the effects of my grandmother's motivation for teaching me.

SHANNON NICHOLS

"Proficiency"

In the following literacy narrative, Shannon Nichols, a student at Wright State University, describes her experience taking the standardized writing proficiency test that high school students in Ohio must pass to graduate. She wrote this essay for a college writing course, where her audience included her classmates and instructor.

The first time I took the ninth-grade proficiency test was in March of eighth grade. The test ultimately determines whether students may receive a high school diploma. After months of preparation and anxiety, the pressure was on. Throughout my elementary and middle school years, I was a strong student, always on the honor roll. I never had a GPA below 3.0. I was smart, and I knew it. That is, until I got the results of the proficiency test.

Although the test was challenging, covering reading, writing, math, and citizenship, I was sure I had passed every part. To my surprise, I did pass every part—except writing. "Writing! Yeah right! How did I manage to fail writing, and by half a point, no less?" I thought to myself in disbelief. Seeing my test results brought tears to my eyes. I honestly could not believe it. To make matters worse, most of my classmates, including some who were barely passing eighth-grade English, passed that part.

Until that time, I loved writing just as much as I loved math. It was one of my strengths. I was good at it, and I enjoyed it. If anything, I thought I might fail citizenship. How could I have screwed up writing? I surely spelled every word correctly, used good grammar, and even used big words in the proper context. How could I have failed?

Finally I got over it and decided it was no big deal. Surely I would pass the next time. In my honors English class I worked diligently, passing with an A. By October I'd be ready to conquer that writing test. Well, guess what? I failed the test again, again with only 4.5 of the 5 points needed to pass. That time I did cry, and even went to my English teacher, Mrs. Brown, and asked, "How can I get A's in all my English classes but fail the writing part of the proficiency test twice?" She couldn't answer my question. Even my friends and classmates were confused. I felt like a failure. I had disappointed my family and seriously let myself down. Worst of all, I still couldn't figure out what I was doing wrong.

I decided to quit trying so hard. Apparently—I told myself—the people grading the tests didn't have the slightest clue about what constituted good writing. I continued to excel in class and passed the test on the third try. But I never again felt the same love of reading and writing.   5

This experience showed me just how differently my writing could be judged by various readers. Obviously all my English teachers and many others enjoyed or at least appreciated my writing. A poem I wrote was put on television once. I must have been a pretty good writer. Unfortunately the graders of the ninth-grade proficiency test didn't feel the same, and when students fail the test, the state of Ohio doesn't offer any explanation.

After I failed the test the first time, I began to hate writing, and I started to doubt myself. I doubted my ability and the ideas I wrote

rhetorical situations　　genres　　processes　　strategies　　research mla/apa　　media/ design

about. Failing the second time made things worse, so perhaps to protect myself from my doubts, I stopped taking English seriously. Perhaps
because of that lack of seriousness, I earned a 2 on the Advanced Placement English Exam, barely passed the twelfth-grade proficiency test,
and was placed in developmental writing in college. I wish I knew why
I failed that test, because then I might have written what was expected
on the second try, maintained my enthusiasm for writing, and continued to do well.

*Nichols's narrative focuses on her emotional reaction to failing a test that she
should have passed easily. The contrast between her demonstrated writing ability and her repeated failures creates a tension that captures readers' attention.
We want to know what will happen to her.*

For five
more literacy
narratives,
see
CHAPTER 50.

Key Features / Literacy Narratives

A well-told story.   As with most narratives, those about literacy often
set up some sort of situation that needs to be resolved. That need for resolution makes readers want to keep reading. We want to know whether
Nichols ultimately will pass the proficiency test. Some literacy narratives
simply explore the role that reading or writing played at some time in
someone's life—assuming, perhaps, that learning to read or write is a
challenge to be met.

Vivid detail.   Details can bring a narrative to life for readers by giving
them vivid mental images of the sights, sounds, smells, tastes, and textures of the world in which your story takes place. The details you use
when describing something can help readers picture places, people, and
events; dialogue can help them hear what is being said. We get a picture
of the only treasure Bragg has ever known through the details he provides:
"a water-damaged Faulkner," "a paperback with two naked women on the
cover," books "wrapped in fake leather." Similarly, we hear a three-year-
old's exasperation through his own words: "I'd like to see a menu." Dialogue can help bring a narrative to life.

Some indication of the narrative's significance. By definition, a literacy narrative tells something the writer remembers about learning to read or write. In addition, the writer needs to make clear why the incident matters to him or her. You may reveal its significance in various ways. Nichols does it when she says she no longer loves to read or write. Bragg is more direct when he tells us he would not trade the books for a gold monkey. The trick is to avoid tacking onto the end a statement about your narrative's significance as if it were a kind of moral of the story. Bragg's narrative would have far less power if he'd said, "Thus did my father teach me to value books of all kinds."

A GUIDE TO WRITING A LITERACY NARRATIVE

Choosing a Topic

In general, it's a good idea to focus on a single event that took place during a relatively brief period of time. For example:

- any early memory about writing or reading that you recall vividly
- someone who taught you to read or write
- a book or other text that has been significant for you in some way
- an event at school that was interesting, humorous, or embarrassing
- a writing or reading task that you found (or still find) difficult or challenging
- a memento that represents an important moment in your literacy development (perhaps the start of a **LITERACY PORTFOLIO**)
- the origins of your current attitudes about writing or reading
- perhaps more recent challenges: learning to write instant messages, learning to write email appropriately, learning to construct a Web page

234–35

Make a list of possible topics, and then choose one that you think will be interesting to you and to others — and that you're willing to share with others. If several seem promising, try them out on a friend or classmate.

rhetorical situations | genres | processes | strategies | research mla/apa | media/ design

Or just choose one and see where it leads; you can switch to another if need be. If you have trouble coming up with a topic, try **FREEWRITING, LISTING, CLUSTERING,** or **LOOPING**.

199–202

Considering the Rhetorical Situation

◼ **PURPOSE**	Why do you want to tell this story? To share a memory with others? To fulfill an assignment? To teach a lesson? To explore your past learning? Think about the reasons for your choice and how they will shape what you write.

3–4

◼ **AUDIENCE**	Are your readers likely to have had similar experiences? Would they tell similar stories? How much explaining will you have to do to help them understand your narrative? Can you assume that they will share your attitudes toward your story, or will you have to work at making them see your perspective? How much about your life are you willing to share with this audience?

5–8

◼ **STANCE**	What attitude do you want to project? Affectionate? Neutral? Critical? Do you wish to be sincere? serious? humorously detached? self-critical? self-effacing? something else? How do you want your readers to see you?

12–14

◼ **MEDIA / DESIGN**	Will your narrative be in print? presented orally? on a Web site? Will photos or other illustrations help you present your subject? Is there a typeface that conveys the right tone?

15–17

Generating Ideas and Text

Good literacy narratives share certain elements that make them interesting and compelling for readers. Remember that your goals are to tell the story as clearly and vividly as you can and to convey the meaning the incident has for you today. Start by writing out what you remember about the setting and those involved, perhaps trying out some of the methods in the chapter on GENERATING IDEAS AND TEXT. You may also want to INTERVIEW a teacher or parent who figures in your narrative.

199–204
350–52

Describe the setting. Where does your narrative take place? List the places where your story unfolds. For each place, write informally for a few minutes, DESCRIBING what you remember:

285–93

- *What do you see?* If you're inside, what color are the walls? What's hanging on them? What can you see out any windows? What else do you see? Books? Lined paper? Red ink? Are there people? Places to sit?

- *What do you hear?* A radiator hissing? Air conditioners? Leaves rustling? The wind howling? Rain? Someone reading aloud? Shouts? Cheers? Children playing? Music? The zing of an instant message arriving?

- *What do you smell?* Sweat? White paste? Perfume? Incense? Food cooking?

- *How and what do you feel?* Nervous? Happy? Cold? Hot? A scratchy wool sweater? Tight shoes? Rough wood on a bench?

- *What do you taste?* Gum? Mints? Graham crackers? Juice? Coffee?

Think about the key people. Narratives include people whose actions play an important role in the story. In your literacy narrative, you are probably one of those people. A good way to develop your understanding of the people in your narrative is to write about them:

285–93

- *Describe each person in a paragraph or so.* What do the people look like? How do they dress? How do they speak? Quickly? Slowly? With an accent? Do they speak clearly, or do they mumble? Do they use any distinctive words or phrases? You might begin by DESCRIBING their movements, their posture, their bearing, their facial expressions. Do they have a distinctive scent?

294–98

- *Recall (or imagine) some characteristic dialogue.* A good way to bring people to life and move a story along is with DIALOGUE, to let readers hear

them rather than just hearing about them. Try writing six to ten lines of dialogue between two people in your narrative. If you can't remember an actual conversation, make up one that could have happened. (After all, you are telling the story, and you get to decide how it is to be told.) If you don't recall a conversation, try to remember (and write down) some of the characteristic words or phrases that the people in your narrative used.

Write about "what happened."   At the heart of every good narrative is the answer to the question "What happened?" The action in a literacy NARRATIVE may be as dramatic as winning a spelling bee or as subtle as a conversation between two friends; both contain action, movement, or change that the narrative tries to capture for readers. A good story dramatizes the action. Try SUMMARIZING the action in your narrative in a paragraph—try to capture what happened. Use active and specific verbs (*pondered*, *shouted*, *laughed*) to describe the action as vividly as possible.

304–12

321–22

Consider the significance of the narrative.   You need to make clear the ways in which any event you are writing about is significant for you now. Write a page or so about the meaning it has for you. How did it change or otherwise affect you? What aspects of your life now can you trace to that event? How might your life have been different if this event had not happened or had turned out differently? Why does this story matter to you?

Ways of Organizing a Literacy Narrative

Start by OUTLINING the main events in your narrative. Then think about how you want to tell the story. Don't assume that the only way to tell your story is just as it happened. That's one way—starting at the beginning of the action and continuing to the end. But you could also start in the middle—or even at the end. Shannon Nichols, for example, could have begun her narrative by telling how she finally passed the proficiency test and then gone back to tell about the times she tried to pass it, even as she was an A student in an honors English class. Several ways of organizing a narrative follow.

203–04

[Chronologically, from beginning to end]

[Beginning in the middle]

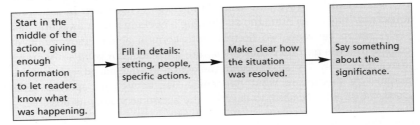

[Beginning at the end]

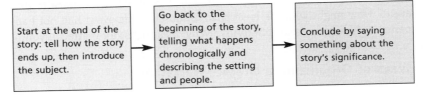

Writing Out a Draft

205–07 ○

Once you have generated ideas and thought about how you want to organize your narrative, it's time to begin **DRAFTING**. Do this quickly—try to write a complete draft in one sitting, concentrating on getting the story on paper or screen and on putting in as much detail as you can. Some writers find it helpful to work on the beginning or ending first.

Draft a beginning. A good narrative grabs readers' attention right from the start. Here are some ways of beginning; you can find more advice in the chapter on **BEGINNING AND ENDING.**

239–49

- *Jump right in.* Sometimes you may want to get to the main action as quickly as possible. Nichols, for example, begins as she takes the ninth-grade proficiency test for the first time.

- *Describe the context.* You may want to provide any background information at the start of your narrative, as I decided to do, beginning by explaining how my grandmother taught me to read.

- *Describe the setting, especially if it's important to the narrative.* Bragg begins by describing the small Alabama town where his father lived.

Draft an ending. Think about what you want your readers to read last. An effective ending helps them understand the meaning of your narrative. Here are some possibilities; look also at the chapter on **BEGINNING AND ENDING.**

239–49

- *End where your story ends.* It's up to you to decide where a narrative ends. Bragg's story ends with him standing in front of a pile of books; mine ends several years after it begins, with my graduation from college.

- *Say something about the significance of your narrative.* Nichols observes that she no longer loves to read or write, for example. The trick is to touch upon the narrative's significance without stating it too directly, like the moral of a fable.

- *Refer back to the beginning.* My narrative ends with my grandmother watching me graduate from college; Nichols ends by contemplating the negative effects of failing the proficiency test.

- *End on a surprising note.* Bragg catches our attention when his father gives him the boxes of books—and leaves us with a complicated image to ponder.

Come up with a title. A good title indicates something about the subject of your narrative—and makes readers want to take a look. Nichols's title states her subject, "Proficiency," but she also puts the word in quotes, calling it into question in a way that might make readers wonder—and read on. I focus on the significance of my narrative: "How I Learned about the Power of Writing." Bragg takes his title from something memorable his father said: "It's all over but the shoutin.' " See the chapter on **GUIDING YOUR READER** for more advice on titles.

250–54

Considering Matters of Design

You'll probably write your narrative in paragraph form, but think about the information you're presenting and how you can design it to enhance your story and appeal to your audience.

454–55

- What would be an appropriate **TYPEFACE**? Something serious, like Times Roman? Something whimsical, like Comic Sans? Something else?

456–57

- Would it help your readers if you added **HEADINGS** in order to divide your narrative into shorter sections?

458–62

- Would photographs or other **VISUALS** show details better than you can describe them with words alone? If you're writing about learning to read, for example, you might scan in an image of one of the first books you read in order to help readers picture it. Or if your topic is learning to write, you could include something you wrote.

Getting Response and Revising

The following questions can help you study your draft with a critical eye. **GETTING RESPONSE** from others is always good, and these questions can guide their reading, too. Make sure they know your purpose and audience.

213–14

- Do the title and first few sentences make readers want to read on? If not, how else might you begin?

- Does the narrative move from beginning to end clearly? Does it flow, and are there effective transitions? Does the narrative get sidetracked at any point?

- Is anything confusing?
- Is there enough detail, and is it interesting? Is there enough information about the setting and the people? Can readers picture the characters and sense what they're like as people? Would it help to add some dialogue, so that readers can "hear" them? Will they be able to imagine the setting?
- Have you made the situation meaningful enough to make readers wonder and care about what will happen?
- Do you narrate any actions clearly? vividly? Does the action keep readers engaged?
- Is the significance of the narrative clear?
- Does the narrative end in a satisfying way? What are readers left thinking?

The preceding questions should identify aspects of your narrative you need to work on. When it's time to **REVISE,** make sure your text appeals to your audience and achieves your purpose as successfully as possible.

○ 214–16

Editing and Proofreading

Readers equate correctness with competence. Once you've revised your draft, follow these guidelines for **EDITING** a narrative:

○ 219–22
◆ 304–12
◆ 254

- Make sure events are **NARRATED** in a clear order and include appropriate time markers, **TRANSITIONS,** and summary phrases to link the parts and show the passing of time.
- Be careful that verb tenses are consistent throughout. If you write your narrative in the past tense ("he *taught* me how to use a computer"), be careful not to switch to the present ("So I *look* at him and *say* . . . ") along the way.
- Check to see that verb tenses correctly indicate when an action took place. If one action took place before another action in the past, you should use the past perfect tense: "I forgot to dot my i's, a mistake I *had made* many times."

294–98 ◆

- Punctuate **DIALOGUE** correctly. Whenever someone speaks, surround the speech with quotation marks ("No way," I said.). Periods and commas go inside quotation marks; exclamation points and question marks go inside if they're part of the quotation, outside if they're part of the whole sentence:

    Inside: Opening the door, Ms. Cordell announced, "Pop quiz!"
    Outside: It wasn't my intention to announce, "I hate to read"!

222–23 ○

- **PROOFREAD** your finished narrative carefully before turning it in.

Taking Stock of Your Work

- How well do you think you told the story?
- What did you do especially well?
- What could still be improved?
- How did you go about coming up with ideas and generating text?
- How did you go about drafting your narrative?
- Did you use photographs or any other graphics? What did they add? Can you think of graphics you might have used?
- How did others' responses influence your writing?
- What would you do differently next time?

224–35 ○

See Chapter 27 if you are required to submit your literacy narrative as part of a writing **PORTFOLIO**.

147–52 ▲
168–73 ▲

> See also **MEMOIRS** (Chapter 15), a kind of narrative that focuses more generally on a significant event from your past, and **REFLECTIONS** (Chapter 18), a kind of essay for thinking about a topic in writing.

■ rhetorical situations　▲ genres　○ processes　◆ strategies　● research mla/apa　□ media/design

Both *Time* and *U.S. News and World Report* cover the same events, but each magazine interprets them differently. All toothpaste ads claim to make teeth "the whitest." Saddam Hussein was supporting terrorists—or he wasn't, depending on which politician is speaking. Those are but three examples that demonstrate why we need to be careful, analytical readers of magazines and newspapers, ads, political documents, even textbooks. Not only does text convey information, but it also influences how and what we think. We need to read, then, to understand not only what texts say but also how they say it. Because understanding how texts say what they say is so crucial, assignments in many disciplines ask you to analyze texts. You may be asked to analyze sensory imagery in James Joyce's "Araby" for a literature class or, for an art history course, to analyze the use of color and space in Edward Hopper's *Nighthawks*. In a statistics course, you might analyze a set of data—a numerical text—to find the standard deviation from the mean. This chapter offers detailed guidelines for writing an essay that closely examines a text both for what it says and for how it does so, with the goal of demonstrating for readers how—and how well—the text achieves its effects. We'll begin with three good examples.

Readings

DAVID S. RUBIN

It's the Same Old Song

In this analysis of a painting, David Rubin, curator of visual arts at the Contemporary Arts Center in New Orleans, analyzes how a painting uses themes from the Eagles' song "Hotel California" to critique California culture. This analysis comes from a book that accompanied a museum exhibition on rock music's influence on contemporary art.

> Whether one has been consciously or subliminally affected by the music, the mention of "Respect," "Hotel California," or "Stayin' Alive," to name a few of the song titles appropriated by artists, conjures up instant associations and pangs of nostalgia. Yet, when attached to an artwork, such titles may take on any number of new meanings, at times reflective of the musical source, but often equally remote from it. . . .

Alfred Leslie, Hotel California *(Wadsworth Atheneum, Hartford, Connecticut)*

Initially an abstract expressionist painter, Alfred Leslie turned to figuration in the 1960s because he felt that "modern art had, in a sense, killed figure painting. Painting the figure could become the most challenging subject one could undertake." By the 1970s, Leslie had developed a distinctive figural style in which subjects are shown in frontal, confrontational poses, at close range, and bathed in sharp, dramatic lighting that was inspired by baroque artists such as Caravaggio. While many of Leslie's paintings deal with events drawn from personal experience, such as his self-portraits and a cycle of paintings concerning the death of a friend, poet Frank O'Hara, others, such as *Hotel California* (1980), are purely fictional.

As with all of Leslie's paintings, the figures in *Hotel California* are based on drawings structured on a geometric grid—a useful formal device for developing stiff, awkward poses. Although they remain anonymous, the man and woman depicted are a generic breed of displaced traveler. They arrive in Los Angeles in search of Eden only to find it as described in the Eagles song. As [sociologist Robert G.] Pielke explains, "The 'hotel' is obviously a metaphorical reference to California and the state of mind that accompanies it. After checking in for the night, a traveler comes to the realization that 'this could be Heaven or this could be Hell'; it turns out to be both. On the one hand it's 'such a lovely place,' but on the other 'we are all prisoners here of our own device' " (189). Leslie, who is a New Yorker, communicates this vision of California through incongruity of scale between the figures and the setting, which is a broad vista with expansive blue skies, as well as through carefully articulated iconographic details, such as the styles of clothing and luggage, the Pepsi can, and the *Hotel California* album cover, shown propped against a wall. Taken together, these minutiae present a disconcerting time capsule of Los Angeles in the 1970s.

Work Cited

Pielke, Robert G. <u>You Say You Want a Revolution: Rock Music in American Culture</u>. Chicago: Nelson-Hall, 1986.

Rubin focuses on several textual elements in the painting: the relative size of people and setting, "iconographic details"; in addition, he discusses contextual elements, including the lyrics of the song that inspired the painting and the artist's method, as evidence to support his analysis.

WILLIAM SAFIRE

A Spirit Reborn

Just before the first anniversary of September 11, 2001, New York Times columnist William Safire analyzed the Gettysburg Address for what it meant to Americans after 9/11.

Abraham Lincoln's words at the dedication of the Gettysburg cemetery will be the speech repeated at the commemoration of September 11 by the governor of New York and by countless other speakers across the nation.

The lips of many listeners will silently form many of the famous phrases. "Four score and seven years ago" — a sonorous way of recalling the founding of the nation eighty-seven years before he spoke — is a phrase many now recite by rote, as is "the last full measure of devotion."

But the selection of this poetic political sermon as the oratorical centerpiece of our observance need not be only an exercise in historical evocation, nonpolitical correctness, and patriotic solemnity. What makes this particular speech so relevant for repetition on this first anniversary of the worst bloodbath on our territory since Antietam Creek's waters ran red is this: now, as then, a national spirit rose from the ashes of destruction.

Here is how to listen to Lincoln's all-too-familiar speech with new ears.

In those 236 words, you will hear the word *dedicate* five times. 5 The first two times refer to the nation's dedication to two ideals mentioned in the Declaration of Independence, the original ideal of "liberty" and the ideal that became central to the Civil War: "that all men are created equal."

The third, or middle, *dedication* is directed to the specific consecration of the site of the battle of Gettysburg: "to dedicate a portion of that field as a final resting place." The fourth and fifth times Lincoln repeated *dedicate* reaffirmed those dual ideals for which the dead being honored fought: "to the unfinished work" and then "to the great task remaining before us" of securing freedom and equality.

Those five pillars of dedication rested on a fundament of religious metaphor. From a president not known for his piety — indeed, often

rhetorical situations genres processes strategies research mla/apa media/ design

criticized for his supposed lack of faith — came a speech rooted in the theme of national resurrection. The speech is grounded in conception, birth, death, and rebirth.

Consider the barrage of images of birth in the opening sentence. The nation was "conceived in liberty" and "brought forth" — that is, delivered into life — by "our fathers" with all "created" equal. (In the nineteenth century, both "men" and "fathers" were taken to embrace women and mothers.) The nation was born.

Then, in the middle dedication, to those who sacrificed themselves, come images of death: "final resting place" and "brave men, living and dead."

Finally, the nation's spirit rises from this scene of death: "that this nation, under God, shall have a new birth of freedom." Conception, birth, death, rebirth. The nation, purified in this fiery trial of war, is resurrected. Through the sacrifice of its sons, the sundered nation would be reborn as one.

An irreverent aside: All speechwriters stand on the shoulders of orators past. Lincoln's memorable conclusion was taken from a fine oration by the Reverend Theodore Parker at an 1850 Boston antislavery convention. That social reformer defined the transcendental "idea of freedom" to be "a government of all the people, by all the people, for all the people."

Lincoln, thirteen years later, dropped the "alls" and made the phrase his own. (A little judicious borrowing by presidents from previous orators shall not perish from the earth.) In delivering that final note, the Union's defender is said to have thrice stressed the noun "people" rather than the prepositions "of," "by," and "for." What is to be emphasized is not rhetorical rhythm but the reminder that our government's legitimacy springs from America's citizens; the people, not the rulers, are sovereign. Not all nations have yet grasped that.

Do not listen on September 11 only to Lincoln's famous words and comforting cadences. Think about how Lincoln's message encompasses but goes beyond paying "fitting and proper" respect to the dead and the bereaved. His sermon at Gettysburg reminds "us the living" of our "unfinished work" and "the great task remaining before us" — to resolve that this generation's response to the deaths of thousands of our people leads to "a new birth of freedom."

Safire analyzed Lincoln's text for what it said to Americans on the anniversary of 9/11. His analysis focuses on patterns of specific words and images—he identifies dedicate *as a key term and analyzes how its meaning changes and develops each time it is used. He shows how Lincoln shaped his text around images of birth, death, and resurrection to assert that although a nation's soldiers die, their deaths permit the rebirth of the nation. In doing so, Safire built an argument linking Lincoln's words to current circumstances.*

DOUG LANTRY

"Stay Sweet As You Are": An Analysis of Change and Continuity in Advertising Aimed at Women

Doug Lantry wrote this analysis of three print ads for a first-year writing course at the University of Akron.

Magazine advertisements aimed at American women have a long history of pushing things like makeup, mouthwash, soap, and other products that reinforce men's roles in women's lives. The concept of personal hygiene has been used to convey the message that "catching" a man or becoming a wife is a woman's ultimate goal, and in advertisements from the 1920s, 1930s, and 1950s this theme can be traced through verbal and visual content.

For example, a 1922 ad for Resinol soap urges women to "make that dream come true" by using Resinol (see Fig. 1). The dream is marriage. The premise is that a bad complexion will prevent marriage even if a woman has attributes like wit and grace, which the ad identifies as positive. Blotchy skin, the ad says, will undermine all that. The word *repellent* is used for emphasis and appears in the same sentence as the words *neglected* and *humiliated*, equating the look of the skin with the state of the person within. Of course, Resinol can remedy the condition, and a paragraph of redemption follows the paragraph about being repellent. A treatment program is suggested, and the look and feel of "velvety" skin are only "the first happy effects," with eventual marriage (fulfillment) implied as the ultimate result of using Resinol soap.

rhetorical situations
genres
processes
strategies
research mla/apa
media/ design

Fig. 1.   A 1922 Resinol soap ad.

Visual content supports the mostly verbal ad. In a darkened room, a lone woman peers dreamily into a fireplace, where she sees an apparition of herself as a bride in a white veil, being fulfilled as a person by marriage to a handsome man. She lounges in a soft chair, where the glow of the image in the fireplace lights her up and warms her as much as the comforting fire itself. A smaller image shows the woman washing with Resinol, contentedly working her way toward clear skin and marriage over a water-filled basin suggestive of a vessel of holy water. This image is reinforced by her closed eyes and serene look and by the ad's suggestion that "right living" is a source of a good complexion.

A somewhat less innocent ad appeared more than a decade later, in 1934 (see Fig. 2). That ad, for Lux soap, like the one for Resinol, prescribes a daily hygiene regimen, but it differs significantly from the Resinol message in that it never mentions marriage and uses a clear-skinned movie star as proof of Lux's effectiveness. Instead of touting marriage, Lux teaches that "a girl who wants to break hearts simply must have a tea-rose complexion." Romance, not marriage, is the woman's goal, and competition among women is emphasized because "girls who want to make new conquests . . . [are] *sure* to win out!" by using Lux. Lux's pitch is more sophisticated than Resinol's, appealing to a more emancipated woman than that of the early 1920s and offering a kind of evidence based on science and statistics. The text cites "9 out of 10 glamorous Hollywood stars" and scientists who explain that Lux slows aging, but it declines to cite names, except that of Irene Dunne, the ad's star. The unnamed stars and scientists give the ad an air of untruthfulness, and this sense is deepened by the paradox of the ad's title: "Girls who know this secret always win out." If Lux is a secret, why does it appear in a mass-media publication?

Like Resinol, Lux urges women to seek love and fulfillment by enhancing their outward beauty and suggests that clear skin means having "the charm men can't resist."

The Lux ad's visual content, like Resinol's, supports its verbal message. Several demure views of Irene Dunne emphasize her "pearly-smooth skin," the top one framed by a large heart shape. In all the photos, Dunne wears a feathery, feminine collar, giving her a birdlike appearance: she is a bird of paradise or an ornament. At the bottom of the ad, we see a happy Dunne being cuddled and admired by a man.

The visual and verbal message is that women should strive, through steps actually numbered in the ad, to attain soft, clear skin

Fig. 2.   1934 Lux soap ad.

and hence charm and hence romance. Not surprisingly, the ad uses the language of battle to describe the effects of clear skin: girls who use Lux will "make new conquests!" and "win out!" Similar themes are developed for a younger audience in a 1954 ad for Listerine mouthwash (see Fig. 3). This time the target is no longer grown women but teenage girls: "If you want to win the boys . . . Stay Sweet As You Are!" Because attracting men would be inappropriate for teenagers, boys are the catch of the day in the Listerine ad. The idea of staying sweet means on the surface that girls should have nice breath, but the youthful context of the ad means that for women to be attractive they must stay young and "stay adorable," preferably with the girlish innocence of a teenager. The consequences of not staying sweet are clear: if you don't use Listerine every morning, every night, and before every

IF YOU WANT TO WIN THE BOYS . . .

Stay Sweet As You Are!

There are good times, good friends, and gaiety ahead if you do. And laughter and love . . . and marriage almost before you know it. But if you don't . . . you're headed for boredom and loneliness.

And it's so easy to stay sweet . . . stay adorable . . . if you let Listerine Antiseptic look after your breath. Every morning. Every night. And especially before every date when you want to be at your best. Listerine instantly stops bad breath, and keeps it stopped for hours, usually . . . *four times better than any tooth paste.*

No Tooth Paste Kills Odor Germs Like This . . . Instantly

Listerine Antiseptic does for you what no tooth paste does. Listerine instantly kills bacteria . . . by millions—stops bad breath instantly, and usually for hours on end.

You see, far and away the most common cause of offensive breath is the bacterial fermentation of proteins which are always present in the mouth. *And research shows that your breath stays sweeter longer, depending upon the degree to which you reduce germs in the mouth.*

Listerine Clinically Proved Four Times Better Than Tooth Paste

No tooth paste, of course, is antiseptic. Chlorophyll does not kill germs—but Listerine kills bacteria by millions, gives you lasting antiseptic protection against bad breath.

Is it any wonder Listerine Antiseptic in recent clinical tests averaged at least four times more effective in stopping bad breath odors than the chlorophyll products or tooth pastes it was tested against? With proof like this, it's easy to see why Listerine belongs in your home. Every morning . . . every night . . . before every date, make it a habit to always gargle Listerine, the most widely used antiseptic in the world.

LISTERINE ANTISEPTIC STOPS BAD BREATH
4 times better than any tooth paste

Every week 2 different shows, Radio & Television—"THE ADVENTURES OF OZZIE & HARRIET" See your paper for times and stations

A Product of The Lambert Company

Fig. 3.   Listerine mouthwash ad.

■ rhetorical situations
▲ genres
○ processes
◆ strategies
● research mla/apa
□ media/design

date, "you're headed for boredom and loneliness." If you do use Listerine, there are "good times, good friends, and gaiety ahead."

Like Lux, Listerine relies on science as well as sex. With talk of "the bacterial fermentation of proteins," research, and clinical tests, the mouthwash props up its romantic and sexual claims by proclaiming scientific facts. Listerine is "4 times better than any tooth paste," the ad proclaims. "With proof like this, it's easy to see why Listerine belongs in your home."

Visuals contribute to the message, as in the other ads. The central image is a photo of a perky, seemingly innocent teenage girl playing records on a portable phonograph. A vision of midcentury American femininity, she wears a fitted sweater, a scarf tied at the neck (like a wrapped present?), and a full, long skirt. She sits on the floor, her legs hidden by the skirt; she could be a cake decoration. Leaning forward slightly, she looks toward the reader, suggesting by her broad smile and submissive posture that perhaps kissing will follow when she wins the boys with her sweet breath. The record player affirms the ad's teenage target.

The intended consumers in the Resinol, Lux, and Listerine ads are   10
women, and the message of all three ads is that the product will lead to — and is required for — romantic or matrimonial success. Each ad implies that physical traits are paramount in achieving this success, and the ads' appearance in widely circulated magazines suggests that catching a man (whether or not she marries him) is the ultimate goal of every American woman. While there is a kind of progress over time, the ads' underlying assumptions remain constant. There is evidence of women's increasing sophistication, illustrated in the later ads' use of science and "objective" proof of the products' effectiveness. Women's development as individuals can also be seen in that marriage is not presupposed in the later ads, and in the case of Lux a single woman has a successful career and apparently has her pick of many partners.

Still, one theme remains constant and may be seen as a continuing debilitating factor in women's struggle for true equality in the world of sex roles: pleasing men is the prerequisite for happiness. Despite apparent advances on other levels, that assumption runs through all three ads and is the main selling point. The consumer of Resinol, Lux, and Listerine is encouraged to objectify herself, to become more physically attractive not for her own sake but for someone else's. The women in all three ads are beautifying themselves because they assume they must "make new conquests," "win the boys," and "make that dream come true."

■❚ For five
more textual
analyses, see
CHAPTER 51.

*Lantry summarizes each ad clearly and focuses his analysis on a theme run-
ning through all three ads: the concept that to find happiness, a woman must
be physically attractive to men. He describes patterns of images and language
in all three ads as evidence.*

Key Features / Textual Analysis

A summary of the text.   Your readers may not know the text you are analyzing, so you need to include it or tell them about it before you can analyze
it. Because Safire's text is so well-known, he describes it only briefly as "Abraham Lincoln's words at the dedication of the Gettysburg cemetery." Texts
that are not so well-known require a more detailed summary. Both Rubin
and Lantry include the texts — and images — they analyze and also describe
them in detail.

Attention to the context.   Texts don't exist in isolation: they are influenced by and contribute to ongoing conversations, controversies, or debates,
so to understand the text, you need to understand the larger context. Rubin
describes Leslie's development and names several song titles that visual
artists have "appropriated." Safire notes the source of the phrase "of the
people, by the people, for the people" and is clearly writing in the context
of the United States after 9/11.

A clear interpretation or judgment.   Your goal in analyzing a text is to
lead readers through careful examination of the text to some kind of interpretation or reasoned judgment, generally announced clearly in a thesis
statement. When you interpret something, you explain what you think it
means, as Lantry does when he argues that the consumers of the three
beauty products are encouraged to "objectify" themselves. He might instead
have chosen to judge the effectiveness of the ads, perhaps noting that they
promise the impossible, that no mouthwash, soap, or other product can guarantee romantic "success."

Reasonable support for your conclusions.   Written analysis of a text is
generally supported by evidence from the text itself and sometimes from

rhetorical
situations
genres
processes
strategies
research
mla/apa
media/
design

other sources. The writer might support his or her interpretation by quoting words or passages from a written text or referring to images in a visual text. Safire, for example, looks at Lincoln's repetition of the word "dedicate" in the Gettysburg Address as a way of arguing that the speech was still relevant in 2002, on the anniversary of the 9/11 attacks. Lantry examines patterns of both language and images in his analysis of the three ads. Note that the support you offer for your interpretation need only be "reasonable"—there is never any one way to interpret something.

A GUIDE TO ANALYZING A TEXT

Choosing a Text to Analyze

Most of the time, you will be assigned a text or a type of text to analyze: a poem in a literature class, the work of a political philosopher in a political science class, a speech in a history or communications course, a painting or sculpture in an art class, a piece of music in a music theory course. If you must choose a text to analyze, look for one that suits the demands of the assignment—one that is neither too large or complex to analyze thoroughly (a Dickens novel or a Beethoven symphony is probably too big) nor too brief or limited to generate sufficient material (a ten-second TV news brief or a paragraph from *Fast Food Nation* would probably be too small). Be sure you understand what the assignment asks you to do, and ask your instructor for clarification if you're not sure.

Considering the Rhetorical Situation

■ **PURPOSE**   Why are you analyzing this text? To demonstrate that you understand it? To persuade readers that the text demonstrates a certain point? Or are you using the text as a way to make some other point?

3–4

■ **AUDIENCE**   Are your readers likely to know your text? How much detail will you need to supply?

■ **STANCE**   What interests you about your analysis? Why? What do you know or believe about your topic, and how will your own beliefs affect your analysis?

■ **MEDIA / DESIGN**   Are you writing an essay for a class? to be published in a journal or magazine? something for the Web? If you are analyzing a visual text, you will probably need to include an image of the text.

Generating Ideas and Text

In analyzing a text, your goal is to understand what it says, how it works, and what it means. To do so, you may find it helpful to follow a certain sequence: read, respond, summarize, analyze, and draw conclusions from your analysis.

Read to see what the text says.   Start by reading carefully, to get a sense of what it says. This means first skimming to **PREVIEW THE TEXT**, rereading for the main ideas, then questioning and **ANNOTATING.**

Consider your **INITIAL RESPONSE.** Once you have a sense of what the
text says, what do you think? What's your reaction to the argument, the tone, the language, the images? Do you find the text difficult? puzzling? Do you agree with what the writer says? Disagree? Agree *and* disagree? Your reaction to a text can color your analysis, so start by thinking about how you react—and why. Consider both your intellectual reaction and any emotional reactions. Identify places in the text that trigger or account for those reactions. If you think that you have no particular reaction or response, try to articulate why. Whatever your response, think about what accounts for it.

Next, consolidate your understanding of the text by **SUMMARIZING** (or,
if it's a visual text, **DESCRIBING**) what it says in your own words. You may
find it helpful to **OUTLINE** its main ideas. See, for instance, how Lantry care-

rhetorical situations   genres   processes   strategies   research mla/apa   media/ design

fully described what a soap ad he was analyzing shows and says. Some of this analysis ended up in his essay.

> Several demure views of Irene Dunne emphasize her "pearly-smooth skin," the top one framed by a large heart shape. In all the photos, Dunne wears a feathery, feminine collar, giving her a birdlike appearance: she is a bird of paradise or an ornament. At the bottom of the ad, we see a happy Dunne being cuddled and admired by a man.

Decide what you want to analyze.   Having read the text carefully, think about what you find most interesting or intriguing, and why. Does the language interest you? The imagery? The structure? The argument? The larger context? Something else? You might begin your analysis by exploring what attracted your notice.

Study how the text works.   Texts are made up of several components — words, sentences, images, even punctuation. Visual texts might be made up of images, lines, angles, color, light and shadow, and sometimes words. All these elements can be used in various ways. To analyze them, look for patterns in the way they're used and try to decide what those patterns reveal about the text. How do they affect its message? See the sections on THINKING ABOUT HOW THE TEXT WORKS and IDENTIFYING PATTERNS in Chapter 38 for specific guidelines on examining patterns this way.

◆ 319–24

Then write a sentence or two describing the patterns you've discovered and how they contribute to what the text says.

Analyze the argument.   Every text makes an argument. Both verbal and visual texts make certain assertions and provide some kind of support for those claims. An important part of understanding any text is to recognize its argument — what the writer or artist wants the audience to believe, feel, or do. Consider the text's purpose and audience, identify its thesis, and decide how convincingly it supports that thesis. See the section on ANALYZING THE ARGUMENT for help doing so.

◆ 324–27

Then write a sentence or two summarizing the argument the text makes, along with your reactions to or questions about that argument.

Think about the larger context. Texts are always part of larger, on-going conversations. To analyze a text's role in its larger context, you may need to do additional RESEARCH to determine where the text was originally published, what else was happening or being discussed at the time the text was published or created, and whether or not the text responded directly to other ideas or arguments. You'll find detailed help doing so in the section on THINKING ABOUT THE LARGER CONTEXT in Chapter 38.

Then write a sentence or two describing the larger context surrounding the text and how that context affects your understanding of the text.

Consider what you know about the writer or artist. What you know about the person who created a text can influence your understanding of that text. His or her other work, reputation, stance, and beliefs are all useful windows into understanding a text. See the guidelines on AUTHORS' CREDENTIALS in Chapter 41.

Then write a sentence or two summarizing what you know about the writer and how that information affects your understanding of the text.

Come up with a thesis. When you analyze a text, you are basically arguing that the text should be read in a certain way. Once you've studied the text thoroughly, you need to identify your analytical goal: do you want to show that the text has a certain meaning? Uses certain techniques to achieve its purposes? Tries to influence its audience in particular ways? Relates to some larger context in some significant manner? Should be taken seriously—or not? Something else? Come up with a tentative THESIS to guide your thinking and analyzing—but be aware that your thesis may change as you continue to work.

Ways of Organizing a Textual Analysis

Examine the information you have to see how it supports or complicates your thesis. Look for clusters of related information that you can use to structure an OUTLINE. Your analysis might be structured in at least two ways. You might, as Safire does, discuss patterns or themes that run through the text. Alternatively, you might analyze each text or section of text separately, as Lantry does. Following are graphic representations of some ways of organizing a textual analysis.

329–449

327–28

355

251–52

203–04

■ rhetorical situations ▲ genres ○ processes ◆ strategies ● research mla/apa □ media/ design

[Thematically]

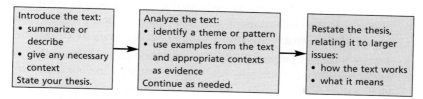

[Part by part, or text by text]

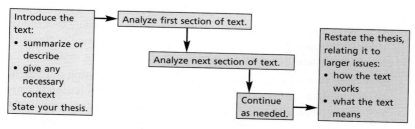

Writing Out a Draft

In drafting your analysis, your goal should be to integrate the various parts into a smoothly flowing, logically organized essay. However, it's easy to get bogged down in the details. Consider writing one section of the analysis first, then another and another until you've drafted the entire middle; then draft your beginning and ending. Alternatively, start by summarizing the text and moving from there to your analysis and then to your ending. However you do it, you need to support your analysis with evidence: from the text itself (as Lantry's analysis of advertisements does), or from **RESEARCH** on the larger context of the text (as Rubin and Safire do).

329–449

Draft a beginning. The beginning of an essay that analyzes a text generally has several tasks: to introduce or summarize the text for your readers, to offer any necessary information on the larger context, and to present your thesis.

321–22
- *Summarize the text.* If the text is one your readers don't know, you need to give a brief **SUMMARY** early on that introduces it to them and shows that you understand it fully. For example, Lantry begins each analysis of a soap advertisement with a brief summary of its content.

- *Provide a context for your analysis.* If there is a larger context that is significant for your analysis, you might mention it in your introduction. Safire does this when he begins his analysis of Lincoln's Gettysburg Address by describing its status as a "centerpiece" of 9/11 commemorations.

- *Introduce a pattern or theme.* If your analysis centers on a certain pattern of textual or contextual elements, you might begin by describing it, as Rubin does in his first sentence when he mentions the "instant associations and pangs of nostalgia" certain song titles evoke.

251–52
- *State your thesis.* Lantry ends his first paragraph by stating the **THESIS** of his analysis: "The concept of personal hygiene has been used to convey the message that 'catching' a man or becoming a wife is a woman's ultimate goal, and in advertisements from the 1920s, 1930s, and 1950s this theme can be traced through verbal and visual content."

239–49
- See Chapter 28 for more advice on **BEGINNING AND ENDING.**

Draft an ending. Think about what you want your readers to take away from your analysis, and end by getting them to focus on those thoughts.

- *Restate your thesis — and say why it matters.* Lantry, for example, ends by pointing out that "one theme remains constant" in all the ads he analyzes: that "pleasing men is the prerequisite for happiness."

- *Say something about the implications of your findings.* If your analysis has any general implications, you might end by stating them as Rubin does: "Taken together, these minutiae present a disconcerting time capsule of Los Angeles in the 1970s."

239–49
- See Chapter 28 for more advice on ways of **BEGINNING AND ENDING.**

Come up with a title. A good title indicates something about the subject of your analysis — and makes readers want to see what you have to

say about it. Rubin's title "It's the Same Old Song," uses a cliché to refer to the "old song" on which the painting he analyzes is based. Safire's title may seem cryptic but would have made sense when it was published, shortly before the first anniversary of 9/11: "A Spirit Reborn." And Lantry's title uses an eye-catching headline from one ad with a clear statement of his essay's content: " 'Stay Sweet As You Are': An Analysis of Change and Continuity in Advertising Aimed at Women." See Chapter 29 on **GUIDING YOUR READER** for more tips on writing titles.

250–54

Considering Matters of Design

- If you cite written text as evidence, be sure to set long quotations and **DOCUMENTATION** according to the style you're using.
- If your essay is lengthy, consider whether **HEADINGS** would make your analysis easier for readers to follow.
- If you're analyzing a visual text, you may need to include a reproduction, along with a caption identifying it.

375–449
456–57

Getting Response and Revising

The following questions can help you study your draft with a critical eye. **GETTING RESPONSE** from others is always good, and these questions can guide their reading, too. Make sure they know your purpose and audience.

213–14

- Is the beginning effective? Does it make a reader want to continue?
- Does the introduction provide an overview of your analysis and conclusions? Is your thesis clear?
- Is the text described or summarized clearly and sufficiently?
- Is the analysis well organized and easy to follow? Do the parts fit together coherently? Does it read like an essay rather than a collection of separate bits of analysis?

- Does each part of the analysis relate to the thesis?
- Is anything confusing or in need of more explanation?
- Are all quotations accurate and correctly documented?
- Is it clear how the analysis leads to the interpretation? Is there adequate evidence to support the interpretation?

214–16 ○
Then it's time to **REVISE.** Make sure your text appeals to your audience and achieves your purpose as successfully as possible.

Editing and Proofreading

Readers equate correctness with competence. Once you've revised your draft, edit carefully:

- Is your thesis clearly stated?
- 239–40 ◆ Does the **BEGINNING** make readers want to read on?
- 358–69 ●
  375–449 ● Check all **QUOTATIONS, PARAPHRASES,** and **SUMMARIES** for accuracy and form. Be sure that each has the required **DOCUMENTATION.**
- 254 ◆ Make sure that your analysis flows clearly from one point to the next and that you use **TRANSITIONS** that help readers move through your text.
- 245 ◆ Does the **ENDING** make clear what your findings mean?
- 222–23 ○ **PROOFREAD** your finished analysis carefully before turning it in.

Taking Stock of Your Work

Take stock of what you've written and learned by writing out answers to these questions:

- How did you go about analyzing the text? What methods did you use—and which ones were most helpful?
- How did you go about drafting your essay?

 rhetorical situations
 genres
 processes
 strategies
● research mla/apa
□ media/ design

- How well did you organize your written analysis? What, if anything, could you do to make it easier to read?

- Did you provide sufficient evidence to support your analysis?

- What did you do especially well?

- What could still be improved?

- Did you use any visuals, and if so, what did they add? Could you have shown the same thing with words?

- How did other readers' responses influence your writing?

- What would you do differently next time?

- Are you pleased with your analysis? What did it teach you about the text you analyzed? Did it make you want to study more works by the same writer or artist?

See also Chapter 14 on **LITERARY ANALYSES** if you are analyzing a work of poetry, fiction, or drama. See Chapter 27 if you are required to submit your analysis as part of a writing **PORTFOLIO.**

▲ 137–46

⬤ 224–35

8   Reporting Information

Many kinds of writing report information. Newspapers report on local and world events; textbooks give information about biology, history, writing; Web sites provide information about products (jcrew.com), people (johnnydepp.com), institutions (smithsonian.org). We write out a lot of information ourselves, from a note we post on our door saying we've gone to choir practice to an essay we're assigned to write for a history class, reporting what we've learned about the state of U.S. diplomacy in the days before the bombing of Pearl Harbor. This chapter focuses on reports that are written to inform readers about a particular topic. Very often this kind of writing calls for some kind of research: you need to know your subject in order to report on it! When you write to report information, you are the expert. This chapter offers guidelines for writing essays that inform. We'll begin with three good examples.

THE 9/11 COMMISSION

The Hijacking of United 175

In 2004, the National Commission on Terrorist Attacks upon the United States published The 9/11 Commission Report, *a detailed account of the "facts and circumstances" of the terrorist attacks on September 11, 2001, with recommendations for "protecting against and preparing for" future terrorist attacks. The audience for the report was the President, Congress, and the American people. To begin, the report lays out the facts of the attacks, one plane at a time. Since it is reporting on an event, the* 9/11 Commission Report *begins with a narrative, relating what the Commission was able to learn about what happened. Here is the report on the hijacking of United 175.*

rhetorical situations

genres

processes

strategies

research mla/apa

media/ design

United Airlines Flight 175 was scheduled to depart for Los Angeles at 8:00. Captain Victor Saracini and First Officer Michael Horrocks piloted the Boeing 767, which had seven flight attendants. Fifty-six passengers boarded the flight.[1]

United 175 pushed back from its gate at 7:58 and departed Logan Airport at 8:14. By 8:33, it had reached its assigned cruising altitude of 31,000 feet. The flight attendants would have begun their cabin service.[2]

The flight had taken off just as American 11 was being hijacked, and at 8:42 the United 175 flight crew completed their report on a "suspicious transmission overheard from another plane (which turned out to have been Flight 11) just after takeoff. This was United 175's last communication with the ground.[3]

The hijackers attacked sometime between 8:42 and 8:46. They used knives (as reported by two passengers and a flight attendant), Mace (reported by one passenger), and the threat of a bomb (reported by the same passenger). They stabbed members of the flight crew (reported by a flight attendant and one passenger). Both pilots had been killed (reported by one flight attendant). The eyewitness accounts came from calls made from the rear of the plane, from passengers originally seated further forward in the cabin, a sign that passengers and perhaps crew had been moved to the back of the aircraft. Given similarities to American 11 in hijacker seating and in eyewitness reports of tactics and weapons, as well as the contact between the presumed team leaders, Atta and Shehhi, we believe the tactics were similar on both flights.[4]

The first operational evidence that something was abnormal on United 175 came at 8:47, when the aircraft changed beacon codes twice within a minute. At 8:51, the flight deviated from its assigned altitude, and a minute later New York air traffic controllers began repeatedly and unsuccessfully trying to contact it.[5]

At 8:52, in Easton, Connecticut, a man named Lee Hanson received a phone call from his son Peter, a passenger on United 175. His son told him: "I think they've taken over the cockpit — An attendant has been stabbed — and someone else up front may have been killed. The plane is making strange moves. Call United Airlines — Tell them it's Flight 175, Boston to LA." Lee Hanson then called the Easton Police Department and relayed what he had heard.[6]

Also at 8:52, a male flight attendant called a United office in San Francisco, reaching Marc Policastro. The flight attendant reported that the flight had been hijacked, both pilots had been killed, a flight attendant had been stabbed, and the hijackers were probably flying the plane. The call lasted about two minutes, after which Policastro and a colleague tried unsuccessfully to contact the flight.[7]

At 8:58, the flight took a heading toward New York City.[8]

At 8:59, Flight 175 passenger Brian David Sweeney tried to call his wife, Julie. He left a message on their home answering machine that the plane had been hijacked. He then called his mother, Louise Sweeney, told her the flight had been hijacked, and added that the passengers were thinking about storming the cockpit to take control of the plane away from the hijackers.[9]

At 9:00, Lee Hanson received a second call from his son Peter: 10

> It's getting bad, Dad — A stewardess was stabbed — They seem to have knives and Mace — They said they have a bomb — It's getting very bad on the plane — Passengers are throwing up and getting sick — The plane is making jerky movements — I don't think the pilot is flying the plane — I think we are going down — I think they intend to go to Chicago or someplace and fly into a building — Don't worry, Dad — If it happens, it'll be very fast — My God, my God.[10]

The call ended abruptly. Lee Hanson had heard a woman scream just before it cut off. He turned on a television, and in her home so did Louise Sweeney. Both then saw the second aircraft hit the World Trade Center.[11]

At 9:03:11, United Airlines Flight 175 struck the South Tower of the World Trade Center.[12] All on board, along with an unknown number of people in the tower, were killed instantly.

Notes

[1] The 56 passengers represented a load factor of 33.33 percent of the airplane's seating capacity of 168, below the 49.22 percent for Flight 175 on Tuesdays in the three-month period prior to September 11, 2001. See UAL report, Flight 175 BOS-LAX Load Factors, undated (from June 1, 2001, to Sept. 11, 2001). Nine passengers holding reservations for Flight 175 did not show for the flight. They were interviewed and cleared by the FBI. FAA report, "Executive Summary," Sept. 12, 2001; FAA report, "Executive Summary, Chronology of a Multiple Hijacking Crisis, September 11, 2001," Sept. 17, 2001; UAL record, Flight 175 ACARS report, Sept. 11, 2001; UAL record, Flight 175 Flight Data Recap, Sept. 11, 2001.

[2] FAA report, "Executive Summary," Sept. 12, 2001; FAA report,

"Executive Summary, Chronology of a Multiple Hijacking Crisis, September 11, 2001," Sept. 17, 2001; NTSB report, "Flight Path Study — United Airlines 175," Feb. 19, 2002; NTSB report, Air Traffic Control Recording — United Airlines Flight 175, Dec. 21, 2001. At or around this time, flight attendants Kathryn Laborie and Alfred Marchand would have begun cabin service in first class; with Amy King and Robert Fangman in business class; and with Michael Tarrou, Amy Jarret, and Alicia Titus in economy class. See UAL report, "Flight 175 Flight Attendant Positions/Jumpseats," undated. United flight attendants, unlike those at American, did not carry cockpit keys. Instead, such keys were stowed in the cabin — on Flight 175, in the overhead bin above seats 1A and 1B in first class. See Don Dillman briefing (Nov. 18, 2003); Bob Jordan briefing (Nov. 20, 2003).

[3] Asked by air traffic controllers at 8:37 to look for an American Airlines 767 (Flight 11), United 175 reported spotting the aircraft at 8:38. At 8:41, the flight crew reported having "heard a suspicious transmission" from another aircraft shortly after takeoff, "like someone keyed the mike and said everyone stay in your seats." See NTSB report, Air Traffic Control Recording — United Airlines Flight 175, Dec. 21, 2001.

[4] See Marc Policastro interview (Nov. 21, 2003); FBI reports of investigation, interview of Lee Hanson, Sept. 11, 2001; interview of Marc Policastro, Sept. 11, 2001; interview of Louise Sweeney, Sept. 28, 2001; interview of Ronald May, Sept 11, 2001. On both American 11 and United 175, Boeing 767 double-aisled aircraft, the hijackers arrayed themselves similarly: two seated in first class close to the cockpit door, the pilot hijacker seated close behind them, and at least one other hijacker seated close behind the pilot hijacker. Hijackers were seated next to both the left and right aisles. On American 77 and United 93, Boeing 757 single-aisle aircraft, the pilot hijacker sat in the first row, closest to the cockpit door. See FBI report, "Summary of Penttbom Investigation," Feb. 29, 2004, pp. 67–69; AAL schematics for Flight 11 and Flight 77; UAL schematics for Flight 175 and Flight 93.

[5] NTSB report, "Flight Path Study — United Airlines 175," Feb. 19, 2002; NTSB report, Air Traffic Control Recording — United Airlines Flight 175, Dec. 21, 2001.

[6] See FBI report of investigation, interview of Lee Hanson, Sept. 11, 2001.

[7] Flight crew on board UAL aircraft could contact the United office in San Francisco (SAMC) simply by dialing *349 on an airphone. See FBI report of investigation, interview of David Price, Jan. 24, 2002. At some

point before 9:00, SAMC notified United's headquarters of the emergency call from the flight attendant. See Marc Policastro interview (Nov. 21, 2003); FBI report of investigation, interview of Marc Policastro, Sept. 11, 2001; Rich Miles interview (Nov. 21, 2003).

[8] NTSB report, "Flight Path Study—United Airlines 175," Feb. 19, 2002.

[9] See FBI reports of investigation, interview of Julie Sweeney, Oct. 2, 2001; interview of Louise Sweeney, Sept. 28, 2001.

[10] See FBI report of investigation, interview of Lee Hanson, Sept. 11, 2001.

[11] See ibid.; interview of Louise Sweeney, Sept. 28, 2001.

[12] NTSB report, "Flight Path Study—United Airlines 175," Feb. 19, 2002.

This report on the events aboard the airliner provides a minute-by-minute narrative, along with direct quotations from passengers as they described the events and came to realize what the hijackers intended to do. The notes provide additional details, including source information; they are reproduced here as they are presented in the original report.

CATHI EASTMAN AND BECKY BURRELL

The Science of Screams: Laws of Physics Instill Thrills in Roller Coasters

The following account, written in 2002 for the Dayton Daily News *by two staff members of a science museum, provides information about how a roller coaster works.*

For roller coasters, being the star of summer amusement park rides certainly has its ups and downs. Ever wonder how they get the energy to deliver thrill after thrill?

A roller coaster uses a motor or other mechanical force to pull or propel the cars to the top of the first hill. After that, it rises and falls, slowing down and speeding up—all on its own.

rhetorical situations   genres   processes   strategies   research mla/apa   media/ design

Whether they're built from wood and ride on steel wheels or follow steel paths on air-cushioned tires, roller coasters work because of two main principles: the laws of conservation of energy and gravity.

The law of conservation of energy states that energy can change from one form to another but cannot be created or destroyed. At rest, a roller coaster represents potential energy, that is, energy that is stored for later use. As the coaster travels to the top of the first hill, it is storing potential energy. That potential energy is then changed into kinetic energy as gravity pulls it down the first hill. Kinetic energy is energy that is being used: in this case, it's the energy caused by motion.

Gravity is the force that pulls all objects in the universe toward one another and that pulls a roller coaster to the bottom of a hill. The farther it goes down the hill, the more potential energy is changed into kinetic energy, which makes the ride go faster.

As it goes up the next hill, kinetic energy is changed back into potential energy and the ride slows down. This changing of kinetic energy to potential energy and back again continues as it continues to go up and down hills. Remember, the energy does not increase, decrease, or disappear; it just changes from one form to the other.

In this brief explanation, the writers define and explain processes to help a general audience understand a complex set of concepts. Their focus on a well-known process—riding a roller coaster—gives them a concrete example with which to illustrate abstract scientific principles. Notice how they use a forecasting statement—"roller coasters work because of two main principles: the laws of conservation of energy and gravity"—to cue readers to the topics they then discuss.

JEFFREY DEROVEN

The Greatest Generation: The Great Depression and the American South

The following essay was written in 2001 by a student for a history course at the Trumbull Campus of Kent State University. It was first published in Etude and Techne, *a journal of Ohio college writing.*

Tom Brokaw called the folks of the mid-twentieth century the greatest generation. So why is the generation of my grandparents seen as this country's greatest? Perhaps the reason is not what they accomplished but what they endured. Many of the survivors feel people today "don't have the moral character to withstand a depression like that."[1] This paper will explore the Great Depression through the eyes of ordinary Americans in the most impoverished region in the country, the American South, in order to detail how they endured and how the government assisted them in this difficult era.

President Franklin D. Roosevelt (FDR) announced in 1938 that the American South "represented the nation's number one economic problem." He commissioned the National Emergency Council to investigate and report on the challenges facing the region. Though rich in physical and human resources, the southern states lagged behind other parts of the nation in economic development.[2]

Poor education in the South was blamed for much of the problem. Young children attending school became too costly for most families. In the Bland family, "when Lucy got to the sixth grade, we had to stop her because there was too much to do."[3] Overcrowding of schools, particularly in rural areas, lowered the educational standards. The short school terms further reduced effectiveness. As Mrs. Abercrombie recalls, "Me and Jon both went to school for a few months but that wa'n't enough for us to learn anything."[4] Without the proper education, the youth of the South entered the work force unprepared for the challenges before them.

Southern industries did not have the investment capital to turn their resources into commodities. Manufacturers were limited to producing goods in the textile and cigarette industries and relied heavily on the cash crops of cotton and tobacco for the economy. Few facilities existed in the South for research that might lead to the development of new industries. Hampered by low wages, low tax revenue, and a high interest rate, Southerners lacked the economic resources to compete with the vast industrial strength of the North. As Abercrombie indicates, "Penalized for being rural, and handicapped in its efforts to industrialize, the economic life of the South has been squeezed to a point where the purchasing power of the southern people does not provide an adequate market for its own industries nor an attractive market for those of the rest of the country."[5] The

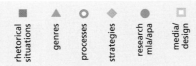

rhetorical situations

genres

processes

strategies

research mla/apa

media/ design

Franklin Delano Roosevelt (1882–1945)
Photo from Bettmann / Corbis

South had an untapped market for production and consumption. However, without adequate capital, it did not have the means to profit from them.

Southern industries paid their employees low wages, which led to a low cost of living. "You could live very cheaply because . . . you couldn't make a great deal of money," remembers Rita Beline."[6] Most families did not have much left for themselves after bills and living expenses. "Nobody had much money, you know," recalls June Atchetce. "Everybody kind of lived at home, had gardens and raised their own produce, raised their own meat and had chickens and eggs and such as that." The needs of the families "were very small as far as purchases were concerned." What they could not grow, they did not have a need for, except for basic staples such as coffee, flour, sugar, and honey. To save on the cost of clothes, families "had a lot of hand-me-downs from the oldest to the baby. We did not throw them away. We patched them up and sent them down the line."[7] Luxury items, like radios, cost too much money, and "only the [aristocrats] had radios because the poor did not stay at home long enough to enjoy them."[8] The fact was that Southerners wanted modern consumer items but did not have the purchasing power to pay for them. "The people of the South need to buy, they want to buy, and they would buy—if they had the money." Without paying laborers a fair wage, industry had forced upon itself a lower living standard, thus perpetuating losses in local revenue resulting in a decline in purchasing power.[9]

The Federal government had to step in and help, as historians David L. Carlton and Peter A. Coclanis note:

> Some of the South's credit difficulties have been slightly relieved in recent years . . . by the Public Works Administration, . . . the Works Progress Administration, [and] the Soil Conservation Service, [which] have brought desperately needed funds into the South.[10]

Along with other New Deal projects like the Tennessee Valley Authority (TVA) and the Civilian Conservation Corps [CCC], President Roosevelt was able to prime the pump into a seemingly dead Southern economy.

Other ways the federal government primed the pump was with the WPA [Works Progress Administration]. This New Deal measure gave jobs to those who wanted to work. Local governments benefited too. The WPA provided new roads, buildings, hospitals, and schools. Rita Beline remembers her "father came very short of money, . . . took a job with the WPA, in which he helped in building a road across a lagoon."[11] President Roosevelt knew "cheap wages mean low buying power."[12] The WPA ensured a fair wage for good work. Warren Addis remembers that "workers were tickled to death with it because it gave so many people jobs. It started out at eight cents an hour for common labor, and it finally went to thirty cents an hour."[13]

FDR also created the CCC. The concept of putting the American youth to work yielded an economic stimulus by having them send home twenty-five dollars a month. That money worked itself back into local economies as families spent the money on needed goods. Young men across the South "left home to go and do this work. They got paid a little bit of money, which they sent home to their families."[14] The CCC created recreation habitats as well. Jefferson Brock recalls, "They came and built brush poles for the fish to live in the lake near my cottage."[15] The CCC became an outlet for young men who could not find work in their hometowns. Jesse Brooks remembers:

> They did a great lot of good. For instance, they built Vogel State Park and raised the wall up on the national cemetery. Just put people to work. Gave them their pride back. A man's not going to feel very good about himself if he can't feed his family. So, that was the

rhetorical situations   genres   processes   strategies   research mla/apa   media/ design

New Deal itself—to put people back to work and get the economy growing again.[16]

The South did not enjoy the United States' economic successes in the early part of the twentieth century and in many ways was a third world country within our own nation. The federal action that fueled the Southern economy during the Great Depression changed the way of life for the better and helped Southerners endure a time of great despair. Programs like the TVA, WPA, and CCC planted the seeds for a prosperous future. I still do not know if they were the greatest generation, but they did overcome tremendous obstacles to bring forth other "greatest generations."

Notes

1. Allen Furline in Kenneth J. Bindas, "Oral History Project," Kent State University, Trumbull Campus, Trumbull, OH. Dr. Bindas has a collection of 476 oral-history interviews from western Georgia and eastern Alabama, from which the information for this paper is derived. (Hereafter cited in Notes as BOHP.)

2. David L. Carlton and Peter A. Coclanis, *Confronting Southern Poverty in the Great Depression: The Report on Economic Conditions of the South with Related Documents* (New York: Bedford/St. Martin's Press, 1996), 92.

3. Vera Bland in BOHP.

4. M. Abercrombie in BOHP.

5. Carlton and Coclanis, *Confronting Southern Poverty*, 76–78.

6. Rita Beline in BOHP.

7. June Romero Atchetce in BOHP.

8. Ruby Girley in BOHP.

9. Carlton and Coclanis, *Confronting Southern Poverty*, 62–65.

10. Ibid., 73.

11. Rita Beline in BOHP.

12. David M. Kennedy, *Freedom from Fear: The American People in Depression and War, 1929–1945* (New York: Oxford University Press, 1999), 346.

13. Warren Addis in BOHP.

14. Jane Berry in BOHP.

15. Jefferson Brock in BOHP.

16. Jesse Brooks in BOHP.

▌▌ For five
more reports,
see
CHAPTER 52.

DeRoven's essay reports information about how the American South got through the Great Depression. His information is based on both library research and interviews with people who lived through the period he describes. He documents his sources according to The Chicago Manual of Style, the preferred style in history classes.

Key Features / Reports

A tightly focused topic. The goal of this kind of writing is to inform readers about something without digressing—and without, in general, bringing in the writer's own opinions. All three examples focus on a particular topic—the hijacking of United 175, the physics of roller coasters, and the Great Depression in the American South—and present information about the topics evenhandedly.

Accurate, well-researched information. Reports usually require some research. The kind of research depends on the topic. Library research to locate scholarly sources may be necessary for some topics—DeRoven, for example, uses an archive available only at his university's library. Other topics may require field research—interviews, observations, and so on. The 9/11 Commission interviewed "more than 1,200 people, in ten countries"—and also reviewed more than 2.5 million pages of documents.

Various writing strategies. Presenting information usually requires various organizing patterns—defining, comparing, classifying, explaining processes, analyzing causes and effects, and so on. Eastman and Burrell explain the process that makes roller coasters work; the portion of the *9/11 Commission Report* reprinted here provides a detailed narrative; DeRoven analyzes some of the causes of the Great Depression in the South.

Clear definitions. Reports need to provide clear definitions of any key terms that their audience may not know. Eastman and Burrell define several terms—"potential energy" and "gravity," among others—as they explain how coasters work.

rhetorical situations genres processes strategies research mla/apa media/ design

Appropriate design.   Reports often combine paragraphs with information presented in lists, tables, diagrams, and other illustrations. When
you're presenting information, you need to think carefully about how to
DESIGN it—numerical data, for instance, can be easier to understand and
remember in a table than in a paragraph. And see how the *9/11 Commission Report* shows us the flight path of United 175 on a map, along with a
minute-by-minute account of the events on the plane (laid out as a list to
make the chronology easy to see).

453–63

United Airlines Flight 175 (UA 175)
Boston to Los Angeles

8:14	Takeoff
8:42	Last radio communication
8:42–8:46	Likely takeover
8:47	Transponder code changes
8:52	Flight attendant notifies UA of hijacking
8:54	UA attempts to contact the cockpit
8:55	New York Center suspects hijacking
9:03:11	Flight 175 crashes into 2 WTC (South Tower)
9:15	New York Center advises NEADS that UA 175 was the second aircraft crashed into WTC
9:20	UA headquarters aware that Flight 175 had crashed into WTC

A GUIDE TO REPORTING INFORMATION

Choosing a Topic

If you are working with an assigned topic, see if you can approach it from an angle that interests you. If you get to choose your topic, the following guidelines should help:

If you get to choose. What interests you? What do you wish you knew more about? The possible topics for informational reports are limitless, but the topics that you're most likely to write well on are those that engage you. They may be academic in nature or reflect your personal interests or both. If you're not sure where to begin, here are some places to start:

- an intriguing technology: file sharing, Google, cell phones, roller coasters
- sports: soccer, snowboarding, ultimate Frisbee, skateboarding, basketball
- an important world event: 9/11, the fall of Rome, the Black Death
- a historical period: the African diaspora, medieval Europe, the Ming dynasty, the Great Depression
- a common object: hooded sweatshirts, gel pens, mascara, Post-it notes
- a significant environmental issue: Arctic oil drilling, the Clean Air Act, mercury and the fish supply
- the arts — hip-hop, outsider art, the J. Paul Getty Museum, Savion Glover, Mary Cassatt

200–01 ○

LIST a few possibilities, and then choose one that you'd like to know more about — and that your audience might find interesting, too. You might start out by phrasing your topic as a question that your research will attempt to answer. For example:

> How is Google different from Yahoo!?
>
> How was the Great Pyramid constructed?
>
> Why did the World Trade Center towers collapse on themselves rather than fall sideways?
>
> What kind of training do football referees receive?

If your topic is assigned. Some assignments are specific: "Explain the physics of roller coasters." If, however, your assignment is broad — "Explain some aspect of the U.S. government" — try focusing on a more limited topic within the larger topic: federalism, majority rule, political parties, states' rights, division of powers. Even if an assignment seems to offer little flexibility, your task is to decide how to research the topic — and sometimes even narrow topics can be shaped to fit your own interests and those of your audience.

Considering the Rhetorical Situation

| ▨ **PURPOSE** | Why are you presenting this information? To teach readers about the subject? To demonstrate your research and writing skills? For some other reason? | 3–4 |

| ▨ **AUDIENCE** | Who will read this report? What does your audience already know about the topic? What background information do they need in order to understand it? Will you need to define any terms? What do you think they want or need to know about it? Why should they care or want to know about it? How can you attract their interest? | 5–8 |

| ▨ **STANCE** | What is your own attitude toward your subject? What interests you most about it? What about it seems important? | 12–14 |

| ▨ **MEDIA / DESIGN** | What medium are you using? What is the best way to present the information? Will it all be in paragraph form, or is there information that is best presented as a chart or a table? Do you need headings? Would diagrams, photographs, or other illustrations help you explain the information? | 15–17 |

Generating Ideas and Text

Good reports share certain features that make them useful and interesting to readers. Remember that your goal is to present information clearly and accurately. Start by exploring your topic.

Explore what you already know about your topic. Write out whatever you know or want to know about your topic, perhaps by **FREEWRITING, LISTING,** or **CLUSTERING.** Why are you interested in this topic? What questions do you have about it? Such questions can help you decide what you'd like to focus on and how you need to direct your research efforts.

199–202

Narrow your topic. To write a good report, you need to narrow your focus—and to narrow your focus, you need to know a fair amount about your subject. If you are assigned to write on a subject like biodiversity, for example, you need to know what it is, what key issues are, and so on. If you do, you can simply list or brainstorm possibilities, choose one, and start your research. If you don't know much about the subject, though, you need to do some research to discover focused, workable topics. This research may shape your thinking and change your focus. Start with **SOURCES** that can give you a general sense of the subject, such as an encyclopedia entry, a magazine article, an Internet site, perhaps an interview with an expert. Your goal at this point is simply to find out what issues your potential topic might include and then to focus your efforts on an aspect of the topic you will be able to cover.

340–53

Come up with a tentative thesis. Once you narrow your topic, write out a statement that explains what you plan to report or explain. A good **THESIS** is potentially interesting (to you and your readers) and limits your topic enough to make it manageable. Eastman and Burrell state their thesis in the form of a direct statement—"roller coasters work because of two main principles: the laws of conservation of energy and gravity"—

251–52

assuming that readers will know that in the essay that follows those two principles will be explained. DeRoven, on the other hand, lays out exactly what will be discussed: "This paper will explore the Great Depression through the eyes of ordinary Americans in the most impoverished region in the country, the American South, in order to detail how they endured and how the government assisted them in this difficult era." At this point, however, you need only a tentative thesis that will help focus any research you do.

Do any necessary research, and revise your thesis. To focus your research efforts, **OUTLINE** the aspects of your topic that you expect to discuss. Identify any aspects that require additional research and **DEVELOP A RESEARCH PLAN.** Expect to revise your outline as you do your research, since more information will be available for some aspects of your topic than others, some may prove irrelevant to your topic, and some may turn out to be more than you need. You'll need to revisit your tentative thesis once you've done any research, to finalize what your statement will be.

203–04
331–39

Ways of Organizing a Report

Reports can be organized in various ways. Here are three common ones:

[Reports on topics that are unfamiliar to readers]

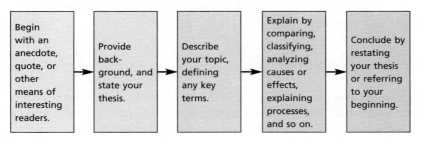

Begin with an anecdote, quote, or other means of interesting readers. → Provide background, and state your thesis. → Describe your topic, defining any key terms. → Explain by comparing, classifying, analyzing causes or effects, explaining processes, and so on. → Conclude by restating your thesis or referring to your beginning.

[Reports on an event]

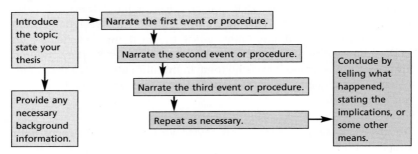

[Reports that compare and contrast]

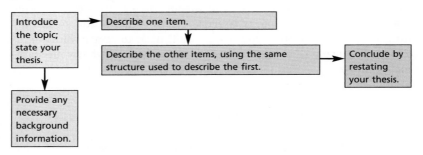

Many reports use a combination of organizational structures; don't be afraid to use whatever method of organization best suits your material and your purpose.

Writing Out a Draft

Once you have generated ideas and thought about how you want to organize your report, it's time to start **DRAFTING**. Do this quickly — try to write a complete draft in one sitting, concentrating on getting the report on paper or screen and on putting in as much detail as you can.

205–07

Writing that reports information often calls for certain writing strategies. The report on the hijacking of United 175, for example, uses **NARRATION**, telling readers what happened, minute by minute. The article about roller coasters requires the **DEFINITION** of concepts such as "gravity" and "conservation of energy." When you're reporting on a topic your readers aren't familiar with, you may wish to **COMPARE** it with something more familiar; you can find useful advice on these and other writing strategies in Part 4 of this book.

304–12
275–84
266–74

Draft a beginning.   Essays that report information often need to begin in a way that will get your audience interested in the topic. Here are a few ways of **BEGINNING**:

239–45

- *Simply state your thesis.* DeRoven begins his essay about "the greatest generation" this way. Opening with a thesis works well when you can assume your readers have enough familiarity with your topic that you don't need to give detailed background information.

- *Open by asking a question.* Eastman and Burrell open this way, asking a question about roller coasters that their report then answers: "Ever wonder how they get the energy to deliver thrill after thrill?"

- *Jump right in.* The writers of the report on the hijacking of United 175 can assume their audience is familiar with the events they are reporting on, so they open by saying simply that "United Airlines Flight 175 was scheduled to depart for Los Angeles at 8:00."

Draft an ending.   Think about what you want your readers to read last. An effective **ENDING** leaves them thinking about your topic.

245–48

- *Summarize your main points.* This is a good way to end when you've presented several key points you want readers to remember. Eastman and Burrell end this way when they write "Remember, the energy does not increase, decrease, or disappear; it just changes from one form to the other."

- *Point out the implications of your report.* DeRoven concludes with a paragraph explaining that "The federal action that fueled the Southern economy during the Great Depression changed the way of life for the better and helped Southerners endure a time of great despair."

- *Frame your report by referring to its introduction.* DeRoven begins and ends his report by mentioning "the greatest generation."

- *Tell what happened.* If you are reporting on an event, you could conclude by telling how it turns out. The report on the hijacking of United 175 ends powerfully by simply saying that "All on board, along with an unknown number of people in the tower, were killed instantly."

Come up with a title. You'll want a title that tells readers something about your subject—and makes them want to know more. Eastman and Burrell, for instance, get our interest in their report on how roller coasters work with the title "The Science of Screams," and tell us something about the subject of their report in a subtitle, "Laws of Physics Instill Thrills in Roller Coasters." See the chapter on **GUIDING YOUR READER** for tips on coming up with titles that are informative and enticing enough to make readers wish to read on.

250–54

Considering Matters of Design

You'll probably write your report in paragraph form, but think about the information you're presenting and how you can design and format it to make it as easy as possible for your readers to understand. You might ask yourself these questions:

454–55

- What is an appropriate **TYPEFACE?** Something serious like Times Roman, something traditional like Courier, something else?

456–57

- Would it help your readers if you divided your report into shorter sections and added **HEADINGS?**

455–56

- Is there any information that would be easier to follow if it were in a **LIST?**

458–60

- Could any of your information be summarized in a **TABLE?**

458–62

- Do you have any data that readers would more easily understand in the form of a bar **GRAPH**, line graph, or pie chart?

rhetorical situations   genres   processes   strategies   research mla/apa   media/design

- Would **ILLUSTRATIONS** — diagrams, photos, drawings, and so on — help you explain anything in your report?

458–62

Getting Response and Revising

The following questions can help you study your draft with a critical eye. **GETTING RESPONSE** from others is always good, and these questions can guide their reading, too. Make sure they know your purpose and audience.

213–14

- Do the title and opening sentences get readers' interest? If not, how might they do so?
- What information does this text provide, and for what purpose?
- Does the introduction explain why this information is being presented? Does it place the topic in a larger context?
- Are all key terms defined?
- As you read, do you have any questions? Is more information or explanation needed? Where might an example help you understand something?
- Is any information presented visually, with a chart, graph, table, drawing, or photograph? If so, is it clear how these illustrations relate to the larger text? Is there any text that would be more easily understood if it were presented visually?
- Does the organization help make sense of the information? Does the text include description, comparison, definition, or any other writing strategies? Does the topic or rhetorical situation call for any particular strategies?
- If the report cites any sources, are they quoted, paraphrased, or summarized effectively (and with appropriate documentation)?
- Does the report end in a satisfying way? What are readers left thinking?

These questions should identify aspects on your report you need to work on. When it's time to **REVISE,** make sure your report appeals to your audience and achieves your purpose as successfully as possible.

214–16

Editing and Proofreading

Readers equate correctness with the writer's competence. Once you've revised your draft, follow these guidelines for **EDITING** a report:

219–22 ○

- Check your use of key terms. Repeating key words is acceptable in reports; synonyms for unfamiliar words may confuse readers while the repetition of key words or the use of clearly identified pronouns can be genuinely helpful.

254 ◆

- Check your use of **TRANSITIONS** to be sure you have them where you need them.

456–57 ☐

- If you have included **HEADINGS,** make sure they're parallel in structure and consistent in design.

458–62 ☐

- Make sure that any photos or other **ILLUSTRATIONS** have captions, that charts and graphs have headings—and that all are referred to in the main text. Have you used white space effectively to separate sections of your report and to highlight graphic elements?

375–449 ●

- Check any **DOCUMENTATION** to see that it follows the appropriate style without mistakes.

222–23 ○

- **PROOFREAD** and spell-check your report carefully.

Taking Stock of Your Work

- How well did you convey the information? Is it complete enough for your audience's needs?
- What strategies did you rely on, and how did they help you achieve your purpose?
- How well did you organize the report?
- How did you go about researching the information for this piece?
- How did you go about drafting this piece?

- Did you use any tables, graphs, diagrams, photographs, illustrations, or other graphics effectively?
- How did others' responses influence your writing?
- What did you do especially well?
- What could still be improved?
- What would you do differently next time?

See Chapter 27 if you are required to submit your report in a writing **PORTFOLIO.** See also Chapter 10 on **ABSTRACTS** if your report requires one; Chapter 13 on **LAB REPORTS,** a kind of report written in the sciences; and Chapter 16 on **PROFILES,** a report based on firsthand research.

● 224–35
▲ 107–11

▲ 127–36

▲ 153–59

9 Arguing a Position

Everything we say or do presents some kind of argument, takes some kind of position. Often we take overt positions: "Everyone in the United States is entitled to affordable health care." "The university needs to offer more language courses." "Ice-T shouldn't have gone into acting." Some scholars claim that everything makes some kind of argument, from yellow ribbons that honor U.S. troops to a yellow smiley face, which might be said to argue for a good day. In college course work, you are constantly called on to argue positions: in an English class, you may argue for a certain interpretation of a poem; in a business course, you may argue for the merits of a flat tax; in a linguistics class, you may argue that English should not be made the official language of the United States. All of those positions are arguable—people of goodwill can agree or disagree with them and present reasons and evidence to support their positions. This chapter provides detailed guidelines for writing an essay that argues a position. We'll begin with three good examples.

Readings

ANNA QUINDLEN
Still Needing the F Word

Anna Quindlen is a columnist for Newsweek, *where this essay appeared in October 2003. In it, she argues that the goals defined by the feminist movement have not yet been achieved.*

Let's use the F word here. People say it's inappropriate, offensive, that it puts people off. But it seems to me it's the best way to begin, when it's simultaneously devalued and invaluable.

rhetorical situations · genres · processes · strategies · research mla/apa · media/design

Feminist. Feminist, feminist, feminist.

Conventional wisdom has it that we've moved on to a postfeminist era, which is meant to suggest that the issues have been settled, the inequities addressed, and all is right with the world. And then suddenly from out of the South like Hurricane Everywoman, a level '03 storm, comes something like the new study on the status of women at Duke University, and the notion that we're post-anything seems absurd. Time to use the F word again, no matter how uncomfortable people may find it.

Fem-i-nism n. 1. Belief in the social, political, and economic equality of the sexes.

That wasn't so hard, was it? Certainly not as hard as being a female   5
undergraduate at Duke, where apparently the operative ruling principle is something described as "effortless perfection," in which young women report expending an enormous amount of effort on clothes, shoes, workout programs, and diet. And here's a blast from the past: they're expected "to hide their intelligence in order to succeed with their male peers."

"Being 'cute' trumps being smart for women in the social environment," the report concludes.

That's not postfeminist. That's prefeminist. Betty Friedan wrote *The Feminine Mystique* exactly forty years ago, and yet segments of the Duke report could have come right out of her book. One seventeen-year-old girl told Friedan, "I used to write poetry. The guidance office says I have this creative ability and I should be at the top of the class and have a great future. But things like that aren't what you need to be popular. The important thing for a girl is to be popular."

Of course, things have changed. Now young women find themselves facing not one but two societal, and self-imposed, straitjackets. Once they obsessed about being the perfect homemaker and meeting the standards of their male counterparts. Now they also obsess about being the perfect professional and meeting the standards of their male counterparts. In the decades since Friedan's book became a best seller, women have won the right to do as much as men do. They just haven't won the right to do as little as men do. Hence, effortless perfection.

While young women are given the impression that all doors are open, all boundaries down, empirical evidence is to the contrary. A study from Princeton issued at the same time as the Duke study showed that faculty women in the sciences reported less satisfaction in their jobs and less of a sense of belonging than their male counterparts. Maybe that's because they made up only 14 percent of the faculty in those disciplines or because one out of four reported their male colleagues occasionally or frequently engaged in unprofessional conduct focusing on gender issues.

[In the 2003 election for governor,] Californians were willing to ignore Arnold Schwarzenegger's alleged career as a serial sexual bigot, despite a total of sixteen women coming forward to say he thought nothing of reaching up your skirt or into your blouse. (Sure, they're only allegations. But it was Arnold himself who said that where there's smoke, there's fire. In this case, there was a conflagration.) The fact that one of the actor's defenses was that he didn't realize this was objectionable—and that voters were OK with that—speaks volumes about enduring assumptions about women. What if he'd habitually publicly humiliated black men, or Latinos, or Jews? Yet the revelation that the guy often demeaned women with his hands was written off as partisan politics and even personal behavior. Personal behavior is when you have a girlfriend. When you touch someone intimately without her consent, it's sexual battery.

The point is not that the world has not changed for women since Friedan's book lobbed a hand grenade into the homes of pseudohappy housewives who couldn't understand the malaise that accompanied sparkling Formica and good-looking kids. Hundreds of arenas, from government office to the construction trades, have opened to working women. Of course, when it leaks out that the Vatican is proposing to scale back on the use of altar girls, it shows that the forces of reaction are always waiting, whether beneath hard hats or miters.

But the world hasn't changed as much as we like to tell ourselves. Otherwise *The Feminine Mystique* wouldn't feel so contemporary. Otherwise Duke University wouldn't find itself concentrating on eating disorders and the recruitment of female faculty. Otherwise the governor-elect of California wouldn't be a guy who thinks it's "playful" to grab and grope, and the voters wouldn't ratify that attitude. Part fair game, part perfection: that's a tough standard for 51 percent of everyone. The first women's rights activists a century ago set out to prove, in Friedan's words, "that woman was not a passive empty mirror." How dispiriting it would be to those long-ago heroines to read

10

of the women at Duke focused on their "cute" reflections in the eyes of others. The F word is not an expletive but an ideal—one that still has a way to go.

Quindlen offers evidence from a variety of sources—feminist scholarship, current events, a research study—to argue her position that the ideals of feminism have still not been met. She adopts an informal tone, which may help readers identify with her as she discusses values they may think they do not share with her. Since this essay appeared in a newsmagazine, Quindlen follows the convention of citing her sources only informally in the text, rather than offering exact citations and a list of references, as academic writers are expected to do.

LAWRENCE LESSIG

Some Like It Hot

This essay on electronic piracy appeared in Wired *magazine in March 2004. Lawrence Lessig is an authority on copyright law. He teaches at Stanford Law School, where he founded its Center for Internet and Society.*

If piracy means using the creative property of others without their permission, then the history of the content industry is a history of piracy. Every important sector of big media today—film, music, radio, and cable TV—was born of a kind of piracy. The consistent story is how each generation welcomes the pirates from the last. Each generation—until now.

The Hollywood film industry was built by fleeing pirates. Creators and directors migrated from the East Coast to California in the early twentieth century in part to escape controls that film patents granted the inventor Thomas Edison. These controls were exercised through the Motion Pictures Patents Company, a monopoly "trust" based on Edison's creative property and formed to vigorously protect his patent rights.

California was remote enough from Edison's reach that filmmakers like Fox and Paramount could move there and, without fear of the law, pirate his inventions. Hollywood grew quickly, and enforcement of federal law eventually spread west. But because patents granted their holders a truly "limited" monopoly of just seventeen years (at that time), the patents had expired by the time enough federal marshals appeared. A new industry had been founded, in part from the piracy of Edison's creative property.

Meanwhile, the record industry grew out of another kind of piracy. At the time that Edison and Henri Fourneaux invented machines for reproducing music (Edison the phonograph; Fourneaux the player piano), the law gave composers the exclusive right to control copies and public performances of their music. Thus, in 1900, if I wanted a copy of Phil Russel's 1899 hit, "Happy Mose," the law said I would have to pay for the right to get a copy of the score, and I would also have to pay for the right to perform it publicly.

But what if I wanted to record "Happy Mose" using Edison's phono-   5
graph or Fourneaux's player piano? Here the law stumbled. If I simply sang the piece into a recording device in my home, it wasn't clear that I owed the composer anything. And more important, it wasn't clear whether I owed the composer anything if I then made copies of those recordings. Because of this gap in the law, I could effectively use someone else's song without paying the composer anything. The composers (and publishers) were none too happy about this capacity to pirate.

In 1909, Congress closed the gap in favor of the composer and the recording artist, amending copyright law to make sure that composers would be paid for "mechanical reproductions" of their music. But rather than simply granting the composer complete control over the right to make such reproductions, Congress gave recording artists a right to record the music, at a price set by Congress, after the composer allowed it to be recorded once. This is the part of copyright law that makes cover songs possible. Once a composer authorizes a recording of his song, others are free to record the same song, so long as they pay the original composer a fee set by the law. So, by limiting musicians' rights—by partially pirating their creative work—record producers and the public benefit.

A similar story can be told about radio. When a station plays a composer's work on the air, that constitutes a "public performance." Copyright law gives the composer (or copyright holder) an exclusive right to public performances of his work. The radio station thus owes the composer money.

rhetorical situations ▲ genres ○ processes ◆ strategies ● research mla/apa □ media/ design

Both photos from Bettmann / Corbis

But when the station plays a record, it is not only performing a copy of the *composer's* work. The station is also performing a copy of the *recording artist's* work. It's one thing to air a recording of "Happy Birthday" by the local children's choir; it's quite another to air a recording of it by the Rolling Stones or Lyle Lovett. The recording artist is adding to the value of the composition played on the radio station. And if the law were perfectly consistent, the station would have to pay the artist for his work, just as it pays the composer.

But it doesn't. This difference can be huge. Imagine you compose a piece of music. You own the exclusive right to authorize public performances of that music. So if Madonna wants to sing your song in public, she has to get your permission.

Imagine she does sing your song, and imagine she likes it a lot. 10 She then decides to make a recording of your song, and it becomes a top hit. Under today's law, every time a radio station plays your song, you get some money. But Madonna gets nothing, save the indirect effect on the sale of her CDs. The public performance of her recording is not a "protected" right. The radio station thus gets to pirate the value of Madonna's work without paying her a dime.

No doubt, one might argue, the promotion artists get is worth more than the performance rights they give up. Maybe. But even if that's the case, this is a choice that the law ordinarily gives to the creator. Instead, the law gives the radio station the right to take something for nothing.

Cable TV, too: When entrepreneurs first started installing cable in 1948, most refused to pay the networks for the content that they hijacked and delivered to their customers — even though they were basically selling access to otherwise free television broadcasts. Cable companies were thus Napsterizing broadcasters' content, but more egregiously than anything Napster ever did — Napster never charged for the content it enabled others to give away.

Broadcasters and copyright owners were quick to attack this theft. As then Screen Actors Guild president Charlton Heston put it, the cable outfits were "free riders" who were "depriving actors of compensation."

Copyright owners took the cable companies to court. Twice the Supreme Court held that the cable companies owed the copyright owners nothing. The debate shifted to Congress, where almost thirty years later it resolved the question in the same way it had dealt with phonographs and player pianos. Yes, cable companies would have to pay for the content that they broadcast, but the price they would have to pay was not set by the copyright owner. Instead, lawmakers set the price so that the broadcasters couldn't veto the emerging technologies of cable. The companies thus built their empire in part upon a piracy of the value created by broadcasters' content.

As the history of film, music, radio, and cable TV suggest, even if 15 some piracy is plainly wrong, not all piracy is. Or at least not in the sense that the term is increasingly being used today. Many kinds of piracy are useful and productive, either to create new content or foster new ways of doing business. Neither our tradition, nor any tradition, has ever banned all piracy.

This doesn't mean that there are no questions raised by the latest piracy concern — peer-to-peer file sharing. But it does mean that we need to understand the harm in P2P sharing a bit more before we condemn it to the gallows.

Like the original Hollywood, P2P sharing seeks to escape an overly controlling industry. And like the original recording and radio indus-

rhetorical situations   genres   processes   strategies   research mla/apa   media/ design

tries, it is simply exploiting a new way of distributing content. But unlike cable TV, no one is selling the content that gets shared on P2P services. This difference distinguishes P2P sharing. We should find a way to protect artists while permitting this sharing to survive.

Much of the "piracy" that file sharing enables is plainly legal and good. It provides access to content that is technically still under copyright but that is no longer commercially available — in the case of music, some four million tracks. More important, P2P networks enable sharing of content that copyright owners want shared, as well as work already in the public domain. This clearly benefits authors and society.

Moreover, much of the sharing — which is referred to by many as piracy — is motivated by a new way of spreading content made possible by changes in the technology of distribution. Thus, consistent with the tradition that gave us Hollywood, radio, the music industry, and cable TV, the question we should be asking about file sharing is how best to preserve its benefits while minimizing (to the extent possible) the wrongful harm it causes artists.

The question is one of balance, weighing the protection of the law 20 against the strong public interest in continued innovation. The law should seek that balance, and that balance will be found only with time.

Lessig argues that the "piracy" that Napster and other peer-to-peer music-sharing services are accused of is similar to that practiced by every other electronic medium in the last one hundred years. He offers a clear definition of piracy and carefully supports his assertions with historical evidence for each one.

ANDY McDONIE

Airport Security: What Price Safety?

Here is an argument written in 2002 by Andy McDonie for his first-year writing course at Wright State University, in Dayton, Ohio.

We all want to feel safe. Most Americans lock their doors at night, lock their cars in parking lots, try to park near buildings or under lights, and wear seat belts. Many invest in expensive security systems, carry pepper spray or a stun gun, keep guns in their homes, or take self-defense classes. Obviously, safety and security are important issues in American life. But there are times when people are unable to protect themselves.

Air travel is one such situation. There is nowhere to run, and no one is allowed to carry weapons that could be used for self-defense on board an aircraft. Therefore, it is important that no one at all be allowed on board an airplane with a gun or any other weapon.

Unfortunately, this is much more easily said than done.

Though airlines and the U.S. government are taking many steps to ensure the safety of passengers, there is still a risk. In light of recent hijackings by militant Islamic Arabs, it would be very easy and economically sensible to target Middle Easterners for security checks at airports and anywhere else security could be an issue. This would allow everyone else who is statistically less likely to be a terrorist to travel more freely without long delays. However, as sensible and economical as this solution could be, it must never be allowed here in the United States.

One airline that targets passengers for security checks based on 5 ethnicity and gender is El Al, Israel's national airline. In "Unfriendly Skies Are No Match for El Al," Vivienne Walt, a writer for *USA Today*, describes her experience flying with this airline. Before anyone gets on any one of El Al's aircraft, he or she has to go through an extensive interview process. The intensity of the process depends on categories into which passengers fit. Jews are in the low-risk category. Most foreigners are medium risk, while travelers with Arabic names are very high-risk. Women traveling alone are considered high risk as well, because authorities fear that a Palestinian lover might plant a bomb in their luggage. Screening passengers takes time; El Al passengers must arrive three hours before their scheduled departure, and even so flights are sometimes delayed because of the screening process.

El Al is secretive about what goes on in its interviews, and company spokespersons admit that the airline will deny boarding privileges to certain ticket holders, but their security record is the best in the world. Since these and other policies took effect over twenty years ago, not one terrorist act has occurred on an El Al plane (Walt 1D–2D). El Al's anti-terrorist system is indisputably effective. But is it ethical?

Here in the United States, airports and airlines are racing to meet new security standards set by the federal government. As travelers are flying and as new regulations are being implemented, more and more air travelers are getting pulled aside for "random" security checks. In my experience, these checks may not be as random as the airports would like the public to think. Since September 11, 2001, I have spent several hours at airport gates and have boarded eight separate flights. Not once have I been delayed at the gate for a random security check. I am a young white male. However, I have seen who does get checked. I have seen some middle-class Caucasians checked, but at least from what I have observed, that is not the norm. Minorities are a target, especially minorities traveling alone. I have seen a seemingly disproportionate number of nonwhites delayed at gates. I have also noticed that women traveling alone or with other women are often picked out.

History has many examples of the U.S. government's suspending or abridging the rights of certain groups during wartime. In the Civil War, Abraham Lincoln suspended the right of habeas corpus (which allows prisoners to have their detention reviewed by a court of law), an act that was later ruled unconstitutional. During the First World War, freedom of speech was restricted by the Supreme Court, which declared, "When a nation is at war, many things that might be said in time of peace are such a hindrance to its effort that their utterance will not be endured so long as men fight and that no Court could regard them as protected by any constitutional right." During the same war, Pittsburgh banned Beethoven's music; the Los Angeles Board of Education forbade discussions of peace in school; and in many states German could not be taught. Perhaps the worst example of American wartime discrimination occurred during World War II, when Japanese Americans had their property seized and were forced to live in internment camps. Lieutenant General John L. DeWitt, one commander enforcing the internment, justified this policy by saying that "in the war in which we are now engaged, racial affiliations are not severed by migration. The Japanese race is an enemy race. . . . A jap is a jap" (O'Brien 419–25).

What can we learn from this grim history? Ben Franklin said that if we sacrifice freedom for security, we get neither. Though safety is important, at what price should it be bought? And if we sacrifice our freedoms for it, are we really safe? It would be easy for most Americans to justify restricting the rights of just one minority group. After all, most people would not be affected. But if we can oppress people from the Middle East during a time of crisis, we can do the same to any other group of people at any time. That is not the way Americans should have to live.

There is an additional point here: not all terrorists are of Middle 10 Eastern descent. If we were to target Middle Easterners for security checks, many Muslims might have difficulty boarding an aircraft, but the Unabomber or Timothy McVeigh would have had little or no trouble. Acts of murder, political turmoil, and terrorism are carried out by persons of all races and nationalities. Focusing on one group might only simplify the process for non-Arab terrorists.

New security measures exist in many European airports. Some use retinal scans, a high-tech way of identifying passengers by scanning their eyes. Most screen checked baggage and match checked baggage to passenger lists. Many airports interview all passengers. According to one German frequent flier, "The level of scrutiny at a checkpoint says a lot about security at the whole airport to me. I feel safer flying to the United States than flying back" (Davis).

Clearly more changes need to be made at airports worldwide. Though it would be more economically sensible to target certain groups, doing so would be unethical. If the rights of one group of people are jeopardized, then the rights of all Americans are jeopardized. Freedom must not be sacrificed for security.

Discriminating against a single group would also be ineffective. Many people of Arab descent would have difficulty boarding an aircraft, but white, black, or Asian terrorists could move through security easily. Targeting certain groups would be easier but less than fair. Instead of focusing on one or more groups, airlines should treat all passengers equally, using technology that is currently available.

Works Cited

Davis, Aaron. "Guarding Europe's Airports—Future of Air Travel Visible in Tight Security Terminal." *San Jose Mercury News*. 22 Nov. 2001: A1+.

O'Brien, Ed. "In War, Is Law Silent?" *Social Education* 65 (2001) 419–25.

Walt, Vivienne. "Unfriendly Skies Are No Match for El Al." *USA Today* 1 Oct. 2001: 1D–2D.

This argument offers a clear statement of its position: people of Middle Eastern descent must not be targeted for airport security checks. McDonie organizes his essay carefully: after introducing the topic, he contrasts El Al's procedures with

rhetorical situations　genres　processes　strategies　research mla/apa　media/ design

those of U.S. air carriers, provides examples of suspended rights in the United States during wartime, presents the core of his argument against targeted searches, and concludes by acknowledging the need for improved security.

For six more arguments, see **CHAPTER 53.**

Key Features / Arguments

A clear and arguable position. At the heart of every argument is a claim with which people may reasonably disagree. Some claims are not arguable because they're completely subjective, matters of taste or opinion ("I hate sauerkraut"), because they are a matter of fact ("The first *Star Wars* movie came out in 1977"), or because they are based on belief or faith ("There is life after death"). To be arguable, a position must reflect one of at least two points of view, making reasoned argument necessary: Internet file sharing should (or should not) be considered fair use; airport security should target certain groups (or should treat everyone the same). In college writing, you will often argue not that a position is correct but that it is plausible — that it is reasonable, supportable, and worthy of being taken seriously.

Necessary background information. Sometimes we need to provide some background on a topic we are arguing so that readers can understand what is being argued. McDonie establishes the need for special measures to ensure airline passengers' safety before launching his argument against targeting specific groups for security checks; Quindlen offers a characterization of the current connotations of the term *feminism* and provides its historical context as context for her argument that it's a term we're "still needing."

Good reasons. By itself, a position does not make an argument; the argument comes when a writer offers reasons to back the position up. There are many kinds of good reasons. Some are a matter of defining — Quindlen bases her argument about feminism on a dictionary definition of the word. Lessig makes his argument by comparing, showing many examples of so-called piracy in other media. McDonie's main reason for his position that we should not target Middle Easterners for airport security checks is that doing so is unethical.

Convincing support for each reason.   It's one thing to give reasons for your position. You then need to offer support for your reasons: facts, statistics, expert testimony, anecdotal evidence, case studies, textual evidence. All three essays use a mix of these types of support. Quindlen uses statistics from a Princeton study to support her claim that women do not yet have job equality in comparison with men; Lessig offers facts from the history of the broadcast media to support his argument for file sharing.

Appeals to readers' values.   Effective arguers try to appeal to readers' values and emotions. Both Quindlen and McDonie appeal to basic values — Quindlen to the value of equality, McDonie to the values of freedom and security. These are deeply held values that we may not think about very much and as a result may see as common ground we share with the writers. And some of Quindlen's evidence appeals to emotion — the examples she offers from Duke University and the state of California are likely to evoke an emotional response in many, if not all, readers.

A trustworthy tone.   Arguments can stand or fall on the way readers perceive the writer. Very simply, readers need to trust the person who's making the argument. One way of winning this trust is by demonstrating that you know what you're talking about. Lessig offers plenty of facts to show his knowledge of copyright history — and he does so in a self-assured tone. There are many other ways of establishing yourself (and your argument) as trustworthy — by showing that you have some experience with your subject (as McDonie does), that you're fair (as Quindlen suggests when she says that "hundreds of arenas . . . have opened to working women"), and of course that you're honest.

Careful consideration of other positions.   No matter how reasonable and careful we are in arguing our positions, others may disagree or offer counterarguments or hold other positions. We need to consider those other views and to acknowledge and, if possible, refute them in our written arguments. Quindlen, for example, acknowledges that women today have more employment opportunities than they did forty years ago, but she refers to the Duke study to refute any argument that women have attained complete equality with men.

A GUIDE TO ARGUING A POSITION

Choosing a Topic

A fully developed argument requires significant work and time, so choosing a topic in which you're interested is very important. Students find that widely debated topics such as "animal rights" or "gun control" can be difficult to write on because they seldom have a personal connection to them. Better topics include those that

- interest you right now,
- are focused, but not too narrowly,
- have some personal connection to your life.

One good way to **GENERATE IDEAS** for a topic that meets those three criteria is to explore your own roles in life.

199–204

Start with your roles in life. On a piece of paper, make four columns with the headings "Personal," "Family," "Public," and "School." Below each heading, **LIST** the roles you play that relate to it. Here is a list one student wrote:

200–01

Personal	Family	Public	School
gamer	son	voter	college student
dog owner	younger	homeless-shelter	work-study
old-car owner	brother	volunteer	employee
male	grandson	American	dorm resident
white		resident	primary-education
middle-class		of Ohio	major

Identify issues that interest you. Think, then, about issues or controversies that may concern you as a member of one or more of those groups. For instance, as a primary-education major, this student cares about the controversy over whether kids should be taught to read by phonics or by whole language methods. As a college student, he cares about the costs of a college education. Issues that stem from these subjects could include the following: Should reading be taught by phonics or whole language? Should college cost less than it does?

Pick four or five of the roles you list. In five or ten minutes, identify issues that concern or affect you as a member of each of those roles. It might help to word each issue as a question starting with *Should*.

Choose one issue to write about. Remember that the issue should be interesting to you and have some connection to your life. It is a tentative choice; if you find later that you have trouble writing about it, simply go back to your list of roles or issues and choose another.

Considering the Rhetorical Situation

3–4	■ **PURPOSE**	Do you want to persuade your audience to do or think something? change their minds? consider alternative views? accept your position as plausible — see that you have thought carefully about an issue and researched it appropriately?
5–8	■ **AUDIENCE**	Who is your intended audience? What do they likely know and believe about this issue? How personal is it for them? To what extent are they likely to agree or disagree with you? Why? What common ground can you find with them?
12–14	■ **STANCE**	How do you want your audience to perceive you? As an authority on your topic? As someone much like them? As calm? reasonable? impassioned or angry? something else? What's your attitude toward your topic, and why?

rhetorical situations ▲ genres ○ processes ◆ strategies ● research mla/apa □ media/design

■ **MEDIA / DESIGN**   What media will you use, and how do your media affect your argument? If you're writing on paper, does your argument call for photos or charts? If you're giving an oral presentation, should you put your reasons and support on slides? If you're writing on the Web, should you add links to counterarguments?

15–17

Generating Ideas and Text

Most essays that successfully argue a position share certain features that make them interesting and persuasive. Remember that your goal is to stake out a position and convince your readers that it is plausible.

Explore what you already know about the issue.   Write out whatever you know about the issue by freewriting or as a **LIST** or **OUTLINE**. Why are you interested in this topic? What is your position on it at this point, and why? What aspect do you think you'd like to focus on? Where do you need to focus your research efforts? This activity can help you discover what more you need to learn. Chances are you'll need to learn a lot more about the issue before you even decide what position to take.

199–201
203–04

Do some research.   At this point, try to get an overview. Start with one **GENERAL SOURCE** of information that will give you a sense of the ins and outs of your issue, one that isn't overtly biased. *Time, Newsweek,* and other national weekly newsmagazines can be good starting points on current issues; encyclopedias are better for issues that are not so current. For some issues, you may need to **INTERVIEW** an expert. For example, one student who wanted to write about chemical abuse of animals at 4H competitions interviewed an experienced show competitor. Use your overview source to find out the main questions your issue raises and to get some idea about the various ways in which you might argue it.

344

351–52

Explore the issue strategically.   Most issues may be argued from many different perspectives. You'll probably have some sense of the different views that exist on your issue, but you should explore multiple perspectives before deciding on your position. The following methods are good ways of exploring issues:

275–84

- As a matter of **DEFINITION**. What is it? How should it be defined? How can *phonics* or *whole language* be defined? How do backers of phonics define it—and how do they define *whole language*? How do advocates of whole language define it—and how do they define *phonics*? Considering these definitions is one way to identify different perspectives on the topic.

260–65

- As a matter of **CLASSIFICATION**. Can the issue be further divided? What categories might it be broken into? Are there different kinds of "phonics" and "whole language"? Do various subcategories suggest various positions or perhaps a way of supporting a certain position? Are there other ways of categorizing the teaching of reading?

266–74

- As a matter of **COMPARISON**. Is one way better than another? Is whole language a better way of teaching children to read than phonics? Is phonics a better way than whole language? Is the answer somewhere in the middle?

299–303

- As a matter of **PROCESS**. Should somebody do something? What? Should teachers use whole language to teach reading? Should they use phonics? Should they use a mix of the two methods?

Reconsider whether the issue can be argued.　Is this issue worth discussing? Why is it important to you and to others? What difference will it make if one position or another prevails? At this point, you want to be sure that your topic is worth arguing about.

Draft a thesis.　Having explored the possibilities, decide your position, and write it out as a complete sentence. For example:

> Pete Rose should not be eligible for the Hall of Fame.
> Reading should be taught using a mix of whole language and phonics.
> Genetically engineered foods should be permitted in the United States.

Qualify your thesis.　Rarely is a position on an issue a matter of being for or against; in most cases, you'll want to qualify your position—in cer-

tain circumstances, with certain conditions, with these limitations, and so on. This is not to say that we should settle, give in, sell out; rather, it is to say that our position may not be the only "correct" one and that other positions may be valid as well. Qualifying your **THESIS** also makes your topic manageable by limiting it. For example:

251–52

> Pete Rose should not be eligible for the Hall of Fame, though he should be permitted to contribute to major league baseball in other ways.
>
> Reading should be taught using a mix of phonics and whole language, but whole language should be the dominant method.
>
> Genetically engineered foods should be permitted in the United States if they are clearly labeled as such.

Some questions for qualifying a thesis

- Can it be true in some cases?
- Can it be true at some times?
- Can it be true for some groups or individuals?
- Can it be true under certain circumstances?

Come up with good reasons. Once you have a thesis, you need to come up with good reasons to convince your readers that it's plausible. Start by stating your position and then answering the question "Why?"

> **Thesis:** Pete Rose should not be eligible for the Hall of Fame. **Why?**
>
> **Underlying reason (because):** He bet on professional baseball games, an illegal practice. **Why?**
>
> **Underlying reason (because):** Professional athletes' gambling on the outcome of games will cause fans to lose faith in professional sports.

As you can see, this exercise can continue indefinitely as the underlying reasons grow more and more general and abstract. You can do the same with other positions:

> **Thesis:** Pete Rose should be eligible for the Hall of Fame. **Why?**
>
> **Underlying reason (because):** He's one of the greatest baseball players of all time. **Why?**

Underlying reason (because): Few players have played with more hustle and passion than Rose.

Write out your position, and then, below it, list several reasons. Think about which reasons are best for your purposes: Which seem the most persuasive? Which are most likely to be accepted by your audience? Which seem to matter the most now? If your list of reasons is short or you think you'll have trouble developing them enough to write an appropriate essay, this is a good time to rethink your topic — before you've invested too much time in it.

Develop support for your reasons.   Next, you have to come up with support for your reasons. Here are some of the ways you can offer support:

- facts
- statistics ("A national study found that X percent of . . . ")
- testimony by authorities and experts ("According to X, . . . ")
- anecdotal evidence ("This happened . . . ")
- scenarios ("What if . . . ?")
- case studies and observation ("This is what happened when . . . ")
- textual evidence ("I found this in . . . ")

Some kinds of support are acceptable to certain audiences but not to others. For example, case studies may be readily accepted in certain social sciences but not in the physical sciences; anecdotes or stories may be accepted as evidence in humanities courses but not in engineering. Some audiences will be persuaded by emotional appeals while others will not. You may well need to consult **SOURCES.**

340–53

Identify other positions.   Now, think about positions that differ from yours and about the reasons people are likely to give for those positions. Be careful to represent their points of view as accurately and fairly as

you can. Then decide whether you need to acknowledge or refute the position.

Acknowledging other positions.   Some positions can't be refuted, but still you need to acknowledge readers' doubts, concerns, and objections to show that you've considered them. Rather than weakening your argument, acknowledging possible objections shows that you've thought about and researched your argument thoroughly. For example, in an essay about his experience growing up homosexual, writer Andrew Sullivan acknowledges that not every young gay man or woman has the same experience: "I should add that many young lesbians and homosexuals seem to have had a much easier time of it. For many, the question of sexual identity was not a critical factor in their life choices or vocation, or even a factor at all." Thus does he qualify his assertions, making his own stance appear to be reasonable. In addition to acknowledging other views, though, you may sometimes shape other views to incorporate them into your own argument.

Refuting other positions.   State the position as clearly and as fairly as you can, and then show why you believe it is wrong. Are the values underlying the position questionable? Is the reasoning flawed? Is the supporting evidence inadequate or faulty? If the argument has some merit but fails on some points, say so, but emphasize its shortcomings. Avoid the **FALLACY** of attacking the person making the argument or bringing up a competing position that no one seriously entertains.

325–27

Ways of Organizing an Argument

Readers need to be able to follow the reasoning of your argument from beginning to end; your task is to lead them from point to point as you build your case. Sometimes you'll want to give all the reasons for your argument first, followed by discussion of any other positions. Alternatively, you might discuss each reason and any counterargument together.

[Reasons to support your argument, followed by counterarguments]

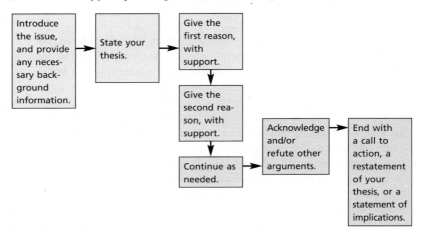

[Reason / counterargument, reason / counterargument]

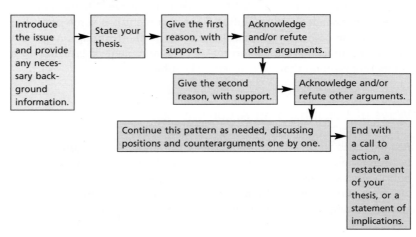

rhetorical situations

genres

processes

strategies

research mla/apa

media/ design

Consider the order in which you discuss your reasons. Usually what comes last is the most emphatic and what comes in the middle is the least emphatic, so you might want to put your most important or strongest reasons first and last.

Writing Out a Draft

Once you have generated ideas, done some research, and thought about how you want to organize your argument, it's time to start **DRAFTING.** Your goal in the initial draft is to develop your argument — you can fill in support and transitions as you revise. You may want to write your first draft in one sitting, so that you can develop your reasoning from beginning to end. Or you may write the main argument first and the introduction and conclusion after you've drafted the body of the essay; many writers find that beginning and ending an essay are the hardest tasks they face. Here is some advice on how you might **BEGIN AND END** your argument:

○ 205–07

◆ 239–49

Draft a beginning.   There are various ways to begin an argument essay, depending on your audience and purpose. Here are a few suggestions.

- *Offer background information.* You may need to give your readers information to help them understand your position. McDonie provides a rationale for Americans' desire to fly safely in dangerous times before stating his own position that safety must not be achieved through selective airport security checks.

- *Define a key term.* You may need to show how you're using certain key words. Lessig, for example, defines piracy as "using the creative property of others without their permission" in his first sentence, a definition that is central to his argument.

- *Begin with something that will get readers' attention.* Quindlen's first sentence does just that: "Let's use the F word here." From there, she goes on to argue that feminism "is not an expletive but an ideal."

- *Explain the context for your position.* All arguments are part of a larger, ongoing conversation, so you might begin by showing how your position fits into the arguments others have made. Quindlen does this in her third paragraph when she refers to the "conventional wisdom" that sees feminism as having accomplished all it set out to accomplish.

Draft an ending.　Your conclusion is the chance to wrap up your argument in such a way that readers will remember what you've said. Here are a few ways of concluding an argument essay.

321–22

- *Summarize your main points.* Especially when you've presented a complex argument, it can help readers to **SUMMARIZE** your main point. McDonie sums up his argument with the sentence "Freedom must not be sacrificed for security."

- *Call for action.* Lessig does this when he concludes by saying the law should seek a balance between copyright law and the need for continued innovation.

- *Frame your argument by referring to the introduction.* Quindlen does this when she ends by saying that "The F word is not an expletive but an ideal—one that still has a way to go."

Come up with a title.　Most often you'll want your title to tell readers something about your topic—and, if possible, to make them want to read on. McDonie covers both bases with his title and subtitle, "Airport Security: What Price Safety?" Quindlen's title doesn't quite tell us what she's writing about, but she probably makes a lot of readers continue reading to see what "Still Needing the F Word" is all about. See the chapter on

250–54

GUIDING YOUR READER for more advice on composing a good title.

Considering Matters of Design

You'll probably write your essay in paragraph form, but think about the information you're presenting and how you can design it in such a way as to make your argument as easy as possible for your readers to understand. Think also about whether any visual elements would be more persuasive than plain words.

454–55

- What would be an appropriate **TYPEFACE**? Something serious like Times Roman? Something traditional like Courier? Something else?

■ rhetorical situations　▲ genres　○ processes　◆ strategies　● research mla/apa　□ media/ design

- Would it help your readers if you divided your argument into shorter sections and added **HEADINGS?**

☐ 456–57

- If you're making several points, would they be easier to follow if you set them off in a **LIST?**

☐ 455–56

- Do you have any supporting evidence that would be easier to understand in the form of a bar **GRAPH,** line graph, or pie chart?

☐ 458–60

- Would **ILLUSTRATIONS** — photos, diagrams, or drawings — add support for your argument?

☐ 458–62

Getting Response and Revising

At this point you need to look at your draft closely, and if possible **GET RESPONSE** from others as well. The following are some questions for looking at an argument with a critical eye.

◯ 213–14

- Is there sufficient background or context?
- Is the thesis clear and appropriately qualified?
- Are the reasons plausible?
- Is there enough support for these reasons? Is that support appropriate?
- Have you cited enough sources, and are these sources credible?
- Can readers follow the steps in your reasoning?
- Have you considered potential objections or other positions? Are there any others that should be addressed?
- Are source materials documented carefully and completely, with in-text citations and a works cited or references section?

Next it's time to **REVISE,** to make sure your argument offers convincing support, appeals to readers' values, and achieves your purpose.

◯ 214–16

Editing and Proofreading

Readers equate correctness with competence. Once you've revised your draft, follow these guidelines for **EDITING** an argument:

◯ 219–22

- Make sure that every assertion you make is well supported.

12–14 ■

- Check to see that your tone is appropriate and consistent throughout, reflects your **STANCE** accurately, and enhances the argument you're making.

254 ◆

- Be sure readers will be able to follow the argument; check to see you've provided **TRANSITIONS** and summary statements where necessary.

358–69 ●
375–449 ●

- Make sure you've smoothly integrated **QUOTATIONS**, **PARAPHRASES**, and **SUMMARIES** from source material into your writing and **DOCUMENTED** them accurately.

458–62 □

- Make sure that **ILLUSTRATIONS** have captions and that charts and graphs have headings—and that all are referred to in the main text.

222–23 ◉

- **PROOFREAD** and spell-check your essay carefully.

Taking Stock of Your Work

Take stock of what you've written by writing out answers to these questions:

- What did you do well in this piece?
- What could still be improved?
- How did you go about researching your topic?
- How did others' responses influence your writing?
- How did you go about drafting this piece?
- Did you use graphic elements (tables, graphs, diagrams, photographs, illustrations) effectively? If not, would they have helped?
- What would you do differently next time?
- What have you learned about your writing ability from writing this piece? What do you need to work on in the future?

224–35 ◉
120–26 ▲
137–46 ▲
160–67 ▲

> See Chapter 27 if you are required to submit your argument as part of a writing **PORTFOLIO**. See also Chapter 12 on **EVALUATIONS**, Chapter 14 on **LITERARY ANALYSES**, and Chapter 17 on **PROPOSALS** for advice on writing those specific types of arguments.

■ rhetorical situations   ▲ genres   ○ processes   ◆ strategies   ● research mla/apa   □ media/design

Abstracts **10**

Abstracts are summaries written to give readers the gist of a report or presentation. Sometimes they are published in conference proceedings or databases. In some academic fields, you may be required to include an abstract in a **REPORT** or as a preview of a presentation you plan to give at an academic or professional conference. Abstracts are brief, typically 100–200 words, sometimes even shorter. Three common kinds are *informative abstracts*, *descriptive abstracts*, and *proposal abstracts*.

▲ 60–81

INFORMATIVE ABSTRACTS

Informative abstracts state in one paragraph the essence of a whole paper about a study or a research project. That one paragraph must mention all the main points or parts of the paper: a description of the study or project, its methods, the results, and the conclusions. Here is an example of the abstract accompanying a seven-page essay that appeared in 2002 in *The Journal of Clinical Psychology*:

> The relationship between boredom proneness and health-symptom reporting was examined. Undergraduate students (N = 200) completed the Boredom Proneness Scale and the Hopkins Symptom Checklist. A multiple analysis of covariance indicated that individuals with high boredom-proneness total scores reported significantly higher ratings on all five subscales of the Hopkins Symptom Checklist (Obsessive–Compulsive, Somatization, Anxiety, Interpersonal Sensitivity, and Depression). The results suggest that boredom proneness may be an important element to consider when assessing symptom reporting. Implications for determining the effects of boredom proneness on psychological- and physical-health symptoms, as well as the application in clinical settings, are discussed.
>
> —Jennifer Sommers and Stephen J. Vodanovich, "Boredom Proneness"

The first sentence states the nature of the study being reported. The next summarizes the method used to investigate the problem, and the following one gives the results: students who, according to specific tests, are more likely to be bored are also more likely to have certain medical or psychological symptoms. The last two sentences indicate that the paper discusses those results and examines the conclusion and its implications.

DESCRIPTIVE ABSTRACTS

Descriptive abstracts are usually much briefer than informative abstracts and provide much less information. Rather than summarizing the entire paper, a descriptive abstract functions more as a teaser, providing a quick overview that invites the reader to read the whole. Descriptive abstracts usually do not give or discuss results or set out the conclusion or its implications. A descriptive abstract of the boredom-proneness essay might simply include the first sentence from the informative abstract plus a final sentence of its own:

> The relationship between boredom proneness and health-symptom reporting was examined. The findings and their application in clinical settings are discussed.

PROPOSAL ABSTRACTS

Proposal abstracts contain the same basic information as informative abstracts, but their purpose is very different. You prepare proposal abstracts to persuade someone to let you write on a topic, do a project, conduct an experiment, or present a paper at a scholarly conference. This kind of abstract is not written to introduce a longer piece but rather to stand alone, and often the abstract is written before the paper itself. Titles and other aspects of the proposal deliberately reflect the theme of the proposed work, and you may use the future tense, rather than the past, to describe work not yet completed. Here is a possible proposal for doing research on boredom:

rhetorical situations | genres | processes | strategies | research mla/apa | media/ design

Undergraduate students will complete the Boredom Proneness Scale and the Hopkins Symptom Checklist. A multiple analysis of covariance will be performed to determine the relationship between boredom-proneness total scores and ratings on the five subscales of the Hopkins Symptom Checklist (Obsessive–Compulsive, Somatization, Anxiety, Interpersonal Sensitivity, and Depression).

Key Features / Abstracts

A summary of basic information. An informative abstract includes enough information to substitute for the report itself, a descriptive abstract offers only enough information to let the audience decide whether to read further, and a proposal abstract gives an overview of the planned work.

Objective description. Abstracts present information on the contents of a report or a proposed study; they do not present arguments about or personal perspectives on those contents. The informative abstract on boredom proneness, for example, offers only a tentative conclusion: "The results *suggest* that boredom proneness *may* be an important element to consider."

Brevity. Although the length of abstracts may vary, journals and organizations often restrict them to 120–200 words — meaning you must carefully select and edit your words.

A BRIEF GUIDE TO WRITING

Considering the Rhetorical Situation

■ **PURPOSE**	Are you giving a brief but thorough overview of a completed study? only enough information to create interest? or a proposal for a planned study or presentation?	3–4
■ **AUDIENCE**	For whom are you writing this abstract? What information about your project will your readers need?	5–8
■ **STANCE**	Whatever your stance in the longer work, your abstract must describe it objectively.	12–14

15–17

■ **MEDIA / DESIGN** How will you set your abstract off from the rest of the paper? If you are publishing it online, will you devote a single Web page to it or make it a preface to the longer work? What format does your audience require?

Generating Ideas and Text

Write the paper first, the abstract last. You can then use the finished work as the guide for the abstract, which should follow the same basic structure. *Exception:* You may need to write a proposal abstract months before the work it describes will be complete.

Copy and paste key statements. If you've already written the work, highlight your thesis objective, or purpose; basic information on your methods; statements f your results; and your conclusion. Copy and paste those sentences into a new document to create a rough version of your abstract.

321–22

Pare down the information to key ideas. SUMMARIZE the report, editing out any nonessential words and details. In your first sentence, introduce the overall scope of your study. Also include any other information that seems crucial to understanding your paper. Avoid phrases that add unnecessary words, such as "It is concluded that." In general, you probably won't want to use "I"; an abstract should cover ideas, not say what you think or will do.

Conform to any requirements. In general, an informative abstract should be at most 10 percent as long as the original and no longer than the maximum length allowed. Descriptive abstracts should be shorter still, and proposal abstracts should conform to the requirements of the organization calling for the proposal.

■ rhetorical situations ▲ genres ○ processes ◆ strategies ● research mla/apa □ media/design

Ways of Organizing an Abstract

[An informative abstract]

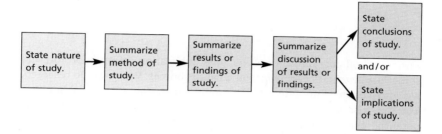

[A descriptive abstract]

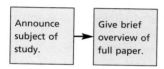

[A proposal abstract]

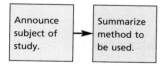

If You Need More Help

See Chapter 23 for guidelines on DRAFTING, Chapter 24 on ASSESSING YOUR DRAFT, Chapter 25 on GETTING RESPONSE AND REVISING, and Chapter 26 on EDITING AND PROOFREADING.

○ 205–07
○ 213–18
○ 219–23

11 Annotated Bibliographies

Annotated bibliographies describe, give publication information for, and sometimes evaluate each work on a list of sources. When we do research, we may consult annotated bibliographies to evaluate potential sources. You may also be assigned to create annotated bibliographies to weigh the potential usefulness of sources and to document your search efforts so that teachers can assess your ability to find, describe, and evaluate sources. There are two kinds of annotations, *descriptive* and *evaluative*; both may be brief, consisting only of phrases, or more formal, consisting of sentences and paragraphs. Sometimes an annotated bibliography is introduced by a short statement explaining its scope.

Descriptive annotations simply summarize the contents of each work, without comment or evaluation. They may be very short, just long enough to capture the flavor of the work, like the following excerpt from a bibliography of books and articles on teen films, published in 1997 in the *Journal of Popular Film and Television*.

MICHAEL BENTON, MARK DOLAN, AND REBECCA ZISCH

Teen Film$

In the introduction to his book *The Road to Romance and Ruin*, Jon Lewis points out that over half of the world's population is currently under the age of twenty. This rather startling fact should be enough to make most Hollywood producers drool when they think of the potential profits from a target movie audience. Attracting the largest demographic group is, after all, the quickest way to box-office success. In fact, almost from its beginning, the film industry has recognized the importance of the teenaged audience, with characters such as Andy Hardy and locales such as Ridgemont High and the 'hood.

rhetorical situations   genres   processes   strategies   research mla/apa   media/ design

Beyond the assumption that teen films are geared exclusively toward teenagers, however, film researchers should keep in mind that people of all ages have attended and still attend teen films. Popular films about adolescents are also expressions of larger cultural currents. Studying the films is important for understanding an era's common beliefs about its teenaged population within a broader pattern of general cultural preoccupations.

This selected bibliography is intended both to serve and to stimulate interest in the teen film genre. It provides a research tool for those who are studying teen films and their cultural implications. Unfortunately, however, in the process of compiling this list we quickly realized that it was impossible to be genuinely comprehensive or to satisfy every interest.

Doherty, Thomas. <u>Teenagers and Teenpics: The Juvenilization of American Movies in the 1950s</u>. Boston: Unwin Hyman, 1988.
Historical discussion of the identification of teenagers as a targeted film market.

Foster, Harold M. "Film in the Classroom: Coping with Teen Pics." <u>English Journal</u> 76 (1987): 86-88.
Evaluation of the potential of using teen films such as <u>Sixteen Candles</u>, <u>The Karate Kid</u>, <u>Risky Business</u>, <u>The Flamingo Kid</u>, and <u>The Breakfast Club</u> to instruct adolescents on the difference between film as communication and film as exploitation.

Paul, William. <u>Laughing, Screaming: Modern Hollywood Horror and Comedy</u>. New York: Columbia UP, 1994.
Critical history and discussion of the "gross-out" movie, discusses <u>Porky's</u> and <u>Carrie</u>.

Rapping, Elayne. "Hollywood's Youth Cult Films." <u>Cineaste</u> 16 (1987-88): 14-19.
Historical and chronological assessment of the image of teenagers and the "cult of youth" in American movies from James Dean to the characters in <u>River's Edge</u>.

Washington, Michael, and Marvin J. Berlowitz. "Blaxploitation Films and High School Youth: Swat Superfly." <u>Jump Cut</u> 9 (1975): 23-24.
Marxist reaction to the trend of youth-oriented black action films. Article seeks to illuminate the negative influences the films have on

high school students by pointing out the false ideas about education, morality, and the black family espoused by the heroes in the films.

These annotations are purely descriptive; the authors express none of their own opinions. They describe works as "historical" or "Marxist" but do not indicate whether they're "good." The bibliography entries are documented in MLA style.

Sometimes annotations go into much more detail and are more formal, as the following entry from a bibliography on censorship in the United States illustrates:

> Downs, Robert Bingham, ed. <u>The First Freedom Today: Critical Issues Relating to Censorship and Intellectual Freedom</u>. Chicago: American Library Association, 1984.
> This book is an anthology of writings about censorship and intellectual freedom in the United States. It gives an overview of the history of the subject and examines some of the key issues in the field, especially those that developed during the 1960s and 1970s. It includes excerpts from Thomas Emerson's writings on the First Amendment and then devotes several chapters to exploring censorship topics, including school textbooks and libraries, obscenity and pornography, the teaching of evolution, and topics of special interest to the press, such as libel, privacy, free press, and fair trial.

Evaluative annotations offer opinions on a source as well as describing it. The following two annotations show how an evaluative annotation can differ from a descriptive one:

DESCRIPTIVE ANNOTATION

> Krakauer, Jon. <u>Under the Banner of Heaven: A Story of Violent Faith</u>. New York: Doubleday, 2003.
> Krakauer explores the beliefs and sometimes violent actions of fundamentalist Mormons in the western United States. He focuses his study on two brothers who murdered the wife and infant daughter of their younger brother, believing they were acting under orders from God. Krakauer claims that the beliefs motivating their actions have created a climate promoting violent actions against nonbelievers.

EVALUATIVE ANNOTATION

Krakauer, Jon. <u>Under the Banner of Heaven: A Story of Violent Faith</u>.
    New York: Doubleday, 2003.
A chilling exploration of the beliefs and sometimes violent actions of funda-
mentalist Mormons in the western United States. Krakauer focuses his study
on two brothers who brutally murdered the wife and infant daughter of
their younger brother, believing they were acting under orders from God.
Krakauer argues that the beliefs that motivated their fanaticism have created a climate that leads to violent actions against nonbelievers and he
invites comparisons with Islamic extremists. The book offers an unflattering
portrait of Mormonism in general, as if all Mormons were somehow com-
plicit in the brothers' extreme actions. It's an implication that's hard to credit.

Key Features / Annotated Bibliographies

A statement of scope.   You need a brief introductory statement to explain
what you're covering. The authors of the bibliography on teen films introduce their bibliography with three paragraphs establishing a context for
the bibliography and announcing their purpose for compiling it.

Complete bibliographic information.   Provide all the information about
the source following one documentation system (**MLA**, **APA**, or another
one) so that your readers or other researchers will be able to find each
source easily.

● 375–449

A concise description of the work.   A good annotation describes each
item as carefully and objectively as possible, giving accurate information
and showing that you understand the source. These qualities will help to
build authority—for you as a writer and for your annotations.

Relevant commentary.   If you write an evaluative bibliography, your
comments should be relevant to your purpose and audience. The best way
to achieve relevance is to consider what questions a potential reader might
have about the sources. The evaluative annotation of the Krakauer book,
for example, assumes readers will want to know more than just what the

book is about and gives some sense of the book's tone and the controversy surrounding it.

Consistent presentation.   All annotations should follow a consistent pattern: if one is written in complete sentences, they should all be. Each annotation in the teen films bibliography, for example, begins with a phrase (not a complete sentence) characterizing the work.

A BRIEF GUIDE TO WRITING

Considering the Rhetorical Situation

<table>
<tr><td>3–4</td><td>■ PURPOSE</td><td>Will your bibliography need to demonstrate the depth or breadth of your research? Will your readers actually track down and use your sources? Do you need or want to convince readers that your sources are good?</td></tr>
<tr><td>5–8</td><td>■ AUDIENCE</td><td>For whom are you compiling this bibliography? What does your audience need or want to know about each source?</td></tr>
<tr><td>12–14</td><td>■ STANCE</td><td>Are you presenting yourself as an objective describer or evaluator? Or are you expressing a particular point of view toward the sources you evaluate?</td></tr>
<tr><td>15–17</td><td>■ MEDIA / DESIGN</td><td>If you are publishing the bibliography online, will you provide links from each annotation to the source itself? Online or off, do you need to distinguish the bibliographic information from the annotation by using a different font?</td></tr>
</table>

Generating Ideas and Text

Decide what sources to include.   You may be tempted to include in a bibliography every source you find or look at. A better strategy is to include only those sources that you or your readers may find potentially useful in

rhetorical situations · genres · processes · strategies · research mla/apa · media/design

researching your topic. For an academic bibliography, you need to consider these qualities:

- *Appropriateness.* Is this source relevant to your topic? Is it a primary source or a secondary source? Is it aimed at an appropriate audience? General or specialized? Elementary, advanced, or somewhere in between?

- *Credibility.* Is the author reputable? Is the publication or publishing company reputable? Do its ideas more or less agree with those in other sources you've read?

- *Balance.* Does the source present enough evidence for its assertions? Does it show any particular bias? Does it present countering arguments fairly?

- *Timeliness.* Is the source recent enough? Does it reflect current thinking or research about the subject?

If you need help **FINDING SOURCES,** see Chapter 40.

340–53

Compile a list of works to annotate. Give the sources themselves in whatever documentation style is required; see the guidelines for **MLA** and **APA** styles in Chapters 45 and 46.

378–416
417–49

Determine what kind of bibliography you need to write. Descriptive or evaluative? Will your annotations be in the form of phrases? complete sentences? paragraphs? The form will shape your reading and note taking. If you're writing a descriptive bibliography, your reading goal will be to understand and capture the writer's message as clearly as possible. If you're writing an evaluative bibliography, your annotations must also include your own comments on the source.

Read carefully. To write an annotation, you must understand the source's argument, but when you are writing an annotated bibliography as part of a **PROPOSAL,** you may have neither the time nor the need to read the whole text. Here's a way of quickly determining whether a source is likely to serve your needs:

160–67

- Check the publisher or sponsor (university press? scholarly journal? popular magazine? Web site sponsored by a reputable organization?).

- Read the preface (of a book), abstract (of a scholarly article), introduction (of an article in a nonscholarly magazine, or a Web site).
- Skim the table of contents or the headings.
- Read the parts that relate specifically to your topic.

Research the writer, if necessary.   If you are required to indicate the writer's credentials, you may need to do additional research. You may find information by typing the writer's name into a search engine or looking up the writer in *Contemporary Authors*. In any case, information about the writer should take up no more than one sentence in your annotation.

285–93 ◆ **Summarize the work in a sentence or two.**   **DESCRIBE** it as objectively as possible: even if you are writing an evaluative annotation, you can evaluate the central point of a work better by stating it clearly first. *If you're writing a descriptive annotation, you're done.*

120–26 ▲ **Establish criteria for evaluating sources.**   If you're **EVALUATING** sources for a project, you'll need to evaluate them in terms of their usefulness for 12–14 ■ your project, their **STANCE,** and their overall credibility.

Write a brief evaluation of the source.   If you can generalize about the worth of the entire work, fine. You may find, however, that some parts are useful while others are not, and what you write should reflect that mix.

Be consistent—in content, sentence structure, and format.

- *Content.* Try to provide about the same amount of information for each entry; if you're evaluating, evaluate each source, not just some sources.
- *Sentence structure.* Use the same style throughout—complete sentences, brief phrases, or a mix.
- 454–55 □ *Format.* Use one documentation style throughout; use consistent **TYPE** for each element in each entry—for example, italicize or underline all book titles.

rhetorical situations ▲ genres ○ processes ◆ strategies ● research mla/apa □ media/ design

Ways of Organizing an Annotated Bibliography

Depending on their purpose, annotated bibliographies may or may not include an introduction. Most annotated bibliographies cover a single topic and so are organized alphabetically by author's or editor's last name. When a work lacks a named author, alphabetize it by the first important word in its title. Consult the documentation system you're using for additional details about alphabetizing works appropriately.

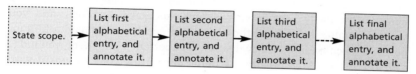

Sometimes an annotated bibliography needs to be organized into several subject areas (or genres, periods, or some other category) and the entries are listed alphabetically within each category. For example, a bibliography about terrorism breaks down into subjects such as "Global Terrorism" and "Weapons of Mass Destruction."

[Multi-category bibliography]

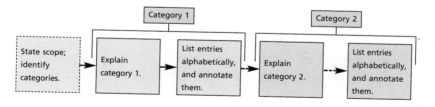

If You Need More Help

See Chapter 23 for guidelines on DRAFTING, Chapter 24 on ASSESSING YOUR DRAFT, Chapter 25 on GETTING RESPONSE AND REVISING, and Chapter 26 on EDITING AND PROOFREADING. See Chapter 27 if you are required to submit your bibliography in a writing PORTFOLIO.

○ 205–35

12 Evaluations

Consumer Reports evaluates MP3 players and laundry detergents. The *Princeton Review* and *US News and World Report* evaluate colleges and universities. You probably consult such sources to make decisions, and you probably evaluate things all the time—when you recommend a film (or not) or a teacher (ditto). An evaluation is at bottom a judgment; you judge something according to certain criteria, supporting your judgment with reasons and evidence. You need to give reasons for evaluating it as you do because often your evaluation will affect your audience's actions: they must see this movie, needn't bother with this book, should be sure to have the Caesar salad at this restaurant, and so on. In the following review, first done for a first-year writing class and later published in the *Dayton Daily News*, Ben Leever offers his evaluation of the TV drama *Dawson's Creek*.

BEN LEEVER

In Defense of Dawson's Creek: Teen Heroes Inspire Youths Seeking Answers

Ever since the Warner Brothers network began airing *Dawson's Creek*, religious and parental advocacy groups alike have criticized its sexually charged dialogue and have deemed it inappropriate for its target audience—teenagers and young adults.

The series, set in a small Massachusetts town and portraying the lives of high-school students, inarguably has embarked on controversial terrain. But rather than quick and thoughtless rebuke, the show deserves more serious analysis and even praise.

The first significant accomplishment of the show has been its commitment not to be a carbon copy of the rich-kids-with-petty-problems format (*Beverly Hills 90210*). Charting a riskier course for teen drama, creator Kevin Williamson has steered the series into delicate issues such as verbally abusive parents, manic depression, and, most recently, homosexuality.

The traditional themes of shows for this age group—maturing friendship, teenage rebellion, and romantic relationships—are still present. Gone, however, is the contrived backdrop of singularly happy, two-parent families living in upper-middle-class America.

One serious issue addressed this season is the "outing" of 17-year-   5
old Jack McPhee (Kerr Smith). In recent episodes, he struggled to find his sexual identity as classmates ridiculed and ostracized him because they suspected him of being gay. Although the writers created an unlikely vehicle for this revelation (a teacher forcing Jack to read out loud a poem he composed), as a recent high-school graduate I can verify that had a similar incident occurred at my alma mater, the response would have been every bit as thoughtless and hurtful.

As the New York *Daily News* recently reported, parents groups claim such issues have no place in shows aimed at teenagers. Brent Bozell, chairman of the Parents Television Council, said: "When you know that your audience is young, you have to know presenting them with such difficult questions is wrong."

Quite to the contrary, it would seem to be wrong to avoid topics such as sex, divorce, and homosexuality when they are clearly the reality of modern society. Bringing these topics to center stage and stimulating discussion would seem a far more effective way of confronting them than denying their existence.

Williamson's greatest success, though, has been the characters he created to deal with these true-to-life scenarios. In an age when highly acclaimed literature proudly portrays the Quentin Tarantino anti-hero, Williamson presents characters not yet enveloped by cynicism, whom we can admire.

Dawson Leery (James Van Der Beek), the show's star, is an excellent student who aspires to be a movie director. In the wake of his parents' recent divorce, he didn't turn to drugs or alcohol but instead fell back on his friends and is now directing a movie he wrote. His co-star, Joey Potter (Katie Holmes), dreams of being an artist while she maintains a stellar grade-point average and works a part-time job. Both characters have difficult home lives, yet both deal with their dilemmas in mature manners that parents could only hope their children imitate.

Dawson's Creek, while better than average, is not by any meas- 10 ure great drama. The dialogue is often needlessly complex and awkward, and the writers haven't escaped many of the clichés that plague teen drama. Yet despite its flaws, the series unabashedly tackles serious issue after serious issue, almost always presenting them from multiple viewpoints. The show's greatest strength is painting backdrops with which all teenagers can identify and then superimposing characters who shine in these difficult scenarios.

At a time when young people can hardly find heroes among their elders, *Dawson's Creek* portrays the nearly unknown heroic teenager. In doing so, the show provides inspiration for a generation desperately seeking answers to questions critics say it should never even address.

▌▌ For five more evaluations, see **CHAPTER 54**.

Leever tells us briefly what the show is about and states his assessment, giving several reasons for his opinion.

Key Features / Evaluations

A concise description of the subject. You should include just enough information to let readers who may not be familiar with your subject understand what it is; the goal is to evaluate, not summarize. Leever quickly describes *Dawson's Creek* as a TV series that focuses on youths in a small town and that contains "sexually charged dialogue."

Clearly defined criteria. You need to determine clear criteria as the basis for your judgment. In reviews or other evaluations written for a broad audience, you can integrate the criteria into the discussion as reasons for your assessment, as Leever does in his evaluation of *Dawson's Creek*. In more formal evaluations, you may need to announce your criteria explicitly. Leever mentions several criteria for evaluating this television show: originality; realism; believable characters willingness to focus on serious, even controversial issues.

A knowledgeable discussion of the subject. To evaluate something credibly, you need to show that you know it yourself and that you've researched what other authoritative sources say. Leever cites many examples, showing his knowledge of the plot and characters of *Dawson's Creek*. He does not cite anyone else's opinion of the show but does refer to what the chairman of the Parents Television Council has said about TV shows that tackle controversial issues.

A balanced and fair assessment. An evaluation is centered on a judgment. Leever concludes that *Dawson's Creek* "while better than average, is not by any measure great" but goes on to say that it "provides inspiration for a generation." It is important that any judgment be balanced and fair. Seldom is something all good or all bad. A fair evaluation need not be all positive or all negative; it may acknowledge both strengths and weaknesses. For example, a movie's soundtrack may be wonderful while the plot is not. Leever is careful to point out some of *Dawson's Creek*'s shortcomings (clichés, dialogue that is often "complex and awkward") even as he judges it good overall.

Well-supported reasons. Your need to give reasons for your judgment. Leever gives several reasons for his positive assessment of *Dawson's Creek*: that it tackles serious issues, that it does not present a "contrived back drop of . . . happy, two-parent families," and that it includes characters "we can admire," and he supports these reasons with examples from the show.

A BRIEF GUIDE TO WRITING

Choose something to evaluate. You can more effectively evaluate a limited subject than a broad one: review certain dishes at a local restaurant rather than the entire menu; review one film or episode rather than all the films by Alfred Hitchcock or all eighty *Star Trek* episodes. The more specific and focused your subject, the better you can write about it.

Considering the Rhetorical Situation

3–4

■ **PURPOSE** Are you writing to affect your audience's opinion of a subject? Do you want to evaluate something to help others decide what to see, do, or buy?

5–8

■ **AUDIENCE** To whom are you writing? What will your audience already know about the subject? What will they expect to learn from your evaluation of it? Are they likely to agree with you or not?

12–14

■ **STANCE** How will you show that you have evaluated the subject fairly and appropriately? Think about the tone you want to use: should it be reasonable? passionate? critical?

15–17

■ **MEDIA / DESIGN** How will you deliver your evaluation? In print? Online? As a speech? Can you show an image or film clip? If you're submitting your text for publication, are there any format requirements?

Generating Ideas and Text

199–200 ○

Explore what you already know. **FREEWRITE** to answer the following questions: What do you know about this subject or subjects like it? What are your initial or gut feelings, and why do you feel as you do? How does this subject reflect or affect your basic values or beliefs? How have others evaluated subjects like this?

Identify criteria. Make a list of criteria you think should be used to evaluate your subject. Think about which criteria will likely be important

5–8 ■
202 ○
202–03 ○

to your **AUDIENCE.** You might find **CUBING** and **QUESTIONING** to be useful processes for thinking about your topic.

Evaluate your subject. Study your subject closely to determine if it meets your criteria. You may want to list your criteria on a sheet of paper with space to take notes, or you may develop a grading scale for each criterion to help stay focused on it. Come up with a tentative judgment.

Compare your subject with others. Often, evaluating something involves COMPARING AND CONTRASTING it with similar things. We judge movies in comparison with the other movies we've seen and french fries with the other fries we've tasted. Sometimes those comparisons can be made informally. For other evaluations, you may have to do research — to try on several pairs of jeans before buying any, for example — to see how your subject compares.

266–74

State your judgment as a tentative THESIS statement. It should be one that balances both pros and cons. "*Fight Club* is a great film — but not for children." "Of the five sport-utility vehicles tested, the Toyota 4Runner emerged as the best in comfort, power, and durability, though not in styling or cargo capacity." Both of these examples offer a judgment but qualify it according to the writer's criteria.

251–52

Anticipate other opinions. I think Adam Sandler is a comic genius whose movies are first-rate. You think Adam Sandler is a terrible actor who makes awful movies. How can I write a review of his latest film that you will at least consider? One way is by acknowledging other opinions — and refuting those opinions as best I can. I may not persuade you to see Adam Sandler's next film, but I can at least demonstrate that by certain criteria he should be appreciated. You may need to RESEARCH how others have evaluated your subject.

329–449

Identify and support your reasons. Write out all the reasons you can think of that will convince your audience to accept your judgment. Review your list to identify the most convincing or important reasons. Then review how well your subject meets your criteria and decide how best to support your reasons: through examples, authoritative opinions, statistics, or something else.

Ways of Organizing an Evaluation

Evaluations are usually organized in one of two ways. One way is to introduce what's being evaluated, followed by your judgment, discussing your criteria along the way. This is a useful strategy if your audience may not be familiar with your subject.

[Start with your subject]

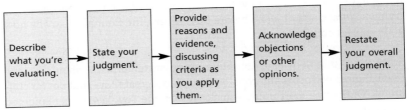

You might also start by identifying your criteria and then follow with a discussion of how your subject meets or doesn't meet those criteria. This strategy foregrounds the process by which you reached your conclusions.

[Start with your criteria]

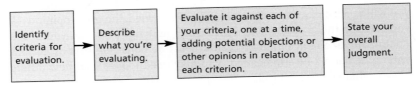

If You Need More Help

205–35 ○

See Chapter 23 for guidelines on **DRAFTING,** Chapter 24 on **ASSESSING YOUR DRAFT,** Chapter 25 on **GETTING RESPONSE AND REVISING,** and Chapter 26 on **EDITING AND PROOFREADING.** See Chapter 27 if you are required to submit your report in a writing **PORTFOLIO.**

Lab Reports **13**

Lab reports describe the procedures and results of experiments in the natural sciences, the social sciences, and engineering. We write reports of lab work in school to show instructors that we have followed certain procedures, achieved appropriate results, and drawn accurate conclusions. On the job, lab reports not only describe what we did and what we learned; they may also present data and interpretations to attempt to persuade others to accept our hypotheses, and they become a record that others may refer to in the future. As an example, here is a lab report written by a student for a psychology class at Wittenberg University.

SARAH THOMAS

The Effect of Biofeedback Training on Muscle Tension and Skin Temperature

Purpose

The purpose of this lab was for subjects to train themselves to increase their skin temperature, measured on the index finger of their non-dominant hand, and to decrease their muscle tension, measured over the frontalis muscle, by using biofeedback training. This study is based on the research of Miller and Brucker (1979), which demonstrated that smooth muscles could experience operant conditioning.

Methods

Subjects

Seven subjects were used in this study: five female and two male. The subjects were the undergraduate students of Dr. Jo Wilson in her honors psychophysiology class at Wittenberg University in Springfield, Ohio. All subjects were in their early twenties.

Apparatus

Equipment used in this lab included an Apple Microlab system configured to measure (1) skin temperature through a thermode taped with paper surgical tape onto the index finger of the subjects' nondominant hand and (2) frontalis muscle tension via three electrodes placed over the frontalis. When subjects' skin temperatures were more than the means for the previous 90-second intervals, the computer emitted a tone. It also emitted a tone when muscle tension in the frontalis was less than the mean of the previous interval. See the procedure section for exact electrode placement specifications.

Materials

Materials used in this lab included paper surgical tape, alcohol to clean off the forehead, conducting gel, wire, electrode collars, and a chair.

Procedure

Upon arriving at the lab, the researchers turned on the Apple Microlab computer. With the aid of Dr. Wilson, subjects had either electrodes attached to their forehead or a thermode attached to the nondominant hand's index finger. The treatment order was random for each subject, and it was reversed for his or her second biofeedback session. The forehead was swiped with alcohol to clean the skin. Electrodes with conducting gel were placed over the frontalis muscle by putting the ground electrode in the center of the forehead and the white electrodes two inches on either side of the center of the forehead. Premeasured electrode collars allowed the researchers to place the conducting gel on the electrodes, peel off the backing on the collar, and place it on the subjects' forehead. The researchers still made sure the electrodes were placed properly. The wire running from the electrodes to the computer was then taped to the subjects' back so it would be out of the way. Subjects were then seated in a comfortable chair with their back to the computer.

Depending on the experimental condition, subjects were told to reduce their frontalis muscle tension by relaxing and even thinking of holding something warm in their hands. They were told that they

would know they were meeting the goal when they heard a tone emitted by the computer.

Each session began with a 90-second baseline period, followed by fifteen 90-second trial periods. During each trial period, a tone was emitted by the computer each time the subjects' frontalis muscle tension was below their mean tension for the previous trial; the tone served as the rewarding stimulus in the operant conditioning paradigm.

When skin temperature was to be measured, a thermode was attached to the index finger of the subjects' nondominant hand with surgical tape. The wire running from the thermode to the computer was taped to the back of their hand so it would be out of their way. Then a 90-second baseline period occurred, followed by fifteen 90-second trial periods. During each trial period, a tone was emitted by the computer each time the subjects' skin temperature was above their mean temperature for the previous trial; once again, the tone served as the rewarding stimulus in the operant conditioning paradigm.

Results

The results of this lab were generally similar (Tables 1 and 2). All subjects demonstrated the ability to increase their skin temperature and decrease the tension in their frontalis muscle in at least one of their sessions. Five subjects were able to increase their skin temperature in both sessions; the same number decreased their muscle tension in both trials.

The majority of subjects (five) were able to both increase the skin temperature of the index finger of their nondominant hand and decrease the tension of their frontalis muscle more during the second trial than the first.

Specifically, subject 7 had atypical results. This subject's overall average skin temperature was less than the baseline value; the subject's overall average muscle tension was more than the baseline value.

Discussion

The bulk of the data collected in this study validated the research of Neal Miller; the subjects appeared to undergo operant conditioning of their smooth muscles in order to relax their frontalis muscles and increase their skin temperatures. Subjects 3 and 6 each failed to do this in one session; subject 7 failed to do this several times. This finding is difficult to explain precisely. It is possible that for subjects 3 and 6, this

Table 1: Skin Temperature in Degrees Fahrenheit during Sessions 1 and 2

	Subject 1	Subject 2	Subject 3	Subject 4	Subject 5	Subject 6	Subject 7
Baseline, Session 1	75.2	77.3	78.5	74.3	78.0	67.7	75.1
Mean skin temp, Session 1	79.3	85.6	78.5	74.4	83.2	73.5	72.6
Mean minus baseline, Session 1	4.1	8.3	0.0	0.1	5.2	5.8	−2.5
Baseline, Session 2	77.9	80.1	69.5	80.9	67.2	73.7	88.0
Mean skin temp, Session 2	79.9	86.3	70.7	84.6	76.8	79.7	88.8
Mean minus baseline, Session 2	2.0	6.2	1.2	3.7	9.6	6.0	0.8
Overall average of mean skin temp minus baseline	3.1	7.3	0.6	1.9	7.4	5.9	−0.85

data was a fluke. For subject 7, it is likely that the subject was simply stressed due to outside factors before arriving for the first trials of EMG and skin temperature, and this stress skewed the data.

The effect of biofeedback training was generally greater as the operant conditioning became better learned. Learning was indicated by the finding that the majority of the subjects performed better on the second trials than on the first trials. This finding shows the effectiveness of biofeedback on reducing factors associated with stress, like muscle ten-

Table 2:   EMG of the Frontalis Muscle in Microvolts for Sessions 1 and 2

	Subject 1	Subject 2	Subject 3	Subject 4	Subject 5	Subject 6	Subject 7
Baseline, Session 1	4.4	4.5	2.8	3.8	7.9	3.1	2.4
Mean EMG, Session 1	2.1	1.4	1.7	3.2	2.0	3.7	3.2
Baseline minus mean, Session 1	2.3	3.1	1.1	0.6	5.9	−0.6	−0.8
Baseline, Session 2	4.1	2.3	3.0	2.9	11.1	6.5	1.9
Mean EMG, Session 2	1.3	1.3	1.4	2.3	2.5	3.2	1.4
Baseline minus mean, Session 2	2.8	1.0	1.6	0.6	8.6	3.3	0.5
Overall average of mean EMG minus baseline	2.6	2.1	1.4	0.6	7.3	1.4	−0.15

sion and low skin temperature; biofeedback's impact is even greater when it is administered over time. The implications of this information are without limits, especially for the treatment of a variety of medical disorders.

There were a few problems with this lab. The subjects all were at different levels of relaxation to begin with. It is impossible to determine the effects of outside events, like exams or other stresses, on their EMG and skin temperature levels. Skin temperature itself could have been altered by cold outside temperatures. Being in a lab may have altered the stress level of some subjects, and noises from outside the lab may have had an effect as well.

If this study were repeated, it would be a good idea to let sub- 15
jects simply be in the lab for a period of time before measures are
taken. This would allow the effect of outside temperature to be minimized. It would also reduce the effect of getting used to the lab,
decreasing the orienting response. Finally, it would also be good to do
the experiment in a soundproof room.

Reference

Miller, N. E., & Brucker, B. S. (1979). A learned visceral response apparently independent of skeletal ones in patients paralyzed by spinal
lesions. In N. Birnbaumer & H. D. Kimmel (Eds.), *Biofeedback and
self-regulation* (pp. 287–304). Hillsdale, NJ: Erlbaum.

*This report includes categories commonly part of lab reports in the natural and
social sciences: purpose, method, results, discussion, and references. Some
reports keep results and discussion in one section; some reports include an
abstract; and some reports include one or more appendices containing tables,
calculations, and other supplemental material, depending on the audience and
publication. In this example, the author assumes that her audience understands
basic terms used in the report, such as frontalis muscle and biofeedback.*

Key Features / Lab Reports

Most lab reports include the following strictly defined parts:

An explicit title. Lab report titles should describe the report factually
and explicitly to let readers know exactly what the report is about and to
provide key words for indexes and search engines. Avoid phrases like "an
Investigation into" or "a Study of" and titles that are clever or cute.
Thomas's title, "The Effect of Biofeedback Training on Muscle Tension
and Skin Temperature," clearly describes the report's subject and includes
the key words needed for indexing (*biofeedback training, muscle tension, skin
temperature*).

rhetorical
situations
genres
processes
strategies
research
mla/apa
media/
design

Abstract.   Some lab reports include a one-paragraph, 100–200-word **ABSTRACT,** a summary of the report's purpose, method, and discussion.

▲ 107–11

Purpose.   Sometimes called an "Introduction," this section describes the reason for conducting the study: Why is this research important? What has been done by others, and how does your work relate to previous work? Why are you doing this research? What will your research tell us?

Methods.   Here you describe how you conducted the study, including the materials and equipment you used and the procedures you followed. This is usually written as a narrative, explaining the process you followed in order to allow others to repeat your study, step-by-step. Your discussion should thoroughly describe the following:

- subjects studied and any necessary contextual information
- apparatus—equipment used, by brand and model number
- materials used
- procedures—including reference to the published work that describes any procedures you used that someone else had already followed; the techniques you used and any modifications you made to them; any statistical methods you used

Results and discussion.   Here you analyze the results and present their implications, explain your logic in accepting or rejecting your initial hypotheses, relate your work to previous work in the field, and discuss the experiment's design and techniques and how they may have affected the results: what did you find out, and what does it mean? In longer reports, you may have two separate sections; "Results" should focus on the factual data you collected by doing the study; "Discussion" should speculate about what the study means: why the results turned out as they did, and what the implications for future studies may be.

References. List works cited in your report, alphabetized by author's last name and using the appropriate documentation style.

Appendices. Appendices are optional, presenting information that is too detailed for the body of the report.

Appropriate format. The design conventions for lab reports vary from discipline to discipline, so you'll need to check to see that yours meets the appropriate requirements. Find out whether any sections need to start their own page, whether you need to include a list of figures, whether you need to include a separate title page—and whether there are any other conventions you need to follow.

A BRIEF GUIDE TO WRITING

Considering the Rhetorical Situation

<table>
<tr>
<td>3–4</td>
<td>■ PURPOSE</td>
<td>Why are you writing? To demonstrate your ability to follow the appropriate methods and make logical inferences? To persuade others that your hypotheses are sound and your conclusions believable? To provide a record of the experiment for others?</td>
</tr>
<tr>
<td>5–8</td>
<td>■ AUDIENCE</td>
<td>Can you assume that your audience is familiar with the field's basic procedures? How routine were your procedures? Which procedures need to be explained in greater detail so your audience can repeat them?</td>
</tr>
<tr>
<td>12–14</td>
<td>■ STANCE</td>
<td>Lab reports need to have an impersonal, analytical stance. Take care not to be too informal, and don't try to be cute.</td>
</tr>
<tr>
<td>15–17</td>
<td>■ MEDIA / DESIGN</td>
<td>Are you planning to deliver your report in print or online? All lab reports have headings; choose a typeface that includes bold or italics so your headings will show clearly.</td>
</tr>
</table>

Generating Ideas and Text

Research your subject.   Researchers do not work in isolation; rather, each study contributes to an ever-growing body of information, and you need to situate your work in that context. **RESEARCH** what studies others have done on the same subject and what procedures those studies followed.

329–449

Take careful notes as you perform your study.   A lab report must be repeatable. Another researcher should be able to duplicate your study exactly, using only your report as a guide, so you must document every method, material, apparatus, and procedure very carefully. Break down procedures and activities into discrete parts, and record them in the order in which they occurred. **ANALYZE CAUSES AND EFFECTS;** think about whether you should **COMPARE** your findings with other studies. Take very careful notes so that you'll be able to **EXPLAIN PROCESSES** you followed.

255–59
266–74
299–303

DRAFT the report a section at a time.   You may find it easiest to start with the "Methods" or "Results" section first, then draft the "Discussion," followed by the "Purpose." Do the "Abstract" last.

205–07

- Write in complete sentences and paragraphs.
- Avoid using the first person *I* or *we*; keep the focus on the study and the actions taken.
- Use the active voice as much as possible ("the rats pushed the lever" rather than "the lever was pushed by the rats").
- Use the past tense throughout the report.
- Place subjects and verbs close together to make your sentences easy to follow.
- Use precise terms consistently throughout the report; don't alternate among synonyms.
- Be sure that each pronoun refers clearly to one noun.

Organizing a Lab Report

Lab reports vary in their details but generally include these sections:

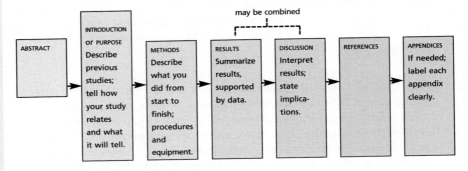

If You Need More Help

205–35 ○

See Chapter 24 on **ASSESSING YOUR DRAFT,** Chapter 25 on **GETTING RESPONSE AND REVISING,** and Chapter 26 on **EDITING AND PROOFREADING.** See Chapter 27 if you are required to submit your report in a writing **PORTFOLIO.**

Literary Analyses 14

Literary analyses are essays in which we examine literary texts closely to understand their messages, interpret their meanings, and appreciate their writers' techniques. You might read *Macbeth* and notice that Shakespeare's play contains a pattern of images of blood. You could explore the distinctive point of view in Ambrose Bierce's story "An Occurrence at Owl Creek Bridge." Or you could point out the differences between Stephen King's *The Shining* and Stanley Kubrick's screenplay based on that novel. In all these cases, you use specific analytical tools to go below the surface of the work to deepen your understanding of how it works and what it means. Here is a sonnet by the nineteenth-century English Romantic poet Percy Bysshe Shelley, followed by one student's analysis of it written for a literature course at Wright State University.

PERCY BYSSHE SHELLEY

Sonnet: "Lift Not the Painted Veil Which Those Who Live"

Lift not the painted veil which those who live
Call Life: though unreal shapes be pictured there,
And it but mimic all we would believe
With colours idly spread,—behind, lurk Fear
And Hope, twin Destinies; who ever weave   5
Their shadows, o'er the chasm, sightless and drear.
I knew one who had lifted it—he sought,
For his lost heart was tender, things to love,
But found them not, alas! nor was there aught

The world contains, the which he could approve. 10
Through the unheeding many he did move,
A splendour among shadows, a bright blot
Upon this gloomy scene, a Spirit that strove
For truth, and like the Preacher found it not.

STEPHANIE HUFF

Metaphor and Society in Shelley's "Sonnet"

In his sonnet "Lift not the painted veil which those who live," Percy Bysshe Shelley introduces us to a bleak world that exists behind veils and shadows. We see that although fear and hope both exist, truth is dishearteningly absent. This absence of truth is exactly what Shelley chooses to address as he uses metaphors of grim distortion and radiant incandescence to expose the counterfeit nature of our world.

The speaker of Shelley's poem presents bold assertions about the nature of our society. In the opening lines of the poem, he warns the reader to "Lift not the painted veil which those who live / Call Life" (1–2). Here, the "painted veil" serves as a grim metaphor for life. More specifically, the speaker equates the veil with what people like to *call* life. In this sense, the speaker asserts that what we believe to be pure reality is actually nothing more than a covering that masks what really lies beneath. Truth is covered by a veil of falsehood and is made opaque with the paint of people's lies.

This painted veil does not completely obstruct our view, but rather distorts what we can see. All that can be viewed through it are "unreal shapes" (2) that metaphorically represent the people that make up this counterfeit society. These shapes are not to be taken for truth. They are unreal, twisted, deformed figures of humanity, people full of falsities and misrepresentations.

Most people, however, do not realize that the shapes and images seen through the veil are distorted because all they know of life is the veil—this life we see as reality only "mimic[s] all we would believe" (3), using "colours idly spread" (4) to create pictures that bear little resemblance to that which they claim to portray. All pure truths are covered up and painted over until they are mere mockeries. The lies that cloak the truth are not even carefully constructed, but are created

idly, with little attention to detail. The paint is not applied carefully, but merely spread across the top. This idea of spreading brings to mind images of paint slopped on so heavily that the truth beneath becomes nearly impossible to find. Even the metaphor of color suggests only superficial beauty — "idly spread" (4) — rather than any sort of pure beauty that could penetrate the surface of appearances.

What really lies behind this facade are fear and hope, both of which "weave / Their shadows, o'er the chasm, sightless and drear" (5–6). These two realities are never truly seen or experienced, though. They exist only as shadows. Just as shadows appear only at certain times of day, cast only sham images of what they reflect, and are paid little attention, so too do these emotions of hope and fear appear only as brief, ignored imitations of themselves when they enter the artificiality of this chasmlike world. Peering into a chasm, one cannot hope to make out what lies at the bottom. At best one could perhaps make out shadows and even that cannot be done with any certainty as to true appearance. The world is so large, so caught up in itself and its counterfeit ways, that it can no longer see even the simple truths of hope and fear. Individuals and civilizations have become sightless, dreary, and as enormously empty as a chasm.

This chasm does not include *all* people, however, as we are introduced to one individual, in line 7, who is trying to bring to light whatever truth may yet remain. This one person, who defies the rest of the world, is portrayed with metaphors of light, clearly standing out among the dark representations of the rest of mankind. He is first presented to us as possessing a "lost heart" (8) and seeking things to love. It is important that the first metaphor applied to him be a heart because this is the organ with which we associate love, passion, and purity. We associate it with brightness of the soul, making it the most radiant spot of the body. He is then described as a "splendour among shadows" (12), his purity and truth brilliantly shining through the darkness of the majority's falsehood. Finally, he is equated with "a bright blot / Upon this gloomy scene" (12–13), his own bright blaze of authenticity burning in stark contrast to the murky phoniness of the rest of the world.

These metaphors of light are few, however, in comparison to those of grim distortion. So, too, are this one individual's radiance and zeal too little to alter the warped darkness they temporarily pierce. This one person, though bright, is not bright enough to light up the rest of civilization and create real change. The light simply confirms the dark falsity that comprises the rest of the world. Shelley gives us one flame of hope, only to reveal to us what little chance it has under the suffocating veil. Both the metaphors of grim distortion and those of radiant incandescence work together in this poem to highlight the world's counterfeit nature.

For five more literary analyses, see **CHAPTER 55.**

Huff focuses her analysis on patterns in Shelley's imagery. In addition, she pays careful attention to individual words and to how, as the poem unfolds, they create a certain meaning. That meaning is her interpretation.

Key Features / Literary Analyses

An arguable thesis. A literary analysis is a form of argument; you are arguing that your analysis of a literary work is valid. Your thesis, then, should be arguable, as Huff's is: "[Shelley] uses metaphors of grim distortion and radiant incandescence to expose the counterfeit nature of our world." A mere summary—"Shelley writes about a person who sees reality and seeks love but never finds it"—would not be arguable and therefore is not a good thesis.

Careful attention to the language of the text. The key to analyzing a text is looking carefully at the language, which is the foundation of its meaning. Specific words, images, metaphors—these are where analysis begins. You may also bring in contextual information, such as cultural, historical, or biographical facts, or you may refer to similar texts. But the words, phrases, and sentences that make up the text you are analyzing are your primary source when dealing with texts. That's what literature teachers mean by "close reading": reading with the assumption that every word of a text is meaningful.

Attention to patterns or themes. Literary analyses are usually built on evidence of meaningful patterns or themes within a text or among several texts. These patterns and themes reveal meaning. In Shelley's poem, images of light and shadow and artifice and reality create patterns of meaning, while the poem's many half rhymes (*live/believe*, *love/approve*) create patterns of sound that may contribute to the overall meaning.

rhetorical situations   genres   processes   strategies   research mla/apa   media/ design

A clear interpretation.   A literary analysis demonstrates the plausibility of its thesis by using evidence from the text and, sometimes, relevant contextual evidence to explain how the language and patterns found there support a particular interpretation. When you write a literary analysis, you show readers one way the text may be read and understood; that is your interpretation.

MLA style.   Literary analyses usually follow MLA style. Even though Huff's essay has no works-cited list, it refers to line numbers using MLA style.

A BRIEF GUIDE TO WRITING

Considering the Rhetorical Situation

■ **PURPOSE**	What do you need to do—show that you have examined the text carefully? offer your own interpretation? demonstrate a particular analytical technique? Or some combination? If you're responding to an assignment, does it specify what you need to do?	3–4
■ **AUDIENCE**	What do you need to do to convince your readers that your interpretation is plausible and based on sound analysis? Can you assume that readers are already familiar with the text you are analyzing, or do you need to tell them about it?	5–8
■ **STANCE**	How can you see your subject through interested, curious eyes—and then step back in order to see what your observations might *mean*?	12–14
■ **MEDIA/DESIGN**	Will your analysis focus on a print text and take the form of a print text? If your subject is a visual or electronic medium, will you need to show significant elements in your analysis? Are you required to follow MLA or some other style?	15–17

Generating Ideas and Text

Look at your assignment. Does it specify a particular kind of analysis? Does it ask you to consider a particular theme? to use any specific critical approaches? Look for any terms that tell you what to do, words like *analyze, compare, interpret,* and so on.

Study the text with a critical eye. When we read a literary work, we often come away with a reaction to it: we like it, we hate it, it made us cry or laugh, it perplexed us. That may be a good starting point for a literary analysis, but students of literature need to go beyond initial reactions, to think about HOW THE TEXT WORKS: What does it *say,* and what does it *do?* What elements make up this text? How do those elements work together or fail to work together? Does this text lead you to think or feel a certain way? How does it fit into a particular context (of history, culture, technology, genre, and so on)?

319–21

Choose a method for analyzing the text. There are various ways to analyze your subject. Three common focuses are on the text itself, on your own experience reading it, and on other cultural, historical, or literary contexts.

- *The text itself.* Trace the development and expression of themes, characters, and language through the work. How do they help to create the overall meaning, tone, or effect for which you're arguing? To do this, you might look at the text as a whole, something you can understand from all angles at once. You could also pick out parts from the beginning, middle, and end as needed to make your case, DEFINING key terms, DESCRIBING characters and settings, and NARRATING key scenes. The example essay about the Shelley sonnet offers a text-based analysis that looks at patterns of images in the poem. You might also examine the same theme in several different works.

275–84
285–93
304–12

- *Your own response as a reader.* Explore the way the text affects you or develops meanings as you read through it from beginning to end. By doing such a close reading, you're slowing down the process to notice how one element of the text leads you to expect something, confirming earlier suspicions or surprises. You build your analysis on your experience of reading the text—as if you were pretending to drive somewhere for the first time, though in reality you know the way intimately. By closely examining the language of the text as you experience it, you explore how it leads you to a set of responses, both intellectual and emotional. If you were responding in this way to the Shelley poem, you might discuss how its first lines suggest that while life is an illusion, a veil, one might pull it aside and glimpse reality, however "drear."

- *Context*. Analyze the text as part of some **LARGER CONTEXT**—as part of a certain time or place in history or as an expression of a certain culture (how does this text relate to the time and place of its creation?), as one of many other texts like it, a representative of a genre (how is this text like or unlike others of its kind? how does it use, play with, or flout the conventions of the genre?). A context-based approach to the Shelley poem might look at Shelley's own philosophical and religious views and how they may have influenced the poem's characterization of the world we experience as illusory, a "veil." 327–28

Read the work more than once.   Reading literature, watching films, or listening to speeches is like driving to a new destination: the first time you go, you need to concentrate on getting there; on subsequent trips, you can see other aspects—the scenery, the curve of the road, other possible routes—that you couldn't pay attention to earlier. When you experience a piece of literature for the first time, you usually focus on the story, the plot, the overall meaning. By experiencing it repeatedly, you can see how its effects are achieved, what the pieces are and how they fit together, where different patterns emerge, how the author crafted the work. To analyze a literary work, then, plan to read it more than once, with the assumption that every part of the text is there for a reason. Focus on details, even on a single detail that shows up more than once: Why is it there? What can it mean? How does it affect our experience of reading or studying a text? Also, look for anomalies, details that *don't* fit the patterns: Why are they part of the text? What can they mean? How do they affect the experience of the text? See the **READING STRATEGIES** chapter for several different methods for reading a text. 313–28

251–52 **Compose a strong thesis.** The THESIS of a literary analysis should be specific, limited, and open to potential disagreement. In addition, it should be analytical, not evaluative: avoid thesis statements that make overall judgments, such as a reviewer might do: "Virginia Woolf's *The Waves* is a failed experiment in narrative" or "No one has equaled the achievement of *The Matrix* trilogy." Rather, offer a way of seeing the text: "The choice presented in Robert Frost's 'The Road Not Taken' ultimately makes no difference"; "The plot of *The Matrix Reloaded* reflects the politics of America after 9/11."

Do a close reading. When you analyze a text, you need to find specific, brief passages that support your interpretation. Then you should interpret those passages in terms of their language, their context, or your reaction to them as a reader. To find such passages, you must read the text closely, questioning it as you go, asking, for example:

- What language provides evidence to support your thesis?
- What does each word (phrase, passage) mean exactly?
- Why does the writer choose *this* language, *these* words? What are the implications or connotations of the language? If the language is dense or difficult, why might the writer have written it that way?
- What images or metaphors are used? What is their effect on the meaning?

322–24 - What PATTERNS of language, imagery, or plot do you see? If something is repeated, what significance does the repetition have?
- How does each word, phrase, or passage relate to what precedes and follows it?
- How does the experience of reading the text affect its meaning?

327–28 - What words, phrases, or passages connect to a larger CONTEXT? What language demonstrates that this work reflects or is affected by that context?
- How do these various elements of language, image, and pattern support your interpretation?

Your analysis should focus on analyzing and interpreting your subject, not simply summarizing or paraphrasing it. Many literary analyses also use the strategy of COMPARING two or more works.

266–74

Find evidence to support your interpretation.   The parts of the text you examine in your close reading become the evidence you use to support your interpretation. Some think that we're all entitled to our own opinions about literature. And indeed we are. But when writing a literary analysis, we're entitled only to our own *well-supported* and *well-argued* opinions. When you analyze a text, you must treat it like any other ARGUMENT: you need to discuss how the text creates an effect or expresses a theme, and then you have to show evidence from the text — significant plot or structural elements; important characters; patterns of language, imagery, or action — to back up your argument.

82–106

Pay attention to matters of style.   Literary analyses have certain conventions for using pronouns and verbs.

- In informal papers, it's okay to use the first person: "I believe Frost's narrator has little basis for claiming that one road is 'less traveled.'" In more formal essays, make assertions directly; claim authority to make statements about the text: "Frost's narrator has no basis for claiming that one road is 'less traveled.'"

- Discuss textual features in the present tense even if quotations from the text are in another tense: "When Nick finds Gatsby's body floating in the pool, he says very little about it: 'the laden mattress moved irregularly down the pool.'" Describe the historical context of the setting in the past tense: "In the 1920s, such estates as Gatsby's were rare."

Cite and document sources appropriately.   Use MLA citation and documentation style unless told otherwise. Format QUOTATIONS properly, and use SIGNAL PHRASES when need be.

378–416
360–63
367–68

Think about format and design.   Brief essays do not require HEADINGS; text divisions are usually marked by TRANSITIONS between paragraphs. In longer papers, though, heads can be helpful.

456–57
254

Organizing a Literary Analysis

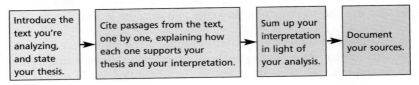

If You Need More Help

205–35 ○ See Chapter 23 for guidelines on **DRAFTING,** Chapter 24 on **ASSESSING YOUR DRAFT,** Chapter 25 on **GETTING RESPONSE AND REVISING,** and Chapter 26 on **EDITING AND PROOFREADING.** See Chapter 27 if you are required to submit your analysis in a writing **PORTFOLIO.**

rhetorical situations

genres

processes

strategies

research mla/apa

media/ design

Memoirs 15

We write memoirs to explore our past—about shopping for a party dress with Grandma, or driving a car for the first time, or breaking up with our first love. *Memoirs* focus on events and people and places that are important to us. We usually have two goals when we write a memoir: to capture an important moment and to convey something about its significance for us. In the following example from *When Broken Glass Floats: Growing Up under the Khmer Rouge* (2001), a woman who grew up in Cambodia during the Vietnam War recalls her first experience of battle.

CHANRITHY HIM

When Broken Glass Floats

In 1969 war comes, and I am only four.

Loud rumbling noises wake me. I fumble in the dark, trying to open the mosquito netting around my bed. I run in the dark toward the living room, searching for my mother and father. *"Mak! Pa!"* I scream with all my might, trying to compete with the raucous sounds.

From the living room, I hear my oldest sister, twelve-year-old Chea, screaming: *"Mak! Pa! Yeakong chol srok Khmer! Yeakong chol srok Khmer!"* The Viet Cong are invading Cambodia! Her voice is itself a blast of terror.

Chea's hysterical warning makes me realize that the raging noise outside could be related to the word I had been wondering about: *war*. More than anything, I want to see my parents. Suddenly the light flips on, revealing my frightened sisters and brothers running around frantically, randomly—as disoriented as ants whose hill has been plowed under.

I see my mother clutching my baby sister, Avy, and my father standing at the wall where he has just turned on the light. I run to stand 5 beside *Mak*. My father reaches out to hold Chea's shoulders. He looks into her eyes and carefully says: "Achea, *koon,* take your brothers and sisters with you and hide in the bunker by the pond. Hunch and walk low, so you won't get hit by bullets. Hurry, *koon Pa!* [father's child]"

My brothers and sisters rush out the doorway, a small, traumatized herd of cattle. I clench my mother's hand, and my body rattles with each echo of gunfire. Carrying Avy and holding on to me, *Mak* hurries toward the door. She can't move quickly, for she is six months pregnant. Artillery explodes outside, and I scream and burst into tears. *Mak* shakes off my hand, then grabs onto it tightly.

"*Pa vea!*" She shouts to my father, who is running from one window to the next, sticking his head out and listening. "What are you doing? You'll get shot! Why aren't you careful? Help me with the children!" *Mak* is scared, and her tone frightens me even more than the artillery roaring in the night air.

Pa shouts back, "I just want to know where the gunfire is coming from."

Mak bends toward me. Her words come as hard and fast as an auctioneer's: "Athy, *koon,* wait for your father here." *Mak* takes Avy downstairs. My heart races when I see that she is scared for my father. After she hurries out, I cry, jumping up and down, anxious for *Pa* to take me to the bunker.

Pa runs over to comfort me, snatches me down from the peak of my hysteria. He carries me to the open bunker, a hole in the sticky clay soil ringed with sandbags. Safe at the bunker, he can't rest. He needs to go back to the house for *Yiey Tot,* his grandmother, who is blind and frail. He takes Chea and Tha with him to help carry her. Above the noise I can hear my great-grandmother's groans.

"Hunch, *koon!*" I hear *Pa* cry. "Don't you hear the flying bullets? Don't worry, *Yiey,* we won't drop you."

I'm relieved when everyone in my family, including Aunt Cheng, *Pa's* younger sister, finally hides by the pond. Lying beside my mother in the cold night, I wonder if everyone is as scared as I am as the bullets whiz over us—a fierce hiss and invisible whisper, so quick you wonder if you really heard it. Flares erupt like lightning, illuminating the dark sky.

So this is war. Will it ever stop?

Finally the gunfire belches its last round. Silence and relief. *Now we can go back home,* I think to myself, ready to be freed from wor-

rhetorical situations　genres　processes　strategies　research mla/apa　media/ design

ries about war. I look forward to the morning. I want to forget the adult world that pulled me from my dreams and into a nightmare.

What I don't know is that there is a world outside Cambodia — a world that will affect me, my family, and Cambodia as a nation. I do not know who owned the guns that night — only that they were aimed at me. It will be years before I begin to understand the causes and effects of war, the political gamesmanship. But by then my family will have become flotsam caught in the heave and thrust of its tide.

I look back now as a survivor educated in America. I've sought out answers to questions I raised as a little girl. Trying to make sense of what happened. Trying to understand the players in the Vietnam conflict and those who took advantage of the situation, pulling Cambodia — the pawn, they called it — into the whirlpool of destruction.

Him's memoir tells, first of all, a gripping story about a child in wartime trying to understand why an innocent family — hers — is being shot at. The significance of the event — for the family and for the world — she makes horrifyingly clear.

▮▮ For five more memoirs, see **CHAPTER 56**.

Key Features / Memoirs

A good story.   Your memoir should be interesting, to yourself and others. It need not be about a world-shaking event, but your topic — and how you write about it — should interest your readers. At the center of most good stories stands a conflict or question to be resolved. The most compelling memoirs feature some sort of situation or problem that needs resolution. That need for resolution is another name for suspense. It's what makes us want to keep reading.

Vivid details.   Details bring a memoir to life by giving readers mental images of the sights, sounds, smells, tastes, and textures of the world in which your story takes place. The goal is to show as well as tell, to take readers there. When Him's sister screams out, *"Mak! Pa! Yeakong chol srok Khmer!"* we don't at first know what she's saying, but we can hear her screaming. A memoir is more than simply a report of what happened; it uses vivid details and dialogue to bring the events of the past to life, much as good fiction brings to life events that the writer makes up or embellishes.

Clear significance. Memories of the past are filtered through our view from the present: we pick out some moments in our lives as significant, some as more important or vivid than others. Over time, our interpretations change, and our memories themselves change.

A good memoir conveys something about the significance of its subject. As a writer, you need to reveal something about what the incident means to you. You don't, however, want to simply announce the significance as if you're tacking on the moral of the story. Him, for example, tells us at the end of the piece that she's trying "to make sense of what happened." She stops short, though, of telling us that that's why she wrote this narrative.

A BRIEF GUIDE TO WRITING

Deciding on a Topic

200–01 ○ **Choose an event to write about.** LIST several events or incidents from your past that you consider significant in some way. They do not have to be earthshaking; indeed, they may involve a quiet moment that only you see as important — a brief encounter with a remarkable person, a visit to a special place, a memorable achievement (or failure), something that makes you laugh whenever you think about it. Writing about events that happened at least a few years ago is often easier than writing about recent events because you can more easily step back and see those events with a clear perspective. To choose the event that you will write about, consider how well you can recall what happened, how interesting it will be to readers, and whether you want to share it with an audience.

Considering the Rhetorical Situation

3–4 ■ **PURPOSE** What important aspect of yourself are you trying to convey? How will this story help your readers (and you yourself) understand you, as you were then and as you are now?

■ **AUDIENCE** Who are your readers? What do you want them to think of you after reading your memoir? How can you help them understand your experience?

5–8

■ **STANCE** What impression do you want to give, and how can your words contribute to that impression? What tone do you want to project? Sincere? Serious? Humorous? Detached? Self-critical?

12–14

■ **MEDIA / DESIGN** Will your memoir be a print document? a speech? Will it be posted on a Web site? Will you include illustrations, audio or video clips, or other visual texts?

15–17

Generating Ideas and Text

Think about what happened. Take a few minutes to write out an account of the incident: **WHAT** happened, **WHERE** it took place, **WHO** else was involved, what was said, how you feel about it, and so on. Can you identify any tension or conflict that will make for a compelling story? If not, you might want to rethink your topic.

202–03

Consider its significance. Why do you still remember this event? What effect has it had on your life? What makes you want to tell someone else about it? Does it say anything about you? What about it might interest someone else? If you have trouble answering these questions, you should probably find another topic. But in general, once you have defined the significance of the incident, you can be sure you have a story to tell — and a reason for telling it.

Think about the details. The best memoirs connect with readers by giving them a sense of what it was like to be there, leading them to experience in words and images what the writer experienced in life. Spend some time **DESCRIBING** the incident, writing what you see, hear, smell, touch, and taste when you envision it. Do you have any photos or memorabilia or other **VISUAL** materials you might include in your memoir? Try writing out **DIALOGUE,** things that were said (or, if you can't recall exactly, things that

285–93
458–62
294–98

might have been said). Look at what you come up with—is there detail
enough to bring the scene to life? anything that might be called vivid? If
you don't have enough detail, you might reconsider whether you recall
enough about the incident to write about it. If you have trouble coming
up with plenty of detail, try **FREEWRITING**, **LISTING**, or **LOOPING**.

199–201

Ways of Organizing Memoirs

[Tell about the event from beginning to end]

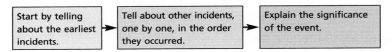

[Start at the end and tell how the event came about]

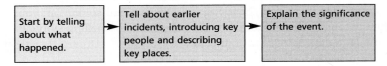

If You Need More Help

205–35

See Chapter 23 for guidelines on **DRAFTING**, Chapter 24 on **ASSESSING YOUR DRAFT**, Chapter 25 on **GETTING RESPONSE AND REVISING**, and Chapter 26 on **EDITING AND PROOFREADING**. See Chapter 27 if you are required to submit your memoir in a writing **PORTFOLIO**.

Profiles are written portraits—of people, places, events, or other things. We find profiles of celebrities, travel destinations, and offbeat festivals in magazines and newspapers, on radio and TV. A profile presents a subject in an entertaining way that conveys its significance, showing us something or someone that we may not have known existed or that we see every day but don't know much about. Here, for example, is an excerpt from a profile of a person. The excerpt is from Bob Merlis's, "Foster Cars: Orphan Makes and the People Who Love Them," an article published in *Automobile* magazine.

BOB MERLIS

Shirley Barnes, M.D.

Her business card reads Shirley Barnes, M.D., and she's a doctor, all right—a Metropolitan Doctor. Her passion is the Nash Metropolitan, the little car produced by Austin of England for American Motors between 1954 and 1962. Barnes is a legend among southern California Met lovers—an icon, a beacon, and a font of useful knowledge and freely offered opinions. She learned to drive on her brother's Met back in 1960 and really hasn't been the same since. She was a professional dancer—tap, ballet, acrobatic—but became a shade-tree mechanic of the highest order mostly out of necessity. Her first Met, a '59 purchased in 1966, needed service and she suffered a rude awakening when she couldn't find anyone willing to work on it. She met an elderly mechanic and became his apprentice. "He couldn't use his hands but he still had the brain," Barnes recalls. . . .

Like Fred Walker [who restores Kaiser-Frazer automobiles], she believes in keeping the cars as original as possible, which flies in the

face of the current trend in Met circles to swap engines . . . and add automatic transmissions. . . . "My conviction is that if you put the right parts on the car, if they stay as stock as possible, you'll do fine."

Barnes tries hard to practice what she preaches in workshops where she teaches other Metheads how to do their own clutch and brake jobs. She has a sixth sense about the cars and can usually diagnose a problem over the phone. Her relationship with Metropolitans is not, strictly speaking, physical. She has an emotional bond with the cars and has given names to most of her personal fleet of thirteen. There's Daisy, the yellow convertible; Sheba, named by her mother-in-law; Misfit, the one she picked up on an April Fools' Day a while back. And Hannibal, Lady Bird, Homer, Omar, Clover, and Hercules, the one geared low, which pulled her trailer (a 1947 teardrop model named Beep-Beep) to Reno and back.

Shirley is completely involved with her cars. "I get upset when they don't run." She's convinced they have hearts and minds of their own. And she says good night to them, individually, before she, herself, turns in, visions of Met-shaped sugarplums dancing tap, acrobatic, or ballet in her head.

This profile starts with an unusual subject — a woman who fixes a kind of car that's no longer even made. The writer goes on to engage our interest by presenting details that help us understand her passion for these cars and her work.

For five more profiles, see **CHAPTER 57**.

Key Features / Profiles

An interesting subject.   The subject may be something unusual, or it may be something very ordinary shown in an intriguing way. You might profile an interesting person (Shirley Barnes, for example, is someone who does something unusual), a place (Barnes's garage, perhaps), an event (a convention or rally for owners of Nash Metropolitans), or an activity (the workshops for other "Metheads").

Any necessary background or context.   A profile usually includes just enough information to let readers know where the subject comes from or why it is what it is. For example, Merlis gives us minimal background on

Shirley Barnes: the Metropolitan is a little car once made in England, and Barnes became a Metropolitan specialist when she started working on hers and fell in love with the cars.

An interesting angle.   A good profile captures its subject from a particular angle. Merlis doesn't try to tell us all about Barnes; rather, he focuses on her as a specialized mechanic, ignoring other aspects of her life. Her relationships, her home, her other interests are irrelevant to Merlis's task: to provide a clear picture of a mechanic who fixes one brand of car.

A firsthand account.   Whether you are writing about a person, place, or event, you need to spend time observing and interacting with your subject. With a person, interacting means watching and conversing. Successful journalists tell us that "following the guy around"—getting a subject to do something and talk about it at the same time—yields excellent material for a profile. When a *Washington Post* writer met Theodor Geisel (Dr. Seuss) before profiling him, she asked him not only to talk about his characters but also to draw one—resulting in a colorful scene (and an illustration) for her profile. With a place or event, interacting may mean visiting and participating, although sometimes you may gather even more information by playing the role of the silent observer.

Engaging details.   You need to include details that bring your subject to life. These may include *specific information* (Shirley Barnes "learned to drive on her brother's Met back in 1960"); *sensory images* ("There's Daisy, the yellow convertible"); *figurative language,* including smile and metaphor ("She's convinced [her cars] have hearts and minds of their own"); *dialogue* (" 'He couldn't use his hands but he still had the brain' "); and *anecdotes* ("she says good night to them, individually"). Choose details that show rather than tell—that let your audience see and hear your subject rather than merely read an abstract description of it. And be sure all the details create some *dominant impression* of your subject; the impression we get of Shirley Barnes, for example, is of a colorful, whimsical person whose connection to Nash Metropolitans is more emotional than technical.

A BRIEF GUIDE TO WRITING

Choosing a Suitable Subject

People, places, events, or activities—whatever you choose, you're likely to write a stronger piece if you choose something that arouses your curiosity but you're not too familiar with, because being too familiar with something can blind you to interesting details. **LIST** five to ten interesting subjects that you can see firsthand. Obviously, you can't profile a person who won't be interviewed or a place or activity that can't be observed. So before you commit to a topic, make sure you'll be able to carry out firsthand research and not find out too late that the people you need to interview aren't willing or that places you need to visit are off-limits.

200–01 ○

Considering the Rhetorical Situation

3–4

■ **PURPOSE**   Why are you writing the profile? What angle will best achieve your purpose? How can you inform *and engage* your audience?

5–8

■ **AUDIENCE**   Who is your audience? How familiar are they with your subject? What expectations of your profile might they have? What background information or definitions do you need to provide? How interested will they be—and how can you get their interest?

12–14

■ **STANCE**   What view of your subject do you expect to present? Sympathetic? Critical? Sarcastic? Will you strive for a carefully balanced perspective?

15–17

■ **MEDIA / DESIGN**   Will your profile be a print document? Will it be published on the Web? Will it be an oral presentation? Can (and should) you include images or any other visuals?

rhetorical situations   genres   processes   strategies   research mla/apa   media/design

Generating Ideas and Text

Visit your subject. If you're writing about an amusement park, go there; if you're profiling the man who runs the carousel, make an appointment to meet and interview him. Get to know your subject—if you profile Ben and Jerry, sample the ice cream! Take along a camera if there's anything you might want to show visually in your profile. Find helpful hints for OBSERVING and INTERVIEWING in the chapter on finding sources.

351–53

Explore what you already know about your subject. Why do you find this subject interesting? What do you know about it now? What do you expect to find out about it from your research? What preconceived ideas about or emotional reactions to this subject do you have? Why do you have them? It may be helpful to try some of the activities in the chapter on GENERATING IDEAS AND TEXT.

199–204

If you're planning to interview someone, prepare questions. Merlis likely asked Shirley Barnes such questions as, "How did you become a mechanic? How did you end up specializing in a car that hasn't been made for forty years? Who influenced you?" See the INTERVIEWING guidelines in Chapter 40 for help with planning questions.

351–52

Do additional research. You may be able to write a profile based entirely on your field research. You may, though, need to do some library or Web RESEARCH as well, to deepen your understanding, get a different perspective, or fill in gaps. Often the people you interview can help you find sources of additional information; so can the sponsors of events and those in charge of places. To learn more about a city park, for instance, contact the government office that maintains it.

329–449

Analyze your findings. Look for patterns, images, recurring ideas or phrases, and engaging details. Compare your preconceptions with your findings. Look for contrasts or discrepancies: between a subject's words and actions, between the appearance of a place and what goes on there, between your expectations and your research findings. Merlis may have expected to meet a mechanic—not a former professional dancer who names each of her cars. You may find the advice in the **READING STRATEGIES** chapter helpful here.

313–28

Come up with an angle.　What's most memorable about your subject? What most interests you? What will interest your audience? Merlis wrote his profile for an automobile magazine, so he focused entirely on Barnes's relationship with cars—and on a female mechanic, a subject that might surprise some readers. Sometimes you'll know your angle from the start; other times you'll need to look further into your topic. You might try **CLUSTERING, CUBING, FREEWRITING,** and **LOOPING,** activities that will help you look at your topic from many different angles.

199–202

Note details that support your angle.　Use your angle to focus your research and generate text. Try **DESCRIBING** your subject as clearly as you can, **COMPARING** your subject with other subjects of its sort, writing **DIALOGUE** that captures your subject. Engaging details will bring your subject to life for your audience. Together, these details should create a dominant impression of your subject.

285–93
266–74
294–98

Ways of Organizing a Profile

[As a narrative]

One common way to organize a profile is by **NARRATING.** For example, if you are profiling a chess championship, you may write about it chronologically, creating suspense as you move from start to finish.

304–12

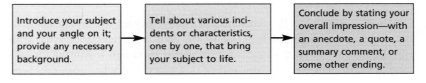

Introduce your subject and your angle on it; provide any necessary background. → Tell about various incidents or characteristics, one by one, that bring your subject to life. → Conclude by stating your overall impression—with an anecdote, a quote, a summary comment, or some other ending.

[As a description]

Sometimes you may organize a profile by DESCRIBING — a person or a place, for instance. The profile of Shirley Barnes is organized this way.

285–93

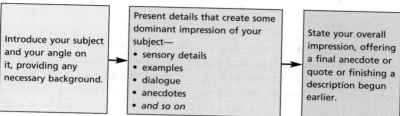

Introduce your subject and your angle on it, providing any necessary background. → Present details that create some dominant impression of your subject—
- sensory details
- examples
- dialogue
- anecdotes
- and so on

→ State your overall impression, offering a final anecdote or quote or finishing a description begun earlier.

If You Need More Help

See Chapter 23 for guidelines on DRAFTING, Chapter 24 on ASSESSING YOUR DRAFT, Chapter 25 on GETTING RESPONSE AND REVISING, and Chapter 26 on EDITING AND PROOFREADING. See Chapter 27 if you are required to submit your profile in a writing PORTFOLIO.

205–35

17 Proposals

Contractors bid on building projects. Musicians and educators apply for grants. Researchers seek funding. Student leaders call for lights on bike paths. You offer to pay half the cost of a car and insurance if your parents will pay the other half. Lovers propose marriage; friends propose sharing dinner and a movie. These are all examples of proposals: ideas put forward for consideration that say, "Here is a solution to a problem" or "This is what ought to be done." All proposals are arguments: when you propose something, you are trying to persuade others to see a problem in a particular way and to accept your solution to the problem. For example, here is a proposal for reducing the costs of higher education, from a lengthy report prepared in 2004 by the Colorado student chapter of the Higher Education Project of the State Public Interest Research Groups (PIRGs). PIRGs are non-partisan, non-profit advocacy groups; this one focuses on increasing aid for college students.

TRACEY KING AND ELLYNNE BANNON

The Burden of Borrowing:
A Proposal for Reducing Student Debt

Higher education is critical to the future success of Americans. In addition to the inherent benefits of a higher education, a college degree is worth 75 percent more than a high school diploma, or more than $1,000,000 over a lifetime in the workforce. However, as college costs continue to swell, students are increasingly shouldering high levels of debt to pay for a college education.

   Thirty-nine percent of student borrowers now graduate with unmanageable levels of debt, meaning that their monthly payments are more than 8 percent of their monthly income. According to new

data from the Department of Education's National Postsecondary Student Aid Study (NPSAS), not only are the majority of students turning to loans to finance college, but debt levels are also escalating. In 1999–2000, 64 percent of students graduated with student-loan debt, and the average student-loan debt has nearly doubled over the past eight years, to $16,928.

There are several possible explanations for increases in student borrowing. First [according to a 2001 report of the Advisory Committee on Student Financial Assistance], the strength of the Pell grant has declined from covering 84 percent of tuition at a four-year public institution in 1975–76 to 39 percent today. While Congress has increased funding in recent years, the Pell grant maximum has not been able to keep up with inflation and rising tuition costs. As a result, low-income students are forced to borrow to cover that unmet need. Second, wealthy families may be shifting more of the cost of college from savings to student loans. Also, as tuition increases faster than inflation and median income, students overall are facing increasing levels of need.

We need to look for solutions that make college more affordable and protect students from unmanageable debt burden. Congress should increase grant-aid funding, reduce the cost of student loans, and provide flexibility within the student loan program to help make college more affordable for all Americans. . . .

Increase grant-aid funding: Federal need-based grant aid provides   5
low-income students with access to a higher education. Without this aid, many low-income students take on unmanageable levels of debt burden or forgo a college education altogether. Recent increases in Pell grant funding may have kept some low-income students from borrowing and slowed the growth of debt levels among those who did borrow. Congress should increase need-based grant funding and, specifically, fully fund the Pell grant program.

Lower the cost of borrowing to students: With the typical senior graduating with $16,928 in federal loan debt, Congress should take the following steps to reduce the cost of borrowing:

- Congress should maintain low interest rates on student loans.

- Congress should pass the Affordable Student Loan Act (H.R. 1622), which would eliminate origination and insurance fees on student loans and save the typical student $677. These savings could be used to pay for tuition, books, and other living expenses.

- Congress should pass a tax credit of up to $1,500 for interest paid on student loans, which would help reduce the burden of debt after graduation.

Continue to provide flexible repayment options to borrowers: Congress should continue to provide flexibility within the student-loan program to help make college more affordable for all Americans. Repayment options such as deferment, loan forgiveness, forbearance, and income-contingent repayment help students who are facing unmanageable debt repay their loans without going into default.

Maintain current loan limits: Congress should not increase loan limits without reducing the current cost of borrowing. Raising loan limits will not solve the access problem. Instead, it will only make the situation worse, with more and more students falling into burdensome debt after college. Congress should continue to work toward increasing access to higher education while protecting students from unmanageable levels of debt.

For five more proposals, see CHAPTER 58.

This proposal clearly defines the problem, offers reasons for the increase in student debt, and proposes a set of actions to deal with the problem. It actually ends with the proposed actions, which function, therefore, as a call to action. Its tone, while forceful, is balanced and reasonable.

Key Features / Proposals

A well-defined problem. Some problems are self-evident or relatively simple, and you would not need much persuasive power to make people act— as with the problem "This university discards too much paper." While some people might see nothing wrong with throwing paper away, most are likely to agree that recycling is a good thing. Other issues are controversial: some people see them as problems while others do not, such as this one: "Motorcycle riders who do not wear helmets risk serious injury and raise health-care costs for everyone." Some motorcyclists believe that wearing or not wearing a helmet is a personal choice; you would have to present arguments to convince your readers that not wearing a helmet is indeed a problem needing a solution. Any written proposal must establish at the outset that there is a problem—and that it's serious enough to require a solution.

A recommended solution. Once you have defined the problem, you need to describe the solution you are suggesting and to explain it in enough detail for readers to understand what you are proposing. Sometimes, as in the student-debt proposal in this chapter, you might suggest several solutions.

A convincing argument for your proposed solution. You need to convince readers that your solution is feasible—and that it is the best way to solve the problem. Sometimes you'll want to explain in detail the steps needed to enact a proposal. See, for example, how the student-loan proposal details *how* Congress could lower the cost of borrowing.

Anticipate questions. You may need to consider any questions readers may have about your proposal—and to show how its advantages outweigh any disadvantages. Had the student-loan proposal been written for a Congressional budget committee, it would have needed to anticipate and answer questions about the costs of the proposed solution.

A call to action. The goal of a proposal is to persuade readers to accept your proposed solution. This solution may include asking readers to take action.

An appropriate tone. Since you're trying to persuade readers to act, your tone is important—readers will always react better to a reasonable, respectful presentation than to anger or self-righteousness.

A BRIEF GUIDE TO WRITING

Deciding on a Topic

Choose a problem that can be solved. When you are assigned to write a proposal for a writing class, you will need to choose a problem to write about. Complex, large problems, such as poverty, hunger, or terrorism, usually require complex, large solutions. Most of the time, focusing on a smaller problem or a limited aspect of a large problem will yield a more manageable proposal. Rather than tackling the problem of world poverty, for example, think about the problem faced by families in your community that have lost jobs and need help until they find employment.

Considering the Rhetorical Situation

3–4

■ **PURPOSE** Do you have a vested interest in the solution your readers adopt, or do you simply want to eliminate the problem, whatever solution might be adopted?

5–8

■ **AUDIENCE** How can you reach your readers? Do you know how receptive or resistant to change they are likely to be? Do they have the authority to enact your proposal?

12–14

■ **STANCE** How can you show your audience that your proposal is reasonable and should be taken seriously? How can you demonstrate your own authority and credibility?

15–17

■ **MEDIA / DESIGN** How will you deliver your proposal? In print? Online? As a speech? Would visuals help you to argue for your proposal?

Generating Ideas and Text

Explore potential solutions to the problem. Many problems can be solved in more than one way, and you need to show your readers that you've examined several potential solutions. You may develop solutions to your problem on your own; more often, though, you'll need to do 329–449 **RESEARCH** to see how others have solved—or tried to solve—similar problems. Don't settle on a single solution too quickly—you'll need to 266–74 **COMPARE** the advantages and disadvantages of several solutions in order to argue convincingly for one.

Decide on the most desirable solution(s). One solution may be head and shoulders above others—but be open to rejecting all the possible solutions on your list and starting over if you need to, or to combining two or more potential solutions in order to come up with an acceptable fix.

rhetorical situations   genres   processes   strategies   research mla/apa   media/ design

Think about why your solution is the best one. Why did you choose your solution? Why will it work better than others? What has to be done to enact it? What will it cost? What makes you think it can be done? Writing out answers to these questions will help you argue for your solution — to show that you have carefully and objectively outlined a problem, analyzed the potential solutions, and weighed their merits — and to show the reasons the solution you propose is the best.

Ways of Organizing a Proposal

You can organize a proposal in various ways, but always you will begin by establishing that there is a problem. You may then consider several solutions before recommending one particular solution. Sometimes, however, you might suggest only a single solution.

[Several possible solutions]

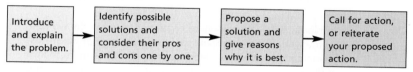

[A single solution]

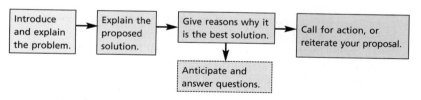

If You Need More Help

See Chapter 23 for guidelines on **DRAFTING,** Chapter 24 on **ASSESSING YOUR DRAFT,** Chapter 25 on **GETTING RESPONSE AND REVISING,** and Chapter 26 on **EDITING AND PROOFREADING.** See Chapter 27 if you are required to submit your proposal in a writing **PORTFOLIO.**

○ 205–35

TOPIC PROPOSALS

Instructors often ask students to write topic proposals to ensure that their topics are appropriate or manageable. If you get your instructor's response to a good proposal before you write it, your finished product will likely be much better than if you try to guess the assignment's demands. Some instructors may also ask for an **ANNOTATED BIBLIOGRAPHY** showing that appropriate sources of information are available—more evidence that the project can be carried out. Here a first-year student proposes a topic for an assignment in a writing course in which she has been asked to take a position on a global issue.

112–19

JENNIFER CHURCH

Biodiversity Loss and Its Effect on Medicine

The loss of biodiversity—the variety of organisms found in the world—is affecting the world every day. Some scientists estimate that we are losing approximately one hundred species per day and that more than a quarter of all species may vanish within fifty years. I recently had the issue of biodiversity loss brought to my attention in a biological sciences course that I am taking this quarter. I have found myself interested in and intrigued by the subject and have found an abundance of information both in books and on the Internet.

In this paper, I will argue that it is crucial for people to stop this rapid loss of our world's biodiversity. Humans are the number-one cause of biodiversity loss in the world. Whether through pollution or toxins, we play a crucial role in the extinction of many different species. For example, 80 percent of the world's medicine comes from biological species and their habitats. One medicine vanishing due to biodiversity loss is TAXOL. Found in the Wollemi pine tree, TAXOL is one of the most promising drugs for the treatment of ovarian and breast cancer. If the Wollemi pine tree becomes extinct, we will lose this potential cure.

I will concentrate primarily on biodiversity and its effects on the medical field. If we keep destroying the earth's biodiversity at the cur-

rent rate, we may lose many opportunities to develop medicines we need to survive. The majority of my information will be found on the Internet, because there are many reliable Web sites from all around the world that address the issue of biodiversity loss and medicine.

Church defines and narrows her topic (from biodiversity loss to the impact of that loss on medicine), discusses her interest, outlines her argument, and discusses her research strategy. Her goal is to convince her instructor that she has a realistic writing project and a clear plan.

Key Features / Topic Proposals

You'll need to explain what you want to write about, why you want to explore it, and what you'll do with your topic. Unless your instructor has additional requirements, here are the features to include:

A concise discussion of the subject.   Topic proposals generally open with a brief discussion of the subject, outlining any important areas of controversy or debate associated with it and clarifying the extent of the writer's current knowledge of it. In its first two paragraphs, Church's proposal includes a concise statement of the topic she wishes to address.

A clear statement of your intended focus.   State what aspect of the topic you intend to write on as clearly as you can, narrowing your focus appropriately. Church does so by stating her intended topic—loss of biodiversity—and then showing how she will focus on the importance of biodiversity to the medical field.

A rationale for choosing the topic.   Tell your instructor why this topic interests you and why you want to write about it. Church both states what made her interested in her topic and hints at a practical reason for choosing it: plenty of information is available.

Mention of resources.   To show your instructor that you can achieve your goal, you need to identify the available research materials.

18 Reflections

Sometimes we write essays just to think about something—to speculate, ponder, probe; to play with an idea, develop a thought; or simply to share something. Reflective essays are our attempt to think something through by writing about it and to share our thinking with others. If such essays make an argument, it is about things we care or think about more than about what we believe to be "true." Have a look at one example by Bernard Cooper, an essayist and novelist who teaches at UCLA and Antioch University/Los Angeles.

BERNARD COOPER

The Fine Art of Sighing

You feel a gradual welling up of pleasure, or boredom, or melancholy. Whatever the emotion, it's more abundant than you ever dreamed. You can no more contain it than your hands can cup a lake. And so you surrender and suck the air. Your esophagus opens, diaphragm expands. Poised at the crest of an exhalation, your body is about to be unburdened, second by second, cell by cell. A kettle hisses. A balloon deflates. Your shoulders fall like two ripe pears, muscles slack at last.

My mother stared out the kitchen window, ashes from her cigarette dribbling into the sink. She'd turned her back on the rest of the house, guarding her own solitude. I'd tiptoe across the linoleum and make my lunch without making a sound. Sometimes I saw her back expand, then heard her let loose one plummeting note, a sigh so long and weary it might have been her last. Beyond our backyard, above telephone poles and apartment buildings, rose the brown horizon of the city; across it glided an occasional bird, or the blimp that advertised Goodyear tires. She might have been drifting into the distance,

rhetorical situations genres processes strategies research mla/apa media/design

or lamenting her separation from it. She might have been wishing she were somewhere else, or wishing she could be happy where she was, a middle-aged housewife dreaming at her sink.

My father's sighs were more melodic. What began as a somber sigh could abruptly change pitch, turn gusty and loose, and suggest by its very transformation that what begins in sorrow might end in relief. He could prolong the rounded vowel of *oy*, or let it ricochet like a echo, as if he were shouting in a tunnel or a cave. Where my mother sighed from ineffable sadness, my father sighed at simple things: the coldness of a drink, the softness of a pillow, or an itch that my mother, following the frantic map of his words, finally found on his back and scratched.

A friend of mine once mentioned that I was given to long and ponderous sighs. Once I became aware of this habit, I heard my father's sighs in my own and knew for a moment his small satisfactions. At other times, I felt my mother's restlessness and wished I could leave my body with my breath, or be happy in the body my breath left behind.

It's a reflex and a legacy, this soulful species of breathing. Listen   5
closely: My ancestors' lungs are pumping like bellows, men towing boats along the banks of the Volga, women lugging baskets of rye bread and pike. At the end of each day, they lift their weary arms in a toast; as thanks for the heat and sting of vodka, their a-h-h's condense in the cold Russian air.

At any given moment, there must be thousands of people sighing. A man in Milwaukee heaves and shivers and blesses the head of the second wife who's not too shy to lick his toes. A judge in Munich groans with pleasure after tasting again the silky bratwurst she ate as a child. Every day, meaningful sighs are expelled from schoolchildren, driving instructors, forensic experts, certified public accountants, and dental hygienists, just to name a few. The sighs of widows and widowers alone must account for a significant portion of the carbon dioxide released into the atmosphere. Every time a girdle is removed, a foot is submerged in a tub of warm water, or a restroom is reached on a desolate road . . . you'd think the sheer velocity of it would create mistrals, siroccos, hurricanes; arrows should be swarming over satellite maps, weathermen talking a mile a minute, ties flapping from their necks like flags.

Before I learned that Venetian prisoners were led across it to their execution, I imagined that the Bridge of Sighs was a feat of invisible engineering, a structure vaulting above the earth, the girders and trusses, the stay ropes and cables, the counterweights and safety rails connecting one human breath to the next.

Cooper explores a common but intriguing subject: the sigh. He begins by describing the physical experience of sighing and then compares two people doing so: his mother, standing at the kitchen window, sighing from disappointment, and his father, sighing with the pleasure of a moment. These memories lead Cooper to realize that his own sighs echo those of his parents and then lead him to reflect on the universality of the sigh. His final paragraph ties the essay together with an image of sighing as a bridge that connects "one human breath to the next."

📖 For five more reflections, see

CHAPTER 59.

Key Features / Reflections

A topic that intrigues you.   A reflective essay has a dual purpose: to ponder something you find interesting or puzzling and to share your thoughts with an audience. Your topic may be anything that interests you. You might write about someone you have never met and are curious about, an object or occurrence that makes you think, a place where you feel comfortable or safe. Your goal is to explore the meaning that the person, object, event, or place has for you in a way that will interest others. One way to do that is by making connections between your personal experience and more general ones that readers may share. Cooper writes about the way he and his parents sigh but in doing so demonstrates the range of emotions that *everyone's* sighs represent.

Some kind of structure.   A reflective essay can be structured in many ways, but it needs to be structured. It may seem to wander, but all its paths and ideas should relate, one way or another. The challenge is to keep your readers' interest as you explore your topic and to leave readers satisfied that the journey was pleasurable, interesting, and profitable. Cooper's essay is carefully structured to move us from particular to general, from the physical sensation of air moving in and out of the body to the abstraction of sighing as a bridge connecting human beings.

Specific details. You'll need to provide specific details to help readers understand and connect with your subject, especially if it's an abstract or unfamiliar one. Cooper's essay offers a wealth of figurative and concrete details: when you sigh, "your shoulders fall like two ripe pears," and "every day, meaningful sighs are expelled from schoolchildren, . . . certified public accountants, and dental hygienists, just to name a few." Anecdotes can bring your subject to life: seeing his mother standing at the kitchen sink, Cooper tells us, "I'd tiptoe across the linoleum and make my lunch without making a sound." Reflections may be about causes, such as why Cooper's mother sighed; comparisons, such as when Cooper compares his two parents' sighs; and examples, such as the simple things that evoke his father's sighs: "the coldness of a drink, the softness of a pillow."

A questioning, speculative tone. In a reflective essay, you are working toward answers, not providing them neatly organized and ready for consumption. So your tone is usually tentative, open; demonstrating willingness to entertain, accept, and reject various ideas as your essay progresses from beginning to end. Cooper achieves such a tone by looking at sighing from several perspectives, never settling on any one of them.

A BRIEF GUIDE TO WRITING

Deciding on a Topic

Choose a subject you want to explore. Write a list of things that you think about, wonder about, find puzzling or annoying. They may be big things—life, relationships—or little things—quirks of certain people's behavior, curious objects, everyday events. Try **CLUSTERING** one or more of those things, or begin by **FREEWRITING** to see what comes to mind as you write.

○ 201–02
○ 199–200

Considering the Rhetorical Situation

■ **PURPOSE**   What's your goal in writing this essay? To introduce a topic that interests you? Entertain? Provoke readers to

3–4

think about something? What aspects of your subject do you want to ponder and reflect on?

5–8   ■ **AUDIENCE**   Who is the audience? How familiar are they with your subject? How will you introduce it in a way that will interest them?

12–14   ■ **STANCE**   What is your attitude toward the topic you plan to explore? Questioning? Playful? Critical? Curious? Something else?

15–17   ■ **MEDIA / DESIGN**   Will your essay be a print document? an oral presentation? Will it be posted on a Web site? Would it help to have any visuals?

Generating Ideas and Text

Explore your subject in detail.   Reflections often start with descriptive 285–93 details. Cooper opens his by **DESCRIBING** the physical feeling of sighing. Those details provide a base for the speculations to come. You may also 260–84 make your point by **DEFINING**, **COMPARING**, even **CLASSIFYING**. Virtually any organizing pattern will help you explore your subject.

Back away.   Ask yourself why your subject matters: why is it important or intriguing or significant? You may try **LISTING** or **OUTLINING** possibilities, 200–01 203–04 or you may want to start **DRAFTING** to see where the writing takes your 205–07 thinking. Your goal is to think on paper (or screen) about your subject, to play with its possibilities.

Think about how to keep readers with you.   Reflections may seem loose or unstructured, but they must be carefully crafted so that readers can follow your train of thought. It's a good idea to sketch out a rough **THESIS** to 251–52 help focus your thoughts. You may not include the thesis in the essay itself, but every part of the essay should in some way relate to it.

rhetorical situations   ▲ genres   ○ processes   ◆ strategies   ● research mla/apa   □ media/design

Ways of Organizing a Reflective Essay

Reflective essays may be organized in many ways because they mimic the way we think, associating one idea with another in ways that make sense but do not necessarily form a "logical" progression. In general, you might consider organizing a reflection using this overall strategy:

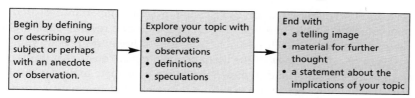

Another way to organize this type of essay is as a series of brief reflections that together create an overall impression:

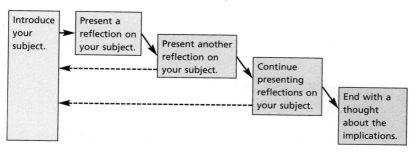

If You Need More Help

See Chapter 23 for GUIDELINES ON DRAFTING, Chapter 24 on ASSESSING YOUR DRAFT, Chapter 25 on GETTING RESPONSE AND REVISING, and Chapter 26 on EDITING AND PROOFREADING. See Chapter 27 if you are required to submit your reflection in a writing PORTFOLIO.

○ 205–35

19 Reviews of Scholarly Literature

Reviews of scholarly literature describe and evaluate important research ("literature") available on a topic. We consult literature reviews when we need an overview of such research. In writing a literature review, your goal is to give an overview of the literature on a topic. You do that by discussing the literature that is most relevant to your topic and your purposes, providing clear and accurate summaries of appropriate source material, and describing relationships among facts and concepts. Here is an example of a literature review that describes two methods of teaching reading. The review was prepared for the North Central Regional Educational Laboratory in 1999.

DEBRA JOHNSON

Balanced Reading Instruction: A Review of the Literature

In the history of education, few topics have sparked such public debate as the teaching of reading. Because reading is at the heart of every child's learning, it has been a principal educational focus for more than a century. Research on reading dates as far back as 1879, when a paper was published on eye movements in reading (Samuels & Kamil, 1984). In the mid-1960s, discussion of appropriate reading instruction gained prominence as a result of published research on models of reading instruction and comparative studies of the U.S. Office of Education's Cooperative Research Program in First Grade Reading Instruction (Venezky, 1984; Samuels & Kamil, 1984). Both of these research efforts sparked widespread interest in all aspects of the reading process, particularly at the beginning stages of learning to read. Two basic views

rhetorical situations • genres • processes • strategies • research mla/apa • media/design of reading instruction grew out of this activity: the skills-based approach (which emphasizes the use of phonics) and the meaning-based approach (which emphasizes reading comprehension and enrichment).

Skills-Based Approach. The skills-based approach to reading was highly influenced by the work of Jeanne S. Chall (Snow, Burns, & Griffin, 1998). In 1967, Chall discussed her efforts to identify effective practices in beginning reading instruction in *Learning to Read: The Great Debate.* She concluded that there are "consistent and substantial advantages to programs that included systematic phonics" (Snow, Burns, & Griffin, 1998). Phonics is an instructional strategy used to teach letter-sound relationships by having readers "sound out" words. In 1990, Marilyn J. Adams extended Chall's work with her review of research, *Beginning to Read: Thinking and Learning About Print.* Like Chall, Adams emphasized that effective reading instruction is based on "direct instruction in phonics, focusing on the orthographic regularities of English" as well as lots of exposure to reading materials and time to practice reading (Snow, Burns, & Griffin, 1998).

In skills-based learning, phonics skills are taught in isolation with the expectation that once letter-sound relationships are learned, meaning will follow. Emphasis is placed on intensive phonics instruction that is highly sequenced. Children learn letter-sound relationships by sounding out words. They learn letter sounds, consonant blends, and long and short vowels. Typically, this approach uses reading programs that offer stories with controlled vocabulary made up of letter-sound relationships and words with which children are already familiar. Writing instruction follows the same vein; children are asked to write only after having achieved mastery in basic spelling skills or when a correct model is provided for them to copy. This type of instruction was widely used in the 1960s and 1970s and today is being promoted as part of the back-to-basics movement.

Meaning-based approach. The meaning-based approach to reading was highly influenced by the work of Kenneth S. Goodman (Samuels & Kamil, 1984). Goodman was a leader in the development of the psycholinguistic perspective, which asserts that readers rely more on the structure and meaning of language rather than on the graphic information from text. He and others also noted that literacy development parallels language development. Goodman's work in miscue analysis and reading process had a tremendous impact on reading instruction, especially with early readers. (In miscue analysis, children are observed while reading orally and observers note where the children substitute words, make additions or omissions, or change the word order. This information is used to determine the strategies that children are using in their reading and to help develop ideas for remediation.) Goodman developed a reading model that became known as the whole-language approach. This approach became popular in the 1980s and has continued through the 1990s.

In contrast to the emphasis on phonics that is promoted by the 5 skills-based approach to reading, the meaning-based approach to reading emphasizes comprehension and meaning in texts. Children focus on the wholeness of words, sentences, paragraphs, and entire books to derive meaning through context. Whole-language advocates stress the importance of children reading high-quality children's literature and using language in ways that relate to their lives, such as daily journals, trade books, letter writing, and writing workshops. Word-recognition skills are taught in the context of reading and writing. Comprehension takes precedence over skills such as spelling. In fact, invented spellings are encouraged when younger children are learning to write their own stories. Children learn phonics skills while they are immersed in reading; they learn to decode words by their context. Whole language also offers a supportive and tolerant atmosphere in which children learn to read.

A common but mistaken view is that whole-language and skills-based instruction are dichotomous. Many educators believed that the whole-language approach would enable children to learn to read and write naturally without direct instruction if they were immersed in a literacy-rich environment (Manzo, 1999; Sherman, 1998; Routman, 1996). Some teachers erroneously interpreted this idea to mean no phonics. However, whole language was never intended to exclude phonics (Sherman, 1998; Routman, 1996). In fact, the teaching of skills in context is one of the key characteristics of whole-language education (Weaver, 1995). Instead of being taught in isolation, skills such as grammar and spelling are embedded in whole-language reading and writing activities and are based on the words that children encounter. In this framework, skills teaching arises as a result of children's needs: meaning and comprehension are emphasized (Strickland, 1998).

rhetorical situations   genres   processes   strategies   research mla/apa   media/design

For years, the works of skills-based and meaning-based researchers were pitted against each other in a media war over the best way to teach reading. Now is the time to find resolution. Recent research, such as *Preventing Reading Difficulties in Young Children* (Snow, Burns, & Griffin, 1998), confirms that the teaching of reading requires solid skill instruction, including phonics and phonemic awareness (awareness of the separate sounds in words), imbedded in enjoyable reading and writing experiences with whole texts to facilitate the construction of meaning. In other words, balanced reading instruction in the classroom combines the best of phonics instruction and the whole-language approach to teach both skills and meaning and to meet the reading needs of individual children. In this combined approach, notes Dieg-mueller (1996), "children are explicitly taught the relationship between letters and sounds in a systematic fashion, but they are being read to and reading interesting stories and writing at the same time."

The current revival of phonics as the cure-all to all reading problems is not the answer to improving reading skills. "Phonics should not be taught as a separate 'subject' with an emphasis on drills and rote memorization," notes the National Association for the Education of Young Children (1996). "The key is a balanced approach and attention to each child's individual needs." In order to accomplish this goal, teachers must keep in mind several key points, notes Strickland (cited in Sherman, 1998): First, teaching phonics is not the same as teaching reading; phonics is merely a tool for readers to use. Second, reading and spelling require much more than just phonics; spelling strategies and word-analysis skills are equally important. Third, memorizing phonics rules does not ensure application of those rules; teaching children how to use phonics is different from teaching them about phonics. Fourth, learners need to see the relevance of phonics for themselves in their own reading and writing.

References

Adams, M. J. (1990). *Beginning to read: Thinking and learning about print.* Cambridge, MA: MIT Press.

Chall, J. S. (1967). *Learning to read: The great debate.* New York: McGraw-Hill.

National Association for the Education of Young Children. (1996). *Phonics and whole language learning: A balanced approach to beginning reading* <http://ericps.crc.uiuc.edu/npin/respar/texts/home/phonics.html>

Samuels, S. J., & Kamil, M. L. (1984). Models of the reading process. In P. D. Pearson, R. Barr, M. L. Kamil, & P. Mosenthal (Eds.), *Handbook of reading research* (Vol. 1, pp. 185–224). New York: Longman.

Sherman, L. (1998, Fall). Seeking common ground. *Northwest Education Magazine* <http://www.nwrel.org/nwedu/fall_98/article2.html>

Snow, C. E., Burns, M. S., & Griffin, P. (Eds.). (1998). *Preventing reading difficulties in young children.* Washington, DC: National Academy Press.

Strickland, D. S. (1998). *Teaching phonics today: A primer for educators.* Newark, DE: International Reading Association.

Venezky, R. L. (1984). The history of reading research. In P. D. Pearson, R. Barr, M. L. Kamil, & P. Mosenthal (Eds.), *Handbook of reading research* (Vol. 1, pp. 3–38). New York: Longman.

The writer begins by establishing a context for the discussion and then focuses on her topic: the controversy between phonics and whole language methods of reading instruction. She defines each method, summarizes the most important literature, and then evaluates the role of each method in reading instruction today. Writing for an audience of educators, she follows APA documentation style. (Because it was written in 1999, its documentation of Internet sources does not include retrieval dates, as would be required now.)

Key Features / Reviews of Scholarly Literature

Careful, thorough research. A review of scholarly literature demands that you research all the major literature on the topic—or at least the major literature available to you, given the time you have.

Accurate, objective summaries of the relevant literature. Readers expect a literature review to objectively summarize the main ideas or conclusions of the texts reviewed.

Critical evaluation of the literature. A literature review offers a considered selection of the most important, relevant, and useful sources of

information on its topic, so you must evaluate each source to decide whether it should be included and then to determine how it advances understanding of the topic.

A clear focus. Because a literature review provides an overview of your topic's main issues and explains the main concepts underlying your research, it must be carefully organized and clearly focused on your specific topic.

A BRIEF GUIDE TO WRITING

Considering the Rhetorical Situation

■ **PURPOSE**	How much information should you provide to explain the scholarly context of your research or argument? What is your primary goal? To show your expertise on the topic? To inform your readers about the literature on a particular topic? To support a topic proposal?	3–4
■ **AUDIENCE**	How much do your readers know about your subject and its scholarly literature? Will you need to provide any background information? What documentation system will your readers expect you to use?	5–8
■ **STANCE**	What is the appropriate tone for your purpose and audience? Do you need to demonstrate your authority? make difficult material accessible?	12–14
■ **MEDIA/DESIGN**	Are you planning to deliver your review in print or online? If you deliver it online, will you provide active links from your review to online literature?	15–17

Generating Ideas and Text

Start early. Selecting, reading, and understanding the most relevant scholarly literature on a topic require time and effort. This is one assignment not to put off until the last minute.

Choose a manageable topic.   Decide what aspect of your topic you're going to research. If you're researching a topic with a vast literature, you'll need to narrow and define the topic to one you can handle. However, you'll also need a topic for which adequate research is available. The narrower your topic, the easier it'll be to do a comprehensive review. After you've done some research, **CLUSTERING** the various facets of your topic may help you narrow your focus.

201–02 ◯

Survey the literature.   Begin by reading—abstracts, first and last paragraphs, charts and graphs—to help decide what's important and what isn't. Look for repeated references to certain studies: the ones that get cited most are probably the most important. The advice in the **READING STRATEGIES** chapter can help you read critically, and you'll also find help in the **EVALUATIONS** chapter developing criteria for deciding what needs to be included and discussed.

313–28 ◆

120–26 ▲

Read easier literature first.   Get to know your way around your topic; understanding its basic terms, techniques, concepts, and controversies will help you tackle more difficult or specialized literature.

Take notes as you read.   While copying and pasting Internet source material can save time, a literature review demands that you summarize and synthesize a lot of material. Consider using a low-tech method: writing notes on 3×5-inch index cards, one card per source, including for each source its thesis or research question, along with a brief **SUMMARY** of its methods or approach, its findings, its conclusions, and **DOCUMENTATION** information. If you gather the documentation information now, you can simply alphabetize the cards and copy their data into your works cited or references section.

366–67 ●

375–449 ●

Look for any patterns, trends, controversies, contradictions.   How do these sources relate to one another? to your topic? Part of your purpose in reviewing the literature is to identify important trends and issues pertaining to your topic—and to summarize such patterns in your review.

Organizing a Review of Scholarly Literature

Reviews of scholarly literature usually organize the literature into sub-groups. See Chapter 31 for help **DIVIDING** your topic into meaningful subtopics.

261–62

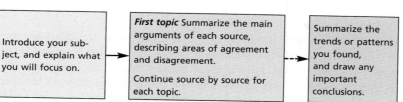

| Introduce your subject, and explain what you will focus on. | **First topic** Summarize the main arguments of each source, describing areas of agreement and disagreement.

Continue source by source for each topic. | Summarize the trends or patterns you found, and draw any important conclusions. |

If You Need More Help

See Chapter 23 for guidelines on **DRAFTING**, Chapter 24 on **ASSESSING YOUR DRAFT**, Chapter 25 on **GETTING RESPONSE AND REVISING**, and Chapter 26 on **EDITING AND PROOFREADING**. See Chapter 27 if you are required to submit your review in a writing **PORTFOLIO**.

205–35

20 Résumés and Application Letters

Résumés summarize our education, work experience, and other accomplishments for prospective employers. Application letters introduce us to those employers. When you send a letter and résumé applying for a job, you are making an argument for why that employer should want to meet you, and perhaps hire you. In a way, the two texts together serve as an advertisement selling your talents and abilities to someone who likely has to sift through many applications to decide whom to invite for an interview. That's why résumés and application letters require a level of care that few other documents do. Résumés and application letters are obviously two very different genres—yet they share one common purpose and are done for the same audience. They also go together in the same envelope or email. Thus, they are presented together in this chapter.

RÉSUMÉS

This chapter covers two kinds of résumés, print ones and scannable ones. *Print résumés* are presented on paper to be read by people. You usually design a print résumé to highlight key information typographically, using italic or bold type for headings, for instance. *Scannable résumés* can be delivered on paper or via email, but they are formatted to be read by a computer. Therefore, you need to use a single typeface without any bold or italics or even indents, and you need to write the résumé using keywords that will hopefully match words in the job descriptions the computer is reading for.

Following are two résumés—the first one print and the second one scannable—both done by one college student applying for an internship before his senior year.

rhetorical situations

genres

processes

strategies

research mla/apa

media/ design

Print Résumé

Samuel Praeger
28 Murphy Lane
Springfield, OH 45399
937-555-2640
spraeger22@webmail.com

OBJECTIVE

To obtain an internship with a public relations firm

EDUCATION
Fall 2002–present

Wittenberg University, Springfield, OH
- B.A. in Psychology expected in May 2006
- Minor in East Asian Studies

EXPERIENCE
2004–present

Department of Psychology, Wittenberg University
Research Assistant
- Collect and analyze data
- Interview research participants

Summer
2004

Landis and Landis Public Relations, Springfield, OH
Events Coordinator
- Organized local charity events
- Coordinated database of potential donors
- Produced two radio spots for event promotion

Summers
2002, 2003

Springfield Aquatic Club, Springfield, OH
Assistant Swim Coach
- Instructed children ages 5–18 in competitive swimming

HONORS
2005

Psi Chi National Honor Society in Psychology

2003–2005

Community Service Scholarship, Wittenberg University

ACTIVITIES

Varsity Swim Team, Ronald McDonald House Fund-raiser

SKILLS

Microsoft Office, SPSS for Windows, Eudora Pro, PowerPoint,
Fluency in Japanese language

REFERENCES

Available upon request

Scannable Résumé

Samuel Praeger

Key words: public relations; event coordination; event promotion; sales; independent worker; responsible; collegiate athletics; Japanese language fluency

Address
28 Murphy Lane
Springfield, OH 45399
Phone: 937-555-2640
E-mail: spraeger22@webmail.com

Education
B.A. in Psychology, Minor in East Asian Studies, Wittenberg University, expected May 2006

Experience
Research Assistant, 2004–present
Wittenberg University, Springfield, OH
Data collection from research participants through interviews. Data entry and analysis, using SPSS statistical software.

Events Coordinator, summer 2004
Landis and Landis Public Relations, Springfield, OH
Organizer of charity events. Coordinator of database. Producer of two radio spots.

Assistant Swim Coach, summers 2002 and 2003
Springfield Aquatic Club, Springfield, OH
Instructor of children ages 5–18 in competitive swimming techniques and rules.

Honors
Psi Chi National Honor Society in Psychology, 2005
Community Service Scholarship, Wittenberg University, 2003–2005

Activities
Varsity Swim Team
Ronald McDonald House Fund-raiser

Skills
Microsoft Office; SPSS for Windows; Eudora Pro; PowerPoint, Fluency in Japanese language

References on request

 rhetorical situations
 genres
 processes
 strategies
 research mla/apa
 media/design

Samuel Praeger's résumé is arranged chronologically, and because he was look-ing for work in a certain field, the résumé is targeted, focusing on his related work and skills and leaving out any references to high school (being in college allows readers to assume graduation from high school, and his past job as a house painter is not relevant). The print version describes his work respon-sibilities using action verbs to highlight what he actually did—produced, instructed, and so on—whereas the scannable version converts the verbs to nouns—producer, instructor. The scannable version is formatted in a single standard typeface, with no italics, boldfacing, or other typographic variation.

Key Features / Résumés

An organization that suits your goals and experience. There are con-ventional ways of organizing a résumé but no one way. You can organ-ize a résumé chronologically or functionally, and it can be targeted or not. A *chronological résumé* is the most general, listing pretty much all your academic and work experience from the most recent to the earli-est. A *targeted résumé* will generally announce the specific goal up top, just beneath your name, and will influence information selectively, showing only the experience and skills relevant to your goal. A *functional résumé* is organized around various kinds of experience and is not chronological. You might write a functional résumé if you wish to demonstrate a lot of experience in more than one area and perhaps if you wish to downplay dates.

Succinct. A résumé should almost always be short—one page if at all possible. Entries should be parallel but do not need to be written in com-plete sentences—"Produced two radio spots," for instance, rather than "I produced two radio spots." *Print résumés* often use action verbs ("instructed," "produced") to emphasize what you accomplished; *scannable résumés* use nouns instead ("instructor," "producer").

A design that highlights key information. It's important for a résumé to look good and to be easy to scan. *On a print résumé*, typography, white space, and alignment matter. Your name should be bold at the top. Major sections should be labeled with headings, all of which should be in one slightly larger or bolder font. And you need to surround each section and the text as a whole with adequate white space to make the parts easy to read—and to make the entire document look professional. *On a scannable résumé,* you should use one standard typeface throughout and *not* use any italics, boldface, bullets, or indents.

A BRIEF GUIDE TO WRITING

Considering the Rhetorical Situation

<table>
<tr>
<td>3–4</td>
<td>■ PURPOSE</td>
<td>Are you seeking a job? an internship? some other position? How will the position for which you're applying affect what you include on your résumé?</td>
</tr>
<tr>
<td>5–8</td>
<td>■ AUDIENCE</td>
<td>What sort of employee is the company or organization seeking? What experience and qualities will the person doing the hiring be looking for?</td>
</tr>
<tr>
<td>12–14</td>
<td>■ STANCE</td>
<td>What personal and professional qualities do you want to convey? Think about how you want to come across—as eager? polite? serious? ambitious?—and choose your words accordingly.</td>
</tr>
<tr>
<td>15–17</td>
<td>■ MEDIA / DESIGN</td>
<td>Are you planning to send your résumé and letter on paper? as an email attachment? in a scannable format? Whatever your medium, be sure both documents are formatted appropriately and proofread carefully.</td>
</tr>
</table>

Generating Ideas and Text for a Résumé

Consider how you want to present yourself.   Begin by gathering the information you will need to include. As you work through the steps of

putting your résumé together, think about the method of organization that works best for your purpose — chronological, targeted, or functional.

- *Contact information.* At the top of your résumé, list your full name, a permanent address (rather than your school address), a permanent telephone number with area code, and your email address (which should sound professional; addresses like *hotbabe334@aol.com* do not make a good first impression on potential employers).

- *Your education.* Start with the most recent: degree (if earned), major (if declared), college attended, and minor (if any). You may want to list your GPA (if it's over 3.0) and any academic honors you've received. If you don't have much work experience, list education first.

- *Your work experience.* As with education, list your most recent job first and work backward. Include job title, organization name, city and state, start and end dates, and responsibilities. Describe them in terms of your duties and accomplishments. If you have extensive work experience in the area in which you're applying, list that first.

- *Community service, volunteer, and charitable activities.* Many high school students are required to perform community service, and many students participate in various volunteer activities that benefit others. List what you've done, and think about the skills and aptitudes that work helped you develop or demonstrate.

- *Other activities, interests, and abilities.* What do you do for fun? What skills do your leisure activities require? (For example, if you play complicated games on the Internet, you probably have a high level of knowledge about computers. You should describe your computer skills in a way that an employer might find useful.)

Define your objective. Are you looking for a particular job for which you should create a targeted résumé? Are you preparing a generic chronological résumé to use in a search for work of any kind? Defining your objective as specifically as possible helps you decide on the form the résumé will take and the information it will include.

Choose contacts.   Whether you list references on your résumé or offer to provide them on request, ask people to serve as references for you before you send out a résumé. It's a good idea to provide each reference with a one-page summary of relevant information about you (for example, give professors a list of courses you took with them, including the grades you earned and the titles of papers you wrote).

Choose your words carefully.   Remember, your résumé is a sales document—you're trying to present yourself as someone worth a second look. Focus on your achievements, using action verbs that say what you've done. If, however, you're composing a scannable résumé, use nouns rather than verbs, and use terms that will function as key words. Key words help the computer match your qualifications to the organization's needs. People in charge of hiring search the database of résumés by entering key words relating to the job for which they are seeking applicants. Key words for a lab technician, for example, might include *laboratory, technician, procedures, subjects, experimental*—among many others. To determine what key words to list on your résumé, read job ads carefully, and use the same words the ads do—as long as they accurately reflect your experience. Be honest—employers expect truthfulness, and embellishing the truth can cause you to lose a job later.

Consider key design elements.   Make sure your résumé is centered on the page and that it looks clean and clear. It's usually best to use a single, simple FONT (serif for print, sans serif for scannable) throughout and to print on white or off-white paper. Limit paper résumés to no more—and no less—than one full page. If you plan to send a scannable résumé or post it on a Web site, create a version that does *not* contain bullets, indents, italics, or underlining, since downloading can cause those elements to get lost or garbled.

454–55 □

Edit and proofread carefully.   Your résumé must be perfect. Show it to others, and proofread again. You don't want even one typo.

Ways of Organizing a Résumé

If you don't have much work experience or if you've just gone back to school to train for a new career, put education before work experience; if you have extensive work experience in the area in which you're applying, list work before education.

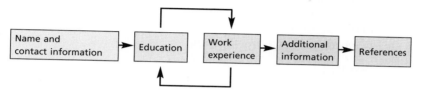

APPLICATION LETTERS

Application letters argue that the writer should be taken seriously as a candidate for a job or some other opportunity. Generally, they are sent together with a résumé, so they don't need to give that much information. They do, however, have to make a favorable impression: the way it's written and presented can get you in for an interview—or not. On the following page is an application letter that Samuel Praeger wrote seeking a position at the end of his junior year. Praeger tailored his letter to one specific reader at a specific organization. The letter cites details, showing that it is not a generic application letter being sent to many possible employers. Rather, it identifies a particular position—the public relations internship—and stresses the fit between his credentials and the position. He also states his availability.

Key Features / Application Letters

A succinct indication of your qualifications. You need to make clear why you're interested in the position or the organization—and at the same time give some sense of why the person you're writing to should at least want to meet you.

street address
city, state zip
date

28 Murphy Lane
Springfield, OH 45399
May 19, 2005

equal space at top and bottom of page, all text aligning at left margin

recipient's name
and title,
organization,
address

Barbara Jeremiah, President
Jeremiah Enterprises
44322 Commerce Way
Worthington, OH 45322

line space

salutation,
with a colon

Dear Ms. Jeremiah:

line space

position
identified

I am writing to apply for the public relations internship advertised in the Sunday, May 18, *Columbus Dispatch*. The success of your company makes me eager to work with you and learn from you.

line space

match between
experience and
job description

My grasp of public relations goes beyond the theories I have learned in the classroom. I worked last summer at Landis and Landis, the Springfield public relations firm, where I was responsible for organizing two charity events that drew over two hundred potential donors each. Since your internship focuses on public relations, my experience in the field should allow me to make a contribution to your company.

availability

I will be available to begin any time after May 23, when the spring term at Wittenberg ends. I enclose my résumé, which provides detailed information about my background. I will phone this week to see if I might arrange an interview.

line space

closing

Sincerely,

4 lines space for signature

Samuel Praeger

sender's name,
typed

Samuel Praeger

rhetorical situations   genres   processes   strategies   research mla/apa   media/design

A reasonable and pleasing tone. When writing to an individual about a job, you need to go beyond simply stating your accomplishments. Through your words, you need to demonstrate that you will be the kind of employee the organization wants. Presentation is also important — your letter should be neat and error free.

A conventional, businesslike format. Application letters typically follow a prescribed format. The most common is the block format shown here. It includes the writer's address, the date, the recipient's name and address, a salutation, the message, a closing, and a signature.

A BRIEF GUIDE TO WRITING

Generating Ideas and Text for Application Letters

Think about exactly what you hope to accomplish. When you're writing an application letter, what do you want? Information? An application form? An interview? A referral? Review your RHETORICAL SITUATION.

1–17

Focus. Application letters are not personal and should not be chatty. Keep them focused: when you're applying for a position, include only information relevant to the position. Don't make your audience wade through irrelevant side issues. Stay on topic.

State the reason for the letter. Unlike essays, which develop a thesis over several paragraphs, or emails, which announce their topic in a subject line, letters need to explicitly introduce their reason for writing, usually in the first paragraph. When you're applying for something, say so in the first sentence: "I am writing to apply for the Margaret Branscomb Peabody Scholarship for students majoring in veterinary science."

Think of your letter as an argument. When you're asking for a job, you're making an ARGUMENT. You're making a claim — that you're qualified for a certain position — and you need to support your claim with reasons and evi-

82–106

dence. Praeger, for example, cites his education and his work experience — and he offers to supply references who will support his application.

Choose an appropriate salutation. If you know the person's name and title, use it: "Dear Professor Turnigan." If you don't know the person's title, one good solution is to address him or her by first and last name: "Dear Julia Turnigan." If, as sometimes happens, you must write to an unknown reader, your options include "To Whom It May Concern" and the more old fashioned "Dear Sir or Madam." Another option might be to omit the salutation completely in such situations and instead use a subject line, for example: "Subject: Public Relations Internship Application." Whenever possible, though, write to a specific person; call the organization and ask whom to write to.

Proofread. Few writing situations demand greater perfection than professional letters — especially application letters. Employers receive dozens, sometimes hundreds, of applications, and often can't look at them all. Typos, grammar errors, and other forms of sloppiness prejudice readers against applications: they're likely to think that if this applicant can't take the time and care to **PROOFREAD,** how badly does he or she want this position? To compete, strive for perfection.

222–23

Ways of Organizing a Letter of Application

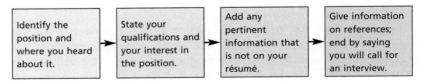

| Identify the position and where you heard about it. | State your qualifications and your interest in the position. | Add any pertinent information that is not on your résumé. | Give information on references; end by saying you will call for an interview. |

If You Need More Help

205–23

See Chapter 23 for guidelines on **DRAFTING,** Chapter 24 on **ASSESSING YOUR DRAFT,** Chapter 25 on **GETTING RESPONSE AND REVISING,** and Chapter 26 on **EDITING.**

part 3

Processes

To create anything, we generally break the work down into a series of steps. We follow a recipe (or the directions on a box) to bake a cake; we break a song down into different parts and the music into various chords to arrange a piece of music. So it is when we write. We rely on various processes to get from a blank page to a finished product. The chapters that follow offer advice on some of these processes—from GENERATING IDEAS to DRAFTING to GETTING RESPONSE to EDITING to COMPILING A PORTFOLIO, and more.

Processes

Collaborating **21**

Whether you're working in a group, participating in a Listserv, or exchanging drafts with a classmate for peer review, you likely spend a lot of time collaborating with others. Even if you do much of your writing sitting alone at a computer, you probably get help from others at various stages in the writing process—and provide help as well. The fact is that two heads can be better than one—and learning to work well with a team is as important as anything you'll learn in college. This chapter offers some guidelines for collaborating successfully with other writers.

Some Ground Rules for Working in a Group

- Make sure everyone is facing everyone else and is physically part of the group. Doing that makes a real difference in the quality of the interactions—think how much better conversation works when you're sitting around a table than it does when you're sitting in a row.

- Thoughtfulness, respect, and tact are key, since most writers (as you know) are sensitive and need to be able to trust those commenting on their work. Respond to the writing of others as you would like others to respond to yours.

- Each meeting needs an agenda—and careful attention paid to time. Appoint one person timekeeper to make sure all necessary work gets done in the available time.

- Appoint another person to be group leader or facilitator. That person needs to make sure everyone gets a chance to speak, no one dominates the discussion, and the group stays on task.

195

rhetorical situations ▪ genres ▲ processes ○ strategies ◆ research mla/apa ● media/ design ◻

321–22

- Appoint a third member of the group to keep a record of the group's discussion. He or she should jot down the major points as they come up and afterward write a **SUMMARY** of the discussion that the group members approve.

Group Writing Projects

Creating a document with a team is common in business and industry and in some academic fields as well. Collaboration of this kind presents new challenges and different kinds of responsibilities. Here are some tips for making group projects work well:

- *Define the task as clearly as possible,* and make sure everyone understands and agrees with the stated goals.
- *Divide the task into parts.* Decide which parts can be done by individuals, which can be done by a subgroup, and which need to be done by everyone together.
- *Assign each group member certain tasks.* Try to match tasks to each person's skills and interests, and divide the work equally.
- *Establish a deadline for each task.* Allow time for unforeseen problems before the project deadline.
- *Try to accommodate everyone's style of working.* Some people value discussion; others want to get right down to the writing. There's no best way to get work done; everyone needs to be conscious that his or her way is not the only way.
- *Work for consensus—not necessarily total agreement.* Everyone needs to agree that the plan is doable and appropriate—if not exactly the way you would do it if you were working alone.
- *Make sure everyone performs.* In some situations, your instructor may help, but in others the group itself may have to develop a way to make sure that the work gets done well and fairly. During the course of the project, it's sometimes helpful for each member of the group to write an assessment both of the group's work and of individual members' contributions.

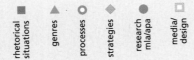

Online Collaboration

Sometimes you'll need or want to work with one or more people online. Working together online offers many advantages, including the ability to collaborate without being in the same place at the same time. Nonetheless, working online presents some challenges that differ from those of face-to-face group work. When sharing writing or collaborating with others online, consider the following suggestions:

- As with all online communication, remember that you need to choose your words carefully to avoid flaming another group member or inadvertently hurting someone's feelings. Without facial expressions, gestures, and other forms of body language and without tone of voice, your words carry all the weight.
- Remember that the **AUDIENCE** for what you write may well extend beyond your group—your work might be forwarded to others, there is no telling who else might read it. ▪ 5–8
- Decide as a group how best to deal with the logistics of exchanging drafts and comments. You can cut and paste text directly into email, send it as an attachment to a message, or post it to a newsgroup or course bulletin board. You may need to use a combination of methods, depending on each group member's access to equipment and software.

Writing Conferences

Conferences with instructors or writing tutors can be an especially helpful kind of collaboration. These one-on-one sessions often offer the most strongly focused assistance you can get—and truly valuable instruction. Here are some tips for making the most of conference time:

- *Come prepared.* Bring all necessary materials, including the draft you'll be discussing, your notes, any outlines—and, of course, any questions.
- *Be prompt.* Your instructor or tutor has set aside a block of time for you, and once that time is up, there's likely to be another student writer waiting.

- *Listen carefully, take notes, discuss your work seriously, and try not to be defensive.* Your instructor or tutor is only trying to help you produce the best piece possible. If you sense that your work is being misunderstood, explain what you're trying to say. Don't get angry! If a sympathetic reader who's trying to help can't understand what you mean, maybe you haven't conveyed your meaning well enough.

- *Reflect on the conference.* Afterward, think about what you learned. What do you have to do now? What have you learned? Think about questions you will ask at your next conference.

rhetorical situations

genres

processes

strategies

research mla/apa

media/ design

Generating Ideas and Text 22

All good writing revolves around ideas. Whether you're writing a job-application letter, a sonnet, or an essay, you'll always spend time and effort generating ideas. Some writers can come up with a topic, put their thoughts in order, and flesh out their arguments in their heads, but most of us need to write down our ideas, play with them, tease them out, and examine them from some distance and from multiple perspectives. This chapter offers activities that can help you do just that. *Freewriting*, *looping*, *listing*, and *clustering* can help you explore what you know about a subject; *cubing* and *questioning* nudge you to consider a subject in new ways; and *outlining*, *letterwriting*, and *discovery drafting* offer ways to generate a text.

Freewriting

An informal method of exploring a subject by writing about it, freewriting ("writing freely") can help you generate ideas and come up with materials for your draft. Here's how to do it:

1. Write as quickly as you can without stopping for 5–10 minutes (or until you fill a page or screen).

2. If you have a subject to explore, write it at the top of the page and then start writing, but if you stray, don't worry—just keep writing. If you don't have a subject yet, just start writing and don't stop until the time is up. If you can't think of anything to say, write that ("I can't think of anything to say") again and again until you do—and you will!

3. Once the time is up, read over what you've written, and underline passages that interest you.

4. Then write some more, starting with one of those underlined passages as your new topic. Repeat the process until you've come up with a usable topic.

Looping

Looping is a more focused version of freewriting; it can help you to explore what you know about a subject. You stop, reflect on what you've written, and then write again, developing your understanding in the process. It's good for clarifying your knowledge of a subject and finding a focus. Here's what you do:

1. Write for 5–10 minutes, jotting down whatever you know about your subject. This is your first loop.

2. Read over what you wrote, and then write a single sentence summarizing the most important or interesting idea. You might try completing one of these sentences: "I guess what I was trying to say was . . . " or "What surprises me most in reading what I wrote is . . . " This will be the start of another loop.

3. Write again for 5–10 minutes, using your summary sentence as your beginning and your focus. Again, read what you've written, and then write a sentence capturing the most important idea—in a third loop.

Keep going until you have enough understanding of your topic to be able to decide on a tentative focus—something you can write about.

Listing

Some writers find it useful to keep lists of ideas that occur to them while they are thinking about a topic. Follow these steps:

1. Write a list of potential topics, leaving space to add ideas that might occur to you later. Don't try to limit your list—include anything that interests you.

2. Look for relationships among the items on your list: what patterns do you see?

3. Finally, arrange the items in an order that makes sense for your purpose and can serve as the beginning of an outline for your writing.

Clustering

Clustering is a way of generating and connecting ideas visually. It's useful for seeing how various ideas relate to one another and for developing subtopics. The technique is simple:

1. Write your topic in the middle of a sheet of paper and circle it.
2. Write ideas relating to that topic around it, circle them, and connect them to the central circle.
3. Write down ideas, examples, facts, or other details relating to each idea, and join them to the appropriate circles.
4. Keep going until you can't think of anything else relating to your topic.

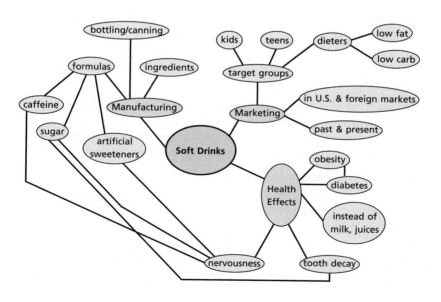

You should end up with various ideas about your topic, and the clusters will allow you to see how they relate. Here's an example of a cluster on the topic of "soft drinks." Note how some ideas link not only to the main topic or related topics but also to other ideas.

Cubing

A cube has six sides. You can examine a topic as you might a cube, looking at it in these six ways:

285–93
- **DESCRIBE** it. What's its color? shape? age? size? What's it made of?

266–74
- **COMPARE** it to something else. What is it similar to or different from?

260–65
- Associate it with other things. What does it remind you of? What connections does it have to other things? How would you **CLASSIFY** it?

255–59
- **ANALYZE** it. How is it made? Where did it come from? Where is it going? How are its parts related?

- Apply it. What is it used for? What can be done with it?

82–106
- **ARGUE** for or against it. Choose a position relating to your subject, and defend it.

Questioning

It's always useful to ask questions, starting with What? Who? When? Where? How? and Why? One method of exploring a topic is asking questions as if the topic were a play. This method is particularly useful for exploring literature, history, the arts, and the social sciences. Start with these questions:

- *What?* What happens? How is it similar to or different from other actions?
- *Who?* Who are the actors? Who are the participants, and who are the spectators? How do the actors affect the action, and how are they affected by it?
- *When?* When does the action take place? How often does it happen? What happens before, after, or at the same time? Would it be different at another time? Does the time have historical significance?

- **Where?** What is the setting? What is the situation, and what makes it significant?

- **Why?** Why did this happen? What are the actors' motives? What end does the action serve?

- **How?** How does the action occur? What are the steps in the process? What techniques are required? What equipment is needed?

Outlining

You may create an *informal outline* by simply listing your ideas and numbering them in the order in which you want to write about them. You might prefer to make a *working outline*, to show the hierarchy of relationships among your ideas. While still informal, a working outline distinguishes your main ideas and your support, often through simple indentation:

First main idea
    Supporting evidence or detail
    Supporting evidence or detail
Second main idea
    Supporting evidence or detail
    Supporting evidence or detail

A *formal outline* shows the hierarchy of your ideas through a system of indenting, numbering, and lettering. Remember that when you divide a point into more specific subpoints, you should have at least two of them—you can't divide something into only one part. Also, try to keep items at each level parallel in structure. Formal outlines work this way:

Thesis statement
    I. First reason
        A. Supporting evidence
            1. Detail of evidence
            2. Detail of evidence
        B. Supporting evidence
    II. Another reason

Writing out a formal outline can be helpful when you're dealing with a complex subject; as you revise your drafts, though, be flexible and ready to change your outline as your understanding of your topic develops.

Letter Writing

Sometimes the prospect of writing a report or essay can be intimidating. You may find that explaining your topic to someone will help you get started. In that case, write a letter to someone you know — your best friend, a parent or grandparent, a sibling — in which you discuss your subject. Explain it in terms that your reader can understand. Use the unsent letter to rehearse your topic; make it a kind of rough draft that you can then revise and develop to suit your actual audience.

Discovery Drafting

Some writers do best by jumping in and writing. Here are the steps to take 205–07 ● if you're ready to write a preliminary **DRAFT**:

1. Write your draft quickly, in one sitting if possible.

2. Assume that you are writing to discover what you want to say and how you need to say it — and that you will make substantial revisions in a later part of the process.

3. Don't worry about grammatical or factual correctness — if you can't think of a word, leave a blank to fill in later. If you're unsure of a date or spelling, put a question mark in parentheses as a reminder to check it later. Just write.

19–192 ▲
> See also each of the **GENRE** chapters for specific
> stategies for generating text in each genre.

rhetorical situations   genres   processes   strategies   research mla/apa   media/ design

Drafting 23

At some point, you need to write out a draft. By the time you begin drafting, you've probably written quite a bit—in the form of notes, lists, outlines, and other kinds of informal writing. This chapter offers some hints on how to write a draft—and reminds you that as you draft, you may well need to get more information, rethink some aspect of your work, or follow new ideas that occur to you as you write.

Establishing a Schedule with Deadlines

Don't wait until the last minute to write. Computers crash, printers jam. Life intervenes in unpredictable ways. You increase your chances of success immensely by setting and meeting deadlines: Research done by ___; rough draft done by ___; revisions done by ___; final draft edited, proofread, and submitted by ___. How much time you need varies with each writing task—but trying to compress everything into twenty-four or forty-eight hours before the deadline is asking for trouble.

Getting Comfortable

When are you at your best? When do you have your best ideas? For major writing projects, consider establishing a schedule that lets you write when you stand the best chance of doing good work. Schedule breaks for exercise and snacks. Find a good place to write, a place where you've got a good surface on which to spread out your materials, good lighting, a comfortable chair, and the right tools (pen, paper, computer) for the job. Often, however, we must make do: you may have to do your drafting in a busy computer lab or classroom. The trick is to make yourself as comfortable as you can manage. Sort out what you *need* from what you *prefer*.

Starting to Write

199–200

All of the above advice notwithstanding, don't worry so much about the trappings of your writing situation that you don't get around to writing. Write. Start by **FREEWRITING,** start with a first sentence, start with awful writing that you know you'll discard later—but write. That's what gets you warmed up and going.

Write quickly in spurts.   Write quickly with the goal of writing a complete draft, or a complete section of a longer draft, in one sitting. If you need to stop in the middle, jot down some notes about where you were headed when you stopped so that you can easily pick up your train of thought when you be in again.

Break down your writing task into small segments.   Big projects can be intimidating. But you can always write one section or, if need be, one paragraph or even a single sentence—and then another and another. It's a little like dieting—if I think I need to lose twenty pounds, I get discouraged and head for the doughnuts; but if I decide that I'll lose one pound and I lose it, well, I'll lose another—*that* I can do.

Expect surprises.   Writing is a form of thinking; the words you write lead you down certain roads and away from others. You may end up somewhere you didn't anticipate. Sometimes that can be a good thing—but sometimes you can write yourself into a dead end or out onto a tangent. Just know that this is natural, part of every writer's experience, and it's okay to double back or follow a new path that opens up before you.

Remember that your writing is not carved in stone.   A first sentence, first page, or first draft represents your attempt to organize into words your thoughts, ideas, feelings, research findings, and more. It's likely that

rhetorical situations | genres | processes | strategies | research mla/apa | media/ design

some of that first try will not achieve your goals. That's okay—having writing on paper or on screen that you can change, add to, and cut means you're part of the way there.

Dealing with Writer's Block

You may sit down to write but find that you can't—nothing occurs to you; your mind is blank. Don't panic; here are some ways to get started writing again:

- Think of the assignment as a problem to be solved. Try to capture that problem in a single sentence: "How do I . . . ?" "What is the best way to . . . ?" "What am I trying to do in . . . ?" Think of a solution to the problem, and then stop thinking about it. If you can't solve it, do something else; give yourself time. Many of us find the solution in the shower, after a good night's sleep.

- Stop trying: take a walk, take a shower, do something else. Come back in a half hour, refreshed.

- Open a window, or get a fresh piece of paper and **FREEWRITE**, or try **LOOPING** or **LISTING**. What are you trying to say? Just let whatever comes come—you may write yourself out of your box.

199–200
200–01

- Try a different medium: try **CLUSTERING**, or draw a chart of what you want to say; draw a picture; doodle.

201–02

- Do some **RESEARCH** on your topic to see what others have said about it.

329–449

- Talk to someone about what you are trying to do; if there's a writing center at your school, talk to a tutor: **GET RESPONSE.** If there's no one to talk to, talk to yourself. It's the act of talking—using your mouth instead of your hands—that can free you up.

213–14

> See the chapter on **GENERATING IDEAS AND TEXT** if you find you need more material. And once you have a draft, see the chapters on **ASSESSING YOUR OWN WRITING** and **GETTING RESPONSE AND REVISING** for help evaluating your draft.

199–204
208–18

24 Assessing Your Own Writing

In school and out, our work is continually assessed by others. Teachers determine whether our writing is strong or weak; supervisors decide whether we merit raises or promotions; even friends and relatives size up the things we do in various ways. As writers, we need to assess our work—to step back and see it with a critical eye. By developing standards of our own and being conscious of the standards others use, we can assess—and shape—our writing, making sure it does what we want it to do. This chapter will help you assess your own written work.

Assessing the Writing You Do for Yourself

We sometimes write not for an audience but for ourselves—to generate ideas, reflect, make sense of things. The best advice on assessing it is *don't*. If you're writing to explore your thoughts, understand a subject, record the events of your day or just for the pleasure of putting words on paper, shut off your internal evaluator. Let the words flow without worrying about them. Let yourself wander without censoring yourself or fretting that what you're writing is incorrect or incomplete or incoherent. That's okay.

199–202 ○ One measure of the success of personal writing is its length. FREEWRITING, journal writing, LISTING, CUBING, and other types of informal writing are like warm-up exercises to limber you up and get you thinking. If you don't give those writing exercises enough time and space, they may not do what you want them to. I've found, for example, that my students' best insights most often appear at the end of their journal entries. Had they stopped before that point, they never would have had those good ideas.

A way to study the ideas in your personal writing is to highlight useful patterns in different colors. For example, academic journals usually

rhetorical situations · genres · processes · strategies · research mla/apa · media/ design

involve some questioning and speculating, as well as summarizing and paraphrasing. Try color coding each of these, sentence by sentence, phrase by phrase: yellow for summaries or paraphrases, green for questions, blue for speculations. Do any colors dominate? If, for example, your text is mostly yellow, you may be restating the course content too much and perhaps need to ask more of your own questions. If you're generating ideas for an essay, you might assign colors to ideas or themes to see which ones are most promising.

Assessing the Writing You Do for Others

What we write for others must stand on its own because we usually aren't present when it is read—we rarely get to explain to readers why we did what we did and what it means. So we need to make our writing as good as we can before we submit, post, display, or publish it. It's a good idea to assess your writing in two stages, first considering how well it meets the needs of your particular rhetorical situation, then studying the text itself to check its focus, argument, and organization. Sometimes some simple questions can get you started:

> What works?
> What still needs work?
> Where do you need to say more (or less)?

Considering the Rhetorical Situation

■ **PURPOSE**　What is your purpose for writing? If you have multiple purposes, list them, and then note which ones are the most important. How does your draft achieve your purpose(s)? If you're writing for an assignment, what are the requirements of the assignment and does your draft meet those requirements?　3–4

■ **AUDIENCE**　To whom are you writing? What do those readers need and expect, as far as you can tell? Does your draft　5–8 answer their needs? Do you define any terms and explain any concepts they won't know?

9–11   ⬛ **GENRE**   What is the genre, and what are the key features of that genre? Does your draft include each of those features?

12–14   ⬛ **STANCE**   Is it clear where you stand on your topic? Does your writing project the personality, voice, and tone that you want? Look at the words you use—how do they represent you as a person?

15–17   ⬛ **MEDIA / DESIGN**   At this point, your text is not likely to be designed, but think about the medium (print? spoken? electronic?) and whether your writing suits it. What design requirements can you anticipate? Lists? Headings? Charts? Visuals?

Examining the Text Itself

Look carefully at your text to see how well it says what you want it to say. Start with the broadest aspect, its focus, and then examine its reasons and evidence, organization, and clarity, in that order. If your writing lacks focus, the revising you'll do to sharpen the focus is likely to change everything else; if it needs more reasons and evidence, the organization may well change.

Consider your focus.   Your writing should have a clear point, and every part of the writing should support that point. Here are some questions that can help you see if your draft is adequately focused:

251–52 ◆
- What is your **THESIS?** Even if it is not stated overtly, you should be able to summarize it for yourself in a single sentence.

- Is your thesis narrow or broad enough to suit the needs and expectations of your audience?

239–45 ◆
- How does the **BEGINNING** focus attention on your main point?

- Does each paragraph support or develop that point? Do any paragraphs or sentences stray from your focus?

- Does the **ENDING** leave readers thinking about your main point? Is there another way of concluding the essay that would sharpen your focus? 245–48

Consider the support you provide for your argument. Your writing needs to give readers enough information to understand your points, follow your argument, and see the logic of your thinking. How much information is enough will vary according to your audience. If they already know a lot about your subject or are likely to agree with your point of view, you may need to give less detail. If, however, they are unfamiliar with your topic or are skeptical about your views, you will probably need to provide much more information to help them understand your position.

- What **REASONS** and **EVIDENCE** do you give to support your thesis? Where might more information be helpful or useful? 93–94
- What key terms and concepts do you **DEFINE?** Are there any other terms your readers might need to have explained? 275–84
- Where might you want more **DESCRIPTION** or other detail? 285–93
- Do you include any **COMPARISONS?** Especially if your readers will not be familiar with your topic, it can help to compare it with something more familiar. 266–74
- If you include **NARRATIVE,** how is it relevant to your point? 304–12
- See Part IV for other useful **STRATEGIES.** 237–328

Consider the organization. As a writer, you need to lead readers through your text, carefully structuring your material so that they will be able to follow your argument.

- Analyze the structure by **OUTLINING** it. An informal outline will do since you mainly need to see the parts, not the details. 203–04
- Does your genre require an abstract, a works cited list, or any other elements?
- What **TRANSITIONS** help readers move from idea to idea and paragraph to paragraph? 254
- Would **HEADINGS** help orient readers? 456–57

Check for clarity. Nothing else matters if readers can't understand what you write. So clarity matters. Following are some questions that can help you see whether your meaning is clear and your text is easy to read:

250–51

- Does your TITLE announce your subject of your text and give some sense of what you have to say? If not, would it strengthen your argument to be more direct?

251–52

- Do you state your THESIS directly? If not, how will readers understand your main point? Try stating your thesis outright, and see if it makes your argument easier to follow.

239–49

- Does your BEGINNING tell readers what they need to understand your text, and does your ENDING help them make sense of what they've just read?

254

- How does each paragraph relate to the ones before and after? Do you make those relationships clear—or do you need to add TRANSITIONS?

- Do you vary your sentences? If all the sentences are roughly the same length and follow the same subject-verb-object pattern, your text probably lacks any clear emphasis and might even be difficult to read.

458–62

- Are VISUALS clearly labeled, positioned near the text they relate to, referred to clearly in the text?

358–69

- If you introduce materials from other SOURCES, have you clearly distinguished quoted, paraphrased, or summarized ideas from your own?

- Have a look at the words you use. Concrete words are generally easier to understand than abstract words. If you use too many abstract words, consider changing some of them to concrete terms. Do you DEFINE all the words that your readers may not know?

275–84

- Does your punctuation make your writing more or less clear? Incorrect punctuation can make writing difficult to follow or, worse, change the intended meaning. As a best-selling punctuation manual reminds us, there's a considerable difference between "eats, shoots, and leaves" and "eats shoots and leaves."

Getting Response and Revising 25

If we want to learn to play a song on the guitar, we play it over and over again until we get it right. If we play basketball or baseball, we likely spend hours shooting foul shots or practicing a swing. Writing works the same way. Making our meaning clear can be tricky, and you should plan on revising and if need be rewriting in order to get it right. When we speak with someone face-to-face or on the phone or write an instant message to a friend, we can get immediate response and adjust or restate our message if we've been misunderstood. When we write, that immediate response is missing, so we need to seek out response from readers to help us revise. This chapter includes a list of things for those readers to consider, along with various strategies for then revising and rewriting.

Getting Response

Sometimes the most helpful eyes belong to others: readers you trust, including trained writing-center tutors. They can often point out problems (and strengths) that you simply cannot see in your own work. Ask your readers to consider the specific elements in the list below, but don't restrict them to those elements. Caution: If a reader says nothing about any of these elements, don't be too quick to assume that you needn't think about them yourself.

- What did you think when you first saw the **TITLE?** Is it interesting? informative? appropriate? Will it attract other readers' attention?

  250–51

- Does the **BEGINNING** grab readers' attention? If so, how does it do so? Does it give enough information about the topic? offer necessary background information? How else might the piece begin?

  239–45

- Is there a clear **THESIS?** What is it?

  251–52

94
375–449

- Is there sufficient **SUPPORT** for the thesis? Is there anywhere you'd like to have more detail? Is the supporting material sufficiently **DOCUMENTED?**

- Does the text have a clear pattern of organization? Does each part relate to the thesis? Does each part follow from the one preceding it? Was the text easy to follow? How might the organization be improved?

245–48

- Is the **ENDING** satisfying? What did it leave you thinking? How else might it end?

12-14

- What is the writer's **STANCE?** Can you tell the writer's attitude toward the subject and audience? What words convey that attitude? Is it consistent throughout?

1–17

- How well does the text address the rest of its **RHETORICAL SITUATION?** Does it meet the needs and expectations of its **AUDIENCE?** Where might readers need more information, guidance, or clarification? Does it achieve its **PURPOSE?** Does every part of the text help achieve the purpose? Could anything be cut? Should anything be added? Does it meet the requirements of its **GENRE?** Should anything be added, deleted, or changed to meet those requirements?

Revising

Once you have studied your draft with a critical eye and hopefully gotten response from other readers, it's time to revise. Major changes may be necessary, and you may need to generate new material or do some rewriting. But assume that your draft is good raw material that you can revise to achieve your purposes. Revision should take place on several levels, from global (whole-text issues) to particular (the details). Work on your draft in that order, starting with the elements that are global in nature and gradually moving to smaller, more particular aspects. This allows you to use your time most efficiently and take care of bigger issues first. In fact, as you deal with the larger aspects of your writing, many of the smaller ones will be taken care of along the way.

Give yourself time to revise. When you have a deadline, set deadlines for yourself that will give you time — preferably several days but as much

as your schedule permits — to work on the text before it has to be delivered. Also, get some distance. Often when you're immersed in a project, you can't see the big picture because you're so busy creating it. If you can, get away from your writing for a while and think about something else. When you return to it, you're more likely to see it freshly. If there's not time to put a draft away for several days or more, even letting it sit overnight or for a few hours can help.

As you revise, assume that nothing is sacred. Bring a critical eye to all parts of a draft, not only to those parts pointed out by your reviewers. Content, organization, sentence patterns, individual words — all are subject to improvement. Be aware that a change in one part of the text may require changes in other parts.

Revise to sharpen your focus.   Examine your **THESIS** to make sure it matches your **PURPOSE** as you now understand it. Read each paragraph to ensure that it contributes to your main point; you may find it helpful to **OUTLINE** your draft to help you see all the parts. If any parts of your draft do not advance your thesis, you need either to modify the parts of the draft that don't match or to revise your thesis to reflect your draft's focus. Read your **BEGINNING AND ENDING** carefully; make sure that the first paragraphs introduce your topic and provide any needed contextual information and that the last paragraphs provide a satisfying conclusion.

 251–52
3–4
 203–04
 239–49

Revise to strengthen the argument.   If readers find some of your claims unconvincing, you need to provide more information or more support. You may need to define terms you've assumed they will understand, offer additional examples, or provide more detail by describing, explaining processes, adding dialogue, or using some other **STRATEGIES.** Make sure you show as well as tell! You might try freewriting, clustering, or other ways of **GENERATING IDEAS AND TEXTS.** If you need to provide additional evidence, you might need to do additional **RESEARCH.**

 237–328
199–204
329–449

Revise to improve the organization.   If you've outlined your draft, number each paragraph, and make sure each one follows from the one before. If anything seems out of place, move it, or if necessary, cut it completely. Check to see if you've included appropriate **TRANSITIONS** or **HEADINGS** to

 254
456–57

help readers move through the text, and add them as needed. Check to make sure your text meets the requirements of the **GENRE** you're writing in.

9–11

Revise for clarity. Be sure readers will be able to understand what you're saying. Look closely at your **TITLE** to be sure it gives a sense of what the text is about, and at your **THESIS** to be sure readers will recognize your main point. If you don't state a thesis directly, consider whether you should. Be sure you provide any necessary background information and **DEFINE** any key terms. Make sure you've integrated any **QUOTATIONS, PARAPHRASES, or SUMMARIES** into your text clearly. Be sure all paragraphs are focused around one main point and that the sentences in each paragraph contribute to that point. Finally, consider whether there are any data that would be more clearly presented in a **CHART, TABLE,** or **GRAPH.**

250–51
251–52
275–84
358–69
458–62

One way to test whether your text is clear is to switch audiences: say what you're trying to say as if you were talking to an eight-year-old. You probably don't want to write that way, but the act of explaining your ideas to a young audience or readers who know nothing about your topic can help you discover any points that may be unclear.

Read and reread and reread. Take some advice from Donald Murray:

> Nonwriters confront a writing problem and look away from the text to rules and principles and textbooks and handbooks and models. Writers look at the text, knowing that the text itself will reveal what needs to be done and what should not yet be done or may never be done. The writer reads and rereads and rereads, standing far back and reading quickly from a distance, moving in close and reading slowly line by line, reading again and again, knowing that the answers to all writing problems lie within the evolving text.
>
> —Donald Murray, *A Writer Teaches Writing*

Rewriting

Some writers find it useful to try rewriting a draft in various ways or from various perspectives just to explore possibilities. Try it! If you find that your original plan works best for your purpose, fine. But you may find that another way will work better. Especially if you're not completely satisfied with your draft, consider the following ways of rewriting. Experiment with your rhetorical situation:

- Rewrite your draft from different points of view, through the eyes of different people perhaps or through the eyes of an animal or even from the perspective of an object. See how the text changes (in the information it presents, its perspective, its voice).

- Rewrite for a different **AUDIENCE.** How might an email detailing a recent car accident be written to a friend, the insurance adjuster, a parent?

5–8

- Rewrite in a different **STANCE.** If the first draft was temperate and judicious, be extreme; if it was polite, be more direct. If the first draft was in standard English, rewrite it in the language your relatives use.

12–14

- Rewrite the draft in a different **GENRE** or **MEDIUM.** Rewrite an essay as a letter, story, poem, speech. Which genre and medium work best to reach your intended audience and achieve your purpose?

9–11
15–16

Ways of rewriting a narrative

- Rewrite one scene completely in **DIALOGUE.**
- Start at the end of the story and work back to the beginning, or start in the middle and fill in the beginning as you work toward the end.

294–98

Ways of rewriting a textual analysis

- **COMPARE** the text you're analyzing with another text (which may be in a completely different genre—film, TV, song lyrics, computer games, poetry, fiction—whatever).

266–74

- Write a parody of the text you're analyzing. Be as silly and as funny as you can while maintaining the structure of the original text. Alternatively, write a parody of your analysis, using evidence from the text to support an outrageous analysis.

Ways of rewriting a report

5–8

- Rewrite for a different **AUDIENCE.** For example, explain a concept to your grandparents; describe the subject of a profile to a visitor from another planet.

- Be silly. Rewrite the draft as if for *The Daily Show* or *The Onion*, or rewrite it as if it were written by Bart Simpson.

Ways of rewriting an argument

82–106

- Rewrite taking another **POSITION.** Argue as forcefully for that position as you did for your actual one, acknowledging and refuting that position. Alternatively, write a rebuttal to your first draft from the perspective of someone with different beliefs.

304–12

- Rewrite your draft as a **STORY**—make it real in the lives of specific individuals. (For example, if you were writing about abortion rights, you could write a story about a young pregnant woman trying to decide what she believes and what to do.) Or rewrite the argument as a fable or parable.

- Rewrite the draft as a letter responding to a hostile reader, trying at least to make him or her understand what you have to say.

- Rewrite the draft as an angry letter to someone, or as a table-thumping dinner-with-the-relatives discussion. Write from the most extreme position possible.

324–27

- Write an **ANALYSIS** of your argument in which you identify, as carefully and as neutrally as you can, the various positions people hold on the issue.

Once you've rewritten a draft in any of these ways, see whether there's anything you can use. Read each draft, considering how it might help you achieve your purpose, reach your audience, convey your stance. Revise your actual draft to incorporate anything you think will make your text more effective.

Editing and Proofreading 26

Your ability to produce clear, error-free writing shows something about your ability as a writer and also leads readers to make assumptions about your intellect, work habits, even your character. Readers of job-application letters and résumés, for example, may reject applications if they contain a single error if only because that's an easy way to narrow the field of potential candidates. In addition, they may well assume that applicants who present themselves sloppily in an application will do sloppy work on the job. This is all to say that you should edit and proof-read your work carefully.

Editing

Editing is the stage when you work on the details of your paragraphs, sentences, words, and punctuation to make your writing as clear, precise, correct—and effective—as possible. Your goal is not to achieve "perfection" (whatever that may be) so much as to make your writing as effective as possible for your particular purpose and audience. Check a good writing handbook for detailed advice, but the following guidelines can help you check your drafts systematically for some common errors with paragraphs, sentences, and words.

Editing paragraphs

- Does each paragraph focus on one point? Does it have a **TOPIC SENTENCE** that announces that point, and if so, where is it located? If it's not the first sentence, should it be? If there's no clear topic sentence, should there be one?

252–53

- Does every sentence in the paragraph relate to the main point of that paragraph? If any sentences do not, consider whether they should be deleted, moved, or revised.

- Is there enough detail to develop the main point of the paragraph? How is the point developed—as a narrative? a definition? some other **STRATEGY?**

237–328

- Where have you placed the most important information—at the beginning? the end? in the middle? The most emphatic spot is at the end, so in general that's where to put information you want readers to remember. The second most emphatic spot is at the beginning.

- Are any paragraphs especially long or short? Consider breaking long paragraphs if there's a logical place to do so—maybe an extended example should be in its own paragraph, for instance. If you have paragraphs of only a sentence or two, see if you can add to them or combine them with another paragraph.

254

- Check the way your paragraphs fit together. Does each one follow smoothly from the one before? Do you need to add any **TRANSITIONS** or other links?

239–45

- Does the **BEGINNING** paragraph catch readers' attention? In what other ways might you begin your text?

245–48

- Does the final paragraph provide a satisfactory **ENDING?** How else might you conclude your text?

Editing sentences

- Is each sentence complete? Does it have someone or something (the subject) performing some sort of action or expressing a state of being (the verb)? Does each sentence begin with a capital letter and end with a period, question mark, or exclamation point?

- Check your use of the active voice ("The choir sang 'Amazing Grace.'") and the passive ("'Amazing Grace' was sung by the choir.") Some kinds of writing call for the passive voice, and sometimes it is more appropriate than the active voice, but in general, you'll do well to edit out any use of the passive voice that's not required.

- Check for parallelism. Items in a list or series should be parallel in form—all nouns (lions, tigers, bears), all verbs (hopped, skipped, jumped), all clauses (he came, he saw, he conquered), and so on.

- Do many of your sentences begin with *it* or *there*? Sometimes these words help introduce a topic, but too often they make your text vague or even conceal needed information. Why write "There are reasons we voted for him" when you can say "We had reasons to vote for him"?

- Are your sentences varied? If they all start with a subject or are all the same length, your writing might be dull and maybe even hard to read. Try varying your sentence openings by adding transitions, introductory phrases, or dependent clauses. Vary sentence lengths by adding detail to some or combining some sentences.

Editing words

- Are you sure of the meaning of every word? Use a dictionary; be sure to look up words whose meanings you're not sure about. And remember your audience—do you use any terms they'll need to have **DEFINED?**   275–84

- Is any of your language too general or vague? Why write that you competed in a race, for example, if you could say you ran the 4 × 200 relay?

- What about the tone? If your stance is serious (or humorous, or critical, or something else), make sure that your words all convey that tone.

- Do all pronouns have clear antecedents? If you write "he" or "they" or "it" or "these," will readers know whom or what the words refer to?

- Have you used any clichés—expressions that are used so frequently that they are no longer fresh? "Live and let live," avoiding something "like the plague," and similar expressions are so predictable that your writing will almost always be better off without them.

- Be careful with the language you use to refer to others. Make sure that your words do not stereotype any individual or group. Mention age, gender, race, religion, sexual orientation, and so on, only if they are relevant to your subject. When referring to an ethnic group, make every effort to use the terms members of the group prefer.

- Edit out language that might be considered sexist. Do you say "he" when you mean "he and she"? Have you used words like *manpower* or *policeman* to refer to people who may be female? If so, substitute less gendered words such as *personnel* or *police officer*. Do your words reflect any gender stereotypes—for example, that all engineers are male, or all schoolteachers female? If you mention someone's gender, is it even necessary? If not, eliminate the unneeded words.

- How many of your verbs are forms of *be*, *do*, and *have*? If you rely too much on these words, try replacing them with more specific verbs. Why write "She did a story" when you could say "She wrote a story"?

- Do you ever confuse *its* and *it's*? Use *it's* when you mean *it is* or *it has*. Use *its* when you mean *belonging to it*.

Proofreading

Proofreading is the final stage of the writing process, the point where you clean up your work to present it to your readers. Proofreading is like checking your appearance in a mirror before going into a job interview: being neat and well groomed looms large in creating a good first impression, and the same principle applies to writing. Misspelled words, missing pages, mixed-up fonts, and other lapses send a negative message about your work—and about you. Most readers excuse an occasional error, but by and large readers are an intolerant bunch: too many errors will lead them to declare your writing—and maybe your thinking—flawed. There goes your credibility. So proofread your final draft with care to ensure that your message is taken as seriously as you want it to be.

Up to this point, you've been told *not* to read individual words on the page and instead to read for meaning. Proofreading demands the opposite: you must slow down your reading so that you can see every word, every punctuation mark.

- Use your computer's grammar checker and spelling checker, but only as a first step, and know that they're not very reliable. Computer pro-

grams don't read writing; instead, they rely on formulas and banks of words, so what they flag (or don't flag) as mistakes may or may not be accurate. If you were to write, "Sea you soon," *sea* would not be flagged as misspelled because it is a word and it's spelled correctly even though it's the wrong word in that sentence.

- To keep your eyes from jumping ahead, place a ruler or piece of paper under each line as you read it. Use your finger or pen or pencil as a pointer.

- Some writers find it helpful to read the text one sentence at a time, beginning with the last sentence and working backward.

- Read your text out loud to yourself—or better, to others, who may *hear* problems you can't see. Alternatively, have someone else read your text aloud to you while you follow along on the page or screen.

- Ask someone else to read your text. The more important the writing is, the more important this step.

- If you find a mistake after you've printed out your text and are unable to print out a corrected version, make the change as neatly as possible in pencil or pen.

27 Compiling a Portfolio

Artists maintain portfolios of their work to show gallery owners, collectors, and other potential buyers. Money managers work with investment portfolios of stocks, bonds, and various mutual funds. And often as part of a writing class, student writers compile portfolios of their work. As with a portfolio of paintings or drawings, a portfolio of writing includes a writer's best work and, sometimes, preliminary and revised drafts of that work, along with a statement by the writer articulating why he or she considers it good. The *why* is as important as the work, for it provides you with an occasion for assessing your overall strengths and weaknesses as a writer. This chapter offers guidelines to help you compile both a *writing portfolio* and a *literacy portfolio*, a project that writing students are sometimes asked to complete as part of a literacy narrative.

Considering the Rhetorical Situation

As with the writing you put in a portfolio, the portfolio itself is generally intended for a particular audience but could serve a number of different purposes. It's a good idea, then, to consider these and the other elements of your rhetorical situation when you begin to compile a portfolio.

<table>
<tr><td>3–4</td><td>■ PURPOSE</td><td>Why are you creating this portfolio? To create a record of your writing? As the basis for a grade in a course? To organize your research? To explore your literacy? For something else?</td></tr>
<tr><td>5–8</td><td>■ AUDIENCE</td><td>Who will read your portfolio? What will your readers expect it to contain? How can you help them understand the context or occasion for each piece of writing you include?</td></tr>
</table>

■ **GENRE** What genres of writing should the portfolio contain? Do you want to demonstrate your ability to write a particular type of writing or in a variety of genres? Will your statement about the portfolio be in the form of a letter or an essay?

9–11

■ **STANCE** How do you want to portray yourself in this portfolio? What items should you include to create this impression? What stance do you want to take in your written assessment of its contents? Thoughtful? Enthusiastic? Something else?

12–14

■ **MEDIA / DESIGN** Will your portfolio be in print? Or will it be electronic? Whichever medium you choose, how can you help readers navigate its contents? What design elements will be most appropriate to your purpose and medium?

15–17

A WRITING PORTFOLIO

What to Include in a Writing Portfolio

A portfolio developed for a writing course typically contains examples of your best work in that course, including any notes, outlines, preliminary drafts, and so on, along with your own assessment of your performance in that course. You might include any of the following items:

- freewriting, outlines, and other work you did to generate ideas
- drafts, rough and revised
- in-class writing assignments
- source material—copies of articles, Web sites, observation notes, interview transcripts, and other evidence of your research
- tests and quizzes
- responses to your drafts
- conference notes, error logs, lecture notes, other course materials
- reflections on your work

What you have included will vary depending on what your instructor asks for. You may be asked to include three of your best papers or everything you've written. You may also be asked to choose certain items for evaluation or perhaps to show work in several different genres. In any case, you will need to choose, and to do that you will need to have criteria for making your choices. Don't base your decision solely on grades (unless grades are one criterion); your portfolio should reflect *your* assessment of your work, not your instructor's. What do you think is your best work? your most interesting work? your most ambitious work? Whatever criteria you use, you are the judge.

Organizing a Portfolio

Your instructor may provide explicit guidelines for organizing your portfolio. If not, here are some guidelines. If you set up a way to organize your writing at the start of the course, you'll be able to keep track of it throughout the course, making your job at term's end much easier. Remember that your portfolio presents you as a writer, presumably at your best. It should be neat, well organized, and easy to navigate.

Paper portfolios.   Choose something in which to gather your work. You might use a two-pocket folder, a three-ring binder, or a file folder, or you may need a box, basket, or some other container to accommodate bulky or odd-shaped items. You might also put your drafts on a computer disk, with each file clearly named.

Label everything. Label each piece at the top of the first page, specifying the assignment, the draft, and the date: "Proposal, Draft 1, 2/12/05"; "Text Analysis, Final Draft, 10/10/05"; "Portfolio Self-Assessment, Final Draft, 12/11/05"—and so on. Write this information neatly on the page, or put it on a Post-it note. For each assignment, arrange your materials chronologically, with your earliest material (freewriting, for example) on the bottom, and each successive item (source materials, say, then your outline, then your first draft, and so on) on top of the last, ending with

rhetorical situations

genres

processes

strategies

research mla/apa

media/ design

your final draft on top. That way readers can see how your writing progressed from earliest work to final draft.

Online portfolios. You might also assemble a Web portfolio that includes a home page with links to your portfolio's contents. Doing this requires that you create Web pages and then make them available on the Web. Some Web-based courseware programs allow you to create a portfolio from the texts you've submitted to the program; others require you to use a Web-authoring program. Microsoft FrontPage, Netscape Composer, or Macromedia Dreamweaver may be available through your school. Road Runner, Tripod, and Yahoo! GeoCities also provide tools for constructing Web pages. You can also use Microsoft Word, Excel, or PowerPoint. The programs available for your use and the requirements for posting your portfolio on the Web vary from school to school and instructor to instructor; ask your instructor or your school's computer help desk for help (and see the chapter on **ELECTRONIC TEXT** for general guidance).

476–84

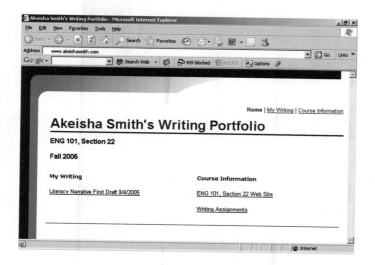

In general, you should first create a basic Web home page using one of those programs. Your home page should include your name, the portfolio's title, the relevant course information, the date, a menu of the contents, and your self-assessment. Below is an example, created with PowerPoint, of the kind of home page you might create early in the course; you can add links as you write new drafts.

Your home page might include a menu of links to each portfolio item, as this one does. Alternatively, you might include links to each piece of writing as you discuss it in your self-assessment—or you could do both. However you guide readers to your writing, be sure to provide a clearly descriptive title for each item. On each page of a final draft, you might create links to preliminary drafts and to work you did generating ideas.

The best way to plan such a portfolio is to make a map of its contents, like the one shown here done for a first-year writing course. Each box represents a different page; each line represents a link from one page to another.

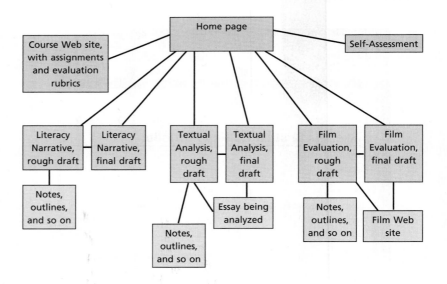

Reflecting on Your Writing Portfolio

The most important part of your portfolio is your written statement reflecting on your work. This is an occasion to step back from the work at hand and examine it with a critical eye. It is also an opportunity to assess your work, and to think about what you're most proud of, what you most enjoyed doing, what you want to improve. It's your chance to think about and say what you've learned. Some instructors may ask you to write out your assessment in essay form; others will want you to put it in letter form, which usually allows for a more relaxed and personal tone. Whatever form it takes, your statement should cover the following ground:

- *An evaluation of each piece of writing in the portfolio.* Consider both strengths and weaknesses, and give examples from your writing to support what you say. What would you change if you had more time? Which is your favorite piece, and why? Which is your least favorite?

- *An assessment of your overall writing performance.* What do you do well? What still needs improvement?

- *A discussion of how the writing you did in this course has affected your development as a writer.* How does the writing in your portfolio compare with writing you did in the past? What do you know now that you didn't know before? What can you do that you couldn't do before?

- *A description of your writing habits and process.* What do you usually do? How well does it work? What techniques seem to help you most, and why? Which seem less helpful? Cite passages from your drafts that support your conclusions.

- *An analysis of your performance in the course.* How did you spend your time? Did you collaborate with others? Did you have any conferences with your instructor? Did you visit the writing center? Consider how these or any other activities contributed to your success.

A SAMPLE SELF-ASSESSMENT

Here is a letter written by Nathaniel Cooney as part of his portfolio for his first-year writing class at Wright State University.

2 June 2004

Dear Reader,

It is my hope that in reading this letter, you will gain an understanding of the projects contained in this portfolio. I enclose three works that I have submitted for an introductory writing class at Wright State University, English 102, Writing in Academic Discourse: an informative report, an argument paper, and a genre project based largely on the content of the argument paper. I selected the topics of these works for two reasons: First, they address issues that I believe to be relevant in terms of both the intended audience (peers and instructors of the course) and the times when they were published. Second, they speak to issues that are important to me personally. Below I present general descriptions of the works, along with my review of their strengths and weaknesses.

My purpose in writing the informative report "Higher Standards in Education Are Taking Their Toll on Students" was to present a subject in a factual manner and to support it with well-documented research. My intent was not to argue a point. However, because I chose a narrowly focused topic and chose information to support a thesis, the report tends to favor one side of the issue over the other. Because as a student I have a personal stake in the changing standards in the formal education system, I chose to research recent changes in higher education and their effects on students. Specifically, I examine students' struggles to reach a standard that seems to be moving farther and farther beyond their grasp.

I believe that this paper could be improved in two areas. The first is a bias that I think exists because I am a student presenting information from the point of view of a student. It is my hope, however, that my inclusion of unbiased sources lessens this problem somewhat and, furthermore, that it presents the reader with a fair and accurate collection of facts and examples that supports the thesis. My second area of concern is the overall balance in the paper between outside sources supporting my own thoughts and outside sources supporting opposing points of view. Rereading the paper, I notice many places where I may have worked too hard to include sources to support my ideas. I do not necessarily see that as a bad thing, however, because, as I stated earlier, the outside sources work to counterbalance my own bias and provide the reader with additional information. I do think, though, that the paper might be improved if I were to reach a better balance between the amount of space dedicated to the expression of my ideas and the amount of space dedicated to the presentation of source materials.

The second paper, "Protecting Animals That Serve," is an argument intended not only to take a clear position on an issue but also to argue for that position and convince the reader that it is a valid one. That issue is the need for legislation guaranteeing that certain rights of service animals be protected. I am blind and use a guide dog. Thus, this issue is especially important to me. During the few months that I have had him, my guide dog has already encountered a number of situations where intentional or negligent treatment by others has put him in danger. At the time I was writing the paper, a bill was being written in the Ohio House of Representatives that, if passed, would protect service animals and establish consequences for those who violated the law. The purpose of the paper, therefore, was to present the reader with information about service animals, establish the need for the legislation in Ohio and nationwide, and argue for passage of such legislation.

I think that the best parts of my argument are the introduction and the conclusion. In particular, I think that the conclusion does a good job of not only bringing together the various points, but also conveying the significance of the issue for me and for others. In contrast, I think that the area most in need of further attention is the body of the paper. While I think the content is strong, I believe the overall organization could be improved. The connections between ideas are unclear in places, particularly in the section that acknowledges opposing viewpoints. This may be due in part to the fact that I had difficulty understanding the reasoning behind the opposing argument.

The argument paper served as a starting point for the genre project, for which the assignment was to revise one paper written for this class in a different genre. My genre project consists of a poster and a brochure. As it was for the argument paper, my primary goal was to convince my audience of the importance of a particular issue and viewpoint—specifically, to convince my audience to support House Bill 369, the bill being introduced in the Ohio Legislature that would create laws to protect the rights of service animals in the state.

Perhaps both the greatest strength and the greatest weakness of the genre project is my use of graphics. Because of my blindness, I was limited in my use of some graphics. Nevertheless, the pictures were carefully selected to capture the attention of readers, and, in part, to appeal to their emotions as they viewed and reflected on the material.

I noticed two other weaknesses in this project. First, I think that in my effort to include the most relevant information in the brochure, I may have included too many details. Because space is limited, brochures generally include only short, simple facts. Although I tried to keep the facts short and simple, I also tried to use the space that I had to provide as much supporting information as I could. This may have resulted in too much information, given the genre. Second, I dedicated one portion of the poster to a poem I wrote. While the thoughts it conveys are extremely impor-

rhetorical situations

genres

processes

strategies

research mla/apa

media/ design

tant to me, I was somewhat unsatisfied with its style. I tried to avoid a simple rhyme scheme, but the words kept making their way back to that format. I kept the poem as it was on the advice of others, but I still believe that it could be better.

Despite its weakness, the poem also adds strength to the project in its last stanzas. There, I ask readers to take a side step for a moment, to consider what their lives would be like if they were directly affected by the issue, and to reflect on the issue from that perspective. I hope that doing so personalized the issue for readers and thus strengthened my argument.

I put a great deal of time, effort, and personal reflection into each project. While I am hesitant to say that they are finished and while I am dissatisfied with some of the finer points, I am satisfied with the overall outcome of this collection of works. Viewing it as a collection, I am also reminded that writing is an evolving process and that even if these works never become exactly what I envisioned them to be, they stand as reflections of my thoughts at a particular time in my life. In that respect, they need not be anything but what they already are, because what they are is a product of who I was when I wrote them. I hope that you find the papers interesting and informative and that as you read them, you, too, may realize their significance.

Respectfully,

Nathaniel J. Cooney

Nathaniel J. Cooney

Enclosures (3)

Cooney describes each of the works he includes and considers their strengths and weaknesses, citing examples from his texts to support his assessment.

A LITERACY PORTFOLIO

As a writing student, you may be asked to think back to the time when you first learned to read and write or to remember significant books or other texts you've read and perhaps to put together a portfolio that chronicles your development as a reader and writer. You may also be asked to put together a literacy portfolio as part of a written narrative assignment.

What you include in such a portfolio will vary depending on what you've kept over the years and what your family has kept. You may have all of your favorite books, stories you dictated to a preschool teacher, notebooks in which you practiced cursive writing. Or you may have almost nothing. What you have or don't have is unimportant in the end: what's important is that you gather what you can and arrange it in a way that shows how you think about your development and growth as a literate person. What has been your experience with reading and writing? What's your earliest memory of learning to write? If you love to read, what led you to love it? Who was most responsible for shaping your writing ability? Those are some of the questions you'll ask if you write a **LITERACY NARRATIVE.** You might also compile a literacy portfolio as a good way to generate ideas and text for that assignment.

21–38

What to Include in a Literacy Portfolio

- school papers
- drawings and doodles from preschool
- favorite books
- photographs you've taken
- drawings
- poems
- letters

rhetorical situations　　genres　　processes　　strategies　　research mla/apa　　media/ design

- journals and diaries
- lists
- reading records or logs
- marriage vows
- legal documents
- speeches you've given
- awards you've received

Organizing a Literacy Portfolio

You may wish to organize your material chronologically, but there are other methods of organization to consider as well. For example, you might group items according to where they were written (at home, at school, at work), by genre (stories, poems, essays, letters, notes), or even by purpose (pleasure, school, work, church, and so on). Arrange your portfolio in the way that best conveys who you are as a literate person. Label each item you include, perhaps with a Post-it note, to identify what it is, when it was written or read, and why you've included it in your portfolio.

Reflecting on Your Literacy Portfolio

- Why did you choose each item?
- Is anything missing? Are there any other important materials that should be here?
- Why is the portfolio arranged as it is?
- What does the portfolio show about your development as a reader and writer?
- What patterns do you see? Are there any common themes you've read or written about? Any techniques you rely on? Any notable changes over time?
- What are the most significant items — and why?

part 4

Strategies

Whenever we write, we draw on many different strategies to articulate what we have to say. We may DEFINE key terms, DESCRIBE people or places, and EXPLAIN how something is done. We may COMPARE one thing to another. Sometimes we may choose a pertinent story to NARRATE, and we may even want to include some DIALOGUE. The chapters that follow offer advice on how to use these AND OTHER BASIC STRATEGIES for developing and organizing the texts you write.

Strategies

Beginning and Ending 28

Whenever we pick up something to read, we generally start by looking at the first few words or sentences to see if they grab our attention, and based on them we decide whether to keep reading. Beginnings, then, are important, both attracting readers and giving them some information about what's to come. When we get to the end of a text, we expect to be left with a sense of closure, of satisfaction—that the story is complete, our questions have been answered, the argument has been made. So endings are important, too. This chapter offers advice on how to write beginnings and endings.

Beginning

How you begin depends on your **RHETORICAL SITUATION,** especially your purpose and audience. Academic audiences generally expect your introduction to establish context, explaining how the text fits into some larger conversation, addresses certain questions, or explores an aspect of the subject. Most introductions also offer a brief description of the text's content, often in the form of a thesis statement. The following opening of an essay about "the greatest generation" does all of this:

1–17

> Tom Brokaw called the folks of the mid-twentieth century the greatest generation. So why is the generation of my grandparents seen as this country's greatest? Perhaps the reason is not what they accomplished but what they endured. Many of the survivors feel people today "don't have the moral character to withstand a depression like that." This paper will explore the Great Depression through the eyes of ordinary Americans in the most impoverished region in the country, the

rhetorical situations genres processes strategies research mla/apa media/ design

American South, in order to detail how they endured and how the government assisted them in this difficult era.

— Jeffrey DeRoven, "The Greatest Generation: The Great Depression and the American South"

If you're writing for a nonacademic audience or genre — for a newspaper or a Web site, for example — your introduction may need to entice your readers to read on by connecting your text to their interests through shared experiences, anecdotes, or some other attention-getting device. Cynthia Bass, writing a newspaper article about the Gettysburg Address on its 135th anniversary, connects that date — the day her audience would read it — to Lincoln's address. She then develops the rationale for thinking about the speech and introduces her specific topic: debates about the writing and delivery of the Gettysburg Address:

> November 19 is the 135th anniversary of the Gettysburg Address. On that day in 1863, with the Civil War only half over and the worst yet to come, Abraham Lincoln delivered a speech now universally regarded as both the most important oration in U.S. history and the best explanation — "government of the people, by the people, for the people" — of why this nation exists.
>
> We would expect the history of an event so monumental as the Gettysburg Address to be well established. The truth is just the opposite. The only thing scholars agree on is that the speech is short — only ten sentences — and that it took Lincoln under five minutes to stand up, deliver it, and sit back down.
>
> Everything else — when Lincoln wrote it, where he wrote it, how quickly he wrote it, how he was invited, how the audience reacted — has been open to debate since the moment the words left his mouth.
>
> — Cynthia Bass, "Gettysburg Address: Two Versions"

Ways of Beginning

Explain the larger context of your topic. Most essays are part of an ongoing conversation, so you might begin by outlining the positions to which your writing responds, as the following example from an essay about prejudice does:

rhetorical situations   genres   processes   strategies   research mla/apa   media/ design

The war on prejudice is now, in all likelihood, the most uncontroversial social movement in America. Opposition to "hate speech," formerly identified with the liberal left, has become a bipartisan piety. In the past year, groups and factions that agree on nothing else have agreed that the public expression of any and all prejudices must be forbidden. On the left, protesters and editorialists have insisted that Francis L. Lawrence resign as president of Rutgers University for describing blacks as "a disadvantaged population that doesn't have that genetic, hereditary background to have a higher average." On the other side of the ideological divide, Ralph Reed, the executive director of the Christian Coalition, responded to criticism of the religious right by calling a press conference to denounce a supposed outbreak of "name-calling, scapegoating, and religious bigotry." Craig Rogers, an evangelical Christian student at California State University, recently filed a $2.5 million sexual-harassment suit against a lesbian professor of psychology, claiming that anti-male bias in one of her lectures violated campus rules and left him feeling "raped and trapped."

In universities and on Capitol Hill, in workplaces and newsrooms, authorities are declaring that there is no place for racism, sexism, homophobia, Christian-bashing, and other forms of prejudice in public debate or even in private thought. "Only when racism and other forms of prejudice are expunged," say the crusaders for sweetness and light, "can minorities be safe and society be fair." So sweet, this dream of a world without prejudice. But the very last thing society should do is seek to utterly eradicate racism and other forms of prejudice.

—Jonathan Rauch, "In Defense of Prejudice"

State your thesis. Sometimes the best beginning is a clear **THESIS** stating your position, like the following statement in an essay arguing that under certain circumstances torture is necessary:

251–52

It is generally assumed that torture is impermissible, a throwback to a more brutal age. Enlightened societies reject it outright, and regimes using it risk the wrath of the United States.

I believe this attitude is unwise. There are situations in which torture is not merely permissible but morally mandatory. Moreover, these situations are moving from the realm of imagination to fact.

—Michael Levin, "The Case for Torture"

Forecast your organization.   You might begin by briefly outlining the way in which you will organize your text. The following example offers background on the subject, an analysis of immigration patterns in the United States, and describes the points that the writer's analysis will discuss:

> This paper analyzes the new geography of immigration during the twentieth century and highlights how immigrant destinations in the 1980s and 1990s differ from earlier settlement patterns. The first part of the analysis uses historical U.S. Census data to develop a classification of urban immigrant "gateways" that describes the ebb and flow of past, present, and likely future receiving areas. The remainder of the analysis examines contemporary trends to explore the recent and rapid settlement of the immigrant population in America's metropolitan gateways.
>
> —Audrey Singer, "The Rise of New Immigrant Gateways"

Offer background information.   If your readers may not know as much as you do about your topic, giving them information to help them understand your position can be important, as David Guterson does in an essay on the Mall of America:

> Last April, on a visit to the new Mall of America near Minneapolis, I carried with me the public-relations press kit provided for the benefit of reporters. It included an assortment of "fun facts" about the mall: 140,000 hot dogs sold each week, 10,000 permanent jobs, 44 escalators and 17 elevators, 12,750 parking places, 13,300 short tons of steel, $1 million in cash disbursed weekly from 8 automatic-teller machines. Opened in the summer of 1992, the mall was built on the 78-acre site of the former Metropolitan Stadium, a five-minute drive from the Minneapolis–St. Paul International Airport. With 4.2 million square feet of floor space—including twenty-two times the retail footage of the average American shopping center—the Mall of America was "the largest fully enclosed combination retail and family entertainment complex in the United States."
>
> —David Guterson, "Enclosed. Encyclopedic. Endured: The Mall of America"

rhetorical situations   genres   processes   strategies   research mla/apa   media/design

275–84

Define key terms or concepts. The success of an argument often hinges on how key terms are DEFINED. You may wish to provide definitions up front, as this page from an advocacy Web site, *Health Care without Harm*, does in a report on the hazards of fragrances in health-care facilities:

> To many people, the word "fragrance" means something that smells nice, such as perfume. We don't often stop to think that scents are chemicals. Fragrance chemicals are organic compounds that volatilize, or vaporize into the air—that's why we can smell them. They are added to products to give them a scent or to mask the odor of other ingredients. The volatile organic chemicals (VOCs) emitted by fragrance products can contribute to poor indoor air quality (IAQ) and are associated with a variety of adverse health effects.
>
> —Health Care without Harm, "Fragrances"

Connect your subject to your readers' interests or values. You'll always want to establish common ground with your readers, and sometimes you may wish to do so immediately, in your introduction, as in this example:

> We all want to feel safe. Most Americans lock their doors at night, lock their cars in parking lots, try to park near buildings or under lights, and wear seat belts. Many invest in expensive security systems, carry pepper spray or a stun gun, keep guns in their homes, or take self-defense classes. Obviously, safety and security are important issues in American life.
>
> —Andy McDonie, "Airport Security: What Price Safety?"

Start with something that will provoke readers' interest. Anna Quindlen opens an essay on feminism with the following eye-opening assertion:

> Let's use the F word here. People say it's inappropriate, offensive, that it puts people off. But it seems to me it's the best way to begin, when it's simultaneously devalued and invaluable.
> Feminist. Feminist, feminist, feminist.
>
> —Anna Quindlen, "Still Needing the F Word"

304–12

Start with an anecdote.   Sometimes a brief **NARRATIVE** helps bring a topic to life for readers. See, for example, how an essay on the dozens, a type of verbal contest played by some African Americans, begins:

> Alfred Wright, a nineteen-year-old whose manhood was at stake on Longwood Avenue in the South Bronx, looked fairly calm as another teenager called him Chicken Head and compared his mother to Shamu the whale.
>
> He fingered the gold chain around his thin neck while listening to a detailed complaint about his sister's sexual abilities. Then he slowly took the toothpick out of his mouth; the jeering crowd of young men quieted as he pointed at his accuser.
>
> "He was so ugly when he was born," Wright said, "the doctor smacked his mom instead of him."
>
> —John Tierney, "Playing the Dozens"

Ask a question.   Instead of a thesis statement, you might open with a question about the topic your text will explore, as this study of the status of women in science does:

> Are women's minds different from men's minds? In spite of the women's movement, the age-old debate centering around this question continues. We are surrounded by evidence of de facto differences between men's and women's intellects — in the problems that interest them, in the ways they try to solve those problems, and in the professions they choose. Even though it has become fashionable to view such differences as environmental in origin, the temptation to seek an explanation in terms of innate differences remains a powerful one.
>
> —Evelyn Fox Keller, "Women in Science: A Social Analysis"

Jump right in.   Occasionally you may wish to start a narrative as close to the key action as possible. See how one writer jumps right into his profile of a blues concert:

> Long Tongue, the Blues Merchant, strolls onstage. His guitar rides side-saddle against his hip. The drummer slides onto the tripod seat behind the drums, adjusts the high-hat cymbal, and runs a quick, off-beat tattoo on the tom-tom, then relaxes. The bass player plugs into the ampli-

fier, checks the settings on the control panel, and nods his okay. Three horn players stand off to one side, clustered, lurking like brilliant sorcerer-wizards waiting to do magic with their musical instruments.

—Jerome Washington, "The Blues Merchant"

Ending

Endings are important because they're the last words readers read. How you end a text will depend in part on your RHETORICAL SITUATION. You may end by wrapping up loose ends, or you may wish to give readers something to think about. Some endings do both, as Cynthia Bass does in her report on the disputes over the Gettysburg Address. In her two final paragraphs, she first summarizes the dispute and then shows its implications:

1–17

> What's most interesting about the Lincoln-as-loser and Lincoln-as-winner versions is how they marshal the same facts to prove different points. The invitation asks Lincoln to deliver "a few appropriate remarks." Whether this is a putdown or a reflection of the protocol of the time depends on the "spin"—an expression the highly politicized Lincoln would have readily understood—which the scholar places on it.
>
> These diverse histories should not in any way diminish the power or beauty of Lincoln's words. However, they should remind us that history, even the history of something as deeply respected as the Gettysburg Address, is seldom simple or clear. This reminder is especially useful today as we watch expert witnesses, in an effort to divine what the founders meant by "high crimes and misdemeanors," club one another with conflicting interpretations of the same events, the same words, the same precedents, and the same laws.

—Cynthia Bass, "Gettysburg Address: Two Versions"

Bass summarizes the dispute about Lincoln's Address and then moves on to discuss the role of scholars in interpreting historical events. Writing during the Clinton impeachment hearings, she concluded by pointing out the way in which expert government witnesses often offer conflicting interpretations of events to suit their own needs. The ending combines several strategies to bring various strands of her essay together, leaving readers to interpret her final words themselves.

Ways of Ending

366–67
Restate your main point.   Sometimes you'll simply **SUMMARIZE** your central idea, as in this example from an essay arguing that we have no "inner" self and that we should be judged by our actions alone:

> The inner man is a fantasy. If it helps you to identify with one, by all means, do so; preserve it, cherish it, embrace it, but do not present it to others for evaluation or consideration, for excuse or exculpation, or, for that matter, for punishment or disapproval.
>   Like any fantasy, it serves your purposes alone. It has no standing in the real world which we share with each other. Those character traits, those attitudes, that behavior—that strange and alien stuff sticking out all over you—*that's the real you!*
>
> —Willard Gaylin, "What You See Is the Real You"

Discuss the implications of your argument.   The following conclusion of an essay on the development of Post-it notes leads readers to consider how failure sometimes leads to innovation:

> Post-it notes provide but one example of a technological artifact that has evolved from a perceived failure of existing artifacts to function without frustrating. Again, it is not that form follows function but, rather, that the form of one thing follows from the failure of another thing to function as we would like. Whether it be bookmarks that fail to stay in place or taped-on notes that fail to leave a once-nice surface clean and intact, their failure and perceived failure is what leads to the true evolution of artifacts. That the perception of failure may take centuries to develop, as in the case of loose bookmarks, does not reduce the importance of the principle in shaping our world.
>
> —Henry Petroski, "Little Things Can Mean a Lot"

304–12
End with an anecdote, maybe finishing a **NARRATIVE** that was begun earlier in your text or adding one that illustrates the implications of your argument. See how Sarah Vowell uses a story to end an essay on students' need to examine news reporting critically:

I looked at Joanne McGlynn's syllabus for her media studies course, the one she handed out at the beginning of the year, stating the goals of the class. By the end of the year, she hoped her students would be better able to challenge everything from novels to newscasts, that they would come to identify just who is telling a story and how that person's point of view affects the story being told. I'm going to go out on a limb here and say that this lesson has been learned. In fact, just recently, a student came up to McGlynn and told her something all teachers dream of hearing. The girl told the teacher that she was listening to the radio, singing along with her favorite song, and halfway through the sing-along she stopped and asked herself, "What am I singing? What do these words mean? What are they trying to tell me?" And then, this young citizen of the republic jokingly complained, "I can't even turn on the radio without thinking anymore."

—Sarah Vowell, "Democracy and Things Like That"

Refer to the beginning. One way to bring closure to a text is to bring up something discussed in the beginning; often the reference adds to or even changes the original meaning. See, for example, how Barbara Kingsolver opens an essay arguing that the American flag symbolizes not only patriotism but also the desire for peace and the right to dissent with this anecdote:

My daughter came home from kindergarten and announced, "Tomorrow we all have to wear red, white, and blue."
"Why?" I asked, trying not to sound anxious.
"For all the people that died when the airplanes hit the buildings."
I said quietly, "Why not wear black, then? Why the colors of the flag, what does that mean?"
"It means we're a country. Just all people together."

She returns to this image at the end, where the final sentence takes on a new meaning:

Shortly after the September attacks, my town became famous for a simple gesture in which some eight thousand people wearing red, white, or blue T-shirts assembled themselves in the shape of a flag on a baseball field and had their photograph taken from above. That picture soon began to turn up everywhere, but we saw it first on our newspaper's front page. Our family stood in silence for a minute looking at that stunningly beautiful photograph of a human flag, trying to know what to make of it. Then my teenager, who has a quick mind for numbers and a sensitive heart, did an interesting thing. She laid her hand over part of the picture, leaving visible more or less five thousand people, and said, "In New York, that many might be dead." We stared at what that looked like — that many innocent souls, particolored and packed into a conjoined destiny — and shuddered at the one simple truth behind all the noise, which was that so many beloved, fragile lives were suddenly gone from us. That is my flag, and that's what it means: We're all just people, together.

— Barbara Kingsolver, "And Our Flag Was Still There"

Propose some action, as in the following conclusion of a report on the consequences of binge drinking among college students:

The scope of the problem makes immediate results of any interventions highly unlikely. Colleges need to be committed to large-scale and long-term behavior-change strategies, including referral of alcohol abusers to appropriate treatment. Frequent binge drinkers on college campuses are similar to other alcohol abusers elsewhere in their tendency to deny that they have a problem. Indeed, their youth, the visibility of others who drink the same way, and the shelter of the college community may make them less likely to recognize the problem. In addition to addressing the health problems of alcohol abusers, a major effort should address the large group of students who are not binge drinkers on campus who are adversely affected by the alcohol-related behavior of binge drinkers.

— Henry Wechsler et al., "Health and Behavioral Consequences of Binge Drinking in College: A National Survey of Students at 140 Campuses"

Considering the Rhetorical Situation

As a writer or speaker, you need to think about the message that you want to articulate, the audience you want to reach, and the larger context you are writing in.

rhetorical situations · genres · processes · strategies · research mla/apa · media/design

■ **PURPOSE**   Your purpose will affect the way you begin and end. If you're trying to persuade readers to do something, you may want to open by clearly stating your thesis and end by calling for a specific action.

3–4

■ **AUDIENCE**   Who do you want to reach, and how does that affect the way you begin and end? You may want to open with an intriguing fact or anecdote to entice your audience to read a profile, for instance, whereas readers of a report may expect it to conclude with a summary of your findings.

5–8

■ **GENRE**   Does your genre require a certain type of beginning or ending? Arguments, for example, often provide a statement of the thesis near the beginning; proposals typically end with a call for some solution.

9–11

■ **STANCE**   What is your stance, and can your beginning and ending help you convey that stance? For example, beginning an argument on the distribution of AIDS medicine to underdeveloped countries with an anecdote may demonstrate concern for the human costs of the disease, whereas starting with a statistical analysis may suggest the stance of a careful researcher. Ending a proposal by weighing the advantages and disadvantages of the solution you propose may make you seem reasonable.

12–14

■ **MEDIA / DESIGN** Your medium may affect the way you begin and end. A web text, for instance, may open with a home page listing a menu of the site—and giving readers a choice of where they will begin. With a print text, you get to decide how it will begin and end.

15–17

See also the **GUIDES TO WRITING** in chapters 6–9 for ways of beginning and ending a **LITERACY NARRATIVE,** an essay **ANALYZING TEXT,** a **REPORT,** or an **ARGUMENT.**

▲ 21–106

29 Guiding Your Reader

Traffic lights, street signs, and lines on the road help drivers find their way. Readers need similar guidance—to know, for example, whether they're reading a report or an argument, an evaluation or a proposal. They also need to know what to expect: What will the report be about? What perspective will it offer? What will this paragraph cover? What about the next one? How do the two paragraphs relate to each other? When you write, you need to provide cues to help your readers navigate your text and understand the points you're trying to make. This chapter offers advice on guiding your reader and, specifically, on using *titles*, *thesis statements*, *topic sentences*, and *transitions*.

Titles

A title serves various purposes, naming a text and providing clues to the content. It also helps readers decide whether they want to read further, so it's worth your while to come up with a title that attracts interest. Some titles include subtitles. You generally have considerable freedom in choosing a title but always you'll want to consider the RHETORICAL SITUATION to be sure your title serves your purpose and appeals to the audience you want to reach.

1–17

Some titles simply announce the subject of the text:

"Black Men and Public Space"
"Ain't I a Woman?"
"Why Colleges Shower Their Students with A's"
Nickel and Dimed

Some titles provoke readers or otherwise entice them to read:

"Kill 'Em! Crush 'Em! Eat 'Em Raw!"
"Thank God for the Atom Bomb"
"What Are Homosexuals For?"

Sometimes writers add a subtitle to explain or illuminate the title:

Aria: Memoir of a Bilingual Childhood
"Health and Behavioral Consequences of Binge Drinking in College: A
    National Survey of Students at 140 Campuses"
"From Realism to Virtual Reality: Images of America's Wars"

Sometimes when you're starting to write, you'll think of a title that helps you generate ideas and write. More often, though, a title is one of the last things you'll write, when you know what you've written and can craft a suitable name for your text.

Thesis Statements

A thesis identifies the topic of your text along with the claim you are making about it. A good thesis helps readers understand an essay. Working to create a sharp thesis can help you focus both your thinking and your writing. Here are three steps for moving from a topic to a thesis statement:

1. State your topic as a question.   You may have an idea for a topic, such as "famine," "gas prices," or "the effects of creatine on athletes." Those may be good topics, but they're not thesis statements, primarily because none of them actually makes a statement. A good way to begin moving from topic to thesis statement is to style your topic as a question:

What can be done to prevent famine in Africa?
What causes fluctuations in gasoline prices?
What are the effects of creatine on athletes?

2. Then turn your question into a position. A thesis statement is an assertion—it takes a stand or makes a claim. Whether you're writing a report or an argument, you are saying, "This is the way I see . . . " or "This is what I believe about . . . " Your thesis statement announces your position on the question you are raising about your topic, so a relatively easy way of establishing a thesis is to answer your own question:

> The most recent famine in Eritrea could have been avoided if certain measures had been taken.
>
> Gasoline prices fluctuate for several reasons.
>
> There are positive as well as negative effects of using creatine to enhance athletic performance.

3. Narrow your thesis. A good thesis is specific, guiding you as you write and showing your audience exactly what your essay will cover. The preceding thesis statements need to be qualified and focused—they need to be made more specific. For example:

> The 1984 famine in Eritrea could have been avoided if farmers had received training in more effective methods and had had access to certain technology and if Western nations had provided more aid more quickly.
>
> Gasoline prices fluctuate because of production procedures, consumer demand, international politics, and oil companies' policies.
>
> When adult athletes use creatine, they become stronger and larger— with no known serious side effects.

Thesis statements are typically positioned at or near the end of the introduction of a text, to let readers know at the outset what you're claiming and what your text will be aiming to prove.

Topic Sentences

Just as a thesis announces your topic and your position, a topic sentence states the subject and focus of a paragraph. Good paragraphs focus on a single point, which is summarized in a topic sentence. Usually, but not always, the topic sentence begins the paragraph:

Graduating from high school or college is an exciting, occasionally even traumatic event. Your identity changes as you move from being a high school teenager to a university student or a worker; your connection to home loosens as you attend school elsewhere, move to a place of your own, or simply exercise your right to stay out later. You suddenly find yourself doing different things, thinking different thoughts, fretting about different matters. As recent high school graduate T. J. Devoe puts it, "I wasn't really scared, but having this vast range of opportunity made me uneasy. I didn't know *what* was gonna happen." Jenny Petrow, in describing her first year out of college, observes, "It's a tough year. It was for all my friends."

—Sydney Lewis, *Help Wanted: Tales from the First Job Front*

Sometimes the topic sentence may come at the end of the paragraph or even at the end of the preceding paragraph, depending on the way the paragraphs relate to one another. Other times a topic sentence will summarize or restate a point made in the previous paragraph, helping readers understand what they've just read as they move on to the next point. See how the linguist Deborah Tannen does this in the first paragraphs of an article on differences in men's and women's conversational styles:

I was addressing a small gathering in a suburban Virginia living room — a women's group that had invited men to join them. Throughout the evening, one man had been particularly talkative, frequently offering ideas and anecdotes, while his wife sat silently beside him on the couch. Toward the end of the evening, I commented that women frequently complain that their husbands don't talk to them. This man quickly concurred. He gestured toward his wife and said, "She's the talker in our family." The room burst into laughter; the man looked puzzled and hurt. "It's true," he explained. "When I come home from work I have nothing to say. If she didn't keep the conversation going, we'd spend the whole evening in silence."

This episode crystallizes the irony that although American men tend to talk more than women in public situations, they often talk less at home. And this pattern is wreaking havoc with marriage.

—Deborah Tannen, "Sex, Lies, and Conversation: Why Is It So Hard for Men and Women to Talk to Each Other?"

Transitions

Transitions help readers move from thought to thought — from sentence to sentence, paragraph to paragraph. You are likely to use a number of transitions as you draft; when you're **EDITING,** you should make a point of checking transitions. Here are some common ones:

219–22

- **To show causes and effects:** accordingly, as a result, because, consequently, hence, so, then, therefore, thus
- **To show comparisons:** also, in the same way, like, likewise, similarly
- **To show contrasts or exceptions:** although, but, even though, however, in contrast, instead, nevertheless, nonetheless, on the contrary, on the one hand . . . on the other hand, still, yet
- **To show examples:** even, for example, for instance, indeed, in fact, of course, such as
- **To show place or position:** above, adjacent to, below, beyond, elsewhere, here, inside, near, outside, there
- **To show sequence:** again, also, and, and then, besides, finally, furthermore, last, moreover, next, too
- **To show time:** after, as soon as, at first, at the same time, before, eventually, finally, immediately, later, meanwhile, next, simultaneously, so far, soon, then, thereafter
- **To signal a summary or conclusion:** as a result, as we have seen, finally, in a word, in any event, in brief, in conclusion, in other words, in short, in the end, in the final analysis, on the whole, therefore, thus, to summarize

453–63

See also Chapter 47 on **PRINT TEXT** for ways of creating visual signals for your readers.

rhetorical situations

genres

processes

strategies

research mla/apa

media/ design

Analyzing Causes and Effects **30**

Analyzing causes helps us think about why something happened, whereas thinking about effects helps us consider what might happen. When we hear a noise in the night, we want to know what caused it. Children poke sticks into holes to see what will happen. Researchers try to understand the causes of diseases. Writers often have occasion to consider causes of effects as part of a larger topic or sometimes as a main focus: in a **PROPOSAL,** we might consider the effects of reducing tuition or the causes of recent tuition increases; in a **MEMOIR,** we might explore why the person we had a date with failed to show up. Often we can only speculate about probable causes or likely effects. In writing about causes and effects, then, we are generally **ARGUING** for those we consider plausible or probable. This chapter will help you analyze causes and effects in writing—and to do so in a way that suits your rhetorical situation.

▲ 160–67
▲ 147–52

▲ 82–106

Determining Plausible Causes and Effects

What causes ozone depletion? sleeplessness? obesity? And what are their effects? Those are of course large, complex topics, but whenever you have reason to ask why something happened or what could happen, there will likely be several possible causes and just as many predictable effects. There may be obvious causes, though often they will be less important than others that are harder to recognize. (Eating too much may be an obvious cause of being overweight, but *why* people eat too much has several less obvious causes: portion size, advertising, lifestyle, and physiological disorders are only a few possibilities.) Similarly, short-term effects are often less important than long-term ones. (A stomachache may be an effect of eating too much candy, but the chemical imbalance that can result from consuming too much sugar is a much more serious effect.)

200–02 ○
203–04 ○
329–449 ●

3–8 ■

LISTING, **CLUSTERING**, and **OUTLINING** are useful processes for analyzing causes. And at times you might need to do some **RESEARCH** to identify possible causes or effects and to find evidence to support your analysis. When you've identified potential causes and effects, you need to analyze them. Which causes and effects are primary? Which seem to be secondary? Which are most relevant to your **PURPOSE** and are likely to convince your **AUDIENCE?** You will probably need to choose from several possible causes and effects for your analysis because you won't want or need to include all of them.

Arguing for Causes or Effects

Once you've identified several possible causes or predictable effects, you need to argue that some are more plausible than others. You must provide convincing support for your argument because you cannot prove that X causes Y or that Y will be caused by Z; you can show only, with good reasons and appropriate evidence, that X is likely to cause Y or that Y will likely follow from Z. See, for example, how an essay on the psychological basis for risk taking speculates about two potential causes for the popularity of extreme sports:

> Studies now indicate that the inclination to take high risks may be hardwired into the brain, intimately linked to arousal and pleasure mechanisms, and may offer such a thrill that it functions like an addiction. The tendency probably affects one in five people, mostly young males, and declines with age. It may ensure our survival, even spur our evolution as individuals and as a species. Risk taking probably bestowed a crucial evolutionary advantage, inciting the fighting and foraging of the hunter-gatherer. . . .
>
> As psychologist Salvadore Maddi, PhD, of the University of California at Davis warns, "High-risk takers may have a hard time deriving meaning and purpose from everyday life." Indeed, this peculiar form of dissatisfaction could help explain the explosion of high-risk sports in America and other postindustrial Western nations. In unstable cultures, such as those at war or suffering poverty, people rarely seek out additional thrills. But in a rich and safety-obsessed country like America, land of guardrails, seat belts, and personal-injury lawsuits, everyday life may have

rhetorical situations   genres   processes   strategies   research mla/apa   media/ design

become too safe, predictable, and boring for those programmed for risk taking.

—Paul Roberts, "Risk"

Roberts suggests that genetics is one likely cause of extreme sports and that an American obsession with safety is perhaps a cause of their growing popularity. Notice, however, that he presents these as likely or possible, not certain, by choosing his words carefully: "studies now *indicate*," "the inclination to take high risks *may* be hardwired." "Risk taking *probably* bestowed a crucial evolutionary advantage," "this dissatisfaction *could help* explain." Like Roberts, you will almost always need to qualify what you say about causes and effects — to say that something *could explain* (rather than saying it "explains") or that it *suggests* (rather than "shows"). Plausible causes and effects can't be proved definitively, so you need to acknowledge that your argument is not the last word on the subject.

Ways of Organizing an Analysis of Causes and Effects

Your analysis of causes and effects may be part of a proposal or some other genre of writing, or you may write a text whose central purpose is to analyze causes or speculate about effects. While there are many ways to organize an analysis of causes and effects, three common ways are to state a cause and then discuss its effects, to state an effect and then discuss its causes, and to identify a chain of causes and effects.

Identify a cause and then discuss its effects.   If you were writing about global warming, you might first show that many scientists fear it will have several effects, including drastic climate changes, the extinction of various kinds of plants, and elevated sea levels.

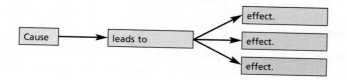

Identify an effect and then trace its causes. If you were writing about school violence, for example, you might argue that it is a result of sloppy dress, informal teacher-student relationships, low academic standards, and disregard for rules.

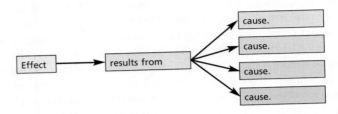

Identify a chain of causes and effects leading from one to another. You may sometimes discuss a chain of causes and effects. If you were writing about the right to privacy, for example, you might consider the case of Megan's law. A convicted child molester raped and murdered a neighborhood child whose name was Megan; the crime caused New Jersey legislators to pass the so-called Megan's law (an effect), which requires that convicted sex offenders be publicly identified. As more states enact versions of Megan's law, concern for the rights of those who are identified is developing—the effect is becoming a cause of further effects.

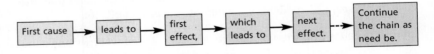

Considering the Rhetorical Situation

As a writer or speaker, you need to think about the message that you want to articulate, the audience you want to reach, and the larger context you are writing in.

3–4   ■ **PURPOSE**   Your purpose may be to analyze causes. But sometimes you'll have another goal that calls for such analysis—

a business report, for example, might need to explain what caused a decline in sales.

■ **AUDIENCE**   Who is your intended audience, and how will analyzing causes help you reach them? Do you need to tell
them why some event happened, or what effects
resulted?

5–8

■ **GENRE**   Does your genre require you to analyze causes? Proposals, for example, often need to consider the effects
of a proposed solution.

9–11

■ **STANCE**   What is your stance, and could analyzing causes or
effects show that stance? Could it help demonstrate
your seriousness, or show that your conclusions are
reasonable?

12–14

■ **MEDIA / DESIGN**   You can rely on words to analyze causes, but sometimes a drawing will help readers *see* how causes lead
to effects.

15–17

See also the **PROCESSES**
chapters (Chapters 21–27) for
help **GENERATING IDEAS,**
DRAFTING, and so on if you
need to write an entire text
whose purpose is to analyze
causes or speculate about
effects.

193–235

31 Classifying and Dividing

Classification and division are ways of organizing information: various pieces of information about a topic may be classified according to their similarities, or a single topic may be divided into parts. We might classify different kinds of flowers as annuals or perennials, for example, and classify the perennials further as dahlias, daisies, roses, and peonies. We might also divide a flower garden into distinct areas: for herbs, flowers, and vegetables. Writers often use classification and division as ways of developing and organizing material. This book, for instance, classifies comparison, definition, description, and several other common ways of thinking and writing as strategies. It divides the information it provides about writing into seven parts: "Rhetorical Situations," "Genres," "Processes," and so on. Each part further divides its material into various chapters. Even if you never write a book, you will have occasion to classify and divide material in **ANNOTATED BIBLIOGRAPHIES**, **LITERATURE REVIEWS**, and essays **ANALYZING TEXTS.** This chapter offers advice for classifying and dividing information for various writing purposes—and to do so in a way that suits your own rhetorical situation.

112–19 ▲
174–81 ▲
137–46 ▲

Classifying

When we classify something, we group it with similar things. A linguist would classify French and Spanish and Italian as Romance languages, for example—and Russian, Polish, and Bulgarian as Slavic languages. In a hilarious (if totally phony) news story from *The Onion* about a church bake

rhetorical situations genres processes strategies research mla/apa media/design

sale, the writer classifies the activities observed there as examples of the seven deadly sins:

> GADSDEN, AL — The seven deadly sins — avarice, sloth, envy, lust, glut-tony, pride, and wrath — were all committed Sunday during the twice-annual bake sale at St. Mary's of the Immaculate Conception Church.
>
> — *The Onion*, "All Seven Deadly Sins
> Committed at Church Bake Sale"

The article goes on to categorize the participants' behavior in terms of the sins, describing one parishioner who commits the sin of pride by bragging about her cookies, others who commit the sin of envy by envying the pop-ularity of the prideful parishioner's baked goods (the consumption of which leads to the sin of gluttony). In all, the article notes, "347 individ-ual acts of sin were committed at the bake sale," and every one of them can be classified as one of the seven deadly sins.

Dividing

As a writing strategy, division is a way of breaking something into parts — and a way of making the information easy for readers to follow and under-stand. See how this example about children's ways of nagging divides their tactics into seven categories:

> James U. McNeal, a professor of marketing at Texas A&M Univer-sity, is considered America's leading authority on marketing to chil-dren. In his book *Kids as Customers* (1992), McNeal provides marketers with a thorough analysis of "children's requesting styles and appeals." He classifies juvenile nagging tactics into seven major categories. A *pleading* nag is one accompanied by repetitions of words like "please" or "mom, mom, mom." A *persistent* nag involves constant requests for the coveted product and may include the phrase "I'm gonna ask just one more time." *Forceful* nags are extremely pushy and may include subtle threats, like "Well, then, I'll go and ask Dad." *Demonstrative* nags are the most high risk, often characterized by full-blown tantrums in public places, breath

holding, tears, a refusal to leave the store. *Sugar-coated* nags promise affection in return for a purchase and may rely on seemingly heartfelt declarations, like "You're the best dad in the world." *Threatening* nags are youthful forms of blackmail, vows of eternal hatred and of running away if something isn't bought. *Pity* nags claim the child will be heartbroken, teased, or socially stunted if the parent refuses to buy a certain item. "All of these appeals and styles may be used in combination," McNeal's research has discovered, "but kids tend to stick to one or two of each that prove most effective . . . for their own parents."

> —Eric Schlosser, *Fast Food Nation: The Dark Side of the All-American Meal*

Here the writer announces the division scheme of "seven major categories." Then he names each tactic and describes how it works. And notice the italics: each nagging tactic is italicized, making it easy to recognize and follow. Take away the italics, and the argument would be less visible.

Creating Clear and Distinct Categories

When you classify or divide, you need to create clear and distinct categories. If you're writing about music, you might divide it on the basis of the genre (hip-hop, rock, classical, gospel), artist (male or female, group or solo), or instruments (violins, trumpets, bongos, guitars). These categories must be distinct, so that no information overlaps or fits into more than one category, and they must include every member of the group you're discussing. The simpler the criteria for selecting the categories, the better. The nagging categories in the example from *Fast Food Nation* are based on only one criterion: a child's verbal behavior.

Highlight your categories. Sometimes you may want to highlight your categories visually to make them easier to follow. Eric Schlosser does that by italicizing each category: the *pleading* nag, the *persistent* nag, the *forceful* nag, and so on. Other **DESIGN** elements—bulleted lists, pie charts, tables, images—might also prove useful.

451–84 ❑

rhetorical situations | genres | processes | strategies | research mla/apa | media/ design

See, for instance, how the humorist Dave Barry uses a two-column list to show two categories of males—"men" and "guys"—in his *Complete Guide to Guys*:

Men	Guys
Vince Lombardi	Joe Namath
Oliver North	Gilligan
Hemingway	Gary Larson
Columbus	Whichever astronaut hit the first golf ball on the moon
Superman	Bart Simpson
Doberman pinschers	Labrador retrievers
Abbott	Costello
Captain Ahab	Captain Kangaroo
Satan	Snidely Whiplash
The pope	Willard Scott
Germany	Italy
Geraldo	Katie Couric

—Dave Barry, *Dave Barry's Complete Guide to Guys: A Fairly Short Book*

Sometimes you might show categories visually, like the illustration on the following page from a news story about the many new varieties of Oreo cookies. In the article, the reporter David Barboza classifies Oreos with words:

There is the Double Delight Oreo . . . , the Uh Oh Oreo (vanilla cookie with chocolate filling), Oreo Cookie Barz, Football Oreos, Oreos Cookies and Creme Pie, Oreos in Kraft Lunchables for kids, and Oreo cookies with a variety of cream fillings (mint, chocolate, coffee) and sizes (six-pack, twelve-pack, snack pack, and more).

**DOUBLE DELIGHT
MINT 'N CREME**
Introduced in 2003

**DOUBLE DELIGHT
PEANUT BUTTER &
CHOCOLATE**
2003

**DOUBLE DELIGHT
COFFEE 'N CREME**
2003

UH OH OREO
(Vanilla cookie, chocolate filling)
2003

CHOCOLATE CREME OREO
2001

FOOTBALL OREO
(Football design on biscuit)
Seasonal

DOUBLE STUFF
1974

ORIGINAL
1912

Piling on the Cookies

*In the Oreo's first eight
decades, Nabisco tried only
a handful of variations on the
original. But in recent years, it
has stretched the line to more
than two dozen by varying the
size, the filling, the biscuit
recipe—nearly everything but
the brand name. Here are some
examples now on store shelves.*

David Barboza, "Permutations Push
Oreo Far Beyond Cookie Aisle"

■ rhetorical situations ▲ genres ○ processes ◆ strategies ● research mla/apa □ media/design

The illustration, for an article that shows Oreos to be a "hyperevolving, perpetually repackaged, category-migrating" cookie, makes that classification easy to see—and gets our attention in the first place.

Considering the Rhetorical Situation

As a writer or speaker, you need to think about the message that you want to articulate, the audience you want to reach, and the larger context you are writing in.

■ **PURPOSE** Your purpose for writing will affect how you classify or divide information. Dave Barry classifies males as "men" and "guys" to get a laugh, whereas J. Crew might divide sweaters into cashmere, wool, and cotton to help shoppers find and buy things from their Web site. *3–4*

■ **AUDIENCE** Who in your audience do you want to reach, and will classifying or dividing your material help them follow your argument? *5–8*

■ **GENRE** Does your genre call for you to categorize or divide information? A long report might need to be divided into sections, for instance. *9–11*

■ **STANCE** Your stance may affect the way you classify information. Dave Barry classifies males as "men" and "guys" to reflect a humorist's stance; if he were a psychologist, he might categorize them as "Oedipal," "hormonal," and "libidinal." *12–14*

■ **MEDIA / DESIGN** You can classify or divide in paragraph form, but sometimes a pie chart or list will show the categories better. *15–17*

See also **CLUSTERING, CUBING,** and **LOOPING,** three methods of **GENERATING IDEAS** that can be especially helpful for classifying material. And see all the **PROCESSES** chapters for guidelines on **DRAFTING, REVISING,** and so on if you need to write a classification essay.

200–02
199–204
193–235

32 Comparing and Contrasting

Comparing things looks at their similarities; contrasting them focuses on their differences. It's a kind of thinking that comes naturally and that we do constantly—for example, comparing Houston with Dallas, PCs with Macs, or three paintings by Renoir. And once we start comparing, we generally find ourselves contrasting—Houston and Dallas have differences as well as similarities.

As a student, you'll often be asked to compare and contrast paintings or poems or other things. As a writer, you'll have cause to compare and contrast in most kinds of writing. In a **PROPOSAL**, for instance, you will need to compare your solution with other possible solutions; or in an **EVALUATION**, such as a movie review, you might contrast the film you're reviewing with some other film. This chapter offers advice on ways of comparing and contrasting things for various writing purposes and for your own rhetorical situations.

160–67
120–26

Most of the time, we compare obviously similar things: cars we might purchase, three competing political philosophies, two versions of a film. Occasionally, however, we might compare things that are less obviously similar. See how John McMurtry, an ex–football player, compares football with war in an essay arguing that the attraction football holds for spectators is based in part on its potential for violence and injury:

> The family resemblance between football and war is, indeed, striking. Their languages are similar: "field general," "long bomb," "blitz," "take a shot," "front line," "pursuit," "good hit," "the draft," and so on. Their principles and practices are alike: mass hysteria, the art of intimidation, absolute command and total obedience, territorial aggression, censorship, inflated insignia and propaganda, blackboard maneuvers and strategies, drills, uniforms, marching bands, and train-

rhetorical situations

genres

processes

strategies

research mla/apa

media/design

ing camps. And the virtues they celebrate are almost identical: hyper-aggressiveness, coolness under fire, and suicidal bravery.

—John McMurtry, "Kill 'Em! Crush 'Em! Eat 'Em Raw!"

McMurtry's comparison helps focus readers' attention on what he's arguing about football in part because it's somewhat unexpected. But the more unlikely the comparison, the more you might be accused of comparing apples and oranges. It's important, therefore, that the things we compare be legitimately compared — as is the case in the following comparison of Ronald Reagan and Arnold Schwarzenegger, two actors who became politicians:

> Like Reagan, Arnold Schwarzenegger made California's governorship his first run for office. Reagan was a few weeks from turning 56 when he took the oath of office in January 1967; Schwarzenegger turned 56 last July. Reagan ousted Democratic Governor Pat Brown; Schwarzenegger's ascent came at the expense of Governor Gray Davis, former chief of staff to Pat's son, Jerry, who succeeded Reagan as governor in 1975.
>
> The parallels go on, like credits at the end of a movie. Reagan evoked "the shining city on the hill"; Schwarzenegger alludes to "the golden dream by the sea" (words probably crafted by the governor's chief wordsmith, Landon Parvin, a Reagan presidential speechwriter). Maybe the eeriest parallel of all: "Arnold" is an anagram of "Ronald."
>
> —Bill Whalen, "Reagan and Schwarzenegger — Parallel Universe?"

No doubt there are contrasts between Reagan and Schwarzenegger as well, but for this piece (which we found on the op-ed page of the *San Francisco Chronicle*), the startling comparisons are the point.

Two Ways of Comparing and Contrasting

Comparisons and contrasts may be organized in two basic ways: block and point by point.

The block method.   One way is to discuss separately each item you're comparing, giving all the information about one item and then all the information about the next item. A report on Seattle and Vancouver, for example, compares the firearm regulations in each city using a paragraph about Seattle and then a paragraph about Vancouver:

> Although similar in many ways, Seattle and Vancouver differ markedly in their approaches to the regulation of firearms. In Seattle, handguns may be purchased legally for self-defense in the street or at home. After a thirty-day waiting period, a permit can be obtained to carry a handgun as a concealed weapon. The recreational use of handguns is minimally restricted.
>
> In Vancouver, self-defense is not considered a valid or legal reason to purchase a handgun. Concealed weapons are not permitted. Recreational uses of handguns (such as target shooting and collecting) are regulated by the province, and the purchase of a handgun requires a restricted-weapons permit. A permit to carry a weapon must also be obtained in order to transport a handgun, and these weapons can be discharged only at a licensed shooting club. Handguns can be transported by car, but only if they are stored in the trunk in a locked box.
>
> —John Henry Sloan et al., "Handgun Regulations, Crime, Assaults, and Homicide: A Tale of Two Cities"

The point-by-point method.　The other way to compare things is to focus on specific points of comparison. A later part of the Seattle-Vancouver study compares the two cities' gun laws and how they're enforced, discussing each point one at a time. (We've underlined each point.) The authors discuss one point, comparing the two cities; then they go on to the next point, again comparing the cities:

> Although they differ in their approach to firearm regulations, both cities aggressively enforce existing gun laws and regulations, and convictions for gun-related offenses carry similar penalties. For example, the commission of a class A felony (such as murder or robbery) with a firearm in Washington State adds a minimum of two years of confinement to the sentence for the felony. In the province of British Columbia, the same offense generally results in one to fourteen years of imprisonment in addition to the felony sentence. Similar percentages of homicides in both communities eventually lead to arrest and

police charges. In Washington, under the Sentencing Reform Act of 1981, <u>murder in the first degree</u> carries a minimum sentence of twenty years of confinement. In British Columbia, first-degree murder carries a minimum sentence of twenty-five years, with a possible judicial parole review after fifteen years. <u>Capital punishment</u> was abolished in Canada during the 1970s. In Washington State, the death penalty may be invoked in cases of aggravated first-degree murder, but no one has been executed since 1963.

Using Graphs and Images to Present Comparisons

Some comparisons can be easier to understand if they're presented visually, as a **CHART**, **GRAPH**, or **ILLUSTRATION**. See how this chart shows comparative information about Vancouver and Seattle that can be easily understood at a glance and clearly categorized. It would be possible to show the same material in paragraph form, but it's much easier to see and read in this chart:

458–62

Seattle and Vancouver: Basic Demographic Information	Seattle, Washington	Vancouver, British Columbia
Population (1980)	493,846	430,826
Unemployment rate	5.8%	6.0%
High-school graduates	79.0%	66.0%
Median household income (U.S. dollars)	$16,254	$16,681

—John Henry Sloan et al., "Handgun Regulations, Crime, Assaults, and Homicide: A Tale of Two Cities"

The following bar graph, from an economics textbook, compares the incomes of various professions in the United States, both with one another and with the average U.S. income (defined as 100 percent). Again, it would be possible to write out this information in a paragraph—but it is much easier to understand it this way:

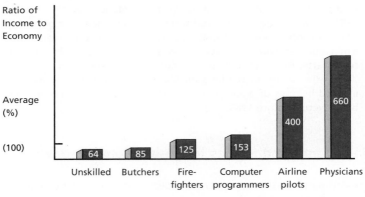

Joseph Stiglitz, *Economics*

Sometimes photographs can make a comparison. The two photos below show a woman before and after she had her hair dyed. The caption suggests that the story is more complicated than the photos alone can tell, however; for the full story, we need words.

"GO BLONDE! 'I tried it before and it came out orange!'" iVillage.com

Lance Jackson, *San Francisco Chronicle*

And here is a composite photograph that illustrates the comparison of Arnold Schwarzenegger with Ronald Reagan on page 267. Just as the article points out some startling similarities between the two actor-politicians, the photograph makes the comparison visual.

Using Figurative Language to Make Comparisons

Another way we make comparisons is with figurative language: words and phrases used in a nonliteral way to help readers see a point. Three kinds of figurative language that make comparisons are similes, metaphors, and analogies. When Robert Burns wrote that his love was "like a red, red rose," he was comparing his love with a rose and evoking an image — in this case, a simile — that helps us understand his feelings for her. A simile makes a comparison using *like* or *as*. In the following example, from an article in the food section of the *New York Times*, a restaurant critic uses several similes (underlined) to help us visualize an unusual food dish:

> Once upon a time, possibly at a lodge in Wyoming, possibly at a butcher shop in Maurice, Louisiana, or maybe even at a plantation in South Carolina, an enterprising cook decided to take a boned chicken, a boned duck, and a boned turkey, stuff them one inside the other <u>like Russian dolls</u>, and roast them. He called his masterpiece turducken. . . .
>
> A well-prepared turducken is a marvelous treat, a free-form poultry terrine layered with flavorful stuffing and moistened with duck fat. When it's assembled, it looks <u>like a turkey</u> and it roasts <u>like a turkey</u>, but when you go to carve it, you can slice through it <u>like a loaf of bread</u>. In each slice you get a little bit of everything: white meat from the breast; dark meat from the legs, duck, carrots, bits of sausage, bread, herbs, juices, and chicken, too.
>
> —Amanda Hesser, "Turkey Finds Its Inner Duck (and Chicken)"

Metaphors make comparisons without such connecting words as *like* or *as*. See how desert ecologist Craig Childs uses a metaphor to help us understand the nature of water during a flood in the Grand Canyon:

> Water splashed off the desert and ran all over the surface, looking for the quickest way down. It was too swift for the ground to absorb. When water flows like this, it will not be clean tap water. It will be <u>a gravy of debris</u>, snatching everything it finds.
>
> —Craig Childs, *The Secret Knowledge of Water*

Calling the water "a gravy of debris" allows us to see the murky liquid as it streams through the canyon.

Analogies are extended similes or metaphors that compare something unfamiliar with something more familiar. Arguing that corporations should not patent parts of human DNA whose function isn't yet clear, a genetics professor uses the familiar image of a library to explain an unfamiliar concept, the patenting of random gene sequences:

It's like having a library of books and randomly tearing pages out. You may know which books the pages came from but that doesn't tell you much about them.

—Peter Goodfellow, quoted in John Vidal and
John Carvel, "Lambs to the Gene Market"

Sometimes analogies are used for humorous effect as well as to make a point, as in this passage from a critique of history textbooks:

Another history text—this one for fifth grade—begins with the story of how Henry B. Gonzalez, who is a member of Congress from Texas, learned about his own nationality. When he was ten years old, his teacher told him he was an American because he was born in the United States. His grandmother, however, said, "The cat was born in the oven. Does that make him bread?"

—Frances FitzGerald, *America Revised: History
Schoolbooks in the Twentieth Century*

The grandmother's question shows how an intentionally ridiculous analogy can be a source of humor—and can make a point memorably.

Considering the Rhetorical Situation

As a writer or speaker, you need to think about the message that you want to articulate, the audience you want to reach, and the larger context you are writing in.

■ **PURPOSE**   Sometimes your purpose for writing will be to compare two or more things. Other times, you may want to compare several things for some other purpose—to compare your views with those of others in an argument essay, or to compare one text with another as you analyze them.   3–4

■ **AUDIENCE**   Who is your audience, and will comparing your topic with a more familiar one help them to follow your argument?   5–8

9–11 ▦ **GENRE**   Does your genre require you to compare something? Evaluations often include comparisons — one book to another, in a review; or ten different cell phones, in *Consumer Reports*.

12–14 ▦ **STANCE**   Your stance may affect any comparisons you make. How you compare two things — evenhandedly, or clearly favoring one over the other, for example — will reflect your stance.

15–17 ▦ **MEDIA / DESIGN**   Some things you will want to compare with words alone (lines from two poems, for instance), but sometimes you may wish to make comparisons visually (two images juxtaposed on a page, or several numbers plotted on a line graph).

199–204 ○

193–235 ○

> See **LOOPING** and **CUBING,** two methods of **GENERATING IDEAS** that can be especially helpful for comparing and contrasting. If you're writing an essay whose purpose is to compare two or more things, see also the **PROCESSES** chapters for help **DRAFTING, REVISING,** and so on.

Defining something says what it is — and what it is not. A terrier, for example, is a kind of dog. A fox terrier is a small dog now generally kept as a pet but once used by hunters to dig for foxes. Happiness is a jelly doughnut, at least according to Homer Simpson. All of those are definitions. As writers, we need to define any terms our readers may not know. And sometimes you'll want to stipulate your own definition of a word in order to set the terms of an **ARGUMENT** — as Homer Simpson does with a definition that's not found in any dictionary. This chapter details strategies for using definitions in your writing, to suit your own rhetorical situations.

▲ 82–106

Formal Definitions

Sometimes to make sure readers understand you, you will need to provide a formal definition. If you are using a technical term that readers are unlikely to know or if you are using a term in a specific way, you need to say then and there what the word means. The word *mutual*, for example, has several dictionary meanings:

mu•tu•al . . .

1a: directed by each toward the other or the others <*mutual* affection> **b:** having the same feelings one for the other <they had long been *mutual* enemies> **c:** shared in common <enjoying their *mutual* hobby> **d:** joint
2: characterized by intimacy
3: of or relating to a plan whereby the members of an organization share in the profits and expenses; *specifically*: of, relating to, or taking the form of an insurance method in which the policyholders constitute the members of the insuring company

— www.Merriam-Webster.com

The first two meanings are commonly understood and probably require no definition. But if you were to use *mutual* in the third sense, it might—depending on your audience. A general audience would probably need the definition; an audience from the insurance industry would not. A Web site that gives basic financial advice to an audience of non-specialists, for instance, offers a specific definition of the term *mutual fund*:

> *Mutual funds* are financial intermediaries. They are companies set up to receive your money and then, having received it, to make investments with the money.
>
> —Bill Barker, "A Grand, Comprehensive Overview to Mutual Funds Investing"

But even writers in specialized fields routinely provide formal definitions to make sure their readers understand the way they are using certain words. See how two writers define the word *stock* as it pertains to their respective (and very different) fields:

> Stocks are the basis for sauces and soups and important flavoring agents for braises. Admittedly, stock making is time consuming, but the extra effort yields great dividends.
>
> —Tom Colicchio, *Think Like a Chef*

> Want to own part of a business without having to show up at its office every day? Or ever? Stock is the vehicle of choice for those who do. Dating back to the Dutch mutual stock corporations of the sixteenth century, the modern stock market exists as a way for entrepreneurs to finance businesses using money collected from investors. In return for ponying up the dough to finance the company, the investor becomes a part owner of the company. That ownership is represented by stock — specialized financial "securities," or financial instruments, that are "secured" by a claim on the assets and profits of a company.
>
> —Fool.com, "Investing Basics: Stocks"

To write a formal definition

- Use words that readers are likely to be familiar with.
- Don't use the word being defined in the definition.

rhetorical situations   genres   processes   strategies   research mla/apa   media/design

- Begin with the word being defined; include the general category to which the term belongs and the attributes that make it different from the others in that category.

For example:

Term	General Category	Distinguishing Attributes
Stock is	a specialized financial "security"	that is "secured" by a claim.
Photosynthesis is	a process	by which plants use sunlight to create energy.
Astronomers are	scientists	who study celestial objects and phenomena.
Adam Sandler,	a comedian,	has starred in several movies, including *The Wedding Singer* and *Punch-Drunk Love.*

Note that the category and distinguishing attributes cannot be stated too broadly; if they were, the definition would be too vague to be useful. It wouldn't be helpful in most circumstances, for example, to say, "Adam Sandler is a man who has acted" or "Photosynthesis is something having to do with plants."

Extended Definitions

Sometimes you need to provide a more detailed definition. Extended definitions may be several sentences long or several paragraphs long and may include pictures or diagrams. Sometimes an entire essay is devoted to defining a difficult or important concept. Here is one writer's extended definition of stem cells:

> By definition, a stem cell is an unspecialized cell that has the ability to divide and renew itself. Under certain conditions, it can generate large numbers of daughter cells and these go on to mature into cells with

special functions, such as beating heart muscle or new bone to heal a fracture.

Stem cells exist naturally in the body. They're in bone marrow and, although rare, in the blood stream. Stem cells also exist in other tissues and organs, such as the liver, pancreas, brain, and maybe even the heart.

Currently, stem cells come from three sources: blastocysts, which are cells isolated from the inner cell mass of a three-to-five-day-old embryo grown in a petri dish in a lab, also called embryonic stem cells; cord blood cells, which are isolated from blood taken from an umbilical cord saved immediately after birth; and adult stem cells, which are collected from a person's own tissues.

—*Cleveland Clinic Magazine*, "The Miracle of Stem Cells"

That definition includes a description of the distinguishing features of stem cells and tells where they are found and where they come from. We can assume that it's written for a general audience, one that doesn't know anything about stem cells.

Abstract concepts often require extended definitions because by nature they are more complicated to define. There are many ways of writing an extended definition, depending in part on the term being defined and on your audience and purpose. The following examples show some of the methods that can be used for composing extended definitions of *democracy*.

Explore the word's origins.   Where did the word come from? When did it first come into use? In the following example, from an essay considering what democracy means in the twenty-first century, the writer started by looking at the word's first known use in English. Though it's from an essay written for a first-year writing course and thus for a fairly general audience, it's a definition that might pique any audience's interest:

According to the *Oxford English Dictionary*, the term *democracy* first appeared in English in a thirteenth-century translation of Aristotle's works—specifically, in his *Politics*, where he stated that the "underlying principle of democracy is freedom" and that "it is customary to say that only in democracies do men have a share in freedom, for that is what every democracy makes its aim." By the sixteenth century, the word was used much as it is now. One writer in 1586, for instance,

defined it in this way: "where free and poore men being the greater number, are lords of the estate."

—Susanna Mejía, "What Does Democracy Mean Now?"

Here's another example, this one written for a scholarly audience, from an essay about women, participation, democracy, and the information age:

> The very word *citizenship* carries with it a connotation of place, a "citizen" being, literally, the inhabitant of a city. Over the years the word has, of course, accumulated a number of associated meanings . . . and the word has come to stand in for such concepts as participation, equality, and democracy. The fact that the concept of locality is deeply embedded in the word *citizen* suggests that it is also fundamental to our current understanding of these other, more apparently abstract words.
>
> In Western thought, the concepts of citizenship, equality, and democracy are closely interlinked and can be traced back to a common source, in Athens in the fifth century B.C. Perhaps it is no accident that it was the same culture which also gave us, in its theater, the concept of the unity of time and space. The Greek city-state has been represented for centuries as the ideal model of democracy, with free and equal access for all citizens to decision making. Leaving aside, for the moment, the question of who was included, and who excluded from this notion of citizenship, we can see that the sense of place is fundamental to this model. Entitlement to participate in the democratic process is circumscribed by geography; it is the inhabitants of the geographical entity of the city-state, precisely defined and bounded, who have the rights to citizenship. Those who are not defined as inhabitants of that specific city-state are explicitly excluded, although, of course, they may have the right to citizenship elsewhere.

—Ursula Huws, "Women, Participation, and
Democracy in the Information Society"

Provide details.   What are its characteristics? What is it made of? See how a historian explores the basic characteristics of democracy in a book written for an audience of historians:

> As a historian I am naturally disposed to be satisfied with the meaning which, in the history of politics, men have commonly attributed to

the word—a meaning, needless to say, which derives partly from the experience and partly from the aspirations of mankind. So regarded, the term *democracy* refers primarily to a form of government, and it has always meant government by the many as opposed to government by the one—government by the people as opposed to government by a tyrant, a dictator, or an absolute monarch. . . . Since the Greeks first used the term, the essential test of democratic government has always been this: the source of political authority must be and remain in the people and not in the ruler. A democratic government has always meant one in which the citizens, or a sufficient number of them to represent more or less effectively the common will, freely act from time to time, and according to established forms, to appoint or recall the magistrates and to enact or revoke the laws by which the community is governed.

—Carl Becker, *Modern Democracy*

Compare it with other words. How is this concept like other similar things? How does it differ? What is it *not* like? **COMPARE AND CONTRAST** it. See how a political science textbook defines a *majoritarian democracy* by comparing its characteristics with those of a *consensual democracy*:

266–74

A majoritarian democracy is one

1. having only two major political parties, not many

2. having an electoral system that requires a bare majority to elect one clear winner in an election, as opposed to a proportional electoral system that distributes seats to political parties according to the rough share of votes received in the election

3. a strong executive (president or prime minister) and cabinet that together are largely independent of the legislature when it comes to exercising the executive's constitutional duties, in contrast to an executive and cabinet that are politically controlled by the parties in the legislature and therefore unable to exercise much influence when proposing policy initiatives.

—Benjamin Ginsberg, Theodore J. Lowi, and Margaret Weir,
We the People: An Introduction to American Politics

And here's an example in which democracy is contrasted with various other forms of governments of the past:

> Caesar's power derived from a popular mandate, conveyed through established republican forms, but that did not make his government any the less a dictatorship. Napoleon called his government a democratic republic, but no one, least of all Napoleon himself, doubted that he had destroyed the last vestiges of the democratic republic.
>
> —Carl Becker, *Modern Democracy*

Give examples. See how the essayist E. B. White defines democracy by giving some everyday examples of considerate behavior, humility, and civic participation — all things he suggests constitute democracy:

> It is the line that forms on the right. It is the don't in don't shove. It is the hole in the stuffed shirt through which the sawdust slowly trickles; it is the dent in the high hat. Democracy is the recurrent suspicion that more than half of the people are right more than half of the time. . . . Democracy is a letter to the editor.
>
> —E. B. White, "Democracy"

White's definition is elegant because he uses examples that his readers will know. His characteristics — metaphors, really — define democracy not as a conceptual way of governing but as an everyday part of American life.

Classify it. Often it is useful to divide or **CLASSIFY** a term. The ways in which democracy unfolds are complex enough to warrant entire textbooks, of course, but the following definition, from the political science textbook, divides democracy into two kinds, representative and direct:

260–65

> A system of government that gives citizens a regular opportunity to elect the top government officials is usually called a representative democracy or republic. A system that permits citizens to vote directly on laws and policies is often called a direct democracy. At the national level, America is a representative democracy in which citizens select government officials but do not vote on legislation. Some states, how-

ever, have provisions for direct legislation through popular referendum. For example, California voters in 1995 decided to bar undocumented immigrants from receiving some state services.

—Benjamin Ginsberg, Theodore J. Lowi, and Margaret Weir,
We the People: An Introduction to American Politics

Stipulative Definitions

Sometimes a writer will stipulate a certain definition, essentially saying, "This is how I'm defining x." Such definitions are not usually found in a dictionary—and at the same time are central to the argument the writer is making. Here is one example, from an essay by Toni Morrison. Describing a scene from a film in which a newly arrived Greek immigrant, working as a shoe shiner in Grand Central Terminal, chases away an African American competitor, Morrison calls the scene an example of "race talk," a concept she then goes on to define:

> This is race talk, the explicit insertion into everyday life of racial signs and symbols that have no meaning other than pressing African Americans to the lowest level of the racial hierarchy. Popular culture, shaped by film, theater, advertising, the press, television, and literature, is heavily engaged in race talk. It participates freely in this most enduring and efficient rite of passage into American culture: negative appraisals of the native-born black population. Only when the lesson of racial estrangement is learned is assimilation complete. Whatever the lived experience of immigrants with African Americans—pleasant, beneficial, or bruising—the rhetorical experience renders blacks as noncitizens, already discredited outlaws.
>
> All immigrants fight for jobs and space, and who is there to fight but those who have both? As in the fishing ground struggle between Texas and Vietnamese shrimpers, they displace what and whom they can. Although U.S. history is awash in labor battles, political fights and property wars among all religious and ethnic groups, their struggles are persistently framed as struggles between recent arrivals and blacks. In race talk the move into mainstream America always means buying into the notion of American blacks as the real aliens. Whatever the

ethnicity or nationality of the immigrant, his nemesis is understood to be African American.

—Toni Morrison, "On the Backs of Blacks"

In this example below, from a book review of Nancy L. Rosenblum's *Membership and Morals: The Personal Uses of Pluralism in America*, published in the *American Prospect*, a magazine for readers interested in political analysis, a Stanford law professor outlines a definition of "the democracy of everyday life":

> Democracy, in this understanding of it, means simply treating people as equals, disregarding social standing, avoiding attitudes of either deference or superiority, making allowances for others' weaknesses, and resisting the temptation to respond to perceived slights. It also means protesting everyday instances of arbitrariness and unfairness—from the rudeness of the bakery clerk to the sexism of the car dealer or the racism of those who vandalize the home of the first black neighbors on the block.

—Kathleen M. Sullivan, "Defining Democracy Down"

Considering the Rhetorical Situation

As a writer or speaker, you need to think about the message that you want to articulate, the audience you want to reach, and the larger context you are writing in.

■ **PURPOSE**   Your purpose for writing will affect any definitions you include. Would writing an extended definition help you explain something? Would stipulating definitions of key terms help you shape an argument? Could an off-beat definition help you entertain your readers?   3–4

■ **AUDIENCE**   What audience do you want to reach, and are there any terms your readers are unlikely to know? Are there terms they might understand differently from the way you're defining them?   5–8

■ **GENRE** Does your genre require you to define terms? Chances are that if you're reporting information you'll need to define some terms, and some arguments rest on the way you define key terms.

■ **STANCE** What is your stance, and do you need to define key terms to show that stance clearly? How you define "fetus," for example, is likely to reveal your stance on abortion.

■ **MEDIA / DESIGN** Your medium will affect the form your definitions take. In a print text, you will need to define terms in your text; if you're giving a speech or presentation, you might also provide images of important terms and their definitions. In an electronic text, you may be able to define terms by linking to an online dictionary definition.

> See also the **PROCESSES** chapters for help **GENERATING IDEAS, DRAFTING, REVISING,** and so on if you are writing a whole essay dedicated to defining a term or concept.

Describing **34**

When we describe something, we indicate what it looks like — and sometimes how it sounds, feels, smells, and tastes. Descriptive details are a way of showing rather than telling, of helping readers see (or hear, smell, and so on) what we're writing about — that the sky is blue, that Miss Havisham is wearing an old yellowed wedding gown, that the chemicals in the beaker have reacted and smell like rotten eggs. You'll have occasion to describe things in most of the writing you do — from describing a favorite hat in a **MEMOIR** to detailing a chemical reaction in a **LAB REPORT**. This chapter will help you work with description — and, in particular, help you think about the use of *detail*, about *objectivity and subjectivity*, about *vantage point*, about creating a clear *dominant impression*, and about using description to fit your rhetorical situation.

▲ 147–52
▲ 127–36

Detail

The goal of using details is to be as specific as possible, providing information that will help your audience imagine the subject or make sense of it. See, for example, how Nancy Mairs, an author with multiple sclerosis, describes the disease in clear, specific terms:

> During its course, which is unpredictable and uncontrollable, one may lose vision, hearing, speech, the ability to walk, control of bladder and/or bowels, strength in any or all extremities, sensitivity to touch, vibration, and/or pain, potency, coordination of movements — the list of possibilities is lengthy and, yes, horrifying. One may also lose one's sense of humor. That's the easiest to lose and the hardest to survive without.
>
> In the past ten years, I have sustained some of these losses. Characteristic of MS are sudden attacks, called exacerbations, followed by remissions, and these I have not had. Instead, my disease has been

slowly progressive. My left leg is now so weak that I walk with the aid of a brace and a cane, and for distances I use an Amigo, a variation on the electric wheelchair that looks rather like an electrified kiddie car. I no longer have much use of my left hand. Now my right side is weakening as well. I still have the blurred spot in my right eye. Overall, though, I've been lucky so far.

—Nancy Mairs, "On Being a Cripple"

Mairs's gruesome list demonstrates, through *specific details*, how the disease affects sufferers generally and her in particular. We know far more after reading this text than we do from the following more general description, from a National Multiple Sclerosis Society brochure:

Multiple sclerosis is a chronic, unpredictable disease of the central nervous system (the brain, optic nerves, and spinal cord). It is thought to be an autoimmune disorder. This means the immune system incorrectly attacks the person's healthy tissue.

MS can cause blurred vision, loss of balance, poor coordination, slurred speech, tremors, numbness, extreme fatigue, problems with memory and concentration, paralysis, and blindness. These problems may be permanent, or they may come and go.

—National Multiple Sclerosis Society, *Just the Facts: 2003–2004*

Specific details are also more effective than labels, which give little meaningful information. Instead of saying that someone is a "moron" or "really smart," it's better to give details so that readers can understand the reasons behind the label: what does this person *do* or *say* that makes him or her deserve this label? See, for example, how the writer of a news story about shopping on the day after Thanksgiving opens with a description of a happy shopper:

Last Friday afternoon, the day ritualized consumerism is traditionally at its most frenetic, Alexx Balcuns twirled in front of a full-length mirror at the Ritz Thrift Shop on West Fifty-seventh Street as if inhabited by the soul of Eva Gabor in *Green Acres*. Ms. Balcuns was languishing in a $795 dyed-mink parka her grandmother had just bought her. Ms. Balcuns is six.

—Ginia Bellafante, "Staying Warm and Fuzzy during Uncertain Times"

rhetorical situations   genres   processes   strategies   research mla/apa   media/ design

The writer might simply have said, "A spoiled child admired herself in the mirror." Instead, she shows her subject twirling and "languishing" in a "$795 dyed-mink parka" and seemingly possessed by the soul of the actress Eva Gabor—all details that create a far more vivid description.

Sensory details help readers imagine sounds, odors, tastes, and physical sensations in addition to sights. In the following example, writer Scott Russell Sanders recalls sawing wood as a child. Note how visual details, odors, and even the physical sense of being picked up by his father mingle to form a vivid scene:

> As the saw teeth bit down, the wood released its smell, each kind with its own fragrance, oak or walnut or cherry or pine—usually pine because it was the softest, easiest for a child to work. No matter how weathered and gray the board, no matter how warped and cracked, inside there was this smell waiting, as of something freshly baked. I gathered every smidgen of sawdust and stored it away in coffee cans, which I kept in a drawer of the workbench. When I did not feel like hammering nails I would dump my sawdust on the concrete floor of the garage and landscape it into highways and farms and towns, running miniature cars and trucks along miniature roads. Looming as huge as a colossus, my father worked over and around me, now and again bending down to inspect my work, careful not to trample my creations. It was a landscape that smelled dizzyingly of wood. Even after a bath my skin would carry the smell, and so would my father's hair, when he lifted me for a bedtime hug.
>
> —Scott Russell Sanders, *The Paradise of Bombs*

Whenever you describe something, you'll select from many possible details you might use. Simply put, to exhaust all of the details to describe something is impossible—and would exhaust your readers as well. To focus your description, you'll need to determine the kinds of details that are appropriate for your subject. They will vary, depending on your **PURPOSE.** See, for example, how the details might differ in three different genres:

3–4

147–52

- For a **MEMOIR** about an event, you might choose details that are significant for you, that evoke the sights, sounds, and meaning of your event.

153–59 ▲
- For a **PROFILE**, you're likely to select details that will reinforce the dominant impression you want to give, that portray the event from the perspective you want readers to see.

127–36 ▲
- For a **LAB REPORT**, you need to give certain specifics—what equipment was used, what procedures were followed, what exactly were the results.

Deciding on a focus for your description can help you see it better, as you'll look for details that contribute to that focus.

Objectivity and Subjectivity

Descriptions can be written with objectivity, with subjectivity, or with a mixture of both. Objective descriptions attempt to be uncolored by personal opinion or emotion. Police reports and much news writing aim to describe events objectively; scientific writing strives for objectivity in describing laboratory procedures and results. See, for example, the following objective account of what happened at the World Trade Center on September 11, 2001:

World Trade Center Disaster — Tuesday, September 11, 2001

On Tuesday, September 11, 2001, at 8:45 a.m. New York local time, One World Trade Center, the north tower, was hit by a hijacked 767 commercial jet airplane loaded with fuel for a transcontinental flight. Two World Trade Center, the south tower, was hit by a similar hijacked jet eighteen minutes later, at 9:03 a.m. (In separate but related attacks, the Pentagon building near Washington, D.C., was hit by a hijacked 757 at 9:43 a.m., and at 10:10 a.m. a fourth hijacked jetliner crashed in Pennsylvania.) The south tower, WTC 2, which had been hit second, was the first to suffer a complete structural collapse, at 10:05 a.m., 62 minutes after being hit itself, 80 minutes after the first impact. The north tower, WTC 1, then also collapsed, at 10:29 a.m., 104 minutes after being hit. WTC 7, a substantial forty-seven-story office building in its own right, built in 1987, was damaged by the collapsing towers, caught fire, and later in the afternoon also totally collapsed.

—GreatBuildingsOnline.com, "World Trade Center"

Subjective descriptions, on the other hand, allow the writer's opinions and emotions to come through. A house can be described as comfortable, with a lived-in look, or as rundown and in need of a paint job and a new roof.

Here's a subjective description of the planes striking the World Trade Center, as told by a woman watching from a nearby building:

> Incredulously, while looking out [the] window at the damage and carnage the first plane had inflicted, I saw the second plane abruptly come into my right field of vision and deliberately, with shimmering intention, thunder full-force into the south tower. It was so close, so low, so huge and fast, so intent on its target that I swear to you, I swear to you, I felt the vengeance and rage emanating from the plane.

> —Debra Fontaine, "Witnessing"

Advertisers regularly use subjective as well as objective description to sell their products, as the ad (on page 290) for a nicotine patch demonstrates. This ad includes an objective description of what makes smoking addictive: "Every time you smoke, the nicotine binds to these little tiny receptors in your brain. Thus, your brain becomes addicted to nicotine." However, it also presents subjective descriptions of the effects of quitting ("if you cut the brain off—well let's just say it gets a little pissed") and the results of buying and using the product: "So your brain's happy. You're happy. Or at least you're happy that your brain's happy."

Vantage Point

Sometimes you'll want or need to describe something from a certain vantage point. Where you locate yourself in relation to what you're describing will determine what you can perceive (and so describe) and what you can't. You may describe your subject from a *stationary vantage point,* from which you (and your readers) see your subject from one angle only, as if you were a camera. This description of one of three photographs that captured a woman's death records only what the camera saw from one angle at one particular moment:

> The first showed some people on a fire escape—a fireman, a woman and a child. The fireman had a nice strong jaw and looked very brave.

The woman was holding the child. Smoke was pouring from the building behind them. A rescue ladder was approaching, just a few feet away, and the fireman had one arm around the woman and one arm reaching out toward the ladder.

—Nora Ephron, "The Boston Photographs"

By contrast, this description of a drive to an Italian villa uses a *moving vantage point*; the writer recounts what he saw as he passed through a gate in a city wall, moving from city to country:

La Pietra — "the stone" — is situated one mile from the Porta San Gallo, an entry to the Old City of Florence. You drive there along the Via Bolognese, twisting past modern apartment blocks, until you come to a gate, which swings open — and there you are, at the upper end of a long lane of cypresses facing a great ocher palazzo; with olive groves spreading out on both sides over an expanse of fifty-seven acres.

There's something almost comically wonderful about the effect: here, the city, with its winding avenue; there, on the other side of a wall, the country, fertile and gray green.

—James Traub, "Italian Hours"

The description of quarries below uses *multiple vantage points* to capture the quarries from many perspectives.

Dominant Impression

With any description, your aim is to create some dominant impression—the overall feeling that the individual details add up to. The dominant impression may be implied, growing out of the details themselves. For example, Scott Russell Sanders's memory of the smell of sawdust creates a dominant impression of warmth and comfort: the "fragrance . . . as of something freshly baked," sawdust "stored . . . away in coffee cans," a young boy "lifted . . . for a bedtime hug." Sometimes, though, a writer will inform readers directly of the dominant impression, in addition to describing it. In an essay about Indiana limestone quarries, Sanders makes the dominant impression clear from the start: "they are battlefields."

> The quarries will not be domesticated. They are not backyard pools; they are battlefields. Each quarry is an arena where violent struggles have taken place between machines and planet, between human ingenuity and brute resisting stone, between mind and matter. Waste rock litters the floor and brim like rubble in a bombed city. The ragged pits might have been the basements of vanished skyscrapers. Stones weighing tens of tons lean against one another at precarious angles, as if they have been thrown there by some gigantic strength and have not yet finished falling. Wrecked machinery hulks in the weeds, grimly rusting, the cogs and wheels, twisted rails, battered engine housings, trackless bulldozers and burst boilers like junk from an armored regiment. Everywhere the ledges are scarred from drills, as if from an artillery barrage or machine-gun strafing. Stumbling onto one of these abandoned quarries and gazing at the ruins, you might be left wondering who had won the battle, men or stone.
>
> —Scott Russell Sanders, *The Paradise of Bombs*

The rest of his description, full of more figurative language ("like rubble in a bombed city," "like junk from an armored regiment," "as if from an artillery barrage or machine-gun strafing") reinforces the direct "they are battlefields" statement.

Organizing Descriptions

You can organize descriptions in many ways. When your description is primarily visual, you will probably organize it spatially: from left to right, top to bottom, outside to inside. If your description uses the other senses, you may begin with the most significant or noteworthy feature and move outward from that center, as Ephron does, or you may create a chronological description of objects as you encounter them, as Traub does in his description of his drive on page 290. You might even pile up details to create a dominant impression, as Sanders and Mairs do.

Considering the Rhetorical Situation

As a writer or speaker, you need to think about the message that you want to articulate, the audience you want to reach, and the larger context you are writing in.

3–4   ■ **PURPOSE**   Your purpose may affect the way you use description. If you're arguing that a government should intervene in another country's civil war, for example, describing the anguish of refugees from that war could make your argument more persuasive. If you're analyzing a painting, you will likely need to describe it.

5–8   ■ **AUDIENCE**   Who is your audience, and will they need detailed description to understand your argument?

9–11   ■ **GENRE**   Does your genre require description? A lab report generally calls for you to describe materials and results;

a memoir about grandma should probably describe her—her smile, her dress, her apple pie.

■ **STANCE**   The way you describe things can help you convey your stance. For example, the details you choose can show you to be objective (or not), careful or casual.

12–14

■ **MEDIA / DESIGN**   Your medium will affect the form your description can take. In a print or spoken text, you will likely rely on words, though you may also include visuals. In an electronic text, you can easily provide links to visuals and so may need fewer words.

15–17

See also **FREEWRITING, CUBING,** and **LISTING,** three methods of **GENERATING IDEAS** that can be especially helpful for developing detailed descriptions. Sometimes you may be assigned to write a whole essay describing something: see the **PROCESSES** chapters for help **DRAFTING, REVISING,** and so on.

199–202

193–235

35 Dialogue

137–59 ▲

Dialogue is a way of adding people's own words to a text, letting readers hear those people's voices—not just what you say about them. **MEMOIRS** and **PROFILES** often include dialogue, and many other genres do as well: **LITERARY ANALYSES** often quote dialogue from the texts they analyze, and

82–106 ▲

essays **ARGUING A POSITION** might quote an authoritative source as support for a claim. This chapter provides brief guidelines for the conventions of paragraphing and punctuating dialogue and offers some good examples of how you can use dialogue most effectively to suit your own rhetorical situations.

Why Add Dialogue?

Dialogue is a way of bringing in voices other than your own, of showing people and scenes rather than just telling about them. It can add color and texture to your writing, making it memorable. Most important, however, dialogue should be more than just colorful or interesting. It needs to contribute to your rhetorical purpose, to support the point you're making. See how dialogue is used in the following excerpt, from a magazine profile of the Mall of America, how it gives us a sense of the place that the journalist's own words could not provide:

> Two pubescent girls in retainers and braces sat beside me sipping coffees topped with whipped cream and chocolate sprinkles, their shopping bags gathered tightly around their legs, their eyes fixed on the passing crowds. They came, they said, from Shakopee—"It's nowhere," one of them explained. The megamall, she added, was "a buzz at first, but now it seems pretty normal. 'Cept my parents are like Twenty Questions every time I want to come here. 'Specially since the shooting."

On a Sunday night, she elaborated, three people had been wounded
when shots were fired in a dispute over a San Jose Sharks jacket. "In the
mall," her friend reminded me. "Right here at megamall. A shooting."
"It's like nowhere's safe," the first added.

> —David Guterson, "Enclosed. Encyclopedic.
> Endured: The Mall of America"

Of course it was the writer who decided whom and what to quote, and
Guterson deliberately chose words that capture the young shoppers'
speech patterns, quoting fragments ("In the *mall*. Right here at megamall.
A shooting"), slang ("a buzz at first," "my parents are like Twenty Questions"), even contractions ('cept, 'specially).

Integrating Dialogue into Your Writing

There are certain conventions for punctuating and paragraphing dialogue:

- *Punctuating*. Enclose each speaker's words in quotation marks, and
  put any end punctuation—periods, question marks, and exclamation
  marks—inside the closing quotation mark. Whether you're transcribing words you heard or making them up, you will sometimes
  need to add punctuation to reflect the rhythm and sound of the
  speech. See, for example, how Chang-Rae Lee adds a comma after *well*
  and italicizes *practice* in the last sentence of the example below, to
  show intonation—and attitude.

- *Paragraphing*. When you're writing dialogue that includes more than
  one speaker, start a new paragraph each time the speaker changes.

- *Signal phrases*. Sometimes you'll need to introduce dialogue with
  SIGNAL PHRASES—"I said," "she asked," and so on—to make clear who
  is speaking. At times, however, the speaker will be clear enough, and
  you won't need any signal phrases.

367–68

Here is a conversation between a mother and her son that illustrates each
of the conventions for punctuating and paragraphing dialogue:

> "Whom do I talk to?" she said. She would mostly speak to me in Korean,
> and I would answer back in English.

"The bank manager, who else?"

"What do I say?"

"Whatever you want to say."

"Don't speak to me like that!" she cried.

"It's just that you should be able to do it yourself," I said.

"You know how I feel about this!"

"Well, maybe then you should consider it *practice*," I answered lightly, using the Korean word to make sure she understood.

—Chang-Rae Lee, "Coming Home Again"

Interviews

Interviews are a kind of dialogue, with different conventions for punctuation. When you're transcribing an interview, give each speaker's name each time he or she speaks, starting a new line but not indenting, and do not use quotation marks. Here are a few lines from an interview that Harold Evans conducted with President Bill Clinton, published in *Talk* magazine shortly before Clinton left office:

> *Talk:* He [Nelson Mandela, president of South Africa and winner of a Nobel Peace Prize] talked to you during impeachment?
>
> **Clinton:** The whole time, yes. He was very loyal to me. He even came here, came a day early, when Congress gave him the gold medal, and came to the White House and attacked what they were doing to me. He helped me in how to think about it, how to deal with it— something I will never forget.
>
> *Talk:* He had his own long years in prison. Was his advice pragmatic about getting through, or spiritual?
>
> **Clinton:** Both. Both. If you read his autobiography, you'll see that. He said basically the only way things like that destroy you is if you give them permission to destroy you.
>
> *Talk:* You get bitter.
>
> **Clinton:** He said as long as you don't—if you're not embittered by this, if you're not angry all the time, if you just let it go, and keep going— then you'll be fine.

—Harold Evans, *Talk*

In preparing the interview for publication, Evans had to add punctuation, which of course was not part of the oral conversation, and he probably deleted pauses and verbal expressions such as *um* and *uh*. At the same time, he kept informal constructions, such as incomplete sentences, which are typical answers to questions ("The whole time, yes."), and repetition used for emphasis ("Both. Both.") to maintain the oral flavor of the interview and to reflect the former president's voice. Evans may also have moved parts of the interview around, to eliminate repetition and keep related subjects together. He identifies President Clinton by name, but since he represents *Talk* magazine, he identifies himself by the magazine's name.

Considering the Rhetorical Situation

As a writer or speaker, you need to think about the message that you want to articulate, the audience you want to reach, and the larger context you are writing in.

▧ **PURPOSE**	Your purpose will affect any use of dialogue. Dialogue can help bring a profile to life, and make it memorable. Interviews with experts or first-hand witnesses can add credibility to a report or argument.	3–4
▧ **AUDIENCE**	Whom do you want to reach, and will dialogue help? Sometimes actual dialogue can help readers hear human voices behind facts or reason.	5–8
▧ **GENRE**	Does your genre require dialogue? If you're evaluating or analyzing a literary work, for instance, you may wish to include dialogue from that work. If you're writing a profile of a person or event, dialogue can help you bring your subject to life. Similarly, an interview with an expert or firsthand witness can add credibility to a report or argument.	9–11
▧ **STANCE**	What is your stance, and can dialogue help you communicate that stance? For example, excerpts of an	12–14

interview may allow you to challenge someone's views and make your own views clear.

15–17

■ **MEDIUM / DESIGN** Your medium will affect the way you present dialogue. In a print text, you will present dialogue through written words. In an oral or electronic text, you might include actual recorded dialogue.

351–52

358–69

See also the guidelines on **INTERVIEWING EXPERTS** for advice on setting up and recording interviews and those on **QUOTING, PARAPHRASING,** and **SUMMARIZING** for help deciding how to integrate dialogue into your text.

rhetorical situations
genres
processes
strategies
research mla/apa
media/ design

Explaining Processes **36**

When you explain a process, you tell how something is (or was) done: how a bill becomes a law, how an embryo develops; or you tell someone how to do something: how to throw a curve ball, how to write a memoir. This chapter focuses on those two kinds of explanations, offering examples and guidelines for explaining a process in writing in a way that works for your rhetorical situation.

Explaining a Process Clearly

Whether the process is simple or complex, you'll need to identify its key stages or steps and explain them one by one, in order. The sequence matters because it allows readers to follow your explanation; it is especially important when you're explaining a process that others are going to follow. Most often you'll explain a process chronologically, from start to finish. **TRANSITIONS** — words like *first*, *next*, *then*, and so on — are often necessary, therefore, to show readers how the stages of a process relate to one another and to indicate time sequences. Finally, you'll find that verbs matter; they indicate the actions that take place at each stage of the process.

254

Explaining How Something Is Done

All processes consist of steps, and when you explain how something is done, you describe each step, generally in order, from first to last. Here, for example, is an explanation of how French fries are made, from an essay published in the *New Yorker:*

Fast-food French fries are made from a baking potato like an Idaho russet, or any other variety that is mealy, or starchy, rather than waxy. The potatoes are harvested, cured, washed, peeled, sliced, and then blanched—cooked enough so that the insides have a fluffy texture but not so much that the fry gets soft and breaks. Blanching is followed by drying, and drying by a thirty-second deep fry, to give the potatoes a crisp shell. Then the fries are frozen until the moment of service, when they are deep-fried again, this time for somewhere around three minutes. Depending on the fast-food chain involved, there are other steps interspersed in this process. McDonald's fries, for example, are briefly dipped in a sugar solution, which gives them their golden-brown color; Burger King fries are dipped in a starch batter, which is what gives those fries their distinctive hard shell and audible crunch. But the result is similar. The potato that is first harvested in the field is roughly 80 percent water. The process of creating a French fry consists, essentially, of removing as much of that water as possible—through blanching, drying, and deep-frying—and replacing it with fat.

—Malcolm Gladwell, "The Trouble with Fries"

Gladwell clearly explains the process of making French fries, showing us the specific steps—how the potatoes "are harvested, cured, washed, peeled, sliced," and so on—and using clear transitions—"followed by," "then," "until," "when"—and action verbs to show the sequence. His last sentence makes his stance clear, pointing out that the process of creating a French fry consists of removing as much of a potato's water as possible "and replacing it with fat."

Explaining How to Do Something

In explaining how to do something, you are giving instruction so that others can follow the process themselves. See how Martha Stewart explains the process of making French fries. She starts by listing the ingredients and then describes the steps:

4 medium baking potatoes
2 tablespoons olive oil
1 1/2 teaspoons salt
1/4 teaspoon freshly ground pepper
malt vinegar (optional)

1. Heat oven to 400 degrees. Place a heavy baking sheet in the oven. Scrub and rinse the potatoes well, and then cut them lengthwise into 1/2-inch-wide batons. Place the potato batons in a medium bowl, and toss them with the olive oil, salt, and pepper.

2. When baking sheet is hot, about 15 minutes, remove from the oven. Place prepared potatoes on the baking sheet in a single later. Return to oven, and bake until potatoes are golden on the bottom, about 30 minutes. Turn potatoes over, and continue cooking until golden all over, about 15 minutes more. Serve immediately.

—Martha Stewart, *Favorite Comfort Food*

Coming from Martha Stewart, the explanation leaves out no details, giving a clear sequence of steps and descriptive verbs that tell us exactly what to do: "heat," "place," "scrub and rinse," and so on. After she gives the recipe, she even goes on to explain the process of *serving* the fries — "Serve these French fries with a bowl of malt vinegar" — and reminds us that "they are also delicious dipped in spicy mustard, mayonnaise, and, of course, ketchup."

Explaining a Process Visually

Some processes are best explained **VISUALLY**, with diagrams or photographs. See, for example, how a cookbook explains one process of shaping dough into a bagel — giving the details in words and then showing us in a drawing how to do it:

458–62

Roll each piece of dough on an unfloured counter into a 12-inch-long rope. Make a ring, overlapping the ends by 2 inches and joining them by pressing down and rolling on the overlap until it is the same thickness as the rest of the dough ring. There will be a 1-inch hole in the center.

1. Rolling the dough into a 12-inch rope

2. Making a ring by twisting one end of the dough over to overlap the other end by 2 inches

3. Pressing down and rolling the dough

Rose Levy Beranbaum, *The Bread Bible*

Considering the Rhetorical Situation

As a writer or speaker, you need to think about the message that you want to articulate, the audience you want to reach, and the larger context you are writing in.

3–4

■ **PURPOSE**   Your purpose for writing will affect the way you explain a process. If you're arguing that we should avoid eating fast food, you might explain the process by which chicken nuggets are made. But to give information about how to fry chicken, you would explain the process quite differently.

5–8

■ **AUDIENCE**   Whom are you trying to reach, and what will you need to provide any special background information? Can they be expected to be interested, or will you first need to interest them in the process?

9–11

■ **GENRE**   Does your genre require you to explain a process? In a lab report, for example, you'll need to explain the processes used in the experiment. You might want to

rhetorical situations   genres   processes   strategies   research mla/apa   media/design

explain the process in a profile of an activity or the process of a solution you are proposing.

■ **STANCE**   If you're giving directions for doing something, you'll want to take a straightforward "do this, then do that" perspective. If you're writing to entertain, you might want to take a clever or amusing stance.
12–14

■ **MEDIA / DESIGN**   Your medium will affect the way you explain a process. In a print text or spoken text, you can use both words and images. On the Web, you may have the option of showing an animation of the process as well.
15–17

See also **LAB REPORTS** if you need to explain the process by which an experiment is carried out; and **PROFILES** if you are writing about an activity that needs to be explained. See **NARRATING** for more advice on organizing an explanation chronologically. Sometimes you may be assigned to write a whole essay or report that explains a process; see **PROCESSES** for help **DRAFTING, REVISING,** and so on.

▲ 127–136

▲ 153–59

◆ 304–12

● 193–235

37 Narrating

82–106 ▲

Narratives are stories. As a writing strategy, a good narrative can lend support to most kinds of writing—in an essay **ARGUING** for Title IX compliance, for example, you might include a brief narrative about an Olympic sprinter who might never have learned to run without Title IX. Or you can bring a **PROFILE** of a favorite coach to life with an anecdote about a pep talk he or she once gave before a championship track meet. Whatever your larger writing purpose, you need to make sure that any narratives you add support that purpose—they should not be inserted simply to tell an interesting story. You'll also need to compose them carefully—to put them in a clear *sequence*, include *pertinent detail*, and make sure they are appropriate to your particular rhetorical situation.

153–59 ▲

Sequencing

When we write a narrative, we arrange events in a particular sequence. Writers typically sequence narratives in chronological order, reverse chronological order, or as a flashback.

Use chronological order.   Often you may tell the story chronologically, starting at the beginning of an event and working through to the end, as Maya Angelou does in this brief narrative from an essay about her high school graduation:

> The school band struck up a march and all classes filed in as had been rehearsed. We stood in front of our seats, as assigned, and on a signal from the choir director, we sat. No sooner had this been accomplished than the band started to play the national anthem. We rose again and sang the song, after which we recited the pledge of allegiance. We

remained standing for a brief minute before the choir director and the principal signaled to us, rather desperately I thought, to take our seats.

—Maya Angelou, "Graduation"

Use reverse chronological order. You may also begin with the final action and work back to the first, as Aldo Leopold does in this narrative about cutting down a tree:

Now our saw bites into the 1890s, called gay by those whose eyes turn cityward rather than landward. We cut 1899, when the last passenger pigeon collided with a charge of shot near Babcock, two counties to the north; we cut 1898, when a dry fall, followed by a snowless winter, froze the soil seven feet deep and killed the apple trees; 1897, another drouth year, when another forestry commission came into being; 1896, when 25,000 prairie chickens were shipped to market from the village of Spooner alone; 1895, another year of fires; 1894, another drouth year; and 1893, the year of "the Bluebird Storm," when a March blizzard reduced the migrating bluebirds to near zero.

—Aldo Leopold, *A Sand County Almanac*

RÉSUMÉS are one genre where we generally use reverse chronological order, listing the most recent jobs or degrees first and then working backward. Notice, too, that we usually write these as narratives—telling what we have done rather than just naming positions we have held: ▲ 182–89

Sept. 2004–present	*Student worker*, Department of Information Management, Central State University, Wilberforce, OH. Compile data and format reports using Excel, Word, and university database programs.
June–Sept. 2004	*Intern*, QuestPro Corporation, West Louisville, KY. Assisted in development of software programs.
Sept. 2003–June 2004	*Bagger*, Ace Groceries, Elba, KY. Bagged customers' purchases.

Use a flashback.   You can sometimes put a flashback in the middle of a narrative, to tell about an incident that illuminates the larger narrative. Terry Tempest Williams does this in an essay about the startling incidence of breast cancer in her family: she recalls a dinnertime conversation with her father right after her mother's death from cancer, when she learned for the first time what caused all of the cancer in her family:

> Over dessert, I shared a recurring dream of mine. I told my father that for years, as long as I could remember, I saw this flash of light in the night in the desert. That this image had so permeated my being, I could not venture south without seeing it again, on the horizon, illuminating buttes and mesas.
>
> "You did see it," he said.
>
> "Saw what?" I asked, a bit tentative.
>
> "The bomb. The cloud. We were driving home from Riverside, California. You were sitting on your mother's lap. She was pregnant. In fact, I remember the date, September 7, 1957. We had just gotten out of the Service. We were driving north, past Las Vegas. It was an hour or so before dawn, when this explosion went off. We not only heard it, but felt it. I thought the oil tanker in front of us had blown up. We pulled over and suddenly, rising from the desert floor, we saw it, clearly, this golden-stemmed cloud, the mushroom. The sky seemed to vibrate with an eerie pink glow. Within a few minutes, a light ash was raining on the car."
>
> I stared at my father. This was new information to me.
>
> —Terry Tempest Williams, "The Clan of the One-Breasted Women"

Williams could have simply announced this information as a fact—but see how much more powerful it is when told in narrative form.

Use time markers.   Time markers help readers follow a sequence of events. The most obvious time markers are those that simply label the time, as the narrative entries in a diary, journal, or log might. For example, here is the final part of the narrative kept in a diary by a doomed Antarctic explorer:

> WEDNESDAY, MARCH 21: Got within eleven miles of depot. Monday night; had to lay up all yesterday in severe blizzard. Today forlorn hope, Wilson and Bowers going to depot for fuel.

MARCH 22 and 23: Blizzard bad as ever—Wilson and Bowers unable to start—tomorrow last chance—no fuel and only one or two [days] of food left—must be near the end. Have decided it shall be natural—we shall march for the depot with or without our effects and die in our tracks.

THURSDAY, MARCH 29: Since the 21st we have had a continuous gale from W.S.W. and S.W. We had fuel to make two cups of tea apiece and bare food for two days on the 20th. Every day we have been ready to start for our depot eleven miles away, but outside the door of the tent it remains a scene of whirling drift. I do not think we can hope for any better things now. We shall stick it out to the end, but we are getting weaker, of course, and the end cannot be far. It seems a pity, but I do not think I can write more. . . .

Last Entry: For God's sake look after our people.

—Robert F. Scott, *Scott's Last Expedition: The Journals*

More often you will integrate time markers into the prose itself, as is done in this narrative about a woman preparing and delivering meals to workers at a cotton gin:

She made her plans meticulously and in secret. <u>One early evening</u> to see if she was ready, she placed stones in two five-gallon pails and carried them three miles to the cotton gin. She rested a little, and then, discarding some rocks, she walked in the darkness to the sawmill five miles farther along the dirt road. <u>On her way back</u> to her little house and her babies, she dumped the remaining rocks along the path.

<u>That same night</u> she worked into the early hours boiling chicken and frying ham. She made dough and filled the rolled-out pastry with meat. At last she went to sleep.

<u>The next morning</u> she left her house carrying the meat pies, lard, an iron brazier, and coals for a fire. <u>Just before lunch</u> she appeared in an empty lot behind the cotton gin. <u>As the dinner noon bell rang</u>, she dropped the savors into boiling fat, and the aroma rose and floated over to the workers who spilled out of the gin, covered with white lint, looking like specters.

—Maya Angelou, *Wouldn't Take Nothing for My Journey Now*

Use transitions. Another way to help readers follow a narrative is with **TRANSITIONS**, words like *first, then, meanwhile, at last*, and so on. See how

◆ 254

the following paragraphs from Langston Hughes's classic essay about meeting Jesus use transitions (and time markers) to advance the action:

> <u>Suddenly</u> the whole room broke into a sea of shouting, <u>as</u> they saw me rise. Waves of rejoicing swept the place. Women leaped in the air. My aunt threw her arms around me. The minister took me by the hand and led me to the platform.
>
> <u>When</u> things quieted down, in a hushed silence, punctuated by a few ecstatic "Amens," all the new young lambs were blessed in the name of God. <u>Then</u> joyous singing filled the room. <u>That night,</u> for the last time in my life but one — for I was a big boy twelve years old — I cried.
>
> —Langston Hughes, "Salvation"

Including Pertinent Detail

When you include a narrative in your writing, you must decide which details you need — and which ones you don't need. For example, you don't want to include so much detail that the narrative distracts the reader from the larger text. You must also decide whether you need to include any background, to set the stage for the narrative. The amount of detail you include depends on your audience and purpose: How much detail does your audience need? How much detail do you need to make your meaning clear? In an essay on the suspicion African American men often face when walking at night, a journalist deliberately inserts a story without setting the stage at all:

> My first victim was a woman — white, well dressed, probably in her late twenties. I came upon her late one evening on a deserted street in Hyde Park, a relatively affluent neighborhood in an otherwise mean, impoverished section of Chicago. As I swung onto the avenue behind her, there seemed to be a discreet, uninflammatory distance between us. Not so. She cast back a worried glance. To her, the youngish black man — a broad six feet two inches with a beard and billowing hair, both hands shoved into the pockets of a bulky military jacket — seemed menacingly close. After a few more quick glimpses, she picked up her

pace and was soon running in earnest. Within seconds she disappeared into a cross street.

—Brent Staples, "Black Men and Public Space"

Words like *victim* and phrases like "came upon her" lead us to assume the narrator is scary and perhaps dangerous. We don't know why he is walking on the deserted street because he hasn't told us: he simply begins with the moment he and the woman encounter each other. For his purposes, that's all the audience needs to know at first, and details of his physical appearance that explain the woman's response come later, after he tells us about the encounter. Had he given us those details at the outset, the narrative would not have been nearly so effective. In a way, Staples lets the story sneak up on us, as the woman apparently felt he had on her.

Other times you'll need to provide more background information, as an MIT professor does when she uses an anecdote to introduce an essay about young children's experiences with electronic toys. First the writer tells us a little about Merlin, the computer tic-tac-toe game that the children in her anecdote play with. As you'll see, the anecdote would be hard to follow without the introduction:

Among the first generation of computational objects was Merlin, which challenged children to games of tic-tac-toe. For children who had only played games with human opponents, reaction to this object was intense. For example, while Merlin followed an optimal strategy for winning tic-tac-toe most of the time, it was programmed to make a slip every once in a while. So when children discovered strategies that allowed them to win and then tried these strategies a second time, they usually would not work. The machine gave the impression of not being "dumb enough" to let down its defenses twice. Robert, seven, playing with his friends on the beach, watched his friend Craig perform the "winning trick," but when he tried it, Merlin did not slip up and the game ended in a draw. Robert, confused and frustrated, threw Merlin into the sand and said, "Cheater. I hope your brains break." He was overheard by Craig and Greg, aged six and eight, who salvaged the by-now very sandy toy and took it upon themselves to set Robert straight. "Merlin doesn't know if it cheats," says Craig. "It doesn't know if you break it, Robert. It's not alive." Greg adds, "It's smart enough to make the right kinds of noises. But it doesn't really know if it loses. And when it cheats, it don't even know it's cheating." Jenny, six, interrupts with disdain: "Greg, to cheat you have to know you are cheating. Knowing is part of cheating."

—Sherry Turkle, "Cuddling Up to Cyborg Babies"

Opening and Closing with Narratives

239–45

Narratives are often useful as **BEGINNINGS** to essays and other kinds of writing. Everyone likes a good story, so an interesting or pithy narrative can be a good way to get your audience's attention. In the following introductory paragraph, a historian tells a gruesome but gripping story to attract our attention to a subject that might not otherwise merit our interest, bubonic plague:

> In October 1347, two months after the fall of Calais, Genoese trading ships put into the harbor of Messina in Sicily with dead and dying men at the oars. The ships had come from the Black Sea port of Caffa (now Feodosiya) in the Crimea, where the Genoese maintained a trading post. The diseased sailors showed strange black swellings about the size of an egg or an apple in the armpits and groin. The swellings oozed blood and pus and were followed by spreading boils and black blotches on the skin from internal bleeding. The sick suffered severe pain and died quickly, within five days of the first symptoms. As the disease spread, other symptoms of continuous fever and spitting of blood appeared instead of the swellings or buboes. These victims coughed and sweated heavily and died even more quickly, within three days or less, sometimes in twenty-four hours. In both types everything that issued from the body—breath, sweat, blood from the buboes and lungs, bloody urine, and blood-blackened excrement—smelled foul. Depression and despair accompanied the physical symptoms, and before the end "death is seen seated on the face."
>
> —Barbara Tuchman, "This Is the End of the World: The Black Death"

Imagine how different the preceding paragraph would be if it weren't in the form of a narrative. Imagine, for example, that Tuchman began by

defining bubonic plague. Would that have gotten your interest? The piece was written for a general audience; how might it have been different if it had been written for scientists? Would they need (or appreciate) the story told here?

Narrative can be a good way of **ENDING** a text, too, by winding up a discussion with an illustration of the main point. Here, for instance, is a concluding paragraph from an essay on American values and Las Vegas weddings.

245–48

> I sat next to one . . . wedding party in a Strip restaurant the last time I was in Las Vegas. The marriage had just taken place; the bride still wore her dress, the mother her corsage. A bored waiter poured out a few swallows of pink champagne ("on the house") for everyone but the bride, who was too young to be served. "You'll need something with more kick than that," the bride's father said with heavy jocularity to his new son-in-law; the ritual jokes about the wedding night had a certain Panglossian character, since the bride was clearly several months pregnant. Another round of pink champagne, this time not on the house, and the bride began to cry. "It was just as nice," she sobbed, "as I hoped and dreamed it would be."
>
> —Joan Didion, "Marrying Absurd"

No doubt Didion makes her points about American values clearly and cogently in the essay. But concluding with this story lets us *see* (and hear) what she is saying about Las Vegas wedding chapels, which sell " 'niceness,' the facsimile of proper ritual, to children who do not know how else to find it, how to make the arrangements, how to do it 'right.' "

Considering the Rhetorical Situation

As a writer or speaker, you need to think about the message that you want to articulate, the audience you want to reach, and the larger context you are writing in.

■ **PURPOSE**   Your purpose will affect the way you use narrative. For example, in an essay about seat belt laws, you might

3–4

tell about the painful rehabilitation of a teenager who was not wearing a seat belt and was injured in an accident in order to persuade readers that seat belts should be mandatory.

5–8 ■ **AUDIENCE** Whom do you want to reach, and do you have an anecdote or other narrative that will help them understand your topic or persuade them that your argument has merit?

9–11 ■ **GENRE** Does your genre require you to include narrative? A memoir about an important event might be primarily narrative, whereas a reflection about an event might focus more on the significance of the event than on what happened.

12–14 ■ **STANCE** What is your stance, and do you have any stories that would help you convey that stance? A funny story, for example, can help create a humorous stance.

15–17 ■ **MEDIA / DESIGN** In a print or spoken text, you will likely be limited to brief narratives, perhaps illustrated with photos or other images. In an electronic text, you might have the option of linking to full-length narratives or visuals available on the Web.

193–235 ○

127–36 ▲

182–89 ▲

See also the **PROCESSES** chapters if you are assigned to write a narrative essay and need help **DRAFTING, REVISING,** and so on. Two special kinds of narratives are **LAB REPORTS** (which use narrative to describe the steps in an experiment from beginning to end) and **RÉSUMÉS** (which essentially tell the story of the work we've done, at school and on the job).

rhetorical situations | genres | processes | strategies | research mla/apa | media/ design

Reading Strategies **38**

We read newspapers to learn about the events of the day. We read cookbooks to find out how to make brownies and textbooks to learn about history, chemistry, and other academic topics. We read short stories for pleasure — and, in literature classes, to analyze plot, setting, character, and theme. And as writers, we read our own drafts to make sure they say what we mean, and we proofread our final drafts to make sure they're correct. In other words, we read in various ways for many different purposes. This chapter offers a number of strategies for reading with a critical eye — from previewing a text to annotating as you read, identifying meaningful patterns, analyzing an argument, and more.

Reading Strategically

Academic reading is challenging because it makes several demands on you at once. Textbooks present new vocabulary and concepts, and picking out the main ideas can be difficult. Scholarly articles present content and arguments you need to understand, and they often assume because readers understand key concepts and vocabulary, they don't generally provide background information. As you read more texts in an academic field and participate in its conversations, the reading will become easier, but in the meantime you can develop strategies that will help you to read carefully and critically.

Different texts require different kinds of effort. Some texts can be read fairly quickly, if you're reading to get a general overview. Most of the time, though, you need to read carefully, matching the pace of your reading to the difficulty of the text. To read with a critical eye, you can't be in too much of a hurry. You'll likely need to skim the text for an overview of the basic ideas and then read carefully. And then you may read the text again. That is true for visual as well as verbal texts—you'll often need to get an overview of a text and then to pay close attention to its details.

Previewing a Text

It's usually a good idea to start by skimming a text: read the title and sub-title, any headings, the first and last paragraphs, the first sentences of all the other paragraphs. Study any illustrations and other visuals. Your goal is to get a sense of where the text is heading. At this point, don't stop to look up unfamiliar words; just underline them or put a mark in the margin, and look them up later.

Considering the Rhetorical Situation

3–4 ■ **PURPOSE**   What is the purpose? To entertain? inform? persuade readers to think something or take some action?

5–8 ■ **AUDIENCE**   Who is the intended audience? Are you a member of that group? If not, should you expect that you'll need to look up unfamiliar terms or concepts or that you'll run into assumptions you don't necessarily share?

9–11 ■ **GENRE**   What is the genre? Is it a report? an argument? an analysis? something else? Knowing the genre can help you anticipate certain key features.

12–14 ■ **STANCE**   Who is the writer, and what is his or her stance? Critical? Curious? Opinionated? Objective? Passionate? Indifferent? Something else? Knowing the stance affects the way you understand a text, whether you're inclined to agree or disagree, to take it seriously, and so on.

15–17 ■ **MEDIA / DESIGN**   What is the medium, and how does it affect the way you read? If it's a print text, do you know anything about the publisher? If it's on the Web, who sponsors the site, and when was it last updated? Are there any design elements — such as headings, summaries, color, or boxes — that highlight key parts of the text?

Thinking about Your Initial Response

It's usually good to read a text first just to get a sense of it. Some readers find it helps to jot down brief notes about their first response to a text, noting their reaction and thinking a little about why they reacted as they did:

- **What are your initial reactions?** Describe both your intellectual reaction and any emotional reaction. Identify places in the text that caused you to react as you did. If you had no particular reaction, note that.

- **What accounts for your reaction?** Do you agree or disagree with the writer or have a different perspective? Why? Are your reactions rooted in personal experiences? positions you hold? particular beliefs? some personal philosophy? As much as possible, you want to keep your opinions from coloring your analysis, so it's important to try to identify those opinions up front — and to give some thought to where they come from.

Annotating

Many readers find it helps to annotate as they read: highlighting key words, phrases, sentences; connecting ideas with lines or symbols; writing comments or questions in the margin; noting anything that seems noteworthy or questionable. Annotate as if you're having a conversation with the author, someone you take seriously but whose words you do not accept without question. Put your part of the conversation in the margin, asking questions, talking back: "What's this mean?" "So what?" "Says who?" "Where's evidence?" "Yes!" "Whoa!" even ☺ or ☹.

What you annotate depends on your PURPOSE or what you're most interested in. If you're analyzing an argument, you would probably underline any THESIS STATEMENT and then the reasons and evidence that support the statement. It might help to restate those ideas in your own words,

3–4

251–52

in the margins—in order to put them in your own words, you need to understand them! If you are looking for meaningful patterns, you might highlight each pattern in a different color and write any questions or notes about it in that color. If you are analyzing a literary text to look for certain elements or themes or patterns, you might highlight key passages that demonstrate those things.

Annotating forces you to read for more than just the surface meaning. Especially when you are going to be writing about or responding to a text, annotating creates a record of things you may want to refer to.

There are some texts that you cannot annotate, of course: library books, materials you read on the Web, and so on. Then you will need to make notes elsewhere, and you might find it useful to keep a reading log for that purpose.

On pages 317–18 is an annotated passage from Lawrence Lessig's essay "Some Like It Hot," included in Chapter 9: These annotations rephrase key definitions, identify the essay's thesis and main ideas, ask questions, and comment on issues raised in the essay. Annotating the entire essay, which appears on pages 85–89, would provide a look at Lessig's ideas and a record of the experience of reading the essay—useful for both understanding it and analyzing it.

Playing the Believing and Doubting Game

200–01
199–200

One way to think about your response to a text is to **LIST** or **FREEWRITE** as many reasons as you can think of for believing what the writer says and then as many as you can for doubting it. First, write as if you agree with everything in the writer's argument; look at the world from his or her perspective, trying to understand the writer's premises and reasons for arguing as he or she does even if you strongly disagree. Then, write as if you doubt everything in the text: try to find every flaw in the argument, every possible way it can be refuted—even if you totally agree with it. Developed by writing theorist Peter Elbow, the believing and doubting game helps you consider new ideas and question ideas you already have—and at the same time see where you stand in relation to the ideas in the text you're reading.

rhetorical situations　　genres　　processes　　strategies　　research mla/apa　　media/ design

If piracy means using the creative property of others without their permission, then the history of the content industry is a history of piracy.
Every important sector of big media today—film, music, radio, and
cable TV—was born of a kind of piracy. The consistent story is how
each generation welcomes the pirates from the last. Each generation—
until now.

　The Hollywood film industry was built by fleeing pirates. Creators
and directors migrated from the East Coast to California in the early
twentieth century in part to escape controls that film patents granted
the inventor Thomas Edison. These controls were exercised through the
Motion Pictures Patents Company, a monopoly "trust" based on Edison's creative property and formed to vigorously protect his patent
rights.

　California was remote enough from Edison's reach that filmmakers like Fox and Paramount could move there and, without fear of the
law, pirate his inventions. Hollywood grew quickly, and enforcement
of federal law eventually spread west. But because patents granted
their holders a truly "limited" monopoly of just seventeen years (at
that time), the patents had expired by the time enough federal marshals appeared. A new industry had been founded, in part from the
piracy of Edison's creative property.

　Meanwhile, the record industry grew out of another kind of piracy.
At the time that Edison and Henri Fourneaux invented machines for
reproducing music (Edison the phonograph; Fourneaux the player
piano), the law gave composers the exclusive right to control copies
and public performances of their music. Thus, in 1900, if I wanted a
copy of Phil Russel's 1899 hit, "Happy Mose," the law said I would have
to pay for the right to get a copy of the score, and I would also have
to pay for the right to perform it publicly.

　But what if I wanted to record "Happy Mose" using Edison's   5
phonograph or Fourneaux's player piano? Here the law stumbled. If I
simply sang the piece into a recording device in my home, it wasn't
clear that I owed the composer anything. And more important, it

*Piracy—
unauthorized use
of the artistic
work of others.*

*"Content
industry"—new
term. Film, music,
and so on?
Doesn't include
books and maga-
zines?*

*Thesis: "Big
media" are all
based on piracy.*

*Hollywood film
industry started
in order to avoid
Edison's patents.
What were they
for? Cameras and
projectors? Is this
true?*

*Record-industry
piracy.*

Player pianos?

wasn't clear whether I owed the composer anything if I then made copies of those recordings. Because of this gap in the law, I could effectively use someone else's song without paying the composer anything. The composers (and publishers) were none too happy about this capacity to pirate.

In 1909, Congress closed the gap in favor of the composer and the recording artist, amending copyright law to make sure that composers would be paid for "mechanical reproductions" of their music. But rather than simply granting the composer complete control over the right to make such reproductions, Congress gave recording artists a right to record the music, at a price set by Congress, after the composer allowed it to be recorded once. This is the part of copyright law that makes cover songs possible. Once a composer authorizes a recording of his song, others are free to record the same song, so long as they pay the original composer a fee set by the law. So, by limiting musicians' rights—by partially pirating their creative work—record producers and the public benefit.

—Lawrence Lessig, "Some Like It Hot"

Is copyright law different for books and other printed matter?

Partial piracy? Not sure about this—when artists use a song, they pay a fee but don't need permission. The composer doesn't have complete control. So it's piracy, but not completely?

Thinking about How the Text Works:
What It Says, What It Does

Sometimes you'll need to think about how a text works, how its parts fit together. You may be assigned to analyze a text, or you may just need to make sense of a difficult text, to think about how the ideas all relate to one another. Whatever your purpose, a good way to think about a text's structure is by **OUTLINING** it, paragraph by paragraph. If you're interested in analyzing its ideas, look at what each paragraph *says*; if, on the other hand, you're concerned with how the ideas are presented, pay attention to what each paragraph *does*.

◯ 203–04

What it says. Write a sentence that identifies what each paragraph says. Once you've done that for the whole text, look for patterns in the topics the writer addresses. Pay attention to the order in which the topics are presented. Also look for gaps, ideas the writer has left unsaid. Such paragraph-by-paragraph outlining of the content can help you see how the writer has arranged ideas and how that arrangement builds an argument or develops a topic. Here, for example, is such an outline of Lawrence Lessig's essay (the numbers on the left refer to the paragraphs):

1	Every major type of media bases its development on piracy, the unauthorized use of artists' work.
2, 3	To escape patents that restricted the copying of innovations in filmmaking, the movie industry moved from the East Coast to California.
4, 5	Copyright law gave composers control over the performance of their music—but because it didn't cover the recording of music and the sale of copies of the recordings, it allowed piracy in the record industry.
6	Congress eventually changed the law, allowing musicians to record a song without the composer's permission if they paid the composer a fee.
7–11	When a radio station plays a song, it pays the composer but not the recording artist, thus pirating the recording artist's work.

12, 13	Cable TV has pirated works, too, by paying networks nothing for their broadcasts — despite protests by broadcasters and copyright owners.
14	Congress eventually extended the copyright law to cable TV, forcing the cable companies to pay for their broadcasts at a price controlled by Congress in order to protect the innovations of the cable industry.
15	The history of the major media industries suggests that piracy is not necessarily "plainly wrong."
16, 17	Peer-to-peer file sharing, like the earlier media-industry innovations, is being used to share artistic content and avoid industry controls, but it differs from the early cable industry in that it is not selling any content.
18	P2P file sharing provides access to music that can no longer be purchased, music that copyright holders want to share, and music that is no longer copyrighted.
19	P2P file sharing, like the earlier innovations, is the result of new technology, and it raises similar questions: how can it best be used without penalizing the artists whose works are "pirated"?
20	Copyright law must balance the protection of artists' works with the innovation in technologies, a process that takes time.

What it does.   Identify the function of each paragraph. Starting with the first paragraph, ask, What does this paragraph do? Does it introduce a topic? provide background for a topic to come? describe something? define something? entice me to read further? Something else? What does the second paragraph do? the third? As you go through the text, you may identify groups of paragraphs that have a single purpose. For an example, look at this functional outline of Lessig's essay (again, the numbers on the left refer to the paragraphs):

1	Defines the key term, *piracy*, and illustrates the thesis using the history of four media industries in the United States.
2, 3	Tells the history of the first medium, film, by focusing on piracy as a major factor in its development.
4–6	Tells the history of the second medium, the recording industry, again by focusing on the role of piracy in its development.

■ rhetorical situations   ▲ genres   ○ processes   ◆ strategies   ● research mla/apa   ▢ media/ design

7–11	Tells the history of the third medium, radio, focusing on the role of piracy in its development.
12–14	Tells the history of the fourth medium, cable TV, focusing on the role of piracy in its development.
15	Offers conclusions about piracy based on the similar roles played by piracy in the histories of the four media.
16, 17	Compares the current controversy over piracy in peer-to-peer file sharing on the Internet with the role of piracy in the earlier media.
18	Describes the benefits of P2P file sharing.
19, 20	Compares those benefits with those of the other media and offers a conclusion in the form of a problem to be solved.

Summarizing

Summarizing a text can help you both to see the relationships among its ideas and to understand what it's saying. When you SUMMARIZE, you restate a text's main ideas in your own words, leaving out most examples and other details. Here's a summary of Lawrence Lessig's essay:

366–67

> The development of every major media industry is based on piracy, the unauthorized use of artists' or inventors' work. First, the film industry flourished by evading restrictions on the copying of innovations in filmmaking. Then, the recording industry benefited from copyright laws that gave composers control over the performance of their music but not over the recording of it or the sale of the recordings. A law passed in 1909 in effect allows musicians to record a song without the composer's permission if they pay the composer a fee. Radio broadcasters benefit from piracy, too, every time they play a song recorded by someone other than the composer: they pay the composer a fee but not the recording artist. Finally, when it first started operating, cable TV benefited from piracy—by paying the networks nothing for their broadcasts. Congress eventually extended the copyright law, forcing cable companies to pay for the content they broadcast—but at a price controlled by Congress so that the networks wouldn't be able to drive the cable companies out of business. Peer-to-peer file sharing, like the early media industries, is being used to share artistic content and avoid indus-

try controls on that sharing. It benefits the public by allowing access to music that is out of print, that copyright holders want to share, and that is no longer copyrighted. Therefore, the public needs to figure out how to make it work without penalizing musicians by pirating their songs. Copyright law must balance the protection of artists' work with the encouragement of technological innovation.

Identifying Patterns

Look for notable patterns in the text: recurring words and their synonyms, as well as repeated phrases, metaphors and other images, and types of sentences. Some writers find it helps to highlight patterns in various colors. Does the author rely on any particular writing **STRATEGIES**: narration? comparison? Something else?

237–328

It might be important to consider the kind of evidence offered: Is it more opinion than fact? nothing but statistics? If many sources are cited, is the information presented in any predominant patterns: as **QUOTATIONS? PARAPHRASES? SUMMARIES?** Are there repeated references to certain experts or sources?

358–69

In visual texts, look for patterns of color, shape, and line. What's in the foreground, and what's in the background? What's completely visible, partly visible, or invisible? In both verbal and visual texts, look for omissions and anomalies: What isn't there that you would expect to find? Is there anything that doesn't really fit in?

If you discover patterns, then you need to consider what, if anything, they mean in terms of what the writer is saying. What do they reveal about the writer's underlying premises and beliefs? What do they tell us about the writer's strategies for persuading us to accept the truth of what he or she is saying?

See how color coding William Safire's essay on the Gettysburg Address reveals several patterns in the language Safire uses. In this excerpt from the essay, which appears in full in Chapter 7, religious references are colored yellow; references to a "national spirit," green; references to life, death, and rebirth, blue; and places where he directly addresses the reader, gray.

But the selection of this poetic political sermon as the oratorical centerpiece of our observance need not be only an exercise. . . . now, as
then, a national spirit rose from the ashes of destruction.

Here is how to listen to Lincoln's all-too-familiar speech with new
ears.

In those 266 words, you will hear the word *dedicate* five times.
. . .

Those five pillars of dedication rested on a fundament of religious
metaphor. From a president not known for his piety — indeed, often
criticized for his supposed lack of faith — came a speech rooted in the
theme of national resurrection. The speech is grounded in conception,
birth, death, and rebirth.

Consider the barrage of images of birth in the opening sentence. . . .

Finally, the nation's spirit rises from this scene of death: "that this
nation, under God, shall have a new birth of freedom." Conception,
birth, death, rebirth. The nation, purified in this fiery trial of war, is
resurrected. Through the sacrifice of its sons, the sundered nation
would be reborn as one. . . .

Do not listen on Sept. 11 only to Lincoln's famous words and comforting cadences. Think about how Lincoln's message encompasses but
goes beyond paying "fitting and proper" respect to the dead and the
bereaved. His sermon at Gettysburg reminds "us the living" of our
"unfinished work" and "the great task remaining before us" — to
resolve that this generation's response to the deaths of thousands of
our people leads to "a new birth of freedom."

The color coding helps us to see patterns in Safire's language, just as Safire
reveals patterns in Lincoln's words. He offers an interpretation of Lincoln's
address as a "poetic political sermon," and the words he uses throughout
support that interpretation. At the end, he repeats the assertion that Lincoln's address is a sermon, inviting us to consider it differently. Targeting
different textual elements, such as commands to the reader ("Consider,"
"Do not listen," "Think about"), offers additional information on how Safire
wishes to position himself in relation to his readers.

Count up the parts.   This is a two-step process: first, you count things:
how many of this, how many of that. Look for words, phrases, or sentences that seem important, or select a few typical paragraphs on which

to focus. After you count, see what you can conclude about the writing. You may want to work with others, dividing up the counting.

- *Count words.* Count one-, two-, three-syllable words, repeated words, active and passive verbs, prepositions, jargon or specialized terms.

- *Count sentences.* Count the number of words in each sentence, the average number of words per sentence; figure the percentage of sentences above and below average; count the number of sentences in each paragraph; count the number of simple sentences, compound sentences, complex sentences, fragments; mark the distinct rhythms (tap out the beat as you read aloud); count repeated phrases.

- *Count paragraphs.* Count the number of paragraphs, the average number of words and sentences per paragraph, the shortest and longest paragraphs; consider the position of the longest and shortest paragraphs; find parallel paragraph structures.

- *Count images.* List, circle, or underline verbal or visual images, similes, metaphors, and other figures of speech. Categorize them by meaning as well as type.

What do your findings tell you about the text? What generalizations can you make about it? Why did the author choose the words or images he or she used and in those combinations? What do those words tell you about the writer—or about his or her stance? Do your findings suggest a strategy, a plan for your analysis? For instance, Safire counts the number of times Lincoln uses *dedicate* and images of birth, death, and rebirth to argue something about Lincoln's speech and what it should mean to Safire's audience on the anniversary of 9/11.

Analyzing the Argument

All texts make some kind of argument, claiming something and then offering reasons and evidence as support for the claim. As a critical reader, you need to look closely at the argument a text makes—you need to recognize all the claims it makes, consider the support it offers for those claims, and decide how you want to respond. What do you think, and why? Here are some of the aspects of a text you'll need to consider when you analyze an argument:

- **What is the claim?** What is the main point the writer is trying to make? Is there a clearly stated THESIS, or is it merely implied?
- **What support does the writer offer for the claim?** What REASONS are given to support the claim? What EVIDENCE backs up those reasons? Facts? Statistics? Testimonials by authorities? Examples? Pertinent anecdotes? Are the reasons plausible and sufficient?
- **How evenhandedly does the writer present the issues?** Is there any mention of counterarguments? If so, how does the writer deal with them? By refuting them? By acknowledging them and responding to them reasonably? Does the writer treat other arguments respectfully? dismissively? Are his or her own arguments appropriately qualified?
- **What authorities or sources of outside information does the writer use?** How are they used? How credible are they? Are they in any way biased or otherwise unreliable? Are they current?
- **How does the writer address you as the reader?** Does the writer assume that readers know something about what is being discussed? Does his or her language include you or exclude you? (Hint: If you see the word *we*, do you feel included?) Do you sense that you and the author share any beliefs or attitudes?

Check for fallacies. Fallacies are arguments that involve faulty reasoning. Because they often seem plausible, they can be persuasive. It is important, therefore, that you question the legitimacy of such reasoning when you run across it.

Philosophers and rhetoricians have identified many kinds of faulty reasoning; here are some of the most common kinds:

- **Ad hominem** arguments attack someone's character rather than addressing the issues. (*Ad hominem* is Latin for "to the man.") It is an especially common fallacy in political discourse and elsewhere: "Jack Turner has no business talking about the way we run things in this city. He's lived here only five years and is just another flaky liberal."

The length of time Turner has lived in the city has no bearing on the worth of his argument; neither does his political stance, which his opponent characterizes unfairly.

- *Bandwagon appeals* argue that because others think or do something, we should, too. For example, an advertisement for a rifle association suggests that "67 percent of voters support laws permitting concealed weapons. You should, too." It assumes that readers want to be part of the group and implies that an opinion that is popular must be correct.

- *Begging the question* is a circular argument. It assumes as a given what is trying to be proved, essentially supporting an assertion with the assertion itself. Consider this statement: "Affirmative action can never be fair or just because you cannot remedy one injustice by committing another." This statement begs the question because to prove that affirmative action is unjust, it assumes that it is an injustice.

- *Either-or* arguments, also called *false dilemmas*, are oversimplifications. Either-or arguments assert that there can be only two possible positions on a complex issue. For example, "Those who oppose our actions in this war are enemies of freedom" inaccurately assumes that if someone opposes the war in question, he or she opposes freedom. In fact, people might have many other reasons for opposing the war.

- *False analogies* compare things that resemble each other in some ways but not in the most important respects. For example: "Trees pollute the air just as much as cars and trucks do." Although it's true that plants emit hydrocarbons, and hydrocarbons are a component of smog, they also produce oxygen, whereas motor vehicles emit gases that combine with hydrocarbons to form smog. Vehicles pollute the air; trees provide the air that vehicles' emissions pollute.

- *Faulty causality,* also known as *post hoc, ergo propter hoc* (Latin for "after this, therefore because of this"), assumes that because one event followed another, the first event caused the second—for example, "Legalizing same-sex marriage in Sweden led to an increase in the number of children born to unwed mothers." The statement contains no evidence to show that the first event caused the second. The birth rate could have been affected by many factors, and same-sex marriage may not even be among them.

- *Hasty generalizations* are conclusions based on insufficient or inappropriately qualified evidence. This summary of a research study is a good example: "Twenty randomly chosen residents of Brooklyn, New York, were asked whether they found graffiti tags offensive; fourteen said yes, five said no, and one had no opinion. Therefore, 70 percent of Brooklyn residents find tagging offensive." In Brooklyn, a part of New York City with a population of over two million, twenty residents is far too small a group from which to draw meaningful conclusions. To be able to generalize, the researcher would have had to survey a much greater percentage of Brooklyn's population.

- *Slippery slope* arguments assert that one event will inevitably lead to another, often cataclysmic event without presenting evidence that such a chain of causes and effects will in fact take place. Here's an example: "If the state legislature passes this 2 percent tax increase, it won't be long before all the corporations in the state move to other states and leave thousands unemployed." According to this argument, if taxes are raised, the state's economy will be ruined — not a likely scenario, given the size of the proposed increase.

Considering the Larger Context

All texts are part of ongoing conversations with other texts that have dealt with the same topic. An essay arguing for handgun trigger locks is part of an ongoing conversation about gun control, which is itself part of a conversation on individual rights and responsibilities. Academic texts document their sources in part to show their relationship to the ongoing scholarly conversations on a particular topic. Academic reading usually challenges you to become aware of those conversations. And in fact, any time you're reading to learn, you're probably reading for some larger context. Whatever your reading goals, being aware of that larger context can help you better understand what you're reading. Here are some specific aspects of the text to pay attention to:

- *Who else cares about this topic?* Especially when you're reading in order to learn about a topic, the texts you read will often reveal which people or groups are part of the conversation — and might be sources of further reading. For example, an essay describing the formation of Mammoth Cave could be of interest to geologists, spelunkers, travel writers, or tourists. If you're reading such an essay while doing research on the cave, you should consider how the audience addressed determines the nature of the information provided — and its suitability as a source for your research.

- *Ideas.* Does the text refer to any concepts or ideas that give you some sense that it's part of a larger conversation? An argument on airport security measures, for example, is part of larger conversations about government response to terrorism, the limits of freedom in a democracy, and the possibilities of using technology to detect weapons and explosives, among others.

- *Terms.* Is there any terminology or specialized language that reflects the writer's allegiance to a particular group or academic discipline? If you run across words like *false consciousness*, *ideology*, and *hegemony*, for example, you might guess the text was written by a Marxist scholar.

- *Citations.* Whom does the writer cite? Do the other writers have a particular academic specialty, belong to an identifiable intellectual school, share similar political leanings? If an article on politics cites Michael Moore and Barbara Ehrenreich in support of its argument, you might assume the writer holds liberal opinions; if it cites Rush Limbaugh and Sean Hannity, the writer is likely a conservative.

354–57

208–23

> See also the chapter on **EVALUATING SOURCES** for help analyzing the reliability of a text, and see the chapters on **ASSESSING YOUR OWN WRITING, GETTING RESPONSE AND REVISING,** and **EDITING AND PROOFREADING** for advice on reading your own writing.

part 5

Doing Research

We do research all the time, for many different reasons. We search the Web for information about a new computer, ask friends about the best place to get coffee, try on several pairs of jeans before deciding which ones to buy. You have no doubt done your share of library research before now, and you probably visited a number of schools' Web sites before deciding which college you wanted to attend. Research, in other words, is something you do every day. The following chapters offer advice on the kind of research you'll need to do for your academic work and, in particular, for research papers and other written documents.

329

Doing Research

Developing a Research Plan

When you need to do research, it's sometimes tempting to jump in and start looking for information right away. To do research well, however—to find appropriate sources and use them wisely—you need to work systematically. You need a research plan. This chapter will help you establish such a plan and then get started.

Establishing a Schedule

Doing research is complex and time-consuming, so it's good to establish a schedule for yourself. Research-based writing projects usually require you to come up with a topic (or to analyze the requirements of an assigned topic). You'll need to do preliminary research to come up with a research question to guide your research efforts. Once you do some serious, focused research to find the information you need, you'll be ready to turn your research question into a tentative thesis and sketch out a rough outline. After doing whatever additional research you need to fill in your outline, you'll write a draft—and get some response to that draft. Perhaps you'll need to do additional research before revising. Finally, you'll need to edit and proofread. And so you'll want to start by establishing a schedule, perhaps using the form on the next page.

Getting Started

Once you have a schedule, you can get started. The sections that follow offer advice on considering your rhetorical situation, coming up with a topic, and thinking about what you already know about it; doing prelim-

rhetorical situations   genres   processes   strategies   research mla/apa   media/ design

Scheduling a Research Project

	Complete by:
Analyze your rhetorical situation.	_____
Choose a possible topic.	_____
Do preliminary research.	_____
Come up with a research question.	_____
Schedule interviews and other field research.	_____
Find and read library and Web sources.	_____
Do any field research.	_____
Come up with a tentative thesis and outline.	_____
Write out a draft.	_____
Get response.	_____
Do any additional research.	_____
Revise.	_____
Prepare a list of works cited.	_____
Edit.	_____
Prepare the final draft.	_____
Proofread.	_____
Submit the final draft.	_____

inary research, and creating a working bibliography; developing a research question, devising a tentative thesis and a rough outline, and keeping track of your sources. The chapters that follow offer guidelines for **FINDING SOURCES** and **EVALUATING SOURCES**.

340–53 ⬤
354–57 ⬤

Considering the Rhetorical Situation

As with any writing task, you need to start by considering your purpose, your audience, and the rest of your rhetorical situation:

rhetorical situations   genres   processes   strategies   research mla/apa   media/design

■ **PURPOSE**   Is this project part of an assignment—and if so, does
                       it specify any one purpose? If not, what is your broad
                       purpose? To inform? argue? entertain? A combination?

3–4

■ **AUDIENCE**   To whom are you writing? What does your audience
                       likely know about your topic, and is there any back-
                       ground information you'll need to provide? What opin-
                       ions or attitudes do your readers likely hold? What
                       kinds of evidence will they find persuasive? How do
                       you want them to respond to your writing?

5–8

■ **GENRE**   Are you writing to report on something? to compose a
                       profile? to make a proposal? an argument? What are
                       the requirements of your genre in terms of the num-
                       ber and kind of sources you must use?

9–11

■ **STANCE**   What is your attitude toward your topic? What
                       accounts for your attitude? How do you want to come
                       across? Curious? Critical? Positive? Something else?

12–14

■ **MEDIA / DESIGN**   What medium will you use? Print? Spoken? Electronic?
                       Will you need to compose any charts, photographs,
                       video, presentation software slides, or other visuals?

15–17

Coming Up with a Topic

If you need to choose a topic, consider your interests. What do you want
to learn about? What do you have questions about? What topics from
your courses have you found intriguing? What community, national, or
global issues do you care about? If your topic is assigned, you still need
to make sure you understand exactly what it asks you to do. Read the
assignment carefully, looking for key words: does it ask you to ANALYZE,
COMPARE, EVALUATE, SUMMARIZE? If the assignment offers broad guidelines
but allows you to choose within them, identify the requirements and the
range of possibilities, and define your topic within those constraints. For

255–59
266–74
120-26
366–67

example, in an American history course, your instructor might ask you to "discuss social effects of the Civil War." To define a suitable topic, you might choose to explore such topics as poverty among Confederate soldiers or former slaveholders, the migration of members of those groups to Mexico or northern cities, the establishment of independent black churches, the growth of sharecropping among former slaves, or the spread of the Ku Klux Klan — to name a few possibilities. Once you have a broad topic, you might try FREEWRITING, LOOPING, LISTING, or CLUSTERING to find an angle to research.

199–202

Narrow the topic.　As you consider possible topics, look to narrow your focus on a topic to make it specific enough for you to research and cover in a paper. For example:

Too general: the environment

Still too general: chemicals harmful to the environment

Better: chemicals i　gasoline that harm the environment

More specific: the effects of the gasoline additive MTBE on water purity

If you limit your topic, you can address it with specific information that you'll be more easily able to find and manage. In addition, a limited topic will be more likely to interest your audience than a broad subject that forces you to use abstract, general statements. For example, it's much harder to write well about "the environment" than it is to address a topic that covers a single environmental issue.

Think about what you know about your topic.　Chances are you already know something about your topic, and articulating that knowledge can help you see possible ways to focus your topic or come up with potential sources of information. FREEWRITING, LISTING, CLUSTERING, and LOOPING are all good ways of tapping your knowledge of your topic. Consider where you might find information about it: Have you read about it in a textbook? heard stories about it on the news? visited Web sites focused on it? Do you know anyone who knows about this topic?

199–202

rhetorical situations　genres　processes　strategies　research mla/apa　media/ design

Doing Some Preliminary Research

Doing some preliminary research can save you time in the long run. Scholarly sources usually focus on narrow, specialized aspects of subjects. To define the focus for your research, you first need to explore sources that will provide an overview of your topic.

One way to begin is to look at **REFERENCE WORKS** — sources that deal with the general topic and that include summaries or overviews of the scholarship in a field. General encyclopedias can give you some background, but they aren't suitable as sources for college work; use them as a starting point, to give you some basic information about your topic and help you see some of the paths you might follow. The same is true of the results you're likely to get from skimming Web sites on the subject. Discipline-specific encyclopedias can be more helpful, as they usually present subjects in much greater depth and provide more scholarly references that might provide starting points for your research. Even if you know a lot about a subject, doing research can open you to new ways of seeing and approaching it, increasing your options for developing and narrowing your topic.

344–45

At this stage, pay close attention to the terms used to discuss your topic. These terms could be keywords that you can use to search for information on your topic in library catalogs, in databases, and on the Web.

Keeping a Working Bibliography

A working bibliography is a record of all the sources you consult. You should keep such a record so that you can find sources easily when you need them and then cite any that you use. You can keep a working bibliography on index cards or in a notebook, or in many cases you can print out or photocopy the data you need. To save time later, include all the bibliographic information you'll need to document the sources you use. If possible, follow the **DOCUMENTATION** style you'll use when you write.

375–449

On the next page is most of the basic information you'll want to include for each source in your working bibliography. Go to wwnorton.com/write/fieldguide for templates you can use to keep track of this information.

Information for a working bibliography

FOR A BOOK

Library call number
Author(s) or editor(s)
Title and subtitle
Publication information: city, publisher, year of publication
Other information: edition, volume number, translator, and so on
If your source is a chapter in a book, include its author, title, and page numbers.

FOR AN ARTICLE IN A PERIODICAL

Author(s)
Title and subtitle
Name of periodical
Volume number, issue number, date
Page numbers

FOR A WEB SOURCE

URL
Author(s) or editor(s) if available
Name of site
Sponsor of site
Date site was first posted or last updated
Date you accessed site
If the source is an article or book reprinted on the Web, include its title, the title and publication information of the periodical or book where it was first published, and any page numbers.

FOR A SOURCE FROM AN ELECTRONIC DATABASE

Publication information for the source
Name of database
Item number, if there is one
Name of subscription service and its URL
Library where you accessed source
Date you accessed source

Coming Up with a Research Question

Once you've surveyed the territory of your topic, you'll likely find that your understanding of your topic has become broader and deeper. You may find that your interests have changed and your research has led to surprises and additional research. That's okay: as a result of exploring avenues you hadn't anticipated, you may well come up with a better topic than the one you'd started with. At some point, though, you need to come up with a research question—a specific question that you will then work to answer through your research.

To write a research question, review your analysis of the **RHETORICAL SITUATION,** to remind yourself of any time constraints or length considerations. Generate a list of questions beginning with What? When? Where? Who? How? Why? Would? Could? and Should? Here, for example, are some questions about the tentative topic "the effects of the gasoline additive MTBE on water purity":

1–17

> *What* are the effects of MTBE on humans and animals?
>
> *When* did MTBE become commonly used as a gasoline additive?
>
> *Where* has MTBE entered the water table?
>
> *Who* wants to ban MTBE, and *who* would benefit from banning it?
>
> *How* widespread is groundwater pollution by MTBE?
>
> *Why* do environmental groups oppose the use of MTBE?
>
> *Would* it be appropriate for the EPA to regulate the use of MTBE?
>
> *Could* substitutes for MTBE maintain clean air without pollution?
>
> *Should* the use of MTBE as a gasoline additive be banned?

Select one question from your list that you find interesting and that suits your rhetorical situation. Use the question to guide your research.

Drafting a Tentative Thesis

Once your research has led you to a possible answer to your research question, try formulating that answer as a tentative **THESIS**. You need not be

251–52

committed to the thesis; in fact, you should not be. The object of your research should be to learn about your topic, not to find information that simply supports what you already think you believe. Your tentative thesis may (and probably will) change as you learn more about your subject, consider the many points of view on it, and reconsider your topic and, perhaps, your goal: what you originally planned to be an informational report may become an argument, or the argument you planned to write may become a report. However tentative, a thesis allows you to move forward by clarifying your purpose for doing research. Here are some tentative thesis statements on the topic of MTBE:

> The EPA should regulate the use of MTBE.
>
> Substitutes for MTBE can maintain clean air without causing pollution.
>
> The use of MTBE as a gasoline additive should be banned.

As with a research question, a tentative thesis should guide your research efforts — but be ready to revise it as you learn still more about your topic. Research should be a process of inquiry, in which you approach your topic with an open mind, ready to learn and possibly change. If you hold too tightly to a tentative thesis, you risk selecting only that research and evidence that supports your view, making your writing biased and unconvincing.

Creating a Rough Outline

203–04 ◯

After you've created a tentative thesis, write out a rough **OUTLINE** for your research paper. Your rough outline can be a simple list of topics you want to explore, something that will help you structure your research efforts and organize your notes and other materials. As you read your sources, you can use your outline to keep track of what you need to find and where the information you do find fits into your argument. Then you'll be able to see if you've covered all the ideas you intended to explore — or whether you need to rethink the categories on your outline.

Keeping Track of Your Sources

- *Staple together copies and printouts of print materials.* It's easy for individual pages to get shuffled or lost on a desk or in a backpack. Keep a stapler handy, and fasten pages together as soon as you copy them or print them out.

- *Store Web site URLs* as *favorites* (in Internet Explorer) or *bookmarks* (in Netscape Navigator).

- *Label everything.* Label your copies with the source's author and title.

- *Highlight sections you plan to use.* When you sit down to draft, your goal will be to find what you need quickly, so as soon as you decide you might use a source, highlight the paragraphs or sentences that you think you'll use. If your instructor wants copies of your sources to see how you used them, you've got them ready.

- *Use your rough outline to keep track of what you've got.* In the margin of each highlighted section, write the number or letter to which the section corresponds. (It's a good idea to write it in the same place consistently so you can flip through a stack of copies and easily see what you've got.) Alternatively, attach sticky notes to each photocopy, using a different color for each main heading in your outline.

- *Keep everything in a file folder or box.* That way, even though your research material may not look organized, it will all be in one place — and if you highlight, number, and use sticky notes, your material will be organized and you'll be better prepared to write a draft. This folder or box will also serve you well if you are required to create a portfolio that includes your research notes, photocopies of sources, and drafts.

See the guidelines on **FINDING SOURCES** once you're ready to move on to in-depth research and those on **EVALUATING SOURCES** for help thinking critically about the sources you find.

340–57

40 Finding Sources

To analyze media coverage of the 2004 Democratic National Convention, you examine news stories and blogs published at the time. To write an essay interpreting a poem by Maya Angelou, you study the poem and read several critical interpretations in literary journals. To write a report on career opportunities in psychology, you interview a graduate of your university who is working in a psychology clinic. In each of these cases, you go beyond your own knowledge to consult additional sources of information.

This chapter offers guidelines for locating a range of sources — print and online, general and specialized, published and firsthand. Keep in mind that as you do research, finding and **EVALUATING SOURCES** are two activities that usually take place simultaneously. So this chapter and the next one go hand in hand.

354–57

Kinds of Sources

Primary and secondary sources.   Your research will likely lead you to both primary and secondary sources. *Primary sources* include historical documents, literary works, eyewitness accounts, field reports, diaries, letters, and lab studies, as well as any original research you do through interviews, observation, experiments, or surveys. *Secondary sources* include scholarly books and articles, reviews, biographies, textbooks, and other works that interpret or discuss primary sources. Novels and poems are

340

primary sources; articles interpreting them are secondary sources. The Declaration of Independence is a primary historical document; a historian's description of the events surrounding the Declaration's writing is secondary. A published report of scientific findings is primary; a critique of that report is secondary.

Whether a work is considered primary or secondary sometimes depends on your topic and purpose: if you're analyzing a poem, a critic's article interpreting the poem is a secondary source—but if you're investigating that critic's work, the article would be a primary source for your study.

Primary sources are useful because they offer firsthand accounts, whereas secondary sources can help you understand and evaluate primary source material.

Print and online sources.   Some sources are available only in print; some are available only online. But many print sources are also available on the Web. You'll find print sources in your school's library, but chances are that many of the books in your library's reference section will also be available online. And when it comes to finding sources, it's likely that you'll *search* for most sources online, through the library's Web site. In general, there are four kinds of sources you'll want to consult, each of which is discussed in this chapter:

GENERAL REFERENCE WORKS, for encyclopedias, dictionaries, and the like

THE LIBRARY CATALOG, for books

INDEXES AND DATABASES, for periodicals

SEARCH ENGINES AND SUBJECT DIRECTORIES, for material on the Web

344

345–46

346–49

349–50

On the next page is a sample search page from the catalog of one university library. This catalog, like most, allows you to search by book title, journal title, author, subject, call number, and keyword. In addition, the links at the top of the page permit you to search through various indexes and databases and take advantage of interlibrary loan (for materials that your library doesn't have) and various tutorials.

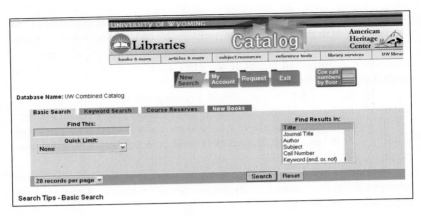

Part of a library catalog search page.

Searching Electronically

Whether you're searching for books, articles in periodicals, or material available on the Web, chances are you'll conduct much of your search electronically. Most materials produced since the 1980s can be found electronically, most library catalogs are online, and most periodical articles can be found by searching electronic indexes and databases. In each case, you can search for authors, titles, or subjects.

When you're searching for subjects, you'll need to come up with *keywords* that will lead you to the information you're looking for. Usually if you start with only one keyword, you'll end up with far too many results — tens of thousands of references when you're searching the Web — so the key to searching efficiently is to come up with keywords that will focus your searches on the information you need. Some search engines will let you enter more than one word and will identify only those sources that contain all the words you entered. Other search engines will let you type in more than one word and will identify those sources that contain at least one of those words but not necessarily all of them. Most search engines

have "advanced search" options that will help you focus your research. Specific commands will vary among search engines and within databases, but here are some of the most common ones:

- Type quotation marks around words to search for an exact phrase— "Thomas Jefferson"—unless you're using a search engine that includes a field to search for exact phrases, in which case you won't need the quotation marks. If your exact-phrase search doesn't yield good results, try removing the quotation marks.

- Type AND to find sources that include more than one keyword: Jefferson AND Adams. Some search engines require a plus sign instead: +Jefferson+Adams.

- Type OR if you're looking for sources that include one of several terms: Jefferson OR Adams OR Madison.

- Type NOT to find sources *without* a certain word: Jefferson NOT Adams. Some search engines call for a minus sign (actually, a hyphen) instead: +Jefferson-Adams will result in sources in which the name Jefferson appears but the name Adams does not.

- Type an asterisk—or some other symbol—to search for words in different forms—teach* will yield sources containing *teacher* and *teaching*, for example. Check the search engine's search tips to find out what symbol to use.

- Some search engines allow you to ask questions in conversational language: What did Thomas Jefferson write about slavery?

- Be more general (*education Japan* instead of *secondary education Japan*) when you get too few sources; be more specific (*homeopathy* instead of *medicine*) when you get far too many sources.

- If you don't get results with one set of keywords, substitute synonyms (if *folk medicine* doesn't generate much information, try *home remedy*). Or look through the sources that turn up in response to other terms to see what keywords you might use in subsequent searches. Searching requires flexibility, in the words you use and the methods you try.

Reference Works

The reference section of your school's library is the place to find encyclopedias, dictionaries, atlases, almanacs, bibliographies, and other reference works in print. Many of these sources are also online and can be accessed from any computer that is connected to the Internet. Others are available only in the library. Remember, though, that whether in print or online, reference works are only a starting point, a place where you can get an overview of your topic.

General reference works. Consult encyclopedias for general background information on a subject, dictionaries for definitions of words, atlases for maps and geographic data, and almanacs for statistics and other data on current events. These are some works you might consult:

The New Encyclopaedia Britannica

The Columbia Encyclopedia

Webster's Third New International Dictionary

Oxford English Dictionary

National Geographic Atlas of the World

Statistical Abstract of the United States

The World Almanac and Book of Facts

Specialized reference works. You can also go to specialized reference works, which provide in-depth information on a single field or topic. These may also include authoritative bibliographies, leading you to more specific works. A reference librarian can refer you to specialized encyclopedias in particular fields; but you'll find a list of some at wwnorton.com/write/fieldguide.

Bibliographies. Bibliographies provide an overview of what has been published on a topic, listing published works along with the information you'll need to find each work. Some are annotated with brief summaries of each work's contents. You'll find bibliographies at the end of scholarly articles and books, and you can also find book-length bibliographies, both

in the reference section of your library and online. Check with a reference librarian for bibliographies on your research topic.

Books / Searching the Library Catalog

The library catalog is your primary source for finding books. Most library catalogs are computerized and can be accessed through the library's Web site. You can search by author, title, subject, or keyword. The image below shows the result of a keyword search for material on art in Nazi Germany. This search revealed that the library has nineteen books on the topic; to access information on each one, the researcher must simply click on the title. The second image shows complete information for one source: bibliographic data about author, title, and publication; call

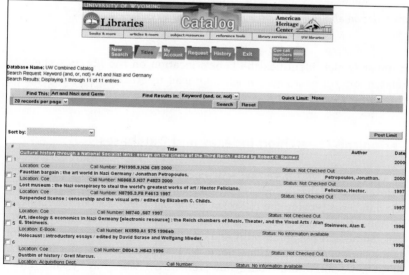

List of books on a library catalog screen.

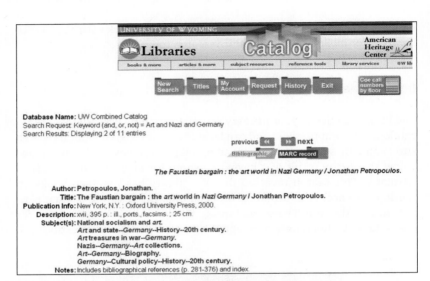

Information about a book on a library catalog screen.

number (which identifies the book's location on the library's shelves); related subject headings (which may lead to other useful materials in the library) — and more.

Periodicals / Searching Indexes and Databases

To find journal and magazine articles, you will need to search periodical indexes and databases. Indexes provide listings of articles organized by topics; databases provide the full texts. Some databases also include indexes of bibliographic citations, which you may use to track down the actual articles. Some indexes are in print and can be found in the reference section of the library; many are online. Some databases are available for free; most of the more authoritative ones, however, are available only by subscription and so must be accessed through a library.

Print indexes.   You'll need to consult print indexes to find articles published before the 1980s. Here are six useful ones:

> *The Readers' Guide to Periodical Literature* (print, 1900–; online, 1983–)
>
> *Magazine Index* (print, 1988–; online via InfoTrac, 1973–)
>
> *The New York Times Index* (print and online, 1851–)
>
> *Humanities Index* (print, 1974–; online, 1984–)
>
> *Social Sciences Index* (print, 1974–; online, 1983–)
>
> *General Science Index* (print, 1978–; online, 1984–)

General electronic indexes and databases.   A reference librarian can help you determine which databases will be most helpful to you, but here are some useful ones:

Academic Search Premier is a multidisciplinary index and database containing the full text of articles in more than 3,600 journals and indexing of over 8,000 journals, with abstracts of their articles.

EBSCOhost provides interlinked databases of abstracts and full-text articles from a variety of periodicals.

FirstSearch offers access to more than 10 million full-text, full-image articles in dozens of databases covering many disciplines.

InfoTrac offers over 15 million full-text articles in a broad spectrum of disciplines and on a wide variety of topics from over 5,000 scholarly and popular periodicals, including the *New York Times*.

JSTOR archives scanned copies of entire publication runs of scholarly journals in many disciplines, but it does not include current issues of the journals.

LexisNexis Academic Universe contains full-text publications and articles from a large number of sources — newspapers, business and legal resources, medical texts, and reference sources such as *The World Almanac* and the Roper public opinion polls.

MasterFile Premier provides full-text articles from more than 1,900 general reference, business, consumer health, general science, and multicultural periodicals as well as indexing of another 2,510 periodicals and abstracts of their articles.

ProQuest provides access to full-text articles from thousands of periodicals and newspapers from 1986 to the present, with many entries updated daily.

SIRS Researcher contains records of articles from selected domestic and international newspapers, magazines, journals, and government publications.

Single-subject indexes and databases. These are just a sample of what's available; check with a reference librarian for indexes and databases in the subject you're researching.

America: History and Life indexes scholarly literature on the history of the United States and Canada.

American Humanities Index contains bibliographic references to more than 1,000 journals dealing with the humanities.

BIOSIS Previews provides abstracts and indexes for more than 5,500 sources on biology, botany, zoology, environmental studies, and agriculture.

ERIC is the U.S. Department of Education's Educational Resource Information Center database.

Historical Abstracts includes abstracts of articles on the history of the world, excluding the United States and Canada, since 1450.

MLA International Bibliography indexes scholarly articles on modern languages, literature, folklore, and linguistics.

PsychINFO indexes scholarly literature in a number of disciplines relating to psychology.

Web-based indexes and databases. The following are freely available on the Internet:

Infomine contains "useful Internet resources such as databases, electronic journals, electronic books, bulletin boards, mailing lists, online library card catalogs, articles, directories of researchers, and many other types of information."

rhetorical situations　genres　processes　strategies　research mla/apa　media/design

Librarians' Index to the Internet is "a searchable, annotated subject directory of more than 14,000 Internet resources selected and evaluated by librarians for their usefulness to users of public libraries."

The World Wide Web Virtual Library is a catalog of Web sites on a wide range of subjects, compiled by volunteers with expertise in particular subject areas.

CSA: Hot Topics Series provides comprehensive information on current issues in biomedicine, engineering, the environment, the social sciences, and the humanities, with an overview of each subject, key citations with abstracts, and links to Web sites.

The Voice of the Shuttle: Web Site for Humanities Research offers information on subjects in the humanities, organized to mirror the way the humanities are organized for research and teaching as well as the way they are adapting to social, cultural, and technological changes.

The Library of Congress offers online access to information on a wide range of subjects, including academic subjects, as well as prints, photographs, and government documents.

Education Index is an annotated guide to education-related sites on the Web, sorted by subject and life stage.

JURIST is a university-based online gateway to authoritative legal instruction, information, and scholarship.

The Web

The Web provides access to countless sites containing information posted by governments, educational institutions, organizations, businesses, and individuals. Web sites are different from other sources in several ways: (1) they often provide entire texts, not just citations of texts, (2) their content varies greatly in its reliability, and (3) they are not stable: what you see on a site today may be different (or gone) tomorrow. Anyone who wants to can post texts on the Web, so you need to **EVALUATE** carefully what you find there.

354–57

Because it is so vast and dynamic, finding what you want on the Web can be a challenge. The primary way of finding information on the Web is with a search engine. There are several ways of searching the Web:

- *Keyword searches.* Google, HotBot, AltaVista, Lycos, and Yahoo! all scan the Web looking for keywords that you specify.

- *Subject directories.* Google, Yahoo! and some other search engines offer directories that arrange information by topics, much like a library cataloging system. Such directories allow you to broaden or narrow your search if you need to—for example, a search for "birds" can be broadened to "animals" or narrowed to "blue-footed booby."

- *Metasearches.* MetaCrawler, Vivísimo, SurfWax, and Dogpile are metasearch engines that allow you to use several search engines simultaneously.

- *Academic searches.* You may find more suitable results for academic writing at Google Scholar (scholar.google.com), a search engine that finds scholarly literature, including peer-reviewed papers, technical reports, and abstracts, or at Scirus (scirus.com), which finds peer-reviewed documents on scientific, technical, and medical topics.

Each search engine and metasearch engine has its own protocols for searching; most have an "advanced search" option that will help you search more productively. Remember, though, that you need to be careful about evaluating sources that you find on the Web because the Web is unregulated and no one independently verifies the information posted on its sites.

Doing Field Research

Sometimes you'll need to do your own research, to go beyond the information you find in published sources and gather data by doing field research. Two kinds of field research you might want to consider are interviews and observations.

rhetorical situations   genres   processes   strategies   research mla/apa   media/ design

Interviewing experts.   Some kinds of writing—a profile of a living person, for instance—almost require that you conduct an interview. And sometimes you may just need to find information that you haven't been able to find in published sources. To get firsthand information on the experience of serving as a soldier in Iraq, you might interview your cousin who served a tour of duty there, or to find current research on pesticide residues in food, you might need to interview a toxicologist. Whatever your goal, you can conduct interviews face-to-face, over the telephone, or by mail or email. In general, you will want to use interviews to find information you can't find elsewhere. Below is some advice on planning and conducting an interview.

Before the interview

1. Once you identify someone you want to interview, email or phone to ask for an appointment, stating your **PURPOSE** for the interview and what you hope to learn.
2. Once you've set up the appointment, send a note or email confirming the time and place. If you wish to record the interview, be sure to ask for permission to do so. If you plan to conduct the interview by mail or email, state when you will send your questions.
3. Write out questions. Plan questions that invite extended response: "What accounts for the recent spike in gasoline prices?" forces an explanation, whereas "Is the recent spike in gas prices a direct result of global politics?" is likely to elicit only a yes or a no.

At the interview

4. Record the full name of the person you interview, along with the date, time, and place of the interview; you'll need this information to cite and document the interview accurately.
5. Take notes, even if you are recording the interview.
6. Keep track of time: don't take more than you agreed to beforehand unless both of you agree to keep talking. End by saying thank you and offering to provide a copy of your final product.

After the interview

7. Flesh out your notes with details as soon as possible after the interview, while you still remember them.

8. Be sure to send a thank-you note or email.

Observation. Some writing projects are based on information you get by observing something. For a sociology paper, you may observe how students behave in large lectures. For an education course, you may observe one child's progress as a writer over a period of time. The following advice can help you conduct observations.

Before observing

3–4

1. Think about your research **PURPOSE:** What are you looking for? What do you expect to find? How will your presence as an observer affect what you observe? What do you plan to do with what you find?

2. If necessary, set up an appointment. You may need to ask permission of the people you wish to observe. Be honest and open about your goals and intentions; college students doing research assignments are often welcomed where others may not be.

While observing

3. You may want to divide each page of your notepaper down the middle vertically and write only on the left side of the page, reserving the right side for information you will fill in later.

285–88

4. Note **DESCRIPTIVE** details about the setting. What do you see? What do you hear? Do you smell anything? Get down details about color, shape, size, sound, and so on. Consider photographing or making a sketch of what you see.

285–93

5. Who is there, and what are they doing? **DESCRIBE** what they look like, and make notes about what they say. Note any significant demographic details—about gender, race, occupation, age, dress, and so on.

304–12

6. What is happening? Who's doing what? What's being said? Note down these kinds of **NARRATIVE** details.

After observing

7. As soon as possible after you complete your observations, use the right side of your pages to fill in gaps and note additional details.

8. **ANALYZE** your notes, looking for patterns. Did some things appear or happen more than once? Did anything stand out? surprise or puzzle you? What did you learn?

255–59

> See **EVALUATING SOURCES** for help determining their usefulness. See also Chapter 42 for help taking notes on your sources.

354–57

41 Evaluating Sources

Searching the *Health Source* database for information on the incidence of meningitis among college students, you find seventeen articles. A Google search on the same topic produces over ten thousand hits. How do you decide which sources to read? This chapter presents advice on evaluating sources — first to determine whether a source is useful for your purposes and then to read with a critical eye the ones you choose.

Considering the Reliability of Print and Online Sources

Books and journals that have been published in print have most likely been evaluated by editors, publishers, or expert reviewers before publication. Magazines and newspapers have probably been fact-checked; not so most Web sites — anyone who wishes to post something on the Web can do so. In addition, Web sources come and go, and are easily changed. So print sources are always more stable and often more trustworthy.

Considering Whether a Source Serves Your Purpose

3–4 ■ Think about your **PURPOSE.** Are you trying to persuade readers to believe or do something? To inform them about something? If the former, it will be especially important to find sources representing various stances; if the latter, you may need sources that are more factual or informative. Recon-
5–8 ■ sider your **AUDIENCE.** What kinds of sources will they find persuasive? If you're writing for readers in a particular field, what counts as evidence in that field? Following are some questions that can help you select useful sources:

rhetorical situations   genres   processes   strategies   research mla/apa   media/ design

- *Is it relevant?* How does the source relate to your purpose? What will it add to your work? Look at the title and at any introductory material—a preface, abstract, or introduction—to see what it covers.

- *What are the author's credentials?* What are the author's qualifications to write on the subject? Is he or she associated with a particular position on the issue? If the source is a book or a periodical, see whether it mentions other works this author has written. If it's a Web site, see whether an author is identified. If one is, you might do a Web search to see what else you can learn about him or her.

- *What is the stance?* Consider whether a source covers various points of view or advocates one particular point of view. Does its title suggest a certain slant? If it's a Web site, you might check to see whether it includes links to other sites of one or many perspectives. You'll want to consult sources with a variety of viewpoints.

- *Who is the publisher?* If it's a book, what kind of company published it; if an article, what kind of periodical did it appear in? Books published by university presses and articles in scholarly journals are reviewed by experts before they are published. Books and articles written for general audiences typically do not undergo rigorous review—and they may lack the kind of in-depth discussion that is useful to the researcher of an academic work.

- *If it's a Web site, who is the sponsor?* Is the site maintained by an organization? an interest group? a government agency? an individual? If the site doesn't give this information, look for clues in the URL: *edu* is used mostly by colleges and universities, *gov* by government agencies, *org* by nonprofit organizations, *mil* by the military, and *com* by commercial organizations.

- *What is the level?* Can you understand the material? Texts written for a general audience might be easier to understand but are not likely to be authoritative enough for academic work. Texts written for scholars will be more authoritative but may be hard to comprehend.

- *When was it published?* See when books and articles were published. Check to see when Web sites were last updated. (If the site lists no date, see if links to other sites still work.) Recent does not necessarily mean better—some topics may require very current information whereas others may call for older sources.

- **Is it *available*?** Is it a source you can get hold of? If it's a book and your school's library doesn't have it, can you get it through interlibrary loan?

- **Does it *include other useful information*?** Is there a bibliography that might lead you to other sources? How current are the sources it cites?

Reading Sources with a Critical Eye

82–106 ▲
- **What ARGUMENTS does the author make?** Does the author present a number of different positions, or does he or she argue for a particular position? Do you need to **ANALYZE THE ARGUMENT?**
324–27 ◆

- **How *persuasive* do you find the argument?** What reasons and evidence does the author provide in support of any position(s)? Are there citations or links—and if so, are they credible? Is any evidence presented without citations? Do you find any of the author's assumptions questionable? How thoroughly does he or she consider opposing arguments?

12–14 ■
- **What is the author's STANCE?** Does the author strive for objectivity, or does the language reveal a particular bias? Is the author associated with a special interest that might signal a certain perspective? Does he or she consider opposing views? Do the sources cited reflect multiple viewpoints, or only one?

- **Does the *publisher* bring a certain stance to the work?** Book publishers, periodicals, or Web sites that are clearly liberal or conservative or advance a particular agenda will likely express views reflecting their
12–14 ■
  STANCE.

- **Do you recognize ideas you've run across in other sources?** Does it leave out any information that other sources include?

- **Does this source support or challenge your own position—or does it do both?** Does it support your thesis? offer a different argument altogether? Does it represent a position you may need to **ACKNOWLEDGE** or
100–01 ▲

■ rhetorical situations ▲ genres ○ processes ◆ strategies ● research mla/apa □ media/ design

REFUTE? Don't reject a source that challenges your views; your sources should reflect a variety of views on your topic, showing that you've considered the subject thoroughly.

▲ 101

• *What can you tell about the intended AUDIENCE and PURPOSE?* Are you a member of the audience addressed—and if not, does that affect the way you interpret what you read? Is the main purpose to inform readers about a topic or to argue a certain point?

■ 3–8

> See QUOTING, PARAPHRASING, AND SUMMARIZING for help in taking notes on your sources and deciding how to use them in your writing. See also ACKNOWLEDGING SOURCES, AVOIDING PLAGIARISM for advice on giving credit to the sources you use.

● 358–74

42 Quoting, Paraphrasing, and Summarizing

In an oral presentation about the rhetoric of Abraham Lincoln, you quote a memorable line from the Gettysburg Address. For an essay on the Tet Offensive in the Vietnam War, you paraphrase arguments made by several commentators and summarize some key debates about that war. Like all writers, you work with the ideas and words of others. This chapter will help you with the specifics of quoting, paraphrasing, and summarizing source materials that you wish to use in your writing.

Taking Notes

When you find material you think will be useful, take careful notes. How do you determine how much or how little to record? You need to write down enough information so that when you refer to it later, you will be reminded of the main points, and you need to keep a precise record of where the information comes from.

- *Use index cards, a computer file, or a notebook,* labeling each entry with the information that will allow you to keep track of where it comes from—author, title, and the pages or the URL. You needn't write down full bibliographic information (you can abbreviate author's name and title) since you'll include that information in your **WORKING BIBLIOGRAPHY.**

335–36

- *Take notes in your own words, and use your own sentence patterns.* If you make a note that is a detailed **PARAPHRASE**, label it as such so that you'll know to provide appropriate **DOCUMENTATION** if you use it.

363–66
375–449

rhetorical situations · genres · processes · strategies · research mla/apa · media/design

- *If you find wording that you'd like to quote*, be sure to enclose it in quotation marks to distinguish your source's words from your own. Double-check your notes to be sure any quoted material is accurately quoted—and that you haven't accidentally PLAGIARIZED your sources.

370–74

- *Label each note with a subject heading.*

Here's an example of one writer's notes:

Source: Steingraber, "Pesticides" (976)

— 1938: pathbreaking experiments showed that dogs exposed to aromatic amines developed cancer of the bladder.

— aromatic amines: chemicals used in coal-derived synthetic dyes

— Mauve the first synthetic dye—invented in 1854—then synthetic dyes replaced most natural dyes made with plants

— Bladder cancer common among textile workers who used dyes

— Steingraber: "By the beginning of the twentieth century, bladder cancer rates among this group of workers had skyrocketed, and the dog experiments helped unravel this mystery."

— 1921: International Labor Organization labels a.a. as carcinogenic (before experiments)

— Dog experiments also helped explain: early 20th century: metal workers, machinists, and workers in the tire industry developed bladder cancer—cutting oils contained aromatic amines to inhibit rust used a.a. accelerants.

— Sandra Steingraber: biologist and ecologist

Deciding Whether to Quote, Paraphrase, or Summarize

When it comes time to DRAFT, you'll need to decide *how* to use the sources you've found—in other words, whether to quote, paraphrase, or summarize. You might follow this rule of thumb: QUOTE texts when the wording is worth repeating or makes a point so well that no rewording will do it

205–07

360–63

363–66

justice, when you want to cite the exact words of a known authority on your topic, when his or her opinions challenge or disagree with those of others, or when the source is one you want to emphasize. **PARAPHRASE** sources that are not worth quoting but contain details you need to include.

366–67

SUMMARIZE longer passages whose main points are important but whose details are not.

Quoting

Quoting a source is a way of weaving someone else's exact words into your text. You need to reproduce the source exactly, though you can modify it to omit unnecessary details (with ellipses) or to make it fit smoothly into your text (with brackets). You also need to distinguish quoted material from your own by enclosing short quotations in quotation marks and setting off longer quotes as a block.

Incorporate short quotations into your text, enclosed in quotation marks. If you are following MLA style, this rule holds for four typed lines or fewer; if you are following APA style, short means no more than forty words.

> Gerald Graff argues that colleges make the intellectual life seem more opaque than it needs to be, leaving many students with "the misconception that the life of the mind is a secret society for which only an elite few qualify."

If you are quoting three lines or less of poetry, run them in with your text, enclosed in quotation marks. Separate lines with slashes, leaving one space on each side of the slashes.

> Emma Lazarus almost speaks for the Statue of Liberty with the words inscribed on its pedestal: "Give me your tired, your poor, / Your huddled masses yearning to breathe free, / The wretched refuse of your teeming shore."

rhetorical situations　　genres　　processes　　strategies　　research mla/apa　　media/ design

Set off long quotations block style.   If you are using MLA style, set off quotations of five or more typed lines by indenting the quote one inch (or ten spaces) from the left margin. If you are using APA style, indent quotes of forty or more words one-half inch (or five spaces) from the left margin. In either case, do not use quotation marks, and put any parenthetical citation *after* any end punctuation.

> Nonprofit organizations such as Oxfam and Habitat for Humanity rely on visual representations of the poor. What better way to get our attention, asks Diana George:
>
>> In a culture saturated by the image, how else do we convince Americans that — despite the prosperity they see all around them — there is real need out there? The solution for most nonprofits has been to show the despair. To do that they must represent poverty as something that can be seen and easily recognized: fallen down shacks and trashed out public housing, broken windows, dilapidated porches, barefoot kids with stringy hair, emaciated old women and men staring out at the camera with empty eyes. (210)

If you are quoting four or more lines of poetry, they need to be set off block style in the same way.

Indicate any omissions with ellipses.   You may sometimes delete words from a quotation that are unnecessary for your point. Insert three ellipsis marks (leaving a space before the first and after the last one) to indicate the deletion. If you omit a sentence or more in the middle of a quotation, put a period before the three ellipsis dots.

> Faigley points out that Gore's "Information Superhighway" metaphor "associated the economic prosperity of the 1950s and . . . 1960s facilitated by new highways with the potential for vast . . . commerce to be conducted over the Internet" (253).

> According to Welch, "Television is more acoustic than visual. . . . One can turn one's gaze way from the television, but one cannot turn one's ears from it without leaving the area where the monitor leaks its aural signals into every corner" (102).

Indicate additions or changes with brackets. Sometimes you'll need to change or add words in a quote—to make the quote fit grammatically within your sentence, for example, or to add a comment. In the following example, the writer changes the passage "one of our goals" to fit the grammar of her sentences:

> Writing about the dwindling attention among some composition scholars to the actual teaching of writing, Susan Miller notes that "few discussions of writing pedagogy take it for granted that one of [their] goals is to teach how to write" (480).

Here's an example of brackets used to add explanatory words to a quotation:

> Barbosa observes that even Buarque's lyrics have long included "many a metaphor of *saudades* [yearning] so characteristic of *fado* music" (207).

A note about punctuating quotes. When you incorporate a quotation into your text, you have to think about the end punctuation in the quoted material and also about any punctuation you need to add when you insert the quote into your own sentence.

Periods and commas. With brief quotations, put periods or commas inside the quotation marks, except when you have a parenthetical citation at the end, in which case you put the period after the parentheses.

> "Country music," Tichi says, "is a crucial and vital part of the American identity" (23).

With long quotes set off block style, however, there are no quotation marks, so the period goes *before* the citation, as shown in the example on page 361.

Question marks and exclamation points. These go *inside* closing quotation marks if they are part of the quoted material but outside when they are not. Notice, however, that when there's a parenthetical citation at the end, it is followed by a period.

> Speaking at a Fourth of July celebration in 1852, Frederick Douglass asked, "What have I, or those I represent, to do with your national independence?" (35).

rhetorical situations

genres

processes

strategies

research mla/apa

media/ design

Who can argue with W. Charisse Goodman's observation that media images persuade women that "thinness equals happiness and fulfillment"? (53).

Colons and semicolons. These always go outside the quotation marks.

It's hard to argue with W. Charisse Goodman's observation that media images persuade women that "thinness equals happiness and fulfillment"; nevertheless, American women today are more overweight than ever (53).

Paraphrasing

When you paraphrase, you restate information from a source in your own words, using your own sentence structures. Paraphrase when the source material is important but the original wording is not. Because it includes all the main points of the source, a paraphrase is usually about the same length as the original.

Here is a paragraph about synthetic dyes and cancer, followed by three example paraphrases. The first two demonstrate some of the challenges of paraphrasing:

ORIGINAL SOURCE

In 1938, in a series of now-classic experiments, exposure to synthetic dyes derived from coal and belonging to a class of chemicals called aromatic amines was shown to cause bladder cancer in dogs. These results helped explain why bladder cancers had become so prevalent among dyestuffs workers. With the invention of mauve in 1854, synthetic dyes began replacing natural plant-based dyes in the coloring of cloth and leather. By the beginning of the twentieth century, bladder cancer rates among this group of workers had skyrocketed, and the dog experiments helped unravel this mystery. The International Labor Organization did not wait for the results of these animal tests, however, and in 1921 declared certain aromatic amines to be human carcinogens. Decades later, these dogs provided a lead in understanding why tire-industry workers, as well as machinists and metalworkers, also began falling victim to bladder cancer: aromatic amines had been added to rubbers and cutting oils to serve as accelerants and antirust agents.

—Sandra Steingraber, "Pesticides, Animals, and Humans"

UNACCEPTABLE PARAPHRASE: WORDING TOO CLOSE

<u>Now-classic experiments</u> in 1938 showed that when dogs were exposed to aromatic amines, chemicals used in <u>synthetic dyes derived from coal</u>, they developed bladder cancer. Similar cancers were <u>prevalent among dyestuffs workers</u>, and <u>these</u> experiments <u>helped</u> to <u>explain why</u>. Mauve, a synthetic dye, was invented in 1854, after which <u>cloth and leather</u> manufacturers replaced most of the natural plant-based dyes with synthetic dyes. <u>By the</u> early <u>twentieth century</u>, <u>this group of workers had skyrocketing</u> rates of bladder cancer, a <u>mystery the dog experiments helped to unravel</u>. As early as 1921, though, before the test results proved the connection, the International Labor Organization had labeled <u>certain aromatic amines</u> carcinogenic. Even so, <u>decades later</u> many metalworkers, machinists, and tire-industry workers began developing bladder cancer. The animal tests helped researchers understand that <u>rubbers and cutting oils</u> contained aromatic amines <u>as accelerants and antirust agents</u> (Steingraber 976).

This paraphrase borrows too much of the language of the original or changes it only slightly, as the underlined words and phrases show.

UNACCEPTABLE PARAPHRASE: SENTENCE STRUCTURE TOO CLOSE

In 1938, several pathbreaking experiments showed that being exposed to synthetic dyes that are made from coal and belong to a type of chemicals called aromatic amines caused dogs to get bladder cancer. These results helped researchers identify why cancers of the bladder had become so common among textile workers who worked with dyes. With the development of mauve in 1854, synthetic dyes began to be used instead of dyes based on plants in the dyeing of leather and cloth. By the end of the nineteenth century, rates of bladder cancer among these workers had increased dramatically, and the experiments using dogs helped clear up this oddity. The International

Labor Organization anticipated the results of these tests on animals, though, and in 1921 labeled some aromatic amines carcinogenic. Years later these experiments with dogs helped researchers explain why workers in the tire industry, as well as metalworkers and machinists, also started dying of bladder cancer: aromatic amines had been put into rubbers and cutting oils as rust inhibitors and accelerants (Steingraber 976).

This paraphrase uses original language but follows the sentence structure of Steingraber's text too closely.

ACCEPTABLE PARAPHRASE

Steingraber explains that pathbreaking experiments in 1938 demonstrated that dogs exposed to aromatic amines (chemicals used in coal-derived synthetic dyes) developed cancers of the bladder that were similar to cancers common among dyers in the textile industry. After mauve, the first synthetic dye, was invented in 1854, leather and cloth manufacturers replaced most natural dyes made from plants with synthetic dyes, and by the early 1900s textile workers had very high rates of bladder cancer. The experiments with dogs proved the connection, but years before, in 1921, the International Labor Organization had labeled some aromatic amines carcinogenic. Even so, years later many metalworkers, machinists, and workers in the tire industry started to develop unusually high rates of bladder cancer. The experiments with dogs helped researchers understand that the cancers were caused by aromatic amines used in cutting oils to inhibit rust and in rubbers as accelerants (976).

Some guidelines for paraphrasing

- *Use your own words and sentence structure.* It is acceptable to quote a word or phrase from the original (in quotation marks), but for the most part the words and sentence structures should be your own.

- *Put in quotation marks any of the source's wording that you use.* Quotation marks distinguish the source's words from your own.

- *Indicate the source of your paraphrase.* Although the wording may be yours, the ideas and information come from another source; be sure to name the author and include an **IN-TEXT CITATION** to avoid the possibility of **PLAGIARISM**.

375–88
417–25
370–74

Summarizing

A summary states the main ideas found in a source concisely and in your own words. Unlike a paraphrase, a summary does *not* present all the details so it is generally as brief as possible. Summaries may boil down an entire book or essay into a single sentence, or they may take a paragraph or more to present the main ideas. Here, for example, is a summary of the Steingraber paragraph:

> Steingraber explains that experiments with dogs demonstrated that aromatic amines, chemicals used in synthetic dyes, cutting oils, and rubber, cause bladder cancer (976).

In the context of an essay, the summary might take this form:

> Medical researchers have long relied on experiments using animals to expand understanding of the causes of disease. For example, biologist and ecologist Sandra Steingraber notes that in the second half of the nineteenth century, the rate of bladder cancer soared among textile workers. According to Steingraber, experiments with dogs demonstrated that synthetic chemicals in dyes used to color the textiles caused the cancer (976).

Some guidelines for summarizing

- *Include only the main ideas; leave out the details.* A summary should include just enough information to give the reader the gist of the original. It is always much shorter than the original, sometimes even as brief as one sentence.

rhetorical situations · genres · processes · strategies · research mla/apa · media/ design

- *Use your own words.* If you use any words from the original, enclose them in quotation marks.

- *Indicate the source.* Although the wording may be yours, the ideas and information come from another source. Name the author, either in a signal phrase or parentheses, and include an appropriate **IN-TEXT CITATION** to avoid the possibility of **PLAGIARISM.**

375–88
417–25
370–74

Incorporating Source Materials into Your Text

You need to introduce quotations, paraphrases, and summaries clearly, letting readers know who the author is — and, if need be, something about his or her credentials. Consider this sentence:

> Professor and textbook author Elaine Tyler May argues that many high school history books are too bland to interest young readers (531).

The beginning ("Professor and textbook author Elaine Tyler May argues") functions as a *signal phrase*, telling readers who is making the assertion and why she has the authority to speak on the topic — and making clear that everything between the signal phrase and the parenthetical citation comes from that source. Since the signal phrase names the author, the parenthetical citation includes only the page number; had there been no mention of the author, she would have been named in the parentheses as in the following example:

> Even some textbook authors believe that many high school history books are too bland to interest young readers (May 531).

Signal phrases.   A signal phrase tells readers who says or believes something. The verb you use can be neutral — *says* or *thinks* — or it can suggest something about the **STANCE** — the source's or your own. The above example about the textbook author uses the verb *claims*, suggesting that what she says is arguable (or that the writer believes it is). How

12–14

would it change your understanding if the signal verb were *observes* or *suggests*?

Some common signal verbs

acknowledges	claims	disagrees	observes
admits	comments	disputes	points out
advises	concludes	emphasizes	reasons
agrees	concurs	grants	rejects
argues	confirms	illustrates	reports
asserts	contends	implies	responds
believes	declares	insists	suggests
charges	denies	notes	thinks

Verb tenses. MLA and APA have different conventions regarding the verbs that introduce signal phrases. MLA requires present-tense verbs (*writes, asserts, notes*) in signal phrases to introduce a work you are quoting, paraphrasing, or summarizing.

> In *Poor Richard's Almanack*, Benjamin Franklin <u>notes</u>, "He that cannot obey, cannot command" (739).

If, however, you are referring to the act of writing something rather than simply quoting someone's words, you might not use the present tense. The writer of the following sentence focuses on the year in which the source was written—therefore, the verb is necessarily in the past tense:

> Back in 1941, Kenneth Burke <u>wrote</u> that "the ethical values of work are in its application of the competitive equipment to cooperative ends" (316).

If you are following APA style, use the past tense or present-perfect tense to introduce sources composed in the past.

> Dowdall, Crawford, and Wechsler (1998) <u>observed</u> that women attending women's colleges are less likely to engage in binge drinking than are women who attend coeducational colleges (p. 713).

rhetorical situations · genres · processes · strategies · research mla/apa · media/ design

APA requires the present tense, however, to discuss the results of an experiment or to explain conclusions that are generally agreed on.

> The findings of this study <u>suggest</u> that excessive drinking has serious consequences for college students and their institutions.

> The authors of numerous studies <u>agree</u> that smoking and drinking among adolescents are associated with lower academic achievement.

See the section on **ACKNOWLEDGING SOURCES, AVOIDING PLAGIARISM** for help in giving credit to the sources you use. See also the **SAMPLE RESEARCH PAPERS** to see how sources are cited in MLA and APA styles.

370–74

407–16

438–49

43 Acknowledging Sources, Avoiding Plagiarism

Whenever you do research-based writing, you find yourself entering a conversation—reading what many others have had to say about your topic, figuring out what you yourself think, and then putting what you think in writing—"putting in your oar," as the rhetorician Kenneth Burke once wrote. As a writer, you need to *acknowledge* any words and ideas that come from others—to give credit where credit is due, to recognize the various authorities and many perspectives you have considered, to show readers where they can find your sources, and to situate your own arguments in the ongoing conversation. Using other people's words and ideas without acknowledgment is *plagiarism,* a serious academic and ethical offense. This chapter will show you how to acknowledge the materials you use and avoid plagiarism.

Acknowledging Sources

When you insert in your text information that you've obtained from others, your reader needs to know where your source's words or ideas begin and end. Therefore, you should introduce a source by naming the author in a **SIGNAL PHRASE,** and follow it with a brief parenthetical **IN-TEXT CITATION** or by naming the author in a parenthetical citation. (You need only a brief citation here, since your readers will find full bibliographic information in your list of **WORKS CITED** [MLA] or **REFERENCES** [APA].)

367–68
375–88
417–25
388–407
426–38

Sources that need acknowledgment. You almost always need to acknowledge any information that you get from a specific source. Material you should acknowledge includes the following:

rhetorical situations   genres   processes   strategies   research mla/apa   media/ design

- *Direct quotations.* Any words that you quote from another source must be enclosed in quotation marks, cited with brief bibliographic information in parentheses, and introduced with a signal phrase that tells who wrote it and provides necessary contextual information, as in the following sentence:

  > In a dissenting opinion on the issue of racial preferences in college admissions, Supreme Court justice Ruth Bader Ginsburg argues, "The stain of generations of racial oppression is still visible in our society, and the determination to hasten its removal remains vital" (*Gratz v. Bollinger*).

- *Arguable statements and information that may not be common knowledge.* If you state something about which there is disagreement or for which arguments can be made, cite the source of your statement. If in doubt about whether you need to give the source of an assertion, provide it. As part of an essay on "fake news" programs like *The Daily Show*, for example, you might make the following assertion:

  > The satire of *The Daily Show* complements the conservative bias of Fox News, since both have abandoned the stance of objectivity maintained by mainstream news sources, notes Michael Hoyt, executive editor of the *Columbia Journalism Review* (43).

Others might argue with the contention that the Fox News Channel offers biased reports of the news, so the source of this assertion needs to be acknowledged. In the same essay, you might present information that should be cited because it's not widely known, as in this example:

  > According to a report by the Pew Research Center, 21 percent of Americans under thirty got information about the 2004 presidential campaign primarily from "fake news" and comedy shows like *The Daily Show* and *Saturday Night Live* (2).

- *The opinions and assertions of others.* When you present the ideas, opinions, and assertions of others, cite the source. You may have rewritten the concept in your own words, but the ideas were generated by someone else and must be acknowledged, as they are here:

> Social philosopher David Boonin, writing in the *Journal of Social Philosophy*, asserts that logically, laws banning marriage between people of different races are not discriminatory since everyone of each race is affected equally by them. Laws banning same-sex unions are discriminatory, however, since they apply only to people with a certain sexual orientation (256).

- *Any information that you didn't generate yourself.* If you did not do the research or compile the data yourself, cite your source. This goes for interviews, statistics, graphs, charts, visuals, photographs — anything you use that you did not create. If you create a chart using data from another source, you need to cite that source.

- *Collaboration with and help from others.* In many of your courses and in work situations, you'll be called on to work with others. You may get help with your writing at your school's writing center or from fellow students in your writing courses. Acknowledging such collaboration or assistance, in a brief informational note, is a way of giving credit—and saying thank you. See guidelines for writing notes in the **MLA** and **APA** sections of this book.

388 ●
425 ●

Sources that don't need acknowledgment.   Widely available information and common knowledge do not require acknowledgment. What constitutes common knowledge may not be clear, however. When in doubt, provide a citation, or ask your instructor whether the information needs to be cited. You generally do not need to cite the following sources:

- *Information that most readers are likely to know.* You don't need to acknowledge information that is widely known or commonly accepted as fact. For example, in a literary analysis, you wouldn't cite a source saying that Harriet Beecher Stowe wrote *Uncle Tom's Cabin;* you can assume your readers already know that. On the other hand, you should cite the source from which you got the information stating that the book was first published in installments in a magazine and then, with revisions, in book form, because that information isn't common knowledge. As you do research in areas you're not familiar with, be aware that what constitutes common knowledge isn't always clear; the history of the novel's publication would be known to Stowe scholars and would likely need no acknowledgment in an essay written for them. In this case, too, if you aren't sure whether to acknowledge information, do so.

- *Information and documents that are widely available.* If a piece of information appears in several sources or reference works or if a document has been published widely, you needn't cite a source for it. For example, the date when astronauts Neil Armstrong and Buzz Aldrin landed a spacecraft on the moon can be found in any number of reference works. Similarly, the Declaration of Independence and the Gettysburg Address are reprinted in thousands of sources, so the ones where you found them need no citation.

- *Well-known quotations.* These include such famous quotations as Lady Macbeth's "Out, damned spot!" and John F. Kennedy's "Ask not what your country can do for you; ask what you can do for your country." Be sure, however, that the quotation is correct; Winston Churchill is said to have told a class of schoolchildren, "Never, ever, ever, ever, ever, ever, ever give up. Never give up. Never give up. Never give up." His actual words, however, taken from a longer speech, are much different and begin "Never give in."

- *Material that you created or gathered yourself.* You need not cite photographs that you took, graphs that you composed, or material from an interview or data from an experiment or survey that you conducted—though you should make sure readers know that the work is yours.

A good rule of thumb: *when in doubt, cite your source.* You're unlikely to be criticized for citing too much—but you may invite charges of plagiarism by citing too little.

Avoiding Plagiarism

When you use the words or ideas of others, you need to acknowledge who and where the material came from; if you don't credit those sources, you are guilty of plagiarism. Plagiarism is often committed unintentionally— as when a writer paraphrases someone else's ideas in language that is close to the original. It is essential, therefore, to know what constitutes plagiarism: (1) using another writer's words or ideas without in-text citation and documentation, (2) using another writer's exact words without quotation marks, and (3) paraphrasing or summarizing someone else's ideas using language or sentence structures that are too close to theirs.

358–59

To avoid plagiarizing, take careful **NOTES** as you do your research, clearly labeling as quotations any words you quote directly and being careful to use your own words and sentence structures in paraphrases and summaries. Be sure you know what source material you must **DOCUMENT**,

375–449
426–38
388–407

and give credit to your sources, both in the text and in a list of **REFERENCES** or **WORKS CITED**. Be especially careful with material found online—copying source material right into a document you are writing is all too easy to do. You must acknowledge information you find on the Web just as you must acknowledge all other source materials.

And you must recognize that plagiarism has consequences. Scholars' work will be discredited if it too closely resembles another's. Journalists found to have plagiarized lose their jobs, and students routinely fail courses or are dismissed from their school when they are caught cheating— all too often by submitting as their own essays that they have purchased from online "research" sites. If you're having trouble completing an assignment, seek assistance. Talk with your instructor, or if your school has a writing center, go there for advice on all aspects of your writing, including acknowledging sources and avoiding plagiarism.

In everyday life, we are generally aware of our sources: "I read it in the *Post*." "Amber told me it's your birthday." "If you don't believe me, ask Mom." Saying how we know what we know and where we got our information is part of establishing our credibility and persuading others to take what we say seriously.

The goal of a research project is to study a topic, combining what we learn from sources with our own thinking and then composing a written text. When we write up the results of a research project, we cite the sources we use, usually by quoting, paraphrasing, or summarizing, and we acknowledge those sources, telling readers where the ideas came from. The information we give about sources is called documentation, and we provide it not only to establish our credibility as researchers and writers but also so that our readers, if they wish to, can find the sources themselves.

UNDERSTANDING DOCUMENTATION STYLES

The Norton Field Guide covers the documentation styles of the Modern Language Association (MLA) and the American Psychological Association (APA). MLA style is used chiefly in the humanities; APA is used mainly in the social sciences. Both are two-part systems, consisting of (1) brief in-text parenthetical documentation for quotations, paraphrases, or summaries and (2) more-detailed documentation in a list of sources at the end of the text. MLA and APA require that the end-of-text documentation provide the following basic information about each source you cite:

- author, editor, or organization providing the information
- title of work
- place of publication
- name of organization or company that published it
- date when it was published
- for online sources, date when you accessed the source

MLA and APA are by no means the only documentation styles. Many other publishers and organizations have their own style, among them the University of Chicago Press and the Council of Science Editors. We focus on MLA and APA here because those are styles that college students are often required to use. On the following page are examples of how the two parts — the brief parenthetical documentation in your text and the more detailed information at the end — correspond. The top of the next page shows the two parts according to the MLA system; the bottom, the two parts according to the APA system.

As the examples show, when you cite a work in your text, you can name the author either in a signal phrase or in parentheses. If you name the author in a signal phrase, give the page number(s) in parentheses; when the author's name is not given in a signal phrase, include it in parentheses.

The examples here and throughout this book are color-coded to help you see the crucial parts of each citation: tan for author and editor, yellow for title, and green for publication information: city of publication, name of publisher, year of publication, page number(s), and so on. Comparing the MLA and APA styles of listing works cited or references reveals some differences: MLA includes an author's first name while APA gives only the initial; MLA puts the date at the end while APA places it right after the author's name; MLA underlines titles of long works while APA italicizes them; MLA capitalizes most of the words in the title and subtitle while APA capitalizes only the first words of each. Overall, however, the styles provide similar information: each gives author, title, and publication data.

author   title   publication

MLA Style

IN-TEXT DOCUMENTATION

As Lester Faigley puts it, "The world has become a bazaar from which to shop for an individual 'lifestyle' " (12).

As one observer suggests, "The world has become a bazaar from which to shop for an individual 'lifestyle' " (Faigley 12).

WORKS-CITED DOCUMENTATION

Faigley, Lester. Fragments of Rationality: Postmodernity and the Subject of Composition. Pittsburgh: U of Pittsburgh P, 1992.

APA Style

IN-TEXT DOCUMENTATION

As Faigley (1992) suggested, "The world has become a bazaar from which to shop for an individual 'lifestyle'" (p. 12).

As one observer has noted, "The world has become a bazaar from which to shop for an individual 'lifestyle'" (Faigley, 1992, p. 12).

REFERENCE-LIST DOCUMENTATION

Faigley, L. (1992). *Fragments of rationality: Postmodernity and the subject of composition.* Pittsburgh, PA: University of Pittsburgh Press.

45 MLA Style

Modern Language Association style calls for (1) brief in-text documentation and (2) complete documentation in a list of works cited at the end of your text. The models in this chapter draw on the *MLA Handbook for Writers of Research Papers*, 6th edition, by Joseph Gibaldi (2003). Additional information is available at www.mla.org.

A DIRECTORY TO MLA STYLE

author   title   publication

author   title   publication

MLA IN-TEXT DOCUMENTATION

Brief documentation in your text makes clear to your reader what you took from a source and where in the source you found the information.

In your text, you have three options for citing a source: quoting, paraphrasing, and summarizing. As you cite each source, you will need to decide whether or not to name the author in a signal phrase — "as Toni Morrison writes" — or in parentheses — "(Morrison 24)."

The first examples in this chapter show basic in-text citations of a work by one author. Variations on those examples follow. All of the examples are color-coded to help you see how writers using MLA style work authors and page numbers — and sometimes titles — into their texts. The examples also illustrate the MLA style of using quotation marks around titles of short works and underlining titles of long works. (Your instructor may prefer italics to underlining; find out if you're not sure.)

1. AUTHOR NAMED IN A SIGNAL PHRASE

If you mention the author in a signal phrase, put only the page number(s) in parentheses. Do not write *page* or *p*.

McCullough describes John Adams as having "the hands of a man accustomed to pruning his own trees, cutting his own hay, and splitting his own firewood" (18).

McCullough describes John Adams's hands as those of someone used to manual labor (18).

2. AUTHOR NAMED IN PARENTHESES

If you do not mention the author in a signal phrase, put his or her last name in parentheses along with the page number(s). Do not use punctuation between the name and the page number(s).

> Adams is said to have had "the hands of a man accustomed to pruning his own trees, cutting his own hay, and splitting his own firewood" (McCullough 18).

> One biographer describes John Adams as someone who was not a stranger to manual labor (McCullough 18).

Whether you use a signal phrase and parentheses or parentheses only, try to put the parenthetical citation at the end of the sentence or as close as possible to the material you've cited without awkwardly interrupting the sentence. Notice that in the first example above, the parenthetical reference comes after the closing quotation marks but before the period at the end of the sentence.

3. TWO OR MORE WORKS BY THE SAME AUTHOR

If you cite multiple works by one author, you have four choices. You can mention the author in a signal phrase and give the title and page reference in parentheses. Give the full title if it's brief; otherwise, give a short version.

> Kaplan insists that understanding power in the Near East requires "Western leaders who know when to intervene, and do so without illusions" (Eastward 330).

You can mention both author and title in a signal phrase and give only the page reference in parentheses.

> In Eastward to Tartary, Kaplan insists that understanding power in the Near East requires "Western leaders who know when to intervene, and do so without illusions" (330).

You can indicate author, title, and page reference only in parentheses, with a comma between author and title.

author   title   publication

> Understanding power in the Near East requires "Western leaders who know when to intervene, and do so without illusions" (Kaplan, Eastward 330).

Or you can mention the title in a signal phrase and give the author and page reference in parentheses.

> Eastward to Tartary argues that understanding power in the Near East requires "Western leaders who know when to intervene, and do so without illusions" (Kaplan 330).

4. AUTHORS WITH THE SAME LAST NAME

If your works-cited list includes works by authors with the same last name, you need to give the author's first name in any signal phrase or the author's first initial in the parenthetical reference.

> Edmund Wilson uses the broader term imaginative, whereas Anne Wilson chooses the narrower adjective magical.

> Imaginative applies not only to modern literature (E. Wilson) but also to writing of all periods, whereas magical is often used in writing about Arthurian romances (A. Wilson).

5. AFTER A BLOCK QUOTATION

When quoting more than three lines of poetry, more than four lines of prose, or dialogue from a drama, set off the quotation from the rest of your text, indenting it one inch (or ten spaces) from the left margin. Do not use quotation marks. Place any parenthetical documentation *after* the final punctuation.

> In Eastward to Tartary, Kaplan captures ancient and contemporary Antioch for us:
>
>> At the height of its glory in the Roman-Byzantine age, when it had an amphitheater, public baths, aqueducts, and sewage pipes, half a million people lived in Antioch. Today the

population is only 125,000. With sour relations between Turkey and Syria, and unstable politics throughout the Middle East, Antioch is now a backwater—seedy and tumbledown, with relatively few tourists. I found it altogether charming. (123)

6. TWO OR MORE AUTHORS

For a work by two or three authors, name all the authors, either in a signal phrase or in the parentheses.

Carlson and Ventura's stated goal is to introduce Julio Cortázar, Marjorie Agosín, and other Latin American writers to an audience of English-speaking adolescents (v).

For a work with four or more authors, you have the option of mentioning all their names or just the name of the first author followed by *et al.*, which means "and others."

One popular survey of American literature breaks the contents into sixteen thematic groupings (Anderson, Brinnin, Leggett, Arpin, and Toth A19-24).

One popular survey of American literature breaks the contents into sixteen thematic groupings (Anderson et al. A19-24).

7. ORGANIZATION OR GOVERNMENT AS AUTHOR

If the author is an organization, cite the organization either in a signal phrase or in parentheses. It's acceptable to shorten long names.

The U.S. government can be direct when it wants to be. For example, it sternly warns, "If you are overpaid, we will recover any payments not due you" (Social Security Administration 12).

8. AUTHOR UNKNOWN

If you don't know the author of a work, as you won't with many reference books and with most newspaper editorials, use the work's title or a shortened version of the title in the parentheses.

author   title   publication

The explanatory notes at the front of the literature encyclopedia point out that writers known by pseudonyms are listed alphabetically under those pseudonyms (<u>Merriam-Webster's</u> vii).

A powerful editorial in last week's paper asserts that healthy liver donor Mike Hurewitz died because of "frightening" faulty postoperative care ("Every Patient's Nightmare").

9. LITERARY WORKS

When referring to literary works that are available in many different editions, cite the page numbers from the edition you are using, followed by information that will let readers of any edition locate the text you are citing.

NOVELS

Give the page and chapter number.

In <u>Pride and Prejudice,</u> Mrs. Bennett shows no warmth toward Jane and Elizabeth when they return from Netherfield (105; ch. 12).

VERSE PLAYS

Give the act, scene, and line numbers; separate them with periods.

Macbeth continues the vision theme when he addresses the Ghost with "Thou hast no speculation in those eyes / Which thou dost glare with" (3.3.96-97).

POEMS

Give the part and the line numbers (separated by periods). If a poem has only line numbers, use the word *line(s)* in the first reference.

Whitman sets up not only opposing adjectives but also opposing nouns in "Song of Myself" when he says, "I am of old and young, of the foolish as much as the wise, / . . . a child as well as a man" (16.330-32).

One description of the mere in <u>Beowulf</u> is "not a pleasant place!" (line 1372). Later, the label is "the awful place" (1378).

10. WORK IN AN ANTHOLOGY

If you're citing a work that is included in an anthology, name the author(s) of the work, not the editor of the anthology—either in a signal phrase or in parentheses.

> "It is the teapots that truly shock," according to Cynthia Ozick in her essay on teapots as metaphor (70).

> In In Short: A Collection of Creative Nonfiction, readers will find both an essay on Scottish tea (Hiestand) and a piece on teapots as metaphors (Ozick).

11. SACRED TEXT

When citing sacred texts such as the Bible or the Qur'an, give the title of the edition used, and in parentheses give the book, chapter, and verse (or their equivalent), separated by periods. MLA style recommends that you abbreviate the names of the books of the Bible in parenthetical references.

> The wording from The New English Bible follows: "In the beginning of creation, when God made heaven and earth, the earth was without form and void, with darkness over the face of the abyss, and a mighty wind that swept over the surface of the waters" (Gen. 1.1-2).

12. MULTIVOLUME WORK

If you cite more than one volume of a multivolume work, each time you cite one of the volumes, give the volume *and* the page numbers in parentheses, separated by a colon.

> Sandburg concludes with the following sentence about those paying last respects to Lincoln: "All day long and through the night the unbroken line moved, the home town having its farewell" (4: 413).

If your works-cited list includes only a single volume of a multivolume work, the only number you need to give in your parenthetical reference is the page number.

13. TWO OR MORE WORKS CITED TOGETHER

If you're citing two or more works closely together, you will sometimes need to provide a parenthetical citation for each one.

> Tanner (7) and Smith (viii) have looked at works from a cultural perspective.

If the citation allows you to include both in the same parentheses, separate the references with a semicolon.

> Critics have looked at both Pride and Prejudice and Frankenstein from a cultural perspective (Tanner 7; Smith viii).

14. SOURCE QUOTED IN ANOTHER SOURCE

When you are quoting text that you found quoted in another source, use the abbreviation *qtd. in* in the parenthetical reference.

> Charlotte Brontë wrote to G. H. Lewes: "Why do you like Miss Austen so very much? I am puzzled on that point" (qtd. in Tanner 7).

15. WORK WITHOUT PAGE NUMBERS

For works without page numbers, give paragraph or section numbers, using the abbreviation *par.* or *sec.* If you are including the author's name in the parenthetical reference, add a comma.

> Russell's dismissals from Trinity College at Cambridge and from City College in New York City are seen as examples of the controversy that marked the philosopher's life (Irvine, par. 2).

16. AN ENTIRE WORK

If your text is referring to an entire work rather than a part of it, identify the author in a signal phrase or in parentheses. There's no need to include page numbers.

> Kaplan considers Turkey and Central Asia explosive.

> At least one observer considers Turkey and Central Asia explosive (Kaplan).

NOTES

Sometimes you may need to give information that doesn't fit into the text itself—to thank people who helped you, provide additional details, or refer readers to other sources not cited in your text. Such information can be given in a *footnote* (at the bottom of the page) or an *endnote* (on a separate page with the heading *Notes* just before your works-cited list. Put a superscript number at the appropriate point in your text, signaling to readers to look for the note with the corresponding number. If you have multiple notes, number them consecutively throughout your paper.

TEXT

> This essay will argue that small liberal arts colleges should not recruit athletes and, more specifically, that giving student athletes preferential treatment undermines the larger educational goals.[1]

NOTE

> [1]I want to thank all those who have contributed to my thinking on this topic, especially my classmates and my teachers Marian Johnson and Diane O'Connor.

MLA LIST OF WORKS CITED

A works-cited list provides full bibliographic information for every source cited in your text. The list should be alphabetized by authors' last names (or sometimes by editors' or translators' names). Works that do not have an identifiable author or editor are alphabetized by title. See pages 415–16 for a sample works-cited list.

Books

BASIC FORMAT FOR A BOOK

For most books, you'll need to provide information about the author; the title and any subtitle; and the place of publication, publisher, and date. You'll find this information on the book's title page and copyright page.

Greenblatt, Stephen. <u>Will in the World: How Shakespeare Became Shakespeare</u>. New York: Norton, 2004.

A FEW DETAILS TO NOTE

- **TITLES**: capitalize the first and last words of titles, subtitles, and all principal words. Do not capitalize *a, an, the, to,* or any prepositions or coordinating conjunctions unless they begin a title or subtitle.
- **PLACE OF PUBLICATION**: If more than one city is given, use only the first.
- **PUBLISHER**: Use a shortened form of the publisher's name (Norton for W. W. Norton & Company, Princeton UP for Princeton University Press).
- **DATES**: If more than one year is given, use the most recent one.

1. ONE AUTHOR

Author's Last Name, First Name. <u>Title</u>. Publication City: Publisher, Year of publication.

Miller, Susan. <u>Assuming the Positions: Cultural Pedagogy and the Politics of Commonplace Writing</u>. Pittsburgh: U of Pittsburgh P, 1998.

When the title of a book itself contains the title of another book (or other long work), do not underline that title.

Walker, Roy. <u>Time Is Free: A Study of</u> Macbeth. London: Dakers, 1949.

Include the author's middle name or initials. When the title of a book contains the title of a short work, the title of the short work should be enclosed in quotation marks, and the entire title should be underlined.

Thompson, Lawrance Roger. <u>"Fire and Ice": The Art and Thought of Robert Frost</u>. New York: Holt, 1942.

2. TWO OR MORE WORKS BY THE SAME AUTHOR(S)

Give the author's name in the first entry, and then use three hyphens in the author slot for each of the subsequent works, listing them alphabetically by the first important word of each title (see page 390).

Author's Last Name, First Name. <u>Title That Comes First Alphabetically.</u> Publication City: Publisher, Year of publication.

---. <u>Title That Comes Next Alphabetically</u>. Publication City: Publisher, Year of publication.

Kaplan, Robert D. <u>The Coming Anarchy: Shattering the Dreams of the Post Cold War</u>. New York: Random, 2000.

---. <u>Eastward to Tartary: Travels in the Balkans, the Middle East, and the Caucasus</u>. New York: Random, 2000.

3. TWO AUTHORS

First Author's Last Name, First Name, and Second Author's First and Last Names. <u>Title</u>. Publication City: Publisher, Year of publication.

Malless, Stanley, and Jeffrey McQuain. <u>Coined by God: Words and Phrases That First Appear in the English Translations of the Bible</u>. New York: Norton, 2003.

4. THREE AUTHORS

First Author's Last Name, First Name, Second Author's First and Last Names, and Third Author's First and Last Names. <u>Title</u>. Publication City: Publisher, Year of publication.

Sebranek, Patrick, Verne Meyer, and Dave Kemper. <u>Writers INC: A Guide to Writing, Thinking, and Learning</u>. Burlington: Write Source, 1990.

5. FOUR OR MORE AUTHORS

You may give each author's name or the name of the first author only, followed by *et al.*, Latin for "and others."

First Author's Last Name, First Name, Second Author's First and Last Names, Third Author's First and Last Names, and Final Author's First and Last Names. <u>Title</u>. Publication City: Publisher, Year of publication.

Anderson, Robert, John Malcolm Brinnin, John Leggett, Gary Q. Arpin, and Susan Allen Toth. <u>Elements of Literature: Literature of the United States</u>. Austin: Holt, 1993.

First Author's Last Name, First Name, et al. <u>Title</u>. Publication City: Publisher, Year of publication.

Anderson, Robert, et al. <u>Elements of Literature: Literature of the United States</u>. Austin: Holt, 1993.

6. ORGANIZATION OR GOVERNMENT AS AUTHOR

Sometimes the author is a corporation or government organization.

Organization Name. <u>Title</u>. Publication City: Publisher, Year of publication.

Diagram Group. <u>The Macmillan Visual Desk Reference</u>. New York: Macmillan, 1993.

National Assessment of Educational Progress. <u>The Civics Report Card</u>. Princeton: ETS, 1990.

7. ANTHOLOGY

Editor's Last Name, First Name, ed. <u>Title</u>. Publication City: Publisher, Year of publication.

Hall, Donald, ed. <u>The Oxford Book of Children's Verse in America</u>. New York: Oxford UP, 1985.

If there is more than one editor, list the first editor last-name-first and the others first-name-first.

Kitchen, Judith, and Mary Paumier Jones, eds. <u>In Short: A Collection of Brief Creative Nonfiction</u>. New York: Norton, 1996.

8. WORK(S) IN AN ANTHOLOGY

> Author's Last Name, First Name. "Title of Work." Title of Anthology.
>> Ed. Editor's First and Last Names. Publication City: Publisher, Year of
>> publication. Pages.

> Achebe, Chinua. "Uncle Ben's Choice." The Seagull Reader: Literature.
>> Ed. Joseph Kelly. New York: Norton, 2005. 23-27.

To document two or more selections from one anthology, list each selection by author and title, followed by a cross-reference to the anthology. In addition, include on your works-cited list an entry for the anthology itself (see no. 7 on page 391).

> Author's Last Name, First Name. "Title of Work." Anthology Editor's Last
>> Name. Pages.

> Hiestand, Emily. "Afternoon Tea." Kitchen and Jones. 65-67.

> Ozick, Cynthia. "The Shock of Teapots." Kitchen and Jones. 68-71.

9. AUTHOR AND EDITOR

Start with the author if you've cited the text itself.

> Author's Last Name, First Name. Title. Ed. Editor's First and Last Names.
>> Publication City: Publisher, Year of publication.

> Austen, Jane. Emma. Ed. Stephen M. Parrish. New York: Norton, 2000.

Start with the editor if you've cited his or her work.

> Editor's Last Name, First Name, ed. Title. By Author's First and Last Names.
>> Publication City: Publisher, Year of publication.

> Parrish, Stephen M., ed. Emma. By Jane Austen. New York: Norton, 2000.

10. NO AUTHOR OR EDITOR

> Title. Publication City: Publisher, Year of publication.

> 2004 New York City Restaurants. New York: Zagat, 2003.

11. TRANSLATION

Start with the author to emphasize the work itself.

> Author's Last Name, First Name. <u>Title</u>. Trans. Translator's First and Last
>   Names. Publication City: Publisher, Year of publication.

> Dostoevsky, Fyodor. <u>Crime and Punishment</u>. Trans. Richard Pevear and
>   Larissa Volokhonsky. New York: Vintage, 1993.

Start with the translator to emphasize the translation.

> Translator's Last Name, First Name, trans. <u>Title</u>. By Author's First and Last
>   Names. Publication City: Publisher, Year of publication.

> Pevear, Richard, and Larissa Volokhonsky, trans. <u>Crime and Punishment</u>.
>   By Fyodor Dostoevsky. New York: Vintage, 1993.

12. FOREWORD, INTRODUCTION, PREFACE, OR AFTERWORD

> Part Author's Last Name, First Name. Name of Part. <u>Title of Book</u>.
>   By Author's First and Last Names. Publication City: Publisher, Year
>   of publication. Pages.

> Tanner, Tony. Introduction. <u>Pride and Prejudice</u>. By Jane Austen.
>   London: Penguin, 1972. 7-46.

13. MULTIVOLUME WORK

If you cite all the volumes of a multivolume work, give the number of volumes after the title.

> Author's Last Name, First Name. <u>Title of Complete Work</u>. Number of vols.
>   Publication City: Publisher, Year of publication.

> Sandburg, Carl. <u>Abraham Lincoln: The War Years</u>. 4 vols. New York:
>   Harcourt, 1939.

If you cite only one volume, give the volume number after the title.

> Sandburg, Carl. <u>Abraham Lincoln: The War Years</u>. Vol. 2. New York:
>   Harcourt, 1939.

14. BOOK IN A SERIES

Editor's Last Name, First Name, ed. Title of Book. By Author's First and
Last Names. Series Title abbreviated. Publication City: Publisher, Year
of publication.

Hunter, J. Paul, ed. Frankenstein. By Mary Shelley. Norton Critical Ed.
New York: Norton, 1996.

15. SACRED TEXT

If you have cited a specific edition of a religious text, you need to include
it in your works-cited list.

Title. Editor's First and Last Names, ed. (if any) Publication City:
Publisher, Year of publication.

The New English Bible with the Apocrypha. New York: Oxford UP, 1971.

The Torah: A Modern Commentary. W. Gunther Plaut, ed. New York:
Union of American Hebrew Congregations, 1981.

16. EDITION OTHER THAN THE FIRST

Author's Last Name, First Name. Title. Name or number of ed. Publication
City: Publisher, Year of publication.

Gibaldi, Joseph. MLA Handbook for Writers of Research Papers. 6th ed.
New York: MLA, 2003.

Hirsch, E. D., Jr., ed. What Your Second Grader Needs to Know:
Fundamentals of a Good Second-Grade Education. Rev. ed. New
York: Doubleday, 1998.

17. REPUBLISHED WORK

Give the original publication date after the title, followed by the publication information of the republished edition.

> Author's Last Name, First Name. <u>Title</u>. Year of original edition.
> Publication City: Current Publisher, Year of republication.

Bierce, Ambrose. <u>Civil War Stories</u>. 1909. New York: Dover, 1994.

Periodicals

BASIC FORMAT FOR AN ARTICLE

For most articles, you'll need to provide information about the author, the article title and any subtitle, the periodical title, any volume or issue number, the date, and inclusive page numbers.

> Weinberger, Jerry. "Pious Princes and Red-Hot Lovers: The Politics of
> Shakespeare's <u>Romeo and Juliet</u>." <u>Journal of Politics</u> 65 (2003): 370-75.

A FEW DETAILS TO NOTE

- **AUTHORS**: If there is more than one author, list the first author last-name-first and the others first-name-first.
- **TITLES**: Capitalize the first and last words of titles and subtitles and all principal words. Do not capitalize *a, an, the, to,* or any prepositions or coordinating conjunctions unless they begin a title or subtitle. For periodical titles, omit any initial *A, An,* or *The.*
- **DATES**: Abbreviate the names of months except for May, June, or July: Jan., Feb., Mar., Apr., Aug., Sept., Oct., Nov., Dec. Journals paginated by volume or issue call only for the year (in parentheses).
- **PAGES**: If an article does not fall on consecutive pages, give the first page with a plus sign (55+).

18. ARTICLE IN A JOURNAL PAGINATED BY VOLUME

> Author's Last Name, First Name. "Title of Article." <u>Title of Journal</u>
> Volume (Year): Pages.

Bartley, William. "Imagining the Future in <u>The Awakening</u>." <u>College English</u> 62 (2000): 719-46.

19. ARTICLE IN A JOURNAL PAGINATED BY ISSUE

Author's Last Name, First Name. "Title of Article." <u>Title of Journal</u> Volume.Issue (Year): Pages.

Weaver, Constance, Carol McNally, and Sharon Moerman. "To Grammar or Not to Grammar: That Is <u>Not</u> the Question!" <u>Voices from the Middle</u> 8.3 (2001): 17-33.

20. ARTICLE IN A MONTHLY MAGAZINE

Author's Last Name, First Name. "Title of Article." <u>Title of Magazine</u> Month Year: Pages.

Fellman, Bruce. "Leading the Libraries." <u>Yale Alumni Magazine</u> Feb. 2002: 26-31.

21. ARTICLE IN A WEEKLY MAGAZINE

Author's Last Name, First Name. "Title of Article." <u>Title of Magazine</u> Day Month Year: Pages.

Cloud, John. "Should SATs Matter?" <u>Time</u> 12 Mar. 2001: 62+.

22. ARTICLE IN A DAILY NEWSPAPER

Author's Last Name, First Name. "Title of Article." <u>Name of Newspaper</u> Day Month Year: Pages.

Springer, Shira. "Celtics Reserves Are Whizzes vs. Wizards." <u>Boston Globe</u> 14 Mar. 2005: D4+.

If you are documenting a particular edition of a newspaper (indicated on the front page), specify the edition (late ed., natl. ed., etc.) in between the date and the section and page reference.

Margulius, David L. "Smarter Call Centers: At Your Service?" <u>New York Times</u> 14 Mar. 2002, late ed.: G1+.

author   title   publication

23. UNSIGNED ARTICLE

"Title of Article." <u>Name of Publication</u> Day Month Year: Page(s).

"Laura Bush Ponders Trip to Afghanistan." <u>New York Times</u> 2 Dec. 2003:
   A22.

24. EDITORIAL

"Title." Editorial. <u>Name of Publication</u> Day Month Year: Page.

"Gas, Cigarettes Are Safe to Tax." Editorial. <u>Lakeville Journal</u> 17 Feb.
   2005: A10.

25. LETTER TO THE EDITOR

Author's Last Name, First Name. "Title (if any)." Letter. <u>Name of
   Publication</u> Day Month Year: Page.

Festa, Roger. "Social Security: Another Phony Crisis." Letter. <u>Lakeville
   Journal</u> 17 Feb. 2005: A10.

26. REVIEW

Author's Last Name, First Name. "Title (if any) of Review." Rev. of <u>Title
   of Work</u>, by Author's First and Last Names. <u>Title of Periodical</u> Day
   Month Year: Pages.

Lahr, John. "Night for Day." Rev. of <u>The Crucible</u>, by Arthur Miller. <u>New
   Yorker</u> 18 Mar. 2002: 149-51.

Electronic Sources

BASIC FORMAT FOR AN ELECTRONIC SOURCE

Not every electronic source gives you all the data that MLA would like to
see in a works-cited entry. Ideally, you will be able to list the author's
name, the title, any information about print publication, information about

electronic publication (title of site, editor, date of first electronic publication and/or most recent revision, name of the sponsoring institution), date of access, and URL. Of those nine pieces of information, you will find seven in the following example.

> Johnson, Charles W. "How Our Laws Are Made." Thomas: Legislative Information on the Internet 31 Jan. 2000. Lib. of Congress. 5 Apr. 2005 <http://thomas.loc.gov/home/holam.txt>.

A FEW DETAILS TO NOTE

- **AUTHORS:** If there is more than one author, list the first author last-name-first and the others first-name-first.

- **TITLES:** Capitalize the first and last words of titles and subtitles, and all principal words. Do not capitalize *a, an, the, to,* or any prepositions or coordinating conjunctions unless they begin a title or subtitle. For periodical titles, omit any initial *A, An,* or *The*.

- **DATES:** Abbreviate the names of months except for May, June, or July: Jan., Feb., Mar., Apr., Aug., Sept., Oct., Nov., Dec. Although MLA asks for the date when materials were first posted or most recently updated, you won't always be able to find that information. You'll also find that it will vary—you may find only the year, not the day and month. The date you must include is the date on which you accessed the electronic source.

- **URL:** Give the address of the Web site in angle brackets. When a URL will not fit on one line, break it only after a slash (and do not add a hyphen). If a URL is very long, consider giving the URL of the site's home page or search page instead. Also keep in mind that if you are accessing an online source through a library's subscription to a database provider (such as EBSCO), you may not see the URL itself. In that case, end your documentation with a period after your access date.

27. PROFESSIONAL WEB SITE

> Title of Site. Ed. Editor's First and Last Names. Date posted or last updated. Sponsoring Institution. Day Month Year of access <URL>.

Stanford Encyclopedia of Philosophy. Ed. Edward N. Zalta. 2003.
Metaphysics Research Lab, Center for the Study of Language and
Information, Stanford U. 25 July 2004 <http://plato.stanford.edu>.

28. PERSONAL WEB SITE

Author's Last Name, First Name. Home page. Date posted or last
updated. Day Month Year of access <URL>.

Chomsky, Noam. Home page. 25 July 2004 <http://web.mit.edu/
linguistics/www.chomsky.home.html>.

29. HOME PAGE FOR AN ACADEMIC DEPARTMENT

Academic Department. Dept. home page. School. Day Month Year of
access <URL>.

English Language and Literatures. Dept. home page. Wright State U
College of Liberal Arts. 12 Mar. 2003 <http://www.cola.wright.edu/
Dept/ENG/Index.htm>.

30. ONLINE BOOK OR PART OF A BOOK

Author's Last Name, First Name. "Title of Short Work." Title of
Long Work. Original year of publication. Database. Date of
electronic publication. Day Month Year of access <URL>.

Anderson, Sherwood. "The Philosopher." Winesburg, Ohio. 1919.
Bartleby.com: Great Books Online. 1999. 7 Apr. 2002 <http://
www.bartleby.com/156/5.html>.

31. ARTICLE IN AN ONLINE PERIODICAL OR DATABASE

If a source does not number pages or paragraphs, follow the year with a
period instead of a colon. Some periodicals have dates; others have volume
and issue numbers instead—volume 10, issue 3 should be listed as 10.3, followed by the year (in parentheses). See the next page for examples.

FROM A PERIODICAL'S WEB SITE

Author's Last Name, First Name. "Title of Article." Title of Periodical
    Date or Volume.Issue (Year): Pages or pars. Day Month Year of
    access <URL>.

Landsburg, Steven E. "Putting All Your Potatoes in One Basket:
    The Economic Lessons of the Great Famine." Slate 13 Mar.
    2001. 15 Mar. 2001 <http://slate.msn.com/Economics/01-03-13/
    Economics.asp>.

FROM A DATABASE PROVIDER

Author's Last Name, First Name. "Title of Article." Title of Periodical Date
    or Volume.Issue (Year): Pages or pars. Database. Database provider.
    Library. Day Month Year of access <URL>.

Bowman, James. "Moody Blues." American Spectator June 1999: 64-65.
    Academic Search Premier. EBSCO. Paul Laurence Dunbar Lib., Wright
    State U. 15 Mar. 2005 <http://epnet.com>.

32. DOCUMENT ACCESSED THROUGH AOL OR OTHER SUBSCRIPTION SERVICE

Note the *keyword* you used or the *path* you followed.

Author's Last Name, First Name. "Title of Document." Title of Longer
    Work. Date of work. Service. Day Month Year of access.
    Keyword: Word.

Stewart, Garrett. "Bloomsbury." World Book Online. 2003. America
    Online. 13 Mar. 2003. Keyword: Worldbook.

Author's Last Name, First Name. "Title of Document." Title of Longer
    Work. Date of work. Service. Day Month Year of access. Path:
    Sequence of Topics.

Hamashige, Hope. "New Pope's Election to Be Shrouded in Ritual, Secrecy." <u>National Geographic News</u>. 1 Apr. 2005. America Online. 25 Apr. 2005. Path: Research and Learning; History; History of Pope Selection.

33. EMAIL

Writer's Last Name, First Name. "Subject Line." Email to the author. Day Month Year of message.

Smith, William. "Teaching Grammar—Some Thoughts." Email to the author. 19 Nov. 2004.

34. POSTING TO AN ELECTRONIC FORUM

Writer's Last Name, First Name. "Title of Posting." Online posting. Day Month Year of posting. Name of Forum. Day Month Year of access <URL>.

Schafer, Judith Kelleher. "Re: Manumission." Online posting. 27 Jan. 2004. H-Net List on Slavery. 29 Jan. 2004 <http://h-net.msu.edu/cgi-bin/logbrowse.pl?trx=lm&list=H-Slavery>.

35. CD-ROM

FOR A SINGLE-ISSUE CD-ROM

<u>Title</u>. CD-ROM. Any pertinent information about the edition, release, or version. Publication City: Publisher, Year of publication.

<u>Othello</u>. CD-ROM. Princeton: Films for the Humanities and Sciences, 1998.

If you are citing only part of the CD-ROM, name the part as you would a part of a book.

"Snow Leopard." <u>Encarta Encyclopedia 1999</u>. CD-ROM. Seattle: Microsoft, 1998.

FOR A PERIODICAL ON A CD-ROM

Author's Last Name, First Name. "Title of Article." <u>Title of Periodical</u>.
    Date or Volume.Issue (Year): Page. <u>Database</u>. CD-ROM. Database
    provider. Month Year of CD-ROM.

Hwang, Suein L. "While Many Competitors See Sales Melt, Ben &
    Jerry's Scoops Out Solid Growth." <u>Wall Street Journal</u>. 25 May 1993:
    B1. <u>ABI-INFORM</u>. CD-ROM. Proquest. June 1993.

Other Kinds of Sources

This section shows how to prepare works-cited entries for categories other
than books, periodicals, and writing found on the Web and CD-ROMs. The
categories are in alphabetical order. Two of them—art and cartoon—cover
works that do not originate on the Web but make their way there. From
these examples, you can figure out a documentation style for any texts
that you may come across on the Web.

A FEW DETAILS TO NOTE

- **AUTHORS:** If there is more than one author, list the first author last-
  name-first and the others first-name-first. Do likewise if you begin an
  entry with performers, speakers, and so on.

- **TITLES:** Capitalize the first and last words of titles and subtitles, and
  all principal words. Do not capitalize *a*, *an*, *the*, *to*, or any prepositions
  or coordinating conjunctions unless they begin a title or subtitle. For
  periodical titles, omit any initial *A*, *An*, or *The*.

- **DATES:** Abbreviate the names of months except for May, June, or July:
  Jan., Feb., Mar., Apr., Aug., Sept., Oct., Nov., Dec. Journals paginated
  by volume or issue need only the year (in parentheses).

36. ADVERTISEMENT

Product or Company. Advertisement. <u>Title of Periodical</u> Date or
    Volume.Issue (Year): Page.

Empire BlueCross BlueShield. Advertisement. <u>Fortune</u> 8 Dec. 2003: 208.

37. ART

> Artist's Last Name, First Name. <u>Title of Art</u>. Year. Institution, City.

Van Gogh, Vincent. <u>The Potato Eaters</u>. 1885. Van Gogh Museum,
  Amsterdam.

ART ON THE WEB

Warhol, Andy. <u>Self-Portrait</u>. 1979. J. Paul Getty Museum, Los Angeles.
  29 Mar. 2005 <http://getty.edu/art/collections/objects/oll4421.html>.

38. CARTOON

> Artist's Last Name, First Name. "Title of Cartoon (if titled)." Cartoon. <u>Title
> of Periodical</u> Date or Volume.Issue (Year): Page.

Chast, Roz. "The Three Wise Men of Thanksgiving." Cartoon. <u>New Yorker</u>
  1 Dec. 2003: 174.

CARTOON ON THE WEB

Fairrington, Brian. Cartoon. <u>Arizona Republic</u> 6 Apr. 2002. 7 Apr. 2002
  <http://cagle.slate.msn.com/politicalcartoons/pccartoons/archives/
  fairrington.asp???Action=Get!>.

39. DISSERTATION

Treat a published dissertation as you would a book, but after its title, add
the abbreviation *Diss.*, the name of the institution, and the date of the dissertation. If the dissertation is published by University Microfilms International (UMI), include the order number, as in the example below.

> Author's Last Name, First Name. <u>Title</u>. Diss. Institution, Year.
> Publication City: Publisher, Year.

Goggin, Peter N. <u>A New Literacy Map of Research and Scholarship in
  Computers and Writing</u>. Diss. Indiana U of Pennsylvania, 2000. Ann
  Arbor: UMI, 2001. 9985587.

For unpublished dissertations, put the title in quotation marks and end with the degree-granting institution and the year.

> Kim, Loel. "Students Respond to Teacher Comments: A Comparison of Online Written and Voice Modalities." Diss. Carnegie Mellon U, 1998.

40. FILM, VIDEO, OR DVD

> <u>Title</u>. Dir. Director's First and Last Names. Perf. Lead Actors' First and Last Names. Distributor, Year of release.

> <u>Casablanca</u>. Dir. Michael Curtiz. Perf. Humphrey Bogart, Ingrid Bergman, and Claude Rains. Warner, 1942.

If it's a video or DVD, give that information before the name of the distributor.

> <u>Easter Parade</u>. Dir. Charles Walters. Perf. Judy Garland and Fred Astaire. DVD. MGM, 1948.

41. INTERVIEW

BROADCAST INTERVIEW

> Subject's Last Name, First Name. Interview. <u>Title of Program</u>. Network. Station, City. Day Month Year.

> Gates, Henry Louis, Jr. Interview. <u>Fresh Air</u>. NPR. WNYC, New York. 9 Apr. 2002.

PUBLISHED INTERVIEW

> Subject's Last Name, First Name. Interview. or "Title of Interview." <u>Title of Periodical</u> Date or Volume.Issue (Year): Pages.

> Brzezinski, Zbigniew. "Against the Neocons." <u>American Prospect</u> Mar. 2005: 26-27.

> Stone, Oliver. Interview. <u>Esquire</u> Nov. 2004: 170.

PERSONAL INTERVIEW

Subject's Last Name, First Name. Personal interview. Day Month Year.

Berra, Yogi. Personal interview. 17 June 2001.

42. LETTER

UNPUBLISHED LETTER

Author's Last Name, First Name. Letter to the author. Day Month Year.

Quindlen, Anna. Letter to the author. 11 Apr. 2002.

PUBLISHED LETTER

Letter Writer's Last Name, First Name. Letter to First and Last Names.
    Day Month Year of letter. Title of Book. Ed. Editor's First and
    Last Names. Publication City: Publisher, Year of publication. Pages.

White, E. B. Letter to Carol Angell. 28 May 1970. Letters of E. B. White.
    Ed. Dorothy Lobarno Guth. New York: Harper, 1976. 600.

43. MAP

Title of Map. Map. Publication City: Publisher, Year of publication.

Toscana. Map. Milan: Touring Club Italiano, 1987.

44. MUSICAL COMPOSITION

Composer's Last Name, First Name. "Title of Short Composition." or Title
    of Long Composition. Year of composition (optional).

Ellington, Duke. "Mood Indigo." 1931.

If you are identifying a composition by form, number, key, and opus, do
not underline that information or enclose it in quotation marks.

Beethoven, Ludwig van. String quartet no. 13 in B flat, op. 130. 1825.

45. MUSIC RECORDING

> Artist's Last Name, First Name. <u>Title of Long Work</u>. Other pertinent details about the artists. Manufacturer, Year of release.

> Beethoven, Ludwig van. <u>Missa Solemnis</u>. Perf. Westminster Choir and New York Philharmonic. Cond. Leonard Bernstein. Sony, 1992.

Whether you list the composer, conductor, or performer first depends on where you want to place the emphasis. If you are citing a specific song, put it in quotation marks before the name of the recording, which should be underlined.

> Brown, Greg. "Canned Goods." <u>The Live One</u>. Red House, 1995.

46. ORAL PRESENTATION

> Speaker's Last Name, First Name. "Title of Lecture." Sponsoring Institution. Site, City. Day Month Year.

> Cassin, Michael. "Nature in the Raw—The Art of Landscape Painting." Berkshire Institute for Lifetime Learning. Clark Art Institute, Williamstown. 24 Mar. 2005.

47. PAPER FROM PROCEEDINGS OF A CONFERENCE

> Author's Last Name, First Name. "Title of Paper." <u>Title of Conference Proceedings</u>. Date, City. Ed. Editor's First and Last Names. Publication City: Publisher, Year. Pages.

> Zolotow, Charlotte. "Passion in Publishing." <u>A Sea of Upturned Faces: Proceedings of the Third Pacific Rim Conference on Children's Literature</u>. 1986, Los Angeles. Ed. Winifred Ragsdale. Metuchen: Scarecrow P, 1989. 236-49.

48. PERFORMANCE

> <u>Title</u>. By Author's First and Last Names. Other appropriate details about the performance. Site, City. Day Month Year.

<u>Medea</u>. By Euripedes. Dir. Jonathan Kent. Perf. Diana Rigg. Longacre
Theatre, New Haven. 10 Apr. 1994.

49. TELEVISION OR RADIO PROGRAM

"Title of Episode." <u>Title of Program</u>. Other appropriate information
about the writer, director, actors, etc. Network. Station, City.
Day Month Year of broadcast.

"Stirred." <u>The West Wing</u>. Writ. Aaron Sorkin. Dir. Jeremy Kagan. Perf.
Martin Sheen. NBC. WPTV, West Palm Beach. 3 Apr. 2002.

SAMPLE RESEARCH PAPER, MLA STYLE

Dylan Borchers wrote the following essay, which reports information, for
a first-year writing course. It is formatted according to the guidelines of
the *MLA Handbook for Writers of Research Papers*, 6th edition (2003). While
the MLA guidelines are used widely in literature and other disciplines in
the humanities, exact documentation requirements may vary from discipline to discipline and course to course. If you're unsure about what your
instructor wants, ask for clarification.

½"

Borchers   1

1"

Dylan Borchers

Professor Bullock

English 102, Section 4

20 January 2004

Against the Odds:

Harry S. Truman and the Election of 1948

"Thomas E. Dewey's Election as President Is a Foregone Conclusion," read a headline in the New York Times during the presidential election race between incumbent Democrat Harry S. Truman and his Republican challenger, Thomas E. Dewey. Earlier, Life magazine had put Dewey on its cover with the caption "The Next President of the United States" (qtd. in "1948 Truman-Dewey Election"). In a Newsweek survey of fifty prominent political writers, each one predicted Truman's defeat, and Time correspondents declared that Dewey would carry 39 of the 48 states (Donaldson 210). Nearly every major media outlet across the United States endorsed Dewey and lambasted Truman. As historian Robert H. Ferrell observes, even Truman's wife, Bess, thought he would be beaten (270).

1"   1"

The results of an election are not so easily predicted, as the famous photograph on page 2 shows. Not only did Truman win the election, but he won by a significant margin, with 303 electoral votes and 24,179,259 popular votes, compared to Dewey's 189 electoral votes and 21,991,291 popular votes (Donaldson 204-07). In fact, many historians and political analysts argue that Truman

Borchers   2

Fig. 1. President Harry S. Truman holds up an Election Day edition of the <u>Chicago Daily Tribune</u>, which mistakenly announced "Dewey Defeats Truman." St. Louis, 4 Nov. 1948 (Rollins).

Insert illustra-
tions close to the
text to which
they relate. Label
with figure num-
ber, caption, and
parenthetical
source citation.

would have won by an even greater margin had third-party Progressive candidate Henry A. Wallace not split the Democratic vote in New York State and Dixiecrat Strom Thurmond not won four states in the South (McCullough 711). Although Truman's defeat was heavily predicted, those predictions themselves, Dewey's passiveness as a campaigner, and Truman's zeal turned the tide for a Truman victory.

    In the months preceding the election, public opinion polls predicted that Dewey would win by a large margin. Pollster Elmo Roper stopped polling in September, believing there was no reason to continue, given a seemingly inevitable Dewey landslide. Although the margin narrowed as the election drew near, the other

Indent para-
graphs $\frac{1}{2}$-inch or
5 spaces.

Give the author and page numbers in parentheses when no signal phrase is used.

pollsters predicted a Dewey win by at least 5 percent (Donaldson 209). Many historians believe that these predictions aided the president in the long run. First, surveys showing Dewey in the lead may have prompted some of Dewey's supporters to feel overconfident about their candidate's chances and therefore to stay home from the polls on Election Day. Second, these same surveys may have energized Democrats to mount late get-out-the-vote efforts ("1948 Truman-Dewey Election"). Other analysts believe that the overwhelming predictions of a Truman loss also kept at home some Democrats who approved of Truman's policies but saw a Truman loss as inevitable. According to political analyst Samuel Lubell, those Democrats may have saved Dewey from an even greater defeat (Hamby, Man of the People 465). Whatever the impact on the voters, the polling numbers had a decided effect on Dewey.

Historians and political analysts alike cite Dewey's overly cautious campaign as one of the main reasons Truman was able to achieve victory. Dewey firmly believed in public opinion polls. With all indications pointing to an easy victory, Dewey and his staff believed that all he had to do was bide his time and make no foolish mistakes. Dewey himself said, "When you're leading, don't talk"

If you quote text quoted in another source, cite that source in a parenthetical reference.

(qtd. in McCullough 672). Each of Dewey's speeches was well-crafted and well-rehearsed. As the leader in the race, he kept his remarks faultlessly positive, with the result that he failed to deliver a solid message or even mention Truman or any of Truman's policies. Eventually, Dewey began to be perceived as aloof and stuffy. One

Borchers　4

observer compared him to the plastic groom on top of a wedding cake (Hamby, "Harry S. Truman"), and others noted his stiff, cold demeanor (McCullough 671-74).

　　As his campaign continued, observers noted that Dewey seemed uncomfortable in crowds, unable to connect with ordinary people. And he made a number of blunders. One took place at a train stop when the candidate, commenting on the number of children in the crowd, said he was glad they had been let out of school for his arrival. Unfortunately for Dewey, it was a Saturday ("1948: The Great Truman Surprise"). Such gaffes gave voters the feeling that Dewey was out of touch with the public.

　　Again and again through the autumn of 1948, Dewey's campaign speeches failed to address the issues, with the candidate declaring that he did not want to "get down in the gutter" (qtd. in McCullough 701). When told by fellow Republicans that he was losing ground, Dewey insisted that his campaign not alter its course. Even <u>Time</u> magazine, though it endorsed and praised him, conceded that his speeches were dull (McCullough 696). According to historian Zachary Karabell, they were "notable only for taking place, not for any specific message" (244). Dewey's numbers in the polls slipped in the weeks before the election, but he still held a comfortable lead over Truman. It would take Truman's famous whistle-stop campaign to make the difference.

　　Few candidates in U.S. history have campaigned for the presidency with more passion and faith than Harry Truman. In the

If you cite two or more works closely together, provide a parenthetical citation for each one.

autumn of 1948, he wrote to his sister, "It will be the greatest campaign any President ever made. Win, lose, or draw, people will know where I stand" (91). For thirty-three days, Truman traveled the nation, giving hundreds of speeches from the back of the <u>Ferdinand Magellan</u> railroad car. In the same letter, he described the pace: "We made about 140 stops and I spoke over 147 times, shook hands with at least 30,000 and am in good condition to start out again tomorrow for Wilmington, Philadelphia, Jersey City, Newark, Albany and Buffalo" (91). McCullough writes of Truman's campaign:

> No President in history had ever gone so far in quest of support from the people, or with less cause for the effort, to judge by informed opinion. . . . As a test of his skills and judgment as a professional politician, not to say his stamina and disposition at age sixty-four, it would be like no other experience in his long, often difficult career, as he himself understood perfectly. More than any other event in his public life, or in his presidency thus far, it would reveal the kind of man he was. (655)

He spoke in large cities and small towns, defending his policies and attacking Republicans. As a former farmer and relatively late bloomer, Truman was able to connect with the public. He developed an energetic style, usually speaking from notes rather than from a prepared speech, and often mingled with the crowds that met his train. These crowds grew larger as the campaign

Set off quotations of four or more lines by indenting 1 inch (or 10 spaces).

Put parenthetical references after final punctuation in block quotations.

Borchers   6

progressed. In Chicago, over half a million people lined the streets as he passed, and in St. Paul the crowd numbered over 25,000. When Dewey entered St. Paul two days later, he was greeted by only 7,000 supporters ("1948 Truman-Dewey Election"). Reporters brushed off the large crowds as mere curiosity seekers wanting to see a president (McCullough 682). Yet Truman persisted, even if he often seemed to be the only one who thought he could win. By going directly to the American people and connecting with them, Truman built the momentum needed to surpass Dewey and win the election.

The legacy and lessons of Truman's whistle-stop campaign continue to be studied by political analysts, and politicians today often mimic his campaign methods by scheduling multiple visits to key states, as Truman did. He visited California, Illinois, and Ohio 48 times, compared with 6 visits to those states by Dewey. Political scientist Thomas M. Holbrook concludes that his strategic campaigning in those states and others gave Truman the electoral votes he needed to win (61, 65).

The 1948 election also had an effect on pollsters, who, as Elmo Roper admitted, "couldn't have been more wrong" (qtd. in Karabell 255). Life magazine's editors concluded that pollsters as well as reporters and commentators were too convinced of a Dewey victory to analyze the polls seriously, especially the opinions of undecided voters (Karabell 256). Pollsters assumed that undecided voters would vote in the same proportion as decided voters -- and that

If you cite a work with no known author, use the title in your parenthetical reference.

Borchers   7

turned out to be a false assumption (Karabell 258). In fact, the
lopsidedness of the polls might have led voters who supported
Truman to call themselves undecided out of an unwillingness to
associate themselves with the losing side, further skewing the polls'
results (McDonald, Glynn, Kim, and Ostman 152). Such errors led
pollsters to change their methods significantly after the 1948
election.

In a work by four or more authors, either cite them all or name the first one followed by et al.

After the election, many political analysts, journalists, and
historians concluded that the Truman upset was in fact a victory for
the American people, who, the New Republic noted, "couldn't be
ticketed by the polls, knew its own mind and had picked the rather
unlikely but courageous figure of Truman to carry its banner" (qtd.
in McCullough 715). How "unlikely" is unclear, however; Truman
biographer Alonzo Hamby notes that "polls of scholars consistently
rank Truman among the top eight presidents in American history"
(Man of the People 641). But despite Truman's high standing, and
despite the fact that the whistle-stop campaign is now part of our
political landscape, politicians have increasingly imitated the style
of the Dewey campaign, with its "packaged candidate who ran so as
not to lose, who steered clear of controversy, and who made a good
show of appearing presidential" (Karabell 266). The election of 1948
shows that voters are not necessarily swayed by polls, but it may
have presaged the packaging of candidates by public relations
experts, to the detriment of public debate on the issues in future
presidential elections.

1"

Borchers   8

Works Cited

Donaldson, Gary A. _Truman Defeats Dewey_. Lexington: UP of
    Kentucky, 1999.

Ferrell, Robert H. _Harry S. Truman: A Life_. Columbia: U of Missouri P,
    1994.

Hamby, Alonzo L., ed. "Harry S. Truman (1945-1953)."
    AmericanPresident.org. 11 Dec. 2003. Miller Center of Public
    Affairs, U of Virginia. 12 Jan. 2004 <http://
    www.americanpresident.org/history/harrytruman>.

---. _Man of the People: A Life of Harry S. Truman_. New York: Oxford
    UP, 1995.

Holbrook, Thomas M. "Did the Whistle-Stop Campaign Matter?" _PS:
    Political Science and Politics_ 35 (2002): 59-66.

Karabell, Zachary. _The Last Campaign: How Harry Truman Won the
    1948 Election_. New York: Knopf, 2000.

McCullough, David. _Truman_. New York: Simon, 1992.

McDonald, Daniel G., Carroll J. Glynn, Sei-Hill Kim, and Ronald E.
    Ostman. "The Spiral of Silence in the 1948 Presidential
    Election." _Communication Research_ 28 (2001): 139-55.

"1948 Truman-Dewey Election." _Electronic Government Project:
    Eagleton Digital Archive of American Politics_. 2004. Eagleton
    Inst. of Politics, Rutgers, State U of New Jersey. 11 Jan. 2004
    <http://www.eagleton.rutgers.edu/>.

Center the
heading.

Double-space
throughout.

Alphabetize the
list by authors'
last names or by
title for works
with no author.

Begin each entry
at the left mar-
gin; indent sub-
sequent lines
$\frac{1}{2}$-inch or 5
spaces.

If you cite more
than one work
by a single
author, list them
alphabetically by
title, and use 3
hyphens instead
of repeating the
author's name
after the first
entry.

Borchers   9

"1948: The Great Truman Surprise." <u>Media and Politics Online</u>
<u>Projects: Media Coverage of Presidential Campaigns</u>. 29 Oct.
2003. Dept. of Political Science and International Affairs,
Kennesaw State U. 11 Jan. 2004 <http://www.kennesaw.edu/
pols.3380/pres/1948.html>.

Rollins, Byron. Untitled photograph. "The First 150 Years: 1948." <u>AP</u>
<u>History</u>. Associated Press. 10 Jan. 2004 <http://www.ap.org/
pages/history/timeline/1948.htm>.

Truman, Harry S. "Campaigning, Letter, October 5, 1948." <u>Harry S.</u>
<u>Truman</u>. Ed. Robert H. Ferrell. Washington: CQ P, 2003. 91.

Check to be sure
that every source
you use is on the
list of works
cited.

APA Style **46**

American Psychological Association (APA) style calls for (1) brief documentation in parentheses near each in-text citation and (2) complete documentation in a list of references at the end of your text. The models in this chapter draw on the *Publication Manual of the American Psychological Association*, 5th edition (2001). Additional information is available at www.apastyle.org.

A DIRECTORY TO APA STYLE

author   title   publication

APA IN-TEXT DOCUMENTATION

Brief documentation in your text makes clear to your reader precisely what you took from a source and, in the case of a quotation, precisely where (usually, on which page) in the source you found the text you are quoting.

Paraphrases and summaries are more common than quotations in APA-style projects. The chapter on quoting, paraphrasing, and summarizing covers all three kinds of citations. It also includes a list of words you can use in signal phrases to introduce quotations, paraphrases, and summaries. As you cite each source, you will need to decide whether to name the author in a signal phrase—"as McCullough (2001) wrote"—or in parentheses—"(McCullough, 2001)."

The first examples in this chapter show basic in-text documentation for a work by one author. Variations on those examples follow. All of the examples are color-coded to help you see how writers using APA style work authors and page numbers—and sometimes titles—into their texts.

1. AUTHOR NAMED IN A SIGNAL PHRASE

If you are quoting, you must give the page number(s). You are not required to give the page number(s) with a paraphrase or a summary, but APA encourages you to do so, especially if you are citing a long or complex work; most of the models in this chapter do include page numbers. Check with your instructors to find out their preferences.

AUTHOR QUOTED

Put the date in parentheses right after the author's name; put the page in parentheses as close to the quotation as possible.

> McCullough (2001) described John Adams as having "the hands of a man accustomed to pruning his own trees, cutting his own hay, and splitting his own firewood" (p. 18).

> John Adams had "the hands of a man accustomed to pruning his own trees, cutting his own hay, and splitting his own firewood," according to McCullough (2001, p. 18).

Notice that in the first example, the parenthetical reference with the page number comes *after* the closing quotation marks but *before* the period at the end of the sentence.

AUTHOR PARAPHRASED

Put the date in parentheses right after the author's name; follow the date with the page.

> McCullough (2001, p. 18) described John Adams's hands as those of someone used to manual labor.

> John Adams's hands were those of a laborer, according to McCullough (2001, p. 18).

2. AUTHOR NAMED IN PARENTHESES

If you do not mention an author in a signal phrase, put his or her name, a comma, and the year of publication in parentheses as close as possible to the quotation, paraphrase, or summary.

AUTHOR QUOTED

Give the author, date, and page in one parentheses, or split the information between two parentheses.

> Adams is said to have had "the hands of a man accustomed to pruning
> his own trees, cutting his own hay, and splitting his own firewood"
> (McCullough, 2001, p. 18).

> One biographer (McCullough, 2001) has said John Adams had "the hands
> of a man accustomed to pruning his own trees, cutting his own hay, and
> splitting his own firewood" (p. 18).

AUTHOR PARAPHRASED OR SUMMARIZED

Give the author, date, and page in one parentheses toward the beginning
or the end of the paraphrase.

> One biographer (McCullough, 2001, p. 18) described John Adams as
> someone who was not a stranger to manual labor.

> John Adams's hands were those of a laborer (McCullough, 2001, p. 18).

3. AUTHORS WITH THE SAME LAST NAME

If your reference list includes more than one person with the same last
name, include initials in all documentation to distinguish the authors from
one another.

> Eclecticism is common in contemporary criticism (J. M. Smith, 1992, p. vii).

> J. M. Smith (1992, p. vii) has explained that eclecticism is common in
> contemporary criticism.

4. AFTER A BLOCK QUOTATION

If a quotation runs forty or more words, set it off from the rest of your
text and indent it one-half inch (or five spaces) from the left margin with-

out quotation marks. Place the page number(s) in parentheses *after* the end punctuation.

> Kaplan (2000) captured ancient and contemporary Antioch for us:
>> At the height of its glory in the Roman-Byzantine age, when it had an amphitheater, public baths, aqueducts, and sewage pipes, half a million people lived in Antioch. Today the population is only 125,000. With sour relations between Turkey and Syria, and unstable politics throughout the Middle East, Antioch is now a backwater—seedy and tumbledown, with relatively few tourists. I found it altogether charming. (p. 123)

5. TWO AUTHORS

Always mention both authors. Use *and* in a signal phrase, but use an ampersand (&) in parentheses.

> Carlson and Ventura (1990, p. v) wanted to introduce Julio Cortázar, Marjorie Agosín, and other Latin American writers to an audience of English-speaking adolescents.

> According to the Peter Principle, "In a hierarchy, every employee tends to rise to his level of incompetence" (Peter & Hull, 1969, p. 26).

6. THREE OR MORE AUTHORS

In the first reference to a work by three to five persons, name all contributors. In subsequent references, name the first author followed by *et al.* Whenever you refer to a work by six or more contributors, name only the first author, followed by *et al.* Use *and* in a signal phrase, but use an ampersand (&) in parentheses.

> Faigley, George, Palchik, and Selfe (2004, p. xii) have argued that where there used to be a concept called *literacy*, today's multitude of new kinds of texts has given us *literacies*.

> It's easier to talk about a good movie than a good book (Sebranek, Meyer, & Kemper, 1990, p. 143).

author　　　　title　　　　publication

Peilen et al. (1990, p. 75) supported their claims about corporate corruption with startling anecdotal evidence.

7. ORGANIZATION OR GOVERNMENT AS AUTHOR

If an organization has a long name that is recognizable by its abbreviation, give the full name and the abbreviation the first time you cite the source. In subsequent citations, use only the abbreviation. If the organization does not have a familiar abbreviation, use the full name each time you refer to it.

FIRST CITATION

(American Psychological Association [APA], 2001)

SUBSEQUENT CITATIONS

(APA, 2001)

8. AUTHOR UNKNOWN

With reference books and newspaper editorials, among other things, you may not know the author of a work. Use the complete title if it is short; if it is long, use the first few words of the title under which the work appears in the reference list.

Webster's New Biographical Dictionary (1988) identifies William James as "American psychologist and philosopher" (p. 520).

A powerful editorial asserted that healthy liver donor Mike Hurewitz died because of "frightening" faulty postoperative care ("Every Patient's Nightmare," 2002).

9. TWO OR MORE CITATIONS IN ONE PARENTHESES

If you need to cite multiple works in the same parentheses, list them in the same order that they appear in your reference list, separated by semicolons.

Many researchers have argued that what counts as "literacy" is not necessarily learned at school (Heath, 1983; Moss, 2003).

10. SOURCE QUOTED IN ANOTHER SOURCE

When you need to cite a source that was quoted in another source, let the reader know that you used a secondary source by adding the words *as cited in*.

> During the meeting with the psychologist, the patient stated repeatedly that he "didn't want to be too paranoid" (as cited in Oberfield & Yasik, 2004, p. 294).

11. WORK WITHOUT PAGE NUMBERS

Instead of page numbers, some electronic works have paragraph numbers, which you should include if you are referring to a specific part of such a source. Use the ¶ symbol or the abbreviation *para*. In sources with neither page nor paragraph numbers, refer readers to a particular part of the source if possible, perhaps indicating a heading and the paragraph under the heading.

> Russell's dismissals from Trinity College at Cambridge and from City College in New York City have been seen as examples of the controversy that marked the philosopher's life (Irvine, 2002, para. 2).

12. AN ENTIRE WORK

You do not need to give a page number if you are directing readers' attention to an entire work. Identify the author in a signal phrase or in parentheses, and cite the year of publication in parentheses.

> Kaplan (2000) considered Turkey and Central Asia explosive.

13. PERSONAL COMMUNICATION

Cite email, telephone conversations, interviews, personal letters, and other personal texts as *personal communication*, along with the person's initial(s), last name, and the date. You do not need to include such personal communications in your reference list.

author   title   publication

The author and editors seriously considered alternative ways of demonstrating documentation styles (F. Weinberg, personal communication, November 14, 2003).

L. Strauss (personal communication, December 6, 2003) told about visiting Yogi Berra when they both lived in Montclair, New Jersey.

NOTES

APA recognizes that there are instances when writers of research papers may need to use *content notes* to give an explanation or information that doesn't fit into the paper proper. To signal a content note, place a superscript numeral in your text at the appropriate point. Your readers will know to look for a note beginning with the same superscript numeral on a separate page with the heading *Notes*, after your paper but before the reference list. If you have multiple notes, number them consecutively throughout your paper. Indent the first line of each note five spaces, and flush all subsequent lines left.

Here is an example showing text and an accompanying content note from a book called *In Search of Solutions: A New Direction in Psychotherapy* (2003).

TEXT WITH SUPERSCRIPT

An important part of working with teams and one-way mirrors is taking the consultation break, as at Milan, BFTC, and MRI.[1]

CONTENT NOTE

[1]It is crucial to note here that, while working within a team is fun, stimulating, and revitalizing, it is not necessary for successful outcomes. Solution-oriented therapy works equally well when working solo.

APA REFERENCE LIST

A reference list provides full bibliographic information for every source cited in your text with the exception of personal communication. This list should be alphabetized by authors' last names (or sometimes by editors' names). Works that do not have an identifiable author or editor are alphabetized by title. See pages 448–49 for a sample reference list.

Books

BASIC FORMAT FOR A BOOK

For most books, you'll need to provide information about the author; the date of publication; the title and any subtitle; and the place of publication and publisher. You'll find this information on the book's title page and copyright page.

> Diamond, J. (1997). *Guns, germs, and steel: The fates of human societies.*
> New York: Norton.

A FEW DETAILS TO NOTE

- **DATES:** If more than one year is given, use the most recent one.
- **TITLES:** Capitalize only the first word and proper nouns and proper adjectives in titles and subtitles.
- **PLACE OF PUBLICATION:** Give city followed by state (abbreviated) or province or country (for example, Dubuque, IA). Omit state, province, or country for larger cities such as London, New York, and Tokyo. If more than one city is given, use the first.
- **PUBLISHER:** Use a shortened form of the publisher's name (Little, Brown for Little, Brown and Company), but retain *Association, Books,* and *Press* (American Psychological Association, Princeton University Press).

1. ONE AUTHOR

> Author's Last Name, Initials. (Year of publication). *Title.* Publication City:
> Publisher.

author   title   publication

Young, K. S. (1998). *Caught in the net: How to recognize the signs of Internet addiction—and a winning strategy for recovery.* New York: Wiley.

2. TWO OR MORE WORKS BY THE SAME AUTHOR

If the works were published in different years, list them chronologically.

Lewis, B. (1995). *The Middle East: A brief history of the last 2,000 years.* New York: Scribner.

Lewis, B. (2003). *The crisis of Islam: Holy war and unholy terror.* New York: Modern Library.

If the works were published in the same year, list them alphabetically by title, adding "a," "b," and so on to the years.

Kaplan, R. D. (2000a). *The coming anarchy: Shattering the dreams of the post cold war.* New York: Random House.

Kaplan, R. D. (2000b). *Eastward to Tartary: Travels in the Balkans, the Middle East, and the Caucasus.* New York: Random House.

3. TWO OR MORE AUTHORS

For two to six authors, use this format.

First Author's Last Name, Initials, Next Author's Last Name, Initials, & Last Author's Last Name, Initials. (Year of publication). *Title.* Publication City: Publisher.

Malless, S., & McQuain, J. (2003). *Coined by God: Words and phrases that first appear in the English translations of the Bible.* New York: Norton.

Sebranek, P., Meyer, V., & Kemper, D. (1990). *Writers INC: A guide to writing, thinking, and learning.* Burlington, WI: Write Source.

For a work by seven or more authors, name just the first six authors. After the sixth name, add the abbreviation *et al.*

4. ORGANIZATION OR GOVERNMENT AS AUTHOR

Sometimes a corporation or government organization is both author and publisher. If so, use the word *Author* as the publisher.

Organization Name or Government Agency. (Year of publication). *Title.* Publication City: Publisher.

Catholic News Service. (2002). *Stylebook on religion 2000: A reference guide and usage manual.* Washington, DC: Author.

U.S. Social Security Administration. (2003). *Social Security: Retirement benefits.* Washington, DC: Author.

5. AUTHOR AND EDITOR

Author's Last Name, Initials. (Year of edited edition). *Title.* (Editor's Initials Last Name, Ed.). Publication City: Publisher. (Original work[s] published year[s])

Douglass, F. (1994). *Autobiographies.* (H. L. Gates, Jr., Ed.). New York: Library of America. (Original works published 1845–1893)

6. EDITED COLLECTION

First Editor's Last Name, Initials, Next Editor's Last Name, Initials, & Final Editor's Last Name, Initials. (Eds.). (Year of edited edition). *Title.* Publication City: Publisher.

Raviv, A., Oppenheimer, L., & Bar-Tal, D. (Eds.). (1999). *How children understand war and peace: A call for international peace education.* San Francisco: Jossey-Bass.

7. WORK IN A COLLECTION

Author's Last Name, Initials. (Year of publication). Title of article or chapter. In Initials Last Name (Ed.), *Title* (pp. pages). Publication City: Publisher.

author   title   publication

Harris, I. M. (1999). Types of peace education. In A. Raviv, L. Oppenheimer, & D. Bar-Tal (Eds.), *How children understand war and peace: A call for international peace education* (pp. 46–70). San Francisco: Jossey-Bass.

8. UNKNOWN AUTHOR

Title. (Year of publication). Publication City: Publisher.

Webster's new biographical dictionary. (1988). Springfield, MA: Merriam-Webster.

If the title page of a work lists the author as *Anonymous,* treat the reference-list entry as if the author's name were Anonymous, and alphabetize it accordingly.

9. EDITION OTHER THAN THE FIRST

Author's Last Name, Initials. (Year). *Title* (name or number ed.). Publication City: Publisher.

Diamond, R. J. (2002). *Instant psychopharmacology* (2nd ed.). New York: Norton.

10. ONE VOLUME OF A MULTIVOLUME WORK

Author's Last Name, Initials. (Year). *Title of whole work: Vol. number. Title of volume.* Publication City: Publisher.

Spiegelman, A. (1986). *Maus: Vol. 1. My father bleeds history.* New York: Random House.

Periodicals

BASIC FORMAT FOR AN ARTICLE

For most articles, you'll need to provide information about the author; the date; the article title and any subtitle, the periodical title; and any volume or issue number and inclusive page numbers. Here is an example of an entry for an article in a journal.

> Ferguson, N. (2005). Sinking globalization. *Foreign Affairs, 84*(2), 64–77.

A FEW DETAILS TO NOTE

- **AUTHORS**: Give each author's last name first followed by initials. When there are seven or more authors, name the first six and add *et al.* after the sixth name.

- **DATES**: For journals, give year only. For magazines and newspapers, give year followed by a comma and then month or month and day. Do not abbreviate months.

- **TITLES**: Capitalize only the first word and proper nouns and proper adjectives in titles and subtitles of articles. Capitalize the first and last words and all principal words of periodical titles. Do not capitalize *a, an, the,* or any prepositions or coordinating conjunctions unless they begin the title of he periodical.

- **VOLUME AND ISSUE**: For journals and magazines, give volume or volume and issue, as explained in more detail below. For newspapers, do not give volume or issue.

- **PAGES**: For a journal or magazine article, do not use *p.* or *pp.* even though you do use that designation for a newspaper article. If an article does not fall on consecutive pages, give all the page numbers (for example, 45, 75–77 for a journal or magazine; pp. C1, C3, C5–C7 for a newspaper).

11. ARTICLE IN A JOURNAL PAGINATED BY VOLUME

> Author's Last Name, Initials. (Year). Title of article. *Title of Journal, volume,* pages.

> Yaffe, K., Fox, P., Newcomer, R., Sands, L., Lindquist, K., Dane, K., et al. (2002). Patient and caregiver characteristics and nursing home placement in patients with dementia. *Journal of American Medical Association, 287,* 2090–2097.

12. ARTICLE IN A JOURNAL PAGINATED BY ISSUE

> Author's Last Name, Initials. (Year). Title of article. *Title of Journal, volume*(issue), pages.

> Weaver, C., McNally, C., & Moerman, S. (2001). To grammar or not to grammar: That is *not* the question! *Voices from the Middle, 8*(3), 17–33.

13. ARTICLE IN A MAGAZINE

If a magazine is published weekly, include the day and the month. If there is a volume number, include it after the magazine title.

> Author's Last Name, Initials. (Year, Month Day). Title of article. *Title of Magazine, volume*, page(s).

> Wagner, R., & Schiermeier, Q. (2002, April 18). Conservationists under fire in the Philippines. *Nature, 416*, 669.

If a magazine is published monthly, include the month(s) only.

> Webster, D. (2002, May). Drawn from prehistory. *Smithsonian, 33*, 100–107.

14. ARTICLE IN A NEWSPAPER

If page numbers are consecutive, separate them with a dash. If not, separate them with a comma.

> Author's Last Name, Initials. (Year, Month Day). Title of article. *Title of Newspaper*, p(p). page(s).

> Schneider, G. (2005, March 13). Fashion sense on wheels. *The Washington Post*, pp. F1, F6.

15. ARTICLE BY AN UNKNOWN AUTHOR

List an article whose author is unknown by the title of the article.

IN A MAGAZINE

Title of article. (Year, Month Day). *Title of Magazine*, *volume*, page(s).

Hot property: From carriage house to family compound. (2004, December). *Berkshire Living*, *1*, 99.

IN A NEWSPAPER

Title of article. (Year, Month Day). *Title of Newspaper*, p(p). page(s).

Accept terror threat, Homeland chief says. (2005, March 15). *The Cincinnati Enquirer*, p. A5.

16. REVIEW

IN A JOURNAL

Author's Last Name, Initials. (Year). Title of review [Review of *Title of Work*]. *Title of Journal*, *volume*(issue), page(s).

Geller, J. L. (2005). The cock and bull of Augusten Burroughs [Review of the books *Running with scissors*, *Dry: A memoir*, and *Magical thinking*]. *Psychiatric Services, 56*, 364–365.

IN A MAGAZINE

Author's Last Name, Initials. (Year, Month Day). Title of review [Review of *Title of Work*]. *Title of Magazine*, *volume*, page(s).

Brandt, A. (2003, October). Animal planet [Review of the book *Intelligence of apes and other rational beings*]. *National Geographic Adventure, 5*, 47.

IN A NEWSPAPER

Author's Last Name, Initials. (Year, Month Day). Title of review [Review
   of *Title of Work*].*Title of Newspaper*, p(p). page(s).

Morris, C. A. (2005, March 24). Untangling the threads of the Enron
   fraud [Review of the book *Conspiracy of fools: A true story*]. *The
   New York Times*, p. B9.

If the review does not have a title, include just the bracketed information
about the work being reviewed.

Jarratt, S. C. (2000). [Review of the book *Lend me your ear:
   Rhetorical constructions of deafness*]. *College Composition
   and Communication, 52*, 300–302.

Electronic Sources

BASIC FORMAT FOR AN ELECTRONIC SOURCE

Not every electronic source gives you all the data that APA would like
to see in a reference entry. Ideally, you will be able to list author's
or editor's name, date of first electronic publication or most recent
revision, title of document, information about print publication if
any, information about electronic publication (title of site, date of your
access of the site or retrieval of the document, name of the sponsoring institution), and URL (address of document or site). Of those
eight pieces of information, you will find seven in the following
example.

Johnson, C. W. (2000). How our laws are made. In *Thomas: Legislative
   information on the Internet*. Retrieved March 5, 2005, from
   the Library of Congress Web site: http://thomas.loc.gov/home/
   holam.txt

A FEW DETAILS TO NOTE

- **AUTHORS**: List all authors last-name-first and initials. When there's more than one author, use an ampersand (&). When there are seven or more authors, name the first six and add *et al.* after the sixth name.

- **TITLES**: For Web sites and electronic documents, articles, or books, capitalize only the first word of titles and subtitles, proper nouns, and proper adjectives; for titles of periodicals, capitalize the first and last words and all principal words of the periodical title, but do not capitalize *a*, *an*, *the*, *to*, or any prepositions or coordinating conjunctions unless they begin a title or subtitle.

- **DATES**: After the author, give the year of the document's original publication on the Web or of its most recent revision. If neither of those years is clear, use *n.d.* to mean "no date"; the date you *must* include comes toward the end of the entry—month (not abbreviated), day, and year that you retrieved the document.

- **URL**: If you do not identify the sponsoring institution ("the Library of Congress Web site" in the example on page 433), you do not need a colon before the URL. Don't include any punctuation at the end of the URL.

17. NONPERIODICAL WEB SITE

COMPLETE SITE

Author's or Editor's Last Name, Initials. (Ed. if appropriate). (Year). *Title of site*. Retrieved Month Day, Year, from URL

Ockerbloom, J. M. (Ed.). (2005). *The online books page*. Retrieved March 28, 2005, from http://digital.library.upenn.edu/books

If you cannot find an author's or editor's name, use the name of the organization that created the Web site. Alternatively, begin with the title of the site, placing it before the year, as in the following example. For the year give the most recent update. The URL should lead to the site's home page.

Mental help net. (2001). Retrieved March 28, 2005, from http://mentalhelp.net

author   title   publication

PART OF SITE

Author's Last Name, Initials. (Year). Title of page or article. In *Title of site*. Retrieved Month Day, Year, from URL

Tucker-Ladd, C. E. (2000). Happiness, depression and self-concept. In *Psychological self-help*. Retrieved March 28, 2005, from http://mentalhelp.net/psyhelp/chap6/

LARGE AND COMPLEX SITE

Introduce the URL by naming the host organization and the relevant collection, department, or institute within the organization.

Author's or Editor's Last Name, Initials. (Ed. if appropriate). (Year). *Title of site*. Retrieved Month Day, Year, from Host Organization Web site: URL

Salda, M. N. (Ed.). (1995). *The little red riding hood project.* Retrieved March 12, 2003, from University of Southern Mississippi, De Grummond Children's Literature Research Collection Web site: http://www.usm.edu/english/fairytales/lrrh/lrrhhome.htm

18. ARTICLE IN AN ONLINE PERIODICAL OR DATABASE

AN ONLINE ARTICLE WITH NO PRINT VERSION

Author's Last Name, Initials. (Year, Month Day). Title of article. *Title of Periodical*. Retrieved Month Day, Year, from URL

Landsburg, S. E. (2001, March 13). Putting all your potatoes in one basket: The economic lessons of the Great Famine. *Slate*. Retrieved March 5, 2005, from http://slate.msn.com/id/102180

AN ARTICLE IN PRINT AND ONLINE

If an article appears online in the same format and with the same content as its print version, simply add *[Electronic version]*; you do not need to give the URL. See the next page for an example.

> Author's Last Name, Initials. (Year, Month Day). Title of article [Electronic version]. *Title of Newspaper*, p(p). page(s).

> Dowd, M. (2002, April 7). Sacred cruelties [Electronic version]. *The New York Times*, p. A30.

Give the retrieval date and the URL if the online version of a periodical article differs from the print version.

> Author's Last Name, Initials. (Year, Month Day). Title of article. *Title of Newspaper*, p. page. Retrieved Month Day, Year, from URL

> Dowd, M. (2002, April 7). Sacred cruelties. *The New York Times*, p. A30. Retrieved April 8, 2002, from http://www.nytimes.com/2002/04/07/opinion/07DOWD.html

AN ONLINE ARTICLE ACCESSED THROUGH A DATABASE

Follow the format for a journal (as below), magazine, newspaper, or other source, but instead of giving the URL, end your retrieval statement with the name of the database.

> Author's Last Name, Initials. (Year). Title of article. *Title of Journal, volume*(issue). Retrieved Month Day, Year, from Name of database.

> White, D. E. (1999). The "Joineriana": Anna Barbauld, the Aikin family circle, and the dissenting public sphere. *Eighteenth-Century Studies, 32*(4). Retrieved March 3, 2002, from Project Muse database.

19. ELECTRONIC DISCUSSION SOURCES

List online postings only if they are archived and can be retrieved.

> Author's Last Name, Initials. (Year, Month Day). Subject line of message [Msg number, if any]. Message posted to Name of Organization electronic mailing list, archived at URL

author   title   publication

Baker, J. (2005, February 15). Huffing and puffing [Msg 89].
　　Message posted to the American Dialect Society electronic
　　mailing list, archived at http://listserv.linguistlist.org/archives/
　　ads-1.html

Do not include email or other nonarchived discussions in your list of
references. Simply cite the sender's name in your text. See no. 13 on
page 424 for guidelines on identifying such sources in your text.

Other Kinds of Sources

20. FILM

Last Name, Initials (Producer), & Last Name, Initials (Director). (Year). *Title*
　　[Motion picture]. Country: Studio.

Wallis, H. B. (Producer), & Curtiz, M. (Director). (1942). *Casablanca*
　　[Motion picture]. United States: Warner.

21. MUSIC RECORDING

Composer's Last Name, Initials. (Year of copyright). Title of song. On *Title
　　of album* [Medium]. City: Label.

Veloso, C. (1997). Na baixado sapateiro. On *Livros* [CD]. Los Angeles:
　　Nonesuch.

If the music is performed by someone other than the composer, put
that information in brackets following the title. When the recording
date is different from the copyright date, put it in parentheses after
the label.

Cahn, S., & Van Heusen, J. (1960). The last dance [Recorded by F. Sinatra].
　　On *Sinatra reprise: The very good years* [CD]. Burbank, CA: Reprise
　　Records. (1991)

22. PROCEEDINGS OF A CONFERENCE

Author's Last Name, Initials. (Year of publication). Title of paper. In *Proceedings Title* (pp. pages). Publication City: Publisher.

Heath, S. B. (1997). Talking work: Language among teens. In *Symposium about Language and Society–Austin* (pp. 27–45). Austin: Department of Linguistics at the University of Texas.

23. TELEVISION PROGRAM

Last Name, Initials (Writer), & Last Name, Initials (Director). (Year). Title of episode [Descriptive label]. In Initials Last Name (Producer), *Series title*. City: Network.

Sorkin, A. (Writer), & Kagan, J. (Director). (2002). Stirred [Television series episode]. In A. Sorkin (Executive Producer), *The west wing*. New York: NBC.

SAMPLE RESEARCH PAPER, APA STYLE

Carolyn Stonehill wrote the following paper for a first-year writing course. It is formatted according to the guidelines of the *Publication Manual of the American Psychological Association*, 5th edition (2001). While APA guidelines are used widely in linguistics and the social sciences, exact requirements may vary from discipline to discipline and course to course. If you're unsure about what your instructor wants, ask for clarification.

author   title   publication

It's in Our Genes   1

Insert a shortened title and page number in the upper-right corner of each page, including the title page.

It's in Our Genes:

The Biological Basis of Human Mating Behavior

Carolyn Stonehill

English 102, Section 22

Professor Bertsch

February 24, 2003

Center the full title, your name, the name and section number of the course, your instructor's name, and the date, unless your instructor requires different information.

Abstract

While cultural values and messages certainly play a part in the process of mate selection, the genetic and psychological predispositions developed by our ancestors play the biggest role in determining to whom we are attracted. Women are attracted to strong, capable men with access to resources to help rear children. Men find women attractive based on visual signs of youth, health, and, by implication, fertility. While perceptions of attractiveness are influenced by cultural norms and reinforced by advertisements and popular media, the persistence of mating behaviors that have no relationship to societal realities suggests that they are part of our biological heritage.

Unless your instructor specifies another length, limit your abstract to 120 words or fewer.

It's in Our Genes:

The Biological Basis of Human Mating Behavior

Consider the following scenario: It's a sunny afternoon on campus, and Jenny is walking to her next class. Out of the corner of her eye, she catches sight of her lab partner, Joey, parking his car. She stops to admire how tall, muscular, and stylishly dressed he is, and she does not take her eyes off him as he walks away from his shiny new BMW. As he flashes her a pearly white smile, Jenny melts, then quickly adjusts her skirt and smooths her hair.

This scenario, while generalized, is familiar: Our attraction to people — or lack of it — often depends on their physical traits. But why this attraction? Why does Jenny respond the way she does to her handsome lab partner? Why does she deem him handsome at all? Certainly Joey embodies the stereotypes of physical attractiveness prevalent in contemporary American society. Advertisements, television shows, and magazine articles all provide Jenny with signals telling her what constitutes the ideal American man. Yet she is also attracted to Joey's new sports car even though she has a new car herself. Does Jenny find this man striking because of the influence of her culture, or does her attraction lie in a more fundamental part of her constitution? Evolutionary psychologists, who apply principles of evolutionary biology to research on the human mind, would say that Jenny's responses in this situation are due largely to mating strategies developed by her prehistoric ancestors. Driven by the need to reproduce and

Center the title.

Double-space the entire paper.

Indent each new paragraph 5 to 7 spaces ($\frac{1}{2}$-inch).

propagate the species, these ancestors of ours formed patterns of mate selection so effective in providing for their needs and those of their offspring that they are mimicked even in today's society. While cultural values and messages clearly play a part in the process of mate selection, the genetic and psychological predispositions developed by our ancestors play the biggest role in determining to whom we are attracted.

Provide headings to help readers follow the organization.

Women's Need to Find a Capable Mate

Pioneering evolutionary psychologist Trivers (as cited in Allman, 1993) observed that having and rearing children requires women to invest far more resources than men because of the length of pregnancy, the dangers of childbirth, and the duration of infants' dependence on their mothers (p. 56). According to Fisher (as cited in

Refer to authors by last name. In general, use the past tense or the present perfect in signal phrases.

Frank, 2001), one of the leading advocates of this theory, finding a capable mate was a huge preoccupation of all prehistoric reproductive women, and for good reason: "A female couldn't carry a baby in one arm and sticks and stones in the other arm and still feed and protect herself on the very dangerous open grasslands, so she began to need a mate to help her rear her young" (p. 85). So because of this it became advantageous for the woman to find a strong, capable man with access to resources, and it became suitable for the man to find a healthy, reproductively sound woman to bear and care for his offspring. According to evolutionary psychologists, these are the bases upon which modern mate selection is founded, and there are many examples of this phenomenon to be found in our own society.

It's in Our Genes   5

One can see now why Jenny might be attracted by Joey's display of resources — his BMW. In our society, men with good job prospects, a respected social position, friends in high places, or any combination thereof have generally been viewed as more desirable mates than those without these things because they signal to women that the men have resources (Buss & Schmitt, 1993, p. 226). Compared with males, females invest more energy in bearing and raising children, so it is most advantageous for females to choose mates with easy access to resources, the better to provide for their children.

Men's Need to Find a Healthy Mate

For men, reproductive success depends mainly on the reproductive fitness of their female counterpart: No amount of available resources can save a baby miscarried in the first month of gestation. Because of this need for a healthy mate, men have evolved a particular attraction "radar" that focuses on signs of a woman's health and youth, markers that are primarily visual (Weiten, 2001, p. 399). Present-day attractiveness ratings are based significantly on this primitive standard: "Some researchers have suggested that cross-cultural standards of beauty reflect an evolved preference for physical traits that are generally associated with youth, such as smooth skin, good muscle tone, and shiny hair" (Boyd & Silk, 2000, p. 625). This observation would explain why women of our time are preoccupied with plastic surgery, makeup, and — in Jenny's case — a quick hair check as a potential date

Use ampersands in parenthetical references — but use and *in signal phrases.*

If the author is not named in a signal phrase, include the name in parentheses, along with the date and (if the work is quoted), the page number.

approaches. As Cunningham, Roberts, Barbee, Druen, and Wu (1995) noted, "A focus on outer beauty may have stemmed from a need for desirable inner qualities," such as health, strength, and fertility, and "culture may build on evolutionary dynamics by specifying grooming attributes that signal successful adaptation" (pp. 262–263).

If an author is named in a signal phrase, include the publication date in parentheses after the name.

The Influence of the Media on Mate Selection

There is, however, a good deal of opposition to evolutionary theory. Some critics say that the messages fed to us by the media are a larger influence on the criteria of present-day mate selection than any sort of ancestral behavior. Advertisements and popular media have long shown Americans what constitutes a physically ideal mate: In general, youthful, well-toned, symmetrical features are considered more attractive than aging, flabby, or lopsided ones. Evolutionary psychologists argue that research has not determined what is cause and what is effect. Cosmides and Tooby (1997) offered the following analogy to show the danger of assigning culture too powerful a causal role:

Indent quotations of 40 or more words 5 to 7 spaces, about $\frac{1}{2}$-inch from the left margin.

> For example, people think that if they can show that there is information in the culture that mirrors how people behave, then *that* is the cause of their behavior. So if they see that men on TV have trouble crying, they assume that their example is *causing* boys to be afraid to cry. But which is cause and which effect? Does the fact that men don't cry much on TV *teach* boys to not cry, or does it merely *reflect* the way boys normally develop? In the absence of research on the particular topic,

It's in Our Genes   7

there is no way of knowing. ("Nature and Nurture: An Adaptationist Perspective," para. 16)

We can hypothesize, then, that rather than media messages determining our mating habits, our mating habits determine the media messages. Advertisers rely on classical conditioning to interest consumers in their products. For instance, by showing an image of a beautiful woman while advertising a beauty product, advertisers hope that consumers will associate attractiveness with the use of that particular product (Weiten, 2001). In order for this method to be effective, however, the images depicted in conjunction with the beauty product must be ones the general public already finds attractive, and an image of a youthful, clear-skinned woman would, according to evolutionary psychologists, be attractive for reasons of reproductive fitness. In short, what some call media influence is not an influence at all but merely a mirror in which we see evidence of our ancestral predispositions.

If Not Media, Then What?

Tattersall (2001), a paleoanthropologist at the American Museum of Natural History, offered another counterargument to the evolutionary theory of mate selection. First, he argued that the behavior of organisms is influenced not only by genetics, economics, and ecology working together (p. 663). Second, he argued that no comparisons can be made between modern human behavior and that of our evolutionary predecessors because the appearance of *Homo sapiens* presented a sudden, qualitative change

To cite a specific part of an unpaginated Web site, count paragraphs from the beginning of the document or, as is done here, from a major heading.

from the Neanderthals—not a gradual evolution of behavioral traits:

> As a cognitive and behavioral entity, our species is truly unprecedented. Our consciousness is an emergent quality, not the result of eons of fine-tuning of a single instrument. And, if so, it is to this recently acquired quality of uniqueness, not to the hypothetical "ancestral environments," that we must look in the effort to understand our often unfathomable behaviors. (p. 665)

The key to Tattersall's argument is this "emergent quality" of symbolic thought; according to his theories, the ability to think symbolically is what separates modern humans from their ancestors and shows the impossibility of sexual selection behaviors having been passed down over millions of years. Our sexual preferences, Tattersall said, are a result of our own recent and species-specific development and have nothing whatsoever to do with our ancestors.

Opponents of the evolutionary theory, though, fail to explain how "unfathomable" mating behaviors can exist in our present society for no apparent or logical reason. Though medicine has advanced to the point where fertility can be medically enhanced, Singh (1993) observed that curvy women are still viewed as especially attractive because they are perceived to possess greater fertility—a perception that is borne out by several studies of female fertility, hormone levels, and waist-to-hip ratio (p. 304). Though

It's in Our Genes   9

more and more women are attending college and achieving high-paying positions, women are still "more likely than men to consider economic prospects a high priority in a mate" (Sapolsky, 2001–2002, p. 18). While cultural norms and economic conditions influence our taste in mates, as Singh (1993) showed in observing that "the degree of affluence of a society or of an ethnic group within a society may, to a large extent, determine the prevalence and admiration of fatness [of women]" (pp. 304–305), we still react to potential mates in ways determined in Paleolithic times. The key to understanding our mating behavior does not lie only in an emergent modern quality, nor does it lie solely in the messages relayed to us by society; rather, it involves as well the complex mating strategies developed by our ancestors.

It's in Our Genes   10

References

Allman, W. F. (1993, July 19). The mating game [Electronic version].
    U.S. News & World Report, 56–63. Retrieved January 27, 2003,
    from SIRS database.

Boyd, R., & Silk, J. B. (2000). *How humans evolved.* (2nd ed.). New York:
    Norton.

Buss, D. M., & Schmitt, D. P. (1993). Sexual strategies theory: An
    evolutionary perspective on human mating. *Psychological
    Review, 100,* 204–232.

Cosmides, L., & Tooby, J. (1997, January 13). *Evolutionary psychology: A
    primer.* Retrieved February 2, 2003, from University of California,
    Santa Barbara, Center for Evolutionary Psychology Web site:
    http://www.psych.ucsb.edu/research/cep/primer.html

Cunningham, M. R., Roberts, A. R., Barbee, A. P., Druen, P. B., & Wu,
    C.-H. (1995). "Their ideas of beauty are, on the whole, the same
    as ours": Consistency and variability in the cross-cultural
    perception of female physical attractiveness. *Journal of
    Personality and Social Psychology, 68,* 261–279.

Frank, C. (2001, February). Why do we fall in — and out of — love? Dr.
    Helen Fisher unravels the mystery. *Biography,* 85–87, 112.
    Retrieved January 31, 2003, from Academic Search Premier
    database.

Sapolsky, R. M. (2001–2002, December–January). What do females
    want? *Natural History,* 18–21. Retrieved January 26, 2003, from
    Academic Search Premier database.

Begin list of references on a new page; center the heading.

Alphabetize the list by author's last name.

Indent all lines after the first line of each entry 5 spaces or ½-inch.

Be sure every source listed is cited in the text; don't list sources consulted but not cited.

It's in Our Genes   11

Singh, D. (1993). Adaptive significance of female physical
attractiveness: Role of waist-to-hip ratio. *Journal of Personality and Social Behavior, 65,* 293–307.

Tattersall, I. (2001). Evolution, genes, and behavior. *Zygon: Journal of Religion & Science, 36,* 657–666. Retrieved February 3, 2003, from the Psychology and Behavioral Sciences Collection database.

Weiten, W. (2001). *Psychology: Themes & variations.* (5th ed.). San Bernardino, CA: Wadsworth.

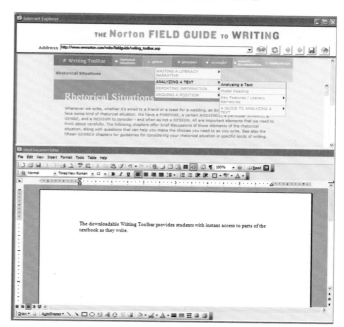

The downloadable Writing Toolbar provides students with instant access to parts of the textbook as they write.

Every new copy of **The Norton Field Guide to Writing** comes with free access to wwnorton.com/write/fieldguide, where you'll find many of the materials in the book online, including chapters on the 4 basic genres (chapters 6–9) and the research and documentation sections. The site contains many other useful resources as well, including model essays, templates and worksheets, a portfolio-keeping tool, and more. A floating toolbar provides students with instant access to key sections of the textbook as they write their assigned papers. The toolbar floats in a window that students can see while writing in Microsoft Word. Important book topics are just a click away.

This registration code offers free access to the site for a full year. Once you register, you can change your password however you wish.

REGISTERING FOR THE WEB SITE:

Go to wwnorton.com/write/fieldguide.

Click on **Register**.

Enter the registration code printed below and follow the instructions to access the site.

Registration Code:

ETAY-QGZQ

Please visit our technical support Web site at
wwnorton.com/web/helpdesk
if you have any difficulties or need further assistance.

If the registration card has been removed from your textbook, visit
wwnorton.com/write/fieldguide
for instructions regarding site access.

part 6

Media / Design

Consciously or not, we design all the texts we write, choosing typefaces, setting up text as lists or charts, deciding whether to add headings — and then whether to center them or flush them left. Sometimes our genre calls for certain design elements — essays begin with titles, letters begin with salutations ("Dear Auntie Em"). Other times we design texts to meet the demands of particular audiences, formatting documentation in MLA or APA or some other style, setting type larger for young children, and so on. And always our designs will depend upon our medium. A memoir might take the form of an essay in a book, be turned into a bulleted list for a PowerPoint presentation, or include links to images or other pages if presented on a Web site. The chapters in this part offer advice for working with PRINT texts, SPOKEN texts, and ELECTRONIC texts.

Media / Design

USA Today reports on a major news story with an article that includes a large photo and a colorful graph; the *New York Times* covers the same story with an article that is not illustrated but has a large headline and a pull quote highlighting one key point. Your psychology textbook includes many photos, tables, charts, and other visuals to help readers understand the subject matter. When you submit an essay for a class, you choose a typeface and you may make the type larger — or smaller — as need be. In all these instances, the message is in some way "designed." This chapter offers advice on designing print texts to suit your purpose, audience, genre, and subject. Much of the advice also holds for **ELECTRONIC TEXTS** and for visuals that accompany **SPOKEN TEXTS**.

476–84
464–75

Considering the Rhetorical Situation

As with all writing tasks, your rhetorical situation affects the way you design a print text.

■ **PURPOSE**   Consider how you can design your text to help achieve your purpose. If you're reporting certain kinds of information, for instance, you may want to present some data in a chart or table; if you're trying to get readers to care about an issue, a photo or pull quote might help you do so.

3–4

■ **AUDIENCE**   Do you need to do anything designwise for your intended audience? Change the type size? Add headings? tables? color?

5–8

rhetorical situations   genres   processes   strategies   research mla/apa   media/ design

9–11

◼ **GENRE** Does your genre have any design requirements? Must (or can) it have headings? illustrations? tables or graphs? a certain size paper?

12–14

◼ **STANCE** How can your design reflect your attitude toward your audience and subject? Do you need a businesslike typeface? Will plotting out statistics on a bar graph make them seem more important than they would seem in the middle of a paragraph? Can you use color?

Some Elements of Design

Whatever your text, you have various design decisions to make. What typeface(s) should you use? How should you arrange your text on the page? Should you include any headings? The following guidelines will help you consider each of these questions.

12–14 ◼

Type. You can choose from among many typefaces, and the one you choose will affect your text—how well readers can read it and how they will perceive your tone and STANCE. Times Roman will make a text look businesslike or academic; *Comic Sans* will make it look playful. For most academic writing, you'll want to use 10- or 11- or 12-point type, and you'll usually want to use a serif face (such as Times Roman or Bookman); which is generally easier to read than a sans serif face (such as Arial, Verdana, or Century Gothic). It's usually a good idea to use a serif face for your main text, reserving sans serif for headings and parts you want to highlight. Decorative typefaces (such as *Magneto*, *Amaze*, Chiller, and *Jokerman*) should be used sparingly and only when they're appropriate for your audience, purpose, and the rest of your RHETORICAL SITUATION. If you use more than one typeface in a text, use each one consistently: one face for HEADINGS, one for captions, one for the main body of your text. And don't go overboard—you won't often have reason to use more than two or, at most, three typefaces in any one text.

1–17 ◼
456–58 ▢

◼ rhetorical situations ▲ genres ○ processes ◆ strategies ● research mla/apa ▢ media/design

Every typeface has regular, **bold**, and *italic* fonts. In general, choose regular for the main text, bold for major headings, and italic for titles of books and other long works and, occasionally, to emphasize words or brief phrases. Avoid italicizing or boldfacing entire paragraphs. If you are following MLA, APA, or some other style, be sure your use of fonts conforms to its requirements.

● 378–416
● 417–49

Finally, consider the line spacing of your text. Generally, academic writing is double-spaced, whereas LETTERS and RÉSUMÉS are usually single-spaced. Some kinds of REPORTS may call for single-spacing; check with your instructor if you're not sure. In addition, you'll often need to add an extra space to set off parts of a text—items in a list, for instance, or headings.

▲ 182–92
▲ 127–36

Layout.   Layout is the way text is arranged on a page. An academic essay, for example, will usually have a title centered at the top, one-inch margins all around, and double-spacing. A text can be presented in paragraphs—or in the form of LISTS, TABLES, CHARTS, GRAPHS, and so on. Sometimes you need to include other elements as well: headings, images and other graphics, captions, lists of works cited.

☐ 455–56
458–60

Paragraphs.   Dividing text into paragraphs focuses information for readers and helps them process the information by dividing it into manageable chunks. If you're writing a story for a newspaper with narrow columns, for example, you'll divide your text into shorter paragraphs than you would if you were writing an academic essay. In general, indent paragraphs five spaces when your text is double-spaced; either indent or skip a line between paragraphs that are single-spaced.

Lists.   Put information into list form that you want to set off and make easily accessible. Number the items in a list when the sequence matters (in instructions, for example); use bullets when the order is not important. Set off lists with an extra line of space above and below, and add extra space between the items on a list if necessary for legibility. Here's an example:

Darwin's theory of how species change through time derives from three postulates, each of which builds on the previous one:

1. The ability of a population to expand is infinite, but the ability of any environment to support populations is always finite.

2. Organisms within populations vary, and this variation affects the ability of individuals to survive and reproduce.

3. The variations are transmitted from parents to offspring.

—Robert Boyd and Joan B. Silk, *How Humans Evolved*

Do not set off text as a list unless there's a good reason to do so, however. Some lists are more appropriately presented in paragraph form, especially when they give information that is not meant to be referred to more than once. In the following example, there is no reason to highlight the information by setting it off in a list—and bad news is softened by putting it in paragraph form:

> I regret to inform you that the Scholarship Review Committee did not approve your application for a Board of Rectors scholarship, for the following reasons: your grade-point average did not meet the minimum requirements; your major is not among those eligible for consideration; and the required letter of recommendation was not received before the deadline.

Presented as a list, that information would be needlessly emphatic.

Headings. Headings make the structure of a text easier to follow and help readers find specific information. Some genres require standard headings—announcing an **ABSTRACT**, for example, or a list of **WORKS CITED**. Other times you will want to use heads to provide an overview of a section of text. You may not need any headings with brief texts, and when you do, you'll probably want to use one level at most, just to announce major topics. Longer texts and information-rich genres, such as pamphlets or detailed **REPORTS**, may require several levels of headings. If you decide to include headings, you will need to decide how to phrase them, what typefaces and fonts to use, and where to position them.

107–11
415–16

127–36

Phrase headings concisely.   Make your headings succinct and parallel in structure. You might make all the headings nouns (**Mushrooms**), noun phrases (**Kinds of Mushrooms**), gerund phrases (**Recognizing Kinds of Mushrooms**), or questions (**How Do I Identify Mushrooms?**). Whatever form you decide on, use it consistently for each heading. Sometimes your

rhetorical situations   genres   processes   strategies   research mla/apa   media/ design

phrasing will depend on your purpose. If you're simply helping readers find information, use brief phrases:

Head	**Forms of Social Groups among Primates**
Subhead	***Solitary Social Groups***
Subhead	***Monogamous Social Groups***

If you want to address your readers directly with the information in your text, consider writing your headings as questions:

How can you identify morels?
Where can you find morels?
How can you cook morels?

Make headings visible.   Headings need to be visible, so consider printing them in a bold, italic, or underlined font—or use a different typeface. For example, you could print your main text in a serif font like Times Roman and your headings in a sans serif font like Arial or make the headings larger than the regular text. When you have several levels of headings, use capitalization, boldface, and italics to distinguish among the various levels. For example:

FIRST-LEVEL HEAD
Second-Level Head
Third-Level Head

Be aware, though, that APA and MLA formats expect headings to be in the same typeface as the main text; APA requires that each level of heading appear in a specific style: all uppercase, uppercase and lowercase, italicized uppercase and lowercase, and so on.

Position headings appropriately.   If you're following **APA** format, center first- and second-level headings. If you're following **MLA** format, align headings at the left margin without any extra space above or below. If you are not following a prescribed format, you get to decide where to position your headings: centered, flush with the left margin, or even alongside the text, in a wide left-hand margin. Position each level of head consistently throughout your text.

417–49
378–416

White space.   Use white space to separate the various parts of a text. In general, use one-inch margins for the text of an essay or report. Unless you're following MLA or APA format, include space above headings, above and below lists, and around photos, graphs, and other images to set them apart from the rest of the text. See the two **SAMPLE RESEARCH PAPERS** in this book for examples of the formats required by MLA and APA.

407–16 ●
438–49 ●

Visuals

Visuals can sometimes help you to make a point in ways that words alone cannot. Be careful, however, that any visuals you use contribute to your point—not simply act as decoration. This section discusses how to use photos, graphs, charts, tables, and diagrams effectively.

Select visuals that are appropriate for your rhetorical situation.   There are various kinds of visuals: photographs, line graphs, bar graphs, pie charts, tables, diagrams, flowcharts, drawings, and more. Which ones you use, if any, will depend on your content, your **GENRE,** and your **RHETORICAL SITUATION.** A newspaper article on housing prices might include a bar graph or line graph, and also some photographs; a report on the same topic written for an economics class would probably have graphs but no photos. See the examples on the facing page, along with advice for using each one.

19–192 ▲
1–17 ■

Some guidelines for using visuals

- Use visuals as part of your text's content, one that is as important as your words to your message. Therefore, avoid clip art, which is usually intended as decoration.
- Position visuals in your text as close as possible to your discussion of the topic to which they relate.
- Number all visuals, using a separate sequence for figures (photos, graphs, and drawings) and tables: *Figure 1, Figure 2; Table 1, Table 2.*
- Refer to the visual before it appears, identifying it and summarizing its point. For example: "As Figure 1 shows, Japan's economy grew dramatically between 1965 and 1980."

rhetorical situations genres processes strategies research mla/apa media/design

Photographs can support an argument, illustrate events and processes, present alternative points of view, and help readers "place" your information in time and space.

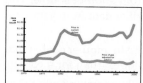

Line graphs are a good way of showing changes in data over time. Each line here shows a different set of data; plotting the two lines together allows readers to compare the data at different points in time.

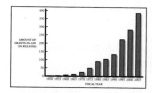

Bar graphs are useful for comparing quantitative data. The bars can be horizontal or vertical.

Pie charts can be used for showing how a whole is divided into parts or how something is apportioned.

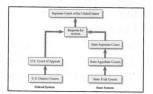

Tables are useful for displaying information concisely, especially when several items are being compared.

Diagrams, flowcharts, and drawings are ways of showing relationships and processes.

- Provide a title or caption for each visual to identify it and explain its significance for your text. For example: "Table 1. Japanese economic output, 1965–80."

375–77 ●

- **DOCUMENT** the source of any visuals you found in another source: "Figure 1. Two Tokyo shoppers display their purchases. (Ochiro, 1967)." Document any tables you create with data from another source. You need not document visuals you create yourself or data from your own experimental or field research.

- Obtain permission to use any visuals you found in another source that will appear in texts you publish in any form other than for a course.

- Label visuals to ensure that your audience will understand what they show. For example, label each section of a pie chart to show what it represents.

When you choose visuals and integrate them into your texts, follow the same procedures you use with other source materials.

Evaluate visuals as you would any text. Make sure visuals relate directly to your subject, support your assertions, and add information that words alone can't provide as clearly or easily. Evaluate visuals as you would other source materials: Is the photographer named? Do charts and graphs identify the source of the data they portray? Where was the visual published? How was the visual used in its original context? Does the information in the visual match, complement, or contradict the information in your other sources?

Include any necessary source information. Make sure visuals are accompanied by background and citation information: graphs and tables should cite the source of the data they present, and captions of photos should identify the photographer and date.

Use visuals ethically. You may want to crop a photograph, cutting it to show only part. See, for example, the photo on the facing page of a young couple in the 1940s and the cropped version that shows only the man's head. You might have reason to crop the photo to accompany a profile or memoir about the man, but you would not want to eliminate the young woman (who later became his wife) from the photo in an account of the

man's life. If you crop or otherwise alter a photograph, keep your purpose in mind.

But altering photographs in a way that misrepresents someone or something is a serious breach of ethics. In 1997, when O. J. Simpson was arrested for the murder of his ex-wife, both *Time* and *Newsweek* used the same mug shot on their covers. *Time*, however, digitally darkened Simpson's skin, making him look "blacker." This sort of manipulation misleads readers, creating visual lies that can inappropriately influence how readers interpret both the text and the subject. If you alter a photo, be sure the image represents the subject accurately—and tell your readers how you have changed it.

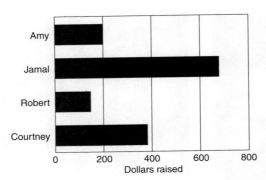

Fig. 1. Fund-raising results for the class gift.

Charts and graphs can mislead, too. Changing the scale on a bar graph, for example, can change the effect of the comparison, making the quantities being compared seem very similar or very different, as the two bar graphs of identical data show in figures 1 and 2.

Depending on th fund-raising goal implied by each bar graph ($800 or $5,000) and the increments of the dollars raised ($200 or $1,000), the two graphs send very different messages, though the dollars raised by each fund-raiser remain the same. Just as you shouldn't edit a quotation or a photograph in a way that might misrepresent its meaning, you should not present data in a way that could mislead readers.

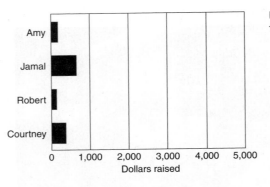

Fig. 2. Fund-raising results for the class gift.

Evaluating a Design

Does the design suit its PURPOSE ?   Do the typeface and any visuals help to convey the text's message, support its argument, or present information? Is there any key information that should be highlighted in a list or chart?

3–4

How well does the design meet the needs of its AUDIENCE ?   Will the overall appearance of the text appeal to the intended readers? Is the typeface large enough for them to read? Are there headings to help them find their way through the text? Are there the kind of visuals they are likely to expect? Are the visuals clearly labeled and referred to in the main text so that readers know why they're there?

5–8

How well does the text meet the requirements of its GENRE ?   Can you tell by looking at the text that it is an academic essay, a lab report, a résumé? Do its typeface, margins, headings, and page layout meet the requirements of **MLA, APA,** or whatever style being followed? Are visuals appropriately labeled and cited?

19–11

378–416
417–49

How well does the design reflect the writer's STANCE ?   Do the page layout and typeface convey the appropriate tone—serious, playful, adventuresome, conservative, and so on? Do the visuals reveal anything about the writer's position or beliefs? For instance, does the choice of visuals show any particular bias?

12–14

48 Spoken Text

In a marketing class, you give a formal presentation as part of a research project. As a candidate for student government, you deliver several speeches to various campus groups. At a good friend's wedding, you make a toast to the married couple. In school and out, you may be called on to speak in public, to compose and deliver spoken texts. This chapter offers guidelines to help you prepare and deliver effective spoken texts, along with the visual aids you often need to include. We'll start with two good examples.

ABRAHAM LINCOLN
Gettysburg Address

Given by the sixteenth president of the United States, at the dedication of the Gettysburg battlefield as a memorial to those who died in the Civil War, this is one of the most famous speeches ever delivered in the United States.

Four score and seven years ago our fathers brought forth on this continent, a new nation, conceived in Liberty, and dedicated to the proposition that all men are created equal.

Now we are engaged in a great civil war, testing whether that nation, or any nation so conceived and so dedicated, can long endure. We are met on a great battle-field of that war. We have come to dedicate a portion of that field, as a final resting place for those who here gave their lives that that nation might live. It is altogether fitting and proper that we should do this.

But, in a larger sense, we can not dedicate—we can not consecrate—we can not hallow—this ground. The brave men, living and

rhetorical situations ▪ genres ▲ processes ○ strategies ◆ research mla/apa ● media/ design □

dead, who struggled here, have consecrated it, far above our poor power to add or detract. The world will little note, nor long remember what we say here, but it can never forget what they did here. It is for us the living, rather, to be dedicated here to the unfinished work which they who fought here have thus far so nobly advanced. It is rather for us to be here dedicated to the great task remaining before us—that from these honored dead we take increased devotion to that cause for which they gave the last full measure of devotion—that we here highly resolve that these dead shall not have died in vain—that this nation, under God, shall have a new birth of freedom—and that government of the people, by the people, for the people, shall not perish from the earth.

You won't likely be called on to deliver such an address, but the techniques Lincoln used—brevity, rhythm, recurring themes—are ones you can use in your own spoken texts. The next example represents the type of spoken text we are sometimes called on to deliver at important occasions in the lives of our families.

JUDY DAVIS

Ours Was a Dad . . .

This short eulogy was given at the funeral of the writer's father, Walter Boock. Judy Davis lives in Davis, California, where she is the principal of North Davis Elementary School.

Elsa, Peggy, David, and I were lucky to have such a dad. Ours was a dad who created the childhood for us that he did not have for himself. The dad who sent us airborne on the soles of his feet, squealing with delight. The dad who built a platform in the peach tree so we could eat ourselves comfortably into peachy oblivion. The dad who assigned us chores and then did them with us. The dad who felt our pain when we skinned our knees.

Ours was the dad who took us camping, all over the U.S. and Canada, but most of all in our beloved Yosemite. The one who awed us with his ability to swing around a full pail of water without spilling a drop and let us hold sticks in the fire and draw designs in the night air with hot orange coals.

Our dad wanted us to feel safe and secure. On Elsa's eighth birthday, we acquired a small camping trailer. One very blustery night in Minnesota, Mom and Dad asleep in the main bed, David suspended in the hammock over them, Peggy and Elsa snuggled in the little dinette bed, and me on an air mattress on the floor, I remember the most incredible sense of well-being: our family all together, so snug, in that little trailer as the storm rocked us back and forth. It was only in the morning that I learned about the tornado warnings. Mom and Dad weren't sleeping; they were praying that when morning came we wouldn't find ourselves in the next state.

Ours was the dad who helped us with homework at the round oak table. He listened to our oral reports, taught us to add by looking for combinations of 10, quizzed us on spelling words, and when our written reports sounded a little too much like the *World Book* encyclopedia, he told us so.

Ours was the dad who believed our round oak table that seated   5
twelve when fully extended should be full at Thanksgiving. Dad called the chaplain at the airbase, asked about homesick boys, and invited them to join our family. Or he'd call International House in Berkeley to see if someone from another country would like to experience an American Thanksgiving. We're still friends with the Swedish couple who came for turkey forty-five years ago. Many people became a part of our extended family around that table. And if twelve around the table were good, then certainly fourteen would be better. Just last fall, Dad commissioned our neighbor Randy to make yet another leaf for the table. There were fourteen around the table for Dad's last Thanksgiving.

Ours was a dad who had a lifelong desire to serve. He delivered Meals on Wheels until he was eighty-three. He delighted in picking up the day-old doughnuts from Mr. Rollen's shop to give those on his route an extra treat. We teased him that he should be receiving those meals himself! Even after walking became difficult for him, he continued to drive and took along an able friend to carry the meals to the door.

Our family, like most, had its ups and downs. But ours was a dad who forgave us our human failings as we forgave him his. He died in

rhetorical situations | genres | processes | strategies | research mla/apa | media/ design

peace, surrounded by love. Elsa, Peggy, David, and I were so lucky to have such a dad.

This eulogy, in honor of the writer's father, provides concrete and memorable details that give the audience a clear image of the kind of man he was. The repetition of the phrase "ours was a dad" provides a rhythm and unity that moves the text forward, and the use of short, conventional sentences makes the text easy to understand—and deliver.

Key Features / Spoken Text

A clear structure. Spoken texts need to be clearly organized so that your audience can follow what you're saying. The **BEGINNING** needs to engage their interest, make clear what you will be talking about, and perhaps forecast the main parts of your talk. The main part of the text should focus on a few main points and only as many as your listeners can be expected to handle. (Remember, they can't go back to reread!) The **ENDING** is especially important: it should leave your audience with something to remember, think about, or do. Davis ends as she begins, saying that she and her sisters and brother "were so lucky to have such a dad." Lincoln ends by challenging his audience to "the great task remaining before us . . . that we . . . resolve that these dead shall not have died in vain—that this nation, under God, shall have a new birth of freedom—and that government of the people, by the people, for the people, shall not perish from the earth."

◆ 239–45

◆ 245–48

Signpost language to keep your audience on track. You may need to provide cues to help your listeners follow your text, especially **TRANSITIONS** that lead them from one point to the next. Sometimes you'll also want to stop and **SUMMARIZE** a complex point to help your audience keep track of your ideas and follow your narrative.

◆ 254

● 366–67

A tone to suit the occasion. Lincoln spoke at a serious, formal event, the dedication of a national cemetery, and his address is formal and even solemn. Davis's eulogy is more informal in tone, as befits a speech given for friends and loved ones. In a presentation to a panel of professors, you probably would want to take an academic tone, avoiding too much slang and speaking in complete sentences. If you had occasion to speak on the very same topic to a neighborhood group, however, you would likely want to speak more casually.

Sound.   Remember that spoken texts have the added element of sound. Be aware of how your words and phrases sound. Even if you're never called on to deliver a Gettysburg Address, you will find that repetition and parallel structure can lend power to a presentation, making it easier to follow — and more likely to be remembered. "We can not dedicate, we can not consecrate — we can not hallow": these are words said more than one hundred years ago, but who among us does not know where they're from? The repetition of "we can not" and the parallel forms of the three verbs are one reason they stay with us. These are structures any writer can use. See how the repetition of "ours was a dad" in Davis's eulogy creates a rhythm that engages listeners and at the same time unifies the text.

Visual aids.   Many times you will want or need to use visuals — Power-Point or other presentation software, transparencies, flip charts, and so on — to present certain information and to highlight key points for your audience.

Considering the Rhetorical Situation

As with any writing, you need to consider your purpose, audience, and the rest of your rhetorical situation:

3–4	■ **PURPOSE**	What is your primary purpose? To inform? persuade? entertain? evoke an emotional response? Something else?
5–8	■ **AUDIENCE**	Think about whom you'll be addressing and how well you know your audience. Will they be interested, or

will you need to get them interested? Are they likely to be friendly? How can you get and maintain their attention, and how can you establish common ground? Will they know about your subject, or will you need to provide background and define key terms?

GENRE   The genre of your text will affect the way you structure it. If you're making an argument, for instance, you'll need to consider counterarguments — and to anticipate questions from members of the audience who hold other opinions. If you're giving a report, you may have reason to prepare handouts with detailed information you don't have time to cover.

9–11

STANCE   Consider the attitude you want to express — is it serious? thoughtful? passionate? well-informed? funny? something else? — and choose your words accordingly.

12–14

Delivering a Spoken Text

The success of a spoken text often hinges on how you deliver it. As you practice delivering your spoken texts, bear in mind the following points.

Speak clearly.   When delivering a spoken text, your first goal is to be understood by your audience. If listeners miss important words or phrases because you don't form your words distinctly, your talk will not succeed. Make sure your pace matches your audience's needs — sometimes you may need to speak slowly to explain complex material; other times you may need to speed up to keep an audience's attention.

Pause for emphasis.   In writing, you have white space and punctuation to show readers where an idea or discussion ends. When speaking, you need to be the one to pause to signal the end of a thought, to give listeners a moment to consider something you've said, or to get them ready for a surprising or amusing statement.

Avoid reading your presentation. Speech textbooks often advise that you never read your speech. For some of us, though, that's just not possible. If you can speak well from notes or an outline, great—you're likely to do well. If you must have a complete text in front of you, though, try to write it as if you were talking. Then, practice by reading it into a tape recorder; listen for spots that sound as if you're reading, and work on your delivery to sound more relaxed.

Stand up straight, and look at your audience. Try to maintain some eye contact with your audience. If that's uncomfortable, fake it: pick a spot on the wall just above the head of a person in the last row of chairs, and focus on it. You'll appear as if you're looking at your audience even if you're not looking them in the eye. And if you stand up straight, you'll project the sense that you have confidence in what you're saying. If you appear to believe in your words, others will, too.

Use gestures for emphasis. If you're not used to speaking in front of a group, you may let your nervousness show by holding yourself stiffly, elbows tucked in. To overcome some of that nervousness, take some deep breaths, try to relax, move your arms as you would if you were talking to a friend. Use your hands for emphasis. Most public speakers use one hand to emphasize points and both to make larger gestures. Watch politicians on C-SPAN to see how people who speak on a regular basis use their hands and bodies as part of their overall delivery.

Practice. Practice, practice, and then practice some more. Pay particular attention to how much time you have—and don't go over your time limit.

Visual Aids

When you give an oral presentation, you'll often want or need to include some visuals to help listeners follow what you're saying. Especially when you're presenting complex information, it helps to let them see it as well as hear it. Remember, though, that visuals are a means of conveying information, not mere decoration.

Deciding on the appropriate visual. Presentation software, overhead transparencies, flip charts, and posters are some of the most common kinds of visuals. Presentation software and overhead transparencies are useful for listing main points and for projecting illustrations, tables, and graphs. Overhead transparencies, like whiteboards and chalkboards, allow you to create visuals as you speak. Sometimes you'll want to distribute handouts to provide lists of works cited or copies of any slides you show.

Whatever you decide to use, make sure that the necessary equipment is available — and that it works. If at all possible, check out the room and the equipment before you give your presentation. If you bring your own equipment, make sure electrical outlets are in reach of your power cords.

Also make sure that your visuals will be seen. You may have to rearrange the furniture or the screen in the room to make sure everyone can see. And finally: *have a backup plan.* Computers fail; projector bulbs burn out; marking pens run dry. Whatever visuals you plan, have an alternative plan in case any of these things happen.

Using presentation software. Programs such as Microsoft PowerPoint allow you to create slides that you then project via a computer. These programs enable you to project graphs, charts, photographs, sound — and plain text. Here are some tips for using presentation software effectively:

- *Use* LISTS *rather than paragraphs.* Use slides to emphasize your main points, not to reproduce your talk onscreen. Be aware that you can project the list all at once or one item at a time. □ 455–56

- *Don't put too much information on a slide.* How many bulleted points you include will depend on how long each one is, but you want to be sure that you don't include more words than listeners will be able to read as you present each slide.

- *Be sure your* TYPE *is large enough for your audience to read it.* In general, you don't want to use any type smaller than 18 points, and you'll want something larger than that for headings. Projected slides are easier to read in sans serif fonts like Arial, Helvetica, and Tahoma instead of serif fonts like Times Roman. Avoid using all caps — all-capped text is hard to read. □ 454–55

- *Choose colors carefully.* Your text must contrast strongly with the background. Dark text on a light background is easier to read than the reverse. And remember that not everyone sees all colors; be sure your audience does not need to recognize colors in order to get your meaning. Red-green contrasts are especially hard to see and should be avoided.

- *Use bells and whistles sparingly, if at all.* Presentation software offers lots of decorative backgrounds, letters that fade in or dance across the screen, and, literally, bells and whistles. These can be more distracting than helpful; avoid using them unless they help you make your point.

- *Mark your text.* In your notes, mark each place where you need to click a mouse to call up the next slide.

On the facing page are two slides from a PowerPoint presentation that Dylan Borchers created for an oral presentation based on his essay exploring the U.S. presidential election campaign of 1948 (see pages 408–16). These slides offer an outline of Borchers' main points; the speech itself fills in the details. The design is simple and uncluttered, and the large font and high contrast between type and background make the slides easy to read, even from across a large room.

Overhead transparencies.   Transparency slides can hold more information than slides created with presentation software, but someone must place each transparency on the projector one at a time. To minimize the number of slides you will need, you can place a lot of information on each transparency and use a blank sheet of paper to cover and reveal each point as you discuss it (see an example on page 474). Here are some tips for using overhead transparencies effectively:

- *Use a white background and large type.* If you're typing your text, use black type. Use type that is at least 18 points, and use larger type for headings. As with presentation software, fonts like Arial and Tahoma are easiest to read from a distance. If you're making handwritten transparencies, you might write in several colors.

Dewey

- Appeared overconfident
- Ran a lackluster, "safe" campaign
- Was perceived as stuffy and aloof
- Made several blunders
- Would not address issues

Truman

- Conducted whistle-stop campaign
- Made hundreds of speeches
- Spoke energetically
- Connected personally with voters
- Focused on key states

Slides made with presentation software

> # Dewey
>
> - Appeared overconfident
> - Ran a lackluster, "safe" campaign
> - Was perceived as stuffy and aloof
> - Made several blunders
> - Would not address issues
>
> # Truman
>
> - Conducted whistle-stop campaign
> - Made hundreds of speeches
> - Spoke energetically
> - Connected personally with voters
> - Focused on key states

An overhead transparency

- *Write legibly and large.* If you want to write as you speak and have trouble writing in a straight line, place a sheet of lined paper under the blank slide. Use a blank sheet to cover any unused part of the slide so that you don't smudge the ink on the slide as you write.

- *Position slides carefully.* You might want to mark the top right corner of each transparency to make sure you put it where it needs to go on

the projector. And have someplace to put the transparencies before and after you use them.

See the sample transparency slide on page 474. You might compare it with the PowerPoint slides on page 473 — you'll see that it provides identical information.

Handouts.   When you want to give your audience information they can refer to later — reproductions of your visuals, bibliographic information about your sources, printouts of your slides — do so in the form of a handout. Refer to the handout in your presentation, but unless it includes material your audience needs to consult as you talk, don't distribute the handouts until you are finished. Clearly label everything you give out, including your name and the date and title of the presentation.

See also the guidelines in Chapter 47 on **DESIGNING PRINT TEXT** for additional help creating visuals. If you are working with a group, see Chapter 21 on **COLLABORATING.**

▫ 453–63

◯ 195–98

49 Electronic Text

College singing groups create Web sites to publicize their concerts and sell their CDs. Political commentators post their opinions on blogs; readers of the blogs post responses. Job seekers post scannable résumés. And almost everyone sends email, every day, rain or shine. These are just some of the electronic texts you may have occasion to write. These texts differ in a few obvious ways from print texts—Web sites open with home pages rather than with plain introductory paragraphs, for instance—but like print texts, they have certain key features and are composed in the context of particular rhetorical situations. This chapter offers some very basic advice for thinking about the rhetorical situations and key features of texts that you post online.

Considering the Rhetorical Situation

As with any writing task, you need to consider your particular rhetorical situation when you write something to post online. In fact, you may need to consider it especially carefully, since the makeup of an online audience is pretty much impossible to predict—there's no telling who might read what you write or how efficient your readers' computer systems will be at dealing with different types and sizes of files.

3–4   ■ **PURPOSE**   Why are you writing—to fulfill an assignment? answer a question? find or provide information? get in touch with someone? In email, you may want to state your topic, and even your purpose, in the subject line. On a Web site, you will need to make the site's purpose clear on its home page.

rhetorical situations   genres   processes   strategies   research mla/apa   media/ design

■ **AUDIENCE**

What kind of readers are you aiming to reach, and what might they be expecting from you? What are they likely to know about your topic, and what information will you need to provide? What are their technical limitations — can they receive files the size of the one you want to send? If you're constructing a Web site, what kind of home page will appeal to your intended audience?

    What do you want them to do — read what you write? forward what you write to others? write something themselves? Remember, however, that you can never be sure where your original readers will forward your email or who will visit a Web site; don't put any writing online that you don't feel comfortable having lots of different people read.

5–8

■ **GENRE**

Are you reporting information? evaluating something? arguing a point? proposing an action?

9–11

■ **STANCE**

What overall impression do you want to convey? If you're constructing a Web site for a group, how does the group wish to be seen? Should the site look academic? hip? professional? If you want to demonstrate a political stance, remember that the links you provide can help you to do so. (Remember too that if you want to show a balanced political stance, the links should reflect a range of different viewpoints.)

12–14

■ **DESIGN**

Your medium will affect your design choices. If you're writing email, you'll want to format it to be as simple as possible — different colors and fonts are not necessarily recognized by every email program, so it's best to write in black type using a standard font. It's best also to keep your paragraphs short so readers can see each point without a lot of scrolling. If you're constructing a Web site, you'll need to create a consistent design scheme using color and type to signal key parts of the site.

15–17

Key Features / Email

Email is such a constant form of communicating that it can feel and read more like talking than writing. But writing it is, and it has certain features and conventions that readers expect and that writers need to be aware of.

An explicit subject line.   Your subject line should state your topic clearly: "Reminder: emedia meeting at 2" rather than "Meeting" or "Hi." People get so much email that they need to see a reason to read yours. In addition, most computer viruses are sent via unsolicited email messages, so many people delete all messages from unknown senders or with suspicious or vague subject lines. A clear subject line increases the chances that your message will be read.

A tone appropriate to the situation.   Email messages should be written in the same tone you'd use if you were writing the same text on paper. You can be informal when writing to friends, but you should be more formal when writing to people you don't know, especially in professional or academic contexts (to your boss or your instructor). Be aware that your tone starts with your salutation (*Hi Lisa* to a friend, *Dear Professor Alikum* to a teacher). And of course your tone is reflected in the register and conventions of your writing. You can use email shorthand with friends (gtg, cul8r), but professional and academic email should observe professional and academic conventions (complete sentences, correct spelling and punctuation).

Brevity.   Email works best when it's brief. Short paragraphs are easier to read on screen than long ones—you don't want readers to have to do too much scrolling to see the point you're trying to make. When you need to email a longer text, you may want to send it as an attachment that readers can open separately. If you don't know for sure whether your recipients will be able to open an attachment, check with them first before sending it.

Speed and reach.   This one's not a textual feature as much as it is a reminder to be careful before you hit *send*. Email travels so fast—and can be so easily forwarded to people you never imagined would read what

rhetorical situations | genres | processes | strategies | research mla/apa | media/ design

you've written—that you want to be good and sure that your email neither says something you'll regret later (don't send email when you're
angry!) nor includes anything you don't want the whole world, or at least
part of it, reading (don't put confidential or sensitive information in email).

Key Features / Web Sites

The writing you do for the Web differs from that which you do on paper,
in the way that you organize and present it—and in the way your readers will approach what you write. Here are some of the features that characterize most Web sites, along with general advice to help you think about
each feature when you write for the Web.

A home page.   The home page functions much like the first page of an
essay, giving the name of the site, indicating something about its purpose,
and letting readers know what they'll find on the site. It also gives the name
of the site's author or sponsor and includes information about when the
site was last updated. Plan the text for a home page so that it fits on one
screen, and make it simple enough graphically that it downloads quickly.

A clear organizational structure.   Web texts are presented as a number
of separate pages, and when you compose a Web site you need to organize the pages so that readers can get to them. Unlike print text, in which
the writer determines where a text begins and ends and what order it follows in between, most Web texts are organized so that readers can choose
which pages they'll look at and in what order. There's no sure way that
you can know what sequence they'll follow. Here are three common ways
of organizing a Web site:

As a sequence.   A simple way to organize a site is as a linear sequence
of pages.

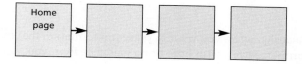

Use this organization if you want readers to view pages in a specific sequence. Though it still doesn't guarantee that they'll follow your sequence, it certainly increases the chances that they'll do so.

As a hierarchy. A hierarchical design groups related Web pages in the same way an outline organizes related topics in an essay.

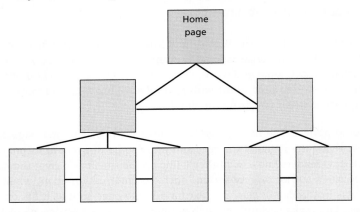

Use a hierarchy to guide readers through complex information while allowing them to choose what to read within categories.

As a web. A web design allows readers to view pages in just about any order they wish.

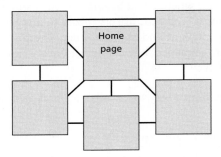

Use a web design when you want to present information that readers can browse for themselves, with little or no guidance from you.

rhetorical situations genres processes strategies research mla/apa media/ design

An explicit navigation system. Just as a book has a table of contents, so a Web site has a navigation menu. The navigation menu shows what's on your site, usually in a menu of the main parts that readers can click on to get to the pages. The navigation menu should appear in the same place on every page. One item on the menu should be a button that lets readers return to the home page.

A consistent design. Design is important — for creating a visual tone for the site, highlighting features or information, and providing a clear focus and emphasis. You need to create a clear color scheme (all links in one color, for example, to distinguish them from the rest of the text) and a consistent **PAGE DESIGN** (for example, a navigation bar at the top of each page and a background color that stays the same and doesn't detract from the content); in addition, you need to use **TYPE** consistently (for example, one font for the main text, another for the headings).

454–58

454–55

You can also use color and type to create emphasis or to highlight particular types of information. Though you can't know which pages readers will go to, careful site design can help you control what's on the page they'll see first. You can also include **IMAGES** — drawings, photos, maps, and the like. Be sure, however, that the illustrations you include support or add to your point, and that they are not mere decoration. Take care also that you don't include so many graphics that the site takes a long time to open.

458–62

Finally, your design should reflect the appropriate tone and **STANCE.** Formal, informal, academic, whimsical, whatever — your choice of type and color and images can convey this stance.

12–14

Links. Web sites include links among the pages on the site as well as to material elsewhere on the Web. Links allow you to bring material from other sources into your text — you can link to the **DEFINITION** of a key term, for instance, rather than defining it yourself, or you can link to a **SOURCE** rather than summarizing or paraphrasing it. You can also provide a list of links to related sites. When you're writing a text for a Web site, you can link to some of the details, giving readers the choice of whether they want or need to see an illustration, detailed description, map, and so on. For example, page 482 shows how my literacy narrative (on pages 25–27) might look as a Web text.

275–84
340–53

Amanda K. Hartman was born in 1882 in West Virginia. She left home at 14 for Cleveland, Ohio, where she worked as a seamstress. In her 30's she married Frederick Hartman, a German immigrant. Together they had one child, Louise. After her husband's death in 1955, Amanda obtained a realtor's license and sold real estate for many years.

She read widely, preferring Greek and Roman history and philosophy. Between 1952 and 1956, she and her husband shared a large house with my parents, giving her ample opportunity to read to me. She taught me to read by reading to me for hours on end, every day. She died at the age of 93.

My family was blue-collar, working-class, and — my grandmother excepted — not very interested in books or reading. But my parents took pride in my achievement and told stories about my precocious literacy, such as the time at a restaurant when the waitress bent over as I sat in my booster chair and asked, "What would you like, little boy?" I'm told I gave her a withering look and said, "I'd like to see a menu."

There was a more serious aspect to reading so young, however. At that time the murder trial of Dr. Sam Sheppard, a physician whose wife had been bludgeoned to death in their house, was the focus of lurid coverage in the Cleveland newspapers. Daily news stories recounted the grisly details of both the murder and the trial testimony, in which Sheppard maintained his innocence. (The story would serve as the inspiration for the TV series and Harrison Ford movie, The Fugitive.)

Sample Web text, with links

How text on the Web links to details from other sources. As the text on the facing page shows, links from my narrative might include a brief biography of my grandmother, *Court TV's* account of the Sheppard murder case, a site presenting excerpts of news coverage of the trial, and a poster from *The Fugitive.* Such links allow me to stay focused on my own narrative while offering readers the opportunity to explore issues mentioned in my story in as much depth as they want.

A Sample Site

Here and on page 484 are examples from a home page, a content page, and a linked page from a Web site created by Colleen James, a student at Illinois State University, as part of an online portfolio of work for a course in hypertext.

Home page

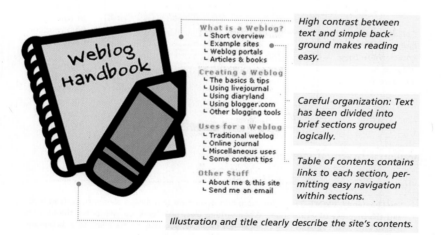

High contrast between text and simple background makes reading easy.

Careful organization: Text has been divided into brief sections grouped logically.

Table of contents contains links to each section, permitting easy navigation within sections.

Illustration and title clearly describe the site's contents.

Contents page

Explicit navigation system: Links to pages in the site appear at the same place on each page.

Color is used to show headings and links.

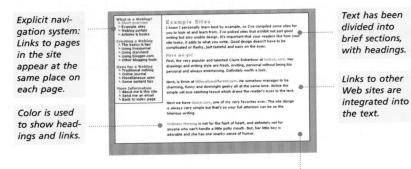

Text has been divided into brief sections, with headings.

Links to other Web sites are integrated into the text.

Background doesn't interfere with reading.

Linked page

Consistent design helps readers know where they are and how to navigate the site.

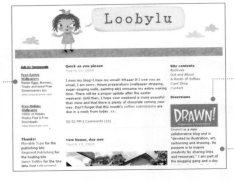

Links to other parts of the site help readers navigate.

High contrast between text and simple background makes reading easy.

english.ilstu.edu/students/cejames/final/

See Chapter 47, **PRINT TEXT**, for more information on text design elements, such as fonts and effective use of white space. When writing electronic texts, be aware that the way you use various **STRATEGIES** may change—for example, you may create a link to a dictionary definition of a term instead of defining it within the text.

453–63 ◨
237–328 ◆

rhetorical situations
genres
processes
strategies
research mla/apa
media/ design

part 7

Readings

"Read, read, read. Read everything — trash, classics, good and bad, and see how they do it." So said the American writer William Faulkner, and on the following pages you will find an anthology of readings that show how Faulkner, Zora Neale Hurston, David Sedaris, Joan Didion, and many other writers "do it." Read on, and pay attention to how these writers use the **KEY FEATURES** and **STRATEGIES** that you yourself are learning to use. The anthology includes readings in ten **GENRES;** you'll find a menu of the readings on the inside back cover of the book.

Readings

Literacy Narratives **50**

rhetorical
situations

genres

processes

strategies

research
mla/apa

media/
design

readings

TANYA BARRIENTOS

Se Habla Español

Tanya Barrientos is a columnist and feature writer for the Philadelphia Inquirer. *The following essay appeared in a 2004 issue of* Latina, *a bilingual magazine published by and for Latinas. It was adapted from an essay of the same title that was published in* Border-Line Personalities: A New Generation of Latinas Dish on Sex, Sass, and Cultural Shifting *(2004). In this piece, Barrientos recounts her struggles as a Latina who is not fluent in Spanish. She takes her title from a phrase often seen in store windows, announcing that "Spanish is spoken" there.*

THE MAN ON THE OTHER END of the phone line is telling me the classes I've called about are first-rate: native speakers in charge, no more than six students per group. I tell him that will be fine and yes, I've studied a bit of Spanish in the past. He asks for my name and I supply it, rolling the double "r" in "Barrientos" like a pro. That's when I hear the silent snag, the momentary hesitation I've come to expect at this part of the exchange. Should I go into it again? Should I explain, the way I have to half a dozen others, that I am Guatemalan by birth but *pura gringa* by circumstance?

This will be the sixth time I've signed up to learn the language my parents speak to each other. It will be the sixth time I've bought workbooks and notebooks and textbooks listing 501 conjugated verbs in alphabetical order, in hopes that the subjunctive tense will finally take root in my mind. In class I will sit across a table from the "native speaker," who will wonder what to make of me. "Look," I'll want to say (but never do). "Forget the dark skin. Ignore the obsidian eyes. Pretend I'm a pink-cheeked, blue-eyed blonde whose name tag says 'Shannon.'" Because that is what a person who doesn't innately know the difference between *corre, corra,* and *corrí* is supposed to look like, isn't it?

I came to the United States in 1963 at age 3 with my family and immediately stopped speaking Spanish. College-educated and seamlessly bilingual when they settled in west Texas, my parents (a psychology professor and an artist) wholeheartedly embraced the notion of

the American melting pot. They declared that their two children would speak nothing but *inglés*. They'd read in English, write in English, and fit into Anglo society beautifully.

It sounds politically incorrect now. But America was not a hyphenated nation back them. People who called themselves Mexican Americans or Afro-Americans were considered dangerous radicals, while law-abiding citizens were expected to drop their cultural baggage at the border and erase any lingering ethnic traits.

To be honest, for most of my childhood I liked being the brown girl 5 who defied expectations. When I was 7, my mother returned my older brother and me to elementary school one week after the school year had already begun. We'd been on vacation in Washington, D.C., visiting the Smithsonian, the Capitol, and the home of Edgar Allan Poe. In the Volkswagen on the way home, I'd memorized "The Raven," and I would recite it with melodramatic flair to any poor soul duped into sitting through my performance. At the school's office, the registrar frowned when we arrived.

"You people. Your children are always behind, and you have the nerve to bring them in late?"

"My children," my mother answered in a clear, curt tone, "will be at the top of their classes in two weeks."

The registrar filed our cards, shaking her head.

I did not live in a neighborhood with other Latinos, and the public school I attended attracted very few. I saw the world through the clear, cruel vision of a child. To me, speaking Spanish translated into being poor. It meant waiting tables and cleaning hotel rooms. It meant being left off the cheerleading squad and receiving a condescending smile from the guidance counselor when you said you planned on becoming a lawyer or a doctor. My best friends' names were Heidi and Leslie and Kim. They told me I didn't seem "Mexican" to them, and I took it as a compliment. I enjoyed looking into the faces of Latino store clerks and waitresses and, yes, even our maid and saying *"Yo no hablo español."* It made me feel superior. It made me feel American. It made me feel white. I thought if I stayed away from Spanish, stereotypes would stay away from me.

Then came the backlash. During the two decades when I'd worked 10 hard to isolate myself from the stereotype I'd constructed in my own head, society shifted. The nation changed its views on ethnic identity. College professors started teaching history through African American and Native American eyes. Children were told to forget about the melting pot and picture America as a multicolored quilt instead. Hyphens suddenly had muscle, and I was left wondering where I fit in.

The Spanish language was supposedly the glue that held the new Latino community together. But in my case it was what kept me apart. I felt awkward among groups whose conversations flowed in and out of Spanish. I'd be asked a question in Spanish and I'd have to answer in English, knowing this raised a mountain of questions. I wanted to call myself Latina, to finally take pride, but it felt like a lie. So I set out to learn the language that people assumed I already knew.

> If I stayed away from Spanish, stereotypes would stay away from me.

After my first set of lessons, I could function in the present tense. "*Hola, Paco. ¿Qué tal? ¿Qué color es tu cuaderno? El mío es azul.*" My vocabulary built quickly, but when I spoke, my tongue felt thick inside my mouth — and if I needed to deal with anything in the future or the past, I was sunk. I enrolled in a three-month submersion program in Mexico and emerged able to speak like a sixth-grader with a solid C average. I could read Gabriel García Márquez with a Spanish-English dictionary at my elbow, and I could follow 90 percent of the melodrama on any given telenovela. But true speakers discover my limitations the moment I stumble over a difficult construction, and that is when I get the look. The one that raises the wall between us. The one that makes me think I'll never really belong. Spanish has become a litmus test showing how far from your roots you've strayed.

My bilingual friends say I make too much of it. They tell me that my Guatemalan heritage and unmistakable Mayan features are enough to legitimize my membership in the Latin American club. After all, not all Poles speak Polish. Not all Italians speak Italian. And as this nation grows more and more Hispanic, not all Latinos will share one language. But I don't believe them.

There must be other Latinas like me. But I haven't met any. Or, I should say, I haven't met any who have fessed up. Maybe they are secretly struggling to fit in, the same way I am. Maybe they are hiring tutors and listening to tapes behind locked doors, just like me. I wish we all had the courage to come out of our hiding places and claim our rightful spot in the broad Latino spectrum. Without being called hopeless gringas. Without having to offer apologies or show remorse.

If it will help, I will go first.

Aquí estoy. Spanish-challenged and *pura* Latina.   15

Engaging with the Text

1. Tanya Barrientos gives her article a Spanish **TITLE**. How does this prepare you for the subject of the article? What does this title lead you to believe about Barrientos's feelings about Spanish? Is that impression supported by the rest of the article? Why or why not?
250–51

2. Barrientos **BEGINS** her essay with an anecdote about signing up for a Spanish class. What is the effect of beginning with this anecdote? Does it attract your interest? How does it prepare you for the rest of the essay?
239–45

3. Barrientos tells of learning to read and write in Spanish. One key feature of a literacy narrative is an indication of the narrative's **SIGNIFICANCE**. For her, what is the significance of learning that language? Why is it so important to her?
30

4. Barrientos peppers her essay with Spanish words and phrases, without offering any English translation. What does this tell you about her **STANCE**? Would her stance seem different if she'd translated the Spanish? Why or why not?
12–14

5. *For Writing.* As Barrientos notes, language plays a big part in her identity. Think about the languages you speak. If you speak only English, think about what kind of accent you have. (If you think you don't have one, consider how someone from a different region might hear you.) Does the language you speak or accent you have change according to the situation? Does it change according to how you perceive yourself? Write an essay **REFLECTING** on the way you speak and how it affects (or is affected by) your identity.
168–73

FREDERICK DOUGLASS

Learning to Read

One of the foremost leaders of the abolitionist movement,
Frederick Douglass (1818–1895) was born into slavery. He escaped in
1838 and went on to become one of America's first great black speakers,
providing a powerful voice against racial injustice. He published the
antislavery newspaper The North Star *and served as an adviser to*
President Lincoln during the Civil War. The following literacy narrative
comes from Douglass's autobiography, Narrative of the Life of
Frederick Douglass, an American Slave, Written by Himself
(1845).

I LIVED IN MASTER HUGH'S FAMILY ABOUT SEVEN YEARS. During this time, I succeeded in learning to read and write. In accomplishing this, I was compelled to resort to various stratagems. I had no regular teacher. My
mistress, who had kindly commenced to instruct me, had, in compliance with the advice and direction of her husband, not only ceased to
instruct, but had set her face against my being instructed by any one
else. It is due, however, to my mistress to say of her, that she did not
adopt this course of treatment immediately. She at first lacked the
depravity indispensable to shutting me up in mental darkness. It was
at least necessary for her to have some training in the exercise of irre-
sponsible power, to make her equal to the task of treating me as though
I were a brute.

My mistress was, as I have said, a kind and tender-hearted woman;
and in the simplicity of her soul she commenced, when I first went to
live with her, to treat me as she supposed one human being ought to
treat another. In entering upon the duties of a slaveholder, she did not
seem to perceive that I sustained to her the relation of a mere chattel,
and that for her to treat me as a human being was not only wrong, but
dangerously so. Slavery proved as injurious to her as it did to me. When
I went there, she was a pious, warm, and tender-hearted woman. There
was no sorrow or suffering for which she had not a tear. She had bread

for the hungry, clothes for the naked, and comfort for every mourner that came within her reach. Slavery soon proved its ability to divest her of these heavenly qualities. Under its influence, the tender heart became stone, and the lamblike disposition gave way to one of tiger-like fierceness. The first step in her downward course was in her ceasing to instruct me. She now commenced to practise her husband's precepts. She finally became even more violent in her opposition than her husband himself. She was not satisfied with simply doing as well as he had commanded; she seemed anxious to do better. Nothing seemed to make her more angry than to see me with a newspaper. She seemed to think that here lay the danger. I have had her rush at me with a face made all up of fury, and snatch from me a newspaper, in a manner that fully revealed her apprehension. She was an apt woman; and a little experience soon demonstrated, to her satisfaction, that education and slavery were incompatible with each other.

From this time I was most narrowly watched. If I was in a separate room any considerable length of time, I was sure to be suspected of having a book, and was at once called to give an account of myself. All this, however, was too late. The first step had been taken. Mistress, in teaching me the alphabet, had given me the *inch*, and no precaution could prevent me from taking the *ell*.[1]

The plan which I adopted, and the one by which I was most successful, was that of making friends of all the little white boys whom I met in the street. As many of these as I could, I converted into teachers. With their kindly aid, obtained at different times and in different places, I finally succeeded in learning to read. When I was sent of errands, I always took my book with me, and by going one part of my errand quickly, I found time to get a lesson before my return. I used also to carry bread with me, enough of which was always in the house, and to which I was always welcome; for I was much better off in this regard than many of the poor white children in our neighborhood. This bread I used to bestow upon the hungry little urchins, who, in return, would

---

1. Unit of length equal to 45 inches; the reference here is to the proverb "Give him an inch and he'll take an ell."

give me that more valuable bread of knowledge. I am strongly tempted to give the names of two or three of those little boys, as a testimonial of the gratitude and affection I bear them; but prudence forbids; — not that it would injure me, but it might embarrass them; for it is almost an unpardonable offence to teach slaves to read in this Christian country. It is enough to say of the dear little fellows, that they lived on Philpot Street, very near Durgin and Bailey's ship-yard. I used to talk this matter of slavery over with them. I would sometimes say to them, I wished I could be as free as they would be when they got to be men. "You will be free as soon as you are twenty-one, *but I am a slave for life!* Have not I as good a right to be free as you have?" These words used to trouble them; they would express for me the liveliest sympathy, and console me with the hope that something would occur by which I might be free.

I was now about twelve years old, and the thought of being *a slave for life* began to bear heavily upon my heart. Just about this time, I got hold of a book entitled "The Columbian Orator." Every opportunity I got, I used to read this book. Among much of other interesting matter, I found in it a dialogue between a master and his slave. The slave was represented as having run away from his master three times. The dialogue represented the conversation which took place between them, when the slave was retaken the third time. In this dialogue, the whole argument in behalf of slavery was brought forward by the master, all of which was disposed of by the slave. The slave was made to say some very smart as well as impressive things in reply to his master — things which had the desired though unexpected effect; for the conversation resulted in the voluntary emancipation of the slave on the part of the master.

In the same book, I met with one of Sheridan's mighty speeches on and in behalf of Catholic emancipation.[2] These were choice documents to me. I read them over and over again with unabated interest. They gave tongue to interesting thoughts of my own soul, which had fre-

5

---

2. Richard Brinsley Sheridan (1751–1815), Irish playwright and statesman. The speech Douglass refers to here, arguing for the abolition of laws that denied civil liberties to Roman Catholics in Great Britain and Ireland, was actually made by Arthur O'Connor, an Irish patriot.

quently flashed through my mind, and died away for want of utterance. The moral which I gained from the dialogue was the power of truth over the conscience of even a slaveholder. What I got from Sheridan was a bold denunciation of slavery, and a powerful vindication of human rights. The reading of these documents enabled me to utter my thoughts, and to meet the arguments brought forward to sustain slavery; but while they relieved me of one difficulty, they brought on another even more painful than the one of which I was relieved. The more I read, the more I was led to abhor and detest my enslavers. I could regard them in no other light than a band of successful robbers, who had left their homes, and gone to Africa, and stolen us from our homes, and in a strange land reduced us to slavery. I loathed them as being the meanest as well as the most wicked of men. As I read and contemplated the subject, behold! that very discontentment which Master Hugh had predicted would follow my learning to read had already come, to torment and sting my soul to unutterable anguish. As I writhed under it, I would at times feel that learning to read had been a curse rather than a blessing. It had given me a view of my wretched condition, without the remedy. It opened my eyes to the horrible pit, but to no ladder upon which to get out. In moments of agony, I envied my fellow-slaves for their stupidity. I have often wished myself a beast. I preferred the condition of the meanest reptile to my own. Any thing, no matter what, to get rid of thinking! It was this everlasting thinking of my condition that tormented me. There was no getting rid of it. It was pressed upon me by every object within sight or hearing, animate or inanimate. The silver trump of freedom had roused my soul to eternal wakefulness. Freedom now appeared, to disappear no more forever. It was heard in every sound, and seen in every thing. It was ever present to torment me with a sense of my wretched condition. I saw nothing without seeing it, I heard nothing without hearing it, and felt nothing without feeling it. It looked from every star, it smiled in every calm, breathed in every wind, and moved in every storm.

I often found myself regretting my own existence, and wishing myself dead; and but for the hope of being free, I have no doubt but that I should have killed myself, or done something for which I should have been killed. While in this state of mind, I was eager to hear any one speak of slavery. I was a ready listener. Every little while, I could hear something about the abolitionists. It was some time before I found what the word meant. It was always used in such connections as to make it an interesting word to me. If a slave ran away and succeeded in getting clear, or if a slave killed his master, set fire to a barn, or did any thing very wrong in the mind of a slaveholder, it was spoken of as the fruit of *abolition*. Hearing the word in this connection very often, I set about learning what it meant. The dictionary afforded me little or no help. I found it was "the act of abolishing"; but then I did not know what was to be abolished. Here I was perplexed. I did not dare to ask any one about its meaning, for I was satisfied that it was something they wanted me to know very little about. After a patient waiting, I got one of our city papers, containing an account of the number of petitions from the north, praying for the abolition of slavery in the District of Columbia, and of the slave trade between the States. From this time I understood the words *abolition* and *abolitionist,* and always drew near when that word was spoken, expecting to hear something of importance to myself and fellow-slaves. The light broke in upon me by degrees. I went one day down on the wharf of Mr. Waters; and seeing two Irishmen unloading a scow of stone, I went, unasked, and helped them. When we had finished, one of them came to me and asked me if I were a slave. I told him I was. He asked, "Are ye a slave for life?" I told him that I was. The good Irishman seemed to be deeply affected by the statement. He said to the other that it was a pity so fine a little fellow as myself should be a slave for life. He said it was a shame to hold me. They both advised me to run away to the north; that I should find friends there, and that I should be free. I pretended not to be interested in what they said, and treated them as if I did not understand them; for I feared they might be treacherous. White men have been known to encourage slaves to escape, and then, to get the reward, catch them and return them to their masters. I was afraid that these seemingly good men might use me so; but I nevertheless remembered their advice, and from that time I resolved to run away. I looked forward to a time at which it would be safe for me to escape. I was too young to think of doing so immediately; besides, I wished to learn how to write, as I might have occasion to write my

own pass. I consoled myself with the hope that I should one day find a good chance. Meanwhile, I would learn to write.

The idea as to how I might learn to write was suggested to me by being in Durgin and Bailey's ship-yard, and frequently seeing the ship carpenters, after hewing, and getting a piece of timber ready for use, write on the timber the name of that part of the ship for which it was intended. When a piece of timber was intended for the larboard side, it would be marked thus — "L." When a piece was for the starboard side, it would be marked thus — "S." A piece for the larboard side forward, would be marked thus — "L. F." When a piece was for starboard side forward, it would be marked thus — "S. F." For larboard aft, it would be marked thus — "L. A." For starboard aft, it would be marked thus — "S. A." I soon learned the names of these letters, and for what they were intended when placed upon a piece of timber in the shipyard. I immediately commenced copying them, and in a short time was able to make the four letters named. After that, when I met with any boy who I knew could write, I would tell him I could write as well as he. The next word would be, "I don't believe you. Let me see you try it." I would then make the letters which I had been so fortunate as to learn, and ask him to beat that. In this way I got a good many lessons in writing, which it is quite possible I should never have gotten in any other way. During this time, my copy-book was the board fence, brick wall, and pavement; my pen and ink was a lump of chalk. With these, I learned mainly how to write. I then commenced and continued copying the Italics in Webster's Spelling Book, until I could make them all without looking on the book. By this time, my little Master Thomas had gone to school, and learned how to write, and had written over a number of copy-books. These had been brought home, and shown to some of our near neighbors, and then laid aside. My mistress used to go to class meeting at the Wilk Street meetinghouse every Monday afternoon, and leave me to take care of the house. When left thus, I used to spend the time in writing in the spaces left in Master Thomas's copy-book, copying what he had written. I continued to do this until I could write a hand very similar to that of Master Thomas. Thus, after a long, tedious effort for years, I finally succeeded in learning how to write.

Engaging with the Text

1. Frederick Douglass notes that within the mindset of a slaveholder "education and slavery were incompatible with each other." What does Douglass mean by this observation? What does his experience suggest about the relationship between literacy (reading and writing) and freedom?

30

2. What is the **SIGNIFICANCE** of Douglass's tale? Why do you think the story of how he learned to read and write was important to him? Though times have changed since Douglass wrote his autobiography, it is still read today. What is its significance today? How is it seen differently today from when it was first published?

285–93
285–88
291–92

3. In the beginning of this text, Douglass **DESCRIBES** his mistress and her role in his education. What **DETAILS** does he offer about her, and what **DOMINANT IMPRESSION** do they create? How do you think Douglass felt about her at the time that he wrote this narrative? Cite examples from the text in your response.

29
30

4. Although Douglass's text was written over one hundred and fifty years ago, it nevertheless exhibits the same features that distinguish literacy narratives written today — a **WELL-TOLD STORY**, **VIVID DETAILS**, and some indication of the narrative's **SIGNIFICANCE**. Choose one of those features and discuss how it helps make this a powerful and effective literacy narrative.

5. *For Writing.* Think about your own experience learning to read and write. Did you want to learn, or was it simply expected of you? Did you in any way teach yourself, or did you learn from a schoolteacher or a relative? Write your own **LITERACY NARRATIVE**, considering how you learned to read and write.

21–38

MALCOLM X

Literacy Behind Bars

Best known as a militant black nationalist leader who rose to global fame as an advocate for Pan-Africanism (a movement that aims to unite all people of African descent), Malcolm X was born Malcolm Little in 1925. He replaced the name Little, which he considered a slave name, with the letter X to represent his lost African tribal name. Founder of the Muslim Mosque Inc. and the Organization of Afro-American Unity, Malcolm X was assassinated by political rivals on February 21, 1965. The following narrative comes from his autobiography, The Auto-biography of Malcolm X (1965), which he wrote with Alex Haley.

MANY WHO TODAY HEAR ME somewhere in person, or on television, or those who read something I've said, will think I went to school far beyond the eighth grade. This impression is due entirely to my prison studies.

It had really begun back in the Charlestown Prison,[1] when Bimbi first made me feel envy of his stock of knowledge. Bimbi had always taken charge of any conversation he was in, and I had tried to emulate him. But every book I picked up had few sentences which didn't contain anywhere from one to nearly all of the words that might as well have been in Chinese. When I just skipped those words, of course, I really ended up with little idea of what the book said. So I had come to the Norfolk Prison Colony still going through only book-reading motions. Pretty soon, I would have quit even these motions, unless I had received the motivation that I did.

I saw that the best thing I could do was get hold of a dictionary — to study, to learn some words. I was lucky enough to reason also that I should try to improve my penmanship. It was sad. I couldn't even write in a straight line. It was both ideas together that moved me to request a dictionary along with some tables and pencils from the Norfolk Prison Colony school.

---

1. Near Boston, Massachusetts.

Malcolm X, 1964. Time Life Pictures / Getty Images.

I spent two days just riffling uncertainly through the dictionary's pages. I'd never realized so many words existed! I didn't know *which* words I needed to learn. Finally, just to start some kind of action, I began copying.

In my slow, painstaking, ragged handwriting, I copied into my tablet everything printed on that first page, down to the punctuation marks.

I believe it took me a day. Then, aloud, I read back, to myself, everything I'd written on the tablet. Over and over, aloud, to myself, I read my own handwriting.

I woke up the next morning, thinking about those words — immensely proud to realize that not only had I written so much at one time, but I'd written words that I never knew were in the world. Moreover, with a little effort, I also could remember what many of these words meant. I reviewed the words whose meanings I didn't remember. Funny thing, from the dictionary first page right now, that "aardvark" springs to my mind. The dictionary had a picture of it, a long-tailed, long-eared, burrowing African mammal, which lives off termites caught by sticking out its tongue as an anteater does for ants.

I was so fascinated that I went on — I copied the dictionary's next page. And the same experience came when I studied that. With every succeeding page, I also learned of people and places and events from history. Actually the dictionary is like a miniature encyclopedia. Finally the dictionary's A section had filled a whole tablet — and I went on into the B's. That was the way I started copying what eventually became the entire dictionary. It went a lot faster after so much practice helped me to pick up handwriting speed. Between what I wrote in my tablet, and writing letters, during the rest of my time in prison I would guess I wrote a million words.

I suppose it was inevitable that as my word-base broadened, I could for the first time pick up a book and read and now begin to understand what the book was saying. Anyone who has read a great deal can imagine the new world that opened. Let me tell you something: from then until I left that prison, in every free moment I had, if I was not reading in the library, I was reading on my bunk. You couldn't have gotten me out of books with a wedge. Between Mr. Muhammad's teachings, my correspondence, my visitors — usually Ella and Reginald — and my reading of books, months passed without my even thinking about being imprisoned. In fact, up to then, I never had been so truly free in my life.

As you can imagine, especially in a prison where there was heavy emphasis on rehabilitation, an inmate was smiled upon if he demonstrated an unusually intense interest in books. There was a sizable number of well-read inmates, especially the popular debaters. Some were said by many to be practically walking encyclopedias. They were almost celebrities. No university would ask any student to devour literature as I did when this new world opened to me, of being able to read and *understand.*

I read more in my room than in the library itself. An inmate who was known to read a lot could check out more than the permitted maximum number of books. I preferred reading in the total isolation of my own room.

When I had progressed to really serious reading, every night at about ten P.M. I would be outraged with the "lights out." It always seemed to catch me right in the middle of something engrossing.

Fortunately, right outside my door was a corridor light that cast a glow into my room. The glow was enough to read by, once my eyes adjusted to it. So when "lights out" came, I would sit on the floor where I could continue reading in that glow.

At one-hour intervals the night guards paced past every room. Each time I heard the approaching footsteps, I jumped into bed and feigned sleep. And as soon as the guard passed, I got back out of bed onto the floor area of that light-glow, where I would read for another fifty-eight minutes — until the guard approached again. That went on until three or four every morning. Three or four hours of sleep a night was enough for me. Often in the years in the streets I had slept less than that. [. . .]

I have often reflected upon the new vistas that reading opened to me. I knew right there in prison that reading had changed forever the course of my life. As I see it today, the ability to read awoke inside me some long dormant craving to be mentally alive. I certainly wasn't seeking any degree, the way a college confers a status symbol upon its students. My homemade education gave me, with every additional book

that I read, a little bit more sensitivity to the deafness, dumbness, and blindness that was afflicting the black race in America. Not long ago, an English writer telephoned me from London, asking questions. One was, "What's your alma mater?" I told him, "Books." You will never catch me with a free fifteen minutes in which I'm not studying something I feel might be able to help the black man. [. . .]

Every time I catch a plane, I have with me a book that I want to read — and that's a lot of books these days. If I weren't out here every day battling the white man, I could spend the rest of my life reading, just satisfying my curiosity — because you can hardly mention anything I'm not curious about. I don't think anybody ever got more out of going to prison than I did. In fact, prison enabled me to study far more intensively than I would have if my life had gone differently and I had attended some college. I imagine that one of the biggest troubles with colleges is there are too many distractions, too much panty-raiding, fraternities, and boola-boola and all of that. Where else but in a prison could I have attacked my ignorance by being able to study intensely sometimes as much as fifteen hours a day.

Engaging with the Text

1. In **DESCRIBING** how he felt after learning to read and write more fluently, Malcolm X states that even though he was in prison, he "never had been so truly free in [his] life." There is a certain irony that anyone would feel free while incarcerated. Consider the relationship between literacy and freedom.

   285–93

2. How would you characterize Malcolm X's **STANCE?** Where in his narrative is this stance made most explicit? Point to specific words and phrases that convey his stance.

   12–14

3. As he describes his efforts to learn to read and write, do you think Malcolm X is **OBJECTIVE, SUBJECTIVE,** or a mixture of both? Give examples from the text to support your answer. Why do you think he chose to write that way?

   288–89

30 ▲

4. Discuss the **SIGNIFICANCE** of Malcolm X's narrative, and by implication the significance of learning to read and write. What lessons does his experience teach us about the power of reading and writing?

5. *For Writing.* Malcolm X advocates reading as an excellent road to education, but a college education consists of far more than reading. Write a **LITERACY NARRATIVE** looking at the role that reading has played in your education so far. Consider the kinds of texts you've read — those you've been assigned to read, and also those you yourself have chosen to read. Consider also the other kinds of work you've done at school — lectures you've attended, exams you've taken, discussions you've participated in, essays you've written, blogs you've created. How important is reading compared with this other work?

21–38 ▲

AMY TAN

Mother Tongue

Amy Tan is the author of novels, children's books, and essays. Her essays have been published in Life *and* Threepenny Review; *her short stories have appeared in* McCall's, Atlantic Monthly, *and other magazines. She is best known for her novel* The Joy Luck Club *(1989), which examines the lives of and the relationships between four Chinese American daughters and their mothers. The following selection was first delivered as a talk at a symposium on language in San Francisco in 1989.*

I AM NOT A SCHOLAR OF ENGLISH OR LITERATURE. I cannot give you much more than personal opinions on the English language and its variations in this country or others.

I am a writer. And by that definition, I am someone who has always loved language. I am fascinated by language in daily life. I spend a great deal of my time thinking about the power of language — the way it can evoke an emotion, a visual image, a complex idea, or a simple truth. Language is the tool of my trade. And I use them all — all the Englishes I grew up with.

Recently, I was made keenly aware of the different Englishes I do use. I was giving a talk to a large group of people, the same talk I had already given to half a dozen other groups. The nature of the talk was about my writing, my life, and my book, *The Joy Luck Club.* The talk was going along well enough, until I remembered one major difference that made the whole talk sound wrong. My mother was in the room. And it was perhaps the first time she had heard me give a lengthy speech, using the kind of English I have never used with her. I was saying things like, "The intersection of memory upon imagination" and "There is an aspect of my fiction that relates to thus-and-thus" — a speech filled with carefully wrought grammatical phrases, burdened, it suddenly seemed to me, with nominalized forms, past perfect tenses, conditional phrases, all the forms of standard English that I had learned in school and through books, the forms of English I did not use at home with my mother.

Just last week, I was walking down the street with my mother, and I again found myself conscious of the English I was using, the English I do use with her. We were talking about the price of new and used furniture and I heard myself saying this: "Not waste money that way." My husband was with us as well, and he didn't notice any switch in my English. And then I realized why. It's because over the twenty years we've been together I've often used the same kind of English with him, and sometimes he even uses it with me. It has become our language of intimacy, a different sort of English that relates to family talk, the language I grew up with.

So you'll have some idea of what this family talk I heard sounds 5 like, I'll quote what my mother said during a recent conversation which I videotaped and then transcribed. During this conversation, my mother was talking about a political gangster in Shanghai who had the same last name as her family's, Du, and how the gangster in his early years wanted to be adopted by her family, which was rich by comparison. Later, the gangster became more powerful, far richer than my mother's family, and one day showed up at my mother's wedding to pay his respects. Here's what she said in part:

"Du Yusong having business like fruit stand. Like off the street kind. He is Du like Du Zong — but not Tsung-ming Island people. The local people call putong, the river east side, he belong to that side local people. That man want to ask Du Zong father take him in like become own family. Du Zong father wasn't look down on him, but didn't take seriously, until that man big like become a mafia. Now important person, very hard to inviting him. Chinese way, came only to show respect, don't stay for dinner. Respect for making big celebration, he shows up. Mean gives lots of respect. Chinese custom. Chinese social life that way. If too important won't have to stay too long. He come to my wedding. I didn't see, I heard it. I gone to boy's side, they have YMCA dinner. Chinese age I was nineteen."

You should know that my mother's expressive command of English belies how much she actually understands. She reads the *Forbes* report, listens to *Wall Street Week*, converses daily with her stockbroker, reads all of Shirley MacLaine's books with ease — all kinds of things I can't begin to understand. Yet some of my friends tell me they understand 50 percent of what my mother says. Some say they understand 80 to 90 percent. Some say they understand none of it, as if she were speaking pure Chinese. But to me, my mother's English is perfectly clear, perfectly natural. It's my mother tongue. Her language, as I hear it, is vivid, direct, full of observation and imagery. That was the language that helped shape the way I saw things, expressed things, made sense of the world.

Lately, I've been giving more thought to the kind of English my mother speaks. Like others, I have described it to people as "broken" or "fractured" English. But I wince when I say that. It has always bothered me that I can think of no way to describe it other than "broken," as if it were damaged and needed to be fixed, as if it lacked a certain wholeness and soundness. I've heard other terms used, "limited English," for example. But they seem just as bad, as if everything is limited, including people's perceptions of the limited English speaker.

I know this for a fact, because when I was growing up, my mother's "limited" English limited *my* perception of her. I was ashamed of her English. I believed that her English reflected the quality of what she had to say. That is, because she expressed them imperfectly her thoughts were imperfect. And I had plenty of empirical evidence to support me: the fact that people in department stores, at banks, and at restaurants did not take her seriously, did not give her good service, pretended not to understand her, or even acted as if they did not hear her.

My mother has long realized the limitations of her English as well. 10 When I was fifteen, she used to have me call people on the phone to pretend I was she. In this guise, I was forced to ask for information or even to complain and yell at people who had been rude to her. One time it was a call to her stockbroker in New York. She had cashed out her small portfolio and it just so happened we were going to go to New York the next week, our very first trip outside California. I had to get on the phone and say in an adolescent voice that was not very convincing, "This is Mrs. Tan."

And my mother was standing in the back whispering loudly, "Why he don't send me check, already two weeks late. So mad he lie to me, losing me money."

And then I said in perfect English, "Yes, I'm getting rather concerned. You had agreed to send the check two weeks ago, but it hasn't arrived."

Then she began to talk more loudly. "What he want, I come to New York tell him front of his boss, you cheating me?" And I was trying to calm her down, make her be quiet, while telling the stockbroker, "I can't tolerate any more excuses. If I don't receive the check immediately, I am going to have to speak to your manager when I'm in New York next week." And sure enough, the following week there we were in front of this astonished stockbroker, and I was sitting there red-faced and quiet, and my mother, the real Mrs. Tan, was shouting at his boss in her impeccable broken English.

We used a similar routine just five days ago, for a situation that was far less humorous. My mother had gone to the hospital for an appointment, to find out about a benign brain tumor a CAT scan had revealed a month ago. She said she had spoken very good English, her best English, no mistakes. Still, she said, the hospital did not apologize when they said they had lost the CAT scan and she had come for nothing. She said they did not seem to have any sympathy when she told them she was anxious to know the exact diagnosis, since her husband and son had both died of brain tumors. She said they would not give her any more information until the next time and she would have to make another appointment for that. So she said she would not leave until the doctor called her daughter. She wouldn't budge. And when the doctor finally called her daughter, me, who spoke in perfect English — lo and behold — we had assurances the CAT scan would be found, promises that a conference call on Monday would be held, and apologies for any suffering my mother had gone through for a most regrettable mistake.

I think my mother's English almost had an effect on limiting my 15 possibilities in life as well. Sociologists and linguists probably will tell you that a person's developing language skills are more influenced by peers. But I do think that the language spoken in the family, especially in immigrant families which are more insular, plays a large role in shaping the language of the child. And I believe that it affected my results on achievement tests, IQ tests, and the SAT. While my English skills were never judged as poor, compared to math, English could not be considered my strong suit. In grade school I did moderately well, getting perhaps B's, sometimes B-pluses, in English and scoring perhaps in the sixtieth or seventieth percentile on achievement tests. But those scores were not good enough to override the opinion that my true abilities lay in math and science, because in those areas I achieved A's and scored in the ninetieth percentile or higher.

This was understandable. Math is precise; there is only one correct answer. Whereas, for me at least, the answers on English tests were always a judgment call, a matter of opinion and personal experience. Those tests were constructed around items like fill-in-the-blank sentence completion, such as, "Even though Tom was _____, Mary thought he was _____." And the correct answer always seemed to be the most bland combinations of thoughts, for example, "Even though Tom was shy, Mary thought he was charming," with the grammatical structure "even though" limiting the correct answer to some sort of semantic opposites, so you wouldn't get answers like, "Even though Tom was foolish, Mary thought he was ridiculous." Well, according to my mother, there were very few limitations as to what Tom could have been and what Mary might have thought of him. So I never did well on tests like that.

The same was true with word analogies, pairs of words in which you were supposed to find some sort of logical, semantic relationship — for example, "*Sunset* is to *nightfall* as _____ is to _____." And here you would be presented with a list of four possible pairs, one of which showed the same kind of relationship: *red* is to *stoplight, bus* is to *arrival, chills* is to *fever, yawn* is to *boring*. Well, I could never think that way. I knew what the tests were asking, but I could not block out of my mind the images already created by the first pair, "*sunset* is to *nightfall*" — and I would see a burst of colors against a darkening sky, the moon rising, the lowering of a curtain of stars. And all the other pairs of words — red, bus, stoplight, boring — just threw up a mass of confusing images, making it impossible for me to sort out something as logical as saying: "A sunset precedes nightfall" is the same as "a chill precedes a fever." The only way I would have gotten that answer right would have been to imagine an associative situation, for example, my being disobedient and staying out past sunset, catching a chill at night, which turns into feverish pneumonia as punishment, which indeed did happen to me.

I have been thinking about all this lately, about my mother's English, about achievement tests. Because lately I've been asked, as a writer, why there are not more Asian Americans represented in American literature. Why are there few Asian Americans enrolled in creative writing programs? Why do so many Chinese students go into engineering? Well, these are broad sociological questions I can't begin to answer. But I have noticed in surveys — in fact, just last week — that Asian students, as a whole, always do significantly better on math achievement tests than in English. And this makes me think that there are other Asian-American students whose English spoken in the home might also be described as "broken" or "limited." And perhaps they also have teachers who are steering them away from writing and into math and science, which is what happened to me.

Fortunately, I happen to be rebellious in nature and enjoy the challenge of disproving assumptions made about me. I became an English major my first year in college, after being enrolled as pre-med. I started writing nonfiction as a freelancer the week after I was told by my former boss that writing was my worst skill and I should hone my talents toward account management.

But it wasn't until 1985 that I finally began to write fiction. And at 20 first I wrote using what I thought to be wittily crafted sentences, sentences that would finally prove I had mastery over the English language. Here's an example from the first draft of a story that later made its way into *The Joy Luck Club,* but without this line: "That was my mental quandary in its nascent state." A terrible line, which I can barely pronounce.

Fortunately, for reasons I won't get into today, I later decided I should envision a reader for the stories I would write. And the reader I decided upon was my mother, because these were stories about mothers. So with this reader in mind — and in fact she did read my early drafts — I began to write stories using all the Englishes I grew up with: the English I spoke to my mother, which for lack of a better term might be described as "simple"; the English she used with me, which for lack of a better term might

be described as "broken"; my translation of her Chinese, which could certainly be described as "watered down"; and what I imagined to be her translation of her Chinese if she could speak in perfect English, her internal language, and for that I sought to preserve the essence, but neither an English nor a Chinese structure. I wanted to capture what language ability tests can never reveal: her intent, her passion, her imagery, the rhythms of her speech and the nature of her thoughts.

Apart from what any critic had to say about my writing, I knew I had succeeded where it counted when my mother finished reading my book and gave me her verdict: "So easy to read."

Engaging with the Text

1. Amy Tan **BEGINS** by announcing, "I am not a scholar of English . . . I cannot give you much more than personal opinions on the English language and its variations in this country or others." How does this opening set up your expectations for the rest of the essay? Why do you think she chose to begin by denying her own authority? *239–45*

2. Tan writes about the different "Englishes" she speaks. What categories does she **DIVIDE** English into? Why are these divisions important to Tan? How does she say they affect her as a writer? *261–62*

3. Tan wrote this essay for a literary journal. How does writing for a literary **AUDIENCE** affect the language she primarily uses in the essay? What kind of English do you think she believes her audience speaks? Why? Support your answer with quotations from the text. *5–8*

4. How does Tan's **TITLE** — "Mother Tongue" — affect the way you read her argument? What other titles might she have chosen? *250–51*

5. *For Writing.* Explore the differences between the language you speak at home and the languages you use with friends, teachers, employers, and so on. Write an essay that **REFLECTS** on the various languages you speak. If you speak only one language, consider the variations in the ways you speak it — at home, at work, at school, at church, wherever. *168–73*

MIKE ROSE

Potato Chips and Stars

Mike Rose is a professor of social research methodology in the Graduate School of Education and Information Studies at UCLA. A scholar of literacy and education, Rose has published numerous essays and books, including When a Writer Can't Write (1985), Possible Lives (1995), The Mind at Work (2004), *and the award-winning* Lives on the Boundary (1989), *in which this piece first appeared.*

IT'S FUNNY HOW SCANT ARE MY RECOLLECTIONS OF SCHOOL. I remember the red brick building of St. Regina's itself, and the topography of the playground: the swings and basketball courts and peeling benches. There are images of a few students: Erwin Petschaur, a muscular Germany boy with a strong accent; Dave Sanchez, who was good in math; and Sheila Wilkes, everyone's curly-haired heartthrob. And there are two nuns: Sister Monica, the third-grade teacher with beautiful hands for whom I carried a candle and who, to my dismay, had wedded herself to Christ; and Sister Beatrice, a woman truly crazed, who would sweep into class, eyes wide, to tell us about the Apocalypse.

All the hours in class tend to blend into one long, vague stretch of time. What I remember best, strangely enough, are the two things I couldn't understand and over the years grew to hate: grammar lessons and mathematics. I would sit there watching a teacher draw her long horizontal line and her short, oblique lines and break up sentences and put adjectives here and adverbs there and just not get it, couldn't see the reason for it, turned off to it. I would hide by slumping down in my seat and page through my reader, carried along by the flow of sentences in a story. She would test us, and I would dread that, for I always got Cs and Ds. Mathematics was a bit different. For whatever reasons, I didn't learn early math very well, so when it came time for more complicated operations, I couldn't keep up and started daydreaming to avoid my inadequacy. This was a strategy I would rely on as I grew older. I fell further and further behind. A memory: The teacher is faceless and seems very far away. The voice is faint and is discussing an equation written on the board. It is raining, and I am watching the streams of water form patterns on the windows.

I realize now how consistently I defended myself against the lessons I couldn't understand and the people and events of South L.A. that were too strange to view head-on. I got very good at watching a blackboard with minimum awareness. And I drifted more and more into a variety of protective fantasies. I was lucky in that although my parents didn't read or write very much and had no more than a few books around the house, they never debunked my pursuits. And when they could, they bought me what I needed to spin my web.

One early Christmas they got me a small chemistry set. My father brought home an old card table from the secondhand store, and on that table I spread out my test tubes, my beaker, my Erlenmeyer flask, and my gas-generating apparatus. The set came equipped with chemicals, minerals, and various treated papers — all in little square bottles. You could send away to someplace in Maryland for more, and I did, saving pennies and nickels to get the substances that were too exotic for my set, the Junior Chemcraft: Congo red paper, azurite, glycerine, chrome alum, cochineal — this from female insects! — tartaric acid, chameleon paper, logwood. I would sit before my laboratory and play for hours. My father rested on the purple couch in front of me watching wrestling or *Gunsmoke* while I measured powders or heated crystals or blew into solutions that my breath would turn red or pink. I was taken by the blends of names and by the colors that swirled through the beaker. My equations were visual and phonetic. I would hold a flask up to the hall light, imagining the veils of a million atoms dancing. Sulfur and alcohol hung in the air. I wanted to shake down the house.

One day my mother came home from Coffee Dan's with an awful 5 story. The teenage brother of one of her waitress friends was in the hospital. He had been fooling around with explosives in his garage "where his mother couldn't see him," and something happened, and "he blew away part of his throat. For God's sake, be careful," my mother said. "Remember poor Ada's brother." Wow! I thought. How neat! Why couldn't my experiments be that dangerous? I really lost heart when I realized that you could probably eat the chemicals spread across my table.

I knew what I had to do. I saved my money for a week and then walked with firm resolve past Walt's Malts, past the brake shop, across Ninetieth Street, and into Palazolla's market. I bought a little bottle of Alka-Seltzer and ran home. I chipped up the wafers and mixed them into a jar of white crystals. When my mother came home, dog tired, and sat down on the edge of the couch to tell me and Dad about her day, I gravely poured my concoction into a beaker of water, cried something about the unexpected, and ran out from behind my table. The beaker foamed ominously. My father swore in Italian. The second time I tried it, I got something milder — in English. And by my third near-miss with death, my parents were calling my behavior cute. Cute! Who wanted cute? I wanted to toy with the disaster that befell Ada Pendleton's brother. I wanted all those wonderful colors to collide in ways that could blow your voice box right off.

But I was limited by the real. The best I could do was create a toxic antacid. I loved my chemistry set — its glassware and its intriguing labels — but it wouldn't allow me to do the things I wanted to do. St. Regina's had an all-purpose room, one wall of which was lined with old books — and one of those shelves held a row of plastic-covered space novels. The sheen of their covers was gone, and their futuristic portraits were dotted with erasures and grease spots like a meteor shower of the everyday. I remember the rockets best. Long cylinders outfitted at the base with three slick fins, tapering at the other end to a perfect conical point, ready to pierce out of the stratosphere and into my imagination: X-fifteens and Mach 1, the dark side of the moon, the Red Planet, Jupiter's Great Red Spot, Saturn's rings — and beyond the solar system to swirling wisps of galaxies, to stardust.

I would check out my books two at a time and take them home to curl up with a blanket on my chaise longue, reading, sometimes, through the weekend, my back aching, my thoughts lost between galaxies. I became the hero of a thousand adventures, all with intricate plots and the triumph of good over evil, all many dimensions removed from the dim walls of the living room. We were given time to draw in school, so, before long, all this worked itself onto paper. The stories I was reading were

reshaping themselves into pictures. My father got me some butcher paper from Palazzolla's, and I continued to draw at home. My collected works rendered the Horsehead Nebula, goofy space cruisers, robots, and Saturn. Each had its crayon, a particular waxy pencil with mood and meaning: rust and burnt sienna for Mars, yellow for the Sun, lime and rose for Saturn's rings, and bright red for the Jovian spot. I had a little sharpener to keep the points just right. I didn't write any stories; I just read and drew. I wouldn't care much about writing until late in high school.

The summer before the sixth grade, I got a couple of jobs. The first was at a pet store a block or so away from my house. Since I was still small, I could maneuver around in breeder cages, scraping the heaps of parakeet crap from the tin floor, cleaning the water troughs and seed trays. It was pretty awful. I would go home after work and fill the tub and soak until all the fleas and bird mites came floating to the surface, little Xs in their multiple eyes. When I heard about a job selling strawberries door-to-door, I jumped at it. I went to work for a white-haired Chicano named Frank. He would carry four or five kids and dozens of crates of strawberries in his ramshackle truck up and down the avenues of the better neighborhoods: houses with mowed lawns and petunia beds. We'd work all day for seventy-five cents, Frank dropping pairs of us off with two crates each, then picking us up at preassigned corners. We spent lots of time together, bouncing around on the truck bed redolent with strawberries or sitting on a corner, cold, listening for the sputter of Frank's muffler. I started telling the other kids about my books, and soon it was my job to fill up that time with stories.

Reading opened up the world. There I was, a skinny bookworm drawing the attention of street kids who, in any other circumstances, would have had me for breakfast. Like an epic tale-teller, I developed the stories as I went along, relying on a flexible plot line and a repository of heroic events. I had a great time. I sketched out trajectories with my finger on Frank's dusty truck bed. And I stretched out each story's climax, creating cliffhangers like the ones I saw in the Saturday serials. These stories created for me a temporary community.

It was around this time that fiction started leading me circuitously to a child's version of science. In addition to the space novels, St. Regina's library also had half a dozen books on astronomy — *The Golden Book of the Planets* and stuff like that — so I checked out a few of them. I liked what I read and wheedled enough change out of my father to enable me to take the bus to the public library. I discovered star maps, maps of lunar seas, charts upon charts of the solar system and the planetary moons: Rhea, Europe, Callisto, Miranda, Io. I didn't know that most of these moons were named for women — I didn't know classical mythology — but I would say their names to myself as though they had a woman's power to protect: Europa, Miranda, Io . . . The distances between stars fascinated me, as did the sizes of the big telescopes. I sent away for catalogs. Then prices fascinated me too. I wanted to drape my arm over a thousand-dollar scope and hear its motor drive whirr. I conjured a twelve-year-old's life of the astronomer: sitting up all night with potato chips and the stars, tracking the sky for supernovas, humming "Earth Angel" with the Penguins. What was my mother to do but save her tips and buy me a telescope?!

It was a little reflecting job, and I solemnly used to carry it out to the front of the house on warm summer nights, to find Venus or Alpha Centauri or trace the stars in Orion or lock onto the moon. I would lay out my star maps on the concrete, more for their magic than anything else, for I had trouble figuring them out. I was no geometer of the constellations; I was their balladeer. Those nights were very peaceful. I was far enough away from the front door and up enough from the sidewalk to make it seem as if I rested on a mound of dark silence, a mountain in Arizona, perhaps, watching the sky alive with points of light. . . . The flat days, the gang fights — all this receded, for it was now me, the star child, lost in an eyepiece focused on a reflecting mirror that cradled, in its center, a shimmering moon.

Engaging with the Text

1. This piece comes from Mike Rose's book *Lives on the Boundary*, which investigates the shortcomings of remedial education in the United States. In light of the goal of this book, what do you think is the PURPOSE

◼ rhetorical situations   ▲ genres   ○ processes   ◆ strategies   ● research mla/apa   ▢ media/ design   ◫ readings

of this literacy narrative? Why do you think Rose includes it in his book — that is, how does it support a critique of remedial education? How well does this piece achieve its purpose?

2. Elsewhere in this book, Rose observes that some people "describe the classroom as an oasis of possibility." Was this the case for Rose? How does he remember his own time as a student in classrooms? Where did he himself seem to learn best?

3. Well-written literacy narratives often include **VIVID DETAIL.** What kinds of details does Rose **DESCRIBE** in his narrative? What **DOMINANT IMPRESSION** do they create of Rose's childhood and education, and of Rose himself? Point to specific places in the text to support your observations.

▲ 29
◆ 285–93
◆ 291–92

4. Rose describes several different literacies — ways of reading and thinking in grammar, math, chemistry, and astronomy. His narrative shows that he was more successful in learning to read science than grammar or math. Why do you think this was the case? How did science fiction support his abilities in science — and vice versa?

5. *For Writing.* Rose describes several literacies he developed and pursued outside of school: chemistry, where he learned to read chemicals; astronomy, where he learned to read charts and the sky; and science fiction, where he learned to read and tell epic stories. Identify a particular literacy that you have developed outside of school, and write a **LITERACY NARRATIVE** in which you tell about how you first became interested in it, what kinds of materials you read, and what kinds of writing or performance it has led to.

▲ 21–38

51 Textual Analyses

rhetorical situations   genres   processes   strategies   research mla/apa   media/design   readings

DENISE NOE

Parallel Worlds:
The Surprising Similarities (and Differences) of Country-and-Western and Rap

Denise Noe is the community editor for the newsmagazine Caribbean Star *and a writer whose essays have appeared in the* Atlanta Journal-Constitution *and elsewhere. She has also written widely on true crime. The following analysis appeared in 1995 in the* Humanist, *a magazine published by the American Humanist Association that covers such topics as politics, popular culture, science, and religion from a humanist perspective.*

IN ALL OF POPULAR MUSIC TODAY, there are probably no two genres that are more apparently dissimilar than country-and-western and rap: the one rural, white, and southern; the other urban, black, and identified with the two coasts ("New York style" versus "L.A. style"). Yet C&W and rap are surprisingly similar in many ways. In both C&W and rap, for example, lyrics are important. Both types of music tell stories, as do folk songs, and the story is much more than frosting for the rhythm and beat.

The ideologies espoused by these types of music are remarkably similar as well. We frequently stereotype country fans as simple-minded conservatives — "redneck," moralistic super-patriots à la Archie Bunker. But country music often speaks critically of mainstream American platitudes, especially in such highly charged areas as sexual morality, crime, and the Protestant work ethic.

The sexual ethos of C&W and rap are depressingly similar: the men of both genres are champion chauvinists. Country singer Hank Williams, Jr., declares he's "Going Hunting Tonight," but he doesn't need a gun since he's hunting the "she-cats" in a singles bar. Male rappers such as Ice-T, Ice Cube, and Snoop Doggy Dogg are stridently misogynist, with "bitches" and "hos" their trademark terms for half of humanity; their enthusiastic depictions of women raped and murdered are terrifying.

Indeed, the sexism of rap group NWA (Niggaz with Attitude) reached a real-life nadir when one member of the group beat up a woman he thought "dissed" them — and was praised for his brutality by the other members.

On a happier note, both rap and C&W feature strong female voices as well. Women rappers are strong, confident, and raunchy: "I want a man, not a boy / to approach me / Your lame game really insults me. . . . I've got to sit on my feet to come down to your level," taunt lady rappers Entice and Barbie at Too Short in their duet/duel, "Don't Fight the Feeling." Likewise, Loretta Lynn rose to C&W fame with defiant songs like "Don't Come Home a-Drinkin' with Lovin' on Your Mind" and "Your Squaw Is on the Warpath Tonight."

Country music can be bluntly honest about the realities of sex and money — in sharp contrast to the "family values" rhetoric of the right. "Son of Hickory Hollow's Tramp" by Johnny Darrell salutes a mother who works as a prostitute to support her children. "Fancy" by Bobbie Gentry (and, more recently, Reba McEntire) describes a poverty-stricken woman's use of sex for survival and her rise to wealth on the ancient "gold mine." Both tunes are unapologetic about the pragmatic coping strategies of their heroines.

More startling than the resemblances in their male sexism and "uppity" women are the parallels between C&W and rap in their treatment of criminality. Country-and-western music is very far from a rigid law-and-order mentality. The criminal's life is celebrated for its excitement and clear-cut rewards — a seemingly promising alternative to the dull grind of day-to-day labor.

"Ain't got no money / Ain't got no job / Let's find a place to rob," sings a jaunty Ricky Van Shelton in "Crime of Passion." In "I Never Picked Cotton," Roy Clark is more subdued but still unrepentant when he says: "I never picked cotton / like my mother did and my sister did and my brother did / And I'll never die young / working in a coal mine like my daddy did." Waylon Jennings' "Good Ole Boys" boast gleefully of having "hot-wired a city truck / turned it over in the mayor's yard."

Similarly, rap songs like "Gangsta, Gangsta" and "Dopeman" by NWA and "Drama" by Ice-T tell of the thrill and easy money offered by a life of crime. "Drama" records the dizzying high of the thief; "Gangsta,

Gangsta," the rush of adrenaline experienced by a murderer making a quick getaway. Of course, both C&W and rap songs do express the idea that in the long run crime doesn't pay. The sad narrator of Merle Haggard's "Mama Tried" "turned 21 in prison / doing life without parole," while the thief of Ice-T's "Drama" is forced to realize that "I wouldn't be here if I'd fed my brain / Got knowledge from schoolbooks / 'stead of street crooks / Now all I get is penitentiary hard looks."

Though both C&W and rap narrators are often criminals, their attitudes toward law enforcement differ radically. The Irish Rovers' "Wasn't That a Party?" ("that little drag race down on Main Street / was just to see if the cops could run") pokes light-hearted fun at the police, while the Bobby Fuller Four's "I Fought the Law and the Law Won" expresses the most common C&W attitude: an acceptance that criminals must be caught, even if you are one. Neither song displays any anger toward the police, who are, after all, just doing their job.

To rappers, on the other hand, cops are the enemy. Two of the most notorious rap songs are Ice-T's "Cop Killer" and NWA's "Fuck tha Police" (which angrily asserts, "Some police think they have the authority to kill a minority"). Despite ample evidence of police brutality in the inner city, "Fuck tha Police" was almost certainly regarded by nonblack America as a paranoid shriek — until the world witnessed the infamous videotape of several of Los Angeles' finest brutally beating Rodney King while a dozen other "peace officers" nonchalantly looked on. 10

Interestingly, although the C&W view of law enforcement naturally sits better with the general public (certainly with the police themselves), the fact remains that country-and-western music contains a good deal of crime, violence, and casual sex. Yet it is easily accepted by white Americans while rap arouses alarm and calls for labeling. Why?

I believe there are three major reasons. The first, and simplest, is language. Rappers say "bitch," "ho," "fuck," and "motherfucker"; C&W artists don't. Country singers may say, "I'm in the mood to speak some French tonight" (Mary Chapin-Carpenter, "How Do") or "There's two kinds of cherries / and two kinds of fairies" (Merle Haggard, "My Own Kind of Hat"), but they avoid the bluntest Anglo-Saxon terms.

A second reason is race. African-Americans have a unique history of oppression in this country, and rap reflects the inner-city African-

American experience. Then, too, whites expect angry, frightening messages from blacks and listen for them. Many blacks, on the other hand, hope for uplifting messages — and are dismayed when black artists seem to encourage or glorify the drug abuse and violence in their beleaguered communities. Thus, the focus on violence in rap — and the dismissal of same in C&W.

While the differing attitudes toward law enforcement are real enough, much of the difference between violence in country-and-western music and in rap lies not in the songs themselves but in the way they are heard. Thus, when Ice Cube says, "Let the suburbs see a nigga invasion / Point-blank, smoke the Caucasian," many whites interpret that as an incitement to violence. But when Johnny Cash's disgruntled factory worker in "Oney" crows, "Today's the day old Oney gets his," it's merely a joke. Likewise, when Ice Cube raps, "I've got a shotgun and here's the plot / Taking niggas out with the fire of buckshot" ("Gangsta, Gangsta"), he sends shudders through many African-Americans heartbroken by black-on-black violence; but when Johnny Cash sings of an equally nihilistic killing in "Folsom Prison Blues" — "Shot a man in Reno / just to watch him die" — the public taps its feet and hums along. . . . It's just a song, after all.

There is a third — and ironic — reason why rap is so widely attacked: 15
rap is actually closer to mainstream American economic ideology than country-and-western is. While C&W complains about the rough life of honest labor for poor and working-class people, rap ignores it almost entirely. "Work your fingers to the bone and what do you get?" asks Hoyt Axton in a satirical C&W song, then answers sardonically with its title: "Bony Fingers." Likewise, Johnny Paycheck's infamous "Take This Job and Shove It" is a blue-collar man's bitter protest against the rough and repetitive nature of his life's work. Work in C&W is hard and meaningless; it keeps one alive, but leaves the worker with little time or energy left to enjoy life.

Songs by female country singers reinforce this point in a different way; they insist that love (with sex) is more important than affluence. The heroine of Reba McEntire's "Little Rock" says she'll have to "slip [her wedding ring] off," feeling no loyalty to the workaholic husband who

"sure likes his money" but neglects his wife's emotional and physical needs. Jeanne Pruett in "Back to Back" lampoons the trappings of wealth and proclaims, "I'd trade this mansion / for a run-down shack / and a man who don't believe in sleeping back to back."

Rap's protagonists, on the other hand, are shrewd, materialistic, and rabidly ambitious — although the means to their success are officially proscribed in our society. Not for them a "life that moves at a slower pace" (Alabama, "Down Home"); unlike the languorous hero of country-and-western, "catching these fish like they're going out of style" (Hank Williams, Jr., "Country State of Mind"), rap singers and rap characters alike are imbued with the great American determination to get ahead.

Rap's protagonists — drug dealers, burglars, armed robbers, and "gangstas" — live in a society where success is "a fistful of jewelry" (Eazy E, "No More ?s"), "Motorola phones, Sony color TVs" (Ice-T, "Drama"), where "without a BMW you're through" (NWA, "A Bitch Iz a Bitch"). In NWA's "Dopeman," sometimes cited as an antidrug song, the "Dopeman" is the archetypal American entrepreneur: clever, organized, ruthless, and not ruled by impulse — "To be a dopeman you must qualify / Don't get high off your own supply."

The proximity of rap to our success ethic arouses hostility because America is torn by a deep ideological contradiction: we proudly proclaim ourselves a moral (even religious) nation and tout our capitalist economic system. But the reality of a successful capitalist system is that it undermines conventional morality. A glance at the history books shows how our supposedly moral nation heaped rewards upon the aptly named "robber barons": the Rockefellers, Vanderbilts, Carnegies, and Morgans. The crack dealer is a contemporary version of the bootlegger — at least one of whom, Joe Kennedy, Sr., founded America's most famous political dynasty. (Indeed; I would not be surprised if history repeated itself and the son — or daughter — of a drug lord becomes this country's first African-American president.)

Capitalism is unparalleled in its ability to create goods and distrib-   20
ute services, but it is, like the hero of "Drama," "blind to what's wrong." The only real criterion of a person's worth becomes how much money she or he has — a successful crook is treated better than a poor, law-abiding failure.

In short, the laid-back anti-materialism of country-and-western can be dismissed with a shrug, but the rapper is attacked for that unforgivable sin: holding a mirror up to unpleasant truths. And one of them is that amoral ambition is as American as apple pie and the Saturday Night Special.[1]

Engaging with the Text

39–59
266–74

1. Denise Noe **ANALYZES** country-and-western and rap music, **COMPARING AND CONTRASTING** their lyrics and themes. What is her main point?

2. Noe wrote this analysis for a magazine devoted to humanism, which it defines as a "naturalistic and democratic outlook informed by science, inspired by art, and motivated by compassion." How does she appeal to those values? How might her analysis differ had she written it for a business magazine?

50–51

3. What **EVIDENCE** does Noe offer to support her case about the similarities and differences between country-and-western and rap? What other kind of evidence might she have offered?

50

4. What kind of information about **CONTEXT** does Noe provide? Why is this contextual information important in her final analysis of the acceptance of rap and country-and-western music?

39–59

5. *For Writing.* Select two other genres of music that at first glance would seem as different as the two Noe writes about, and **ANALYZE** their lyrics, music, and contexts for any surprising similarities between them. Help readers understand the nature of the differences between the two genres.

---

1. Any cheap, easily obtained handgun.

rhetorical situations　genres　processes　strategies　research mla/apa　media/ design　readings

KATHARINE Q. SEELYE

Lurid Numbers on Glossy Pages!
(Magazines Exploit What Sells)

Katharine Q. Seelye is a reporter for the New York Times, *where she has written widely on the environment and politics. The following article appeared in the* Times *in 2006.*

A TRIP TO THE NEWSSTAND THESE DAYS can be a dizzying descent into a blizzard of numbers. The March issue of *Elle Girl* promises readers "375 excuses to shop." *Harper's Bazaar* offers "783 new ideas to flatter you." *Marie Claire* trumpets not only "71 easy hair and makeup how-tos" but a mind-blowing "1,157 hot looks (all shapes, all sizes, all prices)."

Magazines, particularly the "service" publications aimed at women, have long used numbers as a selling point while helping readers divine what's in, what's hot, what's cool, what's not. But today, these totals, scores, and inventories seem both increasingly random and increasingly, leaping exponentially beyond the sorry single digits of yesteryear to an incalculable proliferation of paths to a better you.

Glamour's March cover takes number-running to a new level, going full tilt with numerals in all cover lines, those blurbs meant to hook the reader at a glance: "7 reasons you will succeed at work," "15 shocking truths about women & food," "25 sexy little secrets of men's bodies," "25 cheap ways to make over your home," to a grand finale of "500 spring looks for all shapes & sizes!"

Men's magazines, too, are buying into the numbers racket.

Field & Stream gives guys "19 ways to get out alive" (Do you really 5 need more than one?) and "50 ways to get your late-season deer." *Blender,* the music magazine, offers "the 50 most awesomely dead rock stars." *Men's Health* boasts on its March cover: "2,143 sexy women confess what they want in bed." (Look closely — it's a poll, not interviews with 2,143 such women.)

Men's Health *magazine, March 2003.*
Courtesy *Men's Health* magazine.

It all adds up to an arms race at the newsstand. The escalating numbers reflect a new reality for monthly magazines as they struggle against hot-selling, celebrity-crazed weeklies and the Internet to maintain their traditional roles as guideposts in an aspirational society and as glossy vehicles for advertisers, particularly those in the multibillion-dollar cosmetics and fashion industries.

Editors sweat to find the perfect number, but admit there is no formula. As Craig Marks, the editor of *Blender,* put it, "It's all voodoo."

Yet certain patterns are evident. One is that bigger is better. "Size matters," Mr. Marks said.

Another is that odd numbers seem to be more believable than even numbers. "The odd number really speaks to authenticity," said Ariel Foxman, editor of *Cargo.* "If it's odd, it can't be made up or shouldn't have been made up." (Editors insist that they use numbers that their writers actually find in their reporting.) And they said that the number 7 seemed to carry a certain appeal, while 13 is to be shunned.

The subject matter often dictates the size of the number. Cynthia 10 Leive, the editor of *Glamour,* said that if the subject was serious, numbers should be avoided. David Zinczenko, editor of *Men's Health,* said that smaller numbers were better for exercise tips, for example, because readers want something manageable. "Saying '35 best exercises' is too many," Mr. Zinczenko said. "But '789 great new tips for summer' is fine. That says value without saying work."

Most editors test their covers in focus groups in an endless search for the magic that will make their magazines fly off the shelves — and to avoid costly mistakes. And many find that numbers, while not solely

responsible for a popular cover, are almost always written large on those that sell best.

Numbers jump out from the clutter of type on the newsstand. They draw the eye and quickly convey value and utility, helping monthlies in particular stay afloat in the rising ride of celebrity obsession.

"Today, the biggest force everyone is dealing with is celebrity magazines," said Kate White, editor of *Cosmopolitan,* the biggest monthly seller in the country. "You're not competing with other people's numbers, you're competing with Brad and Angelina and babies."

Sex still sells, of course, especially when mingled with celebrity. But behind the glamazons and smoldering cover girls, and often in front of them, stand the numbers.

Cosmo sizzles with a sleek Beyoncé Knowles. And in the upper left quadrant, the portion of a magazine that is usually most visible on the newsstand and therefore is considered prime real estate, blares a numeric come-on: "60 sex skills."

That numbers-laden *Glamour* cover features a curvy Sarah Jessica Parker — ringed by numbers. Ms. Leive said that cover with numbers tested better than the same cover without numbers. She also said she used numbers in that case to give readers something to focus on against the busy background.

But numbers are more than a graphic device.

"The arms race took off because people are busy," Ms. Leive said. Numbers, she said, make certain stories "sound like what they are — a fun, quick, informative, quick, entertaining, quick read."

Bonnie Fuller set off the numbers craze a dozen years ago when she was the founding editor of *Marie Claire.*

Ms. Fuller, now the editorial director of American Media, which publishes *Star* magazine, said she started to use numbers because readers shop from magazines and, as a reader, she wanted to look at more stuff; as an editor, she wanted to tell her readers what she had found.

"You're alerting readers that you have the expertise, you've honed down the massive amount of information out there, especially with the Internet, and you won't waste their time," she said.

Lesley Jane Seymour, the current editor of *Marie Claire,* said she periodically muses about dropping the magazine's signature gigantic number that anchors the bottom right of the cover. But readers in focus groups are saying no to zero.

"Readers say, 'I love the number,'" Ms. Seymour said. "It is one of the best-rated cover lines on the magazine. Do we go overboard? Yes, sometimes. But research shows numbers sell."

Compelling covers are essential for newsstand sales, one of the most cut-throat aspects of the publishing business.

"The newsstand market is a vicious one," said Scott Mowbray, editorial director for Time4 Media, which oversees the Time Inc. enthusiast magazines, including *Field & Stream.* "But it's a very good discipline for editors. They're under tremendous pressure and they're using every tool they can and this approach, where you quantify the value, is working right now." 25

Newsstand sales are potentially more lucrative than subscriptions. They require no postage and the reader pays full price. The newsstand is where publishers find new customers. Home subscribers, by definition, already subscribe, probably at a discount. Printing subscription cards and stuffing them into magazines is cheaper than trolling for new subscribers through a direct mail campaign. And newsstand sales contribute to the rate base that publishers can charge for selling ads, said Martin S. Walker, a magazine consultant.

Still, newsstand sales have their own problems. Newsstands have become more crowded and promotional space at checkout counters more expensive, Mr. Walker said.

This new reality is what drove Glenda Bailey, editor of *Harper's Bazaar,* to start producing separate covers of her magazine, one for the newsstand and one for subscribers. The one on the newsstand has more numbers, Ms. Bailey said, because she is trying to capture new readers who may not know what the magazine has to offer; readers who get it at home already know and can take a more leisurely, if not less commercial, approach.

"On the newsstand, the cover is acting as a poster, an ad for what's inside," she said. "The loyal reader is looking for what makes the magazine exceptional."

rhetorical situations | genres | processes | strategies | research mla/apa | media/ design | readings

Mr. Marks of *Blender* said he liked numbers because, like many men, [30]
he likes to rank things. "We've done 'The 500 greatest songs since you
were born,' and '1,001 songs to download' — in case someone did '1,000
songs,' we would have one more."

Jay Rocco, 27, who was thumbing through magazines in Times
Square yesterday and who is a marketer for movies, is one of those guys.
"I pay attention if there's a list, like the best restaurants," Mr. Rocco said.
"Numbers definitely have an effect on me. I consider a point system to
be a good filter and it lets me evaluate something really quickly."

Editors admit to some numbers burnout but say they do not dare
drop them.

"It's such a powerful device, it works over and over and over again,"
said Isobel McKenzie-Price, editor of *All You*, which sells only on newsstands. "As an editor, I often think, 'I can't do this again.' " But, she said,
there are so many drive-by readers, "that what's boring and old hat to
us is new to them."

Kim France, editor of *Lucky*, the women's shopping magazine, which
offers "774 instant wardrobe updates" in its March issue, said that despite
some skepticism, numbers are resurgent. "Five or six years ago, there were
a ton of numbers on covers and people doubted they were working
because there were so many of them," Ms. France said. "Now there's a
numbers creep again. People wouldn't go back to it if it didn't sell."

Engaging with the Text

1. According to Katharine Seelye's **TEXTUAL ANALYSIS,** what role do numbers serve on the covers of magazines? Why does she say that numbers are increasingly showing up on front covers? How much attention
   do you pay to numbers on a magazine cover when you are considering whether to buy it? Do you agree with Seelye's analysis — and if
   not, why not?

   39–59

2. How does the **TITLE** of this article — "Lurid Numbers on Glossy Pages!
   (Magazines Exploit What Sells)" — reflect the author's **STANCE?** Is it an
   effective title? Why or why not?

   250–51
   12–14

3. This article appeared in the business section of the *New York Times*. How has the **AUDIENCE** affected the way Seelye **ANALYZES** the magazine covers? How might she have analyzed the same covers for an article for the arts section of the *Times*?

5–8

39–59

4. Seelye incorporates numerous **QUOTATIONS** in her article, all of which seem to come from **INTERVIEWS.** Why do you think Seelye chose to limit her research to interviews? Is this effective? What additional **SOURCES** could she have used, if any?

360–62

351–52

340–41

5. *For Writing.* Seelye focuses her analysis on one feature of popular magazine covers. Identify one other common feature — bold typefaces, photographs of famous people, bright colors, shocking quotations — and **ANALYZE** and **COMPARE** how that feature is used on several different magazines. What role does it serve and how is it related to the nature of the publication and its intended audience? Restrict your analysis to one kind of magazine (e.g., sports, teen, women's, fitness, gossip, music, news, science, computers), so that you can focus on how that practice functions for one kind of **AUDIENCE.**

39–59

266–74

5–8

PETER STIGLIN

Seeing as Believing:
The Paintings of Judith Belzer

Peter Stiglin edits and writes for Orion Online, *an online magazine published by the Orion Society, an organization that aims "to inform, inspire, and engage individuals in grassroots organizations in becoming a significant force for healing nature and community." The following analysis of Judith Belzer's art appeared in* Orion Online *in 2003.*

We only see what we look at. To look is an act of choice.
— JOHN BERGER

THE AMOUNT OF VISUAL INFORMATION to which Americans are subjected daily is, to no one's surprise, numbing. The sheer volume of it requires us to take in everything as a whole, absorbing much while actually *seeing* very little. In many areas of our lives we rely on passive information, "given" information, adding up to what we *think* we know about ourselves and our world. The intimacy of primary experience is more and more often deferred, becoming less necessary, even less desirable.

This circumstance is perhaps nowhere more in evidence than in our perception of nature. On a drive through the countryside we view nature — hills and streams, trees and color, light and vistas — all at once, an approach that offers neither access *nor* intimacy. "One of the broad lessons I've learned about nature is that it's very fragmented," comments Judith Belzer. "Up close it is very chaotic. You can't see it as a whole without falling back on conventions, like *wilderness,* or *the sublime.* But if you can learn to look again — starting with the particulars of this place, this time — you can put aside the abstractions and begin to find your own order."

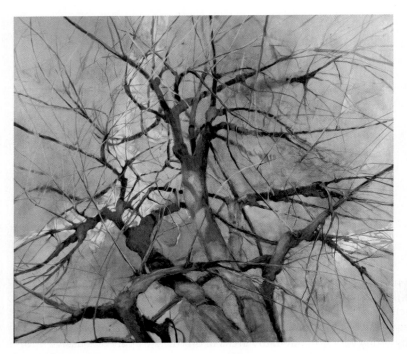

Judith Belzer, Twining Branches #1. Judith Belzer's work courtesy Berry-Hill Galleries, Inc., New York.

Our language offers no singular representation of the profound symbiosis between people and nature. We are linguistically, it seems, forever separate. With its power to reach beyond words, however, art can sometimes propose a worldview more harmonious with the richness of life on this planet, one that enjoins us to bridge the chasm of Eden, that first sin of separation. Attempts by traditional landscape painting to address this breach have been only partially satisfying: the artist's recreation is based on an initial intimacy with nature, but what is often

Judith Belzer, Remnants #6. Judith Belzer's work courtesy Berry-Hill Galleries, Inc., New York.

Judith Belzer, Fall Begins #3. Judith Belzer's work courtesy Berry-Hill Galleries, Inc., New York.

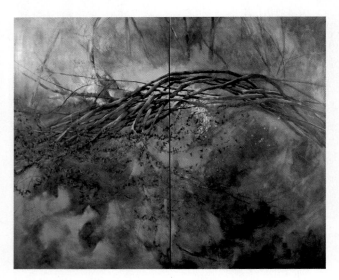

Judith Belzer, New Leaves #5. Judith Belzer's work courtesy Berry-Hill Galleries, Inc., New York.

Judith Belzer, Twining Branches #3. Judith Belzer's work courtesy Berry-Hill Galleries, Inc., New York.

presented to the viewer is a tidy representation of a whole — to be viewed from the outside looking in.

In Judith Belzer's world, remediation — or, more precisely, *rapprochement* — can be found in the selection of the minute, the specific — a branch, a string of leaves — proffering an opening, a ready access point to a secret and mysterious place. *Enter here.*

Like Alice down the rabbit hole, we are taken into the small places, the close spaces, and are brought into intimate relation with what very

little we can see before us, shorn from the whole. "If you can learn to ⁵
immerse yourself in the ordinary things that are very close by," says
the artist, "you start to understand what it means to exist *in* nature.
By establishing a relationship with nature based on particulars — the
way leaves move in space, say, or attach to a branch — you begin to
break our habit of generalizing about nature from a distance. This is
the first step toward changing our approach to the land — and that
starts with seeing."

Engaging with the Text

239–45 ◆   1. Peter Stiglin **OPENS** with an epigraph from philosopher John Berger:
"We only see what we look at. To look is an act of choice." How do
39–59 ▲   Berger's words set the stage for Stiglin's **ANALYSIS** of Judith Belzer's
paintings?

2. According to Stiglin, our language offers no representation of the "profound symbiosis between people and nature. We are linguistically, it
seems, forever separate." What does he mean by this observation?
How do Judith Belzer's paintings, according to Stiglin, bridge the lin-
guistic divide?

50 ▲   3. What is Stiglin's **INTERPRETATION** of Judith Belzer's paintings? Identify
specific passages that reveal this interpretation. How does he support
this interpretation? Do you agree with his interpretation? If not, why
50–51 ▲   not? How might he have offered more **SUPPORT** for his conclusion?

458–62 ☐   4. Although Stiglin includes **PHOTOGRAPHS** of several of Belzer's paintings,
he has not written captions that explain the images or help readers
see anything specific in them. Why do you think he didn't add such
460 ☐   captions? Choose one image and write a **CAPTION** that explains something in the image — and that supports Stiglin's analysis. How does
adding such a caption affect the way readers read the image and the
essay? Do you think it's better to offer such explanation? Why or why
not?

■ rhetorical situations   ▲ genres   ○ processes   ◆ strategies   ● research mla/apa   ☐ media/ design   ❚❚ readings

5. **For Writing.** Think of an artist you like and analyze several of his or her works of art, focusing on patterns or themes you see in the artwork. If possible, interview this artist and ask about his or her artistic goals. Write an essay **ANALYZING** these works of art. You'll want to include some **IMAGES** showing some of the works you analyze, and you may want to quote the artist if you were able to conduct an interview.

▲ 39–59
☐ 458–62

BEVERLY MOSS

Pulpit Talk

Beverly Moss is a professor of English at Ohio State. She has written widely on literacy, community, African-American rhetoric, and the teaching of writing. She is the editor of Literacy Across Communities *(1994) and, with Nels P. Highberg and Melissa Nicolas,* Writing Groups Inside and Outside the Classroom *(2004). The following selection comes from* A Community Text Arises: A Literate Text and a Literacy Tradition in African-American Churches *(2003), Moss's study of the oral and literate traditions of African-American preachers and their congregations. As you read, pay attention to how she uses direct quotations from the discourse she analyzes as examples and support for her analysis.*

THERE WAS MUCH ANTICIPATION about Reverend M.'s arrival to preach the revival. Even though [he] was preaching to a congregation different from his own, it became clear early in [my] fieldwork that he did not consider this congregation totally unfamiliar; nor did he feel the need to abandon many of the strategies that were evident in his home church sermons.

One of the patterns that leaped out at me as I sat in the pew during all the sermons and as I listened to tapes and reviewed fieldnotes was the high level of participation in the sermons by the congregation. Of course, this is a pattern that I had become so familiar with over the years because of its prominence in most African-American churches that I had begun to take it for granted. It is a pattern that almost any discussion of African-American preaching addresses. Just as in the three churches highlighted [earlier], in this church, the congregation and Reverend M. engaged in a call-and-response dialogue. At times during the revival sermons, the feedback from the congregation was so intense that it was impossible to separate speaker from audience. Again, this is not new to African-American churches. Yet it was fascinating to see that this type of collaborative response, this "talking back," was as effective

rhetorical situations   genres   processes   strategies   research mla/apa   media/ design   readings

between Reverend M. and this "new" congregation as it was between Reverend M. and his own congregation. Consider the following exchange from "It's Shoutin' Time":

> When you shout before the battle is over (Preach!)
> It puts things in a proper perspective (Yeah!)
> It puts you in a posture of obedience (Yeah!)
> And it puts things in a proper perspective
> But finally
> When you shout before the battle is fought
> It puts the enemy in confusion (Yeah! That's right!)

The parenthetical expressions, responses from the congregation, do not appear on separate lines because there was little or no pause between the minister's statement and the congregation's response. Often, the congregation's response overlapped with the minister's statement. This type of feedback was typical in the sermons Reverend M. preached to this congregation, as was applause, people standing, cheering, and so on. Practically every sermon Reverend M. preached ended with the majority of the congregation on their feet clapping and talking back to Reverend M.

One of the more interesting highlights of the dialogue or call-and-response collaboration occurred in a sermon within the sermon. In one evening sermon, for example, when Reverend M. discussed how his mother used to talk back to preachers anywhere, he took on the roles of both his mamma and the preacher:

> She be sittin' there sayin' "Well, well," "Don't you see?"
> "Help yourself!" (laughter from congregation)
> "Yes sir"
> "Glory"
> Preacher say "He's a Burden Bearer"
> My mamma say "Yes he is"
> Preacher say "He can make a way"
> My mama say "Yes he can"
> Preacher say "The Lord will provide"
> My mamma say "Yes he will"

This enactment of this mother involved in the dialogue with the preacher not only paralleled the behavior of many in the congregation to whom Reverend M. was preaching at that very moment, but it also established this behavior as a cultural pattern. Note Reverend M.'s preference for direct speech rather than reported or paraphrased speech. His description of his mother was from his memory as a child in Philadelphia. Now, he is standing in front of a congregation in Ohio almost 40 years later engaging them in the same practice, a practice that has become ingrained in the African-American church. Also of note is Reverend M.'s style shift into a form of Vernacular Black English (VBE), a style shift that occurred throughout the sermons when he preached in his own church as well as in the revival sermons. Note, for example, the habitual past tense "she be sittin' there sayin'" and the absence of -s on verb endings in third person singular, "my mamma say" and "the preacher say." Reverend M. shifts from Standard English to VBE when he feels that it fits the topic, when it will make his meaning clearer (for some), when he needs to "bring it to them in a cup they can recognize," or when he needs to "sound Black." At times, the shift is purposeful and, at other times, it just happens. Whenever it happens, it is always rhetorical; that is, it is always meaningful for both Reverend M. and the audience.

Engaging with the Text

39–59 ▲

1. When you **ANALYZE A TEXT**, you are basically arguing that the text should be read in a certain way. What is Beverly Moss's analytical goal in her analysis? What is she trying to show readers about the texts she analyzes?

5–8 ◼

2. Moss wrote this textual analysis for a scholarly **AUDIENCE**, one interested in how discourse works. How might it be different if it were written for the parishioners of Reverend M.'s church?

3. Moss describes the call-and-response practice of the preacher and parishioners as "a cultural pattern." What does she mean by "cultural pattern"? (The common greeting, "How are you?" "Fine, thanks. You?"

is a small example of such a pattern in the United States.) What are some other cultural discourse patterns?

4.　Moss's analysis is based on FIELD RESEARCH, on her own OBSERVATION of Reverend M.'s sermon. What other kinds of RESEARCH might she have included? Why do you think she relied on field research?

● 350–53
● 340–53

5.　**For Writing.** Identify a social gathering such as a religious service, a classroom, a family dinner, or a workplace where you can OBSERVE and analyze the patterns of discourse that take place there. Audio- or videotape several sessions of talk. Transcribe and study the discourse for recurring patterns. Write an essay ANALYZING the patterns you observed. Quote some of the discourse as support for your analysis, and try to INTERPRET what you think it demonstrates about the group and how its members communicate.

● 352–53

▲ 39–59

▲ 50

DIANA GEORGE

Changing the Face of Poverty:
Nonprofits and the Problem of Representation

Diana George is a professor of English at Virgina Polytechnic Institute and State University. She has written widely on culture, writing, and visual representation. She is the editor of Kitchen Cooks, Plate Twirlers, and Troubadours *(1999), a collection of essays by writing program administrators;* Reading Culture *(with John Trimbur, 2004); and* Picturing Texts *(with Lester Faigley, Anna Palchik, and Cynthia Selfe, 2004). The following analysis comes from* Popular Literacy: Studies in Cultural Practices and Poetics *(2001). The endnotes are presented according to* The Chicago Manual of Style, *as they appeared in the original publication.*

Constructively changing the ways the poor are represented in every aspect of life is one progressive intervention that can challenge everyone to look at the face of poverty and not turn away.

— BELL HOOKS, *OUTLAW CULTURE*

ENCLOSED: No Address Labels to Use Up.
No Calendars to Look At.
No Petitions to Sign.

And No Pictures of Starving Children.

Text from the outer envelope of a 1998 Oxfam appeal.

A s I WRITE THIS, Thanksgiving is near. I am about to go out and fill a box with nonperishables for the annual St. Vincent de Paul food drive. Christmas lights already outline some porches. Each day my mailbox is stuffed with catalogs and bills and with appeals from the Native American Scholarship Fund, the Salvation Army, WOJB — Voice of the Anishinabe, the Navaho Health Foundation, the Barbara Kettle Gundlach Shelter Home for Abused Women, Little Brothers Friends of the Elderly, Habitat for Humanity, and more. One *New Yorker* ad for *Children, Inc.* reads, "You don't have to leave your own country to find third-world poverty." Underneath the ad copy, from a black-and-white photo, a young girl in torn and ill-fitting clothes looks directly at the viewer. The copy continues, "In Appalachia, sad faces of children, like Mandy's, will haunt you. There are so many children like her — children who are deprived of the basic necessities right here in America."*

The Oxfam promise that I quote above — to use no pictures of starving children — is surely an attempt to avoid the emotional overload of such images as the one *Children, Inc.* offers. Still, those pictures — those representations of poverty — have typically been one way nonprofits have kept the poor before us. In a culture saturated by the image, how else do we convince Americans that — despite the prosperity they see all around them — there is real need out there? The solution for most nonprofits has been to show the despair. To do that they must represent poverty as something that can be seen and easily recognized: fallen down shacks and trashed out public housing, broken windows, dilapidated porches, barefoot kids with stringy hair, emaciated old women and men staring out at the camera with empty eyes. In such images, poverty is dirt and rags and helplessness. In mail, in magazines, and in newspapers, ads echoing these appeals must vie for our time, attention, and dollars with Eddie Bauer, Nordstrom's, The Gap, and others like them whose polished and attractive images fill our days.

In the pages that follow . . . I examine a particular representation of poverty — publicity videos produced by Habitat for Humanity — in order to suggest that reliance on stereotypes of poverty can, in fact, work against the aims of the organization producing them.

---

*The copy here has been revised, with the author's permission, to reflect the more recent Children, Inc. ad.

You don't have to leave your own country to find third-world poverty.

In Appalachia, sad faces of children, like Mandy's, will haunt you. There are so many children like her— children who are deprived of the basic necessities right here in America.

You can sponsor a boy or girl in need through Children, Inc. Just $24 a month will help provide clothing, shoes, school supplies and food as well as a feeling that someone cares. We'll send you the picture and story of the child you will be helping. Please write, call or visit our website to enroll. Your help will mean so much.

Write to: Children, Inc., 4205 Dover Road, Dept.RB5M6, Richmond, VA 23221-3267 USA

www.children-inc.org
1-800-538-5381

☐ I wish to sponsor a ☐ boy, ☐ girl, in ☐ USA, ☐ Africa, ☐ Latin America, ☐ Middle East, ☐ Asia, ☐ Greatest need.

☐ I will give $24 a month ($288 a year). Enclosed is my gift for a full year ☐, the first month ☐.

☐ I can't sponsor, but I will help $_____ .

Children INCORPORATED
Share in their future

Name _____

Address _____ City _____ State _____ Zip Code _____

☐ Check or Money Order ☐ American Express ☐ Visa ☐ MasterCard   Card No. _____ Expiration Date _____

U.S. gifts are fully tax deductible. Annual financial statements are available on request.

An ad for Children, Inc. Courtesy Children, Inc.

Habitat for Humanity: A Case in Point

I have chosen Habitat for Humanity publicity videos for my focus because Habitat is a popular and far-reaching nonprofit with affiliates not only in the United States but throughout the world. Its goal is not a modest one: Habitat for Humanity aims to eliminate poverty housing from the globe. More than that, Habitat puts housing into the hands of the people who will be housed — into the hands of the homeowners and their neighbors. This is not another program aimed at keeping people in what has become known as the poverty or welfare cycle.

To be very clear, then, I am not criticizing the work of Habitat for   5
Humanity. It is an organization that has done an amazing job of addressing what is, as cofounder Millard Fuller tells us again and again, a worldwide problem. What I would draw attention to, however, is how that problem of inadequate housing and its solution are represented, especially in publicity material produced and distributed by the organization, and how those representations can feed into the troubles that Habitat continues to have as it attempts to change the ways Americans think of helping others. What's more, the kinds of visual arguments Habitat and other nonprofits use to advocate for action or change have become increasingly common tools for getting the message to the public, and yet, I would argue, these messages too often fail to overturn cultural commonplaces that represent poverty as an individual problem that can be addressed on an individual basis. Habitat's catch phrase — A Hand Up, Not a Hand-Out — appeals to a nation that believes anyone can achieve economic security with just the right attitude and set of circumstances.

Habitat's basic program has a kind of elegance. Applicants who are chosen as homeowners put in sweat equity hours to build their home and to help build the homes of others chosen by Habitat. The organization then sells the home to the applicant at cost (that cost held down through Habitat's ability to provide volunteer labor and donated materials) and charges a small monthly mortgage that includes no interest. Unlike public assistance, which is raised or lowered depending on the recipient's circumstances, most Habitat affiliates do not raise mortgage payments when homeowners get better jobs or find themselves in better financial shape. And once the house is paid for, it belongs to the homeowner.

Obviously, in order to run a program like this one, Habitat must produce publicity appeals aimed at convincing potential donors to give time, money, and material. Print ads, public service television and radio spots, commercial appeals linked to products like Maxwell House coffee, and publicity videos meant to be played for churches, volunteer organizations, and even in-flight video appeals on certain airlines are common media for Habitat.

Habitat publicity videos are typically configured as problem-solution arguments. The problem is that too many people have inadequate shelter. The solution is community involvement in a program like Habitat for Humanity. The most common setup for these productions is an opening sequence of images — a visual montage — in which we see black-and-white shots of rural shacks, of men and women clearly in despair, and of thin children in ragged clothing. The voice-over narrative of one such montage tells us the story:

> Poverty condemns millions of people throughout the world to live in deplorable and inhuman conditions. These people are trapped in a cycle of poverty, living in places offering little protection from the rain, wind, and cold. Terrible sanitary conditions make each day a battle with disease and death. And, for this, they often pay over half their income in rent because, for the poor, there are no other choices. Daily, these families are denied a most basic human need: a decent place to live. The reasons for this worldwide tragedy are many. They vary from city to city, country to country, but the result is painfully the same whether the families are in New York or New Delhi.[1]

It is a compelling dilemma.

Organizations like Habitat for Humanity, in order to convey the seriousness of this struggle and, of course, to raise funds and volunteer support for their efforts in addressing it, must produce all sorts of publicity. And in that publicity they must tell us quickly what the problem is and

■ rhetorical situations
▲ genres
○ processes
◆ strategies
● research mla/apa
□ media/ design
📖 readings

what we can do to help. To do that, Habitat gives us a visual representation of poverty, a representation that mirrors the most common understandings of poverty in America.

Now, there is nothing inherently wrong with that representation 10 unless, of course, what you want to do (as Habitat does) is convince the American people to believe in the radical idea that those who have must care for the needs of others, not just by writing a check, but by enabling an entirely different lifestyle. For Americans, it is truly radical to think that our poorer neighbors might actually be allowed to buy a home at no interest and with the donated time and materials of others. It is a radical notion that such a program means that these neighbors then own that house and aren't obliged to do more than keep up with payments in order to continue owning it. And it is a radical idea that Habitat does this work not only in our neighborhoods (not isolated in low-income housing developments) but throughout the world. Habitat International truly believes that we are all responsible for partnering with our neighbors throughout the world so that everyone might eventually have, at least, a simple decent place to live. Like the philosophy behind many nonprofits, Habitat's is not a mainstream notion.

Still, that representation of poverty — clinging as it does to commonplaces drawn from FSA photographs in this century, from Jacob Riis's nineteenth-century photos of urban poverty, and from documentaries of Third World hunger — has serious limitations, which must be obvious to those who remember the moment that the Bush administration* confidently announced that, after looking everywhere, they had discovered no real hunger in the United States. And that myth that poverty cannot/does not actually exist in the heart of capitalism has once again been reinforced in the 1998 Heritage Foundation report in which Robert Rector echoed the perennial argument that there is little true poverty in this country ("Myth").[2] Heritage Foundation's finding

---

*The administration of George H. W. Bush (1989–93). *FSA:* The Farm Security Administration, which hired such prominent photographers as Walker Evans and Dorothea Lange to document rural poverty in the 1930s. *Jacob Riis:* Danish American social reformer (1849–1914).

comes despite figures from the National Coalition for the Homeless ("Myths and Facts About Homelessness"), which tell us that in 1997 nearly one in five homeless people in twenty-nine cities across the United States was employed in a full- or part-time job.[3]

In her call for a changed representation of poverty in America, bell hooks argues that in this culture poverty "is seen as synonymous with depravity, lack and worthlessness." She continues, "I talked with young black women receiving state aid, who have not worked in years, about the issue of representation. They all agree that they do not want to be identified as poor. In their apartments they have the material possessions that indicate success (a VCR, a color television), even if it means that they do without necessities and plunge into debt to buy these items."[4] Hers is hardly a noble image of poverty, but it is a true one and one that complicates the job of an organization like Habitat that must identify "worthy" applicants. This phenomenon of poverty in the center of wealth, in a country with its national mythology of hearty individuals facing the hardness of the Depression with dignity and pride, is certainly a part of what Manning Marable challenges when he asks readers not to judge poverty in the United States by the standards of other countries. Writing of poverty among black Americans, Marable reminds us that "the process of impoverishment is profoundly national and regional."[5] It does little good to compare the impoverished of this country with Third World poverty or, for that matter, with Depression Era poverty.

The solution in these Habitat videos is just as visible and compelling a representation as is the problem. The solution, it seems, is a modern-day barn raising. In clip after clip, Habitat volunteers are shown lined up to raise walls, to hammer nails, to cut boards, to offer each other the "hand up not a hand out," as these publicity messages tell us again and again. Like the barn-raising scene from Peter Weir's *Witness*, framed walls come together against blue skies. People who would normally live in very different worlds come together to help a neighbor. It is all finished in record time: a week, even a day. Volunteers can come together quickly. Do something. Get out just as quickly.

The real trouble with Habitat's representation, then, is twofold: it tells us that the signs of poverty are visible and easily recognized. And it suggests that one of the most serious results of poverty (inadequate shelter) can be addressed quickly with volunteer efforts to bring individuals up and out of the poverty cycle.

Of course, if Habitat works, what could be wrong with the repre-   15
sentation? It is an organization so popular that it receives support from diametrically opposed camps. Newt Gingrich and Jesse Jackson have both pounded nails and raised funds for Habitat. This is what Millard Fuller calls the "theology of the hammer." People might not agree on political parties and they might not agree on how to worship or even what to worship, Fuller says, but they can all agree on a hammer. All can come together to build houses. Or, can they?

As successful as Habitat has been, it is an organization that continues to struggle with such issues as who to choose for housing, how to support potential homeowners, and how to convince affiliates in the United States to tithe a portion of their funds to the real effort of Habitat: eliminating poverty housing throughout the world, not just in the United States. And, even in the United States, affiliates often have trouble identifying "deserving" applicants or convincing local residents to allow Habitat homes to be built in their neighborhoods. There are certainly many cultural and political reasons for these problems, but I would suggest that the way poverty continues to be represented in this country and on tapes like those videos limits our understanding of what poverty is and how we might address it.

That limitation holds true for those caught in poverty as well as those wanting to help. What if, as a potential Habitat applicant, you don't recognize yourself or you refuse to recognize yourself in those representations? As Stanley Aronowitz points out in *The Politics of Identity*, that can happen very easily as class identities, in particular, have become much more difficult to pin down since World War II, especially with an expansion of consumer credit that allowed class and social status to be linked to consumption rather than to professions or even wages. In his discussion of how electronic media construct the *social imaginary*, Aronowitz talks of the working class with few media representations available to them as having fallen into a kind of "cultural homelessness."[6] How much more true is that of the impoverished in this country who may be neither homeless nor ragged, but are certainly struggling every day to feed their families, pay rent, and find jobs that pay more than what it costs for daycare?

I have been particularly interested in this last question because of a difficulty I mentioned earlier, that of identifying appropriate applicants for Habitat homes or even getting some of the most needy families of a given affiliate to apply for Habitat homes. When I showed the video *Building New Lives* to Kim Puuri, a Copper Country Habitat for Humanity homeowner and now member of the affiliate's Homeowner Selection Committee, and asked her to respond, she was very clear in what she saw as the problem:

> When I see those pictures I usually think of Africa or a third-world country and NOT the U.S. It's not that they can't be found here, it's just that you don't publicly see people that bad off other than street people. If they could gear the publicity more to the geographical areas, it may make more of an impact or get a better response from people. It would mean making several videos. It may not be so much of a stereotype, but an association between Habitat and the people they help. People viewing the videos and pictures see the conditions of the people and feel that their own condition may not be that bad and feel they probably wouldn't qualify.[7]

What this Habitat homeowner has noticed is very close to what Stuart Hall describes. That is, the problem with this image, this representation, is not that it is not real enough. The problem has nothing to do with whether or not these are images of poverty as it exists in the world. There is no doubt that this level of poverty does exist in this country and elsewhere despite the Heritage Foundation's attempts to demonstrate otherwise. The problem is that this representation of poverty is a narrow one and functions to narrow the ways we might respond to the poor who do not fit this representation.

The representation I have been discussing is one that insists on constructing poverty as an individual problem that can be dealt with by volunteers on an individual basis. That is the sort of representation common in this country, the sort of representation Paul Wellstone objects to in a recent call to action when he says "We can offer no sin-

gle description of American poverty." What it takes to break through such a representation is first, as Hall suggests, to understand it as a representation, to understand it as a way of imparting meaning. And the only way to contest that representation, to allow for other meanings, other descriptions, is to know more about the many dimensions of poverty in America. "More than 35 million Americans — one out of every seven of our fellow citizens — are officially poor. More than one in five American children are poor. And the poor are getting poorer," Wellstone writes.[8] But we can be certain that much of that poverty is not the sort pictured in those black-and-white images. And if it doesn't *look* like poverty, then how do we address it? How do we identify those "deserving" our help?

Indeed, as Herbert Gans has suggested, the labels we have chosen   20 to place on the poor in this country often reveal more than anything "an ideology of undeservingness," by which we have often elided poverty and immorality or laziness or criminality. "By making scapegoats of the poor for fundamental problems they have not caused nor can change," Gans argues, "Americans can also postpone politically difficult and divisive solutions to the country's economic ills and the need to prepare the economy and polity for the challenges of the twenty-first century."[9] These are tough issues to confront and certainly to argue in a twenty-minute video presentation aimed at raising funds and volunteer support, especially when every piece of publicity must make a complex argument visible.

Notes

1. *Building New Lives* (Americus, Ga.: Habitat for Humanity International). This and other Habitat videos are directed primarily at potential volunteers for the organization or might be used to inform local residents about the work of Habitat.

2. Robert Rector, "The Myth of Widespread American Poverty," *The Heritage Foundation Backgrounder* (18 Sept. 1998), no. 1221. This publication is available on-line at <http://www.heritage.org/library/backgrounder/bg1221es.html>.

3. Cited in Barbara Ehrenreich, "Nickel and Dimed: On (Not) Getting By in America," *Harper's* (January 1999), 44. See also Christina Coburn Herman's *Poverty Amid Plenty: The Unfinished Business of Welfare Reform* NETWORK, A National Social Justice Lobby (Washington, D.C., 1999), from NETWORK's national Welfare Reform Watch Project, which reports that most studies of welfare use telephone surveys even though a substantial percentage of those needing aid do not have phone service (41 percent in the NETWORK survey had no operative phone) and, therefore, are not represented in most welfare reform reports. This report is available on-line at <http://www.network-lobby.org>.

4. bell hooks, "Seeing and Making Culture: Representing the Poor," *Outlaw Culture: Resisting Representations* (New York: 1994), 169.

5. Manning Marable, *How Capitalism Underdeveloped Black America* (Boston: South End Press, 1983), 54.

6. Stanley Aronowitz, *The Politics of Identity: Class, Culture, Social Movements* (New York: Routledge, 1992), 201.

7. Kim Puuri, personal correspondence with author.

8. Paul Wellstone, "If Poverty Is the Question," *Nation* (14 April 1997), 15.

9. Herbert J. Gans, *The War Against the Poor* (New York: Basic Books, 1995), 6–7.

Engaging with the Text

1. How, according to Diana George, is poverty represented by nonprofit agencies such as Habitat for Humanity? What problems does George identify as a result of such representation?

2. George opens her analysis with a bell hooks quote, followed by descriptions of how frequently she encounters charities near Thanksgiving. How do the quote by bell hooks and George's anecdote appeal to different **AUDIENCES?**

3. The Children, Inc. ad that George refers to is reprinted here on p. 544. What does George mean by the "emotional overload" of this image? Why do you think the Oxfam envelope promises not to include images like this?

5–8 ◼

rhetorical situations   genres   processes   strategies   research mla/apa   media/ design   readings

4. What **PURPOSE** does George's textual analysis serve? Where is that purpose made explicit? What other purposes might her essay serve?

   3–4

5. *For Writing.* Identify a print, TV, or Web ad aimed at influencing your opinion on a political or social issue. **ANALYZE** the visuals (drawings, pictures, photographs) and the accompanying words in the ad to describe how the issue is represented. How effectively does the ad meet its goals?

   39–59

52 Reports

rhetorical situations

genres

processes

strategies

research mla/apa

media/ design

readings

LEV GROSSMAN

Meet Joe Blog

Lev Grossman is a book critic and staff writer at Time *magazine as well as the author of two novels,* Codex *(2004) and* Warp *(1997). In 2003, he won the Award for Excellence in Technology Journalism, an award given by the Public Relations Society of America. The following article appeared in* Time *in 2004.*

A **FEW YEARS AGO,** Mathew Gross, 32, was a freelance writer living in tiny Moab, Utah. Rob Malda, 28, was an underperforming undergraduate at a small Christian college in Michigan. Denis Dutton, 60, was a professor of philosophy in faraway Christchurch, New Zealand. Today they are some of the most influential media personalities in the world. You can be one too.

Gross, Malda, and Dutton aren't rich or famous or even conspicuously good-looking. What they have in common is that they all edit blogs: amateur websites that provide news, information and, above all, opinions to rapidly growing and devoted audiences drawn by nothing more than a shared interest or two and the sheer magnetism of the editor's personality. Over the past five years, blogs have gone from an obscure and, frankly, somewhat nerdy fad to a genuine alternative to mainstream news outlets, a shadow media empire that is rivaling networks and newspapers in power and influence. Which raises the question: Who are these folks anyway? And what exactly are they doing to the established pantheon of American media?

Not that long ago, *blogs* were one of those annoying buzz words that you could safely get away with ignoring. The word *blog* — it works as both noun and verb — is short for *Web log*. It was coined in 1997 to describe a website where you could post daily scribblings, journal-style, about whatever you like — mostly critiquing and linking to other articles online that may have sparked your thinking. Unlike a big media outlet, bloggers focus their efforts on narrow topics, often rising to become de facto watchdogs and self-proclaimed experts. Blogs can be about anything: politics, sex, baseball, haiku, car repair. There are blogs about blogs.

Big whoop, right? But it turns out some people actually have interesting thoughts on a regular basis, and a few of the better blogs began drawing sizable audiences. Blogs multiplied and evolved, slowly becoming conduits for legitimate news and serious thought. In 1999 a few companies began offering free make-your-own-blog software, which turbocharged the phenomenon. By 2002, Pyra Labs, which makes software for creating blogs, claimed 970,000 users.

Most of America couldn't have cared less. Until December 2002, that is, when bloggers staged a dramatic show of force. The occasion was Strom Thurmond's 100th birthday party, during which Trent Lott made what sounded like a nostalgic reference to Thurmond's past segregationist leanings.[1] The mainstream press largely glossed over the incident, but when regular journalists bury the lead, bloggers dig it right back up. "That story got ignored for three, four, five days by big papers and the TV networks while blogs kept it alive," says Joshua Micah Marshall, creator of *talkingpointsmemo.com,* one of a handful of blogs that stuck with the Lott story.

Mainstream America wasn't listening, but Washington insiders and media honchos read blogs. Three days after the party, the story was on *Meet the Press.* Four days afterward, Lott made an official apology. After two weeks, Lott was out as Senate majority leader, and blogs had drawn their first blood. Web journalists like Matt Drudge (*drudgereport.com*) had already demonstrated a certain crude effectiveness — witness l'*affaire* Lewinsky[2] — but this was something different: bloggers were offering reasoned, forceful arguments that carried weight with the powers that be.

Blogs act like a lens, focusing attention on an issue until it catches fire, but they can also break stories. On April 21, a 34-year-old blogger and writer from Arizona named Russ Kick posted photographs of coffins

---

1. Strom Thurmond (1902–2003), long-time senator from South Carolina. Trent Lott, senator from Mississippi, former Senate Republican leader until forced to resign from that office in 2002.

2. That is, President Bill Clinton's relations with White House intern Monica Lewinsky, which led to calls for his removal from office.

containing the bodies of soldiers killed in Iraq and Afghanistan and of *Columbia* astronauts.[3] The military zealously guards images of service members in coffins, but Kick pried the photos free with a Freedom of Information Act (FOIA) request. "I read the news constantly," says Kick, "and when I see a story about the government refusing to release public documents, I automatically file an FOIA request for them." By April 23 the images had gone from Kick's blog, *thememoryhole.org,* to the front page of newspapers across the country. Kick was soon getting upwards of four million hits a day.

What makes blogs so effective? They're free. They catch people at work, at their desks, when they're alert and thinking and making decisions. Blogs are fresh and often seem to be miles ahead of the mainstream news. Bloggers put up new stuff every day, all day, and there are thousands of them. How are you going to keep anything secret from a thousand Russ Kicks? Blogs have voice and personality. They're human. They come to us not from some mediagenic anchorbot on an air-conditioned sound stage, but from an individual. They represent — no, they are — the voice of the little guy.

And the little guy is a lot smarter than big media might have you think. Blogs showcase some of the smartest, sharpest writing being published. Bloggers are unconstrained by such journalistic conventions as good taste, accountability, and objectivity — and that can be a good thing. Accusations of media bias are thick on the ground these days, and Americans are tired of it. Blogs don't pretend to be neutral: they're gleefully, unabashedly biased, and that makes them a lot more fun. "Because we're not trying to sell magazines or papers, we can afford to assail our readers," says Andrew Sullivan, a contributor to *Time* and the editor of *andrewsullivan.com.* "I don't have the pressure of an advertising executive telling me to lay off. It's incredibly liberating."

Some bloggers earn their bias the hard way — in the trenches. Military bloggers, or milbloggers in Net patois, post vivid accounts of their tours of Baghdad, in prose covered in fresh flop sweat and powder burns, 10

_____

3. The seven astronauts killed on February 1, 2003, when the space shuttle *Columbia* broke up upon re-entry to Earth's atmosphere.

illustrated with digital photos. "Jason," a National Guardsman whose blog is called *justanothersoldier.com,* wrote about wandering through one of Saddam Hussein's empty palaces. And Iraqis have blogs: a Baghdad blogger who goes by Salam Pax (*dear_raed.blogspot.com*) has parlayed his blog into a book and a movie deal. Vietnam was the first war to be televised; blogs bring Iraq another scary step closer to our living rooms.

But blogs are about much more than war and politics. In 1997 Malda went looking for a "site that mixed the latest word about a new sci-fi movie with news about open-source software. I was looking for a site that didn't exist," Malda says, "so I built it." Malda and a handful of co-editors run *slashdot.org* full time, and he estimates that 300,000 to 500,000 people read the site daily. Six years ago, a philosophy professor in New Zealand named Denis Dutton started the blog Arts & Letters Daily (*artsandlettersdaily.com*) to create a website "where people could go daily for a dose of intellectual stimulation." Now the site draws more than 100,000 readers a month. Compare that with, say, the *New York Review of Books,* which has a circulation of 115,000. The tail is beginning to wag the blog.

Blogs are inverting the cozy media hierarchies of yore. Some bloggers are getting press credentials for this summer's Republican Convention. Three years ago, a 25-year-old Chicagoan named Jessa Crispin started a blog for serious readers called *bookslut.com.* "We give books a better chance," she says. "The *New York Times Book Review* is so boring. We take each book at face value. There's no politics behind it." Crispin's apartment is overflowing with free books from publishers desperate for a mention. As for the *Times,* it's scrutinizing the blogging phenomenon for its own purposes. In January the Gray Lady[4] started up Times on the Trail, a campaign-news website with some decidedly bloglike features; it takes the bold step of linking to articles by competing newspapers, for example. "The *Times* cannot ignore this. I don't think any big media can ignore this," says Len Apcar, editor in chief of the *New York Times* on the Web.

---

4. *The New York Times.*

In a way, blogs represent everything the Web was always supposed to be: a mass medium controlled by the masses, in which getting heard depends solely on having something to say and the moxie to say it.

Unfortunately, there's a downside to this populist sentiment — that is, innocent casualties bloodied by a medium that trades in rumor, gossip, and speculation without accountability. Case in point: Alexandra Polier, better known as the Kerry intern. Rumors of Polier's alleged affair with presidential candidate Senator John Kerry eventually spilled into the blogosphere earlier this year. After Drudge headlined it in February, the blabbing bloggers soon had the attention of tabloid journalists, radio talk-show hosts and cable news anchors. Trouble is, the case was exceedingly thin, and both Kerry and Polier vehemently deny it. Yet the Internet smolders with it to this day.

Some wonder if the backbiting tide won't recede as blogs grow up. 15 The trend now is for more prominent sites to be commercialized. A Manhattan entrepreneur named Nick Denton runs a small stable of bloggers as a business by selling advertising on their sites. So far they aren't showing detectible signs of editorial corruption by their corporate masters — two of Denton's blogs, *gawker.com* and *wonkette.com,* are among the most corrosively witty sites on the Web — but they've lost their amateur status forever.

We may be in the golden age of blogging, a quirky Camelot moment in Internet history when some guy in his underwear with too much free time can take down a Washington politician. It will be interesting to see what role blogs play in the upcoming election. Blogs can be a great way of communicating, but they can keep people apart too. If I read only those of my choice, precisely tuned to my political biases and you read only yours, we could end up a nation of political solipsists, vacuum sealed in our private feedback loops, never exposed to new arguments, never having to listen to a single word we disagree with.

Howard Dean's campaign blog, run by Mathew Gross, may be the perfect example of both the potential and the pitfalls of high-profile blogging. At its peak, *blogforamerica.com* drew 100,000 visitors a day, yet the candidate was beaten badly in the primaries. Still, the Dean model isn't going away. When another political blogger, who goes by the nom de blog Atrios, set up a fund-raising link on his site for Kerry, he raised $25,000 in five days.

You can't blog your way into the White House, at least not yet, but blogs are America thinking out loud, talking to itself, and heaven help the candidate who isn't listening.

Engaging with the Text

60–81 ▲

1. This piece was written as a magazine article, but it basically **REPORTS INFORMATION** to an audience that is assumed to be unfamiliar with the topic. What did you find informative in this piece, and what do you think you'll remember from it?

12–14 ■
5–8 ■

2. How would you characterize Lev Grossman's **STANCE** toward his subject? What in his text reveals his stance? How does his **AUDIENCE**— readers of *Time*—affect his stance? Consider how it might be different for another publication—*BusinessWeek,* for example, or *InStyle.*

250–54 ◆
251–54 ◆

3. Grossman offers various cues throughout the article to **GUIDE READERS,** starting with a title that tells us what the piece is about. What other cues does he offer—a **THESIS STATEMENT? TOPIC SENTENCES? TRANSITIONS?**

4. According to Grossman, "Blogs have voice and personality. They're human. They come to us not from some mediagenic anchorbot on an air-conditioned sound stage, but from an individual. They represent— no, they are—the voice of the little guy." How do blogs relate to mainstream news sources? In what ways do they supplement, challenge, support, or resist mainstream news practices?

60–81 ▲

5. *For Writing.* Locate one or more blogs on a particular subject and **REPORT** on the topics they cover, who participates in them, who edits them, and the degree to which they are flourishing. Consider inserting examples from the blogs to illustrate your report.

■ rhetorical situations
▲ genres
○ processes
◆ strategies
● research mla/apa
□ media/ design
▌▌ readings

ELEANOR J. BADER

Homeless on Campus

Eleanor J. Bader is a freelance writer and an instructor in the English Department at Kingsborough Community College in Brooklyn, New York. She is also the co-author of Targets of Hatred: Anti-Abortion Terrorism *(2001). The following report appeared in 2004 in* The Progressive, *a liberal political magazine. As you read, notice how Bader effectively incorporates specific examples to support the information she reports.*

A ESHA IS A TWENTY-YEAR-OLD at Kingsborough Community College in Brooklyn, New York. Until the fall of 2003, she lived with five people — her one-year-old son, her son's father, her sister, her mother, and her mother's boyfriend — in a three-bedroom South Bronx apartment. Things at home were fine until her child's father became physically abusive. Shortly thereafter, Aesha realized that she and her son had to leave the unit.

After spending thirty days in a temporary shelter, they landed at the city's emergency assistance unit (EAU). "It was horrible," Aesha says. "We slept on benches, and it was very crowded. I was so scared I sat on my bag and held onto the stroller day and night, from Friday to Monday." Aesha and her son spent several nights in the EAU before being sent to a hotel. Sadly, this proved to be a temporary respite. After a few days, they were returned to the EAU, where they remained until they were finally moved to a family shelter in Queens.

Although Aesha believes that she will be able to stay in this facility until she completes her associate's degree, the ordeal of being homeless has taken a toll on her and her studies. "I spend almost eight hours a day on the trains," she says. "I have to leave the shelter at 5:00 a.m. for the Bronx where my girlfriend watches my son for me. I get to her house around 7:00. Then I have to travel to school in Brooklyn — the last stop on the train followed by a bus ride — another two hours away."

Reluctantly, Aesha felt that she had no choice but to confide in teachers and explain her periodic absences. "They've all said that as long as I keep up with the work I'll be OK," she says. But that is not easy for Aesha or other homeless students.

Adriana Broadway lived in ten places, with ten different families,   5 during high school. A native of Sparks, Nevada, Broadway told the LeTendre Education Fund for Homeless Children, a scholarship program administered by the National Association for the Education of Homeless Children and Youth, that she left home when she was thirteen. "For five years, I stayed here and there with friends," she wrote on her funding application. "I'd stay with whoever would take me in and allow me to live under their roof."

Johnny Montgomery also became homeless in his early teens. He told LeTendre staffers that his mother threw him out because he did not get along with her boyfriend. "She chose him over me," he wrote. "Hard days and nights have shaped me." Much of that time was spent on the streets.

Asad Dahir has also spent time on the streets. "I've been homeless more than one time and in more than one country," Dahir wrote on his scholarship application. Originally from Somalia, he and his family fled their homeland due to civil war and ended up in a refugee camp in neighboring Kenya. After more than a year in the camp, he and his thirteen-year-old brother were resettled, first in Atlanta and later in Ohio. There, high housing costs once again rendered the pair homeless.

Broadway, Montgomery, and Dahir are three of the forty-four homeless students from across the country who have been awarded LeTendre grants since 1999. Thanks, in part, to these funds, all three have been attending college and doing well.

But few homeless students are so lucky. "Each year at our national conference, homeless students come forward to share their stories," says Jenn Hecker, the organizing director of the National Student Campaign Against Hunger and Homelessness. "What often comes through is shame. Most feel as though they should be able to cover their costs." Such students usually try to blend in and are reluctant to disclose either their poverty or homelessness to others on campus, she says. Hecker blames rising housing costs for the problem and cites a 2003 survey that

rhetorical situations   genres   processes   strategies   research mla/apa   media/ design   readings

found the median wage needed to pay for a two-bedroom apartment in the United States to be $15.21, nearly three times the federal minimum.

Even when doubled up, students in the most expensive states — Massachusetts, California, New Jersey, New York, and Maryland — are scrambling. "In any given semester, there are four or five families where the head of household is in college," says Beth Kelly, a family service counselor at the Clinton Family Inn, a New York City transitional housing program run by Homes for the Homeless.

Advocates for the homeless report countless examples of students sleeping in their cars and sneaking into a school gym to shower and change clothes. They speak of students who couch surf or camp in the woods — bicycling or walking to classes — during temperate weather. Yet, for all the anecdotes, details about homeless college students are hazy.

"I wish statistics existed on the number of homeless college students," says Barbara Duffield, executive director of the National Association for the Education of Homeless Children and Youth. "Once state and federal responsibility to homeless kids stops — at the end of high school — it's as if they cease to exist. They fall off the map."

Worse, they are neither counted nor attended to.

"Nobody has ever thought about this population or collected data on them because nobody thinks they are a priority to study," says Martha Burt, principal research associate at the Urban Institute.

Critics say colleges are not doing enough to meet — or even recognize — the needs of this group.

"The school should do more," says Aesha. "They have a child care center on my campus, but they only accept children two and up. It would have helped if I could've brought my son to day care at school." She also believes that the college should maintain emergency housing for homeless students.

"As an urban community college, our students are commuters," responds Uda Bradford, interim dean of student affairs at Kingsborough Community College. "Therefore, our student support services are developed within that framework."

"As far as I know, no college has ever asked for help in reaching homeless students," says Mary Jean LeTendre, a retired Department of Education administrator and creator of the LeTendre Education Fund. "Individual colleges have come forward to help specific people, but there is nothing systematic like there is for students in elementary and high school."

"There is a very low awareness level amongst colleges," Duffield adds. "People have this 'you can pull yourself up by your bootstraps' myth about college. There is a real gap between the myth and the reality for those who are trying to overcome poverty by getting an education."

Part of the problem is that the demographics of college attendance have changed. "Most educational institutions were set up to serve fewer, less diverse, more privileged students," says Andrea Leskes, a vice president with the Association of American Colleges and Universities. "As a result, we are not successfully educating all the students who come to college today. This means that nontraditional students — the older, returning ones as well as those from low income or other disenfranchised communities — often receive inadequate support services." 20

"It's not that colleges are not concerned, but attention today is not on serving the poor," says Susan O'Malley, chair of the faculty senate at the City University of New York. "It's not in fashion. During the 1960s, people from all over the country were going to Washington and making a lot of noise. The War on Poverty was influenced by this noise. Now the poor are less visible."

Mary Gesing, a counselor at Kirkwood Community College in Cedar Rapids, Iowa, agrees. "Nothing formal exists for this population, and the number of homeless students on campus is not tracked," she says. Because of this statistical gap, programs are not devised to accommodate homeless students or address their needs.

Despite these programmatic shortfalls, Gesing encounters two to three homeless students — often single parents — each semester. Some became homeless when they left an abuser. Others lost their housing because they could no longer pay for it due to a lost job, the termination of unemployment benefits, illness, the cessation of child support, or drug or alcohol abuse.

rhetorical situations   genres   processes   strategies   research mla/apa   media/design   readings

Kirkwood's approach is a "patchwork system," Gesing explains, and homeless students often drop out or fail classes because no one knows of their plight. "When people don't know who to come to for help they just fade away," she says.

"Without housing, access to a workspace, or access to a shower, 25 students' lives suffer, their grades suffer, and they are more likely to drop classes, if not withdraw entirely from school. I've seen it happen," says Amit Rai, an English professor at a large, public university in Florida. "If seen from the perspective of students, administrators would place affordable housing and full access to health care at the top of what a university should provide."

Yet for all this, individual teachers — as well as administrator and counselors — can sometimes make an enormous difference.

B.R., a faculty member who asked that neither her name nor school be disclosed, has allowed several homeless students to sleep in her office during the past decade. "Although there is no institutional interest or involvement in keeping these students enrolled, a few faculty members really care about the whole student and don't shy away from helping," she says.

One of the students she sheltered lived in the space for three months, whenever she couldn't stay with friends. Like Aesha, this student was fleeing a partner who beat her. Another student had been kicked out of the dorm because her stepfather never paid the bill. She applied for financial assistance to cover the cost, but processing took months. "This student stayed in my office for an entire semester," B.R. says.

A sympathetic cleaning woman knew what was going on and turned a blind eye to the arrangement. "Both students showered in the dorms and kept their toothbrushes and cosmetics in one of the two department bathrooms which I gave them keys to," B.R. adds. "The administration never knew a thing. Both of the students finished school and went on to become social workers. They knew that school would be their saving grace, that knowledge was the only thing that couldn't be snatched."

Engaging with the Text

3–4

1. What do you think is the **PURPOSE** of this report? How does this purpose affect the way the report is written? Point to examples from the text in your response.

60–81

2. This piece basically **REPORTS** on the general topic of homeless college students. What is the author's specific point? How do you know? How else could she have made her point explicit?

245–48

3. Eleanor Bader **ENDS** her essay with a powerful quote from one of her informants, a teacher she calls B.R.: "[The students] knew that school would be their saving grace, that knowledge was the only thing that couldn't be snatched." What does B.R. mean by this observation? In what ways can an education help such students, and in what ways might it be misleading to think that an education alone will solve all of the problems these students face?

304–12

4. Consider the many **NARRATIVES** in this report. Why do you think Bader includes so many narratives? What other kinds of support could she have included?

5. *For Writing.* You may not be aware of services that are readily available on your campus. Do some research to see what services are available at your school, and write a **REPORT** on one of those services. As an alternative, you may want to deliver your report as a Web site.

60–81

rhetorical situations   genres   processes   strategies   research mla/apa   media/ design   readings

ROBB WALSH

Stinkfruit

Once dubbed the "Indiana Jones of food writers," Robb Walsh is the author of several books on travel and food, including Legends of Texas Barbecue *(2002) and* Traveling Jamaica with Knife, Fork, and Spoon *(1995). The following essay comes from* Are You Really Going to Eat That?: Reflections of a Culinary Thrill Seeker *(2003).*

MY THAI HOSTS ARE SMILING and offering encouragement. "Eat some more, go ahead, it grows on you," they're saying. Before me on a plate are several soft, yellow sacs of durian, the sweetest, creamiest fruit I've ever tasted. I have already eaten one of the soft, custardy segments, but the smell of rotten eggs is so overwhelming, I suppress a gag reaction as I take another bite of the second.

I feel a little foolish sitting here in the formal living room of Prabhadpong Vejjajiva, Thailand's former deputy minister of finance. His palatial house, which is located in the middle of a durian plantation in the fruit-growing region of Chanthaburi, is named Barn Kradum Tong, or Golden Button Home. Golden Button is the name of an early-maturing variety of durian that has proven especially profitable for the former government minister. The news that an American is having his first encounter with durian has caused a small crowd to gather. I am the only one in the room with a plate of durian in front of him, and someone is snapping photos while I make my feeble attempts to eat the stuff.

Known as *stinkvrucht* in Dutch, durian is one of those foods that is at first repulsive and yet becomes highly desirable to some people. Watching Westerners experience their first bite of durian is a great source of amusement for Asians. And in this case, my hubris made the scene ever funnier. As a veteran food writer who likes overripe cheeses and brutally hot chile peppers, and has eaten bugs, barnacles, and goat brains in the line of duty, I expected to delight the crowd by eating a whole durian at my first sitting. But to my chagrin, I couldn't eat even two small sections.

Durio zibethinus doesn't look (or smell) like any European fruit I can think of. The husk is about the size of a man's head. With its covering of stout brown thorns, it looks something like a hedgehog. The glossy, malodorous flesh comes in colors ranging from pink to orange. The seeds are contained within the flesh, which fills five interior compartments of the husk. The durian flesh I'm eating is segmented, but not all durians share this feature. Plant explorer Otis W. Barrett described the aroma of durian as containing elements of decayed onion, turpentine, garlic, Limburger cheese and some spicy sort of resin.

Thought to have originated in Borneo or Sumatra, the durian became an important trade item in Burma around four hundred years ago, where it was a favorite of the royal palace. There are hundreds of cultivars of the fruit, but the three major commercial varieties are the early-maturing Golden Button, the mid-season Golden Pillow, and the late-maturing Matong, the last being the favorite of connoisseurs.

Today Thailand and South Vietnam grow most of the world's durian. But to the chagrin of Thai fruit farmers such as Prabhadpong Vejjajiva, buyers throughout Asia are beginning to ask for "Singapore durian." This is the result of a brilliant marketing strategy, he says. The tiny island nation of Singapore is famously adept at filling orders promptly, meeting shipping deadlines, and promoting its products to the rest of the world. Which is why their campaign to sell "Singapore durian" to customers in Japan and elsewhere has met with such success. "But they don't grow any durian in Singapore!" the Thai fruit farmer loudly protests.

To say that durian is very popular in Southeast Asia is an understatement. In Thailand, it is called "the king of fruits." Every year, tourists from Japan and other parts of Asia come to Thailand's fruit-growing regions during the harvest season to participate in durian tours and durian festivals. I imagine it was overzealous durian tourists who caused several airlines in the region to institute their famous "no durian" policies. I have also heard of signs forbidding durian in hotel rooms and on public transportation.

We haven't had much problem with public durian eating in the United States — yet. But be on the lookout, *stinkvrucht* may turn up in your neighborhood any day now. According to the Thai Department of Export Production, the United States is currently the world's largest purchaser of frozen durian. And the market is growing. In 1996, Americans spent about $6.9 million on frozen durian. Last year, that figure rose to around $8.8 million. Frozen durian is sold primarily in Asian markets in major American cities but is considered a poor substitute for the fresh fruit.

So far, efforts to bring fresh durian to the United States have failed. The fruit does not survive the required quarantine process. But Asian-Americans who long for fresh durian shouldn't give up hope. Durian may someday be cultivated in the United States.

A researcher named Surmusk Salakpetch, who is earning a Ph.D. 10 from the University of Hawaii, reports that she has seen durian trees in Hawaii that seemed to be thriving. Salakpetch works at the Chanthaburi Horticultural Research Center, not far from the Golden Button Home plantation. She is the co-author of a Thai publication titled *Technology of Durian Production.* Salakpetch says she has heard that some former sugar cane plantations in Hawaii were being considered as sites for American durian orchards.

If durian farming does come to Hawaii, I wonder whether they will plant the extremely pungent variety that true durian fanciers prefer, or a less aromatic cultivar that Americans might find more palatable. Odorless cultivars of the fruit have already been produced, but they have never gained acceptance. Asians simply like the odoriferous ones better. In fact, Singaporeans and Malaysians are very fond of a preserved form of durian that is even smellier than the fresh variety.

The durian's odor is produced by enzymes that break down two common sulphur-containing amino acids, methionine and cystine, into sulfides and bisulfides that have a very intense smell. To find out more about the chemistry, I call Dr. Ron Buttery, a research chemist at the USDA's Western Research Center in Albany, California. Dr. Buttery points out that there are sulphur compounds in the aroma of many common fruits. In the smell of grapefruit, for instance, there is a tiny amount of a very intense sulphur compound called thio alpha-tepineol, the most potent odorant known. After rummaging around in his files, Dr. Buttery finds a paper on the aroma of durian. According to scientists R. Näf and A. Velluz, there are 43 sulphur compounds in durian. The major ones are ethyl prophyl disulfide, which is also found in onions; dialkyl disulfides, which are found in garlic; and also diethyl disulfide. Similar sulfur compounds are employed by skunks, Buttery notes.

My own reaction to durian surprises me. My disgust is completely involuntary, and there is no getting over it. A Thai friend who lives in the U.S. puts the phenomenon into perspective for me by comparing my reaction to durian to his reaction to cheese. As a child in Thailand, he had never had dairy foods, he says. To him, the smell of cheese is horrible, and as much as he wants to eat foods that contain cheese, he can never get them past his nose.

How does it happen? How do people from particular cultures come to love one smelly food and find another disgusting? I ask Paul Rozin, Ph.D., a professor of psychology at the University of Pennsylvania who specializes in the psychology of biocultural food habits and appreciation.

"Durian and blue cheese both have a rotten smell, which is offensive to most humans," Dr. Rozin says. "But this aversion is not innate. I believe that the disgust reaction comes from a universally acquired aversion that is probably taught in the toilet training process." Infants play with their feces, and animals show no particular aversion to it, Rozin observes. In the socialization process, we learn to feel disgusted by things that smell rotten — especially those, like blue cheese and durian flesh, that are mushy. 15

But the curious thing is that in many cultures, a small subset of rotten-smelling substances become highly favored foods, Rozin says. The category includes cheese for Europeans, fermented fish sauce and durian for Asians, and rotted whale meat for the Inuit — all things that taste much better than they smell. The food itself doesn't have the spoiled quality that the aroma indicates. And we get some pleasure from that — from a situation in which our body tells us no, but our mind tells us it's okay. Rozin calls them "mind over body experiences."

"So it's a form of thrill-seeking?" I ask.

rhetorical situations   genres   processes   strategies   research mla/apa   media/design   readings

"Sure, it's related to thrill-seeking," he says. "But thrill-seeking describes only the process, not the reason why."

"So what's the reason why?" I want to know.

Over and over again, humans develop strong likings for things that 20 are initially aversive, Rozin tells me. Like riding on roller coasters, going to sad movies, and eating blue cheese and durian.

"We're crazy," Rozin chuckles. "What else can I say?"

Engaging with the Text

1. The general subject of this report is, of course, the durian. How does Robb Walsh **FOCUS** the subject to make it interesting? What main point does he make about the durian?

   ▲ 70

2. This report **BEGINS** with Walsh seated in front of a plate of durian, attempting to eat it. How effective is this beginning? There are many other ways it could begin—with a straightforward description of a durian, perhaps, or with facts and figures. Why do you think Walsh opens as he does?

   ◆ 239–45

3. How would you characterize Walsh's **STANCE** toward his subject? Point to language in his report that reveals this stance. What does his stance suggest about Walsh's interest in and relationship with food more generally?

   ▪ 12–14

4. Walsh uses a lot of **DESCRIPTION** to help readers visualize, taste, and, of course, smell the durian. If you were his editor, would you advise him to include a photograph or drawing? Why or why not?

   ◆ 285–93

5. **For Writing.** Identify a food that is associated with your cultural heritage. Research its origins, uses, chemical make-up, availability, and so on, and write a **REPORT** on your findings. Assume that your readers know little about your topic and that you must engage their interest.

   ▲ 60–81

ROD USHER

A Whistle a Day Keeps Globalization Away

Rod Usher is a journalist and a frequent contributor to Time *magazine. He is also the author of* Florid States *(1999), a novel. The following report originally appeared in the London edition of* Time *in 2004.*

MARCIA GARCIA IS AS HIP as any 11-year-old in Seoul, Seattle, or Sydney. Here at the Lomada School on La Gomera, the second-smallest of Spain's seven Canary Islands, she has a cell phone tucked into the waistband of her trousers, which leave a fashionably bare patch of tanned tummy. But Maria and her classmates are also masters of a form of low-tech communication that doesn't require batteries or microwaves. Along with about 1,800 other schoolchildren on this rugged volcanic island, Maria is a student of *El Silbo,* the Gomera whistle, a substitute language based on four consonant and two vowel sounds. At a time when the boom in global communications risks swamping cultures and minority languages, little La Gomera has put its tradition where its mouth is.

Shaping a finger like the letter U and inserting it to one side of the mouth, the islanders learned to communicate across the hills and valleys of the roughly circular island, 26 km at its widest. There were no roads until 1935, and in the central village of Igualero there was only one public phone as late as 1993. Townsfolk used their traditional whistle language to announce, "Call for you, Pedro!"

Today, La Gomera remains home to about 18,000 residents, and tourism is helping to stanch emigration by those no longer able to make a living from farming or fishing. Ferries make the 40-minute trip from Tenerife, and one of the attractions, apart from a rich flora in the cloud-shrouded peaks, the highest of which is just under 1,500 m above sea level, is the chance to hear whistle-speak. When Eugenio Darias was born in 1950, phones were still a novelty. "I learned the *Silbo* playing in the street," he recalls. "If you didn't want to do a lot of climbing up and down to find people, you had to." But as roads, radios, and telephones arrived, the *Silbo* declined to the point where an evolutionary truism — use it or lose it — was about to kick in.

To rescue the tradition, the regional government in 2000 made learning the *Silbo* compulsory, and today Darias teaches it to the 164 students at Lomada School. He coordinates the work of two *Silbo* teachers to cover the island's 14 other schools. Students aged 7 to 14 do half an hour of whistling a week; those under 7 do 15 minutes to acquaint them with the technique. The *Silbo* employs *ch*, *y*, *g* and *k* sounds, plus the vowels *a* and *i*. "The sounds are approximate to spoken Spanish," says Darias. "Some words, such as *catarro* [a cold] and *cacharro* [a cooking utensil], sound much the same, as do *nada* [nothing] and *lana* [wool]. Context tells you which."

To test whether this is all *lana* over the visitor's eyes, Darias is asked 5 to bring in some of his students. Antonio Ramos, Ivan Conrado, twins Paula and Mirta Rodriguez, Maria Garcia and Raico Sanchez do him proud. Maria whistles Antonio's name. He makes a sound that Darias spells out as *fuio*, which in *Silbo* means "What do you want?" She asks him the time. Antonio blasts back that it's 11:30 a.m. Paula Rodriguez is asked to whistle to her twin Mirta: "Have you seen my glasses?" Mirta *silbos* back: "You're wearing them." To the uninitiated, it's all trill and squawk, requiring translation into Spanish by Darias.

Later in the playground, Maria whistles to a boy called Luis. After he gives her the *fuio* acknowledgement she tells him to come and shake a visitor's hand. Luis does so. Teacher Darias explains that coverage depends on topography, wind and the whistler's lungs: "In a valley, the *Silbo* can be heard 2,500 m away." The youngsters at Lomada School are proud of their tradition, which has the advantage of being a secret code. And Maria of the mobile says it still has practical uses. "Say I'm at my grandmother's house and she wants my grandad to bring her some parsley when he returns from their plot 200 m away. I can stand at the door and tell him." *Fuio!* They can't do that in Seoul, Seattle, or Sydney.

In a valley, the *Silbo* can be heard 2,500 m away.

Engaging with the Text

250–51

1. The **TITLE** "A Whistle a Day Keeps Globalization Away" evokes the common saying, "An Apple a Day Keeps the Doctor Away." Why do you think Rod Usher chose this title? To what degree does the allu- 3–4 sion reflect Usher's **PURPOSE?**

237–38

2. Usher gets us interested in his subject in the very first paragraph. How does he do this? What particular **STRATEGY** gets our interest? How else might he have gotten our attention?

245–49
239–45

3. How does Usher **END** his article? How does the conclusion relate back to his **BEGINNING?** What is the effect of this conclusion?

4. This report demonstrates an interesting intersection between the new and the old, between progress and tradition. Maria Garcia, for instance, has a cell phone "tucked into the waistband of her trousers" while she demonstrates the traditional Gomera whistle. What implications can be drawn about the relationship between tradition (old) and invention (new)? What impact might the old (tradition) have on the new (invention) and the new on the old?

5. *For Writing.* Young children often create their own languages, using, for instance, pig Latin or some special code for passing notes. College students often use certain abbreviations or code words as part of their 60–81 language. Write a **REPORT** on some language practice—spoken or writ- ten—that you are familiar with or that you can research by talking 70 with other students. **FOCUS** your report in a way that will interest your reader.

DARA MAYERS

Our Bodies, Our Lives

*Dara Mayers is a freelance writer whose work has been published in
magazines such as* U.S. News and World Report *and* Glamour.
The following report appeared in 2004 in the Ford Foundation Report,
a newsletter for that philanthropic organization.

PUNE, INDIA — When Yogita Kasbe organizes meetings in the slum
areas of this growing city in western India, she provides women with a
forum to discuss the health issues that concern them. She also gives
them a chance to learn about and participate in the development of
microbicides, a new set of products that could enable millions of vulnerable women to protect themselves from H.I.V. Kasbe is a peer counselor who recruits women for the National AIDS Research Institute,
which is conducting the clinical trials for microbicides. Working with
the Global Campaign for Microbicides, based in Washington, D.C., NARI
has developed a method of recruitment that is consistent with the ethical procedures at the heart of the campaign's work.

In the Janawadi slum, Kasbe's meetings sometimes take place in a
small clearing under a streetlight in an alleyway. The conditions are
cramped, but clean, and women sit on the sloping sidewalk. Because
Kasbe is from the neighborhood, it is not difficult for her to gain access
and trust in the community. "First, I'll find one woman I know, and tell
her I want to conduct a group meeting," she says. "I won't initially talk
about H.I.V. I'll talk about cleanliness and hygiene. Once I find one interested woman, I'll ask her to bring a few friends. The turnout, generally,
is good, because people want to know how to improve their health."

When she introduces the topic of H.I.V./AIDS, she finds that
although the women have heard of it, they have received only the most
general information. Kasbe then explains what sexually transmitted
diseases are, what the symptoms of AIDS are, and how to prevent
transmission. Women who are interested in being tested for H.I.V. are
invited to the clinic. If they test negative, Kasbe will inform them of the

benefits and risks of participating in phase-one clinical trials for microbicides. These trials help identify acute side effects and involve a small
number of healthy volunteers. The women must weigh the benefits —
possible protection from sexually transmitted diseases and free medical care during the trials — against the risk of allergic reaction. So far,
reactions have been minimal.

There are 62 microbicide products in development around the
world, designed as gels, lotions, creams, or suppositories that, when
applied vaginally or rectally, will prevent the transmission of H.I.V.
While microbicides may have applicability for gay men as well, they are
being promoted specifically for women and will ultimately be available
in both contraceptive and non-contraceptive forms. Because they are
undetectable to men, microbicides have the added benefit of giving
women the power to protect themselves without requiring their partner's knowledge or acquiescence. Married women are the fastest growing group of people being infected with H.I.V. in India, which soon will
outpace South Africa as the country with the world's highest infection
rate.

"The original conception of the AIDS challenge in the developing 5
world was that it was a supply-line problem," says Lori Heise, director
of the Global Campaign for Microbicides. "There was no discussion of
culture, of women's vulnerability. The fact is, many women in the developing world cannot ask their husbands to use condoms and cannot force
them to be faithful. And even if they can elect to use condoms, they are
forced to make a terrible choice. They can either not have children or
potentially expose themselves to a fatal disease. If all I have to offer is
condoms, I can't even begin the conversation."

Gender inequality in India puts women at great risk. Most women
cannot choose who they will marry, says Jayshodhara Dasgupta, the
coordinator of Sahayog, a resource center on gender and women's health
and rights in Lucknow. In February she attended a workshop on
women's vulnerability to H.I.V./AIDS that was offered as part of the
annual meeting of the Indian Network of Nongovernmental Organizations on H.I.V./AIDS. According to Dasgupta, even suggesting the use of
a condom would make the woman suspect in the eyes of her male part-

ner: "It would imply that she is too informed to be chaste or a virgin. She simply cannot question her husband's sex life. The vast majority of Indian women are very, very far from being able to negotiate safe sex."

The first microbicides are expected to have an effectiveness rate of approximately 40 to 60 percent. But even with limited effectiveness, microbicides are more promising than anything offered to date to limit the spread of H.I.V. in the developing world, according to the Global Campaign and other advocacy groups. Mathematical models developed by the campaign estimate that a 60-percent-effective microbicide, offered in 73 poor countries, would prevent 2.5 million infections over three years and save $2.7 billion in public health-care costs — in addition to $1 billion saved on lost productivity and the cost of training replacement workers.

"Seeta," a mother of two who lives in Janawadi, is a 34-year-old participant in the study being carried out in Pune. She is excited about the potential for microbicides. "Abstinence will not work — our husbands would kick us out of our homes," she says. "And condoms are male controlled. Men decide whether to use them. With microbicides we can rely on ourselves, without depending on men. Current methods are not enough to protect us. The government should make these products available to us. They should promote them. And they should be cheap enough so that poor women can use them. I would advise other women to use the products, and I am telling other women to participate in the trials."

"Ratna," 26, a mother of two, says that she was glad to participate in the microbicide trials, because she wants to take part in the effort to stop the spread of H.I.V. "We will buy it because life is more important than money. It should come as fast as possible onto the market because AIDS is spreading fast." Before participating in the trials, Seeta and Ratna (not their real names) knew nothing about H.I.V.

Promoting community engagement in the process of developing the 10 technology that will give women more power over their personal health and safety is a hallmark of the Global Campaign. For example, in areas where people go through the trash, women could not dispose of the microbicide applicator. Trash pickers would find it and wonder what it

Seeta, one of several uninfected women who volunteered to participate in a study of microbicides. Anita Khemka / Contact Press Images.

was, potentially creating gossip and rumors about them. It is this kind of information that the Global Campaign feels is crucial in the development of microbicides. "These are things that you only find out by working with the communities directly," says Megan Gottemoeller, international programs coordinator for the Global Campaign. "Products need to be developed with the end user in mind, with the cooperation of the users themselves."

The Global Campaign is an umbrella organization with 25 partner organizations and more than 170 endorsing groups. Since 1998 it has promoted the development of microbicides internationally through grass-roots organizing, policy advocacy, lobbying and social science research. However, the campaign's goals go beyond microbicides.

"The origins of the Global Campaign are not in advancing a particular technology," says Gottemoeller. "They are in women's rights and

rhetorical situations

genres

processes

strategies

research mla/apa

media/ design

readings

the gender analysis of women's vulnerability to H.I.V./AIDS. Our ultimate goal is to help people have a range of prevention options that meet their particular needs. We've ended up focusing on microbicides because it is an area of research that is undervalued and underfunded. We saw that there was an opportunity to participate in a more meaningful way than civil society ever has in the scientific process and technology development."

Microbicides are at least five years away from being publicly available. The campaign does not anticipate investment from the pharmaceutical industry until at least one product has blazed the trail through the regulatory process, thereby providing a better idea of the costs of collecting the data necessary for the product to be licensed in the United States. "Virtually all funding for microbicide research is public or from private donors, coming from foundations or the government sector," says Gottemoeller. However, she adds that some small biotech and pharmaceutical companies in India and other developing countries are working with regulatory bodies to guide the process, rather than waiting it out.

Dr. S. M. Mehendale, deputy director of NARI, expresses a sense of urgency. "I believe microbicides would have a very significant impact," he says. "Women are getting infected by their husbands and giving birth to children with H.I.V. Microbicides would really help to break the chain of transmission from men to women, and fewer and fewer babies would be born with H.I.V. The health impact microbicides would have in India would be dramatic."

Advocating for something not yet widely available — and which might prove to be ineffective — poses a difficult challenge for the Global Campaign, but most participants see the campaign for microbicides in the larger context of the struggle for gender equity. "I feel it is essentially a women's rights issue — having equal rights in all areas, including sexual health issues," says Bobby Ramakant, a campaign volunteer who also writes about health issues for the Health and Development Network, a nonprofit based in Thailand that helps disseminate health-related news through electronic discussions forums and newspapers.

"If you want to realize the larger public health goal of protection options for women, you have to address the issue of female empowerment in general," says Ramakant. "Even if 10 years down the line we don't have a microbicide, the campaign for them enables a conversation about the issues and helps to work on gender equality issues. A woman shouldn't have to rely on the mercy of a man to use a condom. If you put microbicides in that context it is definitely a rights issue."

Links to women's organizations, community-based groups, AIDS organizations, research institutions and government agencies have contributed to a remarkable movement for women's health and rights in poor countries, the reach of which extends beyond microbicides. "We have a very, very long way to go," says Dr. Radium Bhattacharya, president of both the Gujarat AIDS Awareness and Prevention Unit and the Indian Network of Nongovernmental Organizations on H.I.V./AIDS. "We have to bring some real structural changes to society. What we are doing now is part of that. We are really breaking the silence about women's health issues."

In a culture in which talking about sex is taboo, conversation about microbicides is in itself a revolutionary step. "Even the idea of a prevention option that women can control changes the minds of women," says Bhattacharya. "The campaign gives women the sense that they have sexual rights. It creates the idea in their minds. Women are starting to understand they have been exploited and are asking for things for themselves. Women are asking for microbicides as fast as they can come. Even just requesting microbicides is a good sign."

The campaign for microbicides has gained some powerful support in India.

"We recognize microbicides as a very important product that can empower women to protect themselves against H.I.V. and other sexually transmitted infections," says Dr. Kamini Walia of the Indian Council of Medical Research. She also voices some common concerns: "The product should be safe, it should be easily accessible, and it should be low-priced."

Ramakant praises the Global Campaign for initiating dialogue to increase awareness about the potential of microbicides. "The Global Campaign has played a key role in bringing people together — researchers, clinicians, NGO communities and donors — in one forum,"

rhetorical situations   genres   processes   strategies   research mla/apa   media/design   readings

he says. "That is a big step. The challenge will be to capture the synergy and channel it to accelerate research and development of microbicides, to pressure donor agencies and government, and to integrate microbicides into family-welfare programs."

Heise calls the campaign a movement on behalf of today's 10- and 11-year-old girls and boys. "With sufficient investment and political will we should have a product available when these young people come of age," she says. "That is my hope, because we cannot afford to lose another entire generation."

Engaging with the Text

1. What is the general topic of this report? Done well, writing that reports information is **TIGHTLY FOCUSED.** What is the specific focus of this report?

   ▲ 70

2. Since this piece was published in the *Ford Foundation Report,* who is the intended **AUDIENCE?** How might this kind of report encourage philanthropic donors? What in this report would make it attractive to those who wish to support this kind of work?

   ■ 5–8

3. How does this report **END?** How would the ending appeal to readers of a *Ford Foundation Report?* What does it leave them thinking? How else might it end?

   ◆ 245–49

4. What does the **IMAGE** contribute to the report? What does it say that words alone cannot?

   □ 458–62

5. *For Writing.* Identify a new medical product and do some research to learn about what it does. Write up a **REPORT** about what the product does, what conditions it cures, whom it's for, and so on.

   ▲ 60–81

53 Arguments

rhetorical situations ▪ genres ▲ processes ○ strategies ◆ research mla/apa ● media/design □ readings ▮

STEPHEN L. CARTER

Just Be Nice

Stephen L. Carter is a professor at Yale Law School and has written extensively on such topics as affirmative action, the judicial confirmation process, and the place of religion in our legal and political cultures. The following argument was written for the Yale Alumni Magazine *in 1998, and was later included in* Civility: Manners, Morals, and the Etiquette of Democracy *(1998).*

WHEN I WAS A CHILD, attending grade school in Washington, D.C., we took classroom time to study manners. Not only the magic words "please" and "thank you" but more complicated etiquette questions, like how to answer the telephone ("Carter residence, Stephen speaking") and how to set the table (we were quizzed on whether knife blades point in or out). And somehow nobody — no children, no parents — objected to what nowadays would surely be viewed as indoctrination.

Today, instruction of this sort is so rare that when a school tries to teach manners to children, it makes news. So when the magazine *U.S. News & World Report* ran a story in 1996 about the decline of civility, it opened with what it must have considered the man-bites-dog vignette — an account of a classroom where young people were taught to be polite. Ironically, this newsworthy curriculum evidently teaches a good deal less about etiquette than we learned back at Margaret M. Amidon Elementary School in the sixties, but that is still a good deal more than children learn in most places. Deportment classes are long gone. Now and then the schools teach some norms of conduct, but almost always about sex, and never the most important ones: *Do not engage in harassment* and *Always use a condom* seem to be the outer limits of their moral capacity. The idea that sex, as a unique human activity, might require a unique morality, different from the general moral rules against physical harm to others and harm to the self, is not one that public schools are prepared to entertain.

Respect for rules of conduct has been lost in the deafening and essentially empty rights-talk of our age. Following a rule of good manners may mean doing something you do not want to do, and the weird rhetoric of our self-indulgent age resists the idea that we have such things as obligations to others. We suffer from what James Q. Wilson has described as the elevation of self-expression over self-control. So when a black student at a Connecticut high school was disciplined in 1996 for wearing pants that drooped (exposing his underwear), not only did he claim a right to wear what he liked, but some community leaders hinted at racism, on the theory that many young African American males dress this way. (The fact that the style is copied from prison garb, which lacks a belt, evidently makes no impression on these particular defenders of the race.)

When I was a child, had my school sought to discipline me, my parents would have assumed the school had good reason. And they probably would have punished me further at home. Unlike many of today's parents, they would not have begun by challenging the teacher or principal who thought I had done wrong. To the student of civility, the relevant difference between that era and the present is the collapse of trust, particularly trust in strangers and in institutions. My parents would have trusted the school's judgment — and thus trusted the school to punish me appropriately — but trust of that kind has largely dissolved. Trust (along with generosity) is at the heart of civility. But cynicism has replaced the healthier emotion of trust. Cynicism is the enemy of civility: it suggests a deep distrust of the motives of our fellow passengers, on trusting others even when there is risk. And so, because we no longer trust each other, we place our trust in the vague and conversation-stifling language of "rights" instead.

Consider again the boy with the droopy pants. To talk about wear-   5
ing a particular set of clothes as a "right" is demeaning to the bloody struggles for such basic rights as the vote and an unsegregated education. But the illusion that all desires are rights continues its insidious spread. At about the same time, a fired waitress at a restaurant not far from Yale, where I teach, announced a "right" to pierce her face with

as many studs and rings as she wishes. And, not long ago, a television program featured an interview with a woman who insisted on the "right" to be as fat as she likes. Rights that are purchased at relatively low cost stand a fair chance of being abused, simply because there is no history behind them, and thus little pressure to use them responsibly — in short, because nobody knows why the right exists. But even a right that possesses a grimly instructive history — a right like freedom of speech — may fall subject to abuse when we forget where it came from.

This proposition helps explain *Cohen v. California,* a 1971 decision in which the Supreme Court overturned the conviction of a young man who wore on his jacket the benign legend F--- THE DRAFT. The case arose as the public language grew vulgar. The 19th and early 20th centuries offered a tradition of public insults that were witty, pointed, occasionally cruel, but not obscene or particularly offensive. Politicians and other public figures competed to demonstrate their cleverness in repartee. (One of my favorites is Benjamin Disraeli's explanation of the difference between a misfortune and a calamity: "If Gladstone fell into the Thames, that would be a misfortune. And if anyone pulled him out, that would be a calamity.") Nowadays the tradition of barbed wit has given way to a witless barbarism, our lazier conversational habit of reaching for the first bit of profanity that comes to mind. The restraint and forethought that are necessary to be clever, even in insult, are what a sacrificed civility demands. When we are lazy about our words, we tell those at whom our vulgarity is directed that they are so far beneath us that they are not worth the effort of stopping to think how best to insult them; we prefer, animal-like, to make the first sound that comes to mind.

In *Cohen v. California,* the justices were unfortunately correct that what the dissenters called "Cohen's absurd and immature antic" was protected by the freedom of speech. But it is important to add that when the framers of the Constitution envisioned the rough-and-tumble world of public argument, they almost certainly imagined heated disagreements against a background of broadly shared values; certainly that was the model offered by John Locke, by then a kind of political folk hero. It is unlikely that the framers imagined a world in which I might feel (morally) free to say the first thing that came into my head. I do think

Cohen was rightly decided, but the danger deserves emphasis: when offensiveness becomes a constitutional right, it is a right without any tradition behind it, and consequently we have no norms to govern its use.

Consider once more the fired waitress. I do not deny that the piercing of one's body conveys, in many cultures, information of great significance. But in America, we have no tradition to serve as guide. No elder stands behind our young to say, "Folks have fought and died for your right to pierce your face, so do it right"; no community exists that can model for a young person the responsible use of the "right"; for the right, even if called self-expression, comes from no source other than desire. If we fail to distinguish desire from right, we will not understand that rights are sensible and wise only within particular contexts that give them meaning. The Constitution protects a variety of rights, but our moral norms provide the discipline in their exercise. Sometimes what the moral norm of civility demands is that we restrain our self-expression for the sake of our community. That is why Isaac Peebles in the nineteenth century thought it wrong for people to sing during a train ride; and why it is wrong to race our cars through the streets, stereos cranked high enough to be sure that everyone we pass has the opportunity to enjoy the music we happen to like; and why it was wrong for Cohen to wear his jacket, and why it is wrong for racists to burn crosses (another harmful act of self-expression that the courts have protected under the First Amendment). And it is why a waitress who encounters the dining public every day in her work must consider the interest of that public as she mulls the proper form of self-expression.

Consequently, our celebration of Howard Stern, Don Imus, and other heroes of "shock radio" might be evidence of a certain loss of moral focus. The proposition that all speech must be protected should not be confused with the very different proposition that all speech must be celebrated. When radio station WABC in New York dismissed a popular talk show host, Bob Grant, who refused to stop making racist remarks on the air, some of his colleagues complained that he was being censored. Lost in the brouhaha was the simple fact that Grant's comments and conduct were reprehensible, and that his abuse of our precious freedoms was nothing to be celebrated.

The point is not that we should rule the offensive illegal, which is why the courts are correct to strike down efforts to regulate speech that some people do not like, and even most speech that hurts; the advantages of yielding to the government so much power over what we say have never been shown to outweigh the dangers. Yet we should recognize the terrible damage that free speech can do if people are unwilling to adhere to the basic precept of civility, that we must sometimes rein in our own impulses — including our impulses to speak hurtful words — for the sake of those who are making the democratic journey with us. The Proverb tells us, "Death and life are in the power of the tongue" (Proverbs 18:21). The implication is that the choice of how to use the tongue, for good or for evil, is ours.

Words are magic. We conjure with them. We send messages, we paint images. With words we report the news, profess undying love, and preserve our religious traditions. Words at their best are the tools of morality, of progress, of hope. But words at their worst can wound. And wounds fester. Consequently, the way we use words matters. This explains why many traditional rules of etiquette, from Erasmus's handbook in the sixteenth century to the explosion of guides to good manners during the Victorian era, were designed to govern how words — those marvelous, dangerous words — should be used. Even the controversial limits on sexual harassment and "hate speech" that have sprouted in our era, limits that often carry the force of law, are really just more rules of civility, more efforts, in a morally bereft age, to encourage us to discipline our desires.

> **How we treat one another is what civility is about.**

My point is not to tell us how to speak. My point is to argue that how we speak is simply one point on a continuum of right and wrong ways to treat one another. And how we treat one another is what civility is about.

Engaging with the Text

251–52 ◆
93 ▲

1. What is Stephen Carter's **THESIS?** What **GOOD REASONS** does he provide to back up his position? Do you accept these reasons? Why or why not?

304–12 ◆

2. How do the **ANECDOTES** about Carter's own experience in grade school and the boy with the droopy pants establish a context for his argument?

3. Carter wrote this piece for the *Yale Alumni Magazine*. What values do you think he assumes that his readers hold? How do you know? How does he appeal to this **AUDIENCE?** Refer to examples in his text.

5–8 ■

4. For Carter, what is the role words play in civility, in how we ought to treat each other? Discuss the power of words as both "tools of morality" and weapons that can "wound." What are the implications of this power for your own speech and writing?

5. *For Writing.* Carter concludes by asserting that "how we treat one another is what civility is all about." What we wear, what we say, even how we move can affect and possibly offend others: wearing a t-shirt bearing a provocative slogan, talking loudly on a cell phone in a public space, putting feet up on the seat in a subway train. Identify other such actions that you or others find offensive. Choose one and write an essay **ARGUING A POSITION** on the issue of its propriety: does it violate norms of civility? How and why (or why not)? You should identify a clear **AUDIENCE** and keep their values in mind as you shape your essay. And remember: whatever position you take, you'll want to consider **OTHER POSITIONS,** including Carter's.

82–106 ▲
5–8 ■
94 ▲

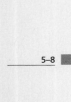

■ ▲ ○ ◆ ● □ ▐▌
rhetorical genres processes strategies research media/ readings
situations   mla/apa design

GREGORY MANTSIOS

Class in America — 2003

Sociologist Gregory Mantsios is the director of the Labor Resource Center at Queens College of the City University of New York. He has written widely on socioeconomic class in America and is the editor of A New Labor Movement for the New Century (1998), a collection of essays. The following argument appeared in Race, Class, and Gender in the United States (2004), a sociology textbook, and the notes are in the style of that publication. As you read, pay attention to how Mantsios identifies four myths about socioeconomic class in America and then structures his argument around them.

PEOPLE IN THE UNITED STATES DON'T LIKE TO TALK ABOUT CLASS. Or so it would seem. We don't speak about class privileges, or class oppression, or the class nature of society. These terms are not part of our everyday vocabulary, and in most circles they are associated with the language of the rhetorical fringe. Unlike people in most other parts of the world, we shrink from using words that classify along economic lines or that point to class distinctions: phrases like "working class," "upper class," and "ruling class" are rarely uttered by Americans.

For the most part, avoidance of class-laden vocabulary crosses class boundaries. There are few among the poor who speak of themselves as lower class; instead, they refer to their race, ethnic group, or geographic location. Workers are more likely to identify with their employer, industry, or occupational group than with other workers, or with the working class.[1]

Neither are those at the other end of the economic spectrum likely to use the word "class." In her study of thirty-eight wealthy and socially prominent women, Susan Ostrander asked participants if they considered themselves members of the upper class. One participant responded, "I hate to use the word 'class.' We are responsible, fortunate people, old families, the people who have something."

Another said, "I hate [the term] upper class. It is so non-upper class to use it. I just call it 'all of us,' those who are wellborn."[2]

It is not that Americans, rich or poor, aren't keenly aware of class 5
differences — those quoted above obviously are; it is that class is not in
the domain of public discourse. Class is not discussed or debated in public because class identity has been stripped from popular culture. The
institutions that shape mass culture and define the parameters of public debate have avoided class issues. In politics, in primary and secondary education, and in the mass media, formulating issues in terms
of class is unacceptable, perhaps even un-American.

There are, however, two notable exceptions to this phenomenon.
First, it is acceptable in the United States to talk about "the middle class."
Interestingly enough, such references appear to be acceptable precisely
because they mute class differences. References to the middle class by
politicians, for example, are designed to encompass and attract the
broadest possible constituency. Not only do references to the middle
class gloss over differences, but these references also avoid any suggestion of conflict or exploitation.

This leads us to the second exception to the class-avoidance phenomenon. We are, on occasion, presented with glimpses of the upper
class and the lower class (the language used is "the wealthy" and "the
poor"). In the media, these presentations are designed to satisfy some
real or imagined voyeuristic need of "the ordinary person." As curiosi-
ties, the ground-level view of street life and the inside look at the rich
and the famous serve as unique models, one to avoid and one to aspire
to. In either case, the two models are presented without causal relation
to each other: one is not rich because the other is poor.

Similarly, when social commentators or liberal politicians draw
attention to the plight of the poor, they do so in a manner that obscures
the class structure and denies class exploitation. Wealth and poverty
are viewed as one of several natural and inevitable states of being: differences are only differences. One may even say differences are the
American way, a reflection of American social diversity.

We are left with one of two possibilities: either talking about class
and recognizing class distinctions are not relevant to U.S. society, or we
mistakenly hold a set of beliefs that obscure the reality of class differences and their impact on people's lives.

rhetorical situations genres processes strategies research mla/apa media/ design readings

Let us look at four common, albeit contradictory, beliefs about the 10 United States.

Myth 1: The United States is fundamentally a classless society. Class distinctions are largely irrelevant today, and whatever differences do exist in economic standing, they are — for the most part — insignificant. Rich or poor, we are all equal in the eyes of the law, and such basic needs as health care and education are provided to all regardless of economic standing.

Myth 2: We are, essentially, a middle-class nation. Despite some variations in economic status, most Americans have achieved relative affluence in what is widely recognized as a consumer society.

Myth 3: We are all getting richer. The American public as a whole is steadily moving up the economic ladder, and each generation propels itself to greater economic well-being. Despite some fluctuations, the U.S. position in the global economy has brought previously unknown prosperity to most, if not all, Americans.

Myth 4: Everyone has an equal chance to succeed. Success in the United States requires no more than hard work, sacrifice, and perseverance: "In America, anyone can become a millionaire; it's just a matter of being in the right place at the right time."

In trying to assess the legitimacy of these beliefs, we want to ask 15 several important questions. Are there significant class differences among Americans? If these differences do exist, are they getting bigger or smaller, and do these differences have a significant impact on the way we live? Finally, does everyone in the United States really have an equal opportunity to succeed?

The Economic Spectrum

Let's begin by looking at difference. An examination of available data reveals that variations in economic well-being are, in fact, immense. Consider the following:

- The wealthiest 1 percent of the American population holds 38 percent of the total national wealth. That is, they own well over one-third of all the consumer durables (such as houses, cars, and stereos) and financial assets (such as stocks, bonds, property, and savings accounts). The richest 20 percent of Americans hold 83 percent of the total household wealth in the country.[3]
- Approximately 241,000 Americans, or approximately three quarters of 1 percent of the adult population, earn more than $1 million *annually*, with many of these individuals earning over $10 million and some earning over $100 million. It would take the average American, earning $34,000 per year, more than 65 *lifetimes* to earn $100 million.[4]

Affluence and prosperity are clearly alive and well in certain segments of the U.S. population. However, this abundance is in contrast to the poverty and despair that is also prevalent in the United States. At the other end of the spectrum:

- Approximately 12 percent of the American population — that is, nearly one of every eight people in this country — live below the official poverty line (calculated in 2001 at $9,214 for an individual and $17,960 for a family of four).[5] Among the poor are over 2.3 million homeless, including nearly 1 million homeless children.[6]
- Approximately one out of every five children in the United States under the age of six lives in poverty.[7]

The contrast between rich and poor is sharp, and with nearly one-third of the American population living at one extreme or the other, it is difficult to argue that we live in a classless society. Big-payoff reality shows, celebrity salaries, and multimillion-dollar lotteries notwithstanding, evidence suggests that the level of inequality in the United States is getting higher. Census data show the gap between the rich and the poor to be the widest since the government began collecting information in 1947[8] and that this gap is continuing to grow. While four out of five households in the United States saw their share of net worth fall between 1992 and 2000, households in the top fifth of the population saw their share increase from 59 percent to 63 percent.[9]

rhetorical
situations   genres   processes   strategies   research
mla/apa   media/
design   readings

Nor is such a gap between rich and poor representative of the rest of the industrialized world. In fact, the United States has by far the most unequal distribution of household income.[10] The income gap between rich and poor in the United States (measured as the percentage of total income held by the wealthiest 20 percent of the population versus the poorest 20 percent) is approximately 11 to 1, one of the highest ratios in the industrialized world. The ratio in Japan and Germany, by contrast, is 4 to 1.[11]

Reality 1: There are enormous differences in the economic standing of the American citizens. A sizable proportion of the U.S. population occupies opposite ends of the economic spectrum. In the middle range of the economic spectrum:

- Sixty percent of the American population holds less than 6 percent of the nation's wealth.[12]
- While the real income of the top 1 percent of U.S. families skyrocketed by 59 percent during the economic boom of the late 1990s, the income of the middle fifth of the population grew only slightly and its share of income (15 percent of the total compared to 48 percent of the total for the wealthiest fifth), actually declined during this same period.[13]
- Regressive changes in governmental tax policies and the weakening of labor unions over the last quarter century have led to a significant rise in the level of inequality between the rich and the middle class. Between 1979 and 2000, the gap in household income between the top fifth and middle fifth of the population rose by 31 percent.[14] During the economic boom of the 1990s, four out of five Americans saw their share of net worth decline, while the top fifth saw their share increase from 59 percent to 63 percent.[15] One prominent economist described economic growth in the United States as a "spectator sport for the majority of American families."[16] Economic decline, on the other hand, is much more "inclusive," with layoffs impacting hardest on middle- and lower-income families — those with fewer resources to fall back on.

The level of inequality is sometimes difficult to comprehend fully by looking at dollar figures and percentages. To help his students visualize the distribution of income, the well-known economist Paul Samuelson asked them to picture an income pyramid made of children's blocks, with each layer of blocks representing $1,000. If we were to construct Samuelson's pyramid today, the peak of the pyramid would be much higher than the Eiffel Tower, yet almost all of us would be within six feet of the ground.[17] In other words, the distribution of income is heavily skewed; a small minority of families take the lion's share of national income, and the remaining income is distributed among the vast majority of middle-income and low-income families. Keep in mind that Samuelson's pyramid represents the distribution of income, not wealth. The distribution of wealth is skewed even further.

Reality 2: The middle class in the United States holds a very small share of the nation's wealth and that share is declining steadily. The gap between rich and poor and between rich and the middle class is larger than it has ever been.

American Life-Styles

At last count, nearly 33 million Americans across the nation lived in unrelenting poverty.[18] Yet, as political scientist Michael Harrington once commented, "America has the best dressed poverty the world has ever known."[19] Clothing disguises much of the poverty in the United States, and this may explain, in part, its middle-class image. With increased mass marketing of "designer" clothing and with shifts in the nation's economy from blue-collar (and often better-paying) manufacturing jobs to white-collar and pink-collar jobs in the service sector, it is becoming increasingly difficult to distinguish class differences based on appearance.[20] The dress-down environment prevalent in the high-tech industry (what one author refers to as the "no-collars movement") has reduced superficial distinctions even further.[21]

Beneath the surface, there is another reality. Let's look at some "typical" and not-so-typical life-styles.

American Profile

Name:	Harold S. Browning
Father:	manufacturer, industrialist
Mother:	prominent social figure in the community
Principal child-rearer:	governess
Primary education:	an exclusive private school on Manhattan's Upper East Side

Note: a small, well-respected primary school where teachers and administrators have a reputation for nurturing student creativity and for providing the finest educational preparation

Ambition: "to become President"

Supplemental tutoring:	tutors in French and mathematics
Summer camp:	sleep-away camp in northern Connecticut

Note: camp provides instruction in the creative arts, athletics, and the natural sciences

Secondary education:	a prestigious preparatory school in Westchester County

Note: classmates included the sons of ambassadors, doctors, attorneys, television personalities, and well-known business leaders

After-school activities: private riding lessons

Ambition: "to take over my father's business"

High-school graduation gift: BMW

(*Continued on next page*)

Family activities:	theater, recitals, museums, summer vacations in Europe, occasional winter trips to the Caribbean
	Note: as members of and donors to the local art museum, the Brownings and their children attend private receptions and exhibit openings at the invitation of the museum director
Higher education:	an Ivy League liberal-arts college in Massachusetts
	Major: economics and political science
	After-class activities: debating club, college newspaper, swim team
	Ambition: "to become a leader in business"
First full-time job (age 23):	assistant manager of operations, Browning Tool and Die, Inc. (family enterprise)
Subsequent employment:	*3 years* — executive assistant to the president, Browning Tool and Die
	Responsibilities included: purchasing (materials and equipment), personnel, and distribution networks
	4 years — advertising manager, Lackheed Manufacturing (home appliances)
	3 years — director or marketing and sales, Comerex, Inc. (business machines)
Present employment (age 38):	executive vice president, SmithBond and Co. (digital instruments)
	Typical daily activities: review financial reports and computer printouts, dictate memoranda, lunch with clients, initiate

(*Continued on next page*)

conference calls, meet with assistants, plan business trips, meet with associates

Transportation to and from work: chauffeured company limousine

Annual salary: $315,000

Ambition: "to become chief executive officer of the firm, or one like it, within the next five to ten years"

Present residence: eighteenth-floor condominium on Manhattan's Upper West Side, eleven rooms, including five spacious bedrooms and terrace overlooking river

Interior: professionally decorated and accented with elegant furnishings, valuable antiques, and expensive artwork

Note: building management provides doorman and elevator attendant; family employs *au pair* for children and maid for other domestic chores

Second residence: farm in northwestern Connecticut, used for weekend retreats and for horse breeding (investment/hobby)

Note: to maintain the farm and cater to the family when they are there, the Brownings employ a part-time maid, groundskeeper, and horse breeder

Harold Browning was born into a world of nurses, maids, and governesses. His world today is one of airplanes and limousines, five-star restaurants, and luxurious living accommodations. The life and life-style of Harold Browning is in sharp contrast to that of Bob Farrell. 25

American Profile

Name:	Bob Farrell
Father:	machinist
Mother:	retail clerk
Principal child-rearer:	mother and sitter
Primary education:	a medium-size public school in Queens, New York, characterized by large class size, outmoded physical facilities, and an educational philosophy emphasizing basic skills and student discipline
	Ambition: "to become President"
Supplemental tutoring:	none
Summer camp:	YMCA day camp
	Note: emphasis on team sports, arts and crafts
Secondary education:	large regional high school in Queens
	Note: classmates included the sons and daughters of carpenters, postal clerks, teaches, nurses, shopkeepers, mechanics, bus drivers, police officers, salespersons
	After-school activities: basketball and handball in school park
	Ambition: "to make it through college"
	High-school graduation gift: $500 savings bond
Family activities:	family gatherings around television set, bowling, an occasional trip to the movie theater, summer Sundays at the public beach

(Continued on next page)

Higher education:	a two-year community college with a technical orientation
	Major: electrical technology
	After-school activities: employed as a part-time bagger in local supermarket
	Ambition: "to become an electrical engineer"
First full-time job (age 19):	service-station attendant
	Note: continued to take college classes in the evening
Subsequent employment:	mail clerk at large insurance firm; manager trainee, large retail chain
Present employment (age 38):	assistant sales manager, building supply firm
	Typical daily activities: demonstrate products, write up product orders, handle customer complaints, check inventory
	Transportation to and from work: city subway
	Annual salary: $39,261
	Ambition: "to open up my own business"
	Additional income: $6,100 in commissions from evening and weekend work as salesman in local men's clothing store
Present residence:	the Farrells own their own home in a working-class neighborhood in Queens

Bob Farrell and Harold Browning live very differently: the life-style of one is privileged; that of the other is not so privileged. The differences are class differences, and these differences have a profound impact on the way they live. They are differences between playing a game of handball in the park and taking riding lessons at a private stable; watching a movie on television and going to the theater; and taking the subway to work and being driven in a limousine. More important, the difference in class determines where they live, who their friends are, how well they are educated, what they do for a living, and what they come to expect from life.

Yet, as dissimilar as their life-styles are, Harold Browning and Bob Farrell have some things in common; they live in the same city, they work long hours, and they are highly motivated. More important, they are both white males.

Let's look at someone else who works long and hard and is highly motivated. This person, however, is black and female.

	American Profile
Name:	Cheryl Mitchell
Father:	janitor
Mother:	waitress
Principal child-rearer:	grandmother
Primary education:	large public school in Ocean Hill-Brownsville, Brooklyn, New York
	Note: rote teaching of basic skills and emphasis on conveying the importance of good attendance, good manners, and good work habits; school patrolled by security guards
	Ambition: "to be a teacher"
Supplemental tutoring:	none
Summer camp:	none

(Continued on next page)

rhetorical situations　genres　processes　strategies　research mla/apa　media/ design　readings

Secondary education:	large public school in Ocean Hill-Brownsville
	Note: classmates included sons and daughters of hairdressers, groundskeepers, painters, dressmakers, dishwashers, domestics
	After-school activities: domestic chores, part-time employment as babysitter and housekeeper
	Ambition: "to be a social worker"
	High-school graduation gift: corsage
Family activities:	church-sponsored socials
Higher education:	one semester of local community college
	Note: dropped out of school for financial reasons
First full-time job (age 17):	counter clerk, local bakery
Subsequent employment:	file clerk with temporary-service agency, supermarket checker
Present employment (age 38):	nurse's aide at a municipal hospital
	Typical daily activities: make up hospital beds, clean out bedpans, weigh patients and assist them to the bathroom, take temperature readings, pass out and collect food trays, feed patients who need help, bathe patients, and change dressings
	Annual salary: $15,820
	Ambition: "to get out of the ghetto"
Present residence:	three-room apartment in the South Bronx, needs painting, has poor ventilation, is in a high-crime area
	Note: Cheryl Mitchell lives with her four-year-old son and her elderly mother

When we look at the lives of Cheryl Mitchell, Bob Farrell, and Harold Browning, we see life-styles that are very different. We are not looking, however, at economic extremes. Cheryl Mitchell's income as a nurse's aide puts her above the government's official poverty line.[22] Below her on the income pyramid are 33 million poverty-stricken Americans. Far from being poor, Bob Farrell has an annual income as an assistant sales manager that puts him well above the median income level — that is, more than 50 percent of the U.S. population earns less money than Bob Farrell.[23] And while Harold Browning's income puts him in a high-income bracket, he stands only a fraction of the way up Samuelson's income pyramid. Well above him are the 241,000 individuals whose annual salary exceeds $1 million. Yet Harold Browning spends more money on his horses than Cheryl Mitchell earns in a year.

Reality 3: Even ignoring the extreme poles of the economic spectrum, we find enormous class differences in the life-styles among the haves, the have-nots, and the have-littles.   30

Class affects more than life-style and material well-being. It has a significant impact on our physical and mental well-being as well.

Researchers have found an inverse relationship between social class and health. Lower-class standing is correlated to higher rates of infant mortality, eye and ear disease, arthritis, physical disability, diabetes, nutritional deficiency, respiratory disease, mental illness, and heart disease.[24] In all areas of health, poor people do not share the same life chances as those in the social class above them. Furthermore, lower-class standing is correlated with a lower quality of treatment for illness and disease. The results of poor health and poor treatment are borne out in the life expectancy rates within each class. Researchers have found that the higher your class standing, the higher your life expectancy. Conversely, they have also found that within each age group, the lower one's class standing, the higher the death rate; in some age groups, the figures are as much as two and three times as high.[25]

Reality 4: From cradle to grave, class standing has a significant impact on our chances for survival.

The lower one's class standing, the more difficult it is to secure appropriate housing, the more time is spent on the routine tasks of everyday life,

the greater is the percentage of income that goes to pay for food and other basic necessities, and the greater is the likelihood of crime victimization.[26] Class can accurately predict chances for both survival and success.

Class and Educational Attainment

School performance (grades and test scores) and educational attainment 35 (level of schooling completed) also correlate strongly with economic class. Furthermore, despite some efforts to make testing fairer and schooling more accessible, current data suggest that the level of inequity is staying the same or getting worse.

In his study for the Carnegie Council on Children twenty-five years ago, Richard De Lone examined the test scores of over half a million students who took the College Board exams (SATs). His findings were consistent with earlier studies that showed a relationship between class and scores on standardized tests; his conclusion: "the higher the student's social status, the higher the probability that he or she will get higher grades."[27] Fifteen years after the release of the Carnegie report, College Board surveys reveal data that are no different: test scores still correlate strongly with family income.

Average Combined Scores by Income (440 to 1600 scale)[28]

Family Income	Median Score
More than $100,000	1130
$80,000 to $100,000	1082
$70,000 to $80,000	1058
$60,000 to $70,000	1043
$50,000 to $60,000	1030
$40,000 to $50,000	1011
$30,000 to $40,000	986
$20,000 to $30,000	954
$10,000 to $20,000	907
less than $10,000	871

These figures are based on the test results of 1,302,903 SAT takers in 1999.

A little more than twenty years ago, researcher William Sewell showed a positive correlation between class and overall educational achievement. In comparing the top quartile (25 percent) of this sample to the bottom quartile, he found that students from upper-class families were twice as likely to obtain training beyond high school and four times as likely to attain a postgraduate degree. Sewell concluded: "Socioeconomic background . . . operates independently of academic ability at every stage in the process of educational attainment."[29]

Today, the pattern persists. There are, however, two significant changes. On the one hand, the odds of getting into college have improved for the bottom quartile of the population, although they still remain relatively low compared to the top. On the other hand, the chances of completing a college degree have deteriorated markedly for the bottom quartile. Researchers estimate the chances of completing a four-year college degree (by age 24) to be nineteen times as great for the top 25 percent of the population as it is for the bottom 25 percent.[30]

Reality 5: Class standing has a significant impact on chances for educational achievement.

Class standing, and consequently life chances, are largely determined at birth. Although examples of individuals who have gone from rags to riches abound in the mass media, statistics on class mobility show these leaps to be extremely rare. In fact, dramatic advances in class standing are relatively infrequent. One study showed that fewer than one in five men surpass the economic status of their fathers.[31] For those whose annual income is in six figures, economic success is due in large part to the wealth and privileges bestowed on them at birth. Over 66 percent of the consumer units with incomes of $100,000 or more have inherited assets. Of these units, over 86 percent reported that inheritances constituted a substantial portion of their total assets.[32]

Economist Harold Wachtel likens inheritance to a series of Monopoly games in which the winner of the first game refuses to relinquish his or her cash and commercial property for the second game. "After all," argues the winner, "I accumulated my wealth and income by my own wits." With such an arrangement, it is not difficult to predict the outcome of subsequent games.[33]

Reality 6: All Americans do not have an equal opportunity to succeed. Inheritance laws ensure a greater likelihood of success for the offspring of the wealthy.

Spheres of Power and Oppression

When we look at society and try to determine what it is that keeps most people down — what holds them back from realizing their potential as healthy, creative, productive individuals — we find institutional forces that are largely beyond individual control. Class domination is one of these forces. People do not choose to be poor or working class; instead, they are limited and confined by the opportunities afford or denied them by a social and economic system. The class structure in the United States is a function of its economic system: capitalism, a system that is based on private rather than public ownership and control of commercial enterprises. Under capitalism, these enterprises are governed by the need to produce a profit for the owners, rather than to fulfill collective needs. Class divisions arise from the differences between those who own and control corporate enterprise and those who do not.

Racial and gender domination are other forces that hold people down. Although there are significant differences in the way capitalism, racism, and sexism affect our lives, there are also a multitude of parallels. And although class, race, and gender act independently of each other, they are at the same time very much interrelated.

On the one hand, issues of race and gender cut across class lines. Women experience the effects of sexism whether they are well-paid professional or poorly paid clerks. As women, they face discrimination and male domination, as well as catcalls and stereotyping. Similarly, a wealthy black man faces racial oppression, is subjected to racial slurs, and is denied opportunities because of his color. Regardless of their class standing, women and members of minority races are constantly dealing with institutional forces that are holding them down precisely because of their gender, the color of their skin, or both. 45

On the other hand, the experiences of women and minorities are differentiated along class lines. Although they are in subordinate posi-

tions vis-à-vis white men, the particular issues that confront women and minorities may be quite different depending on their position in the class structure.

Power is incremental, and class privileges can accrue to individual women and to individual members of a racial minority. At the same time, class-oppressed men, whether they are white or black, have privileges afforded them as men in a sexist society. Similarly, class-oppressed whites, whether they are men or women, benefit from white privilege in a racist society. Spheres of power and oppression divide us deeply in our society, and the schisms between us are often difficult to bridge.

Whereas power is incremental, oppression is cumulative, and those who are poor, black, and female are often subject to all of the forces of class, race, and gender discrimination simultaneously. This cumulative situation is what is meant by the double and triple jeopardy of women and minorities.

Furthermore, oppression in one sphere is related to the likelihood of oppression in another. If you are black and female, for example, you are much more likely to be poor or working class than you would be as a white male. Census figures show that the incidence of poverty varies greatly by race and gender.

Chances of Being Poor in America[34]

White male/ female	White female head*	Hispanic male/ female	Hispanic female head*	Black male/ female	Black female head*
1 in 10	1 in 5	1 in 5	1 in 3	1 in 5	1 in 3

*Persons in families with female householder, no husband present.

In other words, being female and being nonwhite are attributes in our society that increase the chances of poverty and of lower-class standing.

Reality 7: Racism and sexism significantly compound the effects of class in society.

Notes

1. See Jay MacLead, *Ain't No Makin' It: Aspirations and Attainment in a Lower-Income Neighborhood* (Boulder, CO: Westview Press, 1995); Benjamin DeMott, *The Imperial Middle* (New York: Morrow, 1990); Ira Katznelson, *City Trenches: Urban Politics and Patterning of Class in the United States* (New York: Pantheon Books, 1981); Charles W. Tucker, "A Comparative Analysis of Subjective Social Class: 1945–1963," *Social Forces,* no. 46, June 1968, pp. 508–514; Robert Nisbet, "The Decline and Fall of Social Class," *Pacific Sociological Review,* vol. 2, Spring 1959, pp. 11–17; and Oscar Glantz, "Class Consciousness and Political Solidarity," *American Sociological Review,* vol. 23, August 1958, pp. 375–382.

2. Susan Ostander, "Upper-Class Women: Class Consciousness as Conduct and Meaning," in G. William Domhoff, *Power Structure Research* (Beverly Hills, CA: Sage Publications, 1980, pp. 78–79). Also see Stephen Birmingham, *America's Secret Aristocracy* (Boston: Little, Brown, 1987).

3. Lawrence Mishel, Jared Bernstein, and Heather Boushey, *The State of Working America: 2002–03* (Ithaca, NY: ILR Press, Cornell University Press, 2003, p. 277).

4. The number of individuals filing tax returns showing a gross adjusted income of $1 million or more in 2000 was 241,068 (Tax Stats at a Glance, Internal Revenue Service, U.S. Treasury Department, available at www.irs.ustreas.gov/taxstats/article/0,,id=102886,99.html).

5. Bernadette D. Proctor and Joseph Dalaker, "U.S. Census Bureau, Current Population Reports," *Poverty in the United States: 2001* (Washington, DC: U.S. Government Printing Office, 2002, pp. 1–5).

6. Martha Burt, "A New Look at Homelessness in America" (Washington, DC: The Urban Institute, February 2000).

7. Proctor and Dalaker, op. cit., p. 4.

8. Mishel et al., op. cit., p. 53.

9. Mishel et al., ibid., p. 280.

10. Based on a comparison of 19 industrialized states: Mishel et al., ibid., pp. 411–412.

11. See The Center on Budget and Policy Priorities, Economic Policy Institute, "Pulling Apart: State-by-State Analysis of Income Trends," Jan-

uary 2000, fact sheet; "Current Population Reports: Consumer Income" (Washington, DC: U.S. Department of Commerce, 1993); The World Bank, "World Development Report: 1992" (Washington, DC: International Bank for Reconstruction and Development, 1992); The World Bank, "World Development Report 1999/2000," pp. 238–239.

12. Derived from Mishel et al., op. cit., p. 281.

13. Mishel et al., ibid., p. 54.

14. Mishel et al., ibid., p. 70.

15. Mishel et al., ibid., p. 280.

16. Alan Blinder, quoted by Paul Krugman, in "Disparity and Despair," *U.S. News and World Report,* March 23, 1992, p. 54.

17. Paul Samuelson, *Economics,* 10th ed. (New York: McGraw-Hill, 1976, p. 84).

18. Joseph Dalaker, "U.S. Census Bureau, Current Population Reports, series P60–207," *Poverty in the United States: 1998* (Washington, DC: U.S. Government Printing Office, 1999, p. v).

19. Michael Harrington, *The Other America* (New York: Macmillan, 1962, pp. 12–13).

20. Stuart Ewen and Elizabeth Ewen, *Channels of Desire: Mass Images and the Shaping of American Consciousness* (New York: McGraw-Hill, 1982).

21. Andrew Ross, *No-Collar: The Humane Work Place and Its Hidden Costs* (New York: Basic Books, 2002).

22. Based on a poverty threshold for a family of three in 2003 of $15,260.

23. The median income in 2001 was $38,275 for men, $29,214 for women, and $42,228 for households. Carmen DeNavas-Walt and Robert Cleveland, "U.S. Census Bureau, Current Population Reports," *Money Income in the United States: 2001* (Washington, DC: U.S. Government Printing Office, 2002, p. 4).

24. E. Pamuk, D. Makuc, K. Heck, C. Reuben, and K. Lochner, *Socioeconomic Status and Health Chartbook, Health, United States, 1998* (Hyattsville, MD: National Center for Health Statistics, 1998, pp. 145–159); Vincente Navarro, "Class, Race, and Health Care in the United States," in Bersh Berberoglu, *Critical Perspectives in Sociology,* 2nd ed. (Dubuque, IA: Kendall/

rhetorical situations   genres   processes   strategies   research mla/apa   media/ design   readings

Hunt, 1993, pp. 148–156); Melvin Krasner, *Poverty and Health in New York City* (New York: United Hospital Fund of New York, 1989). See also U.S. Dept. of Health and Human Services, *Health Status of Minorities and Low Income Groups*, 1985; and Dan Hughes, Kay Johnson, Sara Rosenbaum, Elizabeth Butler, and Janet Simons, *The Health of America's Children* (The Children's Defense Fund, 1988).

25. E. Pamuk et al., op. cit.; Kenneth Neubeck and Davita Glassberg, *Sociology; A Critical Approach* (New York: McGraw-Hill, 1996, pp. 436–438); Aaron Antonovsky, "Social Class, Life Expectancy, and Overall Mortality," in *The Impact of Social Class* (New York: Thomas Crowell, 1972; pp. 467–491). See also Harriet Duleep, "Measuring the Effect of Income on Adult Mortality Using Longitudinal Administrative Record Data," *Journal of Human Resources*, vol. 21, no. 2, Spring 1986.

26. E. Pamuk et al., op. cit., fig. 20; Dennis W. Roncek, "Dangerous Places: Crime and Residential Environment," *Social Forces*, vol. 60, no. 1, September 1981, pp. 74–96.

27. Richard De Lone, *Small Futures* (New York: Harcourt Brace Jovanovich, 1978, pp. 14–19).

28. Derived from The College Entrance Examination Board, "1999, A Profile of College Bound Seniors: SAT Test Takers"; available at www.collegeboard.org/sat/cbsenior/yr1999/NAT/natbk499.html#income.

29. William H. Sewell, "Inequality of Opportunity for Higher Education," *American Sociological Review*, vol. 36, no. 5, 1971, pp. 793–809.

30. The Mortenson Report on Public Policy Analysis of Opportunity for Postsecondary Education, "Postsecondary Education Opportunity" (Iowa City, IA: September 1993, no. 16).

31. De Lone, op. cit., pp. 14–19.

32. Howard Tuchman, *Economics of the Rich* (New York: Random House, 1973, p. 15).

33. Howard Wachtel, *Labor and the Economy* (Orlando, FL: Academic Press, 1984, pp. 161–162).

34. Derived from Proctor and Dalaker, op. cit., p. 3.

Engaging with the Text

93 ▲

1. Gregory Mantsios offers an either/or **CLAIM**: "Either talking about class and recognizing class distinctions are not relevant to U.S. society, or we mistakenly hold a set of beliefs that obscure the reality of class differences and their impact on people's lives." However, it's clear early on that his argument will focus on one possibility and not the other. What information does he provide that reveals his actual position?

14 ◼

2. Mantsios presents four beliefs about class and labels them "myths." How does his use of this synonym affect his **TONE?** How would you characterize his tone? Give examples from the text.

100 ▲
100–01 ▲

3. How does Mantsios argue against each of the four "myths" he identifies? What evidence does he provide to **SUPPORT** his position? What **OTHER POSITIONS** does he consider? Does he convince you? (If not, why not?)

458–62 ▢
269–71 ◆

4. Mantsios uses **CHARTS** to **COMPARE** the disparate lifestyles of Bob Farrell, Harold Browning, and Cheryl Mitchell. How else might he have presented this information? How do the charts support his claim that class determines "where they live, who their friends are, how well they are educated, what they do for a living, and what they come to expect from life"? Use examples from the essay in your response.

5. **For Writing.** Explore the role of class at your school. For example, what can you learn about the social and economic status of students, faculty, and support staff by examining the cars in the parking lot (and where those lots are located)? Observe a campus social event: Who attends? What do they wear? What campus organization sponsors the event? What norms of behavior are expected at this event? Use the

82–106 ▲

information you collect to **ARGUE A POSITION** on the way social class may affect campus life.

◼ rhetorical situations   ▲ genres   ○ processes   ◆ strategies   ● research mla/apa   ▢ media/ design   📖 readings

SHELBY STEELE

On Being Black and Middle Class

A research fellow at the Hoover Institution, a conservative think tank, Shelby Steele specializes in the study of race relations, multiculturalism, and affirmative action. Like most of his writing, Steele's award-winning collection of essays, The Content of Our Character *(1990), explores issues of race, class, and status in American culture. The following argument appeared in a 1988 issue of* Commentary, *a magazine that specializes in in-depth analyses of current affairs, politics, and culture.*

NOT LONG AGO, a friend of mine, black like myself, said to me that the term "black middle class" was actually a contradiction in terms. Race, he insisted, blurred class distinctions among blacks. If you were black, you were just black and that was that. When I argued, he let his eyes roll at my naiveté. Then he went on. For us, as black professionals, it was an exercise in self-flattery, a pathetic pretension, to give meaning to such a distinction. Worse, the very idea of class threatened the unity that was vital to the black community as a whole. After all, since when had white America taken note of anything but color when it came to blacks? He then reminded me of an old Malcolm X line that had been popular in the sixties. Question: What is a black man with a Ph.D.? Answer: A nigger.

For many years I had been on my friend's side of this argument. Much of my conscious thinking on the old conundrum of race and class was shaped during my high school and college years in the race-charged sixties, when the fact of my race took on an almost religious significance. Progressively, from the mid-sixties on, more and more aspects of my life found their explanation, their justification, and their motivation in race. My youthful concerns about career, romance, money, values, and even styles of dress because a subject to consultation with various oracular sources of racial wisdom. And these ranged from a figure as ennobling as Martin Luther King, Jr., to the underworld elegance of dress I found in jazz clubs on the South Side of Chicago. Everywhere there were signals, and in those days I considered myself so blessed with clarity and direction that I pitied my white classmates who found more embarrassment than guidance in the fact of *their* race. In 1968, inflated by my new power, I took a mischievous delight in calling them culturally disadvantaged.

But now, hearing my friend's comment was like hearing a priest from a church I'd grown disenchanted with. I understood him, but my faith was weak. What had sustained me in the sixties sounded monotonous and off the mark in the eighties. For me, race had lost much of its juju, its singular capacity to conjure meaning. And today, when I honestly look at my life and the lives of many other middle-class blacks I know, I can see that race never fully explained our situation in American society. Black though I may be, it is impossible for me to sit in my single-family house with two cars in the driveway and a swing set in the back yard and *not* see the role class has played in my life. And how can my friend, similarly raised and similarly situated, not see it?

Yet despite my certainty I felt a sharp tug of guilt as I tried to explain myself over my friend's skepticism. He is a man of many comedic facial expressions and, as I spoke, his brow lifted in extreme moral alarm as if I were uttering the unspeakable. His clear implication was that I was being elitist and possibly (dare he suggest?) anti-black — crimes for which there might well be no redemption. He pretended to fear for me. I chuckled along with him, but inwardly I did wonder at myself. Though I never doubted the validity of what I was saying, I felt guilty saying it. Why?

After he left (to retrieve his daughter from a dance lesson) I realized that the trap I felt myself in had a tiresome familiarity and, in a sort of slow-motion epiphany, I began to see its outline. It was like the suddenly sharp vision one has at the end of a burdensome marriage when all the long-repressed incompatibilities come undeniably to light. 5

What became clear to me is that people like myself, my friend, and middle-class blacks generally are caught in a very specific double bind that keeps two equally powerful elements of our identity at odds with each other. The middle-class values by which we were raised — the work ethic, the importance of education, the value of property owner-

ship, of respectability, of "getting ahead," of stable family life, of initiative, of self-reliance, etc. — are, in themselves, raceless and even assimilationist. They urge us toward participation in the American mainstream, toward integration, toward a strong identification with the society — and toward the entire constellation of qualities that are implied in the word "individualism." These values are almost rules for how to prosper in a democratic, free-enterprise society that admirers and rewards individual effort. They tell us to work hard for ourselves and our families and to seek our opportunities whenever they appear, inside or outside the confines of whatever ethnic group we may belong to.

But the particular pattern of racial identification that emerged in the sixties and that still prevails today urges middle-class blacks (and all blacks) in the opposite direction. This pattern asks us to see ourselves as an embattled minority, and it urges an adversarial stance toward the mainstream, an emphasis on ethnic consciousness over individualism. It is organized around an implied separatism.

The opposing thrust of these two parts of our identity results in the double bind of middle-class blacks. There is no forward movement on either plane that does not constitute backward movement on the other. This was the familiar trap I felt myself in while talking with my friend. As I spoke about class, his eyes reminded me that I was betraying race. Clearly, the two indispensable parts of my identity were a threat to each other.

Of course when you think about it, class and race are both similar in some ways and also naturally opposed. They are two forms of collective identity with boundaries that intersect. But whether they clash or peacefully coexist has much to do with how they are defined. Being both black and middle class becomes a double bind when class and race are defined in sharply antagonistic terms, so that one must be repressed to appease the other.

But what is the "substance" of these two identities, and how does 10 each establish itself in an individual's overall identity? It seems to me that when we identify with any collective we are basically identifying with images that tell us what it means to be a member of that collective. Identity is not the same thing as the fact of membership in a collective; it is, rather, a form of self-definition, facilitated by images of what we wish our membership in the collective to mean. In this sense, the images we identify with may reflect the aspirations of the collective more than they reflect reality, and their content can vary with shifts in those aspirations.

But the process of identification is usually dialectical. It is just as necessary to say what we are *not* as it is to say what we are — so that finally identification comes about by embracing a polarity of positive and negative images. To identify as middle class, for example, I must have both passive and negative images of what being middle class entails; then I will know what I should and should not be doing in order to be middle class. The same goes for racial identity.

In the racially turbulent sixties the polarity of images that came to define racial identification was very antagonistic to the polarity that defined middle-class identification. One might say that the positive images of one lined up with the negative images of the other, so that to identify with both required either a contortionist's flexibility or a dangerous splitting of the self. The double bind of the black middle class was in place. . . .

The black middle class has always defined its class identity by means of positive images gleaned from middle- and upper-class white society, and by means of negative images of lower-class blacks. This habit goes back to the institution of slavery itself, when "house" slaves both mimicked the whites they served and held themselves above the "field" slaves. But in the sixties the old bourgeois impulse to dissociate from the lower classes (the "we-they" distinction) backfired when racial identity suddenly called for the celebration of this same black lower class. One of the qualities of a double bind is that one feels it more than sees it, and I distinctly remember the tensions and strange sense of dishonesty I felt in those days as I moved back and forth like a bigamist between the demands of class and race.

Though my father was born poor, he achieved middle-class standing through much hard work and sacrifice (one of his favorite words) and by identifying fully with solid middle-class values — mainly hard work, family life, property ownership, and education for his children (all

four of whom have advanced degrees). In his mind these were not so much values as laws of nature. People who embodied them made up the positive images in his class polarity. The negative images came largely from the blacks he had left behind because they were "going nowhere."

No one in my family remembers how it happened, but as time went on, the negative images congealed into an imaginary character named Sam, who, from the extensive service we put him to, quickly grew to mythic proportions. In our family lore he was sometimes a trickster, sometimes a boob, but always possessed of a catalogue of sly faults that gave up graphic images of everything we should not be. On sacrifice: "Sam never thinks about tomorrow. He wants it now or he doesn't care about it." On work: "Sam doesn't favor it too much." On children: "Sam likes to have them but not to raise them." On money: "Sam drinks it up and pisses it out." On fidelity: "Sam has to have two or three women." On clothes: "Sam features loud clothes. He likes to see and be seen." And so on. Sam's persona amounted to a negative instruction manual in class identity.

I don't think that any of us believed Sam's faults were accurate representations of lower-class black life. He was an instrument of self-definition, not of sociological accuracy. It never occurred to us that he looked very much like the white racist stereotype of blacks, or that he might have been a manifestation of our own racial self-hatred. He simply gave us a counterpoint against which to express our aspirations. If self-hatred was a factor, it was not, for us, a matter of hating lower-class blacks but of hating what we did not want to be.

Still, hate or love aside, it is fundamentally true that my middle-class identity involved a dissociation from images of lower-class black life and a corresponding identification with values and patterns of responsibility that are common to the middle class everywhere. These values sent me a clear message: be both an individual and a responsible citizen; understand that the quality of your life will approximately reflect the quality of effort you put into it; know that individual responsibility is the basis of freedom and that the limitations imposed by fate (whether fair or unfair) are no excuse for passivity.

Whether I live up to these values or not, I know that my acceptance of them is the result of lifelong conditioning. I know also that I share this conditioning with middle-class people of all races and that I can no more easily be free of it than I can be free of my race. Whether all this got started because the black middle class modeled itself on the white middle class is no longer relevant. For the middle-class black, conditioned by these values from birth, the sense of meaning they provide is as immutable as the color of his skin.

I started the sixties in high school feeling that my class-conditioning was the surest way to overcome racial barriers. My racial identity was pretty much taken for granted. After all, it was obvious to the world that I was black. Yet I ended the sixties in graduate school a little embarrassed by my class background and with an almost desperate need to be "black." The tables had turned. I knew very clearly (though I struggled to repress it) that my aspirations and my sense of how to operate in the world came from my class background, yet "being black" required certain attitudes and stances that made me feel secretly a little duplicitous. The inner compatibility of class and race I had known in 1960 was gone.

For blacks, the decade between 1960 and 1969 saw racial identification undergo the same sort of transformation that national identity undergoes in times of war. It became more self-conscious, more narrowly focused, more prescribed, less tolerant of opposition. It spawned an implicit party line, which tended to disallow competing forms of identity. Race-as-identity was lifted from the relative slumber it knew in the fifties and pressed into service in a social and political war against oppression. It was redefined along sharp adversarial lines and directed toward the goal of mobilizing the great mass of black Americans in this warlike effort. It was imbued with a strong moral authority, useful for denouncing those who opposed it and for celebrating those who honored it as a positive achievement rather than as a mere birthright. 20

The form of racial identification that quickly evolved to meet this challenge presented blacks as a racial monolith, a singular people with a common experience of oppression. Differences within the race, no matter how ineradicable, had to be minimized. Class distinctions were

one of the first such differences to be sacrificed, since they not only threatened racial unity but also seemed to stand in contradiction to the principle of equality which was the announced goal of the movement for racial progress. The discomfort I felt in 1969, the vague but relentless sense of duplicity, was the result of a historical necessity that put my race and class at odds, that was asking me to cast aside the distinction of my class and identify with a monolithic view of my race.

If the form of this racial identity was the monolith, its substance was victimization. The civil rights movement and the more radical splinter groups of the late sixties were all dedicated to ending racial victimization, and the form of black identity that emerged to facilitate this goal made blackness and victimization virtually synonymous. Since it was our victimization more than any other variable that identified and unified us, moreover, it followed logically that the purest black was the poor black. It was images of him that clustered around the positive pole of the race polarity; all other blacks were, in effect, required to identify with him in order to confirm their own blackness.

Certainly there were more dimensions to the black experience than victimization, but no other had the same capacity to fire the indignation needed for war. So, again out of historical necessity, victimization became the overriding focus of racial identity. But this only deepened the double bind for middle-class blacks like me. When it came to class we were accustomed to defining ourselves against lower-class blacks and identifying with at least the values of middle-class whites; when it came to race we were now being asked to identify with images of lower-class blacks and to see whites, middle class or otherwise, as victimizers. Negative lining up with positive, we were called upon to reject what we had previously embraced and to embrace what we had previously rejected. To put it still more personally, the Sam figure I had been raised to define myself against had now become the "real" black I was expected to identify with.

The fact that the poor black's new status was only passively earned by the condition of his victimization, not by assertive, positive action, made little difference. Status was status apart from the means by which it was achieved, and along with it came a certain power — the power to define the terms of access to that status, to say who was black and who was not. If a lower-class black said you were not really "black" — a sellout, an Uncle Tom — the judgment was all the more devastating because it carried the authority of his status. And this judgment soon enough came to be accepted by many whites as well.

In graduate school I was once told by a white professor, "Well, but . . . you're not really black. I mean, you're not disadvantaged." In his mind my lack of victim status disqualified me from the race itself. More recently I was complimented by a black student for speaking reasonably correct English, "proper" English as he put it. "But I don't know if I really want to talk like that," he went on. "Why not?" I asked. "Because then I wouldn't be black no more," he replied without a pause.

To overcome his marginal status, the middle-class black had to identify with a degree of victimization that was beyond his actual experience. In college (and well beyond) we used to play a game called "nap matching." It was a game of one-upmanship, in which we sat around outdoing each other with stories of racial victimization, symbolically measured by the naps of our hair. Most of us were middle class and so had few personal stories to relate, but if we could not match naps with our own biographies, we would move on to those legendary tales of victimization that came to us from the public domain.

The single story that sat atop the pinnacle of racial victimization for us was that of Emmett Till, the Northern black teenager who, on a visit to the South in 1955, was killed and grotesquely mutilated for supposedly looking at or whistling at (we were never sure which, though we argued the point endlessly) a white woman. Oh, how we probed his story, finding in his youth and Northern upbringing the quintessential embodiment of black innocence, brought down by a white evil so portentous and apocalyptic, so gnarled and hideous, that it left us with a feeling not far from awe. By telling his story and others like it, we came to *feel* the immutability of our victimization, its utter indigenousness, as a thing on this earth like dirt or sand or water.

Of course, these sessions were a ritual of group identification, a means by which we, as middle-class blacks, could be at one with our race. But why were we, who had only a moderate experience of

25

victimization (and that offset by opportunities our parents never had), so intent on assimilating or appropriating an identity that in so many ways contradicted our own? Because, I think, the sense of innocence that is always entailed in feeling victimized filled us with a corresponding feeling of entitlement, or even license, that helped us endure our vulnerability on a largely white college campus.

In my junior year in college I rode to a debate tournament with three white students and our faculty coach, an elderly English professor. The experience of being the lone black in a group of whites was so familiar to me that I thought nothing of it as our trip began. But then halfway through the trip the professor casually turned to me and, in an isn't-the-world-funny sort of tone, said that he had just refused to rent an apartment in a house he owned to a "very nice" black couple because their color would "offend" the white couple who lived downstairs. His eyebrows lifted helplessly over his hawkish nose, suggesting that he too, like me, was a victim of America's racial farce. His look assumed a kind of comradeship: he and I were above this grimy business of race, though for expediency we had occasionally to concede the world its madness.

My vulnerability in this situation came not so much from the pro- 30 fessor's blindness to his own racism as from his assumption that I would participate in it, that I would conspire with him against my own race so that he might remain comfortably blind. Why did he think I would be amenable to this? I can only guess that he assumed my middle-class identity was so complete and all-encompassing that I would see his action as nothing more than a trifling concession to the folkways of our land, that I would in fact applaud his decision not to disturb propriety. Blind to both his own racism and to me — one blindness serving the other — he could not recognize that he was asking me to betray my race in the name of my class.

His blindness made me feel vulnerable because it threatened to expose my own repressed ambivalence. His comment pressured me to choose between my class identification, which had contributed to my being a college student and a member of the debating team, and my desperate desire to be "black." I could have one but not both; I was double-bound.

Because double binds are repressed there is always an element of terror in them: the terror of bringing to the conscious mind the buried duplicity, self-deception, and pretense involved in serving two masters. This terror is the stuff of vulnerability, and since vulnerability is one of the least tolerable of all human feelings, we usually transform it into an emotion that seems to restore the control of which it has robbed us; most often, that emotion is anger. And so, before the professor had even finished his little story, I had become a furnace of rage. The year was 1967, and I had been primed by endless hours of nap-matching to feel, at least consciously, completely at one with the victim-focused black identity. This identity gave me the license, and the impunity, to unleash upon this professor one of those volcanic eruptions of racial indignation familiar to us from the novels of Richard Wright. Like Cross Damon in *Outsider,* who kills in perfectly righteous anger, I tried to annihilate the man. I punished him not according to the measure of his crime but according to the measure of my vulnerability, a measure set by the cumulative tension of years of repressed terror. Soon I saw the terror in *his* face, as he stared hollow-eyed at the road ahead. My white friends in the back seat, knowing no conflict between their own class and race, were astonished that someone they had taken to be so much like themselves could harbor a rage that for all the world looked murderous.

Though my rage was triggered by the professor's comment, it was deepened and sustained by a complex of need, conflict, and repression in myself of which I had been wholly unaware. Out of my racial vulnerability I had developed the strong need of an identity with which to defend myself. The only such identity available was that of me as victim, him as victimizer. Once in the grip of this paradigm, I began to do far more damage to myself than he had done.

Seeing myself as a victim meant that I clung all the harder to my racial identity, which, in turn, meant that I suppressed my class identity. This cut me off from all the resources my class values might have offered me. In those values, for instance, I might have found the means to a more dispassionate response, the response less of a victim attacked by a victimizer than of an individual offended by a foolish old man. As an individual I might have reported this professor to the college dean.

Or I might have calmly tried to reveal his blindness to him, and possibly won a convert. (The flagrancy of his remark suggested a hidden guilt and even self-recognition on which I might have capitalized. Doesn't confession usually signal a willingness to face oneself?) Or I might have simply chuckled and then let my silence serve as an answer to his provocation. Would not my composure, in any form it might take, deflect into his own heart the arrow he'd shot at me?

Instead, my anger, itself the hair-trigger expression of a long- 35
repressed double bind, not only cut me off from the best of my own resources, it also distorted the nature of my true racial problem. The righteousness of this anger and the easy catharsis it brought buoyed the delusion of my victimization and left me as blind as the professor himself.

As a middle-class black I have often felt myself *contriving* to be "black." And I have noticed this same contrivance in others — a certain stretching away from the natural flow of one's life to align oneself with a victim-focused black identity. Our particular needs are out of sync with the form of identity available to meet those needs. Middle-class blacks need to identify racially; it is better to think of ourselves as black and victimized than not black at all; so we contrive (more unconsciously than consciously) to fit ourselves into an identity that denies our class and fails to address the true source of our vulnerability.

For me this once meant spending inordinate amounts of time at black faculty meetings, though these meetings had little to do with my real racial anxieties or my professional life. I was new to the university, one of two blacks in an English department of over seventy, and I felt a little isolated and vulnerable, though I did not admit it to myself. But at these meetings we discussed the problems of black faculty and students within a framework of victimization. The real vulnerability we felt was covered over by all the adversarial drama the victim/victimized polarity inspired, and hence went unseen and unassuaged. And this, I think, explains our rather chronic ineffectiveness as a group. Since victimization was not our primary problem — the university had long ago opened its doors to us — we had to contrive to make it so, and there is not much energy in contrivance. What I got at these meetings was ultimately an object lesson in how fruitless struggle can be when it is not grounded in actual need.

At our black faculty meetings, the old equation of blackness with victimization was ever present — to be black was to be a victim; therefore, not to be a victim was not to be black. As we contrived to meet the terms of this formula there was an inevitable distortion of both ourselves and the larger university. Through the prism of victimization the university seemed more impenetrable than it actually was, and we more limited in our powers. We fell prey to the victim's myopia, making the university an institution from which we could seek redress but which we could never fully join. And this mind-set often led us to look more for compensations for our supposed victimization than for opportunities we could pursue as individuals.

The discomfort and vulnerability felt by middle-class blacks in the sixties, it could be argued, was a worthwhile price to pay considering the progress achieved during that time of racial confrontation. But what may have been tolerable then is intolerable now. Though changes in American society have made it an anachronism, the monolithic form of racial identification that came out of the sixties is still very much with us. It may be more loosely held, and its power to punish heretics has probably diminished, but it continues to catch middle-class blacks in a double bind, thus impeding not only their own advancement but even, I would contend, that of blacks as a group.

The victim-focused black identity encourages the individual to feel   40 that his advancement depends almost entirely on that of the group. Thus he loses sight not only of his own possibilities but of the inextricable connection between individual effort and individual advancement. This is a profound encumbrance today, when there is more opportunity for blacks than ever before, for it reimposes limitations that can have the same oppressive effect as those the society has only recently begun to remove.

It was the emphasis on mass action in the sixties that made the victim-focused black identity a necessity. But in the eighties and beyond, when racial advancement will come only through a multitude of individual advancements, this form of identity inadvertently adds itself to

rhetorical situations   genres   processes   strategies   research mla/apa   media/ design   readings

the forces that hold us back. Hard work, education, individual initiative, stable family life, property ownership — these have always been the means by which ethnic groups have moved ahead in America. Regardless of past or present victimization, these "laws" of advancement apply absolutely to black Americans also. There is no getting around this. What we need is a form of racial identity that energizes the individual by putting him in touch with both his possibilities and his responsibilities.

It has always annoyed me to hear from the mouths of certain arbiters of blackness that middle-class blacks should "reach back" and pull up those blacks less fortunate than they — as though middle-class status were an unearned and essentially passive condition in which one needed a large measure of noblesse oblige to occupy one's time. My own image is of reaching back from a moving train to lift on board those who have no tickets. A noble enough sentiment — but might it not be wiser to show them the entire structure of principles, efforts, and sacrifice that puts one in a position to buy a ticket any time one likes? This, I think, is something members of the black middle class can realistically offer to other blacks. Their example is not only a testament to possibility but also a lesson in method. But they cannot lead by example until they are released from a black identity that regards that example as suspect, that sees them as "marginally" black, indeed that holds *them* back by catching them in a double bind.

To move beyond the victim-focused black identity we must learn to make a difficult but crucial distinction: between actual victimization, which we must resist with every resource, and identification with the victim's status. Until we do this we will continue to wrestle more with ourselves than with the new opportunities which so many paid so dearly to win.

Engaging with the Text

1. Shelby Steele makes a complex **ARGUMENT** about being black and middle class. What is the primary point that he is arguing? Does he convince you — and if not, why not?

▲ 82–106

275–84

2. Steele refers repeatedly to the "double bind" that middle-class blacks are caught in. How does he DEFINE this double bind — and how does the notion of a double bind affect his argument?

239–45
304–12
251–52

3. Steele BEGINS his essay with an ANECDOTE. What role does this anecdote play in his argument? How does it prepare his audience for his THESIS?

4. In the previous reading, Gregory Mantsios argues that "class-oppressed men, whether they are black or white, have privileges afforded them as men in a sexist society" and that "class-oppressed whites, whether they are men or women, benefit from white privilege in a racist society." In what ways does Steele's essay complicate Mantsios's argument?

5. *For Writing.* How would you characterize your own socioeconomic class and race? What in your life has led you to identify with a particular class and race? What other factors have helped shape your identity? Write an essay in which you take a POSITION on the role class and race have — or have not — played in shaping your identity.

93

rhetorical situations ■
genres ▲
processes ○
strategies ◆
research mla/apa ●
media/ design □
readings ▐▌

DAVID BROOKS

The Triumph of Hope over Self-Interest

David Brooks writes about current affairs and politics as a senior editor at The Weekly Standard, *as a contributing editor at the* Atlantic Monthly *and* Newsweek, *and as a columnist for the* New York Times. *The following essay appeared in the* Times *in 2003.*

WHY DON'T PEOPLE VOTE THEIR OWN SELF-INTEREST? Every few years the Republicans propose a tax cut, and every few years the Democrats pull out their income distribution charts to show that much of the benefits of the Republican plan go to the richest 1 percent of Americans or thereabouts. And yet every few years a Republican plan wends its way through the legislative process and, with some trims and amendments, passes.

The Democrats couldn't even persuade people to oppose the repeal of the estate tax, which is explicitly for the mega-upper class. Al Gore, who ran a populist campaign, couldn't even win the votes of white males who didn't go to college, whose incomes have stagnated over the past decades and who were the explicit targets of his campaign. Why don't more Americans want to distribute more wealth down to people like themselves?

Well, as the academics would say, it's overdetermined. There are several reasons.

People vote their aspirations.

The most telling polling result from the 2000 election was from a *Time* magazine survey that asked people if they are in the top 1 percent of earners. Nineteen percent of Americans say they are in the richest 1 percent and a further 20 percent expect to be someday. So right away you have 39 percent of Americans who thought that when Mr. Gore savaged a plan that favored the top 1 percent, he was taking a direct shot at them.[1]

---

1. In the 2000 presidential campaign, Republican nominee George W. Bush favored a repeal of the estate tax, which affects only the very wealthiest Americans; Democratic nominee Al Gore opposed such a repeal.

It's not hard to see why they think this way. Americans live in a culture of abundance. They have always had a sense that great opportunities lie just over the horizon, in the next valley, with the next job or the next big thing. None of us is really poor, we're just pre-rich.

Americans read magazines for people more affluent than they are (W, *Cigar Aficionado*, *The New Yorker*, *Robb Report*, *Town and Country*) because they think that someday they could be that guy with the tastefully appointed horse farm. Democratic politicians proposing to take from the rich are just bashing the dreams of our imminent selves.

Income resentment is not a strong emotion in much of America.

If you earn $125,000 a year and live in Manhattan, certainly, you are surrounded by things you cannot afford. You have to walk by those buildings on Central Park West with the 2,500-square-foot apartments that are empty three-quarters of the year because the evil owners are mostly living at their other houses in L.A.

But if you are a middle-class person in most of America, you are not 10 brought into incessant contact with things you can't afford. There aren't Lexus dealerships on every corner. There are no snooty restaurants with water sommeliers to help you sort through the bottled *eau*[2] selections. You can afford most of the things at Wal-Mart or Kohl's and the occasional meal at the Macaroni Grill. Moreover, it would be socially unacceptable for you to pull up to church in a Jaguar or to hire a caterer for your dinner party anyway. So you are not plagued by a nagging feeling of doing without.

Many Americans admire the rich.

They don't see society as a conflict zone between the rich and poor. It's taboo to say in a democratic culture, but do you think a nation that watches Katie Couric in the morning, Tom Hanks in the evening and Michael Jordan on weekends harbors deep animosity toward the affluent?

On the contrary. I'm writing this from Nashville, where one of the richest families, the Frists, is hugely admired for its entrepreneurial skill and community service. People don't want to tax the Frists — they want to elect them to the Senate. And they did.

---

2. Water (French).

Nor are Americans suffering from false consciousness. You go to a town where the factories have closed and people who once earned $14 an hour now work for $8 an hour. They've taken their hits. But odds are you will find their faith in hard work and self-reliance undiminished, and their suspicion of Washington unchanged.

Americans resent social inequality more than income inequality.   15
As the sociologist Jennifer Lopez has observed: "Don't be fooled by the rocks that I got, I'm just, I'm just Jenny from the block." As long as rich people "stay real," in Ms. Lopez's formulation, they are admired. Meanwhile, middle-class journalists and academics who seem to look down on megachurches, suburbia, and hunters are resented. Americans see the tax debate as being waged between the economic elite, led by President Bush, and the cultural elite, led by Barbra Streisand, and they are going to side with Mr. Bush, who could come to any suburban barbershop and fit right in.

Most Americans do not have Marxian categories in their heads.
This is the most important reason Americans resist wealth redistribution, the reason that subsumes all others. Americans do not see society as a layer cake, with the rich on top, the middle class beneath them and the working class and underclass at the bottom. They see society as a high school cafeteria, with their community at one table and other communities at other tables. They are pretty sure that their community is the nicest, and filled with the best people, and they have a vague pity for all those poor souls who live in New York City or California and have a lot of money but no true neighbors and no free time.

All of this adds up to a terrain incredibly inhospitable to class-based politics. Every few years a group of millionaire Democratic presidential aspirants pretends to be the people's warriors against the overclass. They look inauthentic, combative rather than unifying. Worst of all, their basic message is not optimistic.

They haven't learned what Franklin and Teddy Roosevelt and even   20 Bill Clinton knew: that you can run against rich people, but only those who have betrayed the ideal of fair competition. You have to be more hopeful and growth-oriented than your opponent, and you cannot imply that we are a nation tragically and permanently divided by income. In the gospel of America, there are no permanent conflicts.

Engaging with the Text

1. David Brooks begins with a question that drives his argument: "Why don't more Americans want to distribute more wealth down to people like themselves?" What **REASONS** does he give to answer this question and what evidence does he offer to **SUPPORT** those reasons?

   93, 99–100
   94, 100
   272–73

2. Brooks offers two **ANALOGIES** to help explain why Americans do not vote for their own self-interest: "Americans do not see society as a layer cake with the rich on top, the middle class beneath them and the working class and underclass at the bottom." Instead, "they see society as a high school cafeteria." What two different views of society do these analogies reveal? How do these two analogies **SUPPORT** Brooks's point about class-based politics?

   94, 100

3. What is the **PURPOSE** of Brooks's argument? Where is this purpose made clear? Does his argument achieve its purpose? If not, why not?

   3–4

4. Brooks makes his own views very clear, but of course there are other views on this topic. What **OTHER POSITIONS** does he consider? What other views might he consider? Does he convince you to accept his argument — and if not, why not?

   94, 100–101

5. *For Writing.* Do you agree with what Brooks contends about the "triumph of hope over self-interest"? Write a letter to the editor of the *Times*, agreeing, disagreeing, or both. Be sure to offer **REASONS** for what you believe.

   93, 99–100

MAGGIE CUTLER

Whodunit — The Media?

*Maggie Cutler is one of several pen names used by Lynn Phillips, a jour-
nalist who has written widely on politics, the media, sex, and women.
She also writes a biweekly satirical column called "The Secret Life of
Maggie Cutler" for Nerve.com. The following essay appeared in a 2001
issue of* The Nation, *a liberal magazine dedicated to "the discussion of
political and social questions" in "a really critical spirit."*

WILL GIRLS IMITATE THE NEW, KICKASS HEROINES in the Japanese animé
Cardcaptors? Will the impressionable 12-year-olds exposed to trailers for
MGM's *Disturbing Behavior* forever after associate good teen behavior
with lobotomies? Did Nine Inch Nails and the video game *DOOM* inspire
the Trenchcoat Mafia's bloodbath at Columbine? Thousands of studies
have been done to try to answer variants of the question: Does media
violence lead to real-life violence, making children more antisocial and
aggressive?

Like most complex issues, discussions about the impact of media
violence on children suffer from that commonest of media problems:
fudge. Almost any simple statement on the subject obscures the complexity of the facts, half-facts, and "results suggest" findings of the past
forty years. The right-wing Parents Television Council, for example,
announces that the per-hour rate in the United States of sexual and violent material and coarse language combined almost tripled from 1989
to 1999. But while PTC president Brent Bozell castigates the media for
lowering standards of acceptable speech and behavior, he doesn't mention that in the final years of this avalanche of dreck the juvenile crime
rate *dropped* more than 30 percent. Or, again, in August 1999 the Senate
Judiciary Committee, headed by Orrin Hatch, reported confidently that
"Television alone is responsible for 10 percent of youth violence." Given
the overall juvenile crime count in 1997, the report implied, some 250
murders and 12,100 other violent crimes would not have been committed if it weren't for the likes of *Batman Beyond.*

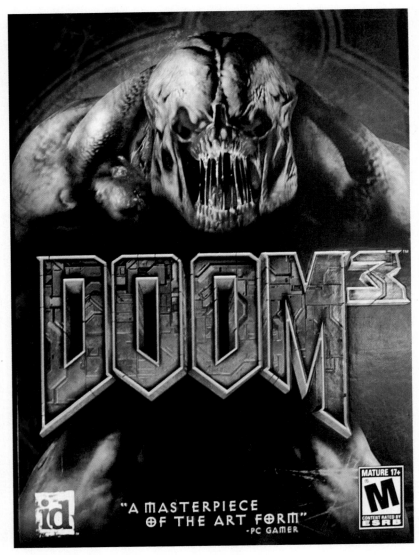

Doom 3, a best-selling video game released in 2004. Getty Images.

But this, of course, is deeply misleading. One of the reasons so many media violence studies have been done is that the phenomenon may be too complex to study conclusively. There's no way, after all, to lock two clones in a black box, feed them different TV, movie, and video-game diets, and open the box years later to determine that, yes, it was definitely those Bruce Lee epics that turned clone A into Jesse Ventura, while clone B's exposure to the movie *Babe* produced a Pee Wee Herman.

It has been hard, in other words, for media violence studies to shake the ambiguity of correlations. Several studies have shown that violent boys tend to watch more TV, choose more violent content, and get more enjoyment out of it. But the studies admittedly can't show exactly how or why that happens. Do temperamentally violent kids seek out shows that express feelings they already have, or are they in it for the adrenaline boost? Do the sort of parents who let kids pig out on gore tend to do more than their share of other hurtful things that encourage violent behavior? To what extent is violent media producing little Johnny's aggression — or inspiring it, making it appear glamorous, righteous, acceptably gratuitous, fun, or "normal" — and to what extent is it merely satisfying little Johnny's greater-than-average longings for the mayhem, vengeance, superhuman power, and sweet revenge that most people, at times, secretly crave?

According to James Garbarino, author of *Lost Boys: Why Our Sons Turn Violent and How We Can Save Them,* it makes no sense to talk about violent media as a direct cause of youth violence. Rather, he says, "it depends": Media violence is a risk factor that, working in concert with others, can exacerbate bad behavior. 5

Like Orrin Hatch's committee, Garbarino estimates the effect of violent media on juvenile violence at about 10 percent, but his ecology-of-violence formulation is far less tidy than the Hatch committee's pop-psych model. Garbarino himself reports in an e-mail that he would like to see media violence treated as a public health problem — damned at its Hollywood source the way sewage treatment plants "reduce the problem of cholera." Nevertheless, his ecology model of how juvenile violence emerges from complex, interacting factors means that hyper-aggressive, "asset poor" kids are likely to be harmed by graphic depictions of violence, while balanced, "asset rich" kids are likely to remain unscathed. A few studies have even found that a "cathartic effect" of media violence makes some kids *less* aggressive. This wide range of individual variance makes policy prescriptions a tricky matter.

The American Psychological Association's Commission on Violence and Youth (1994) mentions violent media as only one among many factors in juvenile violence. It stresses that inborn temperament, early parental abuse or neglect, poverty, cognitive impairment, plus a deficiency of corrective influence or role models in various combinations will put a child at greater risk for violence, both as perpetrator and as victim. The APA found that many damaged kids' lives can be salvaged with early intervention. By the age of 8, these at-risk kids can be identified. Once identified they can be taught skills that enable them to resolve conflicts peacefully. The APA adds that parental guidance along with reducing kids' exposure to graphic violence can help keep them out of the correctional system. But for the kids most at risk, reducing representational violence is obviously no cure. So this past fall, when Senators John McCain and Joseph Lieberman ordered the entertainment industry to stop advertising its nastier products to young children or else face (shudder) regulation, it was fair of media critics to castigate them for exploiting the media violence problem for its bipartisan glow rather than attempting to find the least coercive, most effective ways of keeping children safe and sane.

Perhaps the biggest problem in mitigating the effect of media violence on children is that it's hard to nail down just what "violent media" means to actual kids. As with adult pornography, we all think we know what it is until we have to define it. That's because kids not only process content differently depending on their temperament, background, and circumstances, they seem to process it differently at different ages, too.

A series of often-cited studies known as Winick and Winick (1979) charted distinct stages in media processing abilities. Fairly early, from about 6 until about 10, most — but not all — kids are learning to deal with media much as adults do: interactively rather than passively. In her 1985 book, *Watching* Dallas: *Soap Opera and the Melodramatic Imagination*, Ien Ang of the University of Western Sydney in Australia showed

that different adult viewers rewrote the "messages" of shows to suit their own views. So a wise little girl whose parents discuss media with her might enjoy *Wrestlemania* as an amusing guide to crazy-guys-to-avoid, while an angry, abandoned, slow-witted child is more likely to enter its world of insult and injury with uncritical awe.

At first blush, measures like content labeling would seem to make more sense for the 2-to-6 set because young kids do get confused about reality, fantasy, information, and advertising. But again, what constitutes "violent" content isn't always obvious. The Winicks found that young children whose parents fought a lot responded with more distress to representations of people yelling and screaming — because it seemed real — than to blatant violence for which they had no frame of reference. Should there be a label for "loud and emotional"? And if so, should we slap it on *La Bohème*?

Because representational violence is so hard to define, the recently reported Stanford media effects studies, which focused on third and fourth graders, ducked the problem. The study team, headed by Thomas Robinson, simply worked with teachers, parents, and kids to help children lower their overall media use voluntarily. As a result of the six-month program, which involved classroom instruction, parental support, and peer pressure, kids used media about 30 percent less than usual. And, they found, verbal and physical aggression levels subsequently dropped 25 percent on average. These numbers are being taken especially seriously because they were established "in the field" rather than in the lab, so that the verbal and physical aggression measures was actual, not simulated by, say, asking a child to kick or insult a doll. As media violence studies predicted, the more aggressive kids were to begin with, the more their behavior improved when they consumed less of whatever it was they normally consumed.

Although the Stanford study — perhaps to stay popular with granters — is being promoted as a study on media violence, it is really a study of media overuse, self-awareness, and the rewards of self-discipline. Its clearest finding wasn't that media violence is always harmful but that too much mediated experience seems to impair children's ability to interact well with other people. Follow-up studies at

Stanford will show whether the remarkable benefits of its media reduction program last over a long period. If they do, such classes may be a helpful addition to school curriculums in conjunction, perhaps, with courses in conflict resolution. But in any case, its results demonstrate less the effects of specific content than what could be called "the rule of the real."

The rule of the real says that however strong media influences may be, real life is stronger. Real love, real money, real political events, and real-life, unmediated interpersonal experience all shape kids' lives, minds, and behavior more powerfully than any entertainment products. Even media seen or understood as real — news, documentaries, interviews — will have more impact than that which a kid knows is make-believe. As the Winicks found, kids understand early that cartoon violence is a joke, not a model. Even wrestling, once kids figure out that it's staged, gets processed differently from, say, a schoolyard beating.

Without belittling the importance of media research, it's time that the rule of the real governed policy as well. After all, boys whose dads do hard time tend to end up in jail, while boys who see *Fight Club* tend to end up in film clubs; it's more likely that the Santana High killer decided to shoot up his school after seeing the anniversary coverage of Columbine than because he watched *The Mummy*. Abused young women don't kill their battering husbands because they grew up watching *Charlie's Angels*, and teens who hear no criticism of the Gulf War tend to want another. Given limited energies and resources, if our politicians really wanted to reduce youth violence, they would push to reform prison policies, provide supervised after-school activities for teens, and get early, comprehensive help to high-risk children. As a community, we would do better to challenge the corporate conglomeration of news outlets than to legislate the jugs 'n' jugular quotient in *Tomb Raider*, its labeling, or ad placements — and this is true even though the stuff kids like is often quite nasty, and even though the better part of the scientific establishment now agrees that such excitements are less than benign. But setting priorities like these is hard because, while the real may rule children's lives as it rules our own, it's much more fun to imagine controlling their dreams.

Engaging with the Text

1. What is Maggie Cutler's main CLAIM? Where does she state this claim? What reasons does she give to SUPPORT her claim, and has she convinced you? If not, do you at least accept her argument as plausible?

   ▲ 93
   ▲ 93, 99–100

2. Cutler OPENS her argument with a series of questions. How do these questions prepare readers for her argument? What role do questions play in writing? Where else does she use questions, and to what effect?

   ◆ 239–45

3. "The rule of the real," Cutler writes, "says that however strong media influences may be, real life is stronger." How does the "rule of the real" relate to youth violence? In what ways does this rule complicate the notion that media violence in some way causes youth violence?

4. How would you characterize Cutler's TONE? How does her tone affect the persuasiveness of her argument? Point to examples in her text that reveal that tone.

   ■ 14

5. *For Writing.* Take a POSITION for or against the commonplace assumption that media violence causes actual violence. RESEARCH the issue and use the results of your research to SUPPORT your argument. Make sure to consider and acknowledge in your essay more than one position.

   ▲ 93
   ● 340–53
   ▲ 100

GRANT PENROD

Anti-Intellectualism:
Why We Hate the Smart Kids

The following essay won second place in the 2003–04 Arizona State University Printer's Devil Contest, an annual competition open to all students enrolled in writing classes at Arizona State. Grant Penrod wrote the essay in the fall of 2003 for a first-year composition course.

THE FOOTBALL TEAM FROM MOUNTAIN VIEW HIGH SCHOOL won the Arizona state championship last year. Again. Unbeknownst to the vast majority of the school's student body, so did the Science Bowl Team, the Speech and Debate Team, and the Academic Decathlon team. The football players enjoyed the attentions of an enthralled school, complete with banners, assemblies, and even video announcements in their honor, a virtual barrage of praise and downright deification. As for the three champion academic teams, they received a combined total of around ten minutes of recognition, tacked onto the beginning of a sports assembly. Nearly all of the graduating seniors will remember the name and escapades of their star quarterback; nearly none of them will ever even realize that their class produced Arizona's first national champion in Lincoln-Douglas Debate. After all, why should they? He and his teammates were "just the nerds."

This instance finds plentiful company in the experiences of everyday life; intellectuals constantly see their efforts trivialized in the rush to lavish compliments elsewhere. However, such occurrences present only a faint silhouette of true anti-intellectualism; trivialization seems insignificant when compared with the outright disdain for the educated harbored by much of society. That academia's proponents provoke the wrath of the populace is certain. As an illustration, a commentator under the screen name "ArCaNe" recently posted the following quote on TalkingCock.com, an online discussion board: "Man how I hate nerds . . . if I ever had a tommygun with me . . . I would most probably blow each one of their . . . heads off." Were this statement alone in its extremism, it could be written off a joke. Unfortunately, it represents just one statement along countless similar sites and postings, a veritable cornucopia of evidence attesting to society's distaste for intellectuals. The question, then, is not whether anti-intellectualism exists, but rather why it exists. Several factors seem to contribute to the trend, including social stereotypes, public examples, and monetary obsession. Any or all of these factors can contribute to anti-intellectualism, and the result is a crushing disregard for the lives and achievements of fellow human beings.

Perhaps the most obvious cause of anti-intellectualist tendencies, harmful social stereotypes begin to emerge as early as in high school. The idea of the "geek" or "nerd" of the class is a familiar one to most students, and it is not a pleasant one. One online venter, Dan6erous, describes the image well: "A+ this and . . . got a 1600 on my SAT and got all AP class[es] next year woohoo. That's all these people care about don't they have lives damn nerds." In this respect, the trend to dislike intellectuals stems at least in part from an inescapable perception that concern for grades and test scores excludes the coexistence of normal social activities. Sadly, this becomes somewhat of a self-fulfilling prophecy; "nerds" are excluded from social activity because of their label, and that label in turn intensifies through the resulting lack of social contact. The cycle seems unbreakable. Of course, not all "nerds" are socially excluded; most high school students could readily name a few intelligent people with at least a degree of popularity. The point, though, is that the *image* of intellectualism is disliked as anti-social, and the harms of even a fallacious perception to this effect spread to all of the intelligentsia.

This argument, however, merely accounts for the perpetuation of anti-intellectual feelings. Those feelings must also *originate* somewhere, possibly in the examples set by public figures. Certainly the image presented by modern celebrities suggests that intellectualism has no ties to success and social legitimacy. As an illustration, the Web site Angelfire.com features a compilation of the names of famous high school dropouts ("Noted Individuals"). With such well-known cultural icons as Christina Aguilera, Kid Rock, L. L. Cool J., and Sammy Sosa qualifying for such a list, any drive toward intelligence or education becomes laughable in the eyes of media-inundated young people ("Noted Individuals"). Thus, intellectualism loses the respect that its rigor would otherwise tend to earn it. Uneducated success extends far beyond just singers and sports stars, too; even the current President of the United States presents the image of the success of nonintellectualism. His reputation as a "C" student is widely touted, and his public speeches hardly exonerate his intellectual image. The fact that such a vital public figure can get away with saying things like "It's clearly a budget. It's got a lot of numbers in it," and "There needs to be a wholesale effort against racial profiling, which is illiterate children" reflects rather poorly on the regard in which most Americans hold intelligence ("The Very Long List").

Sadly, the aforementioned examples of uneducated success are even 5 further entrenched by the prodigious wealth of the celebrities involved. For example, Sammy Sosa earned an intimidating eighteen million dollars during the year 2002 ("Sammy Sosa"). Indeed, as a writer for *The Carillon* put it, "In more than a few cases athletes' incomes surpass the gross national product of some third-world countries" (Berjak). In the eyes of an ever-watchful public, just the existence of such amazingly affluent yet strikingly uneducated individuals would seem to call into question the necessity and even legitimacy of intellectualism. Certainly, most of the people effected by these media images are teenagers, but these budding young anti-intellectuals carry the sentiments of education-bashing on into their adult lives as well. As an illustration, Robert T. Kiyosaki (no longer a teenager) claims in his book *If You Want to Be Rich and Happy: Don't Go to School* that education is now merely "an archaic institution that continues to cling to obsolete practices." The tendency to forgo enlightenment for "success" even leaks into the college community now: a recent article by Ethan Bronner states that "in the survey . . . 74.9 percent of freshmen chose being well off as an essential goal while only 40.8 percent selected "developing a philosophy" as a similar goal (Bronner). Indeed, American seems enamored with wealth at the expense of intellectualism. Unfortunately for them, this supposed negative correlation between brains and buying power doesn't even exist; "People holding doctorate degrees earned more than twice the salary of high school graduates" in the year 2000 ("Census").

Regardless of the causes of anti-intellectualism, the effects are clear and devastating; society looks down on those individuals who help it to progress, ostracizing its best and brightest. Some may blame television or general societal degradation for the fall of the educated, but at heart the most disturbing issue involved is the destruction of promising personalities; ignoring intellectuals both in school and later on in life crushes its victims, as illustrated in the following lines:

> My loud and bitter screams aren't being heard
> No one is there to hear them or to care
> They do not come cuz I'm a nerd
> Dealing with this pain is a lot to bear. (F., Casey)

For the sake of the smart kids, we all need to "lay off" a little.

Works Cited

ArCaNe. "Re: A Gifted Student." *TalkingCock.com*. 2 Sept. 2001. 1 Oct. 2003 <http://www.talkingcock.com/html/article.php?sid=416>.

Berjak, Matt. "Money, Contracts, and Switzerland." *The Carillon*. 28 Oct. 1999. 7 Oct. 2003 <http://ursu.uregina.ca/~carillon/99.10.28/sports/money.html>.

Bronner, Ethan. "College Students Value Money Over Mind, Survey Says." *The New York Times Company*. 1998. 7 Oct. 2003 <http://mbhs.bergtraum.k12.ny.us/cybereng/nyt/values.htm>.

"Census 2000: Education." *BermudaSun.org*. 18 Dec. 2002. 7 Oct. 2003 <http://www.bermudasun.org/archives/2002-12-18/01News13/>.

"Dan6erous." *Chilax.com*. 31 Aug. 2003. 1 Oct. 2003 <http://chilax.com/forum/index.php?showtopic=1331&st=60>.

F., Casey. "Untitled." *TeenMag.com*. 2002. 1 Oct. 2003 <http://www.teenmag.com/allaboutyou/poetry/poetry_040902_8.html>.

Kiyosaki, Robert T. "If You Want to Be Rich and Happy: Don't Go to School." *EducationReformBooks.net*. 7 Oct. 2003 <http://educationreformbooks.net/richandhappy.htm>.

"Noted Individuals — High School and Elementary School Dropouts." *Angelfire.com*. 1 Oct. 2003 <http://www.angelfire.com/stars4/lists/dropouts.html>.

"Sammy Sosa." *Forbes.com*. 2002. 7 Oct. 2003 <http://www.forbes.com/celebrities2002/LIROJ0Q.html?passListld=53&passYear=2002&passListType=Person&uniqueld=OJ0Q&dataypte=Person>.

"The Very Long List of Bushisms — Before W. Was (!?) Elected." *Bushisms.com*. 1 Oct. 2003 <http://www.bushisms.com/index1.html>.

Engaging with the Text

94, 100

1. Grant Penrod claims that the effects of anti-intellectualism are "clear and devastating," arguing that society "ostracizes its best and brightest." What **EVIDENCE** does he provide for this argument, and does he convince you? If not, why not?

250–51
5–8
94

2. What does Penrod's **TITLE** tell us about his intended **AUDIENCE?** What values do you think he assumes they hold? How does he **APPEAL** to these readers? Do you think he is successful?

3. Penrod suggests that intellectuals are disliked in part because of the "perception that concern for grades and test scores excludes the coexistence of normal social activities" — and that this becomes a "self-fulfilling prophecy; 'nerds' are excluded from social activity because of their label, and that label in turn intensifies through the resulting lack of social contact." Do you agree? Why, or why not?

94, 100
94, 100–101

4. To support his claim that anti-intellectualism is fueled in part by the media, Penrod names celebrities from sports, music, and politics who became successful without the benefit of an education. Do you agree with Penrod that the success of these celebrities is partly responsible for anti-intellectualism? Why or why not? What **EVIDENCE** could be offered as a **COUNTERARGUMENT?**

260–65

93

93–94,
99–100

5. *For Writing.* Penrod identifies "nerds" as one stereotypical high school group. "Jocks" are another familiar stereotype. How were students **CLASSIFIED** into stereotyped groups at your high school? Were the classifications fair? Who did the classifying? What were the consequences for members of the group and for other students? Write an essay about one of these groups that takes a **POSITION** on what factors motivated the stereotyping. You'll need to support your argument with **REASONS** and **EVIDENCE,** such as facts, statistics, and anecdotes.

Evaluations 54

rhetorical
situations

genres

processes

strategies

research
mla/apa

media/
design

readings

CONSUMER REPORTS

Best Phones:
Basic Features Matter Most

The following evaluation of cell phones appeared in the February 2004 issue of Consumer Reports, *a nonprofit magazine devoted to testing and reporting on consumer goods and services. Because cell phone plans and technology have changed since the evaluation was published, the information it includes is no longer current—but it's a good example of how evaluations can present information. Pay attention to the kind of information that the writer provides to support the evaluation, and to the way that information is designed.*

THE NEWEST CELL PHONES can perform plenty of stunts. You can easily find phones with cameras, cutting-edge games, organizers, Web access, a walkie-talkie, and more. Given the wealth of such appealing features, the ability to make simple phone calls might seem to be an afterthought.

It's not. That's why our tests focused less on the extras and more on the basics to help you get the most from your cellphone service — a phone with high voice quality, decent battery life, and a design that's easy to use. The major developments in this market include these:

- Most cell phones now rely mainly on digital technology, although many have analog circuitry as a backup. Analog serves as a common language and makes it easier for phones from different carriers to use each other's networks. Digital-only phones work longer on a battery charge than digital/analog phones do. On the downside, because the phones use incompatible digital networks, it can be impossible to get service away from your home calling area without analog. You'll have to hope that your carrier has made roaming agreements.

- Phone numbers are portable but phones are not. If you want to switch carriers, you'll need to buy a new phone. That's so, we found, even if you switch to a carrier that uses the same phones as your old one. Case in point: AT&T and Cingular. We bought several models through AT&T, then tried to have them switched to Cingular's service. But AT&T refused to change the codes it had locked into the phones.

- AT&T and Cingular are converting their systems from the older TDMA network to GSM, the technology widely used in Europe and Asia. If you choose either of those carriers, you need to select a phone that will maximize the coverage you get.
- "Push to talk," which lets a cell phone work like a walkie-talkie even for coast-to-coast conversation, is becoming more widely available. Nextel, which pioneered push-to-talk, now has competition from Sprint and Verizon. AT&T is expected to introduce a version this year.

How to Choose

Set your price. You can spend as little as $40 or as much as $600 on a cell phone. You need to begin your selection in the right price tier. Many of the phones we tested fall into the $100-to-$200 tier.

Look first at folding phones. A folding model — what Motorola dubbed the flip phone — has two important designs, we have found. First, the phone is small between calls but opens to a handy size when in use. Second, the folding style puts the microphone close to your mouth for better voice performance.

Be wary of fanciful designs and diminutive keypads. Phones that 5 resemble small sculptures may prove difficult to use. Keys that are small, oddly shaped, or arranged in unusual patterns can be a challenge, especially if you're trying to dial a number in dim light. Our testing includes an evaluation of ease of use. Before you settle on a phone, try one at the store to get a feel for its handiness.

Look for sensible features. Cameras, games, music players, and the like are appealing, fun, even useful for some people. Other features, listed in the Ratings, will prove useful every day. They include:

- Volume controls on the side. They let you change the earpiece volume level without moving the phone too far from your ear. You can't do that if the volume controls are on the keypad.
- A standard headset connector. Most hands-free headsets have a 2.5-mm plug, which fits many phones. Many new GSM phones use proprietary connectors.

CR Quick Recommendations

We've grouped the tested phones by carrier to make it easier for you to find a phone once you've settled on a carrier. Overall, the phones are closely matched in voice quality and sensitivity. We found larger differences in the amount of talk time they offer; the phones for Sprint were the worst in this regard, but still fine for most users.

We have reservations about the extent of coverage on the AT&T and Cingular GSM networks. That's why two of the phones we recommend below in Quick Picks have a backup system for better coverage. We tested the Sony Ericsson T62u, a GSM phone from Cingular, but can't recommend it because it performed erratically. (The T62u is not in the Ratings.)

The phones weigh between 2½ and 4½ ounces and measure 4x2x1 inches, give or take a fraction. Try phones in the store to find a design that works for you.

The **Ratings** rank phones strictly on performance. The Quick Picks consider other factors, such as coverage and value.

QUICK PICKS

Best for Verizon:

1 **LG** $200
3 **LG** $160
4 **Motorola** $200

The LG's (1, 3) are closely matched in performance and features. The Motorola (4) is Verizon's only phone with push-to-talk. All three have a folding case.

Best for Sprint:

8 **Samsung** $100
10 **Sanyo** $230
11 **Nokia** $135

All performed well overall; battery life is their only shortcoming. The Samsung (8) and Nokia (11) have a monochrome display that's usable in bright and dim light. The Sanyo (10) has slightly lower voice quality but includes a camera. Its color display washes out in bright light, we found.

Best for AT&T, Cingular, and T-Mobile:

12 **Siemens** $100
15 **Nokia** $40
21 **Motorola** $100

All three phones offer long battery life and talk time. The Siemens (12) uses GSM technology with TDMA as a backup, to help maximize coverage in AT&T's networks (see box, page 22). The widely available Nokia (15) also has a backup system. If you're signing on with AT&T or Cingular but don't want a GSM phone, then the Motorola (21) is a good choice.

Ratings cell phones

- Availability Most models at stores at least through June.

Excellent Very good Good Fair Poor

Within types, in performance order. Blue key numbers indicate Quick Picks; see box at left.

Key number	Brand & model (Similar models, in small type, comparable to tested model.)	Price	Overall Score	Voice quality	Sensitivity	Talk time (hr.)	Ease of use	Tri-mode	Folding case	Speakerphone	Std. headset connector	Easy-to-mute ringer	Vol. control on side	Camera
VERIZON CDMA PHONES														
1	LG VX6000	$200				3½								
2	Samsung SCH a530	205				3½								
3	LG VX4400	160				3½								
4	Motorola V60p	200				3½								
5	Audiovox CDM-8300	70				3								
6	Motorola T730	165				2½								
7	Motorola V120e	40				3½								
SPRINT CDMA PHONES														
8	Samsung SPH-A460 (SPH-A310 (Verizon))	100				2								
9	Samsung SPH-A600	350				2½								
10	Sanyo SCP-8100	230				2½								
11	Nokia 3585i (3588i (Verizon))	135				2								
AT&T, CINGULAR, AND T-MOBILE GSM PHONES														
12	Siemens S46 (AT&T)	100				5								
13	Panasonic GU87 (AT&T)	300				4½								
14	Siemens S56 A56 (AT&T, Cingular)	150				4½								
15	Nokia 3595 (AT&T, Cingular, T-Mobile)	40				6								
16	Nokia 6800 (AT&T, Cingular)	220				6								
17	Nokia 3650 3600 (AT&T, Cingular, T-Mobile)	300				5								
18	Sony Ericsson T616 (AT&T, Cingular)	180				4½								
AT&T AND CINGULAR TDMA PHONES														
19	Motorola V120T (AT&T)	50				4								
20	Nokia 8265 (AT&T)	150				4½								
21	Motorola V60i V60b (AT&T, Cingular)	100				3½								
22	Nokia 6360 (AT&T)	150				3½								

◨ Discontinued but similar models available. Price is for similar 3588i.

Guide to the Ratings

Overall score is based mainly on voice quality and sensitivity. **Voice quality** covers performance in noisy and quiet environments, for talking and listening; testing was done using live phone calls. **Sensitivity** is a measure of a phone's voice quality when a call is placed using a weak signal. The scores are applicable only within a Ratings group, not between groups. **Talk time** is the average time we think you should expect, based on our tests with strong and weak signals. **Ease of use** takes in the design of the display and keypad and the ease with which we could program and access speed-dial numbers, redial, send or receive text messages, and the like. **Features** columns show which are **tri-mode** (able to operate in digital or analog mode in two frequency bands) and have a **folding case**, built-in **speakerphone**, **standard headset connector**, **easy-to-mute ringer** (lets you mute the ringer and vibrate with the press of one key), **volume control** on the side, or a built-in **camera**. **Price** is the average for a phone purchased from the provider, before rebates or other promotions, in October and November 2003.

FEBRUARY 2004 ◉ CONSUMER REPORTS 23

rhetorical situations

genres

processes

strategies

research mla/apa

media/ design

readings

- An easy-to-mute ringer. Etiquette demands that you keep the phone quiet in restaurants, movies, and other public places. The best phones in this regard can be set to vibrate rather than ring with the push of a single key.

Don't trash your old phone. Phones can be recycled (but be sure to erase names and numbers stored in the memory). Staples and other retailers will take used ones. Some are refurbished and sold in developing countries; others are used for parts. Other recycling programs raise funds for charity, resell phones as alternatives to new ones, or provide phones to the homeless and victims of domestic violence. For more information on recycling, go to *www.collectivegood.com, www.charitablerecycling.com* and *www.recyclewirelessphones.com.*

Engaging with the Text

1. Who is the **AUDIENCE** for this article? How do you think that audience affects the way the article is written?

   5–8

2. What **CRITERIA** does *Consumer Reports* use to evaluate cell phones? Are they adequate? Why or why not? If not, what additional criteria do you think should have been considered? Why?

   122

3. *Consumer Reports* typically summarizes their product evaluations in a **TABLE** at the end of the article. Examine the table titled "Ratings Cell Phones." How does this table function as part of the article? Could the table stand on its own? Why or why not?

   458–62

4. In evaluating goods and services, *Consumer Reports* often offers information that goes beyond product details. What information is included here that is not directly related to the evaluation of cell phones? What does this extra information contribute to the overall argument of the article? Why do you think *Consumer Reports* presents this information?

5. *For Writing.* Select a product that you own — a television, MP3 player, calculator, whatever — and borrow a different brand of the product from a friend. Develop a list of **CRITERIA** and **COMPARE** the two items. Using the results of your comparison, write an **EVALUATION** of both products. Make sure you refer to your criteria and offer **REASONS** for each rating.

   122
   266–74
   120–26
   123

RACHEL FORREST

Craft, Care at Flatbread Company Makes Up for Sparse Menu

A freelance writer and former restaurant owner, Rachel Forrest writes a weekly column on food and wine called "Wine Me Dine Me" for the publication iT *(online at Seacoastonline.com). Her restaurant review column, "Dining Out," appears weekly in* Spotlight *magazine. The following review appeared in the* Portsmouth (NH) Herald *in 2004. Notice how the criteria Forrest uses to evaluate restaurants are implicit throughout the review – and made explicit in the box at the end.*

Here's an all-encompassing philosophy at the Flatbread Company, both at the original Amesbury location and now at the far larger Portsmouth spot (and two others). It has to do with the spirit of good healthy food and honoring those who grow the stuff that goes into it, and those who cook it, serve it, and eat it.

The chicken is free-range, the sausage is made on premises (and nitrate-free, meaning no preservatives), the tomato sauce is homemade, the pizza dough is made with spring water, organic flour, kosher salt, and real cake yeast, the asiago cheese is from Vermont, and the atmosphere is open and friendly and welcoming, in a huge open space with lots of rustic art depicting the produce and philosophy on the walls, and a seat in front of the primitive stone and clay oven where little kids love to sit and watch their food being cooked.

The staff members here are happy and laid-back, with that sort of surfer-dude, slightly hippiesque ease that relaxes, yet they're completely on the ball, offering suggestions about how to arrange one's pizza to accommodate everyone.

We ordered a small homemade sausage flatbread with the nitrate-free maple fennel sausage baked with sundried tomatoes, caramelized onions, mushrooms, garlic oil, parmesan, and herbs ($8.75, the large is $16). On the menu it says that one flatbread is enough for two, but that should be amended to say one large is enough for two. They are kind of small for

the price if measured against other pizza places, but you have to keep in mind the craft that goes into it. Even the sausage is homemade here.

The pizza was great. I could taste each and every element individually and as a whole. The crust is thin and mostly crunchy, but still with a bit of body to it. The sausage is incredible — the wonderful crumbly kind with the sharp spice of fennel and the maple to soften the flavor. The mushrooms were plentiful and fresh and the onions sweet and tender. No grease to run down the arm here — it's all perfectly proportioned.

We also tried a half a plain cheese and herb and half of the veggie special with mozzarella, pine nuts, and lots of basil ($8.25). The pizzas here are all sliced in a grid rather than in the usual wedge slices so be prepared for that. It's not really "foldable" pizza anyway, but it makes it so some of the portions have mostly crust. Since it's not a crust you'll leave on the plate after gobbling up the cheesy bits, it's not a problem. Two of us could have eaten another one of these, so again, I recommend ordering large-sized pizzas.

There aren't many selections on the menu, just eight flatbreads, including a vegan dairy-free variety with caramelized onions, mushrooms, kalamata olives, garlic oil, and herbs ($7.50–$13.50), and Jimmy's Free Range Chicken with the chicken roasted and merged with roasted corn, cilantro, black beans, the herbs, and cheeses, and topped with sour cream and a lime wedge ($9–$16.50). This one is really delicious, but a hard sell to traditionalists.

They also have a Veggie and a Carnivore special daily, including an exotic dry-spiced rubbed pork with a pineapple jerk sauce with dried cranberries and red onions, but there's really not much to choose from, even in the appetizer department with just a salad with organic mesclun and sweet leaf lettuces with organic celery and carrots, and a toasted sesame seaweed in a ginger-tamari vinaigrette ($5.50, with crumbled blue cheese $6.50).

Desserts include homemade brownies and, one of my favorites, hot gingerbread with vanilla ice cream, hot chocolate sauce, and homemade whipped cream ($5.50). It's a big portion with sharp and sweet spices, giving the feeling of being in Grandma's kitchen in winter.

The restaurant serves wine and beer as well as soft drinks and a lemonade sweetened with maple syrup, which gives it a nice flavor boost.

The bar area is a good hang, and there is plenty of space to lounge while waiting for a table, especially on the weekend when they do get slammed.

Although the menu selections may be sparse here (it would be great to see more appetizers) the craft and care that goes into the pizza here is abundant, as is the feeling that by eating here you've entered into a pact with the Earth and with others who live on it to honor what we grow and eat.

Flatbread Company
138 Congress St.
Portsmouth
436-7888
www.flatbreadcompany.com
Hours 11:30 a.m.–10:00 p.m. Seven days a week.

Food**
The all-natural and local farm aspects are appealing, and the pizza has a delicious crispy crust and wonderful ingredients. More appetizer selections would be nice.

Service**
The restaurant is well staffed, and each member knows his or her role, which makes service efficient. Everyone is joyous without being too perky, and very helpful with suggestions.

Ambiance**
The big wide open space keeps short attention spans at bay with all the activity going on, and the action by the primitive oven is entertaining.

Overall**
It's a happy place that honors organic fresh ingredients in both exotic and basic combinations.

About the Ratings
***** — Excellent
**** — Very Good
*** — Good
** — Fair
* — Poor

■ rhetorical situations　▲ genres　○ processes　◆ strategies　● research mla/apa　□ media/ design　📖 readings

Engaging with the Text

1. Rachel Forrest titles her review "Craft, Care at Flatbread Company Makes Up for Sparse Menu." How does this **TITLE** signal the main evaluation of this restaurant?

   250–51

2. Forrest **ENDS** her review by saying that by eating at the Flatbread Company, "you've entered a pact with the Earth and with others who live on it to honor what we grow and eat." Why do you think she chose to end this way? How else might she have concluded?

   245–49

3. Forrest uses a lot of descriptive **DETAIL** in her review. What does she describe, and what details does she include in her descriptions? How effectively do these descriptions **SUPPORT** her evaluation? How do these descriptions relate to her criteria?

   285–88

   123

4. Whether writing about music, restaurants, movies, or books, reviewers are often challenged to be **BALANCED AND FAIR.** Do you think Forrest has achieved that goal here? Why or why not? Point to examples from the review in your response.

   123

5. *For Writing.* Write a review **EVALUATING** a local restaurant. Develop a set of **CRITERIA** on which you'll judge the restaurant (atmosphere, service, quality of food, and so on), rate the restaurant on each of the criteria, and **SUPPORT** your evaluation with specific evidence — from your personal experience there, from the menu, and so on.

   120–26
   122

   123

MICHIKO KAKUTANI

The End of Life As She Knew It

Michiko Kakutani is a book critic at the New York Times. *In 1998, she was awarded the Pulitzer Prize for Criticism. The following review of Joan Didion's memoir,* The Year of Magical Thinking *(2005), appeared in the* Times *in 2005. (A selection from Didion's book is included in Chapter 59, Reflections.)*

IN JOAN DIDION'S WORK, there has always been a fascination with what she once called "the unspeakable peril of the everyday" — the coyotes by the interstate, the snakes in the playpen, the fires and Santa Ana winds of California. In the past, that peril often seemed metaphorical, a product of a theatrical imagination and a sensibility attuned to the emotional and existential fault lines running beneath society's glossy veneer: it was personal but it was also abstract.

There is nothing remotely abstract about what has happened to Ms. Didion in the last two years.

On Christmas Day 2003, her daughter Quintana, who had come down with flulike symptoms, went to the emergency room at Beth Israel North Hospital in New York City. Suffering from pneumonia and septic shock, she was suddenly in the hospital's intensive-care unit, hooked up to a respirator and being given a potent intravenous drug cocktail.

Five days later, Ms. Didion's husband of 40 years, John Gregory Dunne, sat down to dinner in their Manhattan apartment, then abruptly slumped over and fell to the floor. He was pronounced dead — of a massive heart attack — later that evening.

"The Broken Man," what Quintana as a young girl used to call "fear 5 and death and the unknown," had come for her father, even as it had come to wait for her in the I.C.U.

"Life changes fast," Ms. Didion would write a day or two later. "Life changes in the instant. You sit down to dinner and life as you know it ends."

Like those who lost loved ones in the terrorist attacks of 9/11, like those who have lost friends and family members to car accidents, airplane crashes, and other random acts of history, Ms. Didion instantly saw ordinary life morph into a nightmare. She saw a shared existence with shared rituals and shared routines shatter into a million irretrievable pieces.

In her devastating new book, *The Year of Magical Thinking*, Ms. Didion writes about the year she spent trying to come to terms with what happened that terrible December, a year she says that "cut loose any fixed idea I had ever had about death, about illness, about probability and luck, about good fortune and bad, about marriage and children and memory, about grief, about the ways in which people do and do not deal with the fact that life ends, about the shallowness of sanity, about life itself."

Throughout their careers, Ms. Didion and Mr. Dunne wrote about themselves, about their marriage, their nervous breakdowns, the screenplays they worked on together, and the glittering worlds they inhabited in New York and Los Angeles. Writing for both of them was a way to find out what they thought; the construction of a narrative was a means of imposing a pattern on the chaos of life.

And so, almost a year after the twin calamities of December 2003, 10 Ms. Didion began writing this volume. It is an utterly shattering book that gives the reader an indelible portrait of loss and grief and sorrow, all chronicled in minute detail with the author's unwavering reportorial eye. It is also a book that provides a haunting portrait of a four-decade-long marriage, an extraordinarily close relationship between two writers, who both worked at home and who kept each other company almost 24 hours a day, editing each other's work, completing and counterpointing each other's thoughts.

"I could not count the times during the average day when something would come up that I needed to tell him," Ms. Didion writes. "This impulse did not end with his death. What ended was the possibility of response."

Like so many of her fictional heroines, Ms. Didion says she always prized control as a means of lending life at least the illusion of order, and in an effort to cope with what happened to her husband and daughter, she turned to the Internet and to books. "Read, learn, work it up, go to the literature," she writes. "Information is control." She queried doctors, researched the subjects of grief and death, read everything from Emily Post on funeral etiquette to Philippe Ariès's *Western Attitudes toward Death*.

When Quintana suffered a relapse in March 2004 — she collapsed at the Los Angeles airport and underwent emergency neurosurgery at the U.C.L.A. Medical Center for a massive hematoma in her brain — Ms. Didion began researching the doctors' findings. She skimmed the appendices to a book called *Clinical Neuroanatomy* and studied *Intensive Care: A Doctor's Journal* in an effort to learn what questions to ask Quintana's doctors.

During those weeks at U.C.L.A., Ms. Didion says she realized that many of her friends in New York and California "shared a habit of mind usually credited to the very successful": "They believed absolutely in their own management skills. They believed absolutely in the power of the telephone numbers they had at their fingertips, the right doctor, the major donor, the person who could facilitate a favor at State or Justice." For many years, she shared those beliefs, and yet at the same time she says she always understood that "some events in life would remain beyond my ability to control or manage them" and that "some events would just happen. This was one of those events."

Nor could she control her own thoughts. Try as she might to suppress them, memories of her life with Mr. Dunne — of trips they had taken with Quintana to Hawaii, of homes they had lived in Los Angeles and Manhattan, of walks and meals shared — continually bobbed to the surface of her mind, creating a memory "vortex" that pulled her back in time only to remind her of all that she had lost. She began trying to avoid places she might associate with her husband or daughter.

The magical thinking of denial became Ms. Didion's companion. She found herself "thinking as small children think, as if my thoughts or wishes had the power to reverse the narrative, change the outcome." She authorized an autopsy of her husband, reasoning that an autopsy could show what had gone wrong, and if it were something simple —

15

a change in medication, say, or the resetting of a pacemaker — "they might still be able to fix it."

She similarly refused to give away his shoes, reasoning that it would be impossible for him to "come back" without anything to wear on his feet. When she heard that Julia Child had died, she thought: "this was finally working out: John and Julia Child could have dinner together."

In an effort to get her mind around what happened, Ms. Didion ran the events of December 30 through her mind again and again, just as she ran several decades of family life through her mind, looking for a way to de-link the chain of causation. What if they hadn't moved to New York so many years ago? What if Quintana had gone to a different hospital? What if they still lived in Brentwood Park in their two-story Colonial house with the center-hall plan?

Even when Quintana seems to be making a recovery, Ms. Didion finds it difficult to work: she has a panic attack in Boston, trying to cover the Democratic convention, and puts off finishing an article, thinking that without John, she has no one to read it. She feels "fragile, unstable," worried that when her sandal catches on the sidewalk, she will fall and there will be no one to take her to the emergency room. She takes to wearing sneakers about town and begins leaving a light on in the apartment throughout the night.

In this book, the elliptical constructions and sometimes mannered 20 prose of the author's recent fiction give way to stunning candor and piercing details that distinguished her groundbreaking early books of essays, *Slouching Towards Bethlehem* and *The White Album*. At once exquisitely controlled and heartbreakingly sad, *The Year of Magical Thinking* tells us in completely unvarnished terms what it is to love someone and lose him, what it is to have a child fall sick and be unable to help her.

It is a book that tells us how people try to make sense of the senseless and how they somehow go on.

The tragic coda to Ms. Didion's story is not recounted in these pages: the death — from an abdominal infection — of Quintana in August, a year and eight months after she first fell ill and a year and eight months after the death of her father.

Engaging with the Text

239–45

1. Michiko Kakutani waits until the eighth paragraph of her book review to mention the title of the book she's reviewing, Joan Didion's *The Year of Magical Thinking*. How does she **BEGIN** her text, and how does this beginning appeal to readers? What would be the effect had she opened by referring to the book?

359–63

2. Kakutani peppers her review with **QUOTATIONS** from Didion's memoir. What function do these quotations serve? What role, in general, do quotations play in evaluations?

3. Kakutani does not explicitly state her opinion of Didion's book, but how do we know what she thinks? Identify passages that reveal her evaluation.

3–4

4. What is the **PURPOSE** of this review? How do you think this might affect Kakutani's assessment of the book? Does it achieve its purpose? Why or why not?

120–26

123

5. *For Writing.* Write a review **EVALUATING** a book you've read — a novel, a how-to book, a textbook, whatever. Be sure to develop **CRITERIA** to determine the book's strengths and weaknesses and to cite specific examples from the book to support your evaluation.

rhetorical situations   genres   processes   strategies   research mla/apa   media/ design   readings

CRAIG OUTHIER

Potter Power

Craig Outhier is a movie critic whose reviews appear in the Orange County (CA) Register, *the* East Valley (AZ) Tribune, *and the* Colorado Springs Gazette. *He also discusses movies each week on the Arizona radio station KTAR. The following movie review appeared in 2004 in* Get Out, *a free entertainment guide to Arizona published by the East Valley Tribune. As you read, notice how Outhier demonstrates his knowledge of the film industry — and therefore his authority as a film expert — by weaving in information about the movie's director, actors, and characters.*

IN ADDITION TO HIS NEW ADAM'S APPLE, pubescent boy wizard Harry Potter (Daniel Radcliffe) comes equipped with a veritable arsenal of supernatural goodies in *Harry Potter and the Prisoner of Azkaban,* including time travel, omniscient maps, and a majestic horse-bird hybrid that he rides like Funny Cide[1] over the cloud tops.

Unfortunately, Harry's most pressing need goes unmet — specifically, a good family-practice attorney.

As always, this Harry Potter installment — the third in a series based on J. K. Rowling's phenomenally successful children's books — is built around Harry's quest for the truth regarding his dead parents, murdered many years ago by the sinister Lord Valdemort. Just as predictably, Harry is stymied by a tight-lipped adult faculty that inexplicably refuses to surrender its secrets.

Ultimately, this familiar cycle of conceal and reveal grows tiresome. Two hours in, you wish Harry would hire Alan Dershowitz,[2] cite the Freedom of Information Act, and take those cagey stiffs at Hogwarts to court. Anything to give this floundering series a little buoyancy.

---

1. Winner of the Kentucky Derby and the Preakness Stakes in 2003.
2. American lawyer and jurist (b. 1938).

Emma Watson, Rupert Grint, and Daniel Radcliffe in Harry Potter and the Prisoner of Azkaban. Warner Brothers/Courtesy Everett Collection.

Granted, there's more psychological texture here than in previous 5
"Potter" offerings, due chiefly to the fact that it was directed by Alfonso
Cuaron, who also helmed (sarcasm alert!) that other acclaimed kids'
movie, *Y Tu Mamá También*.

Assuming command of the franchise from the competent but
monotonic Chris Columbus,[3] Cuaron brings with him a moodier, more
haroque visual palette to complement the story's portentous themes.
It's like the difference between Mother Goose and Brothers Grimm.
Trained and educated in Mexico, Cuaron is a filmmaker who revels in
details, one who can harness the sensuous energy from the image of,
say, a shriveled sunflower and use it to perfume the next scene.

---

3. Director of *Harry Potter and the Sorcerer's Stone* (2001) and *Harry Potter and the Chamber of Secrets* (2002).

To be sure, something rotten is afoot at Hogwarts, the school for neophyte wizards and witches where Harry — along with pals Ron (Rupert Grint) and Hermione (Emma Watson) — is entering his third year. Now permanently cut off from his abusive, non-magical relatives (in retaliation for an insult against his parents, he turns his uncle's insufferable sister into a human balloon), Harry finds himself facing a more terrifying menace: Sirius Black, the dangerous fugitive wizard who betrayed his parents and orchestrated their death. Played by "Sid and Nancy" nutcase Gary Oldman — who is far too under-used in this movie — Black has escaped from prison and is at large, purportedly hell-bent on killing Harry, too.

Per tradition, Harry is forced to don his invisibility cloak and skulk around to wrest bits of information away from his secretive guardians, but does find an ally in Professor Lupin (David Thewlis from "The Island of Dr. Moreau"), his Defense Against the Dark Arts teacher. Once close to Harry's parents, Lupin confides in Harry his fondness for the deceased Potters and admits that Harry's father was a bit of a rakehell in his youth.

According to fans in the know, this genealogical detail comes to bloom in later "Potter" volumes; explaining, for instance, why Professor Snape (Alan Rickman) harbors such a blistering hatred of young Harry.

However, in the here and now, more questions are posed than answered, including the central mystery of why Harry's parents were murdered in the first place. In the first two movies, the vagaries were tolerable. Now, in the third installment, typically the termination point for most sagas, they have officially been downgraded to tedious.

10

Of course, the elusiveness of the "Potter" stories is by design — Rowling clearly designed Hogwarts to reflect the adult world through a child's eyes; nurturing yet threatening, scholarly yet enigmatic, rife with horrible, wonderful secrets and half-understood rules. Even Dumbledore, the kindly headmaster played by Michael Gambon ("Gosford Park"), stepping in for the late Richard Harris, seems only conveniently interested in Harry's well-being. Harry's new teacher, the tea leaf–reading Professor Trelawney (Emma Thompson), is a near-sighted gypsy who fills his head with paranoid thoughts of death and doom.

All of which is fine for the rank-and-file "Harry" faithful, who are invested enough in the characters — i.e., "Will Ron ever hook up with

Hermione?" — that they can tolerate the ineffectual, snails-clip plot resolution.

The rest of us must find our delights in the movie's bodacious special effects (more seamless than before, including the Quidditch[4] scene), lush production design and generous imagination. It appears that as long as Harry is given neat, audience-pleasing things to ride, eat and incant, he'll stay out of court.

Engaging with the Text

1. What **CRITERIA** does Craig Outhier use to critique the *Harry Potter* movie? How appropriate are these criteria for evaluating films? Would they be appropriate for evaluating other kinds of media? Why or why not?

2. One **PURPOSE** of a movie review is to help moviegoers decide whether or not to see a particular film. Do you think this is Outhier's primary purpose? Why or why not?

3. What does the **IMAGE** contribute to the review? If you've seen the film, would you suggest any other scenes that would tell readers more about the film or its craftsmanship than this one does?

4. How does Outhier **DEMONSTRATE HIS KNOWLEDGE** of films in general, and the Harry Potter film in particular? Point to examples from the review.

5. *For Writing.* Write a review of a movie, television show, or music video. Watch the work that you select more than once, identifying appropriate **CRITERIA**: acting, directing, lighting, sets, music, dialogue — all are potential criteria, but you will probably want to focus on a few. Be sure to cite specific **DETAILS** to support your **EVALUATION**.

123 ▲

3–4 ■

458–62 ◻

123 ▲

123 ▲

285–88 ◆

120–26 ▲

---

4. An imaginary ballgame in the Harry Potter books.

rhetorical situations ■   genres ▲   processes ○   strategies ◆   research mla/apa ●   media/design ◻   readings ▌

PAUL KRUGMAN
California Screaming

Paul Krugman is a professor of economics and international affairs at Princeton University and the author of over twenty books and hundreds of articles on economics. As a columnist for the New York Times, *he writes about international trade, finance, economics, and currency crises. The following piece appeared in the* Times *in December 2000 during the California energy crisis, when rolling blackouts and steep price hikes followed a failed partial deregulation of the energy market there. In deregulation, a government lifts restrictions on an industry in order to encourage competition among businesses. According to prevailing economic theory, this should increase productivity and efficiency, leading to lower prices.*

CALIFORNIA'S DEREGULATED POWER INDUSTRY, in which producers can sell electricity for whatever the traffic will bear, was supposed to deliver cheaper, cleaner power. But instead the state faces an electricity short-age so severe that the governor has turned off the lights on the official Christmas tree — a shortage that has proved highly profitable to power companies, and raised suspicions of market manipulation.

The experience raised questions about deregulation. And more broadly, it is a warning about the dangers of placing blind faith in markets.

True, part of California's problem is an unexpected surge in elec-tricity demand, the byproduct of a booming economy. It's possible that the crisis would have happened even without deregulation.

But probably not. In the bad old days, monopolistic power compa-nies were guaranteed a good profit even if their industry had excess capacity. So they built more capacity than they needed, enough to meet even unexpectedly high demand. But in the deregulated market, where prices fluctuate constantly, companies knew that if they overinvested, prices and profits would plunge. So they were reluctant to build new plants — which is why unexpectedly strong demand has led to short-ages and soaring prices.

Now you could say that in the long run there is nothing wrong with 5
that. Building extra generating capacity was costly, and the costs were
passed on to consumers; while prices may fluctuate in a system with
less slack, on average consumers will pay less. In fact, textbook economics suggests that it's actually a good thing that electricity prices sky-
rocket when supply runs short: that's what gives the power companies
an incentive to invest. And so you could argue that no public intervention is warranted — indeed, that the caps that still place an upper limit
on electricity prices only worsen the problem, that we should rely on
market competition to solve the crisis.

But how competitive is the electricity market? What makes California's power crisis politically explosive is the suspicion that it's not
just about inadequate capacity, but also about artificially inflated prices.

How might market manipulation work? Suppose that it's a hot July,
with air-conditioners across the state running full blast and the power
industry near the limits of its capacity. If some of that capacity suddenly went off line for whatever reason, the resulting shortage would
send wholesale electricity prices sky high. So a large producer could
actually increase its profits by inventing technical problems that shut
down some of its generators, thereby driving up the price it gets on its
remaining output.

Does this really happen? A recent National Bureau of Economic
Research working paper by Severin Borenstein, James Bushnell and
Frank Wolak cites evidence that exactly this kind of market manipulation took place in Britain before 1996 and in California during the summers of 1998 and 1999.

You wouldn't normally expect this to happen in colder months,
when demand is lower. Still, state officials have understandably become
suspicious about California's current power emergency — an emergency
precipitated by the odd fact that about a quarter of the state's generating capacity is off line as the result of either scheduled repairs or
breakdowns.

Maybe California power companies aren't rigging electricity prices. 10
But they clearly have both the means and the incentive to do so — and
you have to wonder why the deregulators didn't worry about this, why

they didn't ask seemingly obvious questions about whether the market they proposed to create would really work as advertised.

And maybe that is the broader lesson of the debacle: Don't rush into a market solution when there are serious questions about whether the market will work. Both economic analysis and British experience should have rung warning bells about California's deregulation scheme; but those warnings were ignored — just as similar warnings are being ignored by enthusiasts for market solutions for everything from prescription drug coverage to education.

Engaging with the Text

1. Examine Paul Krugman's **OPENING** paragraph. How does this paragraph establish the parameters of the situation that Krugman wishes to evaluate? What, for example, does the small piece of information about the official Christmas tree contribute to the picture Krugman paints about the issue of California's deregulated power industry?

   239–45

2. The deregulation of the power industry is a technical topic, and yet Krugman explains the issue clearly, defining terms and explaining processes that readers may not know. This piece was written for the *New York Times* and thus assumes an informed readership. What else, if anything, would need to be **DEFINED** or explained for an **AUDIENCE** of first-year college students in an introduction to economics class?

   275–84
5–8
123

3. What **EVIDENCE** does Krugman supply to **SUPPORT** his speculation that the deregulation of the power industry in California might have led to market manipulation? How convincing is this evidence?

4. What is Krugman's **PURPOSE?** How does the way he **ENDS** reveal this purpose? Does he achieve his purpose? Why or why not?

   3–4
245–49

5. *For Writing.* Write a letter to Krugman agreeing or disagreeing with what he says. Feel free to ask questions if there's anything you think he needs to explain further.

55 Literary Analyses

See also:

STEPHANIE
HUFF
*Metaphor and
Society in
Shelley's
"Sonnet"*
138

rhetorical situations   genres   processes   strategies   research mla/apa   media/ design   readings

PHILIP NEL

Fantasy, Mystery, and Ambiguity

Philip Nel is an English professor at Kansas State University and the author of several books: J. K. Rowling's Harry Potter Novels: A Reader's Guide *(2001),* The Avant-Garde and American Post-modernity: Small Incisive Shocks *(2002), and* Dr. Seuss: American Icon *(2004). The following piece is from his book about the Harry Potter novels, written after the publication of the fourth installment in the series.*

ONE ASPECT OF HARRY POTTER'S APPEAL is that of the apparently ordinary child who turns out to be special — which, surely, is a secret wish of many children. As J. K. Rowling has said, "I was aware when I was writing that this was a very common fantasy for children: 'These boring people cannot be my parents. They just can't be. I'm so much more special than that'" ("Pure Magic"). Like Taran in Lloyd Alexander's chronicles of Prydain (1964–1968), Will Stanton in Susan Cooper's *Dark Is Rising* series (1965–1977), and Lyra Silvertongue in Philip Pullman's *His Dark Materials* trilogy (1995–2000), Harry is special. And, like the children in all these books, he's on a mission. Though Rowling claims that fantasy is her least favorite genre (she prefers the realism of Roddy Doyle), her books owe a lot to the traditions of fantasy. Harry, a classic fantasy hero, is the oppressed child who fights back, proving himself and quashing his enemies. Featuring more than 100 characters, the *Harry Potter* series is an epic fantasy. Though we have only the first four novels by which to judge it, the series has every indication of leading toward a *Last Battle* — to borrow the title of the final Narnia novel — in which the forces of good vanquish the forces of evil.

While they attain the magical skills they will need in the confrontation toward which the narrative pushes them, a fantasy novel's young characters embark on a journey of self-discovery. As does Bilbo Baggins in J. R. R. Tolkien's *The Hobbit* (1937) and Ged in Ursula K. Le Guin's *A Wizard of Earthsea* (1968), Harry Potter gains a deeper understanding of himself as he moves toward the anticipated final battle. Initially worried that his Muggle upbringing will place him at a disadvantage among Hogwarts students, Harry discovers that he does have talents: he's great at flying and a natural Seeker on his house's Quidditch team. Just as we all must come to terms with who we are, Harry also wonders if some of his abilities make him a bad person. A Parselmouth, Harry can talk to snakes, a rare ability he shares with dark wizards like Voldemort and Salazar Slytherin. Possessing the capacity to speak Parseltongue worries Harry, because the Sorting Hat had offered to place him in Slytherin, only sending him to Gryffindor when he kept chanting "Not Slytherin, not Slytherin" (*Philosopher's Stone* 90–91). When he expresses this anxiety, Dumbledore advises, "It is our choices, Harry, that show us what we truly are, far more than our abilities" (*Chamber of Secrets* 245). Dumbledore's moral applies equally well to Ron and Hermione, who also come into their own during the course of the series. At first an overbearing school swot, Hermione grows more comfortable with herself, develops a strong sense of commitment to her friends, and — though she remains the smartest student in her year — learns to resist the impulse to display her intelligence at every available opportunity. Ron has thus far developed less than Hermione or Harry, but he is gradually emerging from the shadow of his older brothers, playing a key role in solving the mysteries of the first three novels and sharing some of Harry's limelight in *Goblet of Fire*.

As in many fantasy novels and fairy tales, the central character is on a quest; however, the narrative of Harry's quest unfolds more like a classic mystery. In the first novel, Harry seeks to protect the Philosopher's Stone; in the second, to stop the basilisk from attacking students; in the third, to elude and to be revenged upon Sirius Black, whom he believes was an accomplice in his parents' murder; and in the fourth, to win the Triwizard Tournament cup. In its effort to highlight Harry's quests, the previous sentence oversimplifies all four novels. Ron and Hermione often join in Harry's quests, and the implicit and explicit nature of each quest changes as Rowling's mystery unfolds. In *Harry Potter and the Philosopher's Stone*, the three characters first wonder what is hidden on the righthand side of the third-floor corridor; upon learning

what it is, they puzzle over who wants it, suspect Snape, and finally decide to protect it themselves. Concurrent with this mystery quest, they also want to know: Who is Nicolas Flamel? Who or what has been attacking the unicorns? Why did Snape seem to be sabotaging Harry's broom at the Quidditch match? At the opening banquet, why did Harry's scar hurt when Snape appeared to be looking at him? Of course, two overriding questions in all of the novels are: How did Harry survive the Avada Kevadra curse that killed both of his parents? And why did Voldemort want to kill Harry in the first place? Harry asks Dumbledore both questions in *Philosopher's Stone*. The Hogwarts headmaster provides a partial answer to the first question when he says that Harry's mother died to save him, and that Voldemort cannot understand a love that powerful. In words that may echo the author's sentiments toward her own late mother, Dumbledore tells Harry, "to have been loved so deeply, even though the person who loved us is gone, will give us some protection for ever" (216). However, Dumbledore does not tell us why Voldemort wanted the Potters dead; that mystery persists.

If the first novel appears to have many mystery plots going at once, it is remarkably simple when compared with the subsequent three. Each of the next three books grows more complex as its mysteries grow more intricate and clever. The final hundred or so pages of *Harry Potter and the Prisoner of Azkaban* — themselves as gripping and elaborate a conclusion to a mystery as one could hope for — prove only to foreshadow the complexity of *Harry Potter and the Goblet of Fire*. In the *Prisoner of Azkaban*'s concluding pages, we witness the arc of Rowling's narrative expanding — an expansion that continues in its sequel. Though the first two novels provide a sense of narrative closure, the next two offer only an emotional resolution, coupled with an uneasy feeling that the dangerous world beyond Hogwarts will continue to bear down upon the young characters. After realizing that their perceptions of several major characters were incorrect, Harry and Hermione listen in disbelief as Dumbledore tells them, "I have no power to make other men see the truth, or to overrule the Minister for Magic" (*Prisoner of Azkaban* 287). Then, in what can only be a reference to the endings of the previous two novels, Harry realizes that he "had grown used to the idea that

Dumbledore could solve anything. He had expected Dumbledore to pull some amazing solution out of the air. But no . . . their last hope was gone" (288). We readers had grown used to the idea that Dumbledore could set things right, too. *Harry Potter and the Goblet of Fire* complicates matters further, revealing corruption in government ministries, the possibilities for global misunderstanding, and the alliance in disarray while Voldemort returns to power.

Underscoring their complexity, the novels view official systems of power skeptically, placing greater faith in unofficial alliances. While not all bureaucrats are corrupt, many officials appear bumbling, misguided, or acting in their own self-interest instead of for the public good. Though Arthur Weasley is kind-hearted and works hard in the Misuse of Muggle Artefacts Office, Ludo Bagman pays more attention to gambling than running the Department of Games and Sports, Cornelius Fudge tends to fudge things (as his name suggests) as Minister for Magic, and Barty Crouch (the Minister for International Magical Co-operation) is more concerned with appearing correct than with being honest or just. Tellingly, when Crouch was head of the Department of Magical Law Enforcement, he sent the innocent Sirius Black to Azkaban without a trial. Unlike the criminal justice system and other official channels of power, the alliance that Dumbledore begins to reassemble in the penultimate chapter of *Harry Potter and the Goblet of Fire* holds more promise. Rowling evinces trust in the greater efficacy of *ad hoc* groups throughout the novels. When school officials either ignore them (*Philosopher's Stone*) or fail to solve the problem (*Chamber of Secrets*), Harry, Ron, and Hermione form their own alliance and solve the problem themselves. Rowling seems more comfortable when power courses through unofficial networks — as if its activist spirit is more democratic than power entrenched in official channels. No stranger to political activism herself, Rowling implies that activists are more worthy of our trust than public officials are.

As the series develops, it grows increasingly interested in questions of power: who has it, who has the right to exercise it over another, who has the moral authority to wield it, and how it should be exercised. Perhaps the most striking example occurs during the nineteenth chapter of *Prisoner of Azkaban,* when Harry intervenes to stop Black and Lupin from killing Pettigrew, the man directly responsible for Voldemort killing Harry's parents. This moment of moral decision-making gives both readers and characters pause: Sirius asks Harry if he's sure, and when Harry explains why he is, he displays a quiet heroism. Harry saves Pettigrew because he does not think his father would want his best friends to become killers (275). Wonderfully, Harry both regrets his noble decision and receives high praise for it. When Pettigrew escapes, Harry accuses himself of helping Voldemort, albeit inadvertently. "I stopped Sirius and Professor Lupin killing Pettigrew! That makes it my fault, if Voldemort comes back!" Dumbledore quietly disagrees: "Hasn't your experience with the Time-Turner taught you anything, Harry? The consequences of our actions are always so complicated, so diverse, that predicting the future is a very difficult business indeed." In addition, Dumbledore notes that in saving Pettigrew, Harry has given Voldemort a deputy who is in Harry's debt. Dumbledore then adds gently, "I knew your father very well, both at Hogwarts and later . . . . He would have saved Pettigrew too, I am sure of it" (311). If Voldemort is interested in power for its own sake, Harry wishes to use his power only when it is *right* to do so. He could have had Pettigrew killed, avenging his parents' deaths, but sensing that vengeance is the wrong motive, he saves Pettigrew's life. In her *New Yorker* essay, Joan Acocella develops a fascinating analysis of power in Rowling's books, arguing that "Each of the novels approaches the problem from a different angle": the first novel is heroic; the second is "secular, topical, political"; the third is psychological; the fourth is more ambitious in its politics, introducing new topics (such as sex) but not yet answering the question of whether power is "reconcilable with goodness" (77–78).

Acocella's analysis reminds us that one of the most compelling aspects of these novels may be their ambiguity. During each novel, we wonder whether characters have done or are doing the right thing; at the end, many questions remain unanswered. During *Harry Potter and the Goblet of Fire,* we wonder if Ludo Bagman is aligned with the dark wizards or merely unscrupulous? At the end of the novel, we know him to be unscrupulous but not bad, though we do not know which side he will end up assisting. A character like Bagman could go either way. In *Prisoner of Azkaban*, after Harry overhears the "facts" (which turn out to be false) that Sirius Black betrayed his parents, we see Harry's dark side. He wants revenge on Black: but will he risk his own life trying to catch him? Harry decides not to, but the incident does call attention to some potential weaknesses that Voldemort could exploit. In future novels, will Harry be able to keep his temper under control? Will his strong resolve be an asset, a hindrance, or a bit of both? Perhaps the fact that these books raise as many questions as they answer accounts — at least in part — for their enormous appeal.

Works Cited

Acocella, Joan. "Under the Spell." *New Yorker* 31 July 2000: 74–78.
Le Guin, Ursula. *A Wizard of Earthsea*. 1968. New York: Bantam, 1975.
"Pure Magic." *CBS Sunday Morning*. Writ. Mark Phillips. CBS. 26 Sept. 1999.
Rowling, J. K. *Harry Potter and the Chamber of Secrets*. London: Bloomsbury, 1998.
———. *Harry Potter and the Goblet of Fire*. London: Bloomsbury, 2000.
———. *Harry Potter and the Philosopher's Stone*. London: Bloomsbury, 1997.
———. *Harry Potter and the Prisoner of Azkaban*. London: Bloomsbury, 1999.
Tolkien, J. R. R. *The Hobbit*. 1937. Rev. ed. New York: Ballantine Books, 1982.

Engaging with the Text

250–51

1. The **TITLE** of this analysis is "Fantasy, Mystery, and Ambiguity." How does this title reflect the organization of the analysis? How effective do you find this organization? Try your hand at writing a different title, one that might provoke readers to read on.

250–54

2. Philip Nel frequently poses questions without answering them. How do they help **GUIDE** readers? Why do you think he doesn't offer answers to these questions?

3. Nel incorporates QUOTATIONS from the Harry Potter novels throughout his analysis. What role(s) do these quotations serve? Point to
   examples from the text in your response.

   ● 359–63

4. Nel claims that the Harry Potter novels are "interested in questions
   of power: who has it, who has the right to exercise it over another,
   who has the moral authority to wield it, and how it should be exercised." Discuss how Nel treats these questions in his ANALYSIS of the
   novels. How significant are these questions for understanding the
   Harry Potter series? What do these questions reveal about Nel's STANCE
   toward the Potter novels?

   ▲ 137–46

   ■ 12–14

5. *For Writing.* Power — who has it, who lacks it, what they do with
   it, how it affects them — is a common thread in many literary
   works. Choose a text you know — a novel, short story, or drama —
   and ANALYZE its treatment of the concept of power.

   ▲ 137–46

STEPHEN GREENBLATT
Shakespeare on Marriage

Stephen Greenblatt is a professor of humanities at Harvard University. A scholar of Renaissance literature, Greenblatt is widely recognized for his contributions to New Historicism, the literary theory that emphasizes understanding literature within its historical context. He is the general editor of The Norton Anthology of English Literature *(2006) and* The Norton Shakespeare *(1997), and is the author of many books on Shakespeare and Renaissance literature. The following analysis is from* Will in the World: How Shakespeare Became Shakespeare *(2004), a biography, written for a general audience, that speculates about his life. Much of the support for the analysis comes from a close reading of Shakespearean texts.*

BIOGRAPHERS EAGER FOR SHAKESPEARE to have had a good marriage have stressed that when he made some money in the theater, he established his wife and family in New Place, the fine house he bought in Stratford; that he must have frequently visited them there; that he chose to retire early and return permanently to Stratford a few years before his untimely death. Some have gone further and assumed that he must have had Anne and the children stay with him for prolonged periods in London. "None has spoken more frankly or justly of the honest joys of 'board and bed,'" wrote the distinguished antiquarian Edgar Fripp, pointing to lines from *Coriolanus*:

> I loved the maid I married; never man
> Sighed truer breath. But that I see thee here,
> Thou noble thing, more dances my rapt heart
> Than when I first my wedded mistress saw
> Bestride my threshold.   (4.5.113–17)

But if these lines were, as Fripp thought, a recollection of the dramatist's own feelings many years before, the recollection was far more bitter than sentimental: they are spoken by the warrior Aufidius, whose rapt heart dances at seeing the hated man he has long dreamed of killing.

It is, perhaps, as much what Shakespeare did *not* write as what he did that seems to indicate something seriously wrong with his marriage. This was an artist who made use of virtually everything that came his way. He mined, with very few exceptions, the institutions and professions and personal relationships that touched his life. He was the supreme poet of courtship: one has only to think of the aging sonneteer and the fair young man, panting Venus and reluctant Adonis, Orlando and Rosalind, Petruccio and Kate, even twisted, perverse Richard III and Lady Anne.[1] And he was a great poet of the family, with a special, deep interest in the murderous rivalry of brothers and in the complexity of father-daughter relations: Egeus and Hermia, Brabanzio and Desdemona, Lear and the fearsome threesome, Pericles and Marina, Prospero and Miranda. But though wedlock is the promised land toward which his comic heroes and heroines strive, and though family fission is the obsessive theme of the tragedies, Shakespeare was curiously restrained in his depictions of what it is actually like to be married.

To be sure, he provided some fascinating glimpses. A few of his married couples have descended into mutual loathing: "O Goneril!" cries the disgusted Albany, in *King Lear*. "You are not worth the dust which the rude wind / Blows in your face." "Milk-livered man!" she spits back at him. "That bear'st a cheek for blows, a head for wrongs: . . . Marry, your manhood! mew!" (4.2.30–32, 51–69). But for the most part, they are in subtler, more complex states of estrangement. Mostly, it's wives feeling neglected or shut out. "For what offence," Kate Percy asks her husband, Harry (better known as Hotspur), in *1 Henry IV*, "have I this fortnight been / A banished woman from my Harry's bed?" She has in point of fact committed no offence — Hotspur is deeply preoccupied with plotting a rebellion — but she is not wrong to feel excluded. Hotspur has chosen to keep his wife in the dark:

---

1. Lovers depicted by Shakespeare in, respectively, the sonnets, the poem *Venus and Adonis*, and the plays *As You Like It, The Taming of the Shrew*, and *Richard III*.

> But hark you, Kate.
> I must not have you henceforth question me
> Whither I go, nor reason whereabout.
> Whither I must, I must; and, to conclude,
> This evening must I leave you, gentle Kate.
>
>   (2.4.32–33, 93–97)

The rebellion is a family affair — Hotspur has been drawn into it by his father and his uncle — but though the fate of his wife will certainly be involved in its outcome, the only knowledge she has of it is from words she has overheard him muttering in his troubled sleep. With bluff, genial misogyny Hotspur explains that he simply does not trust her:

> I know you wise, but yet no farther wise
> Than Harry Percy's wife; constant you are,
> But yet a woman; and for secrecy
> No lady closer, for I well believe
> Thou wilt not utter what thou dost not know.
> And so far will I trust thee, gentle Kate.
>
>   (2.4.98–103)

The words are all good-humored and exuberant, in the way most of the things Hotspur says are, but the marriage they sketch is one at whose core is mutual isolation. (The same play, 1 Henry IV, gives another, more graphic vision of such a marriage in Edmund Mortimer and his Welsh wife: "This is the deadly spite that angers me: / My wife can speak no English, I no Welsh" [3.1.188–89].)

Shakespeare returned to the theme in Julius Caesar, where Brutus's wife, Portia, complains that she has been deliberately shut out of her husband's inner life. Unlike Kate Percy, Portia is not banished from her husband's bed, but her exclusion from his mind leaves her feeling, she says, like a whore:

> Am I yourself
> But as it were in sort or limitation?
> To keep with you at meals, comfort your bed,
> And talk to you sometimes? Dwell I but in the suburbs
> Of your good pleasure? If it be no more,
> Portia is Brutus' harlot, not his wife.
>
>   (2.1.281–86)

The question here and elsewhere in the plays is the degree of intimacy that husbands and wives can achieve, and the answer Shakespeare repeatedly gives is very little.

Engaging with the Text

1. Stephen Greenblatt argues that "it is, perhaps, as much what Shakespeare did *not* write as what he did that seems to indicate something seriously wrong with his marriage." According to Greenblatt, how does Shakespeare portray marriage and what is missing in those portraits?

2. This piece comes from a work Greenblatt wrote for a nonspecialist **AUDIENCE,** one that may or may not be familiar with Shakespeare's plays. How does he make his analysis one that can be understood by someone who has not read those plays?

    5–8

3. Peppered throughout this text are **QUOTATIONS** from Shakespeare's plays. What role do these quotations serve in Greenblatt's analysis?

    359–63

4. How would you characterize Greenblatt's **STANCE?** Cite examples from the text in your response. How does this stance help appeal to his audience? Do you think it suits his subject matter — and if so, how?

    12–14

5. *For Writing.* Select a songwriter who interests you and examine the lyrics of several of his or her songs, focusing on how he or she talks about intimate relationships. **ANALYZE** what the lyrics reveal about the songwriter's feelings about relationships. You'll want to **QUOTE** lyrics from several songs to support your thesis.

    137–46
    359–63

PATRICIA HAMPL

The Invention of Autobiography:
Augustine's Confessions

Patricia Hampl is a professor of English at the University of Minnesota. A widely published poet and essayist, she has also written two memoirs: A Romantic Education (1981), an exploration of her Czech heritage, and Virgin Time: In Search of the Contemplative Life (1992), an account of her journey to understand Catholicism, the religion of her youth. The following analysis comes from I Could Tell You Stories: Sojourns in the Land of Memory (1999), a collection of essays that explores the genre of memoir.

THE FIRST NINE BOOKS of the *Confessions* feel familiar to us. They are what we think of as autobiography. Augustine[1] casts before us incident and vignette, sketch and portrait, stringing these bright gemstones on the story line of his life as he writes his way from his birth in 354 in Thagaste (now Souk Ahras in the hills of eastern Algeria) to the bittersweet period following his baptism when his mother dies at the Roman port of Ostia as she and Augustine and their circle wait to sail home to Africa.

In these nine chapters of his life, Augustine muses about his babyhood, and even beyond that to his time in the womb, searching what a psychologized modern would call "the unconscious" for hints and clues to his nature. He is clearly troubled by the mystery of existence: "I do not know where I came from," he says with surprisingly agnostic wonder.

Augustine begins his great portrait of his devout Berber Christian mother in Book I as he reminds the Lord how he nursed at her breast, taking in, he knows, much more than milk. Monica's personality storms and rainbows over the entire book. She is her son's biggest fan and

---

1. Aurelias Augustinus (354–430), bishop of Hippo and one of the four "Latin Fathers" of the Roman Catholic Church. His *Confessions* (c. 400), often regarded as "the first autobiography," recounts his conversion to Christianity. After his death he was canonized.

greatest nag. She is also "my mother, my incomparable mother!" Her concern about her son verges on obsession. "Like all mothers, though far more than most," Augustine the bishop writes, still confounded after all these years by her passionate attachment, "she loved to have me with her." She follows him to the dock when he is about to leave Africa for Rome, weeping and wailing, begging him either to stay or to take her with him. Finally desperate to be rid of her, he lies about the time of his departure and makes his escape.

A good try, but Monica, of course, gets her way, on earth and in heaven. She follows Augustine to Rome and then to Milan when he secures a plum teaching position there. She prays him into the Church with more than pious wishes: she has a mother's spooky clairvoyance, and assures him she *knows* he will find his way to baptism. Her prophecy climaxes in Book IX during their mutual mystical experience in Ostia.

In marked contrast to his rhapsodic writing about Monica, Augus- 5 tine mentions his father with telling coolness. Patricius was a small-time farmer who remained a pagan until receiving baptism on his deathbed. He was neither a success in life nor a questing soul. He died when Augustine was eighteen and he cast only a faint shadow on his son's consciousness. Augustine was his mother's son, and knew it.

No incident is too small for Augustine in the *Confessions* — provided it has metaphoric value. He is a gifted writer, after all, a pro, and he knows very well that his description of his boyhood theft of pears from a garden — a purely willful act because he didn't even want to eat the pears — rings a change on the first theft in another Garden.

He reports his first prayer — "not to be beaten at school." And reminds God that in response to this first intercession "You did not hear my prayer. . . . " Augustine recalls the harshness of his school days and the cruelty of his teachers with the scorekeeping precision of a true memoirist, immune to the irritating wisdom of forgiving and forgetting. The slap of his boyhood humiliations and the still-tender skin of the adult bishop who recounts them ring down the centuries. "We loved to play," he explains heatedly, appealing to God as if to a referee in a ghostly game of yore, "and we were punished by adults who nonetheless did the same themselves. But whereas the frivolous pursuits of grown-up people are called 'business,' children are punished. . . . Moreover, was the master who flogged me any better himself? If he had been worsted by a fellow-scholar in some pedantic dispute, would he not have been racked by even more bitter jealousy than I was when my opponent in a game of ball got the better of me?" Still arguing his case after all these years.

We see him grow into a young intellectual, sharpening his knives of argument, engaged in his first philosophical battles. The Manichees,[2] a gnostic sect whose dualism greatly appeals to him at first, later become a grave disappointment. He hopscotches from Manicheism to a fashionable skepticism, then into a mystical Neoplatonism[3] that leads him finally to the threshold of the Church. He enumerates his hesitations about Catholicism, and presents the process, both intellectual and spiritual, that leads him finally to the Baptistry in Milan. We feel the circumspection of his mind: After listening carefully to the great bishop Ambrose he says coolly, "I realized that the Catholic faith . . . was in fact intellectually respectable." This is not the response of a credulous seeker, but the balanced judgment of an educated, upwardly mobile provincial intent on climbing in Roman society, a classical Latin scholar still slightly uneasy with the folk elements in biblical texts. The urgency of his search for truth never leaves his story. It is the ground beat of the tale.

But we would not read the *Confessions* down the centuries if they were the testimony of an intellectual's struggles, no matter how passionately told. It is passion itself that makes Augustine alive to us. He insists that we understand this about him: Well after his intellectual questions had been answered, he continues to resist conversion because, to him, baptism means chastity. In fact, the most famous line in the *Confessions* is the prayer of his hot adolescence: "Grant me chastity and self-control, but please not yet."

---

2. Early Christian sect that adhered to a dualistic philosophy, i.e., a worldview that all phenomena are composed of opposites, such as good and evil.

3. Philosophy, modified from the teachings of Plato, that espouses belief in a single source, the One, from which all else emanates, and with which the soul can reunite in trance or ecstasy.

rhetorical situations

genres

processes

strategies

research mla/apa

media/ design

readings

Augustine was not the promiscuous lover of popular imagination 10 — or of his own description. From the age of nineteen he lived in complete and apparently happy fidelity with his girlfriend, a woman of lower rank with whom marriage was not a possibility. We never learn her name. She and Augustine have a child together, a son named Adeodatus (Gift of God) who, like Monica and several youthful friends, compose his intimate circle.

When Augustine does abandon this lover of his youth, it is to make a prudent marriage, a logical career move which Monica promoted. The break is shattering. His girlfriend, he says, "was ripped from my side. . . . So deeply was she engrafted into my heart that it was left torn and wounded and trailing blood." While he waited two years for the girl to whom he was engaged to reach marriageable age, he says, with the crudeness of a broken heart, that he "got myself another woman." But even this indulgence does not help: "The wound inflicted on me by the earlier separation did not heal. . . . After the fever and the immediate acute pain had dulled, it putrefied, and the pain became a cold despair."

Is it possible to read the *Confessions* today with the same urgency that Augustine brought to writing them? This is not simply a modern's self-admiring question about a late fourth-century book's "relevance" to our own secular age. It is a question Augustine would have appreciated, believing as he did in sorting things out for oneself. He refused, for example, to accept the glossy reputation of Faustus, the Manichee sage who proved, when frankly questioned, to be a charming phony. The blunt question of Augustine's appeal to the modern reader must be posed.

The answer lies in Augustine's literary self. With all the theological and cultural differences and all the history that divide us from Augustine's first readers, our recognition of the originality and power of the *Confessions* resides fundamentally in the same place—in his voice. Not because his is a magically "modern" voice from antiquity, somehow chumming up to the reader. In any case, the book isn't written to us.

It is addressed expressly to God. *Magnus es, Domine,* it begins: Great are you, Lord. Augustine claims in the first breath of the *Confessions* that his intention is the innate one — "we humans," he says simply, " . . . long to praise you." But the real voice of the book is one of inquiry. He wants to *know*. At times it is heartbreaking, even comic, to see Augustine struggle with the mystery of existence. "Was there nothing before . . . except the life I lived in my mother's womb?" he asks in Book I. "But then, my God, my sweetness, what came before that? Was I somewhere else? Was I even someone? I have nobody to tell me. . . . Are you laughing at me for asking you these questions?" Augustine is willing to look foolish, even before God, if it will get him below the surface of things. This willingness to risk being a fool for the truth, which is all that literary courage is, keeps Augustine young for the ages.

The habitual way of approaching the *Confessions* is to see Augustine   15 as a penitent, a man gazing with horror at his sinful past from the triumphant refuge of his conversion. Maybe the *Confessions* would have been such a book if Augustine had written them in 387, the year of his baptism and the death of Monica. It was certainly the great high-low year of his existence, the pivot of his life. But it is fully ten years after his baptism (a harrowing adult initiation experience, a true cult act signaling a changed life, not to be confused with the mild christening ceremonies of our own times) when Augustine turns to write the great searching book of his life.

The adjective is significant: What, after all, is a converted Christian properly searching for? Isn't the definition, the whole meaning of religious conversion, precisely that the great answer has been found, that one has moved from uncertainty to conviction? In its ardent, insistent questioning, the *Confessions* is not an ode. Like the Psalms of David, Augustine's great rhapsodic-furious model, it is a call to attention. But then, perhaps to call out to God, to demand a response, is to praise, though not in the pietistic way we routinely mistake as religious. The core of praise, for Augustine, lies in the fact that he, like all human beings, is so thoroughly God's creature that his *confessio*, his life quest for God, can never be finished. He was created to be that creature who beats its fists against the breast of the divine. "For Thou hast made us for Thyself," Augustine says on the first page of the *Confessions*, "and our hearts are restless till they rest in Thee."

Augustine's longing to know is not merely intellectual. He must know as one knows through love — by being known. *Deus, noverim te, noverim me,* he prays. God, let me know You and know myself. Probably no one since Job has inquired of his God as desperately and commandingly. Like Job, Augustine sees prayer as a form of thinking, a way of seeking truth, not a pious form of wishing. But Job is a character in a great primeval tale. Augustine, in the fine paradox of autobiography, is a character in a story *and* the narrator of that character. He bears in his voice the blood-beat of time. He belongs not to myth, but to history. As we do.

Engaging with the Text

1. A **LITERARY ANALYSIS** makes an argument about a text — how it works and/or what it means. What is Patricia Hampl's argument about Augustine's *Confessions?* Restate her **THESIS** in your own words.

   ▲ 137–46
   ◆ 251–52
   ▲ 141

2. Hampl challenges conventional **INTERPRETATIONS** of Augustine's *Confessions* that see him "as a penitent, a man gazing with horror at his sinful past from the triumphant refuge of his conversion." What **EVIDENCE** does she provide to support her analysis?

   ▲ 145

3. Hampl **CLASSIFIES** Augustine's *Confessions* as an autobiography. Could it be called a **MEMOIR?** What key features of an autobiography does she cite to support her classification, and could they be cited as features of a memoir? Why is the classification important?

   ◆ 260–65
   ▲ 147–52

4. Hampl explores why this ancient text continues to be appealing and relevant to contemporary readers, writing, "The answer lies in Augustine's literary self . . . in his voice." What does she means by this claim? How does she illustrate Augustine's "literary self"? What does she mean by "voice"?

5. *For Writing.* Identify a text that has been read by generations of readers (one of Plato's dialogues, perhaps, or Shakespeare's sonnets, or a *Canterbury Tale*) or that is read in high school (*To Kill a Mockingbird, Julius Caesar,* "Stopping by Woods on a Snowy Evening"). Why do you think this text is still read today? Write an **ANALYSIS** of the text that offers an explanation for its enduring popularity — or, conversely, that argues why it should no longer be read.

   ▲ 137–46

LESLIE MARMON SILKO

Language and Literature from a Pueblo Indian Perspective

Poet and fiction writer Leslie Marmon Silko grew up on the Laguna Pueblo Reservation in New Mexico. She is author of a collection of poetry, several novels, and a collection of essays, Yellow Woman and a Beauty of the Spirit: Essays on Native American Life Today *(1996), which addresses the cultural and social contexts that shape her poetry and fiction. The following essay began as a speech and first appeared in print in* English Literature: Opening Up the Canon *(1979), edited by Leslie A. Fiedler and Houston A. Baker. As you read, notice how Silko organizes her analysis and incorporates sample narratives to demonstrate the weblike, nonlinear pattern of Pueblo narratives.*

WHERE I COME FROM, the words most highly valued are those spoken from the heart, unpremeditated and unrehearsed. Among the Pueblo people, a written speech or statement is highly suspect because the true feelings of the speaker remain hidden as she reads words that are detached from the occasion and the audience. I have intentionally not written a formal paper because I want you to *hear* and to experience English in a structure that follows patterns from the oral tradition. For those of you accustomed to being taken from point A to point B to point C, this presentation may be somewhat difficult to follow. Pueblo expression resembles something like a spider's web — with many little threads radiating from the center, crisscrossing each other. As with the web, the structure emerges as it is made and you must simply listen and trust, as the Pueblo people do, that meaning will be made.

My task is a formidable one: I ask you to set aside a number of basic approaches that you have been using, and probably will continue to use, and instead, to approach language from the Pueblo perspective, one that embraces the whole of creation and the whole of history and time.

What changes would Pueblo writers make to English as a language for literature? I have some examples of stories in English that I will use

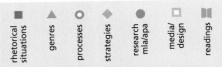

to address this question. At the same time, I would like to explain the importance of storytelling and how it relates to a Pueblo theory of language.

So I will begin, appropriately enough, with the Pueblo Creation story, an all-inclusive story of how life began. In this story, Tséitsínako, Thought Woman, by thinking of her sisters, and together with her sisters, thought of everything that is. In this way, the world was created. Everything in this world was a part of the original creation; the people at home understood that far away there were other human beings, also a part of this world. The Creation story even includes a prophecy, which describes the origin of European and African peoples and also refers to Asians.

This story, I think, suggests something about why the Pueblo people are more concerned with story and communication and less concerned with a particular language. There are at least six, possibly seven, distinct languages among the twenty pueblos of the southwestern United States, for example, Zuñi and Hopi. And from mesa to mesa there are subtle differences in language. But the particular language spoken isn't as important as what a speaker is trying to say, and this emphasis on the story itself stems, I believe, from a view of narrative particular to the Pueblo and other Native American peoples — that is, that language *is* story.

I will try to clarify this statement. At Laguna Pueblo, for example, many individual words have their own stories. So when one is telling a story, and one is using words to tell the story, each word that one is speaking has a story of its own, too. Often the speakers or tellers will go into these word-stories, creating an elaborate structure of stories-within-stories. This structure, which becomes very apparent in the actual telling of a story, informs contemporary Pueblo writing and storytelling as well as the traditional narratives. This perspective on narrative — of story within story, the idea that one story is only the beginning of many stories, and the sense that stories never truly end — represents an important contribution of Native American cultures to the English language.

Many people think of storytelling as something that is done at bedtime, that it is something done for small children. But when I use the term *storytelling,* I'm talking about something much bigger than that. I'm talking about something that comes out of an experience and an understanding of that original view of creation — that we are all part of a whole; we do not differentiate or fragment stories and experiences. In the beginning, Tséitsínako, Thought Woman, thought of all things, and all of these things are held together as one holds many things together in a single thought.

So in the telling (and you will hear a few of the dimensions of this telling) first of all, as mentioned earlier, the storytelling always includes the audience, the listeners. In fact, a great deal of the story is believed to be inside the listener; the storyteller's role is to draw the story out of the listeners. The storytelling continues from generation to generation.

Basically, the origin story constructs our identity — within this story, we know who we are. We are the Lagunas. This is where we come from. We came this way. We came by this place. And so from the time we are very young, we hear these stories, so that when we go out into the world, when one asks who we are, or where we are from, we immediately know: we are the people who came from the north. We are the people of these stories.

In the Creation story, Antelope says that he will help knock a hole 10 in the earth so that the people can come up, out into the next world. Antelope tries and tries; he uses his hooves, but is unable to break through. It is then that Badger says, "Let me help you." And Badger very patiently uses his claws and digs a way through, bringing the people into the world. When the Badger clan people think of themselves, or when the Antelope people think of themselves, it is as people who are of *this* story, and this is *our* place, and we fit into the very beginning when the people first came, before we began our journey south.

Within the clans there are stories that identify the clan. One moves, then, from the idea of one's identity as a tribal person into clan identity, then to one's identity as a member of an extended family. And it is the notion of "extended family" that has produced a kind of story that some distinguish from other Pueblo stories, though Pueblo people do not. Anthropologists and ethnologists have, for a long time, differentiated the types of stories the Pueblos tell. They tended to elevate the old,

sacred, and traditional stories and to brush aside family stories, the family's account of itself. But in Pueblo culture, these family stories are given equal recognition. There is no definite, present pattern for the way one will hear the stories of one's own family, but it is a very critical part of one's childhood, and the storytelling continues throughout one's life. One will hear stories of importance to the family — sometimes wonderful stories — stories about the time a maternal uncle got the biggest deer that was ever seen and brought it back from the mountains. And so an individual's identity will extend from the identity constructed around the family — "I am from the family of my uncle who brought in this wonderful deer and it was a wonderful hunt."

Family accounts include negative stories, too; perhaps an uncle did something unacceptable. It is very important that one keep track of all these stories — both positive and not so positive — about one's own family and other families. Because even when there is no way around it — old Uncle Pete *did* do a terrible thing — by knowing the stories that originate in other families, one is able to deal with terrible sorts of things that might happen within one's own family. If a member of the family does something that cannot be excused, one always knows stories about similar inexcusable things done by a member of another family. But this knowledge is not communicated for malicious reasons. It is very important to understand this. Keeping track of all the stories within the community gives us all a certain distance, a useful perspective, that brings incidents down to a level we can deal with. If others have done it before, it cannot be so terrible. If others have endured, so can we.

The stories are always bringing us together, keeping this whole together, keeping this family together, keeping this clan together. "Don't go away, don't isolate yourself, but come here, because we have all had these kinds of experiences." And so there is this constant pulling together to resist the tendency to run or hide or separate oneself during a traumatic emotional experience. This separation not only endangers the group but the individual as well — one does not recover by oneself.

Because storytelling lies at the heart of Pueblo culture, it is absurd to attempt to fix the stories in time. "When did they tell the stories?"

or "What time of day does the storytelling take place?" — these questions are nonsensical from a Pueblo perspective, because our storytelling goes on constantly: as some old grandmother puts on the shoes of a child and tells her the story of a little girl who didn't wear her shoes, for instance, or someone comes into the house for coffee to talk with a teenage boy who has just been in a lot of trouble, to reassure him that someone else's son has been in that kind of trouble, too. Storytelling is an ongoing process, working on many different levels.

Here's one story that is often told at a time of individual crisis (and   15
I want to remind you that we make no distinctions between types of story — historical, sacred, plain gossip — because these distinctions are not useful when discussing the Pueblo *experience* of language). There was a young man who, when he came back from the war in Vietnam, had saved up his army pay and bought a beautiful red Volkswagen. He was very proud of it. One night he drove up to a place called the King's Bar right across the reservation line. The bar is notorious for many reasons, particularly for the deep *arroyo*[1] located behind it. The young man ran in to pick up a cold six-pack, but he forgot to put on his emergency brake. And his little red Volkswagen rolled back into the *arroyo* and was all smashed up. He felt very bad about it, but within a few days everybody had come to him with stories about other people who had lost cars and family members to that *arroyo,* for instance, George Day's station wagon, with his mother-in-law and kids inside. So everybody was saying, "Well, at least your mother-in-law and kids weren't in the car when it rolled in," and one can't argue with that kind of story. The story of the young man and his smashed-up Volkswagen was now joined with all the other stories of cars that fell into that *arroyo.*

Now I want to tell you a very beautiful little story. It is a very old story that is sometimes told to people who suffer great family or personal loss. This story was told by my Aunt Susie. She is one of the first generation of people at Laguna who began experimenting with English — who began working to make English speak for us — that is, to speak from the heart. (I come from a family intent on getting the stories told.)

---

1. Ravine (Spanish). [*Editor*]

rhetorical situations   genres   processes   strategies   research mla/apa   media/ design   readings

As you read the story, I think you will hear that. And here and there, I think, you will also hear the influence of the Indian school[2] at Carlisle, Pennsylvania, where my Aunt Susie was sent (like being sent to prison) for six years.

This scene is set partly in Acoma, partly in Laguna. Waithea was a little girl living in Acoma and one day she said, "Mother, I would like to have some *yashtoah* to eat." *Yashtoah* is the hardened crust of corn mush that curls up. *Yashtoah* literally means "curled up." She said, "I would like to have some *yashtoah*," and her mother said, "My dear little girl, I can't make you any *yashtoah* because we haven't any wood, but if you will go down off the mesa, down below, and pick up some pieces of wood and bring them home, I will make you some *yashtoah*." So Waithea was glad and ran down the precipitous cliff of Acoma mesa. Down below, just as her mother had told her, there were pieces of wood, some curled, some crooked in shape, that she was to pick up and take home. She found just such wood as these.

She brought them home in a little wicker basket. First she called to her mother as she got home, "*Nayah, deeni!* Mother, upstairs!" The Pueblo people always called "upstairs" because long ago their homes were two, three stories, and they entered from the top. She said, "*Deeni! UPSTAIRS!*" and her mother came. The little girl said, "I have brought the wood you wanted me to bring." And she opened her little wicker basket to lay out the pieces of wood but here they were snakes. They were snakes instead of crooked sticks of wood. And her mother said, "Oh my dear child, you have brought snakes instead!" She said, "Go take them back and put them back just where you got them." And the little girl ran down the mesa again, down below to the flats. And she put those snakes back just where she got them. They were snakes instead and she was very hurt about this and so she said, "I'm not going home. I'm going to *Kawaik*, the beautiful lake place, *Kawaik*, and drown myself in the lake, *byn'yah'nah* [the "west lake"]. I will go there and drown myself."

---

2. The Carlisle Indian Industrial School, federally supported boarding school attended by more than 15,000 Native American children from 1879 to 1918. [*Editor*]

So she started off, and as she passed the Enchanted Mesa near Acoma she met an old man, very aged, and he saw her running, and he said, "My dear child, where are you going?" "I'm going to *Kawaik* and jump into the lake there." "Why?" "Well, because," she said, "my mother didn't want to make any *yashtoah* for me." The old man said, "Oh, no! You must not go my child. Come with me and I will take you home," He tried to catch her, but she was very light and skipped along. And every time he would try to grab her she would skip faster away from him.

The old man was coming home with some wood strapped to his 20 back and tied with yucca. He just let the strap go and let the wood drop. He went as fast as he could up the cliff to the little girl's home. When he got to the place where she lived, he called to her mother. *"Deeni!"* "Come on up!" And he said, "I can't. I just came to bring you a message. Your little daughter is running away. She is going to *Kawaik* to drown herself in the lake there." "Oh my dear little girl!" the mother said. So she busied herself with making the *yashtoah* her little girl liked so much. Corn mush curled at the top. (She must have found enough wood to boil the corn meal and make the *yashtoah*.)

While the mush was cooking off, she got the little girl's clothing, her *manta* dress[3] and buckskin moccasins and all her other garments, and put them in a bundle — probably a yucca bag. And she started down as fast a she could on the east side of Acoma. (There used to be a trail there, you know. It's gone now, but it was accessible in those days.) She saw her daughter way at a distance and she kept calling: "Stsamaku! My daughter! Come back! I've got your *yashtoah* for you." But the little girl would not turn. She kept on ahead and she cried: "My mother, my mother, she didn't want me to have any *yashtoah*. So now I'm going to *Kawaik* and drown myself." Her mother heard her cry and said, "My little daughter, come back here!" "No," and she kept a distance away from her. And they came nearer and nearer to the lake. And she could see her daughter now, very plain. "Come back, my daughter! I have your *yashtoah*." But no, she kept on, and finally she reached the lake and she stood on the edge.

---

3. Square, blanketlike cloth used as a cloak. [*Editor*]

rhetorical situations   genres   processes   strategies   research mla/apa   media/ design   readings

She had tied a little feather in her hair, which is traditional (in death they tie this feather on the head). She carried a feather, the little girl did, and she tied it in her hair with a piece of string, right on top of her head she put the feather. Just as her mother was about to reach her, she jumped into the lake. The little feather was whirling around and around in the depths below. Of course the mother was very sad. She went, grieved, back to Acoma and climbed her mesa home. She stood on the edge of the mesa and scattered her daughter's clothing, the little moccasins, the *yashtoah.* She scattered them to the east, to the west, to the north, to the south. And the pieces of clothing and the moccasions and *yashtoah,* all turned into butterflies. And today they say that Acoma has more beautiful butterflies: red ones, white ones, blue ones, yellow ones. They came from this little girl's clothing.

Now this is a story anthropologists would consider very old. The version I have given you is just as Aunt Susie tells it. You can occasionally hear some English she picked up at Carlisle — words like "precipitous." You will also notice that there is a great deal of repetition, and a little reminder about *yashtoah,* and how it is made. There is a remark about the cliff trail at Acoma — that it was once there, but is there no longer. This story may be told at a time of sadness or loss, but within this story many other elements are brought together. Things are not separated out and categorized; all things are brought together. So that the reminder about the *yashtoah* is valuable information that is repeated — a recipe, if you will. The information about the old trail at Acoma reveals that stories are, in a sense, maps, since even to this day there is little information or material about trails that is passed around with writing. In the structure of this story the repetitions are, of course, designed to help you remember. It is repeated again and again, and then it moves on.

The next story I would like to tell is by Simon Ortiz, from Acoma Pueblo. He is a wonderful poet who also works in narrative. One of the things I find very interesting in this short story is that if you listen very closely, you begin to hear what I was talking about in terms of a story never beginning at the beginning, and certainly never ending. As the Hopis sometimes say, "Well, it has gone this far for a while." There is always that implication of a continuing. The other thing I want you to listen for is the many stories within one story. Listen to the kinds of stories contained within the main story — stories that give one a family identity and an individual identity, for example. This story is called "Home Country":

"Well, it's been a while. I think in 1947 was when I left. My husband had been killed in Okinawa[4] some years before. And so I had no more husband. And I had to make a living. O I guess I could have looked for another man but I didn't want to. It looked like the war had made some of them into a bad way anyway. I saw some of them come home like that. They either got drunk or just stayed around a while or couldn't seem to be satisfied anymore with what was there. I guess now that I think about it, that happened to me although I wasn't in the war not in the Army or even much off the reservation just that several years at the Indian School. Well there was that feeling things were changing not only the men the boys, but things were changing.

"One day the home nurse the nurse that came from the Indian health service was at my mother's home my mother was getting near the end real sick and she said that she had been meaning to ask me a question. I said what is the question. And the home nurse said well your mother is getting real sick and after she is no longer around for you to take care of, what will you be doing you and her are the only ones here. And I said I don't know. But I was thinking about it what she said made me think about it. And then the next time she came she said to me Eloise the government is hiring Indians now in the Indian schools to take care of the boys and girls I heard one of the supervisors saying that Indians are hard workers but you have to supervise them a lot and I thought of you well because you've been taking care of your mother real good and you follow all my instructions. She said I thought of you because you're a good Indian girl and you would be the kind of person for that job. I didn't say anything I had not ever really thought about a job but I kept thinking about it.

"Well my mother she died and we buried her up at the old place the cemetery there it's real nice on the east side of the hill

---

4. Southernmost Japanese island, site of fierce fighting between Japanese and American forces in World War II. [*Editor*]

where the sun shines warm and the wind doesn't blow too much sand around right there. Well I was sad we were all sad for a while but you know how things are. One of my aunties came over and she advised me and warned me about being too sorry about it and all that she wished me that I would not worry too much about it because old folks they go along pretty soon life is that way and then she said that maybe I ought to take in one of my aunties kids or two because there was a lot of them kids and I was all by myself now. But I was so young and I thought that I might do that you know take care of someone but I had been thinking too of what the home nurse said to me about working. Hardly anybody at our home was working at something like that no woman anyway. And I would have to move away.

"Well I did just that. I remember that day very well. I told my aunties and they were all crying and we all went up to the old highway where the bus to town passes by every day. I was wearing an old kind of bluish sweater that was kind of big that one of my cousins who was older had got from a white person a tourist one summer in trade for something she had made a real pretty basket. She gave me that and I used to have a picture of me with it on it's kind of real ugly. Yeah that was the day I left wearing a baggy sweater and carrying a suitcase that someone gave me too I think or maybe it was the home nurse there wasn't much in it anyway either. I was scared and everybody seemed to be sad I was so young and skinny then. My aunties said one of them who was real fat you make sure you eat now make your own tortillas drink the milk and stuff like candies is no good she learned that from the nurse. Make sure you got your letter my auntie said. I had it folded into my purse. Yes I have one too a brown one that my husband when he was still alive one time on furlough he brought it on my birthday it was a nice purse and still looked new because I never used it.

"The letter said that I had a job at Keams Canyon the boarding school there but I would have to go to the Agency first for some papers to be filled and that's where I was going first. The Agency. And then they would send me out to Keams Canyon. I didn't even know where it was except that someone of our relatives said that it was near Hopi. My uncles teased me about watching out for the Hopi men and boys don't let them get too close they said well you know how they are and they were pretty strict too about those things and then they were joking and then they were not too and so I said aw they won't get near to me I'm too ugly and I promised I would be careful anyway.

"So we all gathered for a while at my last auntie's house and then the old man my grandfather brought his wagon and horses to the door and we all got in and sat there for a while until my auntie told her father okay father let's go and shook his elbow because the poor old man was old by then and kind of going to sleep all the time you had to talk to him real loud. I had about ten dollars I think that was a lot of money more than it is now you know and when we got to the highway where the Indian road which is just a dirt road goes off the pave road my grandfather reached into his blue jeans and pulled out a silver dollar and put it into my hand. I was so shocked. We were all so shocked. We all looked around at each other we didn't know where the old man had gotten it because we were real poor two of my uncles had to borrow on their accounts at the trading store for the money I had in my purse but there it was a silver dollar so big and shrinking in my grandfather's hand and then in my hand.

"Well I was so shocked and everybody was so shocked that we all started crying right there at the junction of that Indian road and the pave highway I wanted to be a little girl again running after the old man when he hurried with his long legs to the cornfields or went for water down to the river. He was old then and his eye was turned gray and he didn't do much anymore except drive the wagon and chop a little bit of wood but I just held him and I just held him so tightly.

"Later on I don't know what happened to the silver dollar it had a date of 1907 on it but I kept it for a long time because I guess I wanted to have it to remember when I left my home country. What I did in between then and now is another story but that's the time I moved away,"

is what she said.[5]

There are a great many parallels between Pueblo experiences and those of African and Caribbean peoples — one is that we have all had

25

---

5. Simon J. Ortiz, *Howabah Indians* (Tucson: Blue Moon Press, 1978).

the conqueror's language imposed on us. But our experience with English has been somewhat different in that the Bureau of Indian Affairs schools were not interested in teaching us the canon of Western classics. For instance, we never heard of Shakespeare. We were given Dick and Jane,[6] and I can remember reading that the robins were heading south for the winter. It took me a long time to figure out what was going on. I worried for quite a while about our robins in Laguna because they didn't leave in the winter, until I finally realized that all the big textbook companies are up in Boston and *their* robins do go south in the winter. But in a way, this dreadful formal education freed us by encouraging us to maintain our narratives. Whatever literature we were exposed to at school (which was damn little), at home the storytelling, the special regard for telling and bringing together through the telling, was going on constantly.

And as the old people say, "If you can remember the stories, you will be all right. Just remember the stories." When I returned to Laguna Pueblo after attending college, I wondered how the storytelling was continuing (anthropologists say that Laguna Pueblo is one of the more acculturated pueblos), so I visited an English class at Laguna Acoma High School. I knew the students had cassette tape recorders in their lockers and stereos at home, and that they listened to Kiss and Led Zeppelin and were all informed about popular culture in general. I had with me an anthology of short stories by Native American writers, *The Man to Send Rain Clouds*. One story in the book is about the killing of a state policeman in New Mexico by three Acoma Pueblo men in the early 1950s.[7] I asked the students how many had heard this story and steeled myself for the possibility that the anthropologists were right, that the old traditions were indeed dying out and the students would be ignorant of the story. But instead, all but one or two raised their hands —

---

6. Characters in an early-reading series common in American schools from the 1930s through the 1960s. [*Editor*]

7. See Simon J. Ortiz, "The Killing of a State Cop," in *The Man to Send Rain Clouds*, ed. Kenneth Rosen (New York: Viking Press, 1974), 101–108.

they had heard the story, just as I had heard it when I was young, some in English, some in Laguna.

One of the other advantages that we Pueblos have enjoyed is that we have always been able to stay with the land. Our stories cannot be separated from their geographical locations, from actual physical places on the land. We were not relocated like so many Native American groups who were torn away from their ancestral land. And our stories are so much a part of these places that it is almost impossible for future generations to lose them — there is a story connected with every place, every object in the landscape.

Dennis Brutus has talked about the "yet unborn" as well as "those from the past," and how we are still *all* in *this* place, and language — the storytelling — is our way of passing through or being with them, or being together again. When Aunt Susie told her stories, she would tell a younger child to go open the door so that our esteemed predecessors might bring in their gifts to us. "They are out there," Aunt Susie would say. "Let them come in. They're here, they're here with us *within* the stories."

A few years ago, when Aunt Susie was 106, I paid her a visit, and while I was there she said, "Well, I'll be leaving here soon. I think I'll be leaving here next week, and I will be going over to the Cliff House." She said, "It's going to be real good to get back over there." I was listening, and I was thinking that she must be talking about our house at Paguate Village, just north of Laguna. And she went on, "Well, my mother's sister (and she gave her Indian name) will be there. She has been living there. She will be there and we will be over there, and I will get a chance to write down these stories I've been telling you." Now you must understand, of course, that Aunt Susie's mother's sister, a great storyteller herself, has long since passed over into the land of the dead. But then I realized, too, that Aunt Susie wasn't talking about death the way most of us do. She was talking about "going over" as a journey, a journey that perhaps we can only begin to understand through an appreciation for the boundless capacity of language that, through storytelling, brings us together, despite great distances between cultures, despite great distances in time.

Engaging with the Text

1. Leslie Marmon Silko notes that for Pueblo and other Native American peoples "language is story." What does she mean by this claim? How does she **SUPPORT** this point?

   ▲ 145

2. How does Silko **DEFINE** "storytelling," and why is this definition central to her analysis?

   ◆ 275–84

3. Silko claims that one of the advantages that Pueblos have enjoyed is that "we have always been able to stay with the land. Our stories cannot be separated from their geographical locations, from actual physical places on the land." How do the stories she tells within her essay **SUPPORT** this point? Cite specific examples in your response.

   ▲ 145

4. Silko announces that readers "accustomed to being taken from point A to point B to point C" may find her text difficult to follow. **OUTLINE** the text to see how it is organized. What cues does Silko provide to **GUIDE READERS?**

   ◆ 319–22

   ◆ 250–54

5. *For Writing.* The structure of a literary work is often an excellent subject for analysis, as the way a poem, song, story, novel, or drama is structured strongly influences how we read it and how we interpret it. Choose a literary text you like, and **ANALYZE ITS STRUCTURE.** How does that structure affect the meaning of the text? Alternatively, select one of the stories Silko includes in her essay and analyze its structure. Discuss how it exemplifies the organization of "a spider's web — with many little threads radiating from the center, crisscrossing each other."

   ▲ 137–46

WILLOW D. CRYSTAL

"One of us . . . ":
Concepts of the Private and the Public in "A Rose for Emily"

The following essay was written in 2004 by Willow D. Crystal, a student at Harvard, as a model paper for The Norton Introduction to Literature. *As you read it, notice how Crystal draws on scholarly research to support her claims about the tensions between private and public constructs in Faulkner's "A Rose for Emily." See p. 700 if you want to read the story.*

T HROUGHOUT "A ROSE FOR EMILY," William Faulkner introduces a tension between what is private, or belongs to the individual, and what is public, or the possession of the group. "When Miss Emily Grierson died," the tale begins, "our whole town went to her funeral: the men through a sort of respectful affection for a fallen monument, the women mostly out of curiosity to see the inside of her house . . . " (700). The men of the small town of Jefferson, Mississippi, are motivated to attend Miss Emily's funeral for public reasons; the women, to see "the inside of her house," that private realm which has remained inaccessible for "at least ten years" (700).

This opposition of the private with the public has intrigued critics of Faulkner's tale since the story was first published. Distinctions between the private and the public are central to Lawrence R. Rodgers's argument in his essay " 'We all said, "she will kill herself" ': The Narrator/Detective in William Faulkner's 'A Rose for Emily.' " The very concept of the detective genre demands that "there must be concealed facts that . . . must become clear in the end" (119), private actions which become public knowledge. In her feminist tribute, "A Rose for 'A Rose for Emily,' " Judith Fetterley uses the private-public dichotomy to demonstrate the "grotesque reality" (34) of the patriarchal social system in Faulkner's story. According to Fetterley, Miss Emily's "private life becomes a public document that the town folk feel free to interpret at will" (36). Thus, while critics such as Rodgers and Fetterley offer convincing — if divergent — interpretations of "A Rose for Emily," it is necessary first to understand in Faulkner's eerie and enigmatic story the relationship between the public and the private, and the consequences of this relationship within the story and for the reader.

The most explicit illustration of the opposition between the public and the private occurs in the social and economic interactions between the town of Jefferson, represented by the narrator's "our" and "we," and the reclusive Miss Emily. "Alive," the narrator explains, "Miss Emily had been a tradition, a duty, and a care; a sort of hereditary obligation upon the town, dating from that day in 1894 when Colonel Sartoris, the mayor, . . . remitted her taxes, the dispensation dating from the death of her father on into perpetuity" (700–701). Ironically (and this is one of the prime examples of the complexity of the relationship of private and public in the story), the price of privacy for Miss Emily becomes the loss of that very privacy. Despite — or perhaps because of — her refusal to buy into the community, the citizens of Jefferson determine that it is their "duty," their "hereditary obligation," to oversee her activities. When, for example, Miss Emily's house begins to emit an unpleasant smell, the town officials decide to solve the problem by dusting her property with lime. When she refuses to provide a reason why she wants to buy poison, the druggist scrawls "For rats" (706) across the package, literally and protectively overwriting her silence.

Arguably, the townspeople's actions serve to protect Miss Emily's privacy — by preserving her perceived gentility — as much as they effectively destroy it with their intrusive zeal. But in this very act of protection they reaffirm the town's proprietary relation to the public "monument" that is Miss Emily and, consequently, reinforce her inability to make decisions for herself.

While the communal narrator and Miss Emily appear to be polar opposites — one standing for the public while the other fiercely defends her privacy — the two are united when an outsider such as Homer Barron appears in their midst. If Miss Emily serves as a representation — an icon, an inactive figure in a "tableau," an "idol" — of traditional antebellum southern values, then Homer represents all that is new and different. A "day laborer" (705) from the North, Homer comes to Jefferson to pave the sidewalks, a task which itself suggests the modernization of the town.

The secret and destructive union between these two representational figures implies a complex relationship between the private and the public. When Miss Emily kills Homer and confines his remains to a room in her attic, where, according to Rodgers, "she has been allowed to carry on her illicit love affair in post-mortem privacy" (119), this grotesque act ironically suggests that she has capitulated to the code of gentility that Jefferson imagines her to embody. This code demands the end of a romantic affair which some residents deemed "a disgrace to the town and a bad example to the young people" (706), thus placing tradition and the good of the community above Miss Emily's own wishes. Through its insistence on Miss Emily's symbolic relation to a bygone era, the town — via the narrator — becomes "an unknowing driving force behind Emily's crime" (Rodgers 120). Her private act is both the result of and a support for public norms and expectations.

At the same time, however, the act of murder also marks Miss Emily's corruption of that very code. By killing Homer in private, Miss Emily deliberately flouts public norms, and by eluding explicit detection until after her own death, she asserts the primacy of the private. The murder of the outsider in their midst thus leads Miss Emily to achieve paradoxically both a more complete privacy — a marriage of sorts without a husband — and a role in the preservation of the community.

Yet the elaborate relationship between Jefferson and Miss Emily is not the only way in which Homer's murder may be understood as a casualty of the tension between the public and the private. When Miss Emily kills Homer, Rodgers contends, "from the town's point of view, it was the best thing. . . . Homer represents the kind of unwelcomed resident and ineligible mate the town wants to repel if it is to preserve its traditional arrangements" (125). The people of Jefferson and Miss Emily join in a struggle to "repel" the outside and to ensure a private, inner order and tradition. This complicity creates intriguing parallels between the illicit, fatal union of Homer and Miss Emily and the reunion of the North and the South following the Civil War. In this reformulation of the private and the public, Miss Emily becomes, as Fetterley notes, a "metaphor and mirror for the town of Jefferson" (43). Miss Emily's honor is the townspeople's honor, her preservation their preservation.

Finally, the parallels between Miss Emily's secretive habits and the narrator's circuitous presentation of the story lead to a third dimension of the negotiations between the private and the public in "A Rose for Emily," a dimension in which Faulkner as author and the collective "we" as narrator confront their public consumers, the readers. Told by the anonymous narrator as if retrospectively, "A Rose for Emily" skips forward and back in time, omitting details and deferring revelations to such a degree that many critics have gone to extreme lengths to establish reliable chronologies for the tale. The much-debated "we" remains anonymous and unreachable throughout the tale — maintaining a virtually unbreachable privacy — even as it invites the public (the reader) to participate in the narrator's acts of detection and revelation. Rodgers observes:

> The dramatic distance on display here provides an ironic layer to the narrative. As the observers of the conflict between the teller-of-tale's desire to solve the curious mysteries that surround Emily's life — indeed, his complicity in shaping them — and his undetec-tive-like detachment from her crimes, readers occupy the tantalizing position of having insight into unraveling the mystery which the narrator lacks. (120–21)

The reader is thus a member of the communal "we" — party to the narrator's investigation and Jefferson's voyeuristic obsession with Miss Emily — but also apart, removed to a plane from which "insight" into and observation of the narrator's own actions and motives become possible. The reader, just like Miss Emily, Homer, and the town of Jefferson itself, becomes a crucial element in the tension between the public and the private.

Thus, public and private are, in the end, far from exclusive categories. And for all of its literal as well as figurative insistence on opposition and either/or structures, Faulkner's "A Rose for Emily" enacts the provocative idea of being "[o]ne of us" (709), of being both an individual and a member of a community, both a private entity and a participant in the public sphere.

Works Cited

Faulkner, William. "A Rose for Emily." *The Norton Field Guide to Writing, with Readings.* Ed. Richard Bullock and Maureen Daly Goggin. New York: Norton, 2007. 700–709.

Fetterley, Judith. "A Rose for 'A Rose for Emily.' " *The Resisting Reader: A Feminist Approach to American Fiction.* Bloomington: Indiana UP, 1978. 34–45.

Moore, Gene M. "Of Time and Its Mathematical Progression: Problems of Chronology in Faulkner's 'A Rose for Emily.' " *Studies in Short Fiction* 29 (1992): 195–204.

Rodgers, Lawrence R. " 'We all said, "she will kill herself" ': The Narrator/Detective in William Faulkner's 'A Rose for Emily.' " *Clues: A Journal of Detection* 16 (1995): 117–29.

Engaging with the Text

251–52 1. What is Willow Crystal's **THESIS?** Restate it in your own words. Read "A Rose for Emily" (on pp. 700–709) yourself. Do you agree with Crystal's analysis? Why or why not?

2. Crystal focuses on three examples of the tensions between concepts of public and private. What do these examples contribute to her **ANALYSIS?**

137–46

12–14 3. How would you characterize Crystal's **STANCE** toward Faulkner's story? Identify specific language in her essay that reveals that stance.

367–69 4. How does Crystal **INCORPORATE OTHER SCHOLARSHIP** on Faulkner's story into her analysis? How does she use this scholarship to support her own analysis?

137–46 5. *For Writing.* **ANALYZE** a literary work that intrigues you. You may base a literary analysis on your own reading and thinking about a text.

rhetorical situations   genres   processes   strategies   research mla/apa   media/ design   readings

However, your analysis may be enriched by knowing what others have written about the text as well. **RESEARCH** scholarship on the literary piece to see what other scholars may have said about it. Write an essay that both presents your own analysis and also responds to what others say about the same work. You can agree with what they say, disagree, or both; the important thing is to think about what others say, and to **QUOTE**, **PARAPHRASE**, or **SUMMARIZE** their views in your text.

● 333–57

● 358–69

WILLIAM FAULKNER

A Rose for Emily

William Faulkner (1897–1962) is the author of twenty novels, including The Sound and the Fury *(1929),* As I Lay Dying *(1930), and* Absalom! Absalom! *(1936), as well as many short stories and six books of poetry. He received the Nobel Prize for Literature in 1949 and Pulitzer Prizes in 1954 and 1962. The story "A Rose for Emily" was first published in 1931.*

WHEN MISS EMILY GRIERSON DIED, our whole town went to her funeral: the men through a sort of respectful affection for a fallen monument, the women mostly out of curiosity to see the inside of her house, which no one save an old man-servant — a combined gardener and cook — had seen in at least ten years.

It was a big, squarish frame house that had once been white, decorated with cupolas and spires and scrolled balconies in the heavily lightsome style of the seventies,[1] set on what had once been our most select street. But garages and cotton gins had encroached and obliterated even the august names of that neighborhood; only Miss Emily's house was left, lifting its stubborn and coquettish decay above the cotton wagons and the gasoline pumps — an eyesore among eyesores. And now Miss Emily had gone to join the representatives of those august names where they lay in the cedar-bemused cemetery among the ranked and anonymous graves of Union and Confederate soldiers who fell at the battle of Jefferson.

Alive, Miss Emily had been a tradition, a duty, and a care; a sort of hereditary obligation upon the town, dating from that day in 1894 when Colonel Sartoris, the mayor — he who fathered the edict that no Negro woman should appear on the streets without an apron — remitted her taxes, the dispensation dating from the death of her father on into per-

---

1. The 1870s, the decade after the Civil War (1861–65).

petuity. Not that Miss Emily would have accepted charity. Colonel Sartoris invented an involved tale to the effect that Miss Emily's father had loaned money to the town, which the town, as a matter of business, preferred this way of repaying. Only a man of Colonel Sartoris' generation and thought could have invented it, and only a woman could have believed it.

When the next generation, with its more modern ideas, became mayors and aldermen, this arrangement created some little dissatisfaction. On the first of the year they mailed her a tax notice. February came, and there was no reply. They wrote her a formal letter, asking her to call at the sheriff's office at her convenience. A week later the mayor wrote her himself, offering to call or to send his car for her, and received in reply a note on paper of an archaic shape, in a thin, flowing calligraphy in faded ink, to the effect that she no longer went out at all. The tax notice was also enclosed, without comment.

They called a special meeting of the Board of Aldermen. A deputation waited upon her, knocked at the door through which no visitor had passed since she ceased giving china-painting lessons eight or ten years earlier. They were admitted by the old Negro into a dim hall from which a stairway mounted into still more shadow. It smelled of dust and disuse — a close, dank smell. The Negro led them into the parlor. It was furnished in heavy, leather-covered furniture. When the Negro opened the blinds of one window, a faint dust rose sluggishly about their thighs, spinning with slow motes in the single sun-ray. On a tarnished gilt easel before the fireplace stood a crayon portrait of Miss Emily's father.

They rose when she entered — a small, fat woman in black, with a thin gold chain descending to her waist and vanishing into her belt, leaning on an ebony cane with a tarnished gold head. Her skeleton was small and spare; perhaps that was why what would have been merely plumpness in another was obesity in her. She looked bloated, like a body long submerged in motionless water, and of that pallid hue. Her eyes, lost in the fatty ridges of her face, looked like two small pieces of coal pressed into a lump of dough as they moved from one face to another while the visitors stated their errand.

She did not ask them to sit. She just stood in the door and listened quietly until the spokesman came to a stumbling halt. Then they could hear the invisible watch ticking at the end of the gold chain.

Her voice was dry and cold. "I have no taxes in Jefferson. Colonel Sartoris explained it to me. Perhaps one of you can gain access to the city records and satisfy yourselves."

"But we have. We are the city authorities, Miss Emily. Didn't you get a notice from the sheriff, signed by him?"

"I received a paper, yes," Miss Emily said. "Perhaps he considers   10 himself the sheriff. . . . I have no taxes in Jefferson."

"But there is nothing on the books to show that, you see. We must go by the — "

"See Colonel Sartoris. I have no taxes in Jefferson."

"But, Miss Emily — "

"See Colonel Sartoris." (Colonel Sartoris had been dead almost ten years.) "I have no taxes in Jefferson. Tobe!" The Negro appeared. "Show these gentlemen out."

II

So she vanquished them, horse and foot, just as she had vanquished   15 their fathers thirty years before about the smell. That was two years after her father's death and a short time after her sweetheart — the one we believed would marry her — had deserted her. After her father's death she went out very little; after her sweetheart went away, people hardly saw her at all. A few of the ladies had the temerity to call, but were not received, and the only sign of life about the place was the Negro man — a young man then — going in and out with a market basket.

"Just as if a man — any man — could keep a kitchen properly," the ladies said; so they were not surprised when the smell developed. It was another link between the gross, teeming world and the high and mighty Griersons.

A neighbor, a woman, complained to the mayor, Judge Stevens, eighty years old.

"But what will you have me do about it, madam?" he said.

"Why, send her word to stop it," the woman said. "Isn't there a law?"

"I'm sure that won't be necessary," Judge Stevens said. "It's proba-   20
bly just a snake or a rat that nigger of hers killed in the yard. I'll speak
to him about it."

The next day he received two more complaints, one from a man
who came in diffident deprecation. "We really must do something about
it, Judge. I'd be the last one in the world to bother Miss Emily, but we've
got to do something." That night the Board of Aldermen met — three
gray-beards and one younger man, a member of the rising generation.

"It's simple enough," he said. "Send her word to have her place
cleaned up. Give her a certain time to do it in, and if she don't . . . "

"Dammit, sir," Judge Stevens said, "will you accuse a lady to her
face of smelling bad?"

So the next night, after midnight, four men crossed Miss Emily's
lawn and slunk about the house like burglars, sniffing along the base of
the brickwork and at the cellar openings while one of them performed
a regular sowing motion with his hand out of a sack slung from his
shoulder. They broke open the cellar door and sprinkled lime there, and
in all the outbuildings. As they recrossed the lawn, a window that had
been dark was lighted and Miss Emily sat in it, the light behind her, and
her upright torso motionless as that of an idol. They crept quietly across
the lawn and into the shadow of the locusts that lined the street. After
a week or two the smell went away.

That was when people had begun to feel really sorry for her. Peo-   25
ple in our town, remembering how old lady Wyatt, her great-aunt, had
gone completely crazy at last, believed that the Griersons held themselves a little too high for what they really were. None of the young men
were quite good enough for Miss Emily and such. We had long thought
of them as a tableau; Miss Emily a slender figure in white in the background, her father a spraddled silhouette in the foreground, his back to
her and clutching a horsewhip, the two of them framed by the back-
flung front door. So when she got to be thirty and was still single, we
were not pleased exactly, but vindicated; even with insanity in the family she wouldn't have turned down all of her chances if they had really
materialized.

When her father died, it got about that the house was all that was left to her; and in a way, people were glad. At last they could pity Miss Emily. Being left alone, and a pauper, she had become humanized. Now she too would know the old thrill and the old despair of a penny more or less.

The day after his death all the ladies prepared to call at the house and offer condolence and aid, as is our custom. Miss Emily met them at the door, dressed as usual and with no trace of grief on her face. She told them that her father was not dead. She did that for three days, with the ministers calling on her, and the doctors, trying to persuade her to let them dispose of the body. Just as they were about to resort to law and force, she broke down, and they buried her father quickly.

We did not say she was crazy then. We believed she had to do that. We remembered all the young men her father had driven away, and we knew that with nothing left, she would have to cling to that which had robbed her, as people will.

III

She was sick for a long time. When we saw her again, her hair was cut short, making her look like a girl, with a vague resemblance to those angels in colored church windows — sort of tragic and serene.

The town had just let the contracts for paving the sidewalks, and   30 in the summer after her father's death they began to work. The construction company came with niggers and mules and machinery, and a foreman named Homer Barron, a Yankee — a big, dark, ready man, with a big voice and eyes lighter than his face. The little boys would follow in groups to hear him cuss the niggers, and the niggers singing in time to the rise and fall of picks. Pretty soon he knew everybody in town. Whenever you heard a lot of laughing anywhere about the square, Homer Barron would be in the center of the group. Presently we began to see him and Miss Emily on Sunday afternoons driving in the yellow-wheeled buggy and the matched team of bays from the livery stable.

At first we were glad that Miss Emily would have an interest, because the ladies all said, "Of course a Grierson would not think seri-

rhetorical situations · genres · processes · strategies · research mla/apa · media/ design · readings

ously of a Northerner, a day laborer." But there were still others, older people, who said that even grief could not cause a real lady to forget *noblesse oblige* — without calling it *noblesse oblige*.[2] They just said, "Poor Emily. Her kinsfolk should come to her." She had some kin in Alabama; but years ago her father had fallen out with them over the estate of old lady Wyatt, the crazy woman, and there was no communication between the two families. They had not even been represented at the funeral.

And as soon as the old people said, "Poor Emily," the whispering began. "Do you suppose it's really so?" they said to one another. "Of course it is. What else could . . . " This behind their hands; rustling of craned silk and satin behind jalousies[3] closed upon the sun of Sunday afternoon as the thin, swift clop-clop-clop of the matched team passed: "Poor Emily."

She carried her head high enough — even when we believed that she was fallen. It was as if she demanded more than ever the recognition of her dignity as the last Grierson; as if it had wanted that touch of earthiness to reaffirm her imperviousness. Like when she bought the rat poison, the arsenic. That was over a year after they had begun to say "Poor Emily," and while the two female cousins were visiting her.

"I want some poison," she said to the druggist. She was over thirty then, still a slight woman, though thinner than usual, with cold, haughty black eyes in a face the flesh of which was strained across the temples and about the eyesockets as you imagine a lighthouse-keeper's face ought to look. "I want some poison," she said.

"Yes, Miss Emily. What kind? For rats and such? I'd recom — "   35

"I want the best you have. I don't care what kind."

The druggist named several. "They'll kill anything up to an elephant. But what you want is — "

"Arsenic," Miss Emily said. "Is that a good one?"

"Is . . . arsenic? Yes ma'am. But what you want — "

---

2. The traditional obligation of the nobility to treat the lower classes with respect and generosity (French).

3. Slatted window blinds.

"I want arsenic."   40

The druggist looked down at her. She looked back at him, erect, her face like a strained flag. "Why, of course," the druggist said. "If that's what you want. But the law requires you to tell what you are going to use it for."

Miss Emily just stared at him, her head tilted back in order to look him eye for eye, until he looked away and went and got the arsenic and wrapped it up. The Negro delivery boy brought her the package; the druggist didn't come back. When she opened the package at home there was written on the box, under the skull and bones: "For rats."

IV

So the next day we all said, "She will kill herself"; and we said it would be the best thing. When she had first begun to be seen with Homer Barron, we had said, "She will marry him." Then we said, "She will persuade him yet," because Homer himself had remarked — he liked men, and it was known that he drank with the younger men in the Elk's Club — that he was not a marrying man. Later we said, "Poor Emily," behind the jalousies as they passed on Sunday afternoon in the glittering buggy, Miss Emily with her head high and Homer Barron with his hat cocked and a cigar in his teeth, reins and whip in a yellow glove.

Then some of the ladies began to say that it was a disgrace to the town and a bad example to the young people. The men did not want to interfere, but at last the ladies forced the Baptist minister — Miss Emily's people were Episcopal — to call upon her. He would never divulge what happened during that interview, but he refused to go back again. The next Sunday they again drove about the streets, and the following day the minister's wife wrote to Miss Emily's relations in Alabama.

So she had blood-kin under her roof again and we sat back to watch   45
developments. At first nothing happened. Then we were sure that they were to be married. We learned that Miss Emily had been to the jeweler's and ordered a man's toilet set in silver, with the letters H. B. on each piece. Two days later we learned that she had bought a complete outfit of men's clothing, including a nightshirt, and we said, "They are

married." We were really glad. We were glad because the two female cousins were even more Grierson than Miss Emily had ever been.

So we were not surprised when Homer Barron — the streets had been finished some time since — was gone. We were a little disappointed that there was not a public blowing-off, but we believed that he had gone on to prepare for Miss Emily's coming, or to give her a chance to get rid of the cousins. (By that time it was a cabal, and we were all Miss Emily's allies to help circumvent the cousins.) Sure enough, after another week they departed. And, as we had expected all along, within three days Homer Barron was back in town. A neighbor saw the Negro man admit him at the kitchen door at dusk one evening.

And that was the last we saw of Homer Barron. And of Miss Emily for some time. The Negro man went in and out with the market basket, but the front door remained closed. Now and then we would see her at a window for a moment, as the men did that night when they sprinkled the lime, but for almost six months she did not appear on the streets. Then we knew that this was to be expected too; as if that quality of her father which had thwarted her woman's life so many times had been too virulent and too furious to die.

When we next saw Miss Emily, she had grown fat and her hair was turning gray. During the next few years it grew grayer and grayer until it attained an even pepper-and-salt iron-gray, when it ceased turning. Up to the day of her death at seventy-four it was still that vigorous iron-gray, like the hair of an active man.

From that time on her front door remained closed, save for a period of six or seven years, when she was about forty, during which she gave lessons in china-painting. She fitted up a studio in one of the downstairs rooms, where the daughters and grand-daughters of Colonel Sartoris' contemporaries were sent to her with the same regularity and in the same spirit that they were sent on Sundays with a twenty-five cent piece for the collection plate. Meanwhile her taxes had been remitted.

Then the newer generation became the backbone and the spirit of 50 the town, and the painting pupils grew up and fell away and did not send their children to her with boxes of color and tedious brushes and pictures cut from the ladies' magazines. The front door closed upon the last one and remained closed for good. When the town got free postal delivery Miss Emily alone refused to let them fasten the metal numbers above her door and attach a mailbox to it. She would not listen to them.

Daily, monthly, yearly we watched the Negro grow grayer and more stooped, going in and out with the market basket. Each December we sent her a tax notice, which would be returned by the post office a week later, unclaimed. Now and then we would see her in one of the downstairs windows — she had evidently shut up the top floor of the house — like the carven torso of an idol in a niche, looking or not looking at us, we could never tell which. Thus she passed from generation to generation — dear, inescapable, impervious, tranquil, and perverse.

And so she died. Fell ill in the house filled with dust and shadows, with only a doddering Negro man to wait on her. We did not even know she was sick; we had long since given up trying to get any information from the Negro. He talked to no one, probably not even to her, for his voice had grown harsh and rusty, as if from disuse.

She died in one of the downstairs rooms, in a heavy walnut bed with a curtain, her gray head propped on a pillow yellow and moldy with age and lack of sunlight.

V

The Negro met the first of the ladies at the front door and let them in, with their hushed, sibilant voices and their quick, curious glances, and then he disappeared. He walked right through the house and out the back and was not seen again.

The two female cousins came at once. They held the funeral on the second day, with the town coming to look at Miss Emily beneath a mass of bought flowers, with the crayon face of her father musing profoundly above the bier and the ladies sibilant and macabre; and the very old men — some in their brushed Confederate uniforms — on the porch and the lawn, talking of Miss Emily as if she had been a contemporary of theirs, believing that they had danced with her and courted her perhaps, confusing time with its mathematical progression, as the old do, to whom all the past is not a diminishing road, but, instead, a huge

55

■ rhetorical situations ▲ genres ○ processes ◆ strategies ● research mla/apa ▢ media/ design ▮▮ readings

meadow which no winter ever quite touches, divided from them now by the narrow bottleneck of the most recent decade of years.

Already we knew that there was one room in that region above stairs which no one had seen in forty years, and which would have to be forced. They waited until Miss Emily was decently in the ground before they opened it.

The violence of breaking down the door seemed to fill this room with pervading dust. A thin, acrid pall as of the tomb seemed to lie everywhere upon this room decked and furnished as for a bridal: upon the valance curtains of faded rose color, upon the rose-shaded lights, upon the dressing table, upon the delicate array of crystal and the man's toilet things backed with tarnished silver, silver so tarnished that the monogram was obscured. Among them lay a collar and tie, as if they had just been removed, which, lifted, left upon the surface a pale crescent in the dust. Upon a chair hung the suit, carefully folded; beneath it the two mute shoes and the discarded socks.

The man himself lay in the bed.

For a long while we just stood there, looking down at the profound and fleshless grin. The body had apparently once lain in the attitude of an embrace, but now the long sleep that outlasts love, that conquers even the grimace of love, had cuckolded him. What was left of him, rotted beneath what was left of the nightshirt, had become inextricable from the bed in which he lay; and upon him and upon the pillow beside him lay that even coating of the patient and biding dust.

Then we noticed that in the second pillow was the indentation of 60 a head. One of us lifted something from it, and leaning forward, that faint and invisible dust dry and acrid in the nostrils, we saw a long strand of iron-gray hair.

RITA DOVE

Rita Dove (b. 1952) is a professor of English at the University of Virginia and a former Poet Laureate of the United States. She is the author of eight books of poetry, including Thomas and Beulah *(1986) and* American Smooth *(2004), as well as a book of short stories, a novel, a book of essays, and a play. She has received several awards for her writing, including the Pulitzer Prize in Poetry and the National Humanities Medal. Her poems "Dawn Revisited" and "The First Book" appear in* On the Bus with Rosa Parks *(1999).*

Dawn Revisited

Imagine you wake up
with a second chance: The blue jay
hawks his pretty wares
and the oak still stands, spreading
glorious shade. If you don't look back,   5

the future never happens.
How good to rise in sunlight,
in the prodigal smell of biscuits —
eggs and sausage on the grill.
The whole sky is yours   10

to write on, blown open
to a blank page. Come on,
shake a leg! You'll never know
who's down there, frying those eggs,
if you don't get up and see.   15

rhetorical situations   genres   processes   strategies   research mla/apa   media/design   readings

The First Book

Open it.

Go ahead, it won't bite.
Well . . . maybe a little.

More a nip, like. A tingle.
It's pleasurable, really.   5

You see, it keeps on opening.
You may fall in.

Sure, it's hard to get started;
remember learning to use

knife and fork? Dig in: 10
You'll never reach bottom.

It's not like it's the end of the world —
just the world as you think

you know it.

DYLAN THOMAS

Welsh poet Dylan Thomas (1914–1953) is the author of ten collections of poetry; a radio play, Under Milk Wood *(1954); and several essays and short stories. "Fern Hill" was first published in 1946; "Do Not Go Gentle into That Good Night," in 1952.*

Fern Hill[1]

Now as I was young and easy under the apple boughs
About the lilting house and happy as the grass was green,
    The night above the dingle[2] starry,
      Time let me hail and climb
    Golden in the heydays of his eyes,   5
And honoured among wagons I was prince of the apple towns
And once below a time I lordly had the trees and leaves
      Trail with daisies and barley
    Down the rivers of the windfall light.

And as I was green and carefree, famous among the barns   10
About the happy yard and singing as the farm was home,
    In the sun that is young once only,
      Time let me play and be
    Golden in the mercy of his means,
And green and golden I was huntsman and herdsman, the calves   15
Sang to my horn, the foxes on the hills barked clear and cold,
      And the sabbath rang slowly
    In the pebbles of the holy streams.

All the sun long it was running, it was lovely, the hay
Fields high as the house, the tunes from the chimneys, it was air   20
    And playing, lovely and watery
      And fire green as grass.
    And nightly under the simple stars

---

1. Name of Thomas's aunt's farm in Wales; Thomas spent his boyhood summers there.
2. A small forested valley.

rhetorical situations   genres   processes   strategies   research mla/apa   media/ design   readings

As I rode to sleep the owls were bearing the farm away,
All the moon long I heard, blessed among stables, the night-jars   25
    Flying with the ricks,[3] and the horses
        Flashing into the dark.

And then to awake, and the farm, like a wanderer white
With the dew, come back, the cock on his shoulder: it was all
    Shining, it was Adam and maiden,   30
        The sky gathered again
    And the sun grew round that very day.
So it must have been after the birth of the simple light
In the first, spinning place, the spellbound horses walking warm
    Out of the whinnying green stable   35
        On to the fields of praise.

And honoured among foxes and pheasants by the gay house
Under the new made clouds and happy as the heart was long,
    In the sun born over and over,
        I ran my heedless ways,   40
    My wishes raced through the house high hay
And nothing I cared, at my sky blue trades, that time allows
In all his tuneful turning so few and such morning songs
    Before the children green and golden
        Follow him out of grace,   45

Nothing I cared, in the lamb white days, that time would take me
Up to the swallow thronged loft by the shadow of my hand,
    In the moon that is always rising,
        Nor that riding to sleep
    I should hear him fly with the high fields   50
And wake to the farm forever fled from the childless land.
Oh as I was young and easy in the mercy of his means,
        Time held me green and dying
    Though I sang in my chains like the sea.

---

3. Haystacks. *Night-jars:* birds such as whip-poor-wills that feed on flying insects
after sunset.

Do Not Go Gentle into That Good Night

Do not go gentle into that good night,
Old age should burn and rave at close of day;
Rage, rage against the dying of the light.

Though wise men at their end know dark is right,
Because their words had forked no lightning they   5
Do not go gentle into that good night.

Good men, the last wave by, crying how bright
Their frail deeds might have danced in a green bay,
Rage, rage against the dying of the light.

Wild men who caught and sang the sun in flight,   10
And learn, too late, they grieved it on its way,
Do not go gentle into that good night.

Grave men, near death, who see with blinding sight
Blind eyes could blaze like meteors and be gay,
Rage, rage against the dying of the light.   15

And you, my father, there on the sad height,
Curse, bless, me now with your fierce tears, I pray.
Do not go gentle into that good night.
Rage, rage against the dying of the light.

Memoirs 56

rhetorical situations

genres

processes

strategies

research mla/apa

media/ design

readings

DAVID SEDARIS

Us and Them

Humorist David Sedaris is the author of several collections of personal essays, including Naked *(1997) and* Me Talk Pretty One Day *(2000). He is a frequent commentator on National Public Radio and a playwright whose works include* SantaLand Diaries & Seasons Greetings: 2 Plays *(1998), as well as works coauthored with his sister, Amy Sedaris. In 2001,* Time *magazine named Sedaris "Humorist of the Year." The following essay comes from Sedaris's book-length memoir* Dress Your Family in Corduroy and Denim *(2004).*

WHEN MY FAMILY FIRST MOVED to North Carolina, we lived in a rented house three blocks from the school where I would begin the third grade. My mother made friends with one of the neighbors, but one seemed enough for her. Within a year we would move again and, as she explained, there wasn't much point in getting too close to people we would have to say good-bye to. Our next house was less than a mile away, and the short journey would hardly merit tears or even good-byes, for that matter. It was more of a "see you later" situation, but still I adopted my mother's attitude, as it allowed me to pretend that not making friends was a conscious choice. I could if I wanted to. It just wasn't the right time.

Back in New York State, we had lived in the country, with no sidewalks or streetlights; you could leave the house and still be alone. But here, when you looked out the window, you saw other houses, and people inside those houses. I hoped that in walking around after dark I might witness a murder, but for the most part our neighbors just sat in their living rooms, watching TV. The only place that seemed truly different was owned by a man named Mr. Tomkey, who did not believe in television. This was told to us by our mother's friend, who dropped by one afternoon with a basketful of okra. The woman did not editorialize — rather, she just presented her information, leaving her listener to make of it what she might. Had my mother said, "That's the craziest thing I've ever heard in my life," I assume that the friend would have agreed, and had she said, "Three cheers for Mr. Tomkey," the friend likely would have agreed as well. It was a kind of test, as was the okra.

To say that you did not believe in television was different from saying that you did not care for it. Belief implied that television had a master plan and that you were against it. It also suggested that you thought too much. When my mother reported that Mr. Tomkey did not believe in television, my father said, "Well, good for him. I don't know that I believe in it, either."

"That's exactly how I feel," my mother said, and then my parents watched the news, and whatever came on after the news.

Word spread that Mr. Tomkey did not own a television, and you began 5 hearing that while this was all very well and good, it was unfair of him to inflict his beliefs upon others, specifically his innocent wife and children. It was speculated that just as the blind man develops a keener sense of hearing, the family must somehow compensate for their loss. "Maybe they read," my mother's friend said. "Maybe they listen to the radio, but you can bet your boots they're doing *something*."

I wanted to know what this something was, and so I began peering through the Tomkeys' windows. During the day I'd stand across the street from their house, acting as though I were waiting for someone, and at night, when the view was better and I had less chance of being discovered, I would creep into their yard and hide in the bushes beside their fence.

Because they had no TV, the Tomkeys were forced to talk during dinner. They had no idea how puny their lives were, and so they were not ashamed that a camera would have found them uninteresting. They did not know what attractive was or what dinner was supposed to look like or even what time people were supposed to eat. Sometimes they wouldn't sit down until eight o'clock, long after everyone else had finished doing the dishes. During the meal, Mr. Tomkey would occasionally pound the table and point at his children with a fork, but the moment he finished, everyone would start laughing. I got the idea that he was imitating someone else, and wondered if he spied on us while we were eating.

When fall arrived and school began, I saw the Tomkey children marching up the hill with paper sacks in their hands. The son was one grade lower than me, and the daughter was one grade higher. We never spoke, but I'd pass them in the halls from time to time and attempt to view the world through their eyes. What must it be like to be so ignorant and alone? Could a normal person even imagine it? Staring at an Elmer Fudd lunch box, I tried to divorce myself from everything I already knew: Elmer's inability to pronounce the letter *r*, his constant pursuit of an intelligent and considerably more famous rabbit. I tried to think of him as just a drawing, but it was impossible to separate him from his celebrity.

One day in class a boy named William began to write the wrong answer on the blackboard, and our teacher flailed her arms, saying, "Warning, Will. Danger, danger." Her voice was synthetic and void of emotion, and we laughed, knowing that she was imitating the robot in a weekly show about a family who lived in outer space. The Tomkeys, though, would have thought she was having a heart attack. It occurred to me that they needed a guide, someone who could accompany them through the course of an average day and point out all the things they were unable to understand. I could have done it on weekends, but friendship would have taken away their mystery and interfered with the good feeling I got from pitying them. So I kept my distance.

In early October the Tomkeys bought a boat, and everyone seemed   10 greatly relieved, especially my mother's friend, who noted that the motor was definitely secondhand. It was reported that Mr. Tomkey's father-in-law owned a house on the lake and had invited the family to use it whenever they liked. This explained why they were gone all weekend, but it did not make their absences any easier to bear. I felt as if my favorite show had been canceled.

Halloween fell on a Saturday that year, and by the time my mother took us to the store, all the good costumes were gone. My sisters dressed as witches and I went as a hobo. I'd looked forward to going in disguise to the Tomkey's door, but they were off at the lake, and their house was dark. Before leaving, they had left a coffee can full of gumdrops on the

front porch, alongside a sign reading DON'T BE GREEDY. In terms of Halloween candy, individual gumdrops were just about as low as you could get. This was evidenced by the large number of them floating in an adjacent dog bowl. It was disgusting to think that this was what a gumdrop might look like in your stomach, and it was insulting to be told not to take too much of something you didn't really want in the first place. "Who do these Tomkeys think they are?" my sister Lisa said.

The night after Halloween, we were sitting around watching TV when the doorbell rang. Visitors were infrequent at our house, so while my father stayed behind, my mother, sisters, and I ran downstairs in a group, opening the door to discover the entire Tomkey family on our front stoop. The parents looked as they always had, but the son and daughter were dressed in costumes — she as a ballerina and he as some kind of a rodent with terry-cloth ears and a tail made from what looked to be an extension cord. It seemed they had spent the previous evening isolated at the lake and had missed the opportunity to observe Halloween. "So, well, I guess we're trick-or-treating *now*, if that's okay," Mr. Tomkey said.

I attributed their behavior to the fact that they didn't have a TV, but television didn't teach you everything. Asking for candy on Halloween was called trick-or-treating, but asking for candy on November first was called begging, and it made people uncomfortable. This was one of the things you were supposed to learn simply by being alive, and it angered me that the Tomkeys did not understand it.

"Why of course it's not too late," my mother said. "Kids, why don't you . . . run and get . . . the candy."

"But the candy is gone," my sister Gretchen said. "You gave it away   15
last night."

"Not *that* candy," my mother said. "The other candy. Why don't you run and go get it?"

"You mean *our* candy?" Lisa said. "The candy that we *earned*?"

This was exactly what our mother was talking about, but she didn't want to say this in front of the Tomkeys. In order to spare their feelings, she wanted them to believe that we always kept a bucket of candy lying around the house, just waiting for someone to knock on the door and ask for it. "Go on, now," she said. "Hurry up."

My room was situated right off the foyer, and if the Tomkeys had looked in that direction, they could have seen my bed and the brown paper bag marked MY CANDY. KEEP OUT. I didn't want them to know how much I had, and so I went into my room and shut the door behind me. Then I closed the curtains and emptied my bag onto the bed, searching for whatever was the crummiest. All my life chocolate has made me ill. I don't know if I'm allergic or what, but even the smallest amount leaves me with a blinding headache. Eventually, I learned to stay away from it, but as a child I refused to be left out. The brownies were eaten, and when the pounding began I would blame the grape juice or my mother's cigarette smoke or the tightness of my glasses — anything but the chocolate. My candy bars were poison but they were brand-name, and so I put them in pile no. 1, which definitely would not go to the Tomkeys.

Out in the hallway I could hear my mother straining for something 20 to talk about. "A boat!" she said. "That sounds marvelous. Can you just drive it right into the water?"

"Actually, we have a trailer," Mr. Tomkey said. "So what we do is back it into the lake."

"Oh, a trailer. What kind it is?"

"Well, it's a *boat* trailer," Mr. Tomkey said.

"Right, but is it wooden, or you know . . . I guess what I'm asking is what *style* trailer do you have?"

Behind my mother's words were two messages. The first and most 25 obvious was "Yes, I am talking about boat trailers, but also I am dying." The second, meant only for my sisters and me, was "If you do not immediately step forward with that candy, you will never again experience freedom, happiness, or the possibility of my warm embrace."

I knew that it was just a matter of time before she came into my room and started collecting the candy herself, grabbing indiscriminately, with no regard to my rating system. Had I been thinking straight, I would have hidden the most valuable items in my dresser drawer, but instead, panicked by the thought of her hand on my doorknob, I tore off the wrappers and began cramming the candy bars into my mouth, desperately, like someone in a contest. Most were miniature, which made them easier to accommodate, but still there was only so much room, and it was hard to chew and fit more in at the same time. The headache began immediately, and I chalked it up to tension.

My mother told the Tomkeys she needed to check on something, and then she opened the door and stuck her head inside my room. "What the *hell* are you doing?" she whispered, but my mouth was too full to answer. "I'll just be a moment," she called, and as she closed the door behind her and moved toward my bed, I began breaking the wax lips and candy necklaces pulled from pile no. 2. These were the second-best things I had received, and while it hurt to destroy them, it would have hurt even more to give them away. I had just started to mutilate a miniature box of Red Hots when my mother pried them from my hands, accidentally finishing the job for me. BB-size pellets clattered onto the floor, and as I followed them with my eyes, she snatched up a roll of Necco wafers.

"Not those," I pleaded, but rather than words, my mouth expelled chocolate, chewed chocolate, which fell onto the sleeve of her sweater. "Not those. Not those."

She shook her arm, and the mound of chocolate dropped like a horrible turd upon my bedspread. "You should look at yourself," she said. "I mean, *really* look at yourself."

Along with the Necco wafers she took several Tootsie pops and half a dozen caramels wrapped in cellophane. I heard her apologize to the Tomkeys for her absence, and then I heard my candy hitting the bottom of their bags. 30

"What do you say?" Mrs. Tomkey asked.

And the children answered, "Thank you."

While I was in trouble for not bringing my candy sooner, my sisters were in more trouble for not bringing theirs at all. We spent the early part of the evening in our rooms, then one by one we eased our way back upstairs, and joined our parents in front of the TV. I was the last to arrive, and took a seat on the floor beside the soda. The show was a Western, and even if my head had not been throbbing, I doubt I would have had the wherewithal to follow it. A posse of outlaws crested a rocky hilltop, squinting at a flurry of dust advancing from the horizon, and I thought again of the Tomkeys and of how alone and out of place they had looked in their dopey costumes. "What was up with that kid's tail?" I asked.

"Shhhh," my family said.

For months I had protected and watched over these people, but now, with one stupid act, they had turned my pity into something hard and ugly. The shift wasn't gradual, but immediate, and it provoked an uncomfortable feeling of loss. We hadn't been friends, the Tomkeys and I, but still I had given them the gift of my curiosity. Wondering about the Tomkey family had made me feel generous, but now I would have to shift gears and find pleasure in hating them. The only alternative was to do as my mother had instructed and take a good look at myself. This was an old trick, designed to turn one's hatred inward, and while I was determined not to fall for it, it was hard to shake the mental picture snapped by her suggestion: here is a boy sitting on a bed, his mouth smeared with chocolate. He's a human being, but also he's a pig, surrounded by trash and gorging himself so that others may be denied. Were this the only image in the world, you'd be forced to give it your full attention, but fortunately there were others. This stagecoach, for instance, coming round the bend with a cargo of gold. This shiny new Mustang convertible. This teenage girl, her hair a beautiful mane, sipping Pepsi through a straw, one picture after another, on and on until the news, and whatever came on after the news.

Engaging with the Text

250–51

1. David Sedaris **TITLES** his essay "Us and Them." Whom does this title refer to? With whom are we meant to sympathize — "us" or "them"? How do you know?

149

2. Successful memoirs tell **A GOOD STORY.** Do you think "Us and Them" meets that requirement? Why or why not? Refer to the text in your response.

3. Sedaris describes two handwritten signs from Halloween night. The first is attached to a "coffee can full of gumdrops" telling trick or treaters "DON'T BE GREEDY." The second graces young Sedaris's bag of candy: "MY CANDY. KEEP OUT." What significance do these two signs have in the story? What do they tell us about Sedaris?

4. How would you characterize Sedaris's **STANCE?** What specific passages indicate his attitude about the events he recalls?

    12–14

5. *For Writing.* Recall a time when a person or event taught you something about yourself, something that perhaps you could not fully understand until now. Write a **MEMOIR** that describes the person or narrates the event. Include **VIVID DETAIL** and be sure to make clear what **SIGNIFICANCE** the person or event had in your life.

    147–52

    149

    150

VALERIE STEIKER

Our Mother's Face

Valerie Steiker is an editor at Vogue *and a writer whose essays have appeared in the* New Yorker *and other publications. The following piece is from Steiker's memoir,* The Leopard Hat: A Daughter's Story *(2002), which tells of the lasting influence Steiker's mother had on her life, from her charmed childhood in New York City to the time she spent, in her twenties, at Harvard and in Paris.*

AT THE BEGINNING OF MARCH, my mother's doctor let us know there was truly nothing more he could do for her in the hospital, and my father decided we should bring her home, where she would be more at ease, surrounded by the family and things and memories that she loved. She was happy to come home — we could hear it in her voice as she directed us to pack up her belongings — as if she had worried without telling us that she would never see it again.

The last week of her life I spent at home. It was spring break. My sister and I sat by her bed, talking softly, watching television. We played the sound track to *A Room with a View*[1] over and over, all of us soothed by its ethereal quality. "That's nice," my mother said at one point from her bed. We took turns bringing her things: lunches she couldn't or wouldn't eat, highball glasses filled with 7-Up or ginger ale. She drank constantly. The disease parched her and nothing was enough to quench her thirst.

Although there was a nurse, it was we who administered her pills, careful to take note of the time and to follow the doctor's instructions. At one point, she was in so much pain she threatened to kill herself if we didn't give her another dose of medication. Frantic, we called the doctor so he could tell her we weren't doing anything wrong, and she got on the phone and accused us of all being in a conspiracy to hurt her. My mother, once so full of warmth and love and vitality, had become

---

1. Film (1985) of E. M. Forster's novel.

rhetorical situations   genres   processes   strategies   research mla/apa   media/ design   readings

suspicious, paranoid. The morphine was taking her usual anxieties and feeding them until they grew to monstrous proportions. One afternoon she insisted I escort her to the library. Painted hunter green and filled with books and musical instruments, it was the best-loved room in the house. She explained to me, her voice strict with instruction, that she wanted us to make sure there were no samurai there. Without questioning her, I held her, felt her body's efforts under the peach satin robe as we walked slowly down the hallway, through the bright red foyer where she had so often entertained, and into the library. I turned on the light, and said softly, "See, Mommy? There isn't anyone here." In her quasi-dream state, she seemed satisfied, and we returned to her room. I helped her to her bed, wondering at the speed with which we had all had to surrender our grip on normalcy. . . .

A few days later, Bella came from Belgium. Bella, one of my mother's beloved *tantes,*[2] whom she had been close to ever since she was a child. I went to pick her up at the airport with my uncle, my father's older brother, and on the way back we got caught in traffic on the Fifty-ninth Street Bridge. It seemed inconceivable to me that my mother could die without me, while I was trapped in something so mundane as a traffic jam. When we finally got home, Bella wept over my mother's weakened body, her stark skull, her unblinking, watery eyes. Later she cried to me that she hadn't seen a human being look so ravaged since Auschwitz.[3] None of us knew what to do with ourselves, with the pain — hers and ours — that was everywhere, pervading every available space in the house. With the exception of her bedroom, which was filled with the plastic accoutrements of illness and no longer recognizable as her usual headquarters, the apartment looked as it always had. Only everything was very still. On the tables my mother had arranged so lovingly, the silver-framed photographs of past adventures and delicate porcelain bouquets and figurines sat silently waiting. The couch pillows puffed just so, the tall chairs standing at attention around the dining room

---

2. Aunts (French).

3. Town in Poland that was the site of a Nazi concentration camp in World War II.

table: all was in abeyance. The spirit that had animated each room, every seductive curve of furniture, every woven flowery vine, was withdrawing, its life force waning. She was being taken from us, and nothing, not even our boundless love, could stop the process; no amount of knowledge or money existed that could keep her from going away.

On the morning of the day she died, I looked in the bathroom mirror and ⁵ cried for myself, for the almost unrecognizable girl before me. I didn't get dressed, staying in the same nightshirt I had slept in, which was covered in dark burgundy stripes, and which later I would put away at the back of a shelf, never to be worn again. Whenever I wasn't in my mother's room that day, I spent time cleaning mine. My belongings had gotten out of hand, so I cleaned furiously, folding the clothes that were strewn everywhere and angrily putting books and papers in order on my desk. When the time came — for what, I didn't dare to imagine — I wanted to be ready. A few hours later I got my period. I stared at the clouds of tissue, like pale pink roses, floating in the bowl and took the blood as a benison, a tribute to the children I would have in her memory.

Bella and my father and my sister and I spent that afternoon and evening in my mother's room, holding her hands and stroking her forehead, my sister and I begging her to promise she would watch over us always. In the middle of the night, not knowing what else to do with ourselves, we sat down to play boraco, the family card game, perhaps trying to evoke the Renoir-like afternoons we had spent in Belgian tea gardens together. Just as the cards were laid out, as if she were annoyed by our choosing to play at such a time, the steady rasp of my mother's breathing became jagged, uneven. We flew from the card table and gathered around her bed. It was a sound like something being torn. Ourselves choking, we stroked her face and arms until the last catch in her throat. The life had not flowed out of her; it had been seized.

My father and sister and I drew away from the bed and held one another tightly, a crying circle of three. On the table in her room, there was a nineteenth-century brass lamp: an angel holding up a torch of light. When I looked up from our embrace, the light from next to her bed had cast a silhouette of the angel against the white closet doors,

The author and her mother. Courtesy Pantheon Books and Valerie Steiker.

and I remember thinking to myself that it made perfect sense, that her spirit must have been borne away by angels.

It was about three o'clock in the morning by the time we got into bed. My father slept on the pullout couch in his den — it was too upsetting for him to go into their bedroom without her. Stephanie and I decided to sleep together in my room. As we faced each other in bed, too tired and brokenhearted even to say good night to each other, I watched in amazement as my sister's features became my mother's. I was staring at the face of my mother in my bed, she was right next to me, looking at me lovingly, her eyes melting into mine. Yes, I knew that the undertaker had just come and taken her body away, carrying it on a gurney through the marble lobby where she had so often clipped in her high heels. But this was real. The next morning when I told Stephanie what I had seen as we fell asleep, she looked at me as if I were crazy and then started half laughing, half crying. She had had the exact same experience. She, too, had seen our mother's face, in mine.

Engaging with the Text

3–4   1.   One **PURPOSE** for writing a memoir is to explore our past, to think about people, places, and events that are important to us. What other purpose does Valerie Steiker's memoir serve, both for herself as the writer and us as the readers?

149   2.   What **DETAILS** does Steiker present — of what the apartment looked like, what they ate, what they said, what happened — and what do these reveal about Steiker, and about her feelings for her mother? How does this detailed focus on the mundane create a sense of the profound?

254, 306–08   3.   How does Steiker use **TRANSITIONS** and **TIME MARKERS** to guide readers through the days preceding and following her mother's death? Aside from guiding readers, what is their effect?

147–52   4.   Steiker chose to explore her mother's death through a **MEMOIR.** What
9–11   other **GENRES** might she have used, and how would changing the genre

rhetorical situations   genres   processes   strategies   research mla/apa   media/ design   readings

make the story different? For example, how would it be different as a **REFLECTION?** or a **REPORT?** In what situations would another genre be more appropriate, and why?

168–73, 60–81

5. *For Writing.* Steiker's memoir focuses on the death of her mother as it unfolded in the space of her family's apartment. Identify a place that you hold important in your life and recall an event that occurred there that has some significance for you. Write a **MEMOIR** about the event. Describe the scene in **DETAIL,** helping readers to see, hear, and otherwise sense what it was like. Give details about the key people as well, **DESCRIBING** what they looked like and perhaps including some **DIALOGUE.** Be sure to indicate the **SIGNIFICANCE** of the event in your life.

147–52

149

285–93

294–98

150

HENRY LOUIS GATES JR.

A Giant Step

The director of the W. E. B. Du Bois Institute for African and African American Research at Harvard University, Henry Louis Gates Jr. is a scholar of African American literature and literary criticism. He is the author of The Signifying Monkey: A Theory of Afro-American Literary Criticism *(1988) and one of the general editors of* The Norton Anthology of African American Literature *(1997, second edition 2004). The following essay first appeared in the* New York Times Magazine *in 1990 and was later incorporated in Gates's 1994 autobiography* Colored People: A Memoir.

WHAT'S THIS?" the hospital janitor said to me as he stumbled over my right shoe.

"My shoes," I said.

"That's not a shoe, brother," he replied, holding it to the light. "That's a brick."

It *did* look like a brick, sort of.

"Well, we can throw these in the trash now," he said.　　　　　5

"I guess so."

We had been together since 1975, those shoes and I. They were orthopedic shoes built around molds of my feet, and they had a $2^{1}/_{4}$-inch lift. I had mixed feelings about them. On the one hand, they had given me a more or less even gait for the first time in 10 years. On the other hand, they had marked me as a "handicapped person," complete with cane and special license plates. I went through a pair a year, but it was always the same shoe, black, wide, weighing about four pounds.

It all started 26 years ago in Piedmont, West Virginia, a backwoods town of 2,000 people. While playing a game of touch football at a Methodist summer camp, I incurred a hairline fracture. Thing is, I didn't know it yet. I was 14 and had finally lost the chubbiness of my youth. I was just learning tennis and beginning to date, and who knew where that might lead?

Not too far. A few weeks later, I was returning to school from lunch when, out of the blue, the ball-and-socket joint of my hip sheared apart. It was instant agony, and from that time on nothing in my life would be quite the same.

I propped myself against the brick wall of the schoolhouse, where the school delinquent found me. He was black as slate, twice my size, mean as the day was long and beat up kids just because he could. But the look on my face told him something was seriously wrong, and — bless him — he stayed by my side for the two hours it took to get me into a taxi.

"It's a torn ligament in your knee," the surgeon said. (One of the signs of what I had — a "slipped epithysis" — is intense knee pain, I later learned.) So he scheduled me for a walking cast.

I was wheeled into surgery and placed on the operating table. As the doctor wrapped my leg with wet plaster strips, he asked about my schoolwork.

"Boy," he said, "I understand you want to be a doctor."

I said, "Yessir." Where I came from, you always said "sir" to white people, unless you were trying to make a statement.

Had I taken a lot of science courses?

"Yessir. I enjoy science."

"Are you good at it?"

"Yessir, I believe so."

"Tell me, who was the father of sterilization?"

"Oh, that's easy, Joseph Lister."

Then he asked who discovered penicillin.

Alexander Fleming.

And what about DNA?

Watson and Crick.

The interview went on like this, and I thought my answers might get me a pat on the head. Actually, they just confirmed the diagnosis he'd come to.

He stood me on my feet and insisted that I walked. When I tried, the joint ripped apart and I fell on the floor. It hurt like nothing I'd ever known.

The doctor shook his head. "Pauline," he said to my mother, his voice kindly but amused, "there's not a thing wrong with that child. The problem's psychosomatic. Your son's an overachiever."

Back then, the term didn't mean what it usually means today. In Appalachia, in 1964, "overachiever" designated a sort of pathology: the overstraining of your natural capacity. A colored kid who thought he could be a doctor — just for instance — was headed for a breakdown.

What made the pain abate was my mother's reaction. I'd never, ever heard her talk back to a white person before. And doctors, well, their words were scripture.

Not this time. Pauline Gates stared at him for a moment. "Get his 30 clothes, pack his bags — we're going to the University Medical Center," which was 60 miles away.

Not great news: the one thing I knew was that they only moved you to the University Medical Center when you were going to die. I had three operations that year. I gave my tennis racket to the delinquent, which he probably used to club little kids with. So I wasn't going to make it to Wimbledon. But at least I wasn't going to die, though sometimes I wanted to. Following the last operation, which fitted me for a metal ball, I was confined to bed, flat on my back, immobilized by a complex system of weights and pulleys. It was six weeks of bondage — and bedpans. I spent my time reading James Baldwin, learning to play chess and quarreling daily with my mother, who had rented a small room — which we could ill afford — in a motel just down the hill from the hospital.

I think we both came to realize that our quarreling was a sort of ritual. We'd argue about everything — what time of day it was — but the arguments kept me from thinking about that traction system.

I limped through the next decade — through Yale and Cambridge . . . as far away from Piedmont as I could get. But I couldn't escape the pain, which increased as the joint calcified and began to fuse over the next 15 years. My leg grew shorter, as the muscles atrophied and the ball of the ball-and-socket joint migrated into my pelvis. Aspirin, then Motrin, heating pads and massages, became my traveling companions.

Most frustrating was passing store windows full of fine shoes. I used to dream about walking into one of those stores and buying a pair of shoes. "Give me two pairs, one black, one cordovan," I'd say. "Wrap 'em

rhetorical situations   genres   processes   strategies   research mla/apa   media/ design   readings

up." No six-week wait as with the orthotics in which I was confined. These would be real shoes. Not bricks.

In the meantime, hip-joint technology progressed dramatically. But no surgeon wanted to operate on me until I was significantly older, or until the pain was so great that surgery was unavoidable. After all, a new hip would last only for 15 years, and I'd already lost too much bone. It wasn't a procedure they were sure they'd be able to repeat.

This year, my 40th, the doctors decided the time had come.

I increased my life insurance and made the plunge.

The nights before my operations are the longest nights of my life — but never long enough. Jerking awake, grabbing for my watch, I experience a delicious sense of relief as I discover that only a minute or two have passed. You never want 6 A.M. to come.

And then the door swings open. "Good morning, Mr. Gates," the nurse says. "It's time."

The last thing I remember, just vaguely, was wondering where amnesiac minutes go in one's consciousness, wondering if I experienced the pain and sounds, then forgot them, or if these were somehow blocked out, dividing the self on the operating table from the conscious self in the recovery room. I didn't like that idea very much. I was about to protest when I blinked.

"It's over, Mr. Gates," says a voice. But how could it be over? I had merely *blinked*. "You talked to us several times," the surgeon had told me, and that was the scariest part of all.

Twenty-four hours later, they get me out of bed and help me into a "walker." As they stand me on my feet, my wife bursts into tears. "Your foot is touching the ground!" I am afraid to look, but it is true: the surgeon has lengthened my leg with that gleaming titanium and chrome-cobalt alloy ball-and-socket-joint.

"You'll need new shoes," the surgeon says. "Get a pair of Dock-Sides; they have a secure grip. You'll need a 3/4-inch lift in the heel, which can be as discreet as you want."

I can't help thinking about those window displays of shoes, those elegant shoes that, suddenly, I will be able to wear. Dock-Sides and sneakers, boots and loafers, sandals and brogues. I feel, at last, a furtive sympathy for Imelda Marcos, the queen of soles.

The next day, I walk over to the trash can, and take a long look at   45 the brick. I don't want to seem ungracious or unappreciative. We have walked long miles together. I feel disloyal, as if I am abandoning an old friend. I take a second look.

Maybe I'll have them bronzed.

Engaging with the Text

239–45

147–52

1. Henry Louis Gates Jr. **OPENS** his memoir about something that happened to him when he was fourteen by telling us about what happened to him twenty-six years later. This opening sets up a frame for his **MEMOIR.** What does this frame contribute to your understanding of the earlier event in Gates's life?

5–8

2. Who was Gates's original **AUDIENCE** for this piece? How did he shape this memoir for that audience? Point to examples in your response. How might the text be different had he written it for an audience of doctors? or for an audience of lawyers?

275–84

3. Gates explains that the white doctor used the word "overachiever" to mean something very different from what it means today. How does he **DEFINE** "overachiever"? What is the significance of this definition? What details does he provide to flesh out his definition?

294–98

4. Much of this memoir is told through **DIALOGUE.** Imagine that Gates had simply told what happened, summarizing what was said rather than letting the reader "hear" the key conversations. You might try rewriting the text without dialogue to see the difference. What can you conclude about when and why you might want to use dialogue in your own writing?

147–52

5. *For Writing.* Think of an event from your past that you remember as significant, or perhaps just interesting. Write about this event in a way that tells readers something about yourself. Try to structure your **MEMOIR** as Gates does, juxtaposing the event from your past with one from the present.

RICHARD RODRIGUEZ
None of This Is Fair

Born in California to Mexican immigrants, Richard Rodriguez is a writer whose essays on race, religion, and culture have been widely published. He is also an editor at the Pacific News Service (part of New America Media, a collaboration of ethnic news organizations) and a frequent contributor to The NewsHour with Jim Lehrer. *The following selection comes from his memoir* Hunger of Memory: The Education of Richard Rodriguez *(1982), in which he recounts his education and assimilation into American culture.*

MY PLAN TO BECOME A PROFESSOR OF ENGLISH — my ambition during long years in college at Stanford, then in graduate school at Columbia and Berkeley — was complicated by feelings of embarrassment and guilt. So many times I would see other Mexican-Americans and know we were alike only in race. And yet, simply because our race was the same, I was, during the last years of my schooling, the beneficiary of their situation. Affirmative Action programs had made it all possible. The disadvantages of others permitted my promotion; the absence of many Mexican-Americans from academic life allowed my designation as a "minority student."

For me opportunities had been extravagant. There were fellowships, summer research grants, and teaching assistantships. After only two years in graduate school, I was offered teaching jobs by several colleges. Invitations to Washington conferences arrived and I had the chance to travel abroad as a "Mexican-American representative." The benefits were often, however, too gaudy to please. In three published essays, in conversations with teachers, in letters to politicians and at conferences, I worried the issue of Affirmative Action. Often I proposed contradictory opinions, though consistent was the admission that — because of an early, excellent education — I was no longer a principal victim of racism or any other social oppression. I said that but still I continued to indicate on applications for financial aid that I was a Hispanic-American.

It didn't really occur to me to say anything else, or to leave the question unanswered.

Thus I complied with and encouraged the odd bureaucratic logic of Affirmative Action. I let government officials treat the disadvantaged condition of many Mexican-Americans with my advancement. Each fall my presence was noted by Health, Education, and Welfare department statisticians. As I pursued advanced literary studies and learned the skill of reading Spenser and Wordsworth and Empson,[1] I would hear myself numbered among the culturally disadvantaged. Still, silent, I didn't object.

But the irony cut deep. And guilt would not be evaded by averting my glance when I confronted a face like my own in a crowd. By late 1975, nearing the completion of my graduate studies at Berkeley, I was so wary of the benefits of Affirmative Action that I feared my inevitable success as an applicant for a teaching position. The months of fall — traditionally that time of academic job-searching — passed without my applying to a single school. When one of my professors chanced to learn this in late November, he was astonished, then furious. He yelled at me: Did I think that because I was a minority student jobs would just come looking for me? What was I thinking? Did I realize that he and several other faculty members had already written letters on my behalf? Was I going to start acting like some other minority students he had known? They struggled for success and then, when it was almost within reach, grew strangely afraid and let it pass. Was that it? Was I determined to fail?

I did not respond to his questions. I didn't want to admit to him, 5 and thus to myself, the reason I delayed.

I merely agreed to write to several schools. (In my letter I wrote: "I cannot claim to represent disadvantaged Mexican-Americans. The very fact that I am in a position to apply for this job should make that clear.") After two or three days, there were telegrams and phone calls, invitations to interviews, then airplane trips. A blur of faces and the murmur

---

1. The English poets Edmund Spenser (1552–99) and William Wordsworth (1770–1850), and English literary critic William Empson (1906–84).

of their soft questions. And, over someone's shoulder, the sight of campus buildings shadowing pictures I had seen years before when I leafed through Ivy League catalogues with great expectations. At the end of each visit, interviewers would smile and wonder if I had any questions. A few times I quietly wondered what advantage my race had given me over other applicants. But that was an impossible question for them to answer without embarrassing me. Quickly, several persons insisted that my ethnic identity had given me no more than a "foot inside the door"; at most, I had a "slight edge" over other applicants. "We just looked at your dossier with extra care and we like what we saw. There was never any question of having to alter our standards. You can be certain of that."

In the early part of January, offers arrived on stiffly elegant stationery. Most schools promised terms appropriate for any new assistant professor. A few made matters worse — and almost more tempting — by offering more: the use of university housing; an unusually large starting salary; a reduced teaching schedule. As the stack of letters mounted, my hesitation increased. I started calling department chairmen to ask for another week, then 10 more days — "more time to reach a decision" — to avoid the decision I would need to make.

At school, meantime, some students hadn't received a single job offer. One man, probably the best student in the department, did not even get a request for his dossier. He and I met outside a classroom one day and he asked about my opportunities. He seemed happy for me. Faculty members beamed. They said they had expected it. "After all, not many schools are going to pass up getting a Chicano with a Ph.D. in Renaissance literature," somebody said laughing. Friends wanted to know which of the offers I was going to accept. But I couldn't make up my mind. February came and I was running out of time and excuses. (One chairman guessed my delay was a bargaining ploy and increased his offer with each of my calls.) I had to promise a decision by the 10th; the 12th at the very latest.

On the 18th of February, late in the afternoon, I was in the office I shared with several other teaching assistants. Another graduate student was sitting across the room at his desk. When I got up to leave, he looked over to say in an uneventful voice that he had some big news. He had finally decided to accept a position at a faraway university. It was not a job he especially wanted, he admitted. But he had to take it because there hadn't been any other offers. He felt trapped, and depressed, since his job would separate him from his young daughter.

I tried to encourage him by remarking that he was lucky at least to 10 have found a job. So many others hadn't been able to get anything. But before I finished speaking I realized that I had said the wrong thing. And I anticipated his next question.

"What are your plans?" he wanted to know. "Is it true you've gotten an offer from Yale?"

I said that it was. "Only, I still haven't made up my mind."

He stared at me as I put on my jacket. And smiling, then unsmiling, he asked if I knew that he too had written to Yale. In his case, however, no one had bothered to acknowledge his letter with even a postcard. What did I think of that?

He gave me no time to answer.

"Damn!" he said sharply and his chair rasped the floor as he pushed 15 himself back. Suddenly, it was to *me* that he was complaining. "It's just not right, Richard. None of this is fair. You've done some good work, but so have I. I'll bet our records are just about equal. But when we look for jobs this year, it's a different story. You get all of the breaks."

To evade his criticism, I wanted to side with him. I was about to admit the injustice of Affirmative Action. But he went on, his voice hard with accusation. "It's all very simple this year. You're a Chicano. And I am a Jew. That's the only real difference between us."

His words stung me: there was nothing he was telling me that I didn't know. I had admitted everything already. But to hear someone else say these things, and in such an accusing tone, was suddenly hard to take. In a deceptively calm voice, I responded that he had simplified the whole issue. The phrases came like bubbles to the tip of my tongue: "new blood"; "the importance of cultural diversity"; "the goal of racial integration." These were all the arguments I had proposed several years ago — and had long since abandoned. Of course the offers were unjus-

tifiable. I knew that. All I was saying amounted to a frantic self-defense. I tried to find an end to a sentence. My voice faltered to a stop.

"Yeah, sure," he said. "I've heard all that before. Nothing you say really changes the fact that Affirmative Action is unfair. You see that, don't you? There isn't any way for me to compete with you. Once there were quotas to keep my parents out of certain schools; now there are quotas to get you in and the effect on me is the same as it was for them."

I listened to every word he spoke. But my mind was really on something else. I knew at that moment that I would reject all of the offers. I stood there silently surprised by what an easy conclusion it was. Having prepared for so many years to teach, having trained myself to do nothing else, I had hesitated out of practical fear. But now that it was made, the decision came with relief. I immediately knew I had made the right choice.

My colleague continued talking and I realized that he was simply 20 right. Affirmative Action programs *are* unfair to white students. But as I listened to him assert his rights, I thought of the seriously disadvantaged. How different they were from white, middle-class students who come armed with the testimony of their grades and aptitude scores and self-confidence to complain about the unequal treatment they now receive. I listen to them. I do not want to be careless about what they say. Their rights are important to protect. But inevitably when I hear them or their lawyers, I think about the most seriously disadvantaged, not simply Mexican-Americans, but of all those who do not ever imagine themselves going to college or becoming doctors: white, black, brown. Always poor. Silent. They are not plaintiffs before the court or against the misdirection of Affirmative Action. They lack the confidence (my confidence!) to assume their right to a good education. They lack the confidence and skills a good primary and secondary education provides and which are prerequisites for informed public life. They remain silent.

The debate drones on and surrounds them in stillness. They are distant, faraway figures like the boys I have seen peering down from freeway overpasses in some other part of town.

Engaging with the Text

250–51
1. How did Richard Rodriguez's **TITLE** — "None of This Is Fair" — affect the way you read the essay? What does "this" refer to?

3–4
2. What **PURPOSE** — beyond telling readers something about himself — does Rodriguez's memoir serve? What do readers take away from this essay? What do you think Rodriguez hoped readers would take away?

245–48
3. Look at the way this essay **ENDS.** What is your reaction? How else might it end? Imagine Rodriguez had ended by explaining his decision, or by calling for some kind of action. Would such endings change his message significantly — and if so, how?

4. How would this essay be different if Rodriguez had written it as an op-ed piece, explicitly making an argument about Affirmative Action? As a memoir, it features a good story, vivid detail, and clear signifi-

82–106
cance; what key features would it need to explicitly **ARGUE A POSITION**?

147–52
5. *For Writing*. Write a **MEMOIR** about a difficult or important decision you have had to make. Tell the story of what led to the decision and how you made it, and provide enough detail to bring the decision to life

150
for your readers. Be sure to indicate something about the **SIGNIFICANCE** of the decision for you.

SUSAN JANE GILMAN

Mick Jagger Wants Me

Susan Jane Gilman is a writer whose essays have appeared in several publications, including the New York Times, Ms. *magazine,* Newsday, *and the* Village Voice. *The following selection comes from* Hypocrite in a Pouffy White Dress *(2004), her memoir of growing up "groovy and clueless" in New York City.*

I N NOVEMBER, MICHELLE CAME RUNNING upstairs with a newspaper article. "They're here," she shrieked.

According to the *Daily News*, the Stones[1] were back in New York, putting the finishing touches on their album *Emotional Rescue* at the Electric Lady Studios. From the Yellow Pages, we learned that Electric Lady was on Eighth Street in Greenwich Village. It was 10:00 p.m. on a Thursday night, but clearly, this was not something that could wait until morning.

I told my mother I was going to Michelle's house to bake cookies; she told her mother she was going to mine. Then we both took the C train downtown to West Fourth Street. The studio was one of the most nondescript doorways in all of Greenwich Village. Located next to a movie theater, it was a small, windowless storefront with a small door set in far from the street. Only a small brass plaque saying "electric lady" in lower-case letters distinguished it. You could walk by it a thousand times and never notice.

For the next two hours, Michelle and I stood in front of this doorway, stopping people on the street who looked like they might know something, asking them if they'd seen the Rolling Stones.

After that, we spent every weekend camped out in front of Electric Lady. We'd get downtown at about 10:00 a.m., position ourselves against a car parked right near the entrance, and wait. Michelle would smoke

5

---

1. The Rolling Stones, English rock band popular since the 1960s, fronted by singer Mick Jagger and guitarist Keith Richards.

cigarettes while I, ever the groupie geek, would bring along books and do my homework. We flirted with strangers a bit, if we thought they were "somebody," and took beer from guys on the street. Sometimes Michelle would ring the bell at the entrance and say she was sent over from the *Village Voice* with a package for Keith Richards, but they never let her in.

We fell in with some other hippie-groupie types from Michelle's school who were obsessed with Hendrix, the Doors, Janis Joplin, and Zeppelin as well as the Stones. On the weekends, they often threw "the parents are away" parties out in Flushing, Queens. Since the parties lasted all night, we rarely slept at them; at 3:00 a.m. a bunch of us might try to set up beds on the floor using sofa cushions and towels, but when the sun rose, we'd all be up listening to "Free Bird" and cooking frozen pizza in the kitchen.

Most of the time, none of us knew where we were, or who we were with. People were taking speed, smoking grass, dropping acid, making out with whoever was around: it was a druggie, psychedelic mess. There would be beer and cigarette burns all over the basement floor, cans and paper, little pools of wax where candles had melted down on the coffee tables. Each party, I made out with a different guy. Making out, I'd quickly discovered, was the greatest activity ever invented in the history of the planet. As soon as I started making out with boys on a regular basis, I couldn't believe that vast segments of the human population ever did anything else. How, I wondered, could people possibly pick up their dry cleaning, perform open heart surgery, or teach high school mathematics when *they could be making out instead? What was wrong with this world? Where were people's priorities?*

Yet after eight straight hours of mashing, grinding, and drinking, my lips were always swollen, and by morning, I always felt battered from alcohol. All I ever wanted to do was take a hot shower and slide between the cool, fresh sheets of my own bed. Instead, Michelle and I would take the subway to Greenwich Village and spend a few hours replacing whatever it was we had lost at the party: lipstick, change purses, socks.

We were walking across Eighth Street one of these afternoons when 10 a limousine pulled up in front of Electric Lady.

"Michelle!" I grabbed her hand and we raced across the street. Then we leaned against an Oldsmobile parked right in front of the studio and waited to see who was coming out. We were determined to appear very cool and nonchalant about it.

Two minutes later, the door to Electric Lady swung open and Keith Richards sauntered out with his little blond son in tow. He looked, if this was possible, scraggly and regal. His black hair was tousled and he was wearing a pair of gold-mirrored sunglasses. I sized him up as fast as possible: tight black velvet pants pulled over boots, black jacket, a red-green-yellow scarf slashed around his neck. When he walked into the sunlight, he recoiled a little. Then he spotted me and Michelle, and for a second, he acknowledged us with a nod before staggering toward his limousine.

"Let's go with him. Let's do it, Susie," Michelle whispered. "Let's jump in his limo . . . "

I'd completely jelled. He was walking down the street, and all I could look at was his ass. I was watching his proud legs and his ass, packed into tight black velvet, pull and move, pull and move, with a bit of a jiggle, as he moved toward his car. *That is Keith Richards' ass,* I thought ecstatically. *I am watching Keith Richards' ass.*

Michelle grabbed my wrist and pulled me to the curb. "Let's do it, 15 Susie," she said. "We're really going to do it."

The chauffeur opened the door and Keith's son scuttled in, followed by Keith, who paused for a moment before dipping down into the back seat. He seemed to take one last look at the studio, the street, and the people, and as he did, the sunlight glared off his glasses in flashes of gold. Michelle and I froze. The door slammed, the motor growled, and the limousine veered away from the curb, leaving us standing at the edge of the gutter, shivering, tears running down our faces.

"Keith," we shrieked as the car drove away, "Keith, we love you!"

When it was absolutely out of sight, we started laughing, crying, jumping up and down, and shouting all at once: "We saw Keith! We saw Keith Richards!"

Then Michelle said to me, "I'll bet you anything Mick is still in the studio. We're going to meet him. We'll wait out all night if we have to. But he's ours, Susie. He's finally — f---ing — ours."

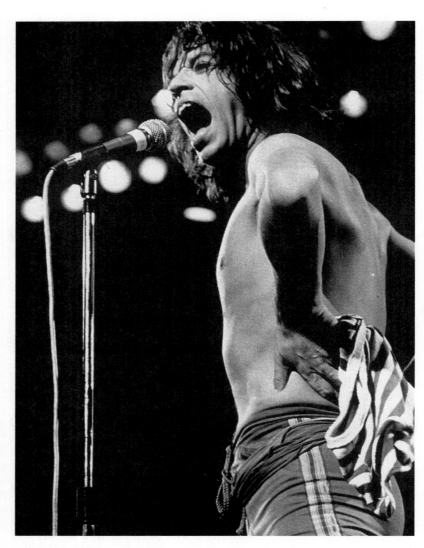

Mick Jagger, 1976. Boccon-Gibod/SIPA.

I should have been thrilled. I should have felt that sweet, heart- 20
pulsing surge of expectation nearing fulfillment. But instead, strangely, I
didn't. Instead, I started to feel something that felt an awful lot like dread.

And then it became instantly clear to me: in my fantasy life with
Mick, I was always beautiful, sexual, confident. I was at dinner parties,
I was in Geometry class. I wasn't waiting outside all night on some urine-
drenched sidewalk, some scraggly kid, some *beggar* ambushing him with
a carnation and an autograph book.

The idea of actually meeting Mick Jagger this way sickened me. How
could I possibly cast myself that way in his eyes? For that matter, how
could I cast myself that way in mine? To be so pathetic and prostrate
before him — Christ, what would I be left with?

I looked at Michelle.

"I can't," I said quietly.

"What? Susie, what are you talking about?" she cried. "This is our 25
dream come true! Mick Jagger is in there! I know it! I'm telling you! We
are meeting Mick Jagger!"

I shook my head. I felt like a jerk, but somehow, I couldn't stop.

"What the hell is wrong with you?" Michelle said.

I looked down and played with the rhinestone buttons on my coat.
For some reason, my eyes started watering. Maybe there *was* something
wrong with me. *I mean, really,* I thought. *Look at me.* Finally, I swallowed.
"Oh, Michelle," I said, "in my dreams, I always meet him at a dinner
party. And somebody introduces us — I don't just come up to him. And
he wants me. Mick Jagger wants *me* — "

Michelle said nothing. She just reached into the pocket of her jeans
jacket and fished out a cigarette. Then, very slowly, she took out her
lighter, flicked it open, and expertly lit her cigarette. When she finally
looked at me, I saw on her face something I hadn't expected: pity. Pity
mixed with just an inkling of fear.

"Um, Susie?" she said carefully, in a tone usually reserved for the 30
senile — or, perhaps, the criminally insane — "Honey? That's a *fantasy*
you're telling me. This?" she waved her hand across Eighth Street. "*This,*
right here? This is real. Mick Jagger is in this recording studio, right here,
right now, and you and I have an opportunity of a lifetime to meet him."

"I'm sorry," I whispered hoarsely. Then I started to cry.

In standard Teenage Girl Culture, this should've been considered a massive betrayal, a pivotal moment that ended our friendship. The fact that it wasn't was a testimony to how close we were. Michelle simply reached over and pushed my hair away from my eyes. "Go home, girl," she said gently. "Go home and take care of yourself."

Engaging with the Text

1. Susan Jane Gilman's **MEMOIR** juxtaposes fantasy with reality — the fantasies of a teenager and the realities of a woman looking back on her youth. How does her mature perspective affect the way she relates her memories? Support your response with examples from the text.

   147–52

2. Although most of Gilman's story is told **CHRONOLOGICALLY,** a brief digression near the beginning tells of typical parties she attended in high school. Why do you think she includes this digression within the larger **NARRATIVE?** How does it contribute to the contrast between fantasy and reality that is such a large part of her story?

   304–05
   304–12

3. Gilman **DESCRIBES** Keith Richards in **VIVID DETAIL.** What **DOMINANT IMPRESSION** of him do these details create?

   285–93
   149
   291–92

4. When it became a very real possibility that Gilman might have an opportunity to meet Mick Jagger, she froze and "started to feel something that felt an awful lot like dread." Why do you think Gilman reacted this way? What does her reaction suggest about the relationship between fantasy and reality? What does it tell us about the **SIGNIFICANCE** of this memoir? Notice that Gilman doesn't announce this significance explicitly. If you were her editor, would you have advised her to make it explicit? Why or why not?

   150

5. *For Writing.* Gilman's **MEMOIR** deals with the clash between fantasy and reality. Write your own memoir, about a time in your life when you managed to, or almost managed to, realize a long-lived desire or fantasy. Try to indicate how that experience lived up to — or did not live up to — the way you had imagined it would be.

   147–52

rhetorical situations   genres   processes   strategies   research mla/apa   media/ design   readings

Profiles **57**

rhetorical situations ■ genres ▲ processes ○ strategies ◆ research mla/apa ● media/design □ readings ▐

KATHLEEN NORRIS

Seeing

Kathleen Norris is a poet and essayist. After graduating from Benning-
ton College, in Vermont, she moved to New York and worked at the
Academy of American Poets, but then settled in Lemmon, South Dakota,
to manage the farm she inherited from her grandmother. There she
wrote a best-selling book, Dakota: A Spiritual Geography *(1993), from*
which this selection is taken. She has also served as a Presbyterian
minister and has been a member of a Benedictine community. Much of
her writing explores religious themes — the poetry collection Little Girls
in Church *(1995), and the nonfiction* Cloister Walk *(1996), among oth-*
ers. As you read the following profile, think about why Norris calls it a
"spiritual geography."

The Midwestern landscape is abstract, and our response to the
geology of the region might be similar to our response to the
contemporary walls of paint in museums. We are forced to live in
our eye.

— MICHAEL MARTONE

Abba Bessarion, at the point of death, said, "The monk ought to
be like the Cherubim and the Seraphim: all eye."

— THE DESERT CHRISTIAN

ONCE, WHEN I WAS DESCRIBING to a friend from Syracuse, New York,
a place on the plains that I love, a ridge above a glacial moraine with a
view of almost fifty miles, she asked, "But what is there to see?"

The answer, of course, is nothing. Land, sky, and the ever changing light. Except for a few signs of human presence — power and telephone lines, an occasional farm building, the glint of a paved road in
the distance — it's like looking at the ocean.

The landscape of western Dakota is not as abstract as the flats of
Kansas, but it presents a similar challenge to the eye that appreciates
the vertical definition of mountains or skyscrapers; that defines beauty

in terms of the spectacular or the busy: hills, trees, buildings, highways, people. We seem empty by comparison.

Here, the eye learns to appreciate slight variations, the possibilities inherent in emptiness. It sees that the emptiness is full of small things, like grasshoppers in their samurai armor clicking and jumping as you pass. This empty land is full of grasses: sedges, switch grass, needle-grass, wheatgrass. Brome can grow waist-high by early summer. Fields of wheat, rye, oats, barley, flax, alfalfa. Acres of sunflowers brighten the land in summer, their heads alert, expectant. By fall they droop like sad children, waiting patiently for the first frost and harvest.

In spring it is a joy to discover, amid snow and mud and pale, with- 5 ered grass, the delicate lavender of pasqueflower blooming on a ridge with a southern exposure. There is variety in the emptiness; the most prosaic pasture might contain hundreds of different wildflowers along with sage, yucca, and prairie cactus. Coulees harbor chokecherry, buf-falo berry, and gooseberry bushes in their gentle folds, along with groves of silvery cottonwoods and Russian olive. Lone junipers often grow on exposed hillsides.

This seemingly empty land is busy with inhabitants. Low to the ground are bullsnakes, rattlers, mice, gophers, moles, grouse, prairie chickens, and pheasant. Prairie dogs are more noticeable, as they denude the landscape with their villages. Badgers and skunk lumber busily through the grass. Jackrabbits, weasels, and foxes are quicker, but the great runners of the Plains are the coyote, antelope, and deer. Mead-owlarks, killdeer, blackbirds, lark buntings, crows, and seagulls dart above the fields, and a large variety of hawks, eagles, and vultures glide above it all, hunting for prey.

Along with the largeness of the visible — too much horizon, too much sky — this land's essential indifference to the human can be unnerving. We had a visitor, a friend from back East who flew into Bis-marck and started a two-week visit by photographing the highway on the way to Lemmon; "Look how far you can see!" he kept exclaiming, trying to capture the whole of it in his camera lens. He seemed relieved to find a few trees in town and in our yard, and did not relish going back out into open country.

One night he called a woman friend from a phone booth on Main Street and asked her to marry him. After less than a week, he decided to cut his visit short and get off the Plains. He and his fiancée broke off the engagement, mutually and amicably, not long after he got home to Boston. The proposal had been a symptom of "Plains fever."

A person is forced inward by the spareness of what is outward and visible in all this land and sky. The beauty of the Plains is like that of an icon; it does not give an inch to sentiment or romance. The flow of the land, with its odd twists and buttes, is like the flow of Gregorian chant that rises and falls beyond melody, beyond reason or human expectation, but perfectly.

Maybe seeing the Plains is like seeing an icon: what seems stern and almost empty is merely open, a door into some simple and holy state.   10

Not long ago, at a difficult time in my life, when my husband was recovering from surgery, I attended a drum ceremony with a Native American friend. Me and boys gathered around the sacred drum and sang a song to ble   it. Their singing was high-pitched, repetitive, solemn, and loud. As they approached the song's end, drumming louder and louder, I realized that the music was also restorative; my two-day headache was gone, my troubles no longer seemed so burdensome.

I wondered how this loud, shrill, holy music, the indigenous song of those who have truly seen the Plains, could be so restful, while the Gregorian chant that I am just learning to sing can be so quiet, and yet as stirring as any drum. Put it down to ecstasy.

Engaging with the Text

155 ▲

1. The best profiles focus on their subject from an **INTERESTING ANGLE.** What would you say Kathleen Norris's angle is?

2. Norris suggests that one has to learn how to see the beauty in "seemingly empty land" where "there is variety in the emptiness." What **ENGAGING DETAILS** does Norris supply to help her reader *see* the beauty of the plains?

155 ▲

rhetorical situations   genres   processes   strategies   research mla/apa   media/design   readings

3. "Seeing the Plains," Norris suggests, "is like seeing an icon: what seems stern and almost empty is merely open, a door into some simple and holy state." What does she mean by this SIMILE? How does this COMPARISON help you understand her view of the landscape?

271–72
266–74

4. Norris's profile of western Dakota might have been written in a different genre — perhaps as a REPORT, or a REFLECTION. Choose one of these genres and decide how this piece would be different. What would remain the same?

60–81,
168–73

5. *For Writing.* Norris's profile of the Dakota plains challenges us to look at our surroundings with care and openness. Select a geographical location that at first glance seems ordinary, and write a PROFILE that DESCRIBES the beauty that can be found in the space. Show readers how one can look with new eyes at something familiar and perhaps taken for granted.

153–59
285–93

NICHOLAS HOWE

Writing Home:
High Street

Nicholas Howe (1953–2006) was a professor of English at the University of California, Berkeley, where his primary work was on the literature and culture of Anglo-Saxon England. His books include The Old English Catalogue Poems *(1985),* Migration and Mythmaking in Anglo-Saxon England *(2002), and the Norton Critical Edition of* Beowulf *(2001). The following profile is of a street in Columbus, Ohio, home of the Ohio State University, where Howe taught before moving to Berkeley. It comes from* Across an Inland Sea: Writing in Place from Buffalo to Berlin *(2003). Before reading Howe's profile, think of a street near your school that you could write about, and read with an eye for the way Howe helps readers to envision a street they've likely never before seen.*

HIGH STREET RUNS THROUGH Columbus, Ohio, as a spine. Its character shifts along its length to reflect the surrounding area: the old downtown with government and commercial offices; the rehabbed gallery district; an amorphous university community; quiet residential neighborhoods with wood-frame houses from the early twentieth century. But it remains always the main street of the city, the north-south line that separates cross-streets into east and west, that serves as the origin point for giving directions. High Street is the main axis for Columbus's grid pattern so that, if you can find it, you are never really lost in the central city. Its name comes from those New Englanders who settled this part of the country after the Revolutionary War, and the occasional anglophile will slip in the definite article as if speaking of an English town: The High Street. But that usage seems almost comic because it is not a street of half-timbered houses, pub signs, and hanging flower baskets.

Over the years the foursquare, though rarely distinguished, brick buildings that line the street have suffered more from botched attempts at modernization than outright neglect. Their slapped-on false facades, out-of-date neon signs, unused upper floors all testify in one way or

High Street, Columbus, Ohio. Photo by Nicholas Howe.

another to their owners' doomed efforts to stem the drift of businesses to the suburbs in the 1950s and 1960s where life was newer and parking easier. Along some stretches, the street has been cut into jaggedly: original buildings were torn down and replaced with one-story strips or supermarkets set far back so shoppers can park in front. This exploitative use of space makes what once had been a symmetrical main street with a trim curbline appear ragged and disconnected. Only in the last several years have zoning regulations been changed to limit setbacks; new buildings must now abut the sidewalk and have their parking lots in the rear, as was the custom in the early 1900s. This return to older practice has become a selling point. A recent for-sale sign on an empty lot along High Street featured a drawing of a typical, early-1900s storefront with signs for imagined businesses that read "Upscale Restaurant" and "Delicious Bakery." A fashionable coffeeshop has just been built on that site with no setback. Even as the building was being finished, it was hard to remember that it was replacing a drive-through beer store that had in turn been a gas station.

The traffic along High Street is steady, sometimes heavy, and always punctuated by buses running north and south. That it has the most regular service in the city, with a bus every seven to ten minutes, is another sign that it is a main drag. In a city that belongs to the car culture of the American heartland, High Street is one of the few places where you will see people walking. Except for several gentrified blocks in the Short North section, with chic restaurants and galleries, much of High Street can still evoke, for those willing to see it, the sense of a small city from early in the twentieth century. But it takes patience to find that city amid the parking lots, the chain drugstores, the fast-food franchises that fill the air with their aromas, the constant flow of traffic that passes along the street without looking at what lines each side.

The few square miles of the world that I know best fall along High Street between Clintonville, the neighborhood of World War I–era houses where I live, and the Ohio State University, where I teach. The distance is about two miles or perhaps forty minutes by foot but I almost never make it in less than an hour because I stop to look in store windows or explore the ways people use the street and its adjacent network of alleys. For ten years or so I have wandered in this neighborhood, buying necessities like food and hardware, spending too much money on used books and cameras, always trying to ease some of the restlessness that comes with a steady life set in one place. Making an alley do the work of the exotic unknown may seem silly, perhaps even pathetic, but it is better for the imagination than reading exploraporn or watching action movies. It gets one out of the house, and that is the first benefit of travel.

Clintonville along High Street is a neighborhood that needs to be 5 walked, not because it is scenic, but because it must be peeled back layer by layer. That way you can see how it has shifted from generation to generation, how it shifts as you walk it day by day. These changes rarely force themselves on you; they can easily be ignored. But paying so little attention to where you live leaves you increasingly unable to appreciate anywhere else, no matter how dramatic. Looked at carefully, though, these two miles of High Street record a changing America. Different moments from the past have left their traces along the street, and they can be read like geological striations or the *pentimento* of an artist's canvas. The painted signs on brick buildings — for long-gone places like Burkart's Economy Stores and a lunchroom called Clinton Villa, or still thriving ones like Schreiner's Hardware and Pace-Hi Beer and Wine Shop — are now so faded as to be barely readable. When they were fresh and garish in their deep colors, these signs must have seemed as arresting as the neon fast-food signs of today. The few that survive along High Street have paled into the brick walls of buildings and no longer catch the eye.

Some of the old back-lit signs that preceded neon remain in place, though the names on them change as tenants come and go. Clintonville Hardware becomes Midwest Photo Exchange, but the sign remains in place. Along this stretch, other buildings have been turned from their original uses as auto showrooms and furniture stores to more improvised purposes, and sheds off of alleys hide old cars soon to be vintage. Nothing here is abandoned in a derelict or wasteful way, nothing here gives cause for fear or even much regret. It's just that people seem to have forgotten to use the upper floors of buildings or the sheds behind them. As life goes on elsewhere, these spaces have lost their purpose.

Wandering around these alleys, down these nooks and crannies, has given density to my life; it has taught me about the uncelebrated persistence of what was built and occupied more than a generation or two ago. I have not lived here long enough to see ghosts turning these corners, nor do I have family ties that run back several generations, as I do in Buffalo. Yet walking these blocks and looking through alleyways behind buildings toward High Street has given me a sense of how the lives passed in a place leave their scars on it. It matters to these wanderings that this is not a "quaint" or "charming" stretch, one gentrified to sterile tastefulness. Instead, it is visibly a mixed-up area with convenience stores, insurance agencies, transmission shops, and a few local bars set beside deeply expert dealers from whom you can purchase a used Ferrari or Mercedes-Benz, an antique Stickley[1] chair, or a new Leica camera. No one planned the neighborhood to be this way, no one has yet driven out the service stores to make room for more boutiques. In an impromptu way, it simply happened, and in happening found its comfortably jumbled character.

Engaging with the Text

1. According to Nicholas Howe, how has High Street changed over the years? What **BACKGROUND** and **CONTEXT** does Howe supply to help his readers understand the changes? How can the character of High Street be described today?

   154–55

2. A good profile generally focuses on an unusual subject, or on something very ordinary shown in an interesting way. How does Howe make a fairly ordinary street in Columbus, Ohio, an **INTERESTING SUBJECT?**

   154

3. According to Howe, what has **CAUSED** the various changes on High Street? Why do you think he addresses these causes in his profile of High Street? What do they contribute to the overall profile?

   255–59

---

   1. Gustav Stickley (1858–1942), American furniture maker and spokesman for the Arts and Crafts movement.

rhetorical situations   genres   processes   strategies   research mla/apa   media/ design   readings

4. Howe tells us that "Clintonville along High Street is a neighborhood that needs to be walked, not because it is scenic, but because it must be peeled back layer by layer." What does he mean by the phrase "layer by layer"? In his **DESCRIPTION** of High Street, how does he peel the layers back for the reader?

◆ 285–93

5. *For Writing.* Select an interesting street, building, or other structure in your neighborhood. Spend some time **OBSERVING** it, do some **RESEARCH** on its history, and write a **PROFILE** that explores how it came to be the way it is today.

● 352–53
● 331–57
▲ 153–59

JOAN DIDION

Georgia O'Keeffe

Joan Didion is a novelist and journalist, the author of several best-selling essay collections, including A Book of Common Prayer *(1977) and* The White Album *(1979). Another selection by Didion appears in Chapter 59, and a review of her memoir* The Year of Magical Thinking *(2005) appears in Chapter 54. The following profile of artist Georgia O'Keeffe, published when O'Keeffe was 92, comes from* The White Album.

"**W**HERE I WAS BORN and where and how I have lived is unimportant," Georgia O'Keeffe told us in the book of paintings and words published in her ninetieth year on earth. She seemed to be advising us to forget the beautiful face in the Stieglitz photographs. She appeared to be dismissing the rather condescending romance that had attached to her by then, the romance of extreme good looks and advanced age and deliberate isolation. "It is what I have done with where I have been that should be of interest." I recall an August afternoon in Chicago in 1973 when I took my daughter, then seven, to see what Georgia O'Keeffe had done with where she had been. One of the vast O'Keeffe "Sky above Clouds" canvases floated over the back stairs in the Chicago Art Institute that day, dominating what seemed to be several stories of empty light, and my daughter looked at it once, ran to the landing, and kept on looking. "Who drew it," she whispered after a while. I told her. "I need to talk to her," she said finally.

My daughter was making, that day in Chicago, an entirely unconscious but quite basic assumption about people and the work they do. She was assuming that the glory she saw in the work reflected a glory in its maker, that the painting was the painter as the poem is the poet, that every choice one made alone — every word chosen or rejected, every brush stroke laid or not laid down — betrayed one's character. *Style is character.* It seemed to me that afternoon that I had rarely seen so instinctive an application of this familiar principle, and I recall being

Georgia O'Keeffe, 1930. Granger Collection.

pleased not only that my daughter responded to style as character but that it was Georgia O'Keeffe's particular style to which she responded: this was a hard woman who had imposed her 192 square feet of clouds on Chicago.

"Hardness" has not been in our century a quality much admired in women, nor in the past twenty years has it even been in official favor for men. When hardness surfaces in the very old we tend to transform it into "crustiness" or eccentricity, some tonic pepperiness to be indulged at a distance. On the evidence of her work and what she has said about it, Georgia O'Keeffe is neither "crusty" nor eccentric. She is simply hard, a straight shooter, a woman clean of received wisdom and open to what she sees. This is a woman who could early on dismiss most of her contemporaries as "dreamy," and would later single out one she liked as "a very poor painter." (And then add, apparently by way of softening the judgment: "I guess he wasn't a painter at all. He had no courage and I believe that to create one's own world in any of the arts takes courage.") This is a woman who in 1939 could advise her admirers that they were missing her point, that their appreciation of her famous flowers was merely sentimental. "When I paint a red hill," she observed coolly in the catalogue for an exhibition that year, "you say it is too bad that I don't always paint flowers. A flower touches almost everyone's heart. A red hill doesn't touch everyone's heart." This is a woman who could describe the genesis of one of her most well-known paintings — the "Cow's Skull: Red, White, and Blue" owned by the Metropolitan — as an act of quite deliberate and derisive orneriness. "I thought of the city men I had been seeing in the East," she wrote. "They talked so often of writing the Great American Novel — the Great American Play — the Great American Poetry. . . . So as I was painting my cow's head on blue I thought to myself, 'I'll make it an American painting. They will not think it great with the red stripes down the sides — Red, White and Blue — but they will notice it.'"

The city men. The men. They. The words crop up again and again as this astonishingly aggressive woman tells us what was on her mind when she was making her astonishingly aggressive paintings. It was

Georgia O'Keeffe, **Red Canna.** University of Arizona Art Museum.

those city men who stood accused of sentimentalizing her flowers: "I made you take time to look at what I saw and when you took time to really notice my flower you hung all your associations with flowers on my flower and you write about my flower as if I think and see what you think and see — and I don't." *And I don't.* Imagine those words spoken, and the sound you hear is *don't tread on me.* "The men" believed it impossible to paint New York, so Georgia O'Keeffe painted New York. "The men" didn't think much of her bright color, so she made it brighter. The men yearned toward Europe so she went to Texas, and then New Mexico. The men talked about Cézanne, "long involved remarks about the 'plastic quality' of his form and color," and took one another's long involved remarks, in the view of this angelic rattlesnake in their midst, altogether too seriously. "I can paint one of those dismal-colored paintings like the men," the woman who regarded herself always as an outsider remembers thinking one day in 1922, and she did: a painting of a shed "all low-toned and dreary with the tree beside the door." She called this act of rancor "The Shanty" and hung it in her next show. "The men seemed to approve of it," she reported fifty-four years later, her contempt undimmed. "They seemed to think that maybe I was beginning to paint. That was my only low-toned dismal-colored painting."

Some women fight and others do not. Like so many successful guer-   5
rillas in the war between the sexes, Georgia O'Keeffe seems to have been equipped early with an immutable sense of who she was and a fairly clear understanding that she would be required to prove it. On the surface her upbringing was conventional. She was a child on the Wisconsin prairie who played with china dolls and painted watercolors with cloudy skies because sunlight was too hard to paint and, with her brother and sisters, listened every night to her mother read stories of the Wild West, of Texas, of Kit Carson and Billy the Kid. She told adults that she wanted to be an artist and was embarrassed when they asked what kind of artist she wanted to be: she had no idea "what kind." She had no idea what artists did. She had never seen a picture that interested her, other than a pen-and-ink Maid of Athens in one of her mother's books, some Mother Goose illustrations printed on cloth, a tablet cover that showed a little girl with pink roses, and the painting of Arabs on horseback that

hung in her grandmother's parlor. At thirteen, in a Dominican convent, she was mortified when the sister corrected her drawing. At Chatham Episcopal Institute in Virginia she painted lilacs and sneaked time alone to walk out to where she could see the line of the Blue Ridge Mountains on the horizon. At the Art Institute in Chicago she was shocked by the presence of live models and wanted to abandon anatomy lessons. At the Art Students League in New York one of her fellow students advised her that, since he would be a great painter and she would end up teaching painting in a girls' school, any work of hers was less important than modeling for him. Another painted over her work to show her how the Impressionists did trees. She had not before heard how the Impressionists did trees and she did not much care.

At twenty-four she left all those opinions behind and went for the first time to live in Texas, where there were no trees to paint and no one to tell her how not to paint them. In Texas there was only the horizon she craved. In Texas she had her sister Claudia with her for a while, and in the late afternoons they would walk away from town and toward the horizon and watch the evening star come out. "That evening star fascinated me," she wrote. "It was in some way very exciting to me. My sister had a gun, and as we walked she would throw bottles into the air and shoot as many as she could before they hit the ground. I had nothing but to walk into nowhere and the wide sunset space with the star. Ten watercolors were made from that star." In a way one's interest is compelled as much by the sister Claudia with the gun as by the painter Georgia with the star, but only the painter left us this shining record. Ten watercolors were made from that star.

Engaging with the Text

1. "Style is character," Joan Didion observes. How does her **PROFILE** of Georgia O'Keeffe support this observation? 153–59

2. Didion includes a number of **QUOTATIONS** in her profile of Georgia O'Keeffe. Why do you think Didion chose so often to quote O'Keeffe 359–63

363–67
directly, rather than **SUMMARIZING** or **PARAPHRASING** her words? You might try paraphrasing one of the quotations to see the difference.

266–74
3. Didion **CONTRASTS** O'Keeffe with "the men." What does she mean by "the men"? What beliefs and personalities does she ascribe to them? How does describing them illuminate aspects of O'Keeffe's character?

4. When this profile was first published, in *The White Album* (1979), it did
458–62
not include any **ILLUSTRATIONS**; we added the two reproduced here. Obviously, this reproduction of *Red Canna* helps readers see one of O'Keeffe's "famous flowers," but what might be the downside of including it here?

5. *For Writing.* Identify someone you know who is an artist, professional
351–52
153–59
or amateur (e.g., a musician, a painter, a quilter, or an actor). **INTERVIEW** that person about the specific art he or she practices. Write a **PROFILE** of the person.

rhetorical situations · genres · processes · strategies · research mla/apa · media/design · readings

JEREMY OLSHAN

Cookie Master

Jeremy Olshan is a reporter with the New York Post *and a freelance writer. His profile of Donald Lau, a man who among other things composes fortunes for fortune cookies, appeared in 2005 in the* New Yorker. *As you read the profile, notice how Olshan incorporates Donald Lau's voice to give readers a sense of who this man is.*

AS A VICE-PRESIDENT AT WONTON FOODS, INC.,** in Long Island City,[1] Donald Lau manages the company's accounts payable and receivable, negotiates with insurers, and, somewhat incidentally, composes the fortunes that go inside the fortune cookies, of which Wonton is the world's largest manufacturer. Each day, Wonton's factory churns out four million Golden Bowl–brand cookies, which are sold to several hundred vendors, who, in turn, sell them to most of the forty thousand Chinese restaurants across the country. Wonton's primacy in the industry and, for that matter, in the gambler's imagination is such that when, in March, five of six lucky numbers printed on a fortune happened to coincide with the winning picks for the Powerball lottery, a hundred and ten people, instead of the usual handful, came forward to claim prizes of around a hundred thousand dollars. Lottery officials suspected a scam until they traced the sequence to a fortune printed with the digits "22-28-32-33-39-40" and Donald Lau's prediction: "All the preparation you've done will finally be paying off."

"We've had winners before, but never this many," Lau said the other day, in his East Williamsburg[2] office, which is furnished with stacks of financial reports and "A Dictionary of American Proverbs." "A computer picks the numbers, not me. If only a computer could also write the fortunes." Lau never expected to become a fortune-cookie writer. After graduating from Columbia with degrees in engineering and business, he

---

1. Section of Queens, a borough of New York City.
2. Section of Brooklyn, a borough of New York City.

joined Bank of America, then ran a company that exported logs from the Pacific Northwest to China. In the early eighties, he was hired by a Chinatown noodle manufacturer, which eventually expanded into fortune cookies. The firm bought the Long Island City plant, and it soon became apparent that its antiquated catalogue of fortunes would have to be updated. ("Find someone as gay as you are," one leftover from the nineteen-forties read.) "We knew we needed to add new sayings," Lau said. "I was chosen because my English was the best of the group, not because I'm poet."

At first, the writing came easily. Finding inspiration in sources ranging from the *I Ching*[3] to the *Post,* Lau cranked out three or four maxims a day, between scrutinizing spreadsheets and monitoring the company's inventory of chow mein. "I'd be on the subway and look up at the signs and think, Hey, that would make a great fortune," he said. (One such adage: "Beware of odors from unfamiliar sources.") "I'd keep a small notebook and jot down whatever came to me. I don't think I ever sat in front of the computer and said, 'I am going to write ten fortunes right now.' It has to come naturally."

Love, riches, power: there is a limited range of experience that can be expressed in one sentence, and, about eleven years into his tenure, Lau began to run out of ideas. He leaned increasingly on traditional Chinese sayings, which offer insight (along the lines of "True gold fears no fire") but not foresight ("Your income will increase"), and in 1995 he gave up altogether. "I've written thousands of fortunes, but the inspiration is gone," Lau said. "Have you heard of writer's block? That is what happened to me."

These days, he cycles selections from his vast oeuvre in and out of circulation. He is worried that readers will notice that the cookies are in reruns, which might result in Wonton's losing its edge on the competition. (This is unlikely. Although there are about forty fortune-cookie companies in the United States, few have Wonton's manufacturing

---

3. Literally, "Book of Changes" (Chinese). The *I Ching* is the oldest of classical Chinese texts; it describes a system of philosophy and statecraft and is often used in divination.

capabilities.) So Lau has decided to bring in new blood. The company will soon advertise for a new fortune writer, and Lau will make the transition to editor. "Maybe when I retire I'll write again — perhaps a book about writing fortunes," he said. Returning to form, he summarized the thrust of the book with two simple axioms. "Don't have too complicated a mind," he said. "Think in ten-word sentences."

Engaging with the Text

1. The cognitive psychologist Jerome Bruner once remarked that "discovery favors the prepared mind." How do Donald Lau's experience and method for writing fortunes bear out this adage? How might this adage serve you in your own writing?

2. Jeremy Olshan includes a number of **ENGAGING DETAILS** about the company for which vice-president Lau works. What function do these details serve in Olshan's profile of Lau?

▲ 155

3. What makes this profile of Lau, a businessman and a food manufacturer, **INTERESTING?** (Or, if you don't find it interesting, why not?) From what **ANGLE** does Olshan approach his subject?

▲ 154–55
▲ 155

4. Olshan wrote this profile for the *New Yorker,* a national magazine that focuses on current events, ideas, and the arts. How might the profile be different had it been written for a food manufacturing magazine? Consider the information it would likely include as well as the way it would be written.

5. *For Writing.* Identify someone with an interesting or offbeat job or hobby. **INTERVIEW** that person, and write a **PROFILE** that helps readers understand how this person began in his or her career or hobby. Use **DIALOGUE** from your interview to help establish the character of your subject.

● 351–52
▲ 153–59
◆ 294–98

SEAN SMITH

Johnny Depp: Unlikely Superstar

Sean Smith is a writer for Newsweek, *where he covers entertainment and the film industry. He was previously the West Coast Editor for* Premiere *magazine. The following profile of actor Johnny Depp was prompted by the release of the film* Pirates of the Caribbean: Dead Man's Chest (2006) *and appeared in the June 26 issue of* Newsweek *that year. Notice that although much of the profile is based on Smith's interview with Depp, Smith also incorporates quotes and other information from other sources.*

FATHERHOOD HAS A WAY of changing people, even iconoclasts. "When I became a dad for the first time, it was like a veil being lifted," Johnny Depp says, as he leans forward, rolling loose tobacco into dark brown paper and using his knee as a table. "I've always loved the process of acting, but I didn't find the occupational hazards particularly rewarding." Occupational hazards like being stalked by paparazzi, mauled by strangers, packaged to sell bubble gum and other side effects of fame. "I can't use the word 'fame' with myself, but yeah," he says. "I just . . . there was a long period of confusion and dissatisfaction, because I didn't understand any of it. There was no purpose to it." He leans back, lights the cigarette, exhales. "I was never horribly self-obsessed or wrapped up in my own weirdness, but when my daughter was born, suddenly there was clarity. I wasn't angry anymore. It was the first purely selfless moment that I had ever experienced. And it was liberating. In that moment, it's like you become something else. The real you is revealed."

The Real Johnny Depp. How long have we searched for him? No one in Hollywood, it's fair to say, has worked harder at *not* being a movie star than Depp has, and yet he has evolved into one of the most adored actors of his generation not in spite of that persistence but because of it. *Pirates of the Caribbean: The Curse of the Black Pearl* may have grossed $653 million worldwide, made Depp a $20 million man and earned him an Oscar nomination, but he still seems an unlikely addition to the A-list. Top-tier stars,

Johnny Depp as Captain Jack Sparrow in Pirates of the Caribbean: Dead Man's Chest *(2006).* © Walt Disney / Courtesy Everett Collection.

even those who are great actors, stay on top by being true to their personas. We pay $10 to see Will Smith or Julia Roberts precisely because they don't surprise us. It's not that they're playing themselves. It's just that the force of their personalities swamps everything else. They're more than actors. They're brands. Depp, 43, is almost pathologically unpredictable. He can be bizarre, hilarious, unsettling—even annoying. But he is never the same. He's the anti-Tom Cruise. "Nothing against Tom, but Johnny may be a bigger star now," says director John Waters, who cast Depp in 1990's *Cry-Baby*. "Nobody is sick of Johnny Depp."

Pirates of the Caribbean: Dead Man's Chest, which opens on July 7, will likely be the highest-grossing movie of the summer. And judging from *Newsweek*'s first look in the editing room, it also promises to be a welcome blast of sunshine in a season when Cruise has crashed and burned, and *The Da Vinci Code* has proved to be a joyless blockbuster. In this second leg of the *Pirates* trilogy—the third installment will be released next summer—lovebirds Will (Orlando Bloom) and Elizabeth (Keira Knightley) are arrested on their wedding day for aiding the escape of Depp's louche Narcissus, Captain Jack Sparrow. To win freedom for his bride and himself, Will must find Captain Jack, get him to hand over his mysterious compass and give it to the wormy Lord Beckett, who plans to use it to rid the world of pirates forever. Jack, meanwhile, has more immediate problems. He owes his soul to undersea Captain Davey Jones, is in danger of being destroyed by a giant sea creature called a *kraken* and has landed on an island of cannibals who have made him their god. Which would be great if the natives didn't make a habit of eating their gods.

Returning director Gore Verbinski, producer Jerry Bruckheimer and team have cranked up the action this time around. One huge set piece includes an elaborate three-way sword fight on a massive water wheel that has snapped off its frame and is rolling at top speed through the jungle. ("It's those moments when you realize how absurd your job is," Depp says. "It's great fun, but it was a bastard to shoot.") Luckily, they've also given Depp plenty of playtime, too. Even more than in the first film, Depp's exaggerated expressions and unexpected line deliveries turn "cute" moments into hilarious ones. At one point, Elizabeth tells Jack, "You're a good man." Depp replies, sloppily, under his breath, "All evidence to the contrary."

Sitting in a bungalow at the Chateau Marmont in Los Angeles, Depp flashes a bit of Captain Jack every time he opens his mouth. Those gold pirate teeth are bonded onto his own. With the shoot for the third *Pirates* resuming in August, Depp figured it was just easier to keep them. "They don't come off until the ride stops," he says, and smiles. "It's a horrible process. I didn't want to go through yanking them off and putting them back on. And it leaves some residue of the character behind." Time slows down when you're with Johnny Depp. He seems like a man who has never rushed to, or from, anywhere in his life. He is chronically late for interviews—sometimes four or five hours, sometimes days—but this time around just a gentlemanly 50 minutes. And once he's with you, he never seems in a hurry to leave. His voice is a soft, low mumble. His body is in almost constant motion—rolling those cigarettes, rubbing an elbow, reaching for a glass—but the rhythm is tranquil and fluid, like a cat licking its paw. He's a calm, almost hypnotic presence. "He's always been true to who he is," says director Tim Burton, who has made five films with Depp, including last year's *Charlie and the Chocolate Factory*. "He's never been ruled by money, or by what people think he should or shouldn't do. Maybe it's just in America, but it seems that if you're passionate about something, it freaks people out. You're considered bizarre or eccentric. To me, it just means you know who you are."

Depp arrived in Hollywood in the early '80s. Despite a physical beauty that had studio executives slobbering to make him into a Romantic Leading Man and hordes of teenage girls (and a few boys) dreaming of touching his hair *just once*, Depp escaped from the Hollywood star machine around 1990, and managed to elude capture for almost two decades. He hid out in strange, sometimes beautiful films, playing unforgettable characters—Edward Scissorhands, Ed Wood, Hunter S. Thompson, Gilbert Grape—in movies that rarely made a dent at the box office. Of the 20 films Depp starred in before 2003, only one, Burton's *Sleepy Hollow*, squeaked past the $100 million mark. Depp got a reputation for being outré and unbankable. "Oh, yeah," he says, then rolls off the list of crimes: "'That guy can't open a film. He does all those weird art movies. He works with directors whose names we can't pronounce.'" He smiles. "But there are worse things they could say."

When news hit years ago that Depp was going to make the first *Pirates*, the buzz around town was that he must be broke, and that after years of taking the artistic high road, he had finally sold out. Depp says he never worried about that. "Never, not once, and I don't know why, because one would think that I would have," he says. "I suppose it's because I feel like I have a voice. The idea of commercial success never bothered me necessarily. What bothered me was *striving* for that, and lying to get that. If I was going to do something, it had to be on my terms—not because I'm some hideous control freak—but because I don't want to live a lie. You really don't want to look back on your life and go, 'I was a complete fraud.'"

The battle to remain authentic has been long and bloody, and it made Depp an angry young man for most of his twenties. Born in Kentucky, the youngest of four kids, and raised in Florida by parents who fought and finally divorced when he was fifteen, Depp dreamed of playing guitar in a band. By sixteen he had dropped out of school and was doing just that, his group opening for acts like Iggy Pop. "It was wonderful," he says. "I couldn't have been happier." But after the band arrived in Los Angeles, Depp found himself broke. A musician he was briefly married to at the time introduced Depp to Nicolas Cage, who suggested that he give acting a try. On little more than a whim, he did, and ended up with a supporting role in *A Nightmare on Elm Street* and a small part in *Platoon*. Still struggling financially, he signed for *21 Jump Street*, a slick TV series about young cops going undercover in high schools. It made Depp a teen idol, and made him miserable just as fast. "Everything flips," he says. "Suddenly, you go into restaurants and people are pointing at you and whispering. You feel spooked by it because that freedom of anonymity is gone. You never get used to that. You'd leave the hotel to go to dinner and there'd be tons of cameras and flashbulbs. 'Smile, Johnny! Smile!'" He looks annoyed by it, even now. "I thought, 'Jesus, I just want to go home.' But there was no home."

Depp was locked into a multiyear contract with the Fox network. "They turned me into this product, and I didn't have a say in it," he says. "You have no voice, you know? I felt like I was a captive." So he lashed out, becoming a disruptive force on the *Jump Street* set in the hope that the network would fire him. "I was the only one who confronted him on what an a--hole he was being," says costar Holly Robinson Peete. "I totally understood his position, but I was over the moon to be a part of this show, and it's hard to come to work every day with someone who is p---ing all over it. So I went into his dressing room and told him how I felt, and right after that he trashed his Winnebago." Peete doesn't have any hard feelings toward Depp, and chalks it up to youth and inexperience. "He's got a really great heart, but he was frustrated," she says. "He just hated the idea of being on a lunch box or some teenage girl's wall."

Finally freed from *Jump Street*, Depp played a succession of iconic loners and dreamers for visionary, unconventional directors, such as Waters, Burton, Jim Jarmusch and Terry Gilliam. But the anger, which Depp calls his "hillbilly rage," never quite dissipated. He was famously arrested for trashing a New York City hotel room in 1994, and while Depp says the incident was blown out of proportion—"I wasn't the Wild Man of Borneo"— he still believed that his fame and success lacked a point, meaning. "I had these sort of self-destructive periods," he says. "We all go through times

10

where we poison ourselves a bit. Looking back on it now, it was simply a waste of time, all the self-medicating and boozing."

Depp was rescued, in part, by Marlon Brando. The two worked together on 1995's *Don Juan DeMarco*, and hit it off at the first rehearsal. "Within minutes, Johnny was in Marlon's lap with, I think, a bottle of gin," says director Jeremy Leven. "And I think he stayed there the whole time." It's easy to imagine the bond between the two men, both actors with unconventional visions, talent to burn and a disdain for art compromised by commerce. "Marlon was a pioneer," Depp says, quietly. "So I wouldn't even put myself in the same thought bubble with him, but he understood a lot of things about me, and was incredibly generous and helpful and caring. Very rarely did we talk about movies or acting, so it wasn't that. He saw me going through stuff that he had been through—my weird hillbilly rage—so yeah, the connection was strong and deep."

But it wasn't until Depp met and fell in love with French actress-singer Vanessa Paradis that everything seemed to fall into place for the actor. After a series of highly public, long-term romances—Sherilyn Fenn, Jennifer Grey, Winona Ryder, Kate Moss—his relationship with Paradis seemed to anchor him. The couple's daughter, Lily-Rose, was born in 1999; their son, Jack, in 2002. Being a father released him from the pressure of finding meaning and identity exclusively in his work. "I think it softened him on one level, and then invigorated him on an artistic one," says Burton. "It's an interesting juxtaposition." Depp himself puts it more directly: "Now I know where home is."

It was Depp's desire to make a movie for his kids that led him to *Pirates.* In a visit to the Disney lot about five years ago, he mentioned to studio chairman Dick Cook that he'd been watching a lot of Disney movies with his daughter, loved them and was hoping to voice a character in a Pixar movie. Cook mentioned that the studio was developing a movie based on the theme-park ride *Pirates of the Caribbean.* "And he got very excited," Cook recalls. "He said, 'Like a real pirate movie? With swords?' And I said, 'Yeah—with swords.' And he said, 'I'm in.'"

As is now well known to *Pirates* fans, studio executives were nonplussed when they began to see the footage of Depp in character. Whereas Captain Jack Sparrow was initially conceived as a young Burt Lancaster, Depp had re-imagined him as a debauched, vain, slightly fey rock star, inspired by Rolling Stones icon Keith Richards and cartoon skunk Pepe Le Pew. "The studio was, like, 'Is he gay? Is he drunk? We don't know *what* he's doing!'" says producer Bruckheimer. "It took a little while to calm everybody down." For his part, Verbinski, the director, loved it. "You know, there's a lot of conspiring that goes on between actors and directors that I think is very healthy," he says. "You should be a little concerned as a director if you're *not* making the studio nervous."

Depp's off-kilter performance, of course, was the very thing that cat-apulted *Pirates* into a cultural phenomenon. "First of all, Johnny is a pirate in real life," says John Waters. "It's the closest part he's ever played to his real self, but the fact that he played it kind of nelly was a big risk." Pause. "If only real gay pirates were that much fun." After decades of being daring and unexpected in daring and unexpected little films, Depp was now staying true to himself in a big summer blockbuster. He didn't have to be an outsider on the outside. He could be an outsider on the inside. "You feel like you have infiltrated the enemy camp, like you got in there some-how and chiseled your name in the castle wall," he says. The huge success of the film "made perfect sense to me on the one hand, and at the same time, it made no sense at all, which I kind of enjoyed." He takes another drag, exhales. "Yeah, it just felt right. Even now, with the dolls and the cereal boxes and snacks and fruit juices, it all just feels fun to me, in a Warholian way. It's absurd. It doesn't get more absurd." Depp's not ready to let go of Captain Jack just yet. "He's a blast to play," he says. "I'll be in a deep, dark depression saying goodbye to him." He laughs. "I'll keep the costume and just prance around the house, entertain the kids." Or the rest of the world. "Maybe '*Pirates* 4, 5 and 6,'" he says. "If they had a good script, why not? I mean, at a certain point, the madness must stop, but for the moment, I can't say that he's done."

These days, Depp and his family divide their time between homes in Los Angeles and France, when they're not on some movie set or other. He says the media perception of him as an expat and wanna-be Frenchman has been overstated. "But, yeah, I love it there," he says. "I've always loved it there. The phones don't ring as much. Movies are never brought up in conversation. I'll take the kids and we'll go out to the trampoline and the swing set, and we'll stop by the garden and see how our tomatoes are

15

rhetorical situations   genres   processes   strategies   research mla/apa   media/ design   readings

doing. You know, old-fart stuff. Good stuff." At last, Depp has learned to quit fighting fate/fame/whatever. "I think everything happened the way it was meant to happen, but I don't know why," he says. "I remember every bump in the road, and I still don't know how I got here. But who am I to ask why? The fact is, this is where I am. So I enjoy it, salute it and keep moving forward." He smiles, a flash of gold. "None of it makes any sense to me, but then, why should it?"

Engaging with the Text

1. Good profiles see their subjects from an **INTERESTING ANGLE.** What do you think is Sean Smith's angle on Johnny Depp? Identify places in the text that make that angle clear.

    ▲ 155

2. Smith **OPENS** his profile of Johnny Depp with an observation: "Fatherhood has a way of changing people, even iconoclasts." How does this opening set the stage for the rest of the profile? Why was having children a turning point in Depp's life? How effective is this opening?

    ◆ 239–45

3. What is Smith's **STANCE** toward Depp, his subject? Point to specific places in the text that reveal this stance.

    ■ 12–14

4. In what ways has Johnny Depp been made into a commodity over the years? How did Depp move from being angry about being commodified—"hat[ing] the idea of being on a lunch box or some teenage girl's wall"—to embracing it, noting that "the dolls and cereal boxes and snacks and fruit juices, it all feels fun to me, in a Warholian way"? How do you feel about this attitude?

5. *For Writing.* Identify a person who is near the top of his or her career (a teacher, a police officer, a business person, an artist—in short, any profession). You might consider finding someone who is in a career you would like to pursue. Interview that person to find out how he or she came to be in the chosen career, how that career has played itself out, and what he or she plans to do next. Write a profile that incorporates **ANECDOTES** and **DIALOGUE** from your subject to help readers understand how that person arrived where he or she is now.

    ◆ 304–12
◆ 294–98

58 Proposals

See also:

rhetorical situations   genres   processes   strategies   research mla/apa   media/ design   readings

DENNIS BARON

Don't Make English Official — Ban It Instead

Dennis Baron is a professor of English and linguistics at the University of Illinois at Urbana-Champaign. His essays on the history of English usage, language legislation, and technology and literacy have been widely published in newspapers and magazines. He is the author of Grammar and Good Taste: Reforming the American Language *(1983) and* The English-Only Question: An Official Language for Americans? *(1992). He also serves as a consultant to policy makers, lawyers, and journalists on questions concerning language. The following proposal originally appeared in the* Washington Post *in 1996.*

CONGRESS IS CONSIDERING, and may soon pass, legislation making English the official language of the United States. Supporters of the measure say that English forms the glue that keeps America together. They deplore the dollars wasted translating English into other languages. And they fear a horde of illegal aliens adamantly refusing to acquire the most powerful language on earth.

On the other hand, opponents of official English remind us that without legislation we have managed to get over ninety-seven percent of the residents of this country to speak the national language. No country with an official language law even comes close. Opponents also point out that today's non-English-speaking immigrants are picking up English faster than earlier generations of immigrants did, so instead of official English, they favor "English Plus," encouraging everyone to speak both English and another language.

I would like to offer a modest proposal to resolve the language impasse in Congress. Don't make English official, ban it instead.

That may sound too radical, but proposals to ban English first surfaced in the heady days after the American Revolution. Anti-British sentiment was so strong in the new United States that a few superpatriots wanted to get rid of English altogether. They suggested replacing English with Hebrew, thought by many in the eighteenth century to be the world's first language, the one spoken in the garden of Eden. French was also considered, because it was thought at the time, and especially by the French, to be the language of pure reason. And of course there was Greek, the language of Athens, the world's first democracy. It's not clear how serious any of these proposals were, though Roger Sherman[1] of Connecticut supposedly remarked that it would be better to keep English for ourselves and make the British speak Greek.

Even if the British are now our allies, there may be some benefit to   5
banning English today. A common language can often be the cause of strife and misunderstanding. Look at Ireland and Northern Ireland, the two Koreas, or the Union and the Confederacy. Banning English would prevent that kind of divisiveness in America today.

Also, if we banned English, we wouldn't have to worry about whose English to make official: the English of England or America? of Chicago or New York? of Ross Perot or William F. Buckley?[2]

We might as well ban English, too, because no one seems to read it much lately, few can spell it, and fewer still can parse it. Even English teachers have come to rely on computer spell checkers.

Another reason to ban English: it's hardly even English anymore. English started its decline in 1066, with the unfortunate incident at Hastings.[3] Since then it has become a polyglot conglomeration of French, Latin, Italian, Scandinavian, Arabic, Sanskrit, Celtic, Yiddish and Chinese, with an occasional smiley face thrown in.

More important, we should ban English because it has become a world language. Remember what happened to all the other world languages: Latin, Greek, Indo-European? One day they're on everybody's tongue; the next day they're dead. Banning English now would save us that inevitable disappointment.

---

1. American revolutionary leader (1721–93), signer of the Declaration of Independence and the U.S. Constitution.

2. Respectively, American industrialist and independent presidential candidate, and conservative political commentator.

3. Port on south coast of England, site of Saxon army's defeat by the invading Norman forces led by William of Normandy (c. 1028–87).

rhetorical situations   genres   processes   strategies   research mla/apa   media/ design   readings

Although we shouldn't ban English without designating a replace-   10
ment for it, there is no obvious candidate. The French blew their chance
when they sold Louisiana. It doesn't look like the Russians are going to
take over this country anytime soon — they're having enough trouble
taking over Russia. German, the largest minority language in the U.S.
until recently, lost much of its prestige after two world wars. Chinese
is too hard to write, especially if you're not Chinese. There's always
Esperanto, a language made up a hundred years ago that is supposed
to bring about world unity. We're still waiting for that. And if you took
Spanish in high school you can see that it's not easy to get large numbers of people to speak another language fluently.

In the end, though, it doesn't matter what replacement language
we pick, just so long as we ban English instead of making it official. Pro-
hibiting English will do for the language what Prohibition did for liquor.
Those who already use it will continue to do so, and those who don't
will want to try out what has been forbidden. This negative psychology
works with children. It works with speed limits. It even worked in the
Garden of Eden.

Engaging with the Text

1. Dennis Baron **BEGINS** his essay by presenting two views on whether
   or not English should be the official language of the United States.
   What is the central problem that both sides are trying to address? Is
   this an effective beginning? Why or why not? How else might he have
   begun?

   239–45

2. Baron offers six **REASONS** for accepting his solution. What are those
   reasons? What is the central point that holds these different reasons
   together? To what degree are we meant to take these reasons seriously?

   93, 325

3. Baron signals that his proposal is meant to be read as satire when he
   writes "I would like to offer a modest proposal to resolve the language
   impasse in Congress. Don't make English official, ban it instead." Here

Baron alludes to Jonathan Swift's "A Modest Proposal," an essay that is a *tour de force* of satire. If we aren't meant to take his proposal at face value — and we aren't — what is the **PURPOSE** of Baron's proposal? What, in other words, is the real argument he is making?

3–4 ■

4. If Baron's purpose is not actually to propose banning English in America, why do you think he chose to use the proposal genre to put forth his argument? What other **GENRES** might he have used?

9–11 ■

5. *For Writing.* Identify a current hotly debated issue in the country, your state, your town, or your school. **PROPOSE** an outlandish solution for the problem and provide a plausible, if ironic, **ARGUMENT** for your solution. Be sure to anticipate — and respond to — possible objections to your proposed solution.

160–65 ▲

163 ▲

STANLEY FISH

Who's in Charge Here?

Stanley Fish is a professor of law and humanities at the College of Law at Florida International University, as well as a scholar of English litera-ture. He is the author of many books, among them Is There a Text in This Class? The Authority of Interpretive Communities *(1980),* Doing What Comes Naturally: Change, Rhetoric, and the Practice of Theory in Literary and Legal Studies *(1989), and* Professional Correctness: Literary Studies and Political Change *(1999). He also writes a monthly column for the* Chronicle of Higher Education, *a publication aimed at educators in colleges and universities. The following proposal appeared in the* Chronicle *in 2005.*

W ELL, I'D GONE AND DONE IT AGAIN. My intentions were good (or so it seemed to me at the time). I had brought the student-evaluation forms with me on the appointed day, but when the class was over, and the students had filed out for the last time, there was the large envelope, unopened.

I threw it in the trash and walked back to my office. In my heart I knew that this behavior of 2004 had its source in 1965, when I was teach-ing at the University of California at Berkeley and first saw *The Slate Sup-plement,* a student-run review of teacher performance on sale at the campus bookstore.

At the time I was struck by the casual cruelty of the entries, espe-cially with respect to younger faculty members whose teaching skills were in the process of being developed. Not long afterward, negative comments from the supplement on the performance of a third-year assistant professor were referred to in the course of his midcareer review.

I protested, saying that if we allowed those unofficial (and unsci-entific) judgments into our discussions, in time they would become part of the official process. And decisions affecting the career and livelihood of countless junior scholars would be inflected by the ill-informed opin-ions of transient students with little or no stake in the enterprise who would be free (because they would be anonymous) to indulge any sense of grievance they happened to harbor in the full knowledge that nothing they said would ever be questioned or challenged.

Nothing like that, a senior colleague assured me solemnly, could 5 ever happen. Faculty members would always be able to distinguish between anecdotal evidence from a questionable source and the hard evidence of publication and research.

The rest, as they say, is history.

It has not been a good history. True, the evaluation forms have been revised and supposedly refined, but in general the revisions have followed political and sociological trends rather than any advance in our understanding of what is and is not good teaching.

In my university, students respond to 27 statements/questions, of which perhaps five or six are obviously and importantly pertinent to the assessment of pedagogical responsibility: "Were examinations and other graded materials returned on a timely basis? Were students tested on materials covered in the course? Was there sufficient feedback on tests and papers? Were course materials well prepared? Did the course unfold as promised in the catalog and syllabus? Was the instructor accessible to students during office hours?"

Other questions might be relevant in some teaching situations, but not in others. "Did the instructor give lectures that facilitated note taking?" (Even in lecture courses this might not be a suitable measure; note taking is not what some lecturers, for reasons they could articulate, wish to provoke.)

Still other questions conflate student and teaching performance, 10 and imply that the latter is always responsible for the former. "Have you learned and understood the subject materials of this course?" You might answer no, but you might also give the same answer to questions like, Did you attend class regularly? Did you read the assignments? Did you spend much time doing research for your final paper?

The majority of the questions encourage and reward behavior that is at best questionable. Were students invited to share their ideas and knowledge? Given that the point of a course is to improve student knowl-

edge, it makes some sense to gauge the extent (or lack) of it at the outset of instruction; but surely one doesn't want student knowledge to be a major ingredient in a course, and as for "sharing" it, that is an activity that belongs in the coffee shop or dorm room, not in a classroom.

And that of course is the issue: Exactly what kind of activity is teaching, after all? Is it therapy? If so, no teacher is licensed to practice it. Is it retail merchandising (in which case it would be appropriate to cater to the consumer's ignorance)? Let's hope not.

Is it civic or democratic conversation? Not if it's done right, although at least one question in the evaluation form suggests otherwise: "Were students encouraged to question and/or challenge the course material?" Imagine the scene: You have spent some time constructing a syllabus and choosing the readings and arranging them in an order that supports or leads to an overarching thesis. But early on, and regularly thereafter, you pause to take a vote — in effect asking, Is this the material you want to study and is this the approach you want me to take? Or, to speak in the vernacular, Are you OK with this?

Well, I guess you could do that, and then adjust your behavior accordingly, but I can't for the life of me see why you would call that teaching.

So there in brief is my brief (not only mine; the points have been 15 made before by many) against student evaluations: They are randomly collected. They are invitations to grind axes without any fear of challenge or discovery. They are based on assumptions that have more to do with pop psychology or self-help or customer satisfaction than with the soundness of one's pedagogy. A whole lot of machinery with a very small and dubious yield.

But don't students have a right to competent and responsible instruction? You bet they do (and this is the only sense I can give to the phrase "student rights"), and that is why I approve of those questions that go right to the heart of what responsible instruction is — course planning, reasonable and rewarding assignments, up-to-date and pertinent readings, generous and helpful feedback, the meeting of curricular expectations, and so on.

Not only are the concerns raised by those questions legitimate, they are too important to be left to the hit-or-miss nonprocedure of the present system.

It would be better if, rather than making complaints anonymously and after the fact, students could report problems to a university office that would assure confidentiality while complaints were being considered by a standing committee. If, in the judgment of that committee, further investigation was warranted, all parties could be informed and invited to a hearing in which everyone would be given an opportunity to speak and respond.

Such procedures already exist to deal with any number of grievances (sexual harassment, discrimination of various kinds), and it would not be that difficult to extend them so that the grievances of those students who feel that an instructor is not doing his or her job could be heard.

No doubt in many colleges and universities a grievance process is already in place, and if it is, there is absolutely no need for the waste of paper and time that now goes into preparing, printing, distributing, collecting, and tabulating forms that report the unfiltered opinions of those who, for whatever reason, decided to express them. 20

To be sure, there would still be a need for teaching evaluations that could legitimately play a role in promotion and tenure decisions. Those evaluations, however, could be provided by the system of peer visitation already used by most departments. It is, after all, a matter of judging professional competence, and who better to do that than a professional, someone who visits your class and assesses what you're doing (or trying to do) in the context of a career-long effort to do the same thing.

Of course you will be more than handicapped if the class your senior colleague visits has a floating population made up of some students who have been there from day one and others who showed up just yesterday, not to mention the absence of those who occupied a seat and a place in your plan of instruction for some weeks before disappearing without notice or explanation.

If those in the room have not been together from the beginning, they will not share an experience and a sustained exploration of issues, and

rhetorical situations   genres   processes   strategies   research mla/apa   media/ design   readings

it may be difficult, if not impossible, to generate the kind of discussion that provides evidence that something educationally valuable is going on. The villain in this piece is the period for adding or dropping a course, which in some universities is extended to the last day of the semester and in many universities is extended through the first six weeks.

I can understand why students, behaving as consumers always do, would want the right to move in and out of classes almost at will, but I cannot understand why faculty members and administrators would grant it to them.

My idea of a good drop-and-add period would be about 20 minutes, 25 but I concede that a week of sampling and shopping might be reasonable. If at the beginning of the second week you know who it is that you're supposed to teach, you have at least a fighting chance of teaching them something.

I am aware of the standard arguments supporting extended drop-and-add periods — students need time to determine whether they have made the right decision, students should be allowed to withdraw from courses for which they feel insufficiently prepared, students should not be forced to continue in a course if the grade they anticipate receiving would negatively impact their grade-point average and therefore jeopardize admission to graduate school — but as far as I can see what they add up to is the desire for a fail-safe education, again a desire I understand, but not one we should gratify.

A colleague who has had much more experience with these matters than I have reports (without endorsing) the question he hears most often when this issue comes up: If students are not doing well in a course, why should we penalize them? If you don't know the answer to that question, you might want to consider another line of work.

Engaging with the Text

1. Stanley Fish tackles two **WELL-DEFINED PROBLEMS**, the first having to do with student evaluations and the second with drop-add periods. How does he establish the problems? What are the **SOLUTIONS** he proposes?

▲ 162

▲ 163

Does he convince you? Do you think the issues he cites are problems? If so, what do you think of his proposed solutions?

_5–8_

2. Consider the **AUDIENCE** for Fish's proposal — readers of the *Chronicle of Higher Education*. How does Fish shape his proposal for the college professors and administrators who read the *Chronicle*? How would you advise him to revise this piece to appeal to an audience of students?

_12–14_

3. How would you characterize Fish's **STANCE?** How does that stance affect his tone and his treatment of counterarguments? How persuasive do you find his tone?

_245–48_

4. Fish **ENDS** by posing a question administrators often hear from parents and students: "If students are not doing well in a course, why should we penalize them?" Rather than answer that question, Fish writes, "If you don't know the answer to that question, you might want to consider another line of work." How effective is this ending? How might this question be answered? Why does Fish believe that those who don't know the answer should stay out of teaching?

_331–57_
_160–65_
_5–8_

5. *For Writing.* Identify a common problem on your campus. **RESEARCH** the problem and write a **PROPOSAL** to address it. Be sure to identify your intended **AUDIENCE** and shape your proposal accordingly.

PETER SINGER

The Singer Solution to World Poverty

*Ethicist Peter Singer is a professor of bioethics in the University Center
for Human Values at Princeton University and a professor in the Center
for Applied Philosophy and Public Ethics at the University of Melbourne
in Australia. The author of eighteen books, among them* Animal Libera-
tion *(revised edition 2001),* One World: Ethics and Globalization
(2002), and The Way We Eat: Why Our Food Choices Matter *(with
Jim Mason, 2006), he is considered one of the founders of the modern
animal rights movement. The following proposal was first published in
1999 in the* New York Times Magazine.

IN THE BRAZILIAN FILM *Central Station,* Dora is a retired schoolteacher
who makes ends meet by sitting at the station writing letters for illiterate people. Suddenly she has an opportunity to pocket $1,000. All she
has to do is persuade a homeless nine-year-old boy to follow her to an
address she has been given. (She is told he will be adopted by wealthy
foreigners.) She delivers the boy, gets the money, spends some of it on
a television set, and settles down to enjoy her new acquisition. Her
neighbor spoils the fun, however, by telling her that the boy was too old
to be adopted — he will be killed and his organs sold for transplanta-
tion. Perhaps Dora knew this all along, but after her neighbor's plain
speaking, she spends a troubled night. In the morning Dora resolves to
take the boy back.

Suppose Dora had told her neighbor that it is a tough world, other
people have nice new TVs too, and if selling the kid is the only way she
can get one, well, he was only a street kid. She would then have become,
in the eyes of the audience, a monster. She redeems herself only by
being prepared to bear considerable risks to save the boy.

At the end of the movie, in cinemas in the affluent nations of the
world, people who would have been quick to condemn Dora if she had
not rescued the boy go home to places far more comfortable than her
apartment. In fact, the average family in the United States spends almost

one-third of its income on things that are no more necessary to them than Dora's new TV was to her. Going out to nice restaurants, buying new clothes because the old ones are no longer stylish, vacationing at beach resorts — so much of our income is spent on things not essential to the preservation of our lives and health. Donated to one of a number of charitable agencies, that money could mean the difference between life and death for children in need.

All of which raises a question: in the end, what is the ethical distinction between a Brazilian who sells a homeless child to organ peddlers and an American who already has a TV and upgrades to a better one — knowing that the money could be donated to an organization that would use it to save the lives of kids in need?

Of course, there are several differences between the two situations   5 that could support different moral judgments about them. For one thing, to be able to consign a child to death when he is standing right in front of you takes a chilling kind of heartlessness; it is much easier to ignore an appeal for money to help children you will never meet. Yet for a utilitarian philosopher like myself — that is, one who judges whether acts are right or wrong by their consequences — if the upshot of the American's failure to donate the money is that one more kid dies on the streets of a Brazilian city, then it is, in some sense, just as bad as selling the kid to the organ peddlers. But one doesn't need to embrace my utilitarian ethic to see that, at the very least, there is a troubling incongruity in being so quick to condemn Dora for taking the child to the organ peddlers while, at the same time, not regarding the American consumer's behavior as raising a serious moral issue.

In his 1996 book *Living High and Letting Die*, the New York University philosopher Peter Unger presented an ingenious series of imaginary examples designed to probe our intuitions about whether it is wrong to live well without giving substantial amounts of money to help people who are hungry, malnourished, or dying from easily treatable illnesses like diarrhea. Here's my paraphrase of one of these examples:

Bob is close to retirement. He has invested most of his savings in a very rare and valuable old car, a Bugatti, which he has not been able to insure. The Bugatti is his pride and joy. In addition to the pleasure he gets from driving and caring for his car, Bob knows that its rising market value means that he will always be able to sell it and live comfortably after retirement. One day when Bob is out for a drive, he parks the Bugatti near the end of a railway siding and goes for a walk up the track. As he does so, he sees that a runaway train, with no one aboard, is running down the railway track. Looking farther down the track, he sees the small figure of a child very likely to be killed by the runaway train. He can't stop the train and the child is too far away to warn of the danger, but he can throw a switch that will divert the train down the siding where his Bugatti is parked. Then nobody will be killed — but the train will destroy his Bugatti. Thinking of his joy in owning the car and the financial security it represents, Bob decides not to throw the switch. The child is killed. For many years to come, Bob enjoys owning his Bugatti and the financial security it represents.

Bob's conduct, most of us will immediately respond, was gravely wrong. Unger agrees. But then he reminds us that we, too, have opportunities to save the lives of children. We can give to organizations like Unicef or Oxfam America. How much would we have to give one of these organizations to have a high probability of saving the life of a child threatened by easily preventable diseases? (I do not believe that children are more worth saving than adults, but since no one can argue that children have brought their poverty on themselves, focusing on them simplifies the issues.) Unger called up some experts and used the information they provided to offer some plausible estimates that include the cost of raising money, administrative expenses, and the cost of delivering aid where it is most needed. By his calculation, $200 in donations would help a sickly two-year-old transform into a healthy six-year-old — offering safe passage through childhood's most dangerous years. To show how practical philosophical argument can be, Unger even tells his readers that they can easily donate funds by using their credit card and calling one of these toll-free numbers: (800) 367-5437 for Unicef; (800) 693-2687 for Oxfam America.

Now you, too, have the information you need to save a child's life. How should you judge yourself if you don't do it? Think again about Bob and his Bugatti. Unlike Dora, Bob did not have to look into the eyes of the child he was sacrificing for his own material comfort. The child was a complete stranger to him and too far away to relate to in an intimate, personal way. Unlike Dora, too, he did not mislead the child or initiate the chain of events imperiling him. In all these respects, Bob's situation resembles that of people able but unwilling to donate to overseas aid and differs from Dora's situation.

If you still think that it was very wrong of Bob not to throw the   10 switch that would have diverted the train and saved the child's life, then it is hard to see how you could deny that it is also very wrong not to send money to one of the organizations listed above. Unless, that is, there is some morally important difference between the two situations that I have overlooked.

Is it the practical uncertainties about whether aid will really reach the people who need it? Nobody who knows the world of overseas aid can doubt that such uncertainties exist. But Unger's figure of $200 to save a child's life was reached after he had made conservative assumptions about the proportion of the money donated that will actually reach its target.

One genuine difference between Bob and those who can afford to donate to overseas aid organizations but don't is that only Bob can save the child on the tracks, whereas there are hundreds of millions of people who can give $200 to overseas aid organizations. The problem is that most of them aren't doing it. Does this mean that it is all right for you not to do it?

Suppose that there were more owners of priceless vintage cars — Carol, Dave, Emma, Fred and so on, down to Ziggy — all in exactly the same situation as Bob, with their own siding and their own switch, all sacrificing the child in order to preserve their own cherished car. Would that make it all right for Bob to do the same? To answer this question affirmatively is to endorse follow-the-crowd ethics — the kind of ethics that led many Germans to look away when the Nazi atrocities were being committed. We do not excuse them because others were behaving no better.

We seem to lack a sound basis for drawing a clear moral line between Bob's situation and that of any reader of this article with $200

to spare who does not donate it to an overseas aid agency. These readers seem to be acting at least as badly as Bob was acting when he chose to let the runaway train hurtle toward the unsuspecting child. In the light of this conclusion, I trust that many readers will reach for the phone and donate that $200. Perhaps you should do it before reading further.

Now that you have distinguished yourself morally from people who put their vintage cars ahead of a child's life, how about treating yourself and your partner to dinner at your favorite restaurant? But wait. The money you will spend at the restaurant could also help save the lives of children overseas! True, you weren't planning to blow $200 tonight, but if you were to give up dining out just for one month, you would easily save that amount. And what is one month's dining out, compared to a child's life? There's the rub. Since there are a lot of desperately needy children in the world, there will always be another child whose life you could save for another $200. Are you therefore obliged to keep giving until you have nothing left? At what point can you stop? 15

Hypothetical examples can easily become farcical. Consider Bob. How far past losing the Bugatti should he go? Imagine that Bob had got his foot stuck in the track of the siding, and if he diverted the train, then before it rammed the car it would also amputate his big toe. Should he still throw the switch? What if it would amputate his foot? His entire leg?

As absurd as the Bugatti scenario gets when pushed to extremes, the point it raises is a serious one: only when the sacrifices become very significant indeed would most people be prepared to say that Bob does nothing wrong when he decides not to throw the switch. Of course, most people could be wrong; we can't decide moral issues by taking opinion polls. But consider for yourself the level of sacrifice that you would demand of Bob, and then think about how much money you would have to give away in order to make a sacrifice that is roughly equal to that. It's almost certainly much, much more than $200. For most middle-class Americans, it could easily be more like $200,000.

Isn't it counterproductive to ask people to do so much? Don't we run the risk that many will shrug their shoulders and say that morality, so conceived, is fine for saints but not for them? I accept that we are unlikely to see, in the near or even medium-term future, a world in which it is normal for wealthy Americans to give the bulk of their wealth to strangers. When it comes to praising or blaming people for what they do, we tend to use a standard that is relative to some conception of normal behavior. Comfortably off Americans who give, say, 10 percent of their income to overseas aid organizations are so far ahead of most of their equally comfortable fellow citizens that I wouldn't go out of my way to chastise them for not doing more. Nevertheless, they should be doing much more, and they are in no position to criticize Bob for failing to make the much greater sacrifice of his Bugatti.

At this point various objections may crop up. Someone may say: "If every citizen living in the affluent nations contributed his or her share I wouldn't have to make such a drastic sacrifice, because long before such levels were reached, the resources would have been there to save the lives of all those children dying from lack of food or medical care. So why should I give more than my fair share?" Another, related objection is that the government ought to increase its overseas aid allocations, since that would spread the burden more equitably across all taxpayers.

Yet the question of how much we ought to give is a matter to be   20 decided in the real world — and that, sadly, is a world in which we know that most people do not, and in the immediate future will not, give substantial amounts to overseas aid agencies. We know, too, that at least in the next year, the United States government is not going to meet even the very modest United Nations–recommended target of 0.7 percent of gross national product; at a moment it lags far below that, at 0.09 percent, not even half of Japan's 0.22 percent or a tenth of Denmark's 0.97 percent. Thus, we know that the money we can give beyond that theoretical "fair share" is still going to save lives that would otherwise be lost. While the idea that no one need do more than his or her fair share is a powerful one, should it prevail if we know that others are not doing their fair share and that children will die preventable deaths unless we do more than our fair share? That would be taking fairness too far.

Thus, this ground for limiting how much we ought to give also fails. In the world as it is now, I can see no escape from the conclusion that each one of us with wealth surplus to his or her essential needs should be giving most of it to help people suffering from poverty so dire as to be life-threatening. That's right: I'm saying that you shouldn't buy that new car, take that cruise, redecorate the house, or get that pricey new suit. After all, a $1,000 suit could save five children's lives.

So how does my philosophy break down in dollars and cents? An American household with an income of $50,000 spends around $30,000 annually on necessities, according to the Conference Board, a nonprofit economic research organization. Therefore, for a household bringing in $50,000 a year, donations to help the world's poor should be as close as possible to $20,000. The $30,000 required for necessities holds for higher incomes as well. So a household making $100,000 could cut a yearly check for $70,000. Again, the formula is simple: Whatever money you're spending on luxuries, not necessities, should be given away.

Now, evolutionary psychologists tell us that human nature just isn't sufficiently altruistic to make it plausible that many people will sacrifice so much for strangers. On the facts of human nature, they might be right, but they would be wrong to draw a moral conclusion from those facts. If it is the case that we ought to do things that, predictably, most of us won't do, then let's face that fact head-on. Then, if we value the life of a child more than going to fancy restaurants, the next time we dine out we will know that we could have done something better with our money. If that makes living a morally decent life extremely arduous, well, then that is the way things are. If we don't do it, then we should at least know that we are failing to live a morally decent life — not because it is good to wallow in guilt but because knowing where we should be going is the first step toward heading in that direction.

When Bob first grasped the dilemma that faced him as he stood by that railway switch, he must have thought how extraordinarily unlucky he was to be placed in a situation in which he must choose between the life of an innocent child and the sacrifice of most of his savings. But he was not unlucky at all. We are all in that situation.

Engaging with the Text

3–4
160–65

1. What is the **PURPOSE** of Peter Singer's proposal? What is he actually **PROPOSING?** What action does he want us to take? Point to passages where his purpose is made explicit.

239–45

2. Singer **OPENS** his essay with reference to the Brazilian film *Central Station* and follows it with a hypothetical scenario. What role do the film and the scenario play in his proposal? What do they contribute to the persuasiveness of his argument? Do you find them effective? Why or why not?

3. Singer argues that "whatever money you're spending on luxuries, not necessities, should be given away." To what degree do you agree with this assumption? How much faith in this claim does Singer himself appear to have?

163

4. What **QUESTIONS** does Singer anticipate? How does he address potential naysayers?

5. *For Writing.* Think of a large societal problem (for example, poverty, pollution, or unemployment) and how the actions of individuals might help alleviate it (volunteering at a food bank, recycling soda cans, restructuring a company to create more positions). Describe the problem and write a **PROPOSAL** for how you and other individuals can help to solve it.

160–65

rhetorical situations   genres   processes   strategies   research mla/apa   media/ design   readings

THE 9/11 COMMISSION

Prevent the Continued Growth of Islamist Terrorism

In November 2002, the National Commission on Terrorist Attacks upon the United States — also known as the 9/11 Commission — was established to investigate the terrorist attacks of September 11, 2001. The ten bipartisan members of the commission issued The 9/11 Commission Report in 2004; their audience was the president, Congress, and the American people. The proposal here is part of a larger recommendation for developing a global strategy to fight terrorism. The endnotes are reproduced here as they appeared in the original report.

IN OCTOBER 2003, REFLECTING ON PROGRESS after two years of waging the global war on terrorism, Defense Secretary Donald Rumsfeld asked his advisers: "Are we capturing, killing or deterring and dissuading more terrorists every day than the madrassas and the radical clerics are recruiting, training, and deploying against us? Does the U.S. need to fashion a broad, integrated plan to stop the next generation of terrorists? The U.S. is putting relatively little effort into a long-range plan, but we are putting a great deal of effort into trying to stop terrorists. The cost-benefit ratio is against us! Our cost is billions against the terrorists' costs of millions."[1]

These are the right questions. Our answer is that we need short-term action on a long-range strategy, one that invigorates our foreign policy with the attention that the President and Congress have given to the military and intelligence parts of the conflict against Islamist terrorism.

Engage the Struggle of Ideas

The United States is heavily engaged in the Muslim world and will be for many years to come. This American engagement is resented. Polls in 2002 found that among America's friends, like Egypt — the recipient

of more U.S. aid for the past 20 years than any other Muslim country —
only 15 percent of the population had a favorable opinion of the United
States. In Saudi Arabia the number was 12 percent. And two-thirds of
those surveyed in 2003 in countries from Indonesia to Turkey (a NATO
ally) were very or somewhat fearful that the United States may attack
them.[2]

Support for the United States has plummeted. Polls taken in Islamic
countries after 9/11 suggested that many or most people thought the
United States was doing the right thing in its fight against terrorism;
few people saw popular support for al Qaeda; half of those surveyed
said that ordinary people had a favorable view of the United States. By
2003, polls showed that "the bottom has fallen out of support for America in most of the Muslim world. Negative views of the U.S. among Muslims, which had been largely limited to countries in the Middle East,
have spread. . . . Since last summer, favorable ratings for the U.S. have
fallen from 61 percent to 15 percent in Indonesia and from 71 percent
to 38 percent among Muslims in Nigeria."[3]

Many of these views are at best uninformed about the United States 5
and, at worst, informed by cartoonish stereotypes, the coarse expression of a fashionable "Occidentalism" among intellectuals who carica-
ture U.S. values and policies. Local newspapers and the few influential
satellite broadcasters — like al Jazeera — often reinforce the jihadist
theme that portrays the United States as anti-Muslim.[4]

The small percentage of Muslims who are fully committed to Usama
Bin Ladin's version of Islam are impervious to persuasion. It is among
the large majority of Arabs and Muslims that we must encourage reform,
freedom, democracy, and opportunity, even though our own promotion
of these messages is limited in its effectiveness simply because we are
its carriers. Muslims themselves will have to reflect upon such basic
issues as the concept of jihad, the position of women, and the place of
non-Muslim minorities. The United States can promote moderation, but
cannot ensure its ascendancy. Only Muslims can do this.

The setting is difficult. The combined gross domestic product of the
22 countries in the Arab League is less than the GDP of Spain. Forty percent of adult Arabs are illiterate, two-thirds of them women. One-third

of the broader Middle East lives on less than two dollars a day. Less than 2 percent of the population has access to the Internet. The majority of older Arab youths have expressed a desire to emigrate to other countries, particularly those in Europe.[5]

In short, the United States has to help defeat an ideology, not just a group of people, and we must do so under difficult circumstances. How can the United States and its friends help moderate Muslims combat the extremist ideas?

Recommendation: The U.S. government must define what the message is, what it stands for. We should offer an example of moral leadership in the world, committed to treat people humanely, abide by the rule of law, and be generous and caring to our neighbors. America and Muslim friends can agree on respect for human dignity and opportunity. To Muslim parents, terrorists like Bin Ladin have nothing to offer their children but visions of violence and death. America and its friends have a crucial advantage — we can offer these parents a vision that might give their children a better future. If we heed the views of thoughtful leaders in the Arab and Muslim world, a moderate consensus can be found.

That vision of the future should stress life over death: individual educational and economic opportunity. This vision includes widespread political participation and contempt for indiscriminate violence. It includes respect for the rule of law, openness in discussing differences, and tolerance for opposing points of view. [10]

Recommendation: Where Muslim governments, even those who are friends, do not respect these principles, the United States must stand for a better future. One of the lessons of the long Cold War was that short-term gains in cooperating with the most repressive and brutal governments were too often outweighed by long-term setbacks for America's stature and interests.

American foreign policy is part of the message. America's policy choices have consequences. Right or wrong, it is simply a fact that American policy regarding the Israeli-Palestinian conflict and American actions in Iraq are dominant staples of popular commentary across the Arab and Muslim world. That does not mean U.S. choices have been wrong. It means those choices must be integrated with America's message of opportunity to the Arab and Muslim world. Neither Israel nor the new Iraq will be safer if worldwide Islamist terrorism grows stronger.

The United States must do more to communicate its message. Reflecting on Bin Ladin's success in reaching Muslim audiences, Richard Holbrooke wondered, "How can a man in a cave outcommunicate the world's leading communications society?" Deputy Secretary of State Richard Armitage worried to us that Americans have been "exporting our fears and our anger," not our vision of opportunity and hope.[6]

Recommendation: Just as we did in the Cold War, we need to defend our ideals abroad vigorously. America does stand up for its values. The United States defended, and still defends, Muslims against tyrants and criminals in Somalia, Bosnia, Kosovo, Afghanistan, and Iraq. If the United States does not act aggressively to define itself in the Islamic world, the extremists will gladly do the job for us.

- Recognizing that Arab and Muslim audiences rely on satellite television and radio, the government has begun some promising initiatives in television and radio broadcasting to the Arab world, Iran, and Afghanistan. These efforts are beginning to reach large audiences. The Broadcasting Board of Governors has asked for much larger resources. It should get them.

- The United States should rebuild the scholarship, exchange, and library programs that reach out to young people and offer them knowledge and hope. Where such assistance is provided, it should be identified as coming from the citizens of the United States.

An Agenda of Opportunity

The United States and its friends can stress educational and economic opportunity. The United Nations has rightly equated "literacy as freedom." 15

- The international community is moving toward setting a concrete goal — to cut the Middle East region's illiteracy rate in half by 2010, targeting women and girls and supporting programs for adult literacy.

- Unglamorous help is needed to support the basics, such as textbooks that translate more of the world's knowledge into local languages and libraries to house such materials. Education about the outside world, or other cultures, is weak.

- More vocational education is needed, too, in trades and business skills. The Middle East can also benefit from some of the programs to bridge the digital divide and increase Internet access that have already been developed for other regions of the world.

Education that teaches tolerance, the dignity and value of each individual, and respect for different beliefs is a key element in any global strategy to eliminate Islamist terrorism.

Recommendation: The U.S. government should offer to join with other nations in generously supporting a new International Youth Opportunity Fund. Funds will be spent directly for building and operating primary and secondary schools in those Muslim states that commit to sensibly investing their own money in public education.

Economic openness is essential. Terrorism is not caused by poverty. Indeed, many terrorists come from relatively well-off families. Yet when people lose hope, when societies break down, when countries fragment, the breeding grounds for terrorism are created. Backward economic policies and repressive political regimes slip into societies that are without hope, where ambition and passions have no constructive outlet.

The policies that support economic development and reform also have political implications. Economic and political liberties tend to be linked. Commerce, especially international commerce, requires ongoing cooperation and compromise, the exchange of ideas across cultures, and the peaceful resolution of differences through negotiation or the rule of law. Economic growth expands the middle class, a constituency for further reform. Successful economies rely on vibrant private sectors, which have an interest in curbing indiscriminate government power. Those who develop the practice of controlling their own economic destiny soon desire a voice in their communities and political societies.

The U.S. government has announced the goal of working toward a Middle East Free Trade Area, or MEFTA, by 2013. The United States has been seeking comprehensive free trade agreements (FTAs) with the Middle Eastern nations most firmly on the path to reform. The U.S.-Israeli FTA was enacted in 1985, and Congress implemented an FTA with Jordan in 2001. Both agreements have expanded trade and investment, thereby supporting domestic economic reform. In 2004, new FTAs were signed with Morocco and Bahrain, and are awaiting congressional approval. These models are drawing the interest of their neighbors. Muslim countries can become full participants in the rules-based global trading system, as the United States considers lowering its trade barriers with the poorest Arab nations.

Recommendation: A comprehensive U.S. strategy to counter terrorism 20 **should include economic policies that encourage development, more open societies, and opportunities for people to improve the lives of their families and to enhance prospects for their children's future.**

Notes

1. DOD memo, Rumsfeld to Myers, Wolfowitz, Pace, and Feith, "Global War on Terrorism," Oct. 16, 2003 (online at www.usatoday.com/news/washington/executive/rumsfeld-memo.htm).

2. For the statistics, see James Zogby, *What Arabs Think: Values, Beliefs, and Concerns* (Zogby International, 2002). For fear of a U.S. attack, see Pew Global Attitudes Project report, *Views of a Changing World: June 2003* (Pew Research Center for the People and the Press, 2003), p. 2. In our interviews, current and former U.S. officials dealing with the Middle East corroborated these findings.

3. For polling soon after 9/11, see Pew Research Center for the People and the Press report, "America Admired, Yet Its New Vulnerability Seen as Good Thing, Say Opinion Leaders; Little Support for Expanding

rhetorical situations   genres   processes   strategies   research mla/apa   media/ design   readings

War on Terrorism" (online at http://people-press.org/reports/print
.php3?ReportID=145). For the quotation, see Pew Global Attitudes Project report, "War with Iraq Further Divides Global Publics But World
Embraces Democratic Values and Free Markets," June 3, 2003 (online at
www.pewtrusts.com/ideas/ideas_item.cfm?content_item_id=1645&
content_type_id=7).

4. For the Occidentalist "creed of Islamist revolutionaries," see, e.g.,
Avishai Margalit and Ian Buruma, *Occidentalism: The West in the Eyes of Its
Enemies* (Penguin Press, 2004).

5. We draw these statistics, significantly, from the U.S. government's working paper circulated in April 2004 to G-8 "sherpas" in preparation for the 2004 G-8 summit. The paper was leaked and published in
Al-Hayat. "U.S. Working Paper for G-8 Sherpas," *Al-Hayat,* Feb. 13, 2004
(online at http://english.daralhayat.com/Spec/02-2004/Article-20040213-
ac40bdaf-c0a8-01ed-004e-5e7ac897d678/story.html).

6. Richard Holbrooke, "Get the Message Out," *Washington Post,* Oct.
28, 2001, p. B7; Richard Armitage interview (Jan. 12, 2004).

Engaging with the Text

1. The 9/11 Commission BEGINS its proposal with a QUOTATION from
   Defense Secretary Donald Rumsfeld. What purpose does this quotation serve? How does it relate to the strategies the Commission outlines?

   239–45
   360–63

2. At the beginning of the report, its authors identify a multi-pronged
   AUDIENCE: "the President of the United States, the United States Congress, and the American people." How do the recommendations in
   this proposal address each audience? Of these audiences, which would
   be considered the primary audience — the one that has the power to
   enact the recommendations? What role can the other audiences play
   in relation to the recommendations?

   5–8

3. According to the proposal, what roles can education, and literacy education in particular, play in the war against terrorism?

160–165, 163

4. As a genre, a **PROPOSAL** includes a clear **CALL TO ACTION.** What actions does this proposal call for? What roles do communication, education, and economic policies play in the calls to action?

5. *For Writing.* Select one of the recommendations outlined in the 9/11 Commission Report, and write a detailed **PROPOSAL** on how to accomplish the goals of that recommendation. Remember that you'll need to establish the **PROBLEM** and present a **CONVINCING ARGUMENT** that your solutions are feasible and represent the best way to solve the problem; and you'll need to **ANTICIPATE AND ANSWER QUESTIONS.**

160–65
162–63
163

rhetorical situations

genres

processes

strategies

research mla/apa

media/ design

readings

HEIDI POLLOCK

You Say You Want a Resolution?

The following proposal was first published in 2003 in h2so4, a magazine "dedicated to provoking thought on politics and philosophy, art and love, without giving up the potential to delight, amuse, and entertain." Heidi Pollock is a frequent contributor.

I HAVE FINALLY MASTERED THE ART of making New Year's resolutions, a skill honed by years of abject failure. Seven years ago I developed a fine-tuned Resolution Philosophy which has proven consistently successful in numerous clinical trials (and tribulations). In the interests of humanitarian aid, I am going to share my hard-won methodology with the world, in the hope that we may forever end the vicious cycle of making vain, fruitless, and doomed resolutions such as "I will lose ten pounds this year," "I will go to the gym three times a week," and "I will not park illegally ever again."

For starters, a New Year's resolution should not be about improving your life; it should be about enriching it in a potentially unpredictable way. The new year provides you with a chance to do new things. Therefore, a New Year's resolution should not be something that you've already thought about doing; it should not be on your existing agenda. "Quit smoking," for instance, doesn't count because the fact that you shouldn't be smoking is old news. A true resolution should be an addition to your life, should expand your horizons and help you grow as a person. It should be process-oriented and not require major psychological or physical changes. A solid resolution should not be too fixated on a specific goal; it should not be subject to a Pass/Fail grade; it should strive for a wide spectrum of achievement(s).

Here are the rules: You should always make three resolutions. This is partly to increase the odds of success, but mostly to direct the focus of enhancement outside the body. The tyranny of "diet" and "gym" resolutions is distinctly unhealty. Resolutions should also be made to benefit your intellectual, emotional, or artistic well-being. Make one resolution in the Health & Lifestyle category, another in the Education/ Practice category and, most importantly, make one resolution in the Project/Task category. This last category is the wildcard designed to help your chances of actually fulfilling at least one of your three resolutions by year's end.

My approach to making New Year's resolutions may strike you as contrived to guarantee success, but I assure you, it isn't. Last year, for example, I couldn't even remember my Education resolution — so, obviously, that was a big failure. I also failed to succeed in the Health category: "Eat one vegetable everyday." I'm a bread/cheese/fruit girl, so this was a bona fide resolution for me, a real challenge. Even after I began to count pea soup, pickles, and red pasta sauce as vegetables, I still failed to live up to this laughably attainable goal. On the plus side, I now have a markedly improved tendency to order entrees that come with "julienned vegetables" instead of "mashed potatoes." I may have failed to meet my goal, but I certainly acquired slightly better dining habits.

Luckily, thanks to my three-resolution rule, I was able to celebrate 5 partial success this year thanks to my Project achievement: "File taxes." Admittedly, this included nine years of back taxes and was therefore a far cry from the simple task you might think. It is also important to note that I resolved to "file" taxes without mentioning the need to "pay" them, thereby increasing the resolution's likelihood of success, if not the IRS's happiness with my substandard citizenship.

Lesson the First: One person's habitual practice is another's daunting resolution. You might find that the laws of this country are motivation enough for filing your taxes, but it certainly wasn't working for me. Never underestimate the value of any resolution, no matter how obvious, unnecessary, trivial, or slight. My friend Susanne, for example, set her Practice resolution one year as "Stop buying new black and grey clothing." Three years ago, her wardrobe contained exactly three things that weren't primarily black or grey; today, the majority of her clothes are of many colors. It's worth noting that the subclauses of her resolution allowed her to replace existing black or grey items as well as permitting her to acquire black or grey items in a "new" clothing category (e.g., the purchase of a new black cardigan was allowed because, although she owned a black turtleneck sweater, a black "heavy" sweater, and a black v-neck "light" sweater, she did not, technically, possess a black cardigan sweater).

Lesson #2: Developing a new habit is more important than attaining an absolute goal. So what if Susanne fudged with the clothing "categories"; her resolution trained her to evaluate her purchasing habits. As for myself, I used to be in the habit of reading constantly, and while I don't have proof, I believe I've slacked off in this regard over the years. This year my Education/Practice resolution is: "Read 2–3 books per month." The goal seems too easily obtainable, even by my lax standards, but the resolution is designed to reinvigorate my reading habit, not to foster my acquisition of specific knowledge. I once resolved to "Take a multivitamin daily" — five years later, I still carry a small plastic vial filled with vitamins to support this acquired habit. (Should you take this habit on, I strongly recommend that you choose vitamins bearing a popular brand-name stamp if you are likely to be a traveler subject to security searches). Of course, under the rubric of my resolution program, "daily" resolutions are actively discouraged, but insofar as they lead to new habits, they can be acceptable.

Lesson #3: Include fail-safes. Although my reading goal is three books per month, if I pick up George Eliot's *Middlemarch* I'm not going to berate myself for squeezing in *The Tao of Pooh* just to make my minimum number. While habit development is decidedly the critical feature of a good resolution, your goal should be attainable. Case in point: I happen to have very lazy bedtime habits, so this year my Health resolution is "Wash face before going to sleep." My intent is to use cleanser and, in an ideal world, moisturizer, but if all I manage to do is splash some cold water near the vicinity of my head, then at least I'll still stand the chance of meeting my stated goal.

Lesson #4: Keep it simple. The "cold water provision" won't just help me achieve the habit formation and goal attainment of "washing my face"; it really represents a much larger and infinitely more important aspect of good resolution making: the theory of greater returns. I happen to know that if I'm standing at a sink, about to slosh some water on my face in an effort to maintain my resolve, I'm highly likely to cave in, locate some cleanser, and actually do some scrubbing. Furthermore, I also know that every time I clean my face I feel guilty about not doing the same for my teeth. Regressing even farther, brushing my teeth often leads to flossing them as well. But what I really know about myself is that there is absolutely no way I could ever, in a million years, possibly "wash my face, brush my teeth, and floss — every single night before going to sleep — for the whole year!" So, I've kept the resolution simple: I'm aiming for cleanser, hoping for floss, but ultimately counting on water to see me through.

Lesson #5: Plan ahead. What I mean by this is plan ahead for your 10 next New Year's Eve and make sure one of your resolutions is entertaining enough to discuss. Pick up a new skill — plumbing, knitting, bird watching, playing the ocarina. Develop a random expertise — opera, knowledge of where the rotating bars are, olive tasting, croquet, formal gardening. Memorize something — poems, star constellations, the common ingredients of shampoo. Vow to write a letter once a month — to a grandparent, a politician, a company that has brought you joy ("Dear Mars, Inc. Thank you for the M&M!"). Read something you normally wouldn't — *Scientific American, Architectural Digest,* Edward Gibbon, *Teen People*. Eat things, visit places, make stuff.

The point: Remember. It is almost impossible in life to master a skill, interest, or knowledge that is completely pointless. If you disagree, then try to prove me wrong! Seriously. I really have no interest in going to a New Year's party next year with a bunch of unimaginative, grumpy, starving, thin people.

Engaging with the Text

239–45

1. Heidi Pollock **BEGINS** by stating her own philosophy about New Year's resolutions. A good New Year's resolution, she tells us, "should be an addition to your life, should expand your horizons and help you grow

rhetorical situations   genres   processes   strategies   research mla/apa   media/ design   readings

as a person. It should be process-oriented and not require major psychological or physical changes." What exactly is she **PROPOSING** — and what is the **PROBLEM** she aims to solve?

160–65, 162

2. Pollock supports her proposal with examples from her own life. How persuasive are these examples?

3. This piece originally appeared in *h2so4*, a magazine whose Web site says that it mixes the "serious and silly, arcane and mundane." Imagine it had been written instead for *Martha Stewart Living* or *Real Simple*, two magazines that offer how-tos and advice for the home. How might it be different? Consider the **TITLE**, for example — how would it be different in one of those magazines? How else might the writing be different?

250–51

4. The **TITLE** is an allusion to a Beatles song; what does it tell readers about the piece? About Pollock's **STANCE**? How does it help establish her **TONE**?

250–51
12–14
14

5. *For Writing.* Identify a practice you engage in (such as studying for tests, shopping on eBay, exercising regularly) that you feel you have mastered. Write a humorous **PROPOSAL** arguing that others should try your method.

160–65

59 Reflections

rhetorical situations   genres   processes   strategies   research mla/apa   media/design   readings

CAMERON STRACHER

In Praise of Zeal

Cameron Stracher is a professor of legal writing at New York Law School, where he publishes the New York Law School Review *and teaches legal scholarship and newsgathering. He is author of a novel,* The Laws of Return *(1996), and a memoir,* Double Billing: A Young Lawyer's Tale of Greed, Sex, Lies, and the Pursuit of a Swivel Chair *(1998). In addition to contributing essays to publications such as the* New York Times *and* Wall Street Journal, *Stracher serves as litigation counsel at CBS. The following reflection appeared in 2004 in the professional magazine* The American Lawyer. *As you read, notice how Stracher uses classification and definition.*

YOU KNOW WHO THEY ARE. They sit in the front of the class, arms raised so high their shoulders threaten to pop, fingers vibrating with manic energy, always ready with an answer. Unloved, unwanted, and occasionally loathed. The gunners.

Every class has one — or five. They compete for teacher's attention, and mark time by the bleating of their voices. Their classmates are both fascinated and repelled. In law school, we played a game called "gunner bingo," in which the object was to arrange gunners on a bingo card, then cross them off as each raised his hand. That was the easy part — the hard part was getting called on by the professor and using the word "bingo" when answering his question. Doing so not only won the admiration of your classmates, but also a substantial pot of money.

While the gunners fired away, we sat in the rear and kept our heads down. Even if we had done the reading, we were silent because being called upon by teacher was not cool. It seemed a betrayal of our peers to flaunt what little knowledge we possessed. Ours was a conspiracy of silence, a confederacy of dunces. Gunner bingo made us feel better about ourselves. We celebrated our ignorance by mocking their knowledge.

Now that I am on the other side of the law school lectern, however, I wonder why I ever found gunners distasteful. Is there something wrong with being prepared? Some tragic flaw associated with classroom participation? As I look over the sullen sleepy heads of most of my students, I am grateful for the flapping hand of the editor in chief of our law review, who has always done the reading and is always prepared to engage in debate over the issues it poses, or at least venture into the quicksand of the Socratic method. Some mornings, teaching is so painful that chewing thumbtacks seems preferable. I've tried threatening, begging, cajoling, and pleading, yet still cannot get my students to speak, though I've not yet tried the ploy of my own contracts professor, who would sit in complete silence until someone raised his hand. I may be a martyr, but I'm not a glutton.

No one loves the teacher's pet, except the teacher. But polishing the   5 apple may shine more than just the surface. It actually correlates with genuine accomplishment. While I've certainly had my share of quiet, brilliant types, I've rarely had the converse: talkative, but stupid. Yes, there is the occasional blabbermouth who just can't get it right; but even he usually ends up learning from his mistakes by the close of the semester. Does this mean smarter students tend to talk more, or does talking more make them smart? Most professors would swear by the latter. After all, isn't that the whole point of the Socratic method? If you make students articulate their thoughts, the rigor required to defend their position will lead them to question their assumptions and, eventually, to knowledge. Students who voluntarily engage in this activity are more likely to learn, and more likely to be open to learning, than those who sit quietly and let others do the work for them.

The backbenching mentality, however, is born young, lives hard, and dies in the practice of law. I remember my first law firm job, where the new associates seemed evenly divided between gunners and backbenchers. (That there were so many of the former should have been my first clue.) The gunners were the ones you saw lunching with the partners, dropping by their offices looking for work, getting chummy with their secretaries, and dressing in matching suspenders or pearls. When a partner called, they came running, rather than blocking their phone calls with caller ID. We mocked their happy puppyitis, but there was a whiff of defensiveness in our denials, a sense that we no longer ruled, a doubt even that we were on the side of might, right, and the British empire.

It all came crashing down for me the first time I drafted a response to a set of interrogatories with a gunner I'll call Pierre. I had never seen an interrogatory before, let alone drafted a response. Pierre, however, had been through several rounds with a partner in another case to whom he had made himself indispensable. Not only was he familiar with the form, he knew the substance: he understood what the plaintiff was attempting to achieve, and how it could best be thwarted. He walked me through the draft, and actually took the time to explain the process and his strategy. Because he was a gunner, I could not publicly acknowledge my gratitude, lest I violate the backbencher's code. But 11 years later I can finally get it off my chest; Thank you, Pierre.

I realized that whatever his motivation, Pierre had clearly learned more than I by working so closely with a partner. Though we were in the same class, his experience put him several years ahead of me. He knew how to practice law, while I was still in the playpen with the torts. More than that, I understood that Pierre's affectation for bow ties and granny glasses was about more than just cozying up to his partnership chances (though it didn't hurt). It was about participating in the process and incorporating his observations into his learning. Rather than refusing to join the club that would have him as a member, Pierre embraced the invitation and became smarter from it. By playing it cool, I had lost a valuable opportunity to gain knowledge I could have used to become a better lawyer.

> By playing it cool, I had lost an opportunity to gain knowledge that could have made me a better lawyer.

I didn't discard my cartoon ties or clunky black shoes immediately, but I smiled at partners when I saw them in the lunchroom, and occasionally said hello. Sometimes I joined them at their table and even answered the phone when they called. I listened as they discussed their cases, and threw in a well-timed question when I was prepared to. I attended practice group luncheons and made intelligent noises, and soon found myself working on interesting cases where I sometimes knew what I was doing. Before long, I saw the way younger associates looked at me — with a mixture of envy and disgust — and I knew I had become what I once loathed.

Pierre moved on, and so did I. By the time I left, my surviving classmates were all gunners. The junior associates who didn't — or wouldn't — play the game just got shoved off the bench. In part, it was self-selection: you don't survive at a law firm by being cynical, unhelpful, scarce. But many others, like me, came to see the wisdom in being an X on the bingo board, counted on to provide an answer without being called upon. For us, it was a chance to be the student we wished we had been: to do the reading and take legible notes, and not to sleep through our classes. It was never too late to start.

These days, I'm proud to say, I kiss ass whenever I can. I also polish apples, lick boots, and call on the gunners whenever I can. It's the least I can do. They need our love and attention. Most of all, we need them.

Engaging with the Text

1. Cameron Stracher learns that being a "gunner" is "about participating in the process and incorporating [one's] observation into [one's] learning." In contrast, "by playing it cool," he "lost a valuable opportunity to gain knowledge." How does active participation help a person learn — or does it?

2. In **DEFINING** what it meant to be a "backbencher," Stracher writes that "ours was a conspiracy of silence, a confederacy of dunces. Gunner bingo made us feel better about ourselves. We celebrated our ignorance by mocking their knowledge." Since there isn't a course in becoming a "backbencher," how and where does one learn the ropes of this very elaborate posture?

3. **REFLECTIONS** can serve various **PURPOSES:** to entertain, to explore an interesting topic, to provoke readers to think about something, to help a writer learn something. What do you think the purpose of Stracher's reflection is? How does he achieve this purpose?

275–84

168–73

3–4

rhetorical situations   genres   processes   strategies   research mla/apa   media/ design   readings

4. How does Stracher use **ANECDOTES?** Select specific passages and explain how they support his overall **THESIS**.

5. *For Writing.* Stracher identifies two groups in school and **CLASSIFIES** them according to their eagerness to participate in class. Based on your own classroom experience, how else might students be classified? Identify two or three other categories, **DEFINE** them, and select the one you currently identify with most closely. Is it the same group you would have identified with in high school? Write an essay **REFLECTING** on your student identity and how it has changed or remained the same over the years.

304–12

251–52

260–61

275–84

168–73

LIZ DUNN

Honk If You're Hoardy

The following reflection first appeared in h2so4, a magazine "dedicated to provoking thought on politics & philosophy, art and love, without thereby giving up the potential to delight, amuse and entertain." Liz Dunn is a frequent contributor to h2so4. As you read her essay, consider the kinds of evidence Dunn provides to explore the question of why she hoards magazines, a condition that makes her, she says, a "maga-zinophile." Also keep in mind that since this piece was written for a general magazine audience, Dunn does not provide the kinds of documentation required in academic writing.

WHEN PEOPLE FIRST SEE THE STACKS of magazines in my apartment, piling up three feet high, all around the perimeter of my living room, they always ask the same question, in the same astonished tone: "Why?"

Instead of answering, I dazzle/horrify them with descriptions of the six huge plastic containers full of hundreds of magazines that I am storing at my parents' house. Of course, my parents are also baffled by my dedication to keeping years and years of various fashion, pop culture, music, and design magazines archived neatly. But they kindly accommodate me, since, as I point out, they have a four-bedroom house and a two-car garage and all I have is a studio apartment.

And since, as I've noted, I don't really answer the question "why?" when asked, the word that lots of people seem to use when describing my compulsion to save magazines is "crazy." They don't see the intrinsic value in these volumes that I do. They don't recognize that each one is filled with well-written coverage of all kinds of key cultural items and issues, plus beautiful photographs of pretty ladies, fancy houses, landscapes, and vistas. Each one has given me pleasure, and so I honor it with a permanent home.

It's like they are little books, packed full of promise. And no one thinks it odd when someone has bookshelves busting full with books in their homes. In fact, when you go to someone's house and notice that they don't have any books, it always seems to point to a void of intelligence or curiosity in that person. I used to save all the books I bought in college, thinking that in my old age I'd fancy a bit of Kierkegaard or Hegel.[1] But when push came to shove in the battle for storage on my shelves, old Soren had to go, to make way for my precious collection of old issues of *Interview,* dating back to when Andy Warhol was still alive and going to parties. What Kierkegaard can teach me about philosophy has ceased to interest me; what Andy Warhol can teach me about his mysterious urban celebrity continues to excite me.

I do, however, have my criteria. I don't save every single magazine that comes my way. For instance, a throwaway magazine like *People* only makes it into the permanent collection if the cover story is a milestone event of interest to me, like Lyle Lovett and Julia Roberts' surprise marriage, Drew Barrymore's first (short-lived) marriage, or the death of Andy Gibb.

The bulk of my collection is as follows: the design magazine *ID,* dating back to 1991; *Paper* magazine, a sort of hipster/scene magazine for New York City that was notable for interviewing up-and-coming superstars before anyone west of NY had heard of them; *Colors,* the Benetton magazine creatively directed by Tibor Kalman; select issues of *Vanity Fair* (the infamous Kurt Cobain–Courtney Love drug issue, Madonna's new baby issue); and issues of well-loved magazines that have gone under, like *Sassy,* a British women's magazine called *Frank,* and the old *Details.* Some magazines I am so enchanted with that I save every issue no matter what the topic or cover story. British *Vogue* is one of those. When I first read its witty stories and discovered its complete fashion coverage, I was hooked and subscribed immediately. With a foreign magazine, the hoarding becomes also somewhat of a money issue: since the issues cost so much, their intrinsic value in my head goes up.

But this isn't just a monetary form of value. I envision my collection taking up space in a future house, one with a big library lined with

---

1. Danish philosopher Søren Kierkegaard (1813–55) and German philosopher Georg Wilhelm Friedrich Hegel (1770–1831). *Andy Warhol:* American artist (1928–87).

bookshelves and walnut paneling. I'll be writing something about an earlier time — 1989, say — and all I'll have to do in order to pick up some period detail is to go to my beloved magazine archives, where I'll be able to find exactly what music, what clothing, what restaurants were hot hot hot. Maybe my magazine archives will even be visited by other magazinophiles who will admire the dedication and perseverance of my hoarding in the face of widespread criticism.

Recently I read a story about a lady who hoarded cats. Poking a bit further into the matter, I found an article in *Psychiatric Times* magazine with all sorts of interesting facts about the psychological disorder of hoarding possessions. Fundamentally, hoarding possessions is defined as "the acquisition of, and failure to discard, possessions that appear to be useless or of limited value." For hoarding to be considered significant, the hoarder's living spaces have to be "sufficiently cluttered so as to preclude activities for which those spaces were designed," and the hoarding must create significant distress or impairment. The article tells us:

> The classic picture of the compulsive hoarder is the individual who saves everything and can throw nothing away. According to Frost and Gross (1993), possessions may be saved by both hoarders and non-hoarders for several different reasons. These include their sentimental value (emotional reasons or reminders of important life events), instrumental value (potential usefulness), or intrinsic value (beauty or attractiveness). The difference between people who hoard possessions and those who do not is that hoarders judge more possessions to have these values.

So you see, I really don't think I qualify as a true psychiatric-diagnosis hoarder. I throw things away, sometimes without even being prompted to! Lately, after years of my father's grumblings about the "ridiculous" magazines, I've taken to going through a bin or two when I'm down for a visit, and weeding out the non-essential issues. Sometimes I have a quandary-moment when I discover something like: a few old issues of *Computer Telephony* magazine with address labels affixed for an old boyfriend, now a successful CEO of a hot new company. Perhaps these will be worth something on eBay one day? According to the experts, a key aspect of hoarding is distorted beliefs about the value of the possessions. But if the possession does have a dollar value that can be verified by online auctions, then who's really crazy here? Are you saying it's me? I can't hear you!

Back to my magazines. Hoarders often identify their collections of stuff as a primary component of their identity, so a removal of or throwing away of possessions can create mourning and sense of loss of self. Some hoarders also express the need to maintain control over possessions. This results in increasing isolation and suspiciousness of others. Like the suspicion that I have towards my family that they are secretly going to throw away all my precious magazines behind my back! That is why I issue repeated warnings and threats about that treasonous crime.

However, in other areas of my life I weed out the outdated and   10 unwanted. When I write little post-it notes to myself, I rush to complete the tasks on the post-it so that I can sooner throw it away. I love using up beauty products and grocery items so that I can throw the used containers away, even if I'm just going to have to replace them again. I do not have any cats.

Plus, after the first three or four years of hoarding all email correspondence, I realized that I would never go back and reread all those emails, and I became a ruthless dealer. A job change forced my hand; faced with backing up three years worth of Eudora correspondence that was chiefly the written equivalent of chatting on the phone, I tossed it all in the "recycle" bin. So I'm not a "crazy" hoarder, no matter what you might think of the magazines lining my living room. Okay?

In fact, this weeding-out process has even bled over into my magazine collecting. Over the years I've gotten more selective about the magazines I keep, and I've gone back into the stacks and looked through and discarded certain volumes that had lost their luster (though these purges are usually motivated by constraints of storage space . . .).

But, looking at the magazines I've chosen to keep, I see something other than the psychiatric definition of a hoarder. These magazines don't form part of my personality. In fact, I think that I am attached to design and fashion magazines because they represent a world beyond me, to which I have no other access; they continue to thrill me and enchant me because they are all I have to connect me to such a world. My emails, my college books, and my post-it notes have given me their messages, I've absorbed them, and either given them permanent residence in my brain or tossed them away. But the magazines are a magical gateway to a sparkling world of designers, celebrities, writers, and artists that remains unknown to me. They are aspirational, my bridge to a foreign land. And so I "hoard" . . . I keep myself surrounded by magazines filled with dreams of everything my life might hold, if only I could assimilate — or store — all the information.

Engaging with the Text

1. What is the central question in Liz Dunn's essay? How does she present and then answer that question?

2. In reflecting on whether she is a "pathological hoarder," Dunn provides a **DEFINITION** and a **DESCRIPTION** of this condition from an article she read in *Psychiatric Times*. How does this information help her support her claim that she does not "qualify as a true psychiatric-diagnosis hoarder"?
275–84
285–93

3. Dunn provides many **SPECIFIC DETAILS** about her magazine collection, including several paragraphs about objects she has no trouble discarding. Why do you think she includes this information? What does it contribute to her reflection?
171

4. Who is the **AUDIENCE** for Dunn's reflection? Identify passages in the essay that provide clues to the intended audience.
5–8

5. *For Writing.* Reflecting on one's own life typically leads one to address questions of "Who am I?" and "Why do I do what I do?" But reflections need not tackle big questions of identity. They often tackle smaller questions in a playful manner. Is there something that others find quirky about you? Write an essay **REFLECTING** on why you do whatever it is that others find unusual. (If you can't think of anything in your own life, perhaps there's something you find quirky about someone else.)
168–73

rhetorical situations | genres | processes | strategies | research mla/apa | media/ design | readings

GEETA KOTHARI

If You Are What You Eat, Then What Am I?

Geeta Kothari's stories and essays have been published in numerous newspapers and journals. She teaches writing at the University of Pittsburgh and is the editor of Did My Mama Like to Dance? and Other Stories About Mothers and Daughters *(1994). The following reflection first appeared in 1999 in the* Kenyon Review, *a literary journal published at Kenyon College. As you read, notice how Kothari incorporates vivid anecdotes to illustrate the competing cultural experiences that complicate her sense of identity.*

To belong is to understand the tacit codes of the people you live
with. —MICHAEL IGNATIEFF, *BLOOD AND BELONGING*

THE FIRST TIME MY MOTHER and I open a can of tuna, I am nine years old. We stand in the doorway of the kitchen, in semidarkness, the can tilted toward daylight. I want to eat what the kids at school eat: bologna, hot dogs, salami — foods my parents find repugnant because they contain pork and meat byproducts, crushed bone and hair glued together by chemicals and fat. Although she has never been able to tolerate the smell of fish, my mother buys the tuna, hoping to satisfy my longing for American food.

Indians, of course, do not eat such things.

The tuna smells fishy, which surprises me because I can't remember anyone's tuna sandwich actually smelling like fish. And the tuna in those sandwiches doesn't look like this, pink and shiny, like an internal organ. In fact, this looks similar to the bad foods my mother doesn't want me to eat. She is silent, holding her face away from the can while peering into it like a half-blind bird.

"What's wrong with it?" I ask.

She has no idea. My mother does not know that the tuna everyone 5
else's mothers made for them was tuna *salad*.

"Do you think it's botulism?"

I have never seen botulism, but I have read about it, just as I have read about but never eaten steak and kidney pie.

There is so much my parents don't know. They are not like other parents, and they disappoint me and my sister. They are supposed to help us negotiate the world outside, teach us the signs, the clues to proper behavior: what to eat and how to eat it.

We have expectations, and my parents fail to meet them, especially my mother, who works full-time. I don't understand what it means, to have a mother who works outside and inside the home; I notice only the ways in which she disappoints me. She doesn't show up for school plays. She doesn't make chocolate-frosted cupcakes for my class. At night, if I want her attention, I have to sit in the kitchen and talk to her while she cooks the evening meal, attentive to every third or fourth word I say.

We throw the tuna away. This time my mother is disappointed. I   10 go to school with tuna eaters. I see their sandwiches, yet cannot explain the discrepancy between them and the stinking, oily fish in my mother's hand. We do not understand so many things, my mother and I.

When we visit our relatives in India, food prepared outside the house is carefully monitored. In the hot, sticky monsoon months in New Delhi and Bombay, we cannot eat ice cream, salad, cold food, or any fruit that can't be peeled. Definitely no meat. People die from amoebic dysentery, unexplained fevers, strange boils on their bodies. We drink boiled water only, no ice. No sweets except for jalebi, thin fried twists of dough in dripping hot sugar syrup. If we're caught outside with nothing to drink, Fanta, Limca, Thums Up (after Coca-Cola is thrown out by Mrs. Gandhi) will do. Hot tea sweetened with sugar, served with thick creamy buffalo milk, is preferable. It should be boiled, to kill the germs on the cup.

My mother talks about "back home" as a safe place, a silk cocoon frozen in time where we are sheltered by family and friends. Back home, my sister and I do not argue about food with my parents. Home is where they know all the rules. We trust them to guide us safely through the maze of city streets for which they have no map, and we trust them to feed and take care of us, the way parents should.

Finally, though, one of us will get sick, hungry for the food we see our cousins and friends eating, too thirsty to ask for a straw, too polite to insist on properly boiled water.

At my uncle's diner in New Delhi, someone hands me a plate of aloo tikki, fried potato patties filled with mashed channa dal and served with a sweet and a sour chutney. The channa, mixed with hot chilies and spices, burns my tongue and throat. I reach for my Fanta, discard the paper straw, and gulp the sweet orange soda down, huge drafts that sting rather than soothe.

When I throw up later that day (or is it the next morning, when a stomachache wakes me from deep sleep?), I cry over the frustration of being singled out, not from the pain my mother assumes I'm feeling as she holds my hair back from my face. The taste of orange lingers in my mouth, and I remember my lips touching the cold glass of the Fanta bottle.

At that moment, more than anything, I want to be like my cousins.

In New York, at the first Indian restaurant in our neighborhood, my father orders with confidence, and my sister and I play with the silverware until the steaming plates of lamb biryani arrive.

What is Indian food? my friends ask, their noses crinkling up.

Later, this restaurant is run out of business by the new Indo-Pak-Bangladeshi combinations up and down the street, which serve similar food. They use plastic cutlery and Styrofoam cups. They do not distinguish between North and South Indian cooking, or between Indian, Pakistani, and Bangladeshi cooking, and their customers do not care. The food is fast, cheap, and tasty. Dosa, a rice flour crepe stuffed with masala potato, appears on the same trays as chicken makhani.

Now my friends want to know, Do you eat curry at home?

One time my mother makes lamb vindaloo for guests. Like dosa, this is a South Indian dish, one that my Punjabi mother has to learn from a cookbook. For us, she cooks everyday food — yellow dal, rice, chapati, bhaji. Lentils, rice, bread, and vegetables. She has never referred to anything on our table as "curry" or "curried," but I know she has made chicken curry for guests. Vindaloo, she explains, is a curry too. I under-

stand then that curry is a dish created for guests, outsiders, a food for people who eat in restaurants.

I look around my boyfriend's freezer one day and find meat: pork chops, ground beef, chicken pieces, Italian sausage. Ham in the refrigerator, next to the homemade bolognese sauce. Tupperware filled with chili made from ground beef and pork.

He smells different from me. Foreign. Strange.

I marry him anyway.

He has inherited blue eyes that turn gray in bad weather, light brown 25 hair, a sharp pointy nose, and excellent teeth. He learns to make chili with ground turkey and tofu, tomato sauce with red wine and portobello mushrooms, roast chicken with rosemary and slivers of garlic under the skin.

He eats steak when we are in separate cities, roast beef at his mother's house, hamburgers at work. Sometimes I smell them on his skin. I hope he doesn't notice me turning my face, a cheek instead of my lips, my nose wrinkled at the unfamiliar, musky smell.

I have inherited brown eyes, black hair, a long nose with a crooked bridge, and soft teeth with thin enamel. I am in my twenties, moving to a city far from my parents, before it occurs to me that jeera, the spice my sister avoids, must have an English name. I have to learn that haldi = turmeric, methi = fenugreek. What to make with fenugreek, I do not know. My grandmother used to make methi roti for our breakfast, cornbread with fresh fenugreek leaves served with a lump of homemade butter. No one makes it now that she's gone, though once in a while my mother will get a craving for it and produce a facsimile ("The cornmeal here is wrong") that only highlights what she's really missing: the smells and tastes of her mother's house.

I will never make my grandmother's methi roti or even my mother's unsatisfactory imitation of it. I attempt chapati; it takes six hours, three phone calls home, and leaves me with an aching back. I have to write translations down: jeera = cumin. My memory is unreliable. But I have always known garam = hot.

If I really want to make myself sick, I worry that my husband will one day leave me for a meat-eater, for someone familiar who doesn't sniff him suspiciously for signs of alimentary infidelity.

Indians eat lentils. I understand this as absolute, a decree from an unidentifiable authority that watches and judges me. 30

So what does it mean that I cannot replicate my mother's dal? She and my father show me repeatedly, in their kitchen, in my kitchen. They coach me over the phone, buy me the best cookbooks, and finally write down their secrets. Things I'm supposed to know but don't. Recipes that should be, by now, engraved on my heart.

Living far from the comfort of people who require no explanation for what I do and who I am, I crave the foods we have shared. My mother convinces me that moong is the easiest dal to prepare, and yet it fails me every time: bland, watery, a sickly greenish yellow mush. These imperfect limitations remind me only of what I'm missing.

But I have never been fond of moong dal. At my mother's table it is the last thing I reach for. Now I worry that this antipathy toward dal signals something deeper, that somehow I am not my parents' daughter, not Indian, and because I cannot bear the touch and smell of raw meat, though I can eat it cooked (charred, dry, and overdone), I am not American either.

I worry about a lifetime purgatory in Indian restaurants where I will complain that all the food looks and tastes the same because they've used the same masala.

Engaging with the Text

1. Geeta Kothari uses food as a way to explore the larger issue of cultural identity. What **SPECIFIC DETAILS** does she include to help her readers understand the pulls of both American and Indian culture? How does she **DESCRIBE** Indian and American food?

▲ 171

◆ 285–93
◆ 250–51

2. A good **TITLE** indicates what the piece is about and makes readers want to read it. How well does this title do those things? How does Kothari answer the question her title asks?

239–45

3. How does Kothari **BEGIN**? Is this an effective beginning? Why or why not? How does it signal to readers what Kothari will address in the rest of the piece?

4. For Kothari, cultural identity shapes, and is shaped by, the foods one eats and the ways one eats them. Her reflection reveals a struggle over two cultures — Indian and American — and she worries that she cannot locate herself fully in either. At the end of her text, she notes: "I worry that this antipathy toward dal signals something deeper, that somehow I am not my parents' daughter, not Indian, and because I cannot bear the touch and smell of raw meat . . . I am not American either." What does it mean to live on the border between two cultures in the ways Kothari describes?

5. *For Writing.* Think about the kinds of foods you grew up with and the ways they were similar or dissimilar to those of your peers. Write an essay **REFLECTING** on the role food has played in your own sense of your cultural heritage and identity.

168–73

rhetorical situations genres processes strategies research mla/apa media/design readings

ZORA NEALE HURSTON

How It Feels to Be Colored Me

*A novelist, folklorist, and anthropologist, Zora Neale Hurston
(1891–1960) was a major figure in the Harlem Renaissance of the early
twentieth century. She is the author of short stories, novels, and books
of nonfiction — including her autobiography, Dust Tracks on a Road
(1942) — but she is best known for the novel Their Eyes Were Watching God (1937). The following essay first appeared in 1928 in The
World Tomorrow, a leftist Christian journal. It was reprinted nearly
fifty years later in a volume of Hurston's writings titled I Love Myself
When I Am Laughing . . . and Then Again When I Am Looking
Mean and Impressive (1979). As you read, notice how Hurston examines her identity from several different social vantage points — race,
region, and gender — to explore the complex question, Who am I?*

I AM COLORED but I offer nothing in the way of extenuating circumstances
except the fact that I am the only Negro in the United States whose
grandfather on the mother's side was *not* an Indian chief.

I remember the very day that I became colored. Up to my thirteenth
year I lived in the little Negro town of Eatonville, Florida. It is exclusively
a colored town. The only white people I knew passed through the town
going to or coming from Orlando. The native whites rode dusty horses,
the Northern tourists chugged down the sandy village road in automo-
biles. The town knew the Southerners and never stopped cane chewing
when they passed. But the Northerners were something else again. They
were peered at cautiously from behind curtains by the timid. The more
venturesome would come out on the porch to watch them go past and
got just as much pleasure out of the tourists as the tourists got out of
the village.

The front porch might seem a daring place for the rest of the town,
but it was a gallery seat for me. My favorite place was atop the gate-
post. Proscenium box for a born first-nighter. Not only did I enjoy the

show, but I didn't mind the actors knowing that I liked it. I usually spoke to them in passing. I'd wave at them and when they returned my salute, I would say something like this: "Howdy-do-well-I-thank-you-where-you-goin'?" Usually automobile or the horse paused at this, and after a queer exchange of compliments, I would probably "go a piece of the way" with them, as we say in farthest Florida. If one of my family happened to come to the front in time to see me, of course negotiations would be rudely broken off. But even so, it is clear that I was the first "welcome-to-our state" Floridian, and I hope the Miami Chamber of Commerce will please take notice.

During this period, white people differed from colored to me only in that they rode through town and never lived there. They liked to hear me "speak pieces" and sing and wanted to see me dance the parse-me-la, and gave me generously of their small silver for doing these things, which seemed strange to me for I wanted to do them so much that I needed bribing to stop. Only they didn't know it. The colored people gave no dimes. They deplored any joyful tendencies in me, but I was their Zora nevertheless. I belonged to them, to the nearby hotels, to the county — everybody's Zora.

But changes came in the family when I was thirteen, and I was sent 5 to school in Jacksonville. I left Eatonville, the town of the oleanders, as Zora. When I disembarked from the river-boat at Jacksonville, she was no more. It seemed that I had suffered a sea change. I was not Zora of Orange County anymore, I was now a little colored girl. I found it out in certain ways. In my heart as well as in the mirror, I became a fast brown — warranted not to rub nor run.

But I am not tragically colored. There is no great sorrow dammed up in my soul, nor lurking behind my eyes. I do not mind at all. I do not belong to the sobbing school of Negrohood who hold that nature somehow has given them a lowdown dirty deal and whose feelings are all hurt about it. Even in the helter-skelter skirmish that is my life, I have seen that the world is to the strong regardless of a little pigmentation more or less. No, I do not weep at the world — I am too busy sharpening my oyster knife.

Someone is always at my elbow reminding me that I am the grand-daughter of slaves. It fails to register depression with me. Slavery is sixty years in the past. The operation was successful and the patient is doing well, thank you. The terrible struggle that made me an American out of a potential slave said "On the line!" The Reconstruction said "Get set!"; and the generation before said "Go!" I am off to a flying start and I must not halt in the stretch to look behind and weep. Slavery is the price I paid for civilization, and the choice was not with me. It is a bully adventure and worth all that I have paid through my ancestors for it. No one on earth ever had a greater chance for glory. The world to be won and nothing to be lost. It is thrilling to think — to know that for any act of mine, I shall get twice as much praise or twice as much blame. It is quite exciting to hold the center of the national stage, with the spectators not knowing whether to laugh or to weep.

The position of my white neighbor is much more difficult. No brown specter pulls up a chair beside me when I sit down to eat. No dark ghost thrusts its leg against mine in bed. The game of keeping what one has is never so exciting as the game of getting.

I do not always feel colored. Even now I often achieve the unconscious Zora of Eatonville before the Hegira.[1] I feel most colored when I am thrown against a sharp white background.

For instance at Barnard. "Beside the waters of the Hudson" I feel   10 my race. Among the thousand white persons, I am a dark rock surged upon, and overswept, but through it all, I remain myself. When covered by the waters, I am; and the ebb but reveals me again.

Sometimes it is the other way around. A white person is set down in our midst, but the contrast is just as sharp for me. For instance, when I sit in the drafty basement that is The New World Cabaret with a white person, my color comes. We enter chatting about any little nothing that we have in common and are seated by the jazz waiters. In the abrupt way that

---

1. Exodus or pilgrimage (Arabic); Hurston refers here to the migration of millions of African Americans from the South to the North in the early twentieth century. *Barnard:* Barnard College in New York City, where Hurston received her B.A. in 1927.

jazz orchestras have, this one plunges into a number. It loses no time in circumlocutions, but gets right down to business. It constricts the thorax and splits the heart with its tempo and narcotic harmonies. This orchestra grows rambunctious, rears on its hind legs and attacks the tonal veil with primitive fury, rending it, clawing it until it breaks through to the jungle beyond. I follow those heathen — follow them exultingly. I dance wildly inside myself; I yell within, I whoop; I shake my assegai above my head, I hurl it true to the mark *yeeeeooww!* I am in the jungle and living in the jungle way. My face is painted red and yellow and my body is painted blue. My pulse is throbbing like a war drum. I want to slaughter something — give pain, give death to what, I do not know. But the piece ends. The men of the orchestra wipe their lips and rest their fingers. I creep back slowly to the veneer we call civilization with the last tone and find the white friend sitting motionless in his seat, smoking calmly.

"Good music they have here," he remarks, drumming the table with his fingertips.

Music. The great blobs of purple and red emotion have not touched him. He has only heard what I felt. He is far away and I see him but dimly across the ocean and the continent that have fallen between us. He is so pale with his whiteness then and I am *so* colored.

At certain times I have no race, I am *me*. When I set my hat at a certain angle and saunter down Seventh Avenue, Harlem City, feeling as snooty as the lions in front of the Forty-Second Street Library, for instance. So far as my feelings are concerned, Peggy Hopkins Joyce[2] on the Boule Mich with her gorgeous raiment, stately carriage, knees knocking together in a most aristocratic manner, has nothing on me. The cosmic Zora emerges. I belong to no race nor time. I am the eternal feminine with its string of beads.

I have no separate feeling about being an American citizen and col- 15
ored. I am merely a fragment of the Great Soul that surges within the boundaries. My country, right or wrong.

---

2. American actress and celebrity (1893–1957). *Boule Mich:* Boulevard St. Michel, a street on the left bank of Paris.

Sometimes, I feel discriminated against, but it does not make me angry. It merely astonishes me. How *can* any deny themselves the pleasure of my company? It's beyond me.

But in the main, I feel like a brown bag of miscellany propped against a wall. Against a wall in company with other bags, white, red and yellow. Pour out the contents, and there is discovered a jumble of small things priceless and worthless. A first-water diamond, an empty spool, bits of broken glass, lengths of string, a key to a door long since crumbled away, a rusty knife-blade, old shoes saved for a road that never was and never will be, a nail bent under the weight of things too heavy for any nail, a dried flower or two still a little fragrant. In your hand is the brown bag. On the ground before you is the jumble it held — so much like the jumble in the bags, could they be emptied, that all might be dumped in a single heap and the bags refilled without altering the content of any greatly. A bit of colored glass more or less would not matter. Perhaps that is how the Great Stuffer of Bags filled them in the first place — who knows?

Engaging with the Text

1. This essay **BEGINS** with an attention-grabbing statement. How does it signal Zora Neale Hurston's **STANCE?** Find other indications in the essay that reveal that stance.

   239–45
   12–14

2. What do you think Hurston's **PURPOSES** were in writing this essay — to explore her topic? entertain? provoke readers? argue a point? something else?

   3–4

3. This essay is filled with references to color. Highlight all the words that refer to colors. Can you **IDENTIFY** any **PATTERNS?** What are some of the things colors are attributed to? Do they in any way relate to her title? What do you think Hurston is saying with all the color imagery?

   322–24

4. Hurston **ENDS** with a **SIMILE** about bags: "brown . . . white, red and yellow . . . a jumble of small things priceless and worthless." How does

   245–48
   271–72

this simile and how do the last four paragraphs relate to her central point about our differences and commonalities?

5. **For Writing.** Think about a time when you realized you were not the same as everyone around you. How did you become aware of your differences? How did you view any differences at the time, and how do you view them today? Write an essay that **REFLECTS** on the same subject Hurston does, how it feels to be you.

168–73 ▲

JOAN DIDION

Grief

A novelist and journalist, Joan Didion is perhaps best known for her col-
lections of essays, including Slouching Toward Bethlehem *(1968),*
The White Album *(1979), and* Political Fictions *(2001). The following*
reflection on grief comes from Didion's memoir, The Year of Magical
Thinking *(2005), which chronicles her experiences of loss and grief*
following the death of her husband. (A review of this book, The End of
Life as She Knew It, *by Michiko Kakutani, is reprinted in Chapter 54.)*
As you read, pay attention to how Didion structures her text, moving
the reader through time from her early childhood to her adulthood and
interweaving her reflections about how to make sense of life after the
loss of a loved one.

GRIEF TURNS OUT TO BE A PLACE none of us know until we reach it. We
anticipate (we know) that someone close to us could die, but we do not
look beyond the few days or weeks that immediately follow such an
imagined death. We misconstrue the nature of even those few days or
weeks. We might expect if the death is sudden to feel shock. We do not
expect this shock to be obliterative, dislocating to both body and mind.
We might expect that we will be prostrate, inconsolable, crazy with loss.
We do not expect to be literally crazy, cool customers who believe that
their husband is about to return and need his shoes. In the version of
grief we imagine, the model will be "healing." A certain forward movement will prevail. The worst days will be the earliest days. We imagine
that the moment to most severely test us will be the funeral, after which
this hypothetical healing will take place. When we anticipate the funeral
we wonder about failing to "get through it," rise to the occasion, exhibit
the "strength" that invariably gets mentioned as the correct response to
death. We anticipate needing to steel ourselves for the moment: will I
be able to greet people, will I be able to leave the scene, will I be able
even to get dressed that day? We have no way of knowing that this will

not be the issue. We have no way of knowing that the funeral itself will be anodyne, a kind of narcotic regression in which we are wrapped in the care of others and the gravity and meaning of the occasion. Nor can we know ahead of the fact (and here lies the heart of the difference between grief as we imagine it and grief as it is) the unending absence that follows, the void, the very opposite of meaning, the relentless succession of moments during which we will confront the experience of meaninglessness itself.

As a child I thought a great deal about meaninglessness, which seemed at the time that most prominent negative feature on the horizon. After a few years of failing to find meaning in the more commonly recommended venues I learned that I could find it in geology, so I did. This in turn enabled me to find meaning in the Episcopal litany, most acutely in the words *as it was in the beginning, is now and ever shall be, world without end,* which I interpreted as a literal description of the constant changing of the earth, the unending erosion of the shores and mountains, the inexorable shifting of the geological structures that could throw up mountains and islands and could just as reliably take them away. I found earthquakes, even when I was in them, deeply satisfying, abruptly revealed evidence of the scheme in action. That the scheme could destroy the works of man might be a personal regret but remained, in the larger picture I had come to recognize, a matter of abiding indifference. No eye was on the sparrow. No one was watching me. *As it was in the beginning, is now and ever shall be, world without end.* On the day it was announced that the atomic bomb had been dropped on Hiroshima those were the words that came immediately to my ten-year-old mind. When I heard a few years later about mushroom clouds over the Nevada test site those were again the words that came to mind. I began waking before dawn, imagining that the fireballs from the Nevada test shots would light up the sky in Sacramento.

Later, after I married and had a child, I learned to find equal meaning in the repeated rituals of domestic life. Setting the table. Lighting the candles. Building the fire. Cooking. All those soufflés, all that crème

rhetorical situations

genres

processes

strategies

research mla/apa

media/ design

readings

caramel, all those daubes and albóndigas and gumbos. Clean sheets, stacks of clean towels, hurricane lamps for storms, enough water and food to see us through whatever geological event came our way. *These fragments I have shored against my ruins,*[1] were the words that came to mind then. These fragments mattered to me. I believed in them. That I could find meaning in the intensely personal nature of my life as a wife and mother did not seem inconsistent with finding meaning in the vast indifference of geology and the test shots; the two systems existed for me on parallel tracks that occasionally converged, notably during earthquakes. In my unexamined mind there was always a point, John's and my death, at which the tracks would converge for a final time. On the Internet I recently found aerial photographs of the house on the Palos Verdes Peninsula in which we had lived when we were first married, the house to which we had brought Quintana home from St. John's Hospital in Santa Monica and put her in her bassinet by the wisteria in the box garden. The photographs, part of the California Coastal Records Project, the point of which was to document the entire California coastline, were hard to read conclusively, but the house as it had been when we lived in it appeared to be gone. The tower where the gate had been seemed intact but the rest of the structure looked unfamiliar. There seemed to be a swimming pool where the wisteria and box garden had been. The area itself was identified as "Portuguese Bend landslide." You could see the slumping of the hill where the slide had occurred. You could also see, at the base of the cliff on the point, the cave into which we used to swim when the tide was at exactly the right flow.

The swell of clear water.

That was one way my two systems could have converged.   5

We could have been swimming into the cave with the swell of clear water and the entire point could have slumped, slipped into the sea around us. The entire point slipping into the sea around us was the kind of conclusion I anticipated. I did not anticipate cardiac arrest at the dinner table.

---

1. Line from T. S. Eliot's poem *The Waste Land* (1922).

Engaging with the Text

1. Joan Didion reflects on what she thought grief would be and how different it turned out to be when her husband died. What role does this contrast — between what she thought would happen and what she actually experienced — play in the way she **STRUCTURES** her thoughts?

   170 ▲

2. How would you characterize Didion's **TONE?** Does it seem appropriate for her topic? Why or why not? How does her tone affect her message?

   13–14 ■

3. How does Didion **DESCRIBE** her "rituals of domestic life"? What specific details does she supply? What **DOMINANT IMPRESSION** of her domestic life is created by these details? Why is that impression important to Didion?

   285–93 ◆
   291–92 ◆

4. What is the **PURPOSE** of Didion's reflection? Where is that purpose made most explicit?

   3–4 ■

5. *For Writing.* Grief is a powerful and sometimes surprising emotion. Think about a time when you experienced a strong emotion — such as grief, anger, or elation. Consider how this emotion affected you, and write an essay that **REFLECTS** on this emotion and your experience of it.

   168–73 ▲

Acknowledgments

IMAGE ACKNOWLEDGMENTS

Every effort has been made to gain permission for images used in this book. Unless otherwise noted, all images not cited in this section have been provided by the editor and authors of this publication. Please contact the publishers with any updated information.

40: Courtesy Alfred Leslie; **45:** From Scholes, Robert, and Nancy R. Comley. *The Practice of Writing.* 3rd ed. New York: St. Martin's Press, 1989; **47:** Courtesy Unilever; **48:** Courtesy Pfizer; **67:** Bettmann/Corbis; **71:** From *The 9/11 Commission Report.* New York: Norton; **87:** (both) Bettmann/Corbis; **227:** screen shot recreated by Kim Yi; **264:** Naum Kazhdan/The *New York Times*; **270:** (top) From Stiglitz, Joseph. *Economics.* New York: Norton; **270:** (bottom) www.ivillage.com; **271:** Lance Jackson/The *San Francisco Chronicle*; **290:** Courtesy Glaxo Smith Kline; **302:** From Beranbaum, Rose Levy. *The Bread Bible.* New York: Norton; **342, 345, 346:** Courtesy of the University of Wyoming Library; **409:** Bettman/Corbis; **459:** (top) Peter Turnley/Corbis; **459:** (second image) From Stiglitz and Walsh. *Principles of Microeconomics.* 3rd ed. New York: Norton; **459:** (third image) From Ginsberg, Lowi, Weir, *We the People.* 5th ed. New York: Norton; **459:** (fourth image) From Stiglitz, Joseph. *Economics.* New York: Norton; **459:** (fifth image) From Maier, Smith, Keyssar, Kevles. *Inventing America.* New York: Norton; **459:** (sixth image) From Ginsberg, Lowi, Weir, *We the People.* 5th ed. New York: Norton; **461:** (top two) Courtesy of the author; **461:** (bottom two) AP/Wide World Photos; **482:** (top) Courtesy of the author; **482:** (top middle) AP/Wide World Photos; **482:** (bottom middle) Courtesy of Dr. R. Standler; **482:** (bottom) Warner Bros./Photofest; **483, 484:** Courtesy Illinois State University, Claire Robertson, www.loobylu.com; **500:** Time/Life Pictures/Getty Images; **526:** Courtesy *Men's Health* magazine; **531–37:** Courtesy Berry-Hill Galleries, Inc., New York; **544:** Courtesy Children, Inc.; **578:** Anita Khemka/Contact Press Images; **630:** Getty Images; **644:** Courtesy *Consumer Reports*; **656:** Warner Brothers/Courtesy Everett Collection; **727:** Courtesy Pantheon Books and Valerie Steiker; **744:** Boccon-Gibod / SIPA; **753:** By Nicholas Howe; **759:** Granger Collection; **761:** © 2006 The Georgia O'Keeffe Museum/Artists Rights Society (ARS), New York. Collection of the University of Arizona Museum of Art, Tucson, Gift of Oliver James; **769:** ©Walt Disney/Courtesy Everett Collection.

TEXT ACKNOWLEDGMENTS

E. J. Bader: "Homeless on Campus," reprinted by permission from *The Progressive.*

Dennis Baron: "Don't Make English Official — Ban It Instead," reprinted by permission of the author.

Tanya Barrientos: "Se Habla Español," from the August 2004 issue of *Latina*. Reprinted by permission of *Latina* magazine.

Dave Barry: "Guys vs. Men" and "Guys vs. Men (Table)" from *Dave Barry's Complete Guide to Guys* by Dave Barry, copyright © 1995 by Dave Barry. Used by permission of Random House, Inc.

Michael Benton, Mark Dolan, and Rebecca Zisch: "Teen Film$: An Annotated Bibliography," from *Journal of Popular Film and Television*, volume 25, pp. 83–88, Summer 1997. Reprinted by permission of the Helen Dwight Reid Educational Foundation. Published by Heldref Publications. © 1997.

Dylan Borchers: "Against the Odds: Harry S. Truman and the Election of 1948," reprinted by permission of the author.

David Brooks: "The Triumph of Hope over Self-Interest," © 2003 by the *New York Times*. Reprinted by permission.

Stephen L. Carter: "Just Be Nice," from pages 66–71 of *Civility: Manners, Morals, and the Etiquette of Democracy*, © 1998 by Stephen L. Carter. Reprinted by permission of Basic Books, a division of Perseus Books, LLC.

Jennifer Church: "Proposal for Biodiversity," reprinted by permission of the author.

Consumer Reports: "Best Phones," copyright © 2004 by Consumers Union of U.S., Inc. Yonkers, NY 10703-1057, a nonprofit organization. Reprinted with permission, from the February 2004 issue of *Consumer Reports* for educational purposes only. No commercial use or reproduction permitted. www.ConsumerReports.org. Please note: Cell phone plans and technology have changed since this information was published, and the information it includes is no longer current. Since it's a good example of how evaluation can present information, permission was granted.

Nathaniel Cooney: "Self-Assessment Portfolio," reprinted by permission of the author.

Bernard Cooper: "The Fine Art of Sighing," from *In Short*. Reprinted by permission of the author.

Maggie Cutler: "Whodunit — the Media?" by Maggie Cutler from the August 19, 2002, issue of *The Nation*. Reprinted by permission of *The Nation*.

Joan Didion: "Georgia O'Keeffe," copyright © 1979 by Joan Didion. Originally published in *The White Album*. Reprinted with permission of the author. Excerpt from *The Year of Magical Thinking* by Joan Didion, copyright © 2005 by Joan Didion. Used by permission of Alfred A. Knopf, a division of Random House, Inc.

Rita Dove: "The First Book" and "Dawn Revisited" from *On the Bus with Rosa Parks* by Rita Dove. Copyright © 1999 by Rita Dove. Used by permission of W. W. Norton & Company.

Liz Dunn: "Honk If You're Hoardy," reprinted by permission of H2so4.

Cathy Eastman and Becky Burrell: "The Science of Screams: Laws of Physics Instill Thrills in Roller Coasters," from the *Dayton Daily News*. Reprinted with permission of the authors.

William Faulkner: "A Rose for Emily," from *Collected Stories of William Faulkner* (New York: Random House, 1950). Reprinted by permission.

Stanley Fish: "Who's in Charge Here?" reprinted by permission of the author.

Rachel Forrest: "Craft, Care at Flatbread Company Makes up for Sparse Menu" reprinted by permission of the author.

Henry Louis Gates Jr.: "A Giant Step," copyright © 1990 by Henry Louis Gates Jr. Originally published in the *New York Times Magazine*. Reprinted by permission of the author.

Diana George: Excerpt from "Changing the Face of Poverty: Nonprofits and the Problem of Representation," by Diana George from *Popular Literacy: Studies in Cultural Practices and Poetics*, ed. John Trimbur, © 2001 by the University of Pittsburgh Press. Reprinted by permission of the University of Pittsburgh Press.

Susan Jane Gilman: excerpt from "Mick Jagger Wants Me," from *Hypocrite in a Pouffy White Dress* by Susan Jane Gilman. Copyright © 2005 by Susan Jane Gilman. By permission of Warner Books, Inc.

Stephen Greenblatt: Excerpt from *Will in the World* by Stephen Greenblatt. Copyright © 2004 by Stephen Greenblatt. Used by permission of W. W. Norton & Company, Inc.

Lev Grossman: "Meet Joe Blog," © 2004 Time Inc. Reprinted by permission.

Patricia Hampl: "The Invention of Autobiography," from *I Could Tell You Stories: Sojourns in the Land of Memory* by Patricia Hampl. Copyright © 1999 by Patricia Hampl. Used by permission of W. W. Norton & Company, Inc.

Amanda Hesser: "Turkey Finds Its Inner Duck," reprinted by permission of the *New York Times*.

Nicholas Howe: "Across An Inland Sea," © 2003 Princeton University Press. Reprinted by permission of Princeton University Press.

Stephanie Huff: "Metaphors and the Counterfeit Nature of Our Society," reprinted by permission of the author.

Zora Neale Hurston: "How It Feels to Be Colored Me," from *I Love Myself When I'm Laughing* by Zora Neale Hurston. Used with the permission of the Estate of Zora Neale Hurston.

Michiko Kakutani: "The End of Life as She Knew It," reprinted by permission of the *New York Times*.

Geeta Kothari: "If You Are What You Eat, Then What Am I?" reprinted by permission of the author.

Paul Krugman: "California Screaming" and "My Economic Plan" reprinted by permission of the *New York Times*.

Doug Lantry: "Stay as Sweet as You Are," reprinted by permission of the author.

Benjamin Leever: "In Defense of *Dawson's Creek*: Series' Teen Heroes Inspire Youth Seeking Answers," from the *Dayton Daily News*. Reprinted by permission of the author.

Lawrence Lessig: "Some Like It Hot-Wired Magazine article," from *Free Culture* by Lawrence Lessig, copyright © 2004 by Lawrence Lessig. Used by permission of The Penguin Press, a division of Penguin Group (USA) Inc.

Andy McDonie: "You'll Love the Way We Fly . . . Maybe," reprinted by permission of the author.

Sarah McGlone: "Effect of Biofeedback Training on Muscle Tension and Skin Temperature," reprinted by permission of the author.

Gregory Mantsios: "Class in America — 2003," from *Race, Class, and Gender in the United States*, ed. Paula Rothenberg. Reprinted by permission of the author.

Dara Mayers: "Our Bodies, Our Lives" from the Ford Foundation report, summer 2004. Reprinted with permission from the Ford Foundation. © Ford Foundation.

Beverly Moss: Excerpt from "Pulpit Talk," from *A Community Text Arises*. Reprinted by permission of Hampton Press.

Philip Nel: "Fantasy, Mystery, and Ambiguity," from *J. K. Rowling's Harry Potter: A Reader's Guide* by Philip Nel. Reprinted by permission of The Continuum International Publishing Group.

Shannon Nichols: "Proficiency," reprinted by permission of the author.

Denise Noe: "Parallel Worlds: The Surprising Similarities (and Differences) of Country-and-Western and Rap," reprinted by permission of the author.

Kathleen Norris: "Seeing," from *Dakota: A Spiritual Geography* by Kathleen Norris. Copyright © 1993 by Kathleen Norris. Reprinted by permission of Houghton Mifflin Company. All rights reserved.

Jeremy Olshan: "Cookie Master," copyright © 2005 Conde Nast Publications. All rights reserved. Originally published in *The New Yorker*. Reprinted by permission.

Craig Outhier: "Potter Power," from the June 3, 2004 issue of *Get Out Magazine*. Reprinted by permission.

Grant Penrod: "Anti-Intellectualism: Why We Hate the Smart Kids," reprinted by permission of the author.

Heidi Pollock: "You Say You Want a Resolution?" reprinted by permission of H2so4.

Anna Quindlen: "Still Needing the F Word," reprinted by permission of International Creative Management, Inc. Copyright © 2003, 2004 by Anna Quindlen.

Richard Rodriguez: "None of This Is Fair," copyright © 1977 by Richard Rodriguez. Reprinted by permission of Georges Borchardt, Inc., on behalf of the author.

Mike Rose: "Potato Chips and Stars," reprinted and edited with permission of The Free Press, a division of Simon & Schuster Adult Publishing Group,

from *Lives on the Boundary: The Struggles and Achievements of America's Underprepared* by Mike Rose. Copyright © 1989 by Mike Rose. All rights reserved.

David S. Rubin: "It's the Same Old Song," from *It's Only Rock and Roll: Rock and Roll Currents in Contemporary Art*. Reprinted by permission of the author.

William Safire: "A Sprit Reborn," reprinted by permission of the *New York Times*.

David Sedaris: "Us and Them," from *Dress Your Family in Corduroy and Denim* by David Sedaris. Copyright © 2004 by David Sedaris. By permission of Little, Brown and Company, Inc.

Katherine Seelye: "Lurid Numbers on Glossy Pages! (Magazines Exploit What Sells)," reprinted by permission of the *New York Times*.

Leslie Marmon Silko: "Language and Literature from a Pueblo Indian Perspective," © 1981 by Leslie Marmon Silko. Reprinted by permission of the Wylie Agency.

Peter Singer: "The Singer Solution to World Poverty," © by Peter Singer. Reprinted by permission of the author.

Sean Smith: "A Pirate's Life," from the June 26, 2006 issue of *Newsweek*. Reprinted by permission.

Shelby Steele: "On Being Black and Middle Class," reprinted with permission of the author. Originally published in *Commentary*, January 1988. Reprinted by permission; all rights reserved.

Valerie Steiker: Excerpt retitled "Our Mother's Face" from *The Leopard Hat: A Daughter's Story* by Valerie Steiker, copyright © 2002 by Valerie Steiker. Used by permission of Pantheon Books, a division of Random House, Inc.

Peter Stiglin: "Seeing as Believing: The Paintings of Judith Belzer," reprinted by permission of Orion Online.

Carolyn Stonehill: "Modern Dating, Prehistoric Style," reprinted by permission of the author.

Cameron Stracher: "In Praise of Zeal" from the August 2004 issue of *The American Lawyer*. Reprinted by permission.

Amy Tan: "Mother Tongue," copyright © 1990 by Amy Tan. First appeared in *The Threepenny Review*. Reprinted by permission of the author and the Sandra Dijkstra Literary Agency.

Dylan Thomas: "Fern Hill" and "Do Not Go Gentle into That Good Night" by Dylan Thomas, from *The Poems of Dylan Thomas*, copyright © 1952 by Dylan Thomas. Reprinted by permission of New Directions Publishing Corporation and David Higham Associates.

Rod Usher: "A Whistle a Day Keeps Globalization Away," © 2004 Time Inc. Reprinted by permission.

Robb Walsh: "Stinkfruit," from *Are You Really Going to Eat That?* by Robb Walsh. Reprinted by permission of Counterpoint, a member of Perseus Books, L.L.C

Bill Whalen: "Reagan's Long Shadow: Reagan and Schwarzenegger — Parallel Universe?" from the *San Francisco Chronicle*. Reprinted by permission of the author.

Malcolm X and Alex Haley: Excerpt from *The Autobiography of Malcolm X* by Malcolm X and Alex Haley, copyright © 1964 by Alex Haley and Malcolm X. Copyright © 1965 by Alex Haley and Betty Shabazz. Used by permission of Random House, Inc.

Glossary / Index*

abstract A GENRE of writing that summarizes a book, an article, or a paper, usually in 100–200 words. Authors in some academic fields must provide, at the top of a report submitted for publication, an abstract of its content. The abstract may then appear in a journal of abstracts, such as *Psychological Abstracts*. An *informative abstract* summarizes a complete report; a briefer *descriptive abstract* works more as a teaser; a standalone *proposal abstract* (also called a TOPIC PROPOSAL) requests permission to conduct research, write on a topic, or present a report at a scholarly conference. Key Features: SUMMARY of basic information • objective description • brevity

---

*This glossary/index defines key terms and concepts, and directs you to pages in the book where you can find specific information on these and other topics. Please note that words set in SMALL CAPITAL LETTERS are themselves defined in the glossary/index.

ad hominem A logical FALLACY that attacks someone's character rather than addresses the issues.

analogies, 272–73

analysis   A GENRE of writing that methodically examines a topic or text by breaking it into its parts and noting how they work in relation to one another. *See* LITERARY ANALYSIS and TEXTUAL ANALYSIS.

analyses, *see* literary analysis; textual analysis

analyzing causes and effects, *see* causes and effects

analyzing text, *see* textual analysis

"And Our Flag Was Still There," 247–48

anecdote   A brief narrative (*see* NARRATE) used to illustrate a point.

anecdotes
    beginnings and, 244
    endings and, 246–47
    narratives and, 244, 309–10

Angelou, Maya, 304–5, 307

annotated bibliography   A GENRE of writing that gives an overview of published research and scholarship on a topic. Each entry includes complete publication information and a SUMMARY or an ABSTRACT for each source. A *descriptive annotation* summarizes the content of a source without commenting on its value; an *evaluative annotation* gives an opinion about the source along with a description of it. Key Features: statement of the scope • complete bibliographic information • relevant commentary • consistent presentation

annotated bibliographies, 112–20
    appropriateness and, 117
    balance and, 117
    careful reading and, 117–18
    complete information, 115
    concise description, 115
    consistency and, 118
    consistent presentation, 116
    credibility and, 117

    descriptive, 112–14
    determining the type of, 117
    evaluating sources, 118
    evaluative, 112, 114, 115
    example of, 112–15
    generating ideas and text, 116–18
    guide to writing, 116–19
    help with, 119
    key features of, 115–16
    organizing, 119
    relevant commentary, 115–16
    researching the writer, 118
    rhetorical situation, 116
    statement of scope, 115
    summarizing the work, 118
    timeliness and, 117

annotating a text, 315–18
    example of, 316–18

"Anti-Intellectualism: Why We Hate the Smart Kids," 636

APA style   A system of documenting sources in the social sciences. APA stands for the American Psychological Association. *See also* DOCUMENTATION.

APA style, 417–49
    in-text documentation, 377, 417, 419–25
    notes, 425
    quotations and, 360–61
    reference list, 377, 418–19, 426–38
        books, 426–30
        electronic sources, 433–37
        other sources, 437–38
        periodicals, 429–33
    sample research paper using, 438–49
    summary of, 375–77
    verb tenses and, 368–69

appendix   A section at the end of a written work for supplementary material that would be distracting in the main part of the text.

authority People or texts that are cited as support for a writer's ARGUMENT. A structural engineer may be quoted as an authority on bridge construction, for example. *Authority* also refers to a quality conveyed by a writer who is knowledgeable about his or her subject.

bandwagon appeal A logical FALLACY that argues for a thought or an action based on the sole defense that others support it.

begging the question A logical FALLACY that goes in a circle, assuming as a given what the writer is trying to prove.

block quotation In a written work, long quotations are set off indented and without quotation marks. in MLA style: set off text more than four typed lines, indented ten spaces (or one inch) from the left margin; in APA style, set off quotes of forty or more words, indented five spaces (or one-half inch) from the left margin. See also QUOTATION.

cause and effect A STRATEGY for analyzing why something occurred or speculating about what its consequences will be. Sometimes cause and effect serves as the ORGANIZING principle for a whole text.

Childs, Craig, 272

chronological order   A way of organizing text that proceeds from the beginning of an event to the end. Reverse chronological order proceeds in the other direction, from the end to the beginning.

chronological ordering, 304–5

Church, Jennifer, 166–67

circular argument, 326

citation   In a text, the act of giving information from a source. A citation and its corresponding parenthetical DOCUMENTATION or footnote or endnote provide minimal information about the source, and complete bibliographic information appears in a list of WORKS CITED or REFERENCES at the end of the text.

claim   A statement that asserts a belief or POSITION. In an ARGUMENT, a claim needs to be stated in a THESIS or clearly implied, and requires support with REASONS and other kinds of EVIDENCE.

"Clan of the One-Breasted Women, The," 306

"Class in America — 2003," 589

classify and divide   A STRATEGY that either groups (classifies) numerous individual items by their similarities (for example, classifying cereal, bread, butter, chicken, cheese, ice cream, eggs, and oil as carbohydrates, proteins, and fats) or breaks (divides) one large category into smaller categories (for example, dividing food into carbohydrates, proteins, and fats). Sometimes classification and/or division serves as the ORGANIZING principle for a whole text.

classifying, 260–61
  creating clear and distinct categories, 262–65
  extended definitions, 281–82
  rhetorical situation, 265

Cleveland Clinic Magazine, 277–78

Clinton, Bill, 245, 296–97

clustering   A PROCESS for GENERATING IDEAS AND TEXT, in which a writer visually connects thoughts by jotting them down and drawing lines between related items.

clustering, 201–2

coherence   The quality that allows an AUDIENCE to follow a text's meaning and to see the connections among ideas, sentences, and paragraphs. Elements that can help to achieve coherence include the title, a clearly stated or implied THESIS, topic sentences, an easy-to-follow organization with clear TRANSITIONS, and parallelism among comparable ideas.

Colicchio, Tom, 276

collaborating   The PROCESS of working with others.

collaboration, 195–98
  acknowledging, 372
  conferences, 197–98
  ground rules for, 195–96
  group projects, 196
  online, 197

color coding, 322–23

"Coming Home Again," 295–96

common ground   Shared values. Writers build common ground with AUDIENCES by acknowledging others' POINTS OF VIEW, seeking areas of compromise, and using language that includes, rather than excludes, those they aim to reach.

compare and contrast   A STRATEGY that highlights the similarities and differences between items. Using the *block method* of comparison-contrast, a writer discusses all the points about one item and then all the same points about the next item; using the *point-by-point method,* a writer discusses one point for both items before going on to discuss the next point for both items, and so on. Sometimes

counterargument In ARGUMENT, an alternative POSITION or objections to the writer's position. The writer of an argument should not only acknowledge counterarguments but also, if at all possible, accept, accommodate, or refute each counterargument.

credibility The sense of trustworthiness that a writer conveys through his or her text.

criteria In EVALUATION, the standards against which something is judged.

cubing A PROCESS for GENERATING IDEAS AND TEXT in which a writer looks at a topic in six ways — to DESCRIBE it, to COMPARE it to something else, to associate it with other things or CLASSIFY it, to analyze it (*see* ANALYSIS), to apply it, and to argue for or against it (*see* ARGUMENT).

define A STRATEGY that gets at the meaning of something. Three main kinds of definitions are the *formal definition,* which may identify the category that something belongs to and tell what distinguishes it from other things in that category: for example, defining a worm as an invertebrate (a category) with a long, rounded body and no appendages (distinguishing features); the *extended definition,* which, as its name suggests, is longer: for example, a paragraph explaining why the antagonist of a story is worm-like; and the *stipulative definition,* which gives a writer's own, particular use of a term: for example, using the term *worm* to refer to a kind of gummy candy. Sometimes definition serves as the ORGAN-IZING principle for a whole text.

describe A STRATEGY that tells how something looks, sounds, smells, feels, or tastes. Effective description creates a clear DOMINANT IMPRESSION built from specific details. Description can be *objective*, *subjective*, or both. Sometimes description serves as the ORGANIZING principle for a whole text.

design The way a text is arranged and presented visually. Elements of design include typeface, color, illustration, layout, and white space. One component of any RHETORICAL SITUATION, design plays an important part in reaching a text's AUDIENCE and achieving its PURPOSE.

dialogue A STRATEGY for adding people's own words to a text.

discovery drafting A PROCESS of DRAFTING something quickly, mostly for the purpose of discovering what one wants to say.

divide *See* CLASSIFY AND DIVIDE.

documentation Publication information about the sources cited in a text. The documentation usually appears in an abbreviated form in parentheses at the point of CITATION or in an endnote or a footnote. Complete documentation usually appears as a list of WORKS CITED or REFERENCES at the end of the text. Documentation styles vary by discipline. For example, Modern Language Association (MLA) style requires an author's complete first name if it appears in a source, whereas American Psychological Association (APA) style requires only the initial of an author's first name.

dominant impression The overall effect created through specific details when a writer DESCRIBES something.

drafting The PROCESS of putting words on paper or screen. Writers often write several drafts, REVISING each until they achieve their goal or reach a deadline. At that point, they submit a finished final draft. *See also* DISCOVERY DRAFTING.

editing The PROCESS of fine-tuning a text — examining each word, phrase, sentence, and paragraph — to be sure that the text is correct and precise and says exactly what the writer intends. *See also* PROOFREADING and REVISING.

either-or argument   A logical FALLACY that oversimplifies to suggest that only two possible positions exist on a complex issue. This fallacy is also
known as a false dilemma.

evaluation   A GENRE of writing that makes a judgment about something—a source, poem, film, restaurant, whatever—based on certain CRITERIA. Key
Features: description of the subject • clearly defined
criteria • knowledgeable discussion of the subject •
balanced and fair assessment

existing knowledge and, 124
generating ideas and text, 124–25
guide to writing, 123–26
help with, 126
key features of, 122–23
knowledgeable discussion of subject, 123
organizing, 125–26
other opinions and, 125
reasons for judgment, 125
rhetorical situation, 124
of sources, *see* evaluating sources
thesis statement, 125
topic for, 123
well-supported reasons, 123

evaluative annotations, 112, 114, 115, 117
see also annotated bibliographies

Evans, Harold, 296–97

evidence   The data you present to support your reasons. Such data may include statistics, calculations, examples, anecdotes, quotations, case studies, or anything else that will convince your reader that your reasons are compelling. Evidence should be sufficient (enough to show that the reasons have merit) and relevant (appropriate to the argument you're making).

examples as transitions, 254

explain a process   A STRATEGY for telling how something is done or how to do something. Sometimes an explanation of a process serves as the ORGANIZING principle for a whole text.

explaining processes, 299–303
    clarity and, 299
    how something is done, 299–300
    how to do something, 300–1
    rhetorical situation, 302–3
    visually, 301–2

extended definitions, 277–82
    classification, 281–82
    comparing to other words, 280–81
    exploring the word's origins, 278–79
    giving examples, 281
    providing details, 279–80

fallacy, logical   Faulty reasoning that can mislead an AUDIENCE. Fallacies include AD HOMINEM, BANDWAGON APPEAL, BEGGING THE QUESTION, EITHER-OR ARGUMENT (also called false dilemma), false analogy, faulty causality (also called POST HOC, ERGO PROPTER HOC), HASTY GENERALIZATION, and SLIPPERY SLOPE.

fallacies, checking for, 325–27

false analogy   A FALLACY comparing things that do resemble each other but that are not alike in the most important respects.

false analogies, 326

false dilemma   See EITHER-OR ARGUMENT.

false dilemmas, 326
"Fantasy, Mystery, and Ambiguity," 663
"Fast Food Nation: The Dark Side of the All-
    American Meal," 261–62
Faulkner, William, 700

faulty causality   A FALLACY that mistakenly assumes the first of two events causes the second. This fallacy is also called POST HOC, ERGO PROPTER HOC.

faulty causality, 326–27
Favorite Comfort Food, 300–301
"Fern Hill," 712

field research   The collection of first-hand data through observation, interviews, and questionnaires or surveys.

field research, 350–53
    interviewing, 351–52
    observing, 352–53

"Fine Art of Sighing, The," 168–71, 172
"First Book, The," 711
FirstSearch, 347
Fish, Stanley, 781
FitzGerald, Frances, 273

flashback   In narrative (NARRATE), an interruption of the main story in order to show an incident that occurred at an earlier time.

flashbacks, 306
Fontaine, Debra, 289
Fool.com, 276

font   A variation of a typeface such as italic and bold.

formal definitions, 275–77
    writing, 276–77
formal outline, 203–4

formal writing   Writing intended to be evaluated by someone such as an instructor or read by an AUDIENCE expecting academic or businesslike argument and presentation. Formal writing should be carefully revised, edited, and PROOFREAD. *See also* INFORMAL WRITING.

Forrest, Rachel, 646
"For Richer," 3–4
"Foster Cars: Orphan Makes and the People Who Love Them," 9–10, 153–59
"Fragrances," 243

freewriting   A PROCESS for GENERATING IDEAS AND TEXT by writing continuously for several minutes without pausing to read what has been written.

freewriting, 199–200

Gates, Henry Louis, Jr., 730
Gaylin, Willard, 246

generating ideas and text   A set of PROCESSES including CLUSTERING, CUBING, DISCOVERY DRAFTING, FREEWRITING, LETTER WRITING, LISTING, LOOPING, OUTLINING, and QUESTIONING.

generating ideas and text, 199–204
    clustering, 201–2
    cubing, 202
    discovery drafting, 204
    freewriting, 199–200
    letter writing, 204
    listing, 200–1
    looping, 200
    outlining, 203–4
    questioning, 202–3
    see also specific genres

genre   A kind of text marked by and expected to have certain key features and to follow certain conventions of style and presentation. In the literary world, readers recognize such genres as the short story and novel (which are expected to have plots) and the poem (which may not have a plot but has other characteristics, such as rhythm); in academic and workplace settings, readers and writers focus on other genres, which also meet expectations in content, style, and appearance. Genres covered in the *Norton Field Guide* include ABSTRACTS, ANNOTATED BIBLIOGRAPHIES, APPLICATION LETTERS, ARGUMENTS, EVALUATIONS, LAB REPORTS, LITERACY NARRATIVES, LITERARY ANALYSES, PROFILES, PROPOSALS, REFLECTIONS, RÉSUMÉS, REPORTS, TEXTUAL ANALYSES, and REVIEWS OF SCHOLARLY LITERATURE.

genre, 9–11, 19–192
    assessing your own writing and, 210
    beginnings and endings and, 249
    causes and effects and, 259
    classifying and dividing and, 265
    comparing and contrasting and, 274
    definitions and, 284
    descriptions and, 292–93
    dialogue and, 297

hasty generalization   A FALLACY that reaches a
conclusion based on insufficient or inappropriately
qualified EVIDENCE.

home page   The introductory page of a Web site.

indexes and databases, 346–49
    general electronic, 347–48
    print indexes, 347
    single-subject, 348
    web-based, 348–49
Infomine, 348

informal writing   Writing not intended to be evaluated, sometimes not even to be read by others. Informal writing is produced primarily to explore ideas or to communicate casually with friends and acquaintances. *See also* FORMAL WRITING.

informative abstracts, 107–8
    organizing, 111
    see also abstracts
Info Trac, 347
"In Praise of Zeal," 809

interpretation   The act of making sense of something or explaining what one thinks it means. Interpretation is the goal of writing a LITERARY ANALYSIS or TEXTUAL ANALYSIS.

interviews
    citing, 405
    dialogue and, 296–97
    as field research, 351–52
    profiles and, 157
in-text documentation
    APA style, 377, 421, 423–29
    MLA style, 377, 378–79, 381–87
introductions, 239–40
    see also beginning
"Invention of Autobiography: Augustine's *Confessions,* The," 674
"Investing Basics: Stocks," 276
"Italian Hours," 290–91
"It's the Same Old Song," 39–41
    analysis of, 50, 55, 57

"Johnny Depp: Unlikely Superstar," 768
Johnson, Debra, 174–78
JSTOR, 347
JURIST, 349
"Just Be Nice," 583
Just the Facts: 2003–2004 (NMSS), 286

Kakutani, Michiko, 650
Keller, Evelyn Fox, 244
Kothari, Geeta, 819

keyword   A term that a researcher inputs when searching databases and the World Wide Web for information.

"Kill 'Em! Crush 'Em! Eat 'Em Raw!" 266–67
King, Tracey, 160–62
Kingsolver, Barbara, 247–48
known audiences, 6
Krugman, Paul, 3–4, 659

labels, 286

lab report   A GENRE of writing that covers the process of conducting an experiment in a controlled setting. Key Features: explicit title • ABSTRACT • PURPOSE • methods • results and discussion • REFERENCES • APPENDIX • appropriate format

lab reports, 127–36
    abstract, 133
    appendices, 134
    drafting, 135
    example of, 127–32
    explicit title, 132
    format, 134
    generating ideas and text, 135
    guide to writing, 134–36
    help with, 136
    key features of, 132–34

layout The way text is arranged on a page or screen — for example, in paragraphs, in lists, on charts, with headings, and so on.

letter writing A PROCESS of GENERATING IDEAS AND TEXT by going through the motions of writing to someone to explain a topic.

link In a Web page, a URL, a word, or image that, when clicked, opens a different page.

listing A PROCESS for GENERATING IDEAS AND TEXT by making lists while thinking about a topic, finding relationships among the notes, and arranging the notes as an outline (*see* OUTLINING).

literacy narrative A GENRE of writing that tells about a writer's experience learning to read or write. Key Features: well-told story • vivid detail • indication of the narrative's significance

literacy portfolio   An organized collection of materials showing examples of one writer's progress as a reader and/or writer.

literary analysis   A GENRE of writing that argues for a particular INTERPRETATION of a literary text—most often fiction, poetry, or drama. *See also* ANALYSIS and TEXTUAL ANALYSIS. Key Features: arguable THESIS • careful attention to the language of the text • attention to patterns or themes • clear interpretation • MLA style

literature   Literary works—including fiction, poetry, drama, and some nonfiction; also, the body of written work produced in a given field.

literature review   *See* REVIEW OF SCHOLARLY LITERATURE.

logical fallacy   *See* FALLACY, LOGICAL.

looping   A PROCESS for GENERATING IDEAS AND TEXT in which a writer writes about a topic quickly for several minutes and summarizes the most important or interesting idea in a sentence, which becomes the beginning of another round of writing and summarizing . . . and so on until finding an angle for a paper.

medium (pl., media)   A means for communicating—for example, in print, with speech, or online. Texts consisting of words are said to use *verbal media,* whereas photographs, films, and sculptures are examples of *visual media* (though some verbal texts include visual images, and some visual texts include words).

memoir   A GENRE that focuses on something significant from the writer's past. Key Features: good story
• vivid details • clear significance

MLA style   A system of documenting sources in the
humanities and fine arts. MLA stands for the Modern
Language Association. (*See also* DOCUMENTATION.)

narrate   A STRATEGY for presenting information as a story, for telling "what happened." It is a pattern most often associated with fiction, but it shows up in all kinds of writing. When used in an essay, a REPORT, or another academic GENRE, a narrative must support a point—not merely tell an interesting story for its own sake. It must also present events in some kind of sequence and include only pertinent detail. Sometimes narrative serves as the ORGANIZING principle for a whole text. See also LITERACY NARRATIVE.

organizing   Arranging parts of a text so that the text as a whole has COHERENCE. The text may use one STRATEGY throughout or may combine several strategies to create a suitable organization.

outlining   A PROCESS for GENERATING IDEAS AND TEXT or for examining a text. An *informal outline* simply lists ideas and then numbers them in the order that they will appear; a *working outline* distinguishes support from main ideas by indenting the former; a *formal outline* is arranged as a series of headings and indented subheadings, each on a separate line, with letters and numerals indicating relative levels of importance.

paraphrase   A rewording of a text in about the same number of words but without using the word order or sentence structure of the original. A paraphrase is generally used when you want to include the details of a passage but do not need to quote it word for word. Like a quotation, a paraphrase requires DOCUMENTATION.

peer review   *See* RESPONDING.

plagiarism   Using another person's words, syntax, or ideas without giving appropriate credit and DOCUMENTATION. Plagiarism is a serious breach of ethics.

poems, 9–10
    citing, 385
    quoting, 361
point-by-point method of comparison, 268–69

point of view   A position from which something is considered.

Pollock, Heidi, 803

portfolio   A collection of writing selected by a writer to show his or her work, sometimes including a statement assessing the work and explaining what it demonstrates.

portfolios, 224–35
    inclusions in, 225–26, 234–35
    literacy, 234–35
    online, 227–28
    organizing, 226–28, 235
    paper, 226–27
    reflecting on, 229–34, 235
    rhetorical situation, 224–25
    sample self-assessment, 230–34

position   A statement that asserts a belief or CLAIM. In an ARGUMENT, a position needs to be stated in a THESIS or clearly implied, and requires support with REASONS and other kinds of EVIDENCE.

post hoc, ergo propter hoc   Latin for "after this, therefore because of this"; also called faulty causality. A FALLACY that assumes the first of two events causes the second.

post hoc, ergo propter hoc, 326–27
"Potato Chips and Stars," 512
"Potter Power," 655

Praeger, Samuel
    application letter of, 189, 190
    résumé of, 183–85
presentation software, 471–72, 473
"Prevent the Continued Growth of Islamist
    Terrorism," 795

primary source   A source such as a literary work, historical document, art, or performance that a researcher examines firsthand. Primary sources also include experiments and FIELD RESEARCH. In writing about the Revolutionary War, a researcher would likely consider the Declaration of Independence a primary source and a textbook's description of the writing of the document a SECONDARY SOURCE.

primary sources, 340–41

print indexes, 347
print résumés, 182–86
    example of, 183
    see also résumés
print sources, 341–42
    reliability of, 354
print text, 453–63
    design elements, 454–58
    evaluating a design, 463
    headings, 456–57
    layout, 455
    lists, 455–56
    paragraphs, 455
    rhetorical situation, 453–54, 458
    typefaces, 454–55
    visuals, see visuals, print text
    white space, 458
proceeding of a conference, citing
    in APA style, 438
    in MLA style, 406

process   In writing, a series of actions that may include GENERATING IDEAS AND TEXT, DRAFTING, REVISING, EDITING, and PROOFREADING a text. See also EXPLAIN A PROCESS.

processes, 193
    explaining, see explaining processes
    see also specific processes

questioning A PROCESS of GENERATING IDEAS AND TEXT about a topic — asking, for example, What? Who? When? Where? How? and Why? or other questions.

quotation Someone's words used exactly as they were spoken or written. Quotation is most effective when the wording is worth repeating or makes a point so well that no rewording will do it justice or when you want to cite someone's exact words or to quote someone whose opinions disagree with others. Quotations need to be acknowledged, with DOCUMENTATION.

responding (to writing) A PROCESS of writing in which a reader responds to a writer's work by giving his or her thoughts about the writer's title, beginning, clarity of THESIS, support and DOCUMENTATION, ORGANIZING, STANCE, treatment of AUDIENCE, achievement of PURPOSE, handling of the GENRE, ending, and other matters.

résumé A GENRE that summarizes someone's academic and employment history, generally written to submit to potential employers. DESIGN and word choice depend on whether a résumé is submitted as a print document or in an electronic or scannable form. Key Features: organization that suits goals and experience • succinctness • design that highlights key information (for print) or that uses only one typeface (for scannable)

review of scholarly literature A GENRE in which, for a given topic, a writer summarizes those scholarly publications ("literature") he or she deems most important. *See also* SCHOLARLY LITERATURE. Key Features: careful, thorough research • accurate, objective SUMMARY of the relevant literature • critical EVALUATION of the literature • clear focus

revising The PROCESS of making substantive changes, including additions and cuts, to a draft so that it contains all the necessary information in an appropriate organization. During revision, a writer generally moves from whole-text issues to details with the goals of sharpening the focus and strengthening the argument.

rewriting A PROCESS of composing a new draft from another perspective — from a different POINT OF VIEW, AUDIENCE, STANCE, GENRE, MEDIUM, sequence, and so on.

rhetorical situation The context within which writing or other communication takes place, including PURPOSE, AUDIENCE, GENRE, STANCE, and MEDIA / DESIGN.

scholarly literature Writing from a scholarly field. *See also* REVIEW OF SCHOLARLY LITERATURE.

secondary source An analysis or INTERPRETATION of a PRIMARY SOURCE. In writing about the Revolutionary War, a researcher would likely consider the Declaration of Independence a PRIMARY SOURCE and

A Directory to MLA Style

A Directory to APA Style

A Menu of Readings